W9-AQK-555

EXPLANATORY NOTES UPON THE NEW TESTAMENT

VOLUME II

EXPLANATORY NOTES UPON THE NEW TESTAMENT

John Wesley

VOLUME II
Romans to Revelation

BAKER BOOK HOUSE
Grand Rapids, Michigan 49506

Reprinted 1981 by
Baker Book House Company
from an undated edition published by
The Wesleyan-Methodist Book-Room, London

Two-volume Set

ISBN: 0-8010-9651-0

Printed in the United States of America

NOTES

ON

ST PAUL'S EPISTLE TO THE ROMANS.

Many of the writings of the New Testament are written in the form of epistles. Such are not only those of St. Paul, James, Peter, Jude, but also both the treatises of St. Luke, and all the writings of St. John. Nay, we have seven epistles herein which the Lord Jesus himself sent by the hand of John to the seven churches; yea, the whole Revelation is no other than an epistle from Him.

Concerning the epistles of St. Paul, we may observe, he writes in a very different manner to those churches which he had planted himself, and to those who had not seen his face in the flesh. In his letters to the former, a loving or sharp familiarity appears, as their behaviour was more or less suitable to the gospel. To the latter, he proposes the pure, unmixed gospel, in a more general and abstract manner.

As to the time wherein he wrote his epistles, it is probable he wrote about the year of Christ, according to the common reckoning,

48	From Corinth,	The Epistle to the Thessalonians.
49	From Phrygia,	To the Galatians.
52	From Ephesus,	The First to the Corinthians.
	From Troas,	The First Epistle to Timothy.
	From Macedonia,	The Second to the Corinthians, and that to Titus.
	From Corinth,	To the Romans.
57	From Rome,	To the Philippians, to Philemon, the Ephesians, and Colossians.
53	From Italy,	To the Hebrews.
66	From Rome,	The Second to Timothy.

As to the general epistles, it seems, St. James wrote a little before his death, which was A. D. 63. St. Peter, who was martyred in the year 67, wrote his latter epistle a little before his death, and not long after his former. St. Jude wrote after him, when the mystery of iniquity was gaining ground swiftly. St. John is believed to have wrote all his epistles a little before his departure. The Revelation he wrote A. D. 96.

That St. Paul wrote this epistle from Corinth we may learn from his commending to the Romans Phebe, a servant of the church of Cenchrea, chap. xvi. 1, a port of Corinth; and from his mentioning the salutations of Caius and Erastus, chap. xvi. 23, who were both Corinthians. Those to whom he wrote seem to have been chiefly foreigners, both Jews and gentiles, whom business drew from other provinces; as appears, both by his writing in Greek, and by his salutations of several former acquaintance.

His chief design herein is to show, 1. That neither the gentiles by the law of nature, nor the Jews by the law of Moses, could obtain justification before God; and that therefore it was necessary for both to seek it from the free mercy of God by faith. 2. That God has an absolute right to show mercy on what terms he pleases, and to withhold it from those who will not accept it on his own terms.

This Epistle consists of five parts:

I. The introduction, C. i. 1—15
II. The proposition briefly proved,
  1. Concerning faith and justification,
  2. Concerning salvation,
  3. Concerning the equality of believers, Jews or gentiles, 16—17
  To these three parts, whereof
    The first is treated of, C. i. 18—iv.
    The second, C. v—viii.
    The third, C. ix.—xi
  not only the treatise itself, but also the exhortation, answers in the same order.
III. The treatise,
  1. Concerning justification, which is,
    (1.) Not by works, for C. i. 18
      The gentiles, C. ii. 1—10
      The Jews, and 11—29
      Both together are under sin, C. iii. 1—20
    (2.) But by faith, 21—31
      as appears by the example of Abraham, and the testimony of David, C. iv. 1—25
  2. Concerning salvation, C. v.—viii.
  3. Concerning the equal privileges of Jewish and gentile believers, C. ix.—xi.
IV. The exhortation, C. xii. 1— 2
  1. Concerning faith and its fruits, love and practical holiness, 3—21
    C. xiii. 1—10
  2. Concerning salvation, 11—14
  3. Of the conjunction of Jews and gentiles, C. xiv. 1—xv. 13
V. The conclusion, 14—xvi. 25

To express the design and contents of this epistle a little more at large: The apostle labours throughout to fix in those to whom he writes a deep sense of the excellency of the gospel, and to engage them to act suitably to it. For this purpose, after a general salutation, chap. i. 1—7, and profession of his affection for them, verses 8—15, he declares he shall not be ashamed openly to maintain the gospel at Rome, seeing it is the powerful instrument of salvation, both to Jews and gentiles, by means of faith, verses 16, 17. And, in order to demonstrate this, he shows,—

1. That the world greatly needed such a dispensation, the gentiles being in a most abandoned state, verses 18—32, and the Jews, though condemning others, being themselves no better, chap. ii. 1—29; as, notwithstanding some cavils, which he obviates, chap. iii. 1—8, their own scriptures testify, verses 9—19. So that all were under a necessity of seeking justification by this method, verses 20—31.

2. That Abraham and David themselves sought justification by faith, and not by works, chap. iv. 1—25.

3. That all who believe are brought into so happy a state, as turns the greatest afflictions into matter of joy, chap. v. 1—11.

4. That the evils brought on mankind by Adam are abundantly recompensed to all that believe in Christ, verses 12—21.

5. That, far from dissolving the obligations to practical holiness, the gospel increases them by peculiar obligations, chap. vi. 1—23.

In order to convince them of these things the more deeply, and to remove their fondness for the Mosaic law, now they were married to Christ by faith in him, chap. vii. 1—6, he shows how unable the motives of the law were to produce that holiness which believers obtain by a living faith in the gospel, chap. vii. 7—25, viii. 1, 2, and then gives a more particular view of those things which rendered the gospel effectual to this great end, verses 3—39.

That even the gentiles, if they believed, should have a share in these blessings, and that the Jews, if they believed not, should be excluded from them, being a point of great importance, the apostle bestows the ninth, tenth, and eleventh chapters in settling it. He begins the ninth chapter by expressing his tender love and high esteem for the Jewish nation, verses 1—5, and then shows,—

1. That God's rejecting great part of the seed of Abraham, yea, and of Isaac too, was undeniable fact, verses 6—13.

2. That God had not chosen them to such peculiar privileges for any kind of goodness either in them or their fathers, verses 14—24.

3. That his accepting the gentiles, and rejecting many of the Jews, had been foretold both by Hosea and Isaiah, verses 25—33.

4. That God had offered salvation to Jews and gentiles on the same terms, though the Jews had rejected it, chap. x. 1—21.

5. That though the rejection of Israel for their obstinacy was general, yet it was not total; there being still a remnant among them who did embrace the gospel, chap. xi. 1—10.

6. That the rejection of the rest was not final, but in the end all Israel should be saved, verses 11—31.

7. That, meantime, even their obstinacy and rejection served to display the unsearchable wisdom and love of God, verses 32—36.

The rest of the epistle contains practical instructions and exhortations. He particularly urges, 1. An entire consecration of themselves to God, and a care to glorify Him by a faithful improvement of their several talents, chap. xii. 1—11. 2. Devotion, patience, hospitality, mutual sympathy, humility, peace, and meekness, verses 12—21. 3. Obedience to magistrates, justice in all its branches, love the fulfilling of the law, and universal holiness, chap. xiii. 1—14. 4. Mutual candour between those who differed in judgment, touching the observance of the Mosaic law, chap. xiv. 1—23, xv. 1—17; in enforcing which he is led to mention the extent of his own labours, and his purpose of visiting the Romans; in the mean time recommending himself to their prayers, verses 18—33. And, after many salutations, chap. xvi. 1—16, and a caution against those who caused divisions, he concludes with a suitable blessing and doxology, verses 17—27.

ROMANS.

CHAPTER I. 1 Paul, a servant of Jesus Christ, called
2 *to be* an apostle, separated to the gospel of God, * Which
he had promised before by his prophets in the holy scrip-
3 tures, Concerning his Son Jesus Christ our Lord, who was
4 of the seed of David according to the flesh; *But* declared
the Son of God with power, according to the Spirit of holi-

* Deut. xviii. 18; Isai. ix. 6, 7; liii. and lxi; Jer. xxiii. 5.

Verse 1. *Paul, a servant of Jesus Christ*—To this introduction the conclusion answers, Romans xv. 15, &c. *Called to be an apostle*—And made an apostle by that calling. While God calls, he makes what he calls. As the Judaizing teachers disputed his claim to the apostolical office, it is with great propriety that he asserts it in the very entrance of an epistle wherein their principles are entirely overthrown. And various other proper and important thoughts are suggested in this short introduction; particularly the prophecies concerning the gospel, the descent of Jesus from David, the great doctrines of his Godhead and resurrection, the sending the gospel to the gentiles, the privileges of Christians, and the obedience and holiness to which they were obliged in virtue of their profession. *Separated*—By God, not only from the bulk of other men, from other Jews, from other disciples, but even from other Christian teachers, to be a peculiar instrument of God in spreading the gospel.

Verse 2. *Which he promised before*—Of old time, frequently, solemnly. And the promise and accomplishment confirm each other.

Verse 3. *Who was of the seed of David according to the flesh*—That is, with regard to his human nature. Both the natures of our Saviour are here mentioned; but the human is mentioned first, because the divine was not manifested in its full evidence till after his resurrection.

Verse 4. *But* powerfully *declared to be the Son of God, according to the Spirit of holiness*—That is, according to his divine nature. *By the resur*

5 ness, by the resurrection from the dead: By whom we have
received grace and apostleship, for obedience to the faith in
6 all nations, for his name: Among whom are ye also the
7 called of Jesus Christ: To all that are in Rome, *who are*
beloved of God, called *and* holy: Grace to you and peace
from God our Father, and the Lord Jesus Christ.
8 First, I thank my God through Jesus Christ for you all,

rection from the dead—For this is both the fountain and the object of our faith; and the preaching of the apostles was the consequence of Christ's resurrection.

Verse 5. *By whom we have received*—I and the other apostles. *Grace and apostleship*—The favour to be an apostle, and qualifications for it. *For obedience to the faith in all nations*—That is, that all nations may embrace the faith of Christ. *For his name*—For his sake; out of regard to him.

Verse 6. *Among whom*—The nations brought to the obedience of faith. *Are ye also*—But St. Paul gives them no pre-eminence above others.

Verse 7. *To all that are in Rome*—Most of these were heathens by birth, verse 13, though with Jews mixed among them. They were scattered up and down in that large city, and not yet reduced into the form of a church. Only some had begun to meet in the house of Aquila and Priscilla. *Beloved of God*—And from his free love, not from any merit of yours, *called* by his word and his Spirit to believe in him, *and* now through faith *holy* as he is holy. *Grace*—The peculiar favour of God. *And peace*—All manner of blessings, temporal, spiritual, and eternal. This is both a Christian salutation and an apostolic benediction. *From God our Father, and the Lord Jesus Christ*—This is the usual way wherein the apostles speak, "God the Father," "God our Father." Nor do they often, in speaking of him, use the word *Lord*, as it implies the proper name of God, *Jehovah*. In the Old Testament, indeed, the holy men generally said, "The Lord our God;" for they were then, as it were, servants; whereas now they are sons: and sons so well know their Father, that they need not frequently mention his proper name. It is one and the same peace, and one and the same grace, which is from God and from Jesus Christ. Our trust and prayer fix on God, as he is the Father of Christ; and on Christ, as he presents us to the Father.

Verse 8. *I thank*—In the very entrance of this one epistle are the traces of all spiritual affections; but of thankfulness above all, with the expression of which almost all St. Paul's epistles begin. He here particularly thanks God, that what otherwise himself should have done, was done at Rome already. *My God*—This very word expresses faith, hope, love, and consequently all true religion. *Through Jesus Christ*—The gifts of God all pass through Christ to us; and all our petitions and thanksgivings pass through Christ to God. *That your faith is spoken of*—In this kind of congratulations St. Paul describes either the whole of Christianity, as Col. i. 3, &c.; or some part of it, as 1 Cor. i. 5. Accordingly

9 that your faith is spoken of through the whole world. For
God, whom I serve with my spirit in the gospel of his Son,
is my witness, how incessantly I make mention of you;
10 Always requesting in my prayers to come unto you, if by
any means now at length I may have a prosperous journey
11 by the will of God. For I long to see you, that I may
impart to you some spiritual gift, that ye may be estab-
12 lished; That is, to be comforted together with you by the
13 mutual faith both of you and me. Now I would not have
you ignorant, brethren, that I have often purposed to come
to you, (though I have been hindered hitherto,) that I
might have some fruit among you also, even as among the

here he mentions the faith of the Romans, suitably to his design, verses 12, 17. *Through the whole world*—This joyful news spreading everywhere, that there were Christians also in the imperial city. And the goodness and wisdom of God established faith in the chief cities; in Jerusalem and Rome particularly; that from thence it might be diffused to all nations.

Verse 9. *God, whom I serve*—As an apostle. *In my spirit*—Not only with my body, but with my inmost soul. *In the gospel*—By preaching it.

Verse 10. *Always*—In all my solemn addresses to God. *If by any means now at length*—This accumulation of particles declares the strength of his desire.

Verse 11. *That I may impart to you*—Face to face, by laying on of hands, prayer, preaching the gospel, private conversation. *Some spiritual gift*—With such gifts the Corinthians, who had enjoyed the presence of St. Paul, abounded, 1 Cor. i. 7, xii. 1, xiv. 1. So did the Galatians likewise, Gal. iii. 5; and, indeed, all those churches which had had the presence of any of the apostles had peculiar advantages in this kind, from the laying on of their hands, Acts xix. 6, viii. 17, &c., 2 Tim. i. 6. But as yet the Romans were greatly inferior to them in this respect; for which reason the apostle, in the twelfth chapter also, says little, if any thing, of their spiritual gifts. He therefore desires to impart some, *that* they *might be established;* for by these was the testimony of Christ confirmed among them. That St. Peter had no more been at Rome than St. Paul, at the time when this epistle was wrote, appears from the general tenor thereof, and from this place in particular: for, otherwise, what St. Paul wishes to impart to the Romans would have been imparted already by St. Peter.

Verse 12. *That is,* I long *to be comforted by the mutual faith both of you and me*—He not only associates the Romans with, but even prefers them before, himself. How different is this style of the apostle from that of the modern court of Rome!

Verse 13. *Brethren*—A frequent, holy, simple, sweet, and yet grand, appellation. The apostles but rarely address persons by their names;

14 other gentiles. I am a debtor both to the Greeks and the
15 barbarians; both to the wise, and to the unwise. Therefore, as much as in me is, I am ready to preach the gospel
16 to you also who are at Rome. For I am not ashamed
of the gospel: for it is the power of God unto salvation to
every one that believeth; both to the Jew, and to the gen-
17 tile. For the righteousness of God is revealed therein from
faith to faith: as it is written, * The just shall live by faith.

* Hab ii. 4.

as, "O ye Corinthians," "O Timotheus." St. Paul generally uses this appellation, "Brethren;" sometimes in exhortation, "My beloved," or, "My beloved brethren;" St. James, "Brethren," "My brethren," "My beloved brethren;" St. Peter and Jude always, "Beloved;" St. John frequently, "Beloved;" once, "Brethren;" oftener than once, "My little children." *Though I have been hindered hitherto*—Either by business, see Romans xv. 22; or persecution, 1 Thess. ii. 2; or the Spirit, Acts xvi. 7. *That I might have some fruit*—Of my ministerial labours. *Even as* I have already had from the many churches I have planted and watered *among the other gentiles.*

Verse 14. *To the Greeks and the barbarians*—He includes the Romans under the Greeks; so that this division comprises all nations. *Both to the wise, and the unwise*—For there were *unwise* even among the Greeks, and *wise* even among the barbarians *I am a debtor* to all—I am bound by my divine mission to preach the gospel to them.

Verse 16. *For I am not ashamed of the gospel*—To the world, indeed, it is folly and weakness, 1 Cor. i. 18; therefore, in the judgment of the world, he ought to be ashamed of it; especially at Rome, the head and theatre of the world. But Paul is not ashamed, knowing *it is the power of God unto salvation to every one that believeth*—The great and gloriously powerful means of saving all who accept salvation in God's own way. As St. Paul comprises the sum of the gospel in this epistle, so he does the sum of the epistle in this and the following verse. *Both to the Jew, and to the gentile*—There is a noble frankness, as well as a comprehensive sense, in these words, by which he, on the one hand, shows the Jews their absolute need of the gospel; and, on the other, tells the politest and greatest nation in the world both that their salvation depended on receiving it, and that the first offers of it were in every place to be made to the despised Jews.

Verse 17. *The righteousness of God*—This expression sometimes means God's eternal, essential righteousness, which includes both justice and mercy, and is eminently shown in condemning sin, and yet justifying the sinner. Sometimes it means that righteousness by which a man, through the gift of God, is made and is righteous; and that, both by receiving Christ through faith, and by a conformity to the essential righteousness of God. St. Paul, when treating of justification, means hereby the righ-

18 For the wrath of God is revealed from heaven against all
ungodliness and unrighteousness of men, who detain the
19 truth in unrighteousness; For what is to be known of God
20 is manifest in them; for God hath showed *it* to them. For
those things of him which are invisible, both his eternal
power and Godhead, are clearly seen from the creation

teousness of faith; therefore called *the righteousness of God,* because God found out and prepared, reveals and gives, approves and crowns it. In this verse the expression means, the whole benefit of God through Christ for the salvation of a sinner. *Is revealed*—Mention is made here, and verse 18, of a twofold revelation,—of wrath and of righteousness: the former, little known to nature, is revealed by the law; the latter, wholly unknown to nature, by the gospel. That goes before, and prepares the way; this follows. Each, the apostle says, *is revealed* at the present time, in opposition to the times of ignorance. *From faith to faith*—By a gradual series of still clearer and clearer promises. *As it is written*—St. Paul had just laid down three propositions: 1. Righteousness is by faith, verse 17: 2. Salvation is by righteousness, verse 16: 3. Both to the Jews and to the gentiles, verse 16. Now all these are confirmed by that single sentence, *The just shall live by faith*—Which was primarily spoken of those who preserved their lives, when the Chaldeans besieged Jerusalem, by believing the declarations of God, and acting according to them. Here it means, He shall obtain the favour of God, and continue therein by believing.

Verse 18. *For*—There is no other way of obtaining life and salvation. Having laid down his proposition, the apostle now enters upon the proof of it. His first argument is, The law condemns all men, as being under sin. None therefore is justified by the works of the law. This is treated of to chap. iii. 20. And hence he infers, Therefore justification is by faith. *The wrath of God is revealed*—Not only by frequent and signal interpositions of divine providence, but likewise in the sacred oracles, and by us, his messengers. *From heaven*—This speaks the majesty of Him whose wrath is revealed, his all-seeing eye, and the extent of his wrath: whatever is under heaven is under the effects of his wrath, believers in Christ excepted. *Against all ungodliness and unrighteousness*—These two are treated of, verses 23, &c. *Of men*—He is speaking here of the gentiles, and chiefly the wisest of them. *Who detain the truth*—For it struggles against their wickedness. *In unrighteousness*—The word here includes ungodliness also.

Verse 19. *For what is to be known of God*—Those great principles which are indispensably necessary to be known. *Is manifest in them; for God hath showed it to them*—By the light which enlightens every man that cometh into the world

Verse 20. *For those things of him which are invisible, are seen*—By the eye of the mind. *Being understood*—They are seen by them, and them only, who use their understanding

of the world, being understood by the things which are
21 made; so that they are without excuse: Because, knowing
God, they did not glorify *him* as God, neither were thankful;
but became vain in their reasonings, and their foolish heart
22 was darkened. Professing to be wise, they became fools,
23 And changed the glory of the incorruptible God into an
image in the likeness of corruptible man, and of birds, and
24 of four-footed creatures, and reptiles. Wherefore God also
gave them up to uncleanness through the desires of their
25 hearts, to dishonour their bodies among themselves: Who
changed the truth of God into a lie, and worshipped and
served the creature above the Creator, who is blessed for
26 ever. Amen. Therefore God gave them up to vile affections: for even their women changed the natural use to that
27 which is against nature: And likewise also men, leaving the
natural use of the woman, burned in their lust toward each

Verse 21. *Because, knowing God*—For the wiser heathens did know that there was one supreme God; yet from low and base considerations they conformed to the idolatry of the vulgar. *They did not glorify him as God, neither were thankful*—They neither thanked him for his benefits, nor glorified him for his divine perfections. *But became vain*—Like the idols they worshipped. *In their reasonings*—Various, uncertain, foolish. What a terrible instance have we of this in the writings of Lucretius! What *vain reasonings*, and how *dark* a heart, amidst so pompous professions of wisdom!

Verse 23. *And changed*—With the utmost folly. Here are three degrees of ungodliness and of punishment: the first is described, verses 21—24; the second, verses 25—27; the third, in the 28th and following verses. The punishment in each case is expressed by *God gave them up*. If a man will not worship God as God, he is so left to himself that he throws away his very manhood. *Reptiles*—Or creeping things; as beetles, and various kinds of serpents.

Verse 24. *Wherefore*—One punishment of sin is from the very nature of it, as verse 27; another, as here, is from vindictive justice. *Uncleanness*—Ungodliness and uncleanness are frequently joined, 1 Thess. iv. 5 as are the knowledge of God and purity. *God gave them up*—By withdrawing his restraining grace.

Verse 25. *Who changed the truth*—The true worship of God. *Into a lie*—False, abominable idolatries. *And worshipped*—Inwardly. *And served*—Outwardly.

Verse 26. *Therefore God gave them up to vile affections*—To which the heathen Romans were then abandoned to the last degree; and none more than the emperors themselves.

Verse 27. *Receiving the just recompence of their error*—Their idolatry.

other; men with men working filthiness, and receiving in
28 themselves the just recompence of their error. And as
they did not like to retain God in *their* knowledge, God gave
them up to an undiscerning mind, to do the things which
29 were not expedient; Filled with all injustice, fornication,
maliciousness, covetousness, wickedness; full of envy, mur-
30 der, contention, deceit, malignity; whisperers, Backbiters,
haters of God, violent, proud, boasters, inventors of evil
31 things, disobedient to parents, Without understanding,
covenant-breakers, without natural affection, implacable,
32 unmerciful. Who knowing the righteous judgment of God,
that they who practise such things are worthy of death, not
only do the same, but have pleasure in those that practise
them.

being punished with that unnatural lust, which was as horrible a dishonour to the body, as their idolatry was to God.

Verse 28. *God gave them up to an undiscerning mind*—Treated of, verse 32. *To do things not expedient*—Even the vilest abominations, treated of verses 29—31.

Verse 29. *Filled with all injustice*—This stands in the first place; *unmercifulness,* in the last. *Fornication*—Includes here every species of uncleanness. *Maliciousness*—The Greek word properly implies a temper which delights in hurting another, even without any advantage to itself.

Verse 30. *Whisperers*—Such as secretly defame others. *Backbiters*—Such as speak against others behind their back. *Haters of God*—That is, rebels against him, deniers of his providence, or accusers of his justice in their adversities; yea, having an inward heart-enmity to his justice and holiness. *Inventors of evil things*—Of new pleasures, new ways of gain, new arts of hurting, particularly in war.

Verse 31. *Covenant-breakers*—It is well known, the Romans, as a nation, from the very beginning of their commonwealth, never made any scruple of vacating altogether the most solemn engagement, if they did not like it, though made by their supreme magistrate, in the name of the whole people. They only gave up the general who had made it, and then supposed themselves to be at full liberty. *Without natural affection*—The custom of exposing their own new-born children to perish by cold, hunger, or wild beasts, which so generally prevailed in the heathen world, particularly among the Greeks and Romans, was an amazing instance of this; as is also that of killing their aged and helpless parents, now common among the American heathens.

Verse 32. *Not only do the same, but have pleasure in those that practise them*—This is the highest degree of wickedness. A man may be hurried by his passions to do the thing he hates; but he that has pleasure in those that do evil, loves wickedness for wickedness' sake. And hereby he encourages them in sin, and heaps the guilt of others upon his own head.

CHAPTER II

CHAP. II. 1 Therefore thou art inexcusable, O man
whosoever thou art that judgest; for in that thou judgest
the other, thou condemnest thyself; for thou that judgest
2 practisest the same things. For we know that the judgment
of God is according to truth against them who practise such
3 things. And thinkest thou this, O man, who judgest them
that practise such things, and doest the same, that thou shalt
4 escape the judgment of God? Or despisest thou the riches
of his goodness and forbearance and longsuffering; not knowing that the goodness of God leadeth thee to repentance?
5 But after thy hardness and impenitent heart treasurest up to
thyself wrath in the day of wrath and revelation and righte-
6 ous judgment of God; Who will * render to every one

* Prov. xxiv. 12.

Verse 1. *Therefore*—The apostle now makes a transition from the gentiles to the Jews, till, at verse 6, he comprises both. *Thou art inexcusable*—Seeing knowledge without practice only increases guilt. *O man*—Having before spoken of the gentile in the third person, he addresses the Jew in the second person. But he calls him by a common appellation, as not acknowledging him to be a Jew. (See verses 17, 28.) *Whosoever thou art that judgest*—Censurest, condemnest. *For in that thou judgest the other*—The heathen. *Thou condemnest thyself; for thou doest the same things*—In effect; in many instances.

Verse 2. *For we know*—Without thy teaching *That the judgment of God*—Not thine, who exceptest thyself from its sentence. *Is according to truth*—Is just, making no exception, verses 5, 6, 11; and reaches the heart as well as the life, verse 16.

Verse 3. *That thou shalt escape*—Rather than the gentile.

Verse 4. *Or despisest thou*—Dost thou go farther still,—from hoping to escape his wrath, to the abuse of his love? *The riches*—The abundance. *Of his goodness, forbearance, and longsuffering*—Seeing thou both hast sinned, dost sin, and wilt sin. All these are afterwards comprised in the single word *goodness*. *Leadeth thee*—That is, is designed of God to lead or encourage thee to it.

Verse 5. *Treasurest up wrath*—Although thou thinkest thou art treasuring up all good things. O what a treasure may a man lay up either way, in this short day of life! *To thyself*—Not to him whom thou judgest. *In the day of wrath, and revelation, and righteous judgment of God*—Just opposite to "the goodness and forbearance and longsuffering" of God. When God shall be *revealed,* then shall also be "revealed" the secrets of men's hearts, verse 16. *Forbearance* and *revelation* respect God, and are opposed to each other; *longsuffering* and *righteous judgment* respect the sinner; *goodness* and *wrath* are words of a more general import.

7 according to his works: To them that by patient continuance
in well-doing seek for glory and honour and immortality,
8 eternal life: But to them that are contentious, and do not
obey the truth, but obey unrighteousness, *shall be* indigna-
9 tion and wrath, Tribulation and anguish, *even* upon every
soul of man who worketh evil, of the Jew first, and also the
10 gentile; But glory, and honour, and peace, *shall be* to every
one who worketh good, to the Jew first, and also to the
gentile.
11 For there is no respect of persons with God. For as
12 many as have sinned without the law shall also perish without the law: and as many as have sinned under the law
13 shall be judged by the law; For not the hearers of the law

Verse 7. *To them that seek for glory*—For pure love does not exclude faith, hope, desire, 1 Cor. xv. 58.

Verse 8. *But to them that are contentious*—Like thee, O Jew, who thus fightest against God. The character of a false Jew is disobedience, stubbornness, impatience. *Indignation and wrath, tribulation and anguish*—Alluding to Psalm lxxviii. 49: "He cast upon them," the Egyptians, "the fierceness of his anger, wrath, and indignation, and trouble;" and finely intimating, that the Jews would in the day of vengeance be more severely punished than even the Egyptians were when God made their plagues so wonderful.

Verse 9. *Of the Jew first*—Here we have the first express mention of the Jews in this chapter. And it is introduced with great propriety. Their having been trained up in the true religion, and having had Christ and his apostles first sent to them, will place them in the foremost rank of the criminals that obey not the truth.

Verse 10. *But glory*—Just opposite to "wrath," from the divine approbation. *Honour*—Opposite to "indignation," by the divine appointment; and *peace* now and for ever, opposed to tribulation and anguish.

Verse 11. *For there is no respect of persons with God*—He will reward every one according to his works. But this is well consistent with his distributing advantages and opportunities of improvement, according to his own good pleasure.

Verse 12. *For as many as have sinned*—He speaks as of the time past, for all time will be past at the day of judgment. *Without the law*—Without having any written law. *Shall also perish without the law*—Without regard had to any outward law; being condemned by the law written in their hearts. The word *also* shows the agreement of the manner of sinning, with the manner of suffering. *Perish*—He could not so properly say, *Shall be judged* without the law.

Verse 13. *For not the hearers of the law are,* even now, *just before God, but the doers of the law shall be justified*—Finally acquitted and rewarded a most sure and important truth, which respects the gentiles also, though

are just with God, but the doers of the law shall be justified.
14 For when the gentiles, who have not the law, do by nature
the things contained in the law, these, not having the law,
15 are a law to themselves: Who show the work of the law
written upon their hearts, their conscience also bearing
witness, and their thoughts among themselves accusing or
16 even defending *them;* In the day when God will judge the
secrets of men by Christ Jesus according to my gospel.
17 But if thou art called a Jew, and restest in the law, and

principally the Jews. St. Paul speaks of the former, verses 14, &c.; of the latter, verses 17, &c. Here is therefore no parenthesis; for the sixteenth verse also depends on the fifteenth, not on the twelfth.

Verse 14. *For when the gentiles*—That is, any of them. St. Paul, having refuted the perverse judgment of the Jews concerning the heathens, proceeds to show the just judgment of God against them. He now speaks directly of the heathens, in order to convince the heathens. Yet the concession he makes to these serves more strongly to convince the Jews. *Do by nature*—That is, without an outward rule; though this also, strictly speaking, is by preventing grace. *The things contained in the law*—The ten commandments being only the substance of the law of nature *These, not having the* written *law, are a law unto themselves*—That is, what the law is to the Jews, they are, by the grace of God, to themselves; namely, a rule of life.

Verse 15. *Who show*—To themselves, to other men, and, in a sense, to God himself. *The work of the law*—The substance, though not the letter, of it. *Written on their hearts*—By the same hand which wrote the commandments on the tables of stone. *Their conscience*—There is none of all its faculties which the soul has less in its power than this. *Bearing witness*—In a trial there are the plaintiff, the defendant, and the witnesses. Conscience and sin itself are witnesses against the heathens. *Their thoughts* sometimes excuse, sometimes condemn, them. *Among themselves*—Alternately, like plaintiff and defendant. *Accusing or even defending them*—The very manner of speaking shows that they have far more room to accuse than to defend.

Verse 16. *In the day*—That is, who show this in the day. Everything will then be shown to be what it really is. In that day will appear the law written in their hearts, as it often does in the present life. *When God shall judge the secrets of men*—On secret circumstances depends the real quality of actions, frequently unknown to the actors themselves, verse 29. Men generally form their judgments, even of themselves merely from what is apparent. *According to my gospel*—According to the tenor of that gospel which is committed to my care. Hence it appears that the gospel also is a law.

Verse 17. *But if thou art called a Jew*—This highest point of Jewish glorying, after a farther description of it interposed, verses 17—20, and refuted, verses 21--24, is itself refuted, verses 25, &c. The description

18 gloriest in God, And knowest *his* will, and discernest the
19 things that differ, being instructed out of the law ; And art
confident that thyself art a guide to the blind, a light
20 of them that are in darkness, An instructer of the ignorant,
a teacher of babes, having the form of knowledge and truth
21 in the law. Thou that teachest another, dost not teach
thyself; thou that proclaimest a man should not steal, dost
22 steal; Thou that sayest a man should not commit adultery,
dost commit adultery ; thou that abhorrest idols, committest
23 sacrilege; Thou that gloriest in the law, by transgress-
24 ing the law dishonourest God. For the name of God
is blasphemed among the gentiles through you,* as it
25 written. Circumcision indeed profiteth, if thou keepest

* Isaiah lii. 5

consists of twice five articles; of which the former five, verses 17, 18, show what he boasts of in himself; the other five, verses 19, 20, what he glories in with respect to others. The first particular of the former five answers to the first of the latter; the second, to the second, and so on. *And restest in the law*—Dependest on it, though it can only condemn thee. *And gloriest in God*—As thy God; and that, too, to the exclusion of others.

Verse 19. *Blind, in darkness, ignorant, babes*—These were the titles which the Jews generally gave the gentiles.

Verse 20. *Having the form of knowledge and truth*—That is, the most accurate knowledge of the truth.

Verse 21. *Thou dost not teach thyself*—He does not teach himself who does not practise what he teaches. *Dost thou steal, commit adultery, commit sacrilege*—Sin grievously against thy neighbour, thyself, God. St. Paul had shown the gentiles, first their sins against God, then against themselves, then against their neighbours. He now inverts the order: for sins against God are the most glaring in an heathen, but not in a Jew. *Thou that abhorrest idols*—Which all the Jews did, from the time of the Babylonish captivity. *Thou committest sacrilege*—Doest what is worse, robbing Him "who is God over all" of the glory which is due to him.

None of these charges were rashly advanced against the Jews of that age; for, as their own historian relates, some even of the priests lived by rapine, and others in gross uncleanness. And as for sacrilegiously robbing God and his altar, it had been complained of ever since Malachi; so that the instances are given with great propriety and judgment.

Verse 25. *Circumcision indeed profiteth*—He does not say, justifies. How far it profited is shown in the third and fourth chapters. *Thy circumcision is become uncircumcision*—Is so already in effect. Thou wilt have no more benefit by it than if thou hadst never received it. The very same observation holds with regard to baptism

the law: but if thou art a transgressor of the law, thy cir-
26 cumcision is become uncircumcision. Therefore if the
uncircumcision keep the righteousness of the law, shall not
27 his uncircumcision be counted for circumcision? Yea, the
uncircumcision that is by nature, fulfilling the law, shall
judge thee, who by the letter and circumcision transgressest
28 the law. For he is not a Jew, who is an outward Jew,
neither *is that* circumcision, which is apparent in the flesh:
29 But he *is* a Jew, who is one inwardly; and circumcision *is*
that of the heart, in the spirit, not in the letter: whose
III. 1 praise is not from men, but from God. What then *is*
the advantage of the Jew? or what the profit of the circum-
2 cision? Much every way: chiefly in that they were intrusted
3 with the oracles of God. For what if some believed not?
4 shall their unbelief disannul the faithfulness of God? God

Verse 26. *If the uncircumcision*—That is, a person uncircumcised. *Keep the law*—Walk agreeably to it. *Shall not his uncircumcision be counted for circumcision*—In the sight of God?

Verse 27. *Yea, the uncircumcision that is by nature*—Those who are, literally speaking, uncircumcised. *Fulfilling the law*—As to the substance of it. *Shall judge thee*—Shall condemn thee in that day. *Who by the letter and circumcision*—Who having the bare, literal, external circumcision, *transgressest the law.*

Verse 28. *For he is not a Jew*—In the most important sense, that is, one of God's beloved people. *Who is one in outward* show only; *neither is that* the true, acceptable *circumcision, which is apparent in the flesh.*

Verse 29. *But he is a Jew*—That is, one of God's people. *Who is one inwardly*—In the secret recesses of his soul. *And* the acceptable *circumcision is that of the heart*—Referring to Deut. xxx. 6; the putting away all inward impurity. This is seated *in the spirit,* the inmost soul, renewed by the Spirit of God. *And not in the letter*—Not in the external ceremony. *Whose praise is not from men, but from God*—The only searcher of the heart.

Verse 1. *What then,* may some say, *is the advantage of the Jew, or of the circumcision*—That is, those that are circumcised, above the gentiles?

Verse 2. *Chiefly in that they were intrusted with the oracles of God*—The scriptures, in which are so great and precious promises. Other prerogatives will follow, Romans ix. 4, 5. St. Paul here singles out this by which, after removing the objection, he will convict them so much the more.

Verse 3. *Shall their unbelief disannul the faithfulness of God*—Will he not still make good his promises to them that do believe?

forbid: let God be true, and every man a liar; as it is written, * That thou mightest be justified in thy saying, and
mightest overcome when thou art judged. But if our
unrighteousness commend the righteousness of God, what
shall we say? *Is* not God unjust who taketh vengeance?
6 (I speak as a man) God forbid: otherwise how should God
7 judge the world? But if the truth of God hath abounded
to his glory through my lie; why am I still judged as a sin-
8 ner? And why may we not (as we are slandered, and as
some affirm us to say) do evil, that good may come? whose
condemnation is just.
9 What then? are we better *than they?* In nowise: for
we have before proved all, both Jews and gentiles, to be
10 under sin; As it is written, † There is none righteous, no,

* Psalm li. 4 † Psalm xiv. 1, &c.

Verse 5. *But*, it may be farther objected, *if our unrighteousness* be subservient to God's glory, is it not unjust in him to punish us for it? *I speak as a man*—As human weakness would be apt to speak.

Verse 6. *God forbid*—By no means. If it were unjust in God to punish that unrighteousness which is subservient to his own glory, *how should God judge the world*—Since all the unrighteousness in the world will then *commend the righteousness of God.*

Verse 7. *But,* may the objector reply, *if the truth of God hath abounded*—Has been more abundantly shown. *Through my lie*—If *my lie*, that is, practice contrary to truth, conduces to the glory of God, by making his truth shine with superior advantage. *Why am I still judged as a sinner*—Can this be said to be any sin at all? Ought I not to do what would otherwise be evil, that so much "good may come?" To this the apostle does not deign to give a direct answer, but cuts the objector short with a severe reproof.

Verse 8. *Whose condemnation is just*—The condemnation of all who either speak or act in this manner. So the apostle absolutely denies the lawfulness of "doing evil," any evil, "that good may come."

Verse 9. *What then*—Here he resumes what he said, verse 1. *Under sin*—Under the guilt and power of it: the Jews, by transgressing the written law; the gentiles, by transgressing the law of nature.

Verse 10. *As it is written*—That all men are under sin appears from the vices which have raged in all ages. St. Paul therefore rightly cites David and Isaiah, though they spoke primarily of their own age, and expressed what manner of men God sees, when he "looks down from heaven;" not what he makes them by his grace. *There is none righteous*—This is the general proposition. The particulars follow: their dispositions and designs, verses 11, 12; their discourse, verses 13, 14; their actions, verses 16—18.

11 **not one**: There is none that understandeth, there is none
12 that seeketh after God. They have all turned aside. they
are together become unprofitable; there is none that doeth
13 good, no, not one. * Their throat *is* an open sepulchre;
with their tongues they have used deceit; the † poison of asps
14 *is* under their lips. ‡ Whose mouth is full of cursing and
15 bitterness: || Their feet *are* swift to shed blood: Destruc-
16 tion and misery are in their ways: And they have not known
17 the way of peace: § The fear of God is not before their
18 eyes. Now we know that whatsoever the law saith, it saith
19 to them that are under the law: that every mouth may be
stopped, and all the world become guilty before God.
20 Therefore no flesh shall be justified in his sight by the
works of the law: for by the law is the knowledge of sin.

* Psalm v. 9. † Psalm cxl. 3. ‡ Psalm x. 7. || Isaiah lix. 7, 8.
§ Psalm xxxvi. 1.

Verse 11. *There is none that understandeth*—The things of God.

Verse 12. *They have all turned aside*—From the good way. *They are become unprofitable*—Helpless, impotent, unable to profit either themselves or others.

Verse 13. *Their throat*—Is noisome and dangerous as *an open sepulchre*. Observe the progress of evil discourse, proceeding out of the heart, through the throat, tongue, lips, till the whole mouth is filled therewith. *The poison of asps*—Infectious, deadly backbiting, tale-bearing, evil-speaking, *is under* (for honey is *on*) *their lips*. An asp is a venomous kind of serpent.

Verse 14. *Cursing*—Against God. *Bitterness*—Against their neighbour

Verse 17. *Of peace*—Which can only spring from righteousness.

Verse 18. *The fear of God is not before their eyes*—Much less is the love of God in their heart.

Verse 19. *Whatsoever the law*—The Old Testament. *Saith, it saith to them that are under the law*—That is, to those who own its authority; to the Jews, and not the gentiles. St. Paul quoted no scripture against them, but pleaded with them only from the light of nature. *Every mouth*—Full of bitterness, verse 14, and yet of boasting, verse 27. *May become guilty*—May be fully convicted, and apparently liable to most just condemnation. These things were written of old, and were quoted by St. Paul, not to *make* men criminal, but to *prove* them so.

Verse 20. *No flesh shall be justified*—None shall be forgiven and accepted of God. *By the works of the law*—On this ground, that he hath kept the law. St. Paul means chiefly the moral part of it, verses 9, 19, ii. 21, &c., 26, which alone is not abolished, verse 31. And it is not without reason, that he so often mentions the works of the law, whether ceremonial or moral; for it was on these only the Jews relied, being

21 But now the righteousness of God is manifested without
22 the law, being attested by the Law and the Prophets; Even
the righteousness of God, by the faith of Jesus Christ, to
23 all and upon all that believe: for there is no difference: For
all have sinned, and are fallen short of the glory of God;
24 And are justified freely by his grace through the redemption
25 which is in Christ Jesus: Whom God hath set forth a propitiation through faith in his blood, for a demonstration
of his righteousness by the remission of past sins, through
26 the forbearance of God: For a demonstration, *I say*, of his

wholly ignorant of those that spring from faith. *For by the law is* only *the knowledge of sin*—But no deliverance either from the guilt or power of it.

Verse 21. *But now the righteousness of God*—That is, the manner of becoming righteous which God hath appointed. *Without the law*—Without that previous obedience which the law requires; without reference to the law, or dependence on it. *Is manifested*—In the gospel. *Being attested by the Law* itself, *and* by *the Prophets*—By all the promises in the Old Testament.

Verse 22. *To all*—The Jews. *And upon all*—The gentiles. *That believe: for there is no difference*—Either as to the need of justification, or the manner of it.

Verse 23. *For all have sinned*—In Adam, and in their own persons; by a sinful nature, sinful tempers, and sinful actions. *And are fallen short of the glory of God*—The supreme end of man; short of his image on earth, and the enjoyment of him in heaven.

Verse 24. *And are justified*—Pardoned and accepted. *Freely*—Without any merit of their own. *By his grace*—Not their own righteousness or works. *Through the redemption*—The price Christ has paid. *Freely by his grace*—One of these expressions might have served to convey the apostle's meaning; but he doubles his assertion, in order to give us the fullest conviction of the truth, and to impress us with a sense of its peculiar importance. It is not possible to find words that should more absolutely exclude all consideration of our own works and obedience, or more emphatically ascribe the whole of our justification to free, unmerited goodness.

Verse 25. *Whom God hath set forth*—Before angels and men. *A propitiation*—To appease an offended God. But if, as some teach, God never was offended, there was no need of this propitiation. And, if so, Christ died in vain. *To declare his righteousness*—To demonstrate not only his clemency, but his justice; even that vindictive justice whose essential character and principal office is, to punish sin. *By the remission of past sins*—All the sins antecedent to their believing.

Verse 26. *For a demonstration of his righteousness*—Both of his justice and mercy. *That he might be just*—Showing his justice on his own Son. *And yet the* merciful *justifier of* every one *that believeth in Jesus* *That he*

righteousness in this present time: that he might be just,
and yet the justifier of him that believeth in Jesus.
27 Where *is* boasting then? It is excluded. By what law?
28 of works? Nay: but by the law of faith. We conclude
then that a man is justified by faith without the works of the
29 law. *Is* God *the God* of the Jews only, and not also of the
30 gentiles? Surely of the gentiles also: Seeing *it is* one God,
who will justify the circumcision by faith, and the uncir-
31 cumcision through *the same* faith. Do we then make void
the law through faith? God forbid: yea, we establish the law.

CHAP. IV. 1 What shall we say then? that our father
2 Abraham hath found according to the flesh? If Abraham

might be just—Might evidence himself to be strictly and inviolably righteous in the administration of his government, even while he is the merciful *justifier of* the sinner *that believeth in Jesus.* The attribute of justice must be preserved inviolate; and inviolate it is preserved, if there was a real infliction of punishment on our Saviour. On this plan all the attributes harmonize; every attribute is glorified, and not one superseded, no, nor so much as clouded.

Verse 27. *Where is* the *boasting then* of the Jew against the gentile? *It is excluded. By what law? of works? Nay*—This would have left room for boasting. *But by the law of faith*—Since this requires all, without distinction, to apply as guilty and helpless sinners, to the free mercy of God in Christ. *The law of faith* is that divine constitution which makes faith, not works, the condition of acceptance.

Verse 28. *We conclude then that a man is justified by faith*—And even by this, not as it is a work, but as it receives Christ; and, consequently, has something essentially different from all our works whatsoever.

Verse 29. *Surely of the gentiles also*—As both nature and the scriptures show.

Verse 30. *Seeing it is one God who*—Shows mercy to both, and by the very same means.

Verse 31. *We establish the law*—Both the authority, purity, and the end of it; by defending that which the law attests; by pointing out Christ, the end of it; and by showing how it may be fulfilled in its purity.

Chapter iv. Having proved it by argument, he now proves by example, and such example as must have greater weight with the Jews than any other. 1. That justification is by faith: 2. That it is free for the gentiles.

Verse 1. *That our father Abraham hath found*—Acceptance with God *According to the flesh*—That is, by works.

Verse 2. The meaning is, If Abraham had been justified by works, he

was justified by works, he hath whereof to glory; but *he*
3 *hath* not in the sight of God. For what saith the scripture?
* Abraham believed God, and it was imputed to him for
4 righteousness. Now to him that worketh, the reward is not
5 reckoned of grace, but of debt. But to him that worketh
not, but believeth on him that justifieth the ungodly, his
6 faith is imputed to him for righteousness. So David also

* Gen. xv. 6.

would have had room to glory. But he had not room to glory. Therefore he was not justified by works.

Verse 3. *Abraham believed God*—That promise of God concerning the numerousness of his seed, Gen. xv. 5, 7; but especially the promise concerning Christ, Gen. xii. 3, through whom all nations should be blessed. *And it was imputed to him for righteousness*—God accepted him as if he had been altogether righteous.

Verse 4. *Now to him that worketh*—All that the law requires, the reward is no favour, but an absolute debt.

These two examples are selected and applied with the utmost judgment and propriety. Abraham was the most illustrious pattern of piety among the Jewish patriarchs. David was the most eminent of their kings. If then neither of these was justified by his own obedience, if they both obtained acceptance with God, not as upright beings who might claim it, but as sinful creatures who must implore it, the consequence is glaring It is such as must strike every attentive understanding, and must affect every individual person.

Verse 5. *But to him that worketh not*—It being impossible he should without faith. *But believeth, his faith is imputed to him for righteousness*—Therefore God's affirming of Abraham, that faith was imputed to him for righteousness, plainly shows that he worked not; or, in other words, that he was not justified by works, but by faith only. Hence we see plainly how groundless that opinion is, that holiness or sanctification is previous to our justification. For the sinner, being first convinced of his sin and danger by the Spirit of God, stands trembling before the awful tribunal of divine justice; and has nothing to plead, but his own guilt, and the merits of a Mediator. Christ here interposes; justice is satisfied; the sin is remitted, and pardon is applied to the soul, by a divine faith wrought by the Holy Ghost, who then begins the great work of inward sanctification. Thus God justifies the ungodly, and yet remains just, and true to all his attributes! But let none hence presume to "continue in sin;" for to the impenitent, God "is a consuming fire." *On him that justifieth the ungodly*—If a man could possibly be made holy before he was justified, it would entirely set his justification aside; seeing he could not, in the very nature of the thing, be justified if he were not, at that very time, ungodly.

Verse 6. *So David also*—David is fitly introduced after Abraham, because he also received and delivered down the promise. *Affirmeth*—A

affirmeth the happiness of the man, to whom God imputeth
7 righteousness without works, * Happy *are* they whose iniqui-
8 ties are forgiven, and whose sins are covered. Happy *is*
9 the man to whom the Lord will not impute sin. *Cometh*
this happiness then on the circumcision *only*, or on the
uncircumcision also? for we say that faith was imputed to
10 Abraham for righteousness. How was it then imputed?
when he was in circumcision, or in uncircumcision? Not in
11 circumcision, but in uncircumcision. And he received the
sign of circumcision, a seal of the righteousness of the faith
which *he had* in uncircumcision: that he might be the
father of all who believe in uncircumcision; that righteous-
12 ness may be imputed to them also: And the father of the

* Psalm xxxii. 1, 2.

man is justified by faith alone, and not by works. *Without works*—That is, without regard to any former good works supposed to have been done by him.

Verse 7. *Happy are they whose sins are covered*—With the veil of divine mercy. If there be indeed such a thing as happiness on earth, it is the portion of that man *whose iniquities are forgiven*, and who enjoys the manifestation of that pardon. Well may he endure all the afflictions of life with cheerfulness, and look upon death with comfort. O let us not contend against it, but earnestly pray that this happiness may be ours!

Verse 9. *This happiness*—Mentioned by Abraham and David. *On the circumcision*—Those that are circumcised only. *Faith was imputed to Abraham for righteousness*—This is fully consistent with our being justified, that is, pardoned and accepted by God upon our believing, for the sake of what Christ hath done and suffered. For though this, and this alone, be the meritorious cause of our acceptance with God, yet faith may be said to be "imputed to us for righteousness," as it is the sole condition of our acceptance. We may observe here, forgiveness, not imputing sin, and imputing righteousness, are all one.

Verse 10. *Not in circumcision*—Not after he was circumcised; for he was justified before Ishmael was born, Gen. xv.; but he was not circumcised till Ishmael was thirteen years old, xvii. 25.

Verse 11. *And*—After he was justified. *He received the sign of circumcision*—Circumcision, which was a sign or token of his being in covenant with God. *A seal*—An assurance on God's part, that he accounted him righteous, upon his believing, before he was circumcised. *Who believe in uncircumcision*—That is, though they are not circumcised.

Verse 12. *And the father of the circumcision*—Of those who are circumcised, and believe as Abraham did. To those who believe not, Abraham is not a father, neither are they his seed.

circumcision to them who not only are of the circumcision,
but also walk in the footsteps of that faith of our father
13 Abraham, which he had in uncircumcision. For the promise, that he should be the heir of the world, *was* not to
Abraham, or to his seed, by the law, but by the righteous-
14 ness of faith. For if they who are of the law *are* heirs, faith
15 is made void, and the promise of no effect: Because the law
worketh wrath: for where no law is, *there is* no transgres-
16 sion. Therefore *it is* of faith, that *it might be* of grace;
that the promise might be firm to all the seed; not only to
that which is of the law, but to that also which is of the faith
17 of Abraham; who is the father of us all, (As it is written,
* I have appointed thee a father of many nations,) before
God in whom he believed, as quickening the dead, and call-
18 ing the things that are not as though they were. Who

* Gen. xvii. 5.

Verse 13. *The promise, that he should be the heir of the world*—Is the same as that he should be "the father of all nations," namely, of those in all nations who receive the blessing. The whole world was promised to him and them conjointly. Christ is the heir of the world, and of all things; and so are all Abraham's seed, all that believe in him with the faith of Abraham.

Verse 14. *If they* only *who are of the law*—Who have kept the whole law. *Are heirs, faith is made void*—No blessing being to be obtained by it; *and* so *the promise* is *of no effect*.

Verse 15. *Because the law*—Considered apart from that grace, which though it was in fact mingled with it, yet is no part of the legal dispensation, is so difficult, and we so weak and sinful, that, instead of bringing us a blessing, it only *worketh wrath;* it becomes to us an occasion of wrath, and exposes us to punishment as transgressors. *Where there is no law* in force, there can be *no transgression* of it.

Verse 16. *Therefore it*—The blessing. *Is of faith, that it might be of grace*—That it might appear to flow from the free love of God, and *that the promise might be firm,* sure, and effectual, *to all the* spiritual *seed of Abraham;* not only Jews, but gentiles also, if they follow his faith.

Verse 17. *Before God*—Though before men nothing of this appeared, those nations being then unborn. *As quickening the dead*—The dead are not dead to him; and even the things that are not, are before God. *And calling the things that are not*—Summoning them to rise into being, and appear before him. The seed of Abraham did not then exist; yet God said, "So shall thy seed be." A man can say to his servant actually existing, Do this; and he doeth it: but God saith to the light, while it does not exist, Go forth; and it goeth.

Verses 18--21 The Apostle shows the power and excellence of that

against hope believed in hope, that he should be the father
of many nations, according to that which was spoken, * So
19 shall thy seed be. And not being weak in faith, he considered not his own body now dead, being about an hundred
20 years old, nor the deadness of Sarah's womb: He staggered
not at the promise of God through unbelief; but was
21 strengthened in faith, giving glory to God; And being fully
assured that, what he had promised, he was able also to
22 perform. And therefore it was imputed to him for righte-
23 ousness. Now it was not written on his account only, that
24 it was imputed unto him; But on ours also, to whom it will
be imputed, if we believe on him who raised up Jesus our
25 Lord from the dead; Who was delivered for our offences,
and was raised for our justification.

CHAP. V. 1 Therefore being justified by faith, we have

* Gen. xv. 5.

faith to which he ascribes justification. *Who against hope*—Against all probability, believed and hoped in the promise. The same thing is apprehended both by faith and hope; by faith, as a thing which God has spoken; by hope, as a good thing which God has promised to us. *So shall thy seed be*—Both natural and spiritual, as the stars of heaven for multitude.

Verse 20. *Giving God* the *glory* of his truth and power.

Verse 23. *On his account only*—To do personal honour to him.

Verse 24. *But on ours also*—To establish us in seeking justification by faith, and not by works; and to afford a full answer to those who say that, "to be justified by works means only, by Judaism; to be justified by faith means, by embracing Christianity, that is, the system of doctrines so called." Sure it is that Abraham could not in this sense be justified either by faith or by works; and equally sure that David (taking the words thus) was justified by works, and not by faith. *Who raised up Jesus from the dead*—As he did in a manner both Abraham and Sarah. *If we believe on him who raised up Jesus*—God the Father therefore is the proper object of justifying faith. It is observable, that St. Paul here, in speaking both of our faith and of the faith of Abraham, puts a part for the whole. And he mentions that part, with regard to Abraham, which would naturally affect the Jews most.

Verse 25. *Who was delivered*—To death. *For our offences*—As an atonement for them. *And raised for our justification*—To empower us to receive that atonement by faith.

Verse 1. *Being justified by faith*—This is the sum of the preceding chapters. *We have peace with God*—Being enemies to God no longer,

2 peace with God through our Lord Jesus Christ: By whom
also we have had access through faith into this grace wherein
3 we stand, and rejoice in hope of the glory of God. And not
only *so*, but we glory in tribulations also: knowing that tri-
4 bulation worketh patience; And patience, experience; and
5 experience, hope: And hope shameth us not; because the
love of God is shed abroad in our hearts by the Holy Ghost
6 which is given unto us. For when we were yet without
7 strength, in due time Christ died for the ungodly. Now onc
will scarce die for a just man: yet perhaps for the good man
8 one would even dare to die. But God recommendeth his

verse 10; neither fearing his wrath, verse 9. We have peace, hope, love, and power over sin, the sum of the fifth, sixth, seventh, and eighth chapters. These are the fruits of justifying faith: where these are not, that faith is not.

Verse 2. *Into this grace*—This state of favour.

Verse 3. *We glory in tribulations also*—Which we are so far from esteeming a mark of God's displeasure, that we receive them as tokens of his fatherly love, whereby we are prepared for a more exalted happiness. The Jews objected to the persecuted state of the Christians as inconsistent with the people of the Messiah. It is therefore with great propriety that the apostle so often mentions the blessings arising from this very thing.

Verse 4. *And patience* works more *experience* of the sincerity of our grace, and of God's power and faithfulness.

Verse 5. *Hope shameth us not*—That is, gives us the highest glorying. We glory in this our hope, *because the love of God is shed abroad in our hearts*—The divine conviction of God's love to us, and that love to God which is both the earnest and the beginning of heaven. *By the Holy Ghost*—The efficient cause of all these present blessings, and the earnest of those to come.

Verse 6. How can we now doubt of God's love? *For when we were without strength*—Either to think, will, or do anything good. *In due time*—Neither too soon nor too late; but in that very point of time which the wisdom of God knew to be more proper than any other. *Christ died for the ungodly*—Not only to set them a pattern, or to procure them power to follow it. It does not appear that this expression, of dying for any one, has any other signification than that of rescuing the life of another by laying down our own.

Verse 7. *A just man*—One who gives to all what is strictly their due *The good man*—One who is eminently holy; full of love, of compassion, kindness, mildness, of every heavenly and amiable temper. *Perhaps—one—would—even—dare to die*—Every word increases the strangeness of the thing, and declares even this to be something great and unusual.

Verse 8. *But God recommendeth*—A most elegant expression. Those are wont to be recommended to us, who were before either unknown to,

love towards us, in that while we were yet sinners, Christ
9 died for us. Much more then, being now justified by his
10 blood, we shall be saved from wrath through him. For if,
being enemies, we were reconciled to God by the death of his
Son, much more, being reconciled, we shall be saved through
11 his life. And not only *so*, but we also glory in God through
our Lord Jesus Christ, by whom we have now received
the reconciliation.
12 Therefore as by one man sin entered into the world, and
death by sin; even so death passed upon all men, in that all
13 sinned: For until the law sin was in the world: but sin is

or alienated from, us. *While we were sinners*—So far from being *good*, that we were not even *just*.

Verse 9. *By his blood*—By his bloodshedding. *We shall be saved from wrath through him*—That is, from all the effects of the wrath of God. But is there then wrath in God? Is not wrath a human passion? And how can this human passion be in God? We may answer this by another question: Is not love a human passion? And how can this human passion be in God? But to answer directly: wrath in man, and so love in man, is a human passion. But wrath in God is not a human passion; nor is love, as it is in God. Therefore the inspired writers ascribe both the one and the other to God only in an analogical sense.

Verse 10. *If*—As sure as · so the word frequently signifies; particularly in this and the eighth chapter. *We shall be saved*—Sanctified and glorified. *Through his life*—Who "ever liveth to make intercession for us."

Verse 11. *And not only so, but we also glory*—The whole sentence, from the third to the eleventh verse, may be taken together thus: We not only "rejoice in hope of the glory of God," *but also* in the midst of tribulations *we glory in God* himself *through our Lord Jesus Christ, by whom we have now received the reconciliation.*

Verse 12. *Therefore*—This refers to all the preceding discourse; from which the apostle infers what follows. He does not therefore properly make a digression, but returns to speak again of sin and of righteousness. *As by one man*—Adam; who is mentioned, and not Eve, as being the representative of mankind. *Sin entered into the world*—Actual sin, and its consequence, a sinful nature. *And death*—With all its attendants. It *entered into the world* when it entered into being; for till then it did not exist. *By sin*—Therefore it could not enter before sin. *Even so*—Namely, by one man. *In that*—So the word is used also, 2 Cor. v. 4. *All sinned*—In Adam. These words assign the reason why death came upon *all men;* infants themselves not excepted, *in that all sinned.*

Verse 13. *For until the law sin was in the world*—*All*, I say, *had sinned, for sin was in the world* long before the written law; *but*, I grant, *sin is not* so much *imputed*, nor so severely punished by God, *where there*

14 not imputed where there is no law. Nevertheless death
reigned from Adam to Moses, even over them that had not
sinned after the likeness of Adam's transgression, who is the
15 figure of him that was to come. Yet not as the offence so
also *is* the free gift. For if by the offence of one many died,
much more the grace of God, and the gift by grace, that
16 of one man, Jesus Christ, hath abounded unto many. And
not as *the loss* by one that sinned, *so is* the gift: for the sentence *was* by one *offence* to condemnation, but the free gift

is no express *law* to convince men of it. Yet that all had sinned, even then, appears in that all died.

Verse 14. *Death reigned*—And how vast is his kingdom! Scarce can we find any king who has as many subjects, as are the kings whom he hath conquered. *Even over them that had not sinned after the likeness of Adam's transgression*—Even over infants who had never sinned, as Adam did, in their own persons; and over others who had not, like him, sinned against an express law. *Who is the figure of him that was to come*—Each of them being a public person, and a federal head of mankind. The one, the fountain of sin and death to mankind by his offence; the other, of righteousness and life by his free gift.

Thus far the apostle shows the agreement between the first and second Adam: afterward he shows the differences between them. The agreement may be summed up thus: As by one man sin entered into the world, and death by sin; so by one man righteousness entered into the world, and life by righteousness. As death passed upon all men, in that all had sinned; so life passed upon all men, (who are in the second Adam by faith,) in that all are justified. And as death through the sin of the first Adam *reigned even over them who had not sinned after the likeness of Adam's transgression;* so through the righteousness of Christ, even those who have not obeyed, after the likeness of his obedience, shall reign in life. We may add, As the sin of Adam, without the sins which we afterwards committed, brought us death; so the righteousness of Christ, without the good works which we afterwards perform, brings us life: although still every good, as well as evil, work, will receive its due reward.

Verse 15. *Yet not*—St. Paul now describes the difference between Adam and Christ; and that much more directly and expressly than the agreement between them. Now the fall and the free gift differ, 1. In amplitude, verse 15. 2. He from whom sin came, and He from whom the free gift came, (termed also "the gift of righteousness,") differ in power, verse 16. 3. The reason of both is subjoined, verse 17. 4. This premised, the offence and the free gift are compared, with regard to their effect, verse 18, and with regard to their cause, verse 19

Verse 16. *The sentence was by one offence to* Adam's *condemnation*—Occasioning the sentence of death to pass upon him, which, by conse-

17 *is* of many offences unto justification. For if through one
man's offence death reigned by one; they who receive the
abundance of grace and of the gift of righteousness shall
18 much more reign in life, by one, *even* Jesus Christ. As
therefore by one offence *the sentence of death came* upon all
men to condemnation; so also by one righteousness *the free*
19 *gift came* upon all men to justification of life. For as by
the disobedience of one man many were constituted sinners,
so by the obedience of one many shall be constituted righte-
20 ous. But the law came in between, that the offence might
abound. Yet where sin abounded, grace did much more
21 abound: That as sin had reigned through death, so grace
also might reign through righteousness to eternal life by
Jesus Christ our Lord.

CHAP. VI. 1 What shall we say then? We will con-

quence, overwhelmed his posterity. *But the free gift is of many offences unto justification*—Unto the purchasing it for all men, notwithstanding many offences.

Verse 17. There is a difference between grace and the gift. *Grace* is opposed to the *offence;* the *gift,* to *death,* being the gift of life.

Verse 18. *Justification of life*—Is that sentence of God, by which a sinner under sentence of death is adjudged to life.

Verse 19. *As by the disobedience of one man many* (that is, all men) *were constituted sinners*—Being then in the loins of their first parent, the common head and representative of them all. *So by the obedience of one*—By his obedience unto death; by his dying for us. *Many*—All that believe. *Shall be constituted righteous*—Justified, pardoned.

Verse 20. *The law came in between*—The offence and the free gift. *That the offence might abound*—That is, the consequence (not the design) of the law's coming in was, not the taking away of sin, but the increase of it. *Yet where sin abounded, grace did much more abound*—Not only in the remission of that sin which Adam brought on us, but of all our own; not only in remission of sins, but infusion of holiness; not only in deliverance from death, but admission to everlasting life, a far more noble and excellent life than that which we lost by Adam's fall.

Verse 21. *That as sin had reigned—so grace also might reign*—Which could not reign before the fall; before man had sinned. *Through righteousness to eternal life by Jesus Christ our Lord*—Here is pointed out the source of all our blessings, the rich and free grace of God. The meritorious cause; not any works of righteousness of man, but the alone merits of our Lord Jesus Christ. The effect or end of all; not only pardon, but life; divine life, leading to glory.

Verse 1. The apostle here sets himself more fully to vindicate his doc-

2 tinue in sin, that grace may abound? God forbid. How
shall we, who are dead to sin, live any longer therein?
3 Know ye not, that as many of us as have been baptized
4 into Jesus Christ have been baptized into his death? Therefore we are buried with him through baptism into death:
that as Christ was raised from the dead by the glory of the
5 Father, so we also should walk in newness of life. For
if we have been planted together in the likeness of his death,
6 we shall be also *in the likeness* of his resurrection: Knowing
this, that our old man is crucified with *him*, that the body
of sin might be destroyed, that we might no longer serve
7 sin. For he that is dead is freed from sin. And we believe,
8 that if we are dead with Christ, we shall also live with him:
9 Knowing that Christ being raised from the dead dieth no

trine from the consequence above suggested, Romans iii. 7, 8. He had then only in strong terms denied and renounced it: here he removes the very foundation thereof.

Verse 2. *Dead to sin*—Freed both from the guilt and from the power of it.

Verse 3. *As many as have been baptized into Jesus Christ have been baptized into his death*—In baptism we, through faith, are ingrafted into Christ; and we draw new spiritual life from this new root, through his Spirit, who fashions us like unto him, and particularly with regard to his death and resurrection.

Verse 4. *We are buried with him*—Alluding to the ancient manner of baptizing by immersion. *That as Christ was raised from the dead by the glory*—Glorious power. *Of the Father, so we also*, by the same power, should rise again; and as he lives a new life in heaven, so we *should walk in newness of life.* This, says the apostle, our very baptism represents to us.

Verse 5. *For*—Surely these two must go together; so that if we are indeed made conformable to his death, we shall also know the power of his resurrection.

Verse 6. *Our old man*—Coeval with our being, and as old as the fall; our evil nature; a strong and beautiful expression for that entire depravity and corruption which by nature spreads itself over the whole man, leaving no part uninfected. This in a believer is *crucified with Christ*, mortified, gradually killed, by virtue of our union with him. *That the body of sin*—All evil tempers, words, and actions. which are the "members" of the "old man," Col. iii. 5, *might be destroyed*

Verse 7. *For he that is dead*—With Christ. *Is freed from* the guilt of past, and from the power of present, *sin*, as dead men from the commands of their former masters.

Verse 8. *Dead with Christ*—Conformed to his death, by dying to sin

10 more; death no more hath dominion over him. For in that
he died, he died to sin once for all: but in that he liveth,
11 he liveth unto God. So reckon ye yourselves to be dead
indeed to sin, but alive to God through Jesus Christ our
12 Lord. Therefore let not sin reign in your mortal body, to
13 obey it in the desires thereof. Neither present your members to sin *as* instruments of unrighteousness: but present
yourselves to God, as alive from the dead, and your mem-
14 bers to God *as* instruments of righteousness. For sin shall
not have dominion over you: for ye are not under the law,
but under grace.

15 What then? shall we sin, because we are not under the
16 law, but under grace? God forbid. Know ye not, that to
whom ye present yourselves servants to obey, his servants
ye are whom ye obey; whether of sin unto death, or of obe-
17 dience unto righteousness? But thanks *be* to God, that,
whereas ye were the servants of sin, ye have *now* obeyed
from the heart the form of doctrine into which ye have been
18 delivered. Being then set free from sin, ye are become the

Verse 10. *He died to sin*—To atone for and abolish it. *He liveth unto God*—A glorious eternal life, such as we shall live also

Verse 12. *Let not sin reign* even *in your mortal body*—It must be subject to death, but it need not be subject to sin.

Verse 13. *Neither present your members to sin*—To corrupt nature, a mere tyrant. *But to God*—Your lawful King.

Verse 14. *Sin shall not have dominion over you*—It has neither right nor power. *For ye are not under the law*—A dispensation of terror and bondage, which only shows sin, without enabling you to conquer it. *But under grace*—Under the merciful dispensation of the gospel, which brings complete victory over it to every one who is under the powerful influences of the Spirit of Christ.

Verse 17. *The form of doctrine into which ye have been delivered*—Literally it is, *The mould into which ye have been delivered;* which, as it contains a beautiful allusion, conveys also a very instructive admonition; intimating that our minds, all pliant and ductile, should be conformed to the gospel precepts, as liquid metals take the figure of the mould into which they are cast.

Verse 18. *Being then set free from sin*—We may see the apostle's method thus far at one view:—

	Chap.	Ver.
1. Bondage to sin	iii.	9
2. The knowledge of sin by the law; a sense of God's wrath; inward death	iii.	20
3. The revelation of the righteousness of God in Christ through the gospel	iii.	21

19 servants of righteousness. I speak after the manner of men
because of the weakness of your flesh: as ye have presented
your members servants to uncleanness and iniquity unto
iniquity; so now present your members servants of righte-
20 ousness unto holiness. For when ye were the servants of sin,
21 ye were free from righteousness. What fruit had ye then
from those things whereof ye are now ashamed? for the end
22 of those things *is* death. But now being made free from
sin, and become servants to God, ye have your fruit unto
23 holiness, and the end everlasting life. For death *is* the
wages of sin; but eternal life *is* the gift of God through
VII. 1 Jesus Christ our Lord. Know ye not, brethren, (for
I speak to them that know the law,) that the law hath domi-

	Chap.	Ver.
4. The centre of all, faith, embracing that righteousness	iii.	22
5. Justification, whereby God forgives all past sin, and freely accepts the sinner	iii.	24
6. The gift of the Holy Ghost; a sense of God's love; new inward life	v.	5
	vi.	4
7. The free service of righteousness	vi.	12

Verse 19. *I speak after the manner of men*—Thus it is necessary that the scripture should let itself down to the language of men. *Because of the weakness of your flesh*—Slowness of understanding flows from the weakness of the flesh, that is, of human nature. *As ye have presented your members servants to uncleanness and iniquity unto iniquity, so now present your members servants of righteousness unto holiness*—*Iniquity* (whereof uncleanness is an eminent part) is here opposed to *righteousness;* and *unto iniquity* is the opposite of *unto holiness. Righteousness* here is a conformity to the divine will; *holiness,* to the whole divine nature. Observe, they who are *servants of righteousness* go on to *holiness;* but they who are *servants to iniquity* get no farther. Righteousness is service, because we live according to the will of another; but liberty, because of our inclination to it, and delight in it.

Verse 20. *When ye were the servants of sin, ye were free from righteousness*—In all reason, therefore, ye ought now to be free from unrighteousness; to be as uniform and zealous in serving God as ye were in serving the devil.

Verse 21. *Those things*—He speaks of them as afar off.

Verse 23. *Death*—Temporal, spiritual, and eternal. *Is the* due *wages of sin; but eternal life is the gift of God*—The difference is remarkable. Evil works merit the reward they receive: good works do not. The former demand wages: the latter accept a free gift.

Verse 1. The apostle continues the comparison between the former and the present state of a believer, and at the same time endeavours to

2 nion over a man as long as it liveth? For the married
woman is bound to *her* husband while he is alive; but if *her*
husband be dead, she is freed from the law of her husband.
3 Therefore if she marry another man while her husband
liveth, she will be called an adulteress: but if her husband
be dead, she is free from that law; so as to be no adulteress,
4 though she marry another man. Therefore, ye also, my
brethren, are become dead to the law by the body of Christ;
that ye might be married to another, *even* to him who was
raised from the dead, that we may bring forth fruit to God.
5 For when we were in the flesh, the motions of sins, which
were by the law, wrought in our members so as to bring
6 forth fruit unto death. But now we are freed from the law,
being dead unto that whereby we were held; so that we
serve in newness of spirit, and not in the oldness of the
letter.
7 What shall we say then? That the law is sin? God

wean the Jewish believers from their fondness for the Mosaic law. *I speak to them that know the law*—To the Jews chiefly here. *As long*—So long, and no longer. *As it liveth*—The law is here spoken of, by a common figure, as a person, to which, as to an husband, life and death are ascribed. But he speaks indifferently of the law being dead to us, or we to it, the sense being the same.

Verse 2. *She is freed from the law of her husband*—From that law which gave him a peculiar property in her.

Verse 4. *Thus ye also*—Are now as free from the Mosaic law as an husband is, when his wife is dead. *By the body of Christ*—Offered up; that is, by the merits of his death, that law expiring with him.

Verse 5. *When ye were in the flesh*—Carnally minded, in a state of nature; before we believed in Christ. *Our sins which were by the law*—Accidentally occasioned, or irritated thereby. *Wrought in our members*—Spread themselves all over the whole man.

Verse 6. *Being dead to that whereby we were held*—To our old husband, the law. *That we might serve in newness of spirit*—In a new, spiritual manner. *And not in the oldness of the letter*—Not in a bare literal, external way, as we did before.

Verse 7. *What shall we say then*—This is a kind of a digression, to the beginning of the next chapter, wherein the apostle, in order to show in the most lively manner the weakness and inefficacy of the law, changes the person and speaks as of himself, concerning the misery of one under the law. This St. Paul frequently does, when he is not speaking of his own person, but only assuming another character, Rom. iii. 5, 1 Cor. x. 30, iv. 6. The character here assumed is that of a man, first ignorant of the law, then under it and sincerely, but ineffectually, striving to serve

forbid. Yea, I should not have known sin, but for the law
I had not known lust, unless the law had said, Thou shalt
8 not covet. But sin, taking occasion by the commandment,
wrought in me all manner of desire. For without the law
9 sin *was* dead. And I was once alive without the law; but
when the commandment came, sin revived, and I died.
10 And the commandment, which *was intended* for life, this I
11 found unto death. For sin taking occasion by the command-
12 ment, deceived me, and by it slew me. So that the law is
holy, and the commandment holy, and just, and good.
13 Was then that which is good made death to me? God

God. To have spoken this of himself, or any true believer, would have been foreign to the whole scope of his discourse; nay, utterly contrary thereto, as well as to what is expressly asserted, Rom. viii. 2. *Is the law sin*—Sinful in itself, or a promoter of sin. *I had not known lust*—That is, evil desire. I had not known it to be a sin; nay, perhaps I should not have known that any such desire was in me: it did not appear, till it was stirred up by the prohibition.

Verse 8. *But sin*—My inbred corruption. *Taking occasion by the commandment*—Forbidding, but not subduing it, was only fretted, and *wrought in me* so much the more *all manner of* evil *desire. For* while I was *without* the knowledge of *the law, sin was dead*—Neither so apparent, nor so active; nor was I under the least apprehensions of any danger from it.

Verse 9. *And I was once alive without the law*—Without the close application of it. I had much life, wisdom, virtue, strength: so I thought. *But when the commandment*—That is, the law, a part put for the whole; but this expression particularly intimates its compulsive force, which restrains, enjoins, urges, forbids, threatens. *Came*—In its spiritual meaning, to my heart, with the power of God. *Sin revived, and I died*—My inbred sin took fire, and all my virtue and strength died away; and I then saw myself to be dead in sin, and liable to death eternal.

Vesse 10. *The commandment which was intended for life*—Doubtless it was originally intended by God as a grand means of preserving and increasing spiritual life, and leading to life everlasting.

Verse 11. *Deceived me*—While I expected life by the law, sin came upon me unawares *and slew* all my hopes.

Verse 12. *The commandment*—That is, every branch of the law. *Is holy, and just, and good*—It springs from, and partakes of, the holy nature of God; it is every way just and right in itself; it is designed wholly for the good of man.

Verse 13. *Was then that which is good made* the cause of evil *to me;* yea, of *death,* which is the greatest of evil? Not so. *But* it was *sin,* which was made death to me, inasmuch as it *wrought death in me* even *by that which is good*—By the good law. *So that sin by the commandment became exceeding sinful*—The consequence of which was, *that* inbred *sin,*

forbid. But sin, that it might appear sin, working death in
me by that which is good; so that sin might by the com-
14 mandment become exceeding sinful. We know that the law
15 is spiritual: but I am carnal, sold under sin. For that
which I do I approve not: for I do not practise what I
16 would; but what I hate, that I do. If then I do what I
17 would not, I consent to the law that *it is* good. Now then
18 it is no more I that do it, but sin that dwelleth in me. For
I know that in me, that is, in my flesh, dwelleth no good
thing: for to will is present with me; but *how* to perform
19 what is good I find not. For the good that I would I do
20 not: but the evil which I would not, that I do. Now if I
do that which I would not, it is no more I that do it, but
21 sin that dwelleth in me. I find then a law, that, when I
22 would do good, evil is present with me. For I delight in
23 the law of God after the inward man: But I see another
law in my members, warring against the law of my mind,
and captivating me to the law of sin which is in my members.

thus driving furiously in spite of the commandment, *became exceeding sinful;* the guilt thereof being greatly aggravated.

Verse 14. *I am carnal*—St. Paul, having compared together the past and present state of believers, that "in the flesh," verse 5, and that "in the spirit," verse 6, in answering two objections, (Is then the law sin? verse 7, and, Is the law death,? verse 13,) interweaves the whole process of a man reasoning, groaning, striving, and escaping from the legal to the evangelical state. This he does from verse 7, to the end of this chapter *Sold under sin*—Totally enslaved; slaves bought with money were absolutely at their master's disposal.

Verse 16. *It is good*—This single word implies all the three that were used before, verse 12, "holy, just, and good."

Verse 17. *It is no more I that* can properly be said to *do it, but* rather *sin that dwelleth in me*—That makes, as it were, another person, and tyrannizes over me.

Verse 18. *In my flesh*—The flesh here signifies the whole man as he is by nature.

Verse 21. *I find then a law*—An inward, constraining power, flowing from the dictate of corrupt nature.

Verse 22. *For I delight in the law of God*—This is more than "I consent to," verse 16. The day of liberty draws near. *The inward man*—Called the mind, verses 23 and 25.

Verse 23. *But I see another law in my members*—Another inward constraining power of evil inclinations and bodily appetites. *Warring against the law of my mind*—The dictate of my mind, which delights in the law of God. *And captivating me*—In spite of all my resistance

24 Wretched man that I am! who shall deliver me from the
25 body of this death? I thank God through Jesus Christ our
Lord. So then I myself with my mind serve the law
VIII. 1 of God; but with my flesh the law of sin. Therefore
there is now no condemnation to those that are in Christ
Jesus, who walk not after the flesh, but after the Spirit.
2 For the law of the Spirit of life in Christ Jesus hath freed
3 me from the law of sin and death. For what the law could
not do, in that it was weak through the flesh, God *hath
done:* sending his own Son in the likeness of sinful flesh
to be a sacrifice for sin, he hath condemned sin in the flesh:
4 That the righteousness of the law might be fulfilled in us,

Verse 24. *Wretched man that I am*—The struggle is now come to the height; and the man, finding there is no help in himself, begins almost unawares to pray, *Who shall deliver me?* He then seeks and looks for deliverance, till God in Christ appears to answer his question. The word which we translate *deliver,* implies *force.* And indeed without this there can be no deliverance. *The body of this death*—That is, this body of death; this mass of sin, leading to death eternal, and cleaving as close to me as my body to my soul. We may observe, the deliverance is not wrought yet.

Verse 25. *I thank God through Jesus Christ our Lord*—That is, God will deliver me through Christ. But the apostle, as his frequent manner is, beautifully interweaves his assertion with thanksgiving; the hymn of praise answering in a manner to the voice of sorrow, "Wretched man that I am!" *So then*—He here sums up the whole, and concludes what he began, verse 7. *I myself*—Or rather *that I,* the person whom I am personating, till this deliverance is wrought. *Serve the law of God with my mind*—My reason and conscience declare for God. *But with my flesh the law of sin*—But my corrupt passions and appetites still rebel. The man is now utterly weary of his bondage, and upon the brink of liberty.

Verse 1. *There is therefore now no condemnation*—Either for things present or past. Now he comes to deliverance and liberty. The apostle here resumes the thread of his discourse, which was interrupted, chap. vii. 7.

Verse 2. *The law of the Spirit*—That is, the gospel. *Hath freed me from the law of sin and death*—That is, the Mosaic dispensation.

Verse 3. *For what the law*—Of Moses. *Could not do, in that it was weak through the flesh*—Incapable of conquering our evil nature. If it could, God needed not to have sent *his own Son in the likeness of sinful flesh*—We with our sinful flesh were devoted to death. But God sending his own Son, in the likeness of that flesh, though pure from sin, *condemned* that *sin* which was *in* our *flesh;* gave sentence, that sin should be destroyed, and the believer wholly delivered from it.

Verse 4. *That the righteousness of the law*—The holiness it required,

5 who walk not after the flesh, but after the Spirit. They
that are after the flesh mind the things of the flesh; but
they that are after the Spirit the things of the Spirit.
6 Now to be carnally minded *is* death; but to be spiritually
7 minded *is* life and peace. Because to be carnally minded *is*
enmity against God: for it is not subject to the law of God,
8 neither indeed can be. So then they who are in the flesh
9 cannot please God. But ye are not in the flesh, but in the
Spirit, if the Spirit of God dwell in you. And if any man
10 have not the Spirit of Christ, he is none of his. Now
if Christ *be* in you, the body indeed *is* dead because of sin;
11 but the Spirit *is* life because of righteousness. And if the

described, verses 5—11. *Might be fulfilled in us, who walk not after the flesh, but after the Spirit*—Who are guided in all our thoughts, words, and actions, not by corrupt nature, but by the Spirit of God. From this place St. Paul describes primarily the state of believers, and that of unbelievers only to illustrate this.

Verse 5. *They that are after the flesh*—Who remain under the guidance of corrupt nature. *Mind the things of the flesh*—Have their thoughts and affections fixed on such things as gratify corrupt nature; namely, on things visible and temporal; on things of the earth, on pleasure, (of sense or imagination,) praise, or riches. *But they who are after the Spirit*—Who are under his guidance. *Mind the things of the Spirit*—Think of, relish, love things invisible, eternal; the things which the Spirit hath revealed, which he works in us, moves us to, and promises to give us.

Verse 6. *For to be carnally minded*—That is, to mind the things of the flesh. *Is death*—The sure mark of spiritual death, and the way to death everlasting. *But to be spiritually minded*—That is, to mind the things of the Spirit. *Is life*—A sure mark of spiritual life, and the way to life everlasting. *And* attended with *peace*—The peace of God, which is the foretaste of life everlasting; and peace with God, opposite to the enmity mentioned in the next verse.

Verse 7. *Enmity against God*—His existence, power, and providence

Verse 8. *They who are in the flesh*—Under the government of it.

Verse 9. *In the Spirit*—Under his government. *If any man have not the Spirit of Christ*—Dwelling and governing in him. *He is none of his*—He is not a member of Christ; not a Christian; not in a state of salvation. A plain, express declaration, which admits of no exception. He that hath ears to hear, let him hear!

Verse 10. *Now if Christ be in you*—Where the Spirit of Christ is, there is Christ. *The body indeed is dead*—Devoted to death. *Because of sin*—Heretofore committed. *But the Spirit is life*—Already truly alive. *Because of righteousness*—Now attained. From verse 13, St. Paul, having finished what he had begun, Romans vi. 1, describes purely the state of believers.

Spirit of him that raised up Jesus from the dead dwell in
you, he that raised up Christ from the dead will also quicken
your mortal bodies by his Spirit that dwelleth in you.
12 Therefore, brethren, we are not debtors to the flesh, to
13 live after the flesh. For if ye live after the flesh, ye shall
die: but if ye through the Spirit mortify the deeds of the
14 flesh, ye shall live. For as many as are led by the Spirit
15 of God, they are the sons of God. For ye have not received
the spirit of bondage again unto fear; but ye have received
16 the Spirit of adoption, whereby we cry, Abba, Father. The
same Spirit beareth witness with our spirits, that we are the
17 children of God: And if children, then heirs; heirs of God,
and joint-heirs with Christ; if we suffer with *him*, that we

Verse 12. *We are not debtors to the flesh*—We ought not to follow it.

Verse 13. *The deeds of the flesh*—Not only evil actions, but evil desires, tempers, thoughts. *If ye mortify*—Kill, destroy these. *Ye shall live*—The life of faith more abundantly here, and hereafter the life of glory.

Verse 14. *For as many as are led by the Spirit of God*—In all the ways of righteousness. *They are the sons of God*—Here St. Paul enters upon the description of those blessings which he comprises, verse 30, in the word *glorified;* though, indeed, he does not describe mere glory, but that which is still mingled with the cross. The sum is, through sufferings to glory.

Verse 15. *For ye*—Who are real Christians. *Have not received the spirit of bondage*—The Holy Ghost was not properly a spirit of bondage, even in the time of the Old Testament. Yet there was something of bondage remaining even in those who then had received the Spirit. *Again*—As the Jews did before. *We*—All and every believer. *Cry*—The word denotes a vehement speaking, with desire, confidence, constancy. *Abba, Father*—The latter word explains the former. By using both the Syriac and the Greek word, St. Paul seems to point out the joint cry both of the Jewish and gentile believers. *The spirit of bondage* here seems directly to mean, those operations of the Holy Spirit by which the soul, on its first conviction, feels itself in bondage to sin, to the world, to Satan, and obnoxious to the wrath of God. This, therefore, and *the Spirit of adoption*, are one and the same Spirit, only manifesting itself in various operations, according to the various circumstances of the persons.

Verse 16. *The same Spirit beareth witness with our spirit*—With the spirit of every true believer, by a testimony distinct from that of his own spirit, or the testimony of a good conscience. Happy they who enjoy this clear and constant!

Verse 17. *Joint heirs*—That we may know it is a great inheritance which God will give us; for he hath given a great one to his Son. *If we suffer with him*—Willingly and cheerfully, for righteousness' sake. This is a new proposition, referring to what follows.

18 may also be glorified with *him.* For I reckon that the
sufferings of the present time *are* not worthy *to be compared*
19 with the glory which shall be revealed in us. For the
earnest expectation of the creation waiteth for the revelation
20 of the sons of God. For the creation was made subject to
21 vanity, not willingly, but by him who subjected *it,* In hope
that the creation itself shall be delivered from the bondage
of corruption into the glorious liberty of the children of God.
22 For we know that the whole creation groaneth together and
23 travaileth together until now. And not only *they,* but even
we ourselves, who have the firstfruits of the Spirit, even we
ourselves groan within ourselves, waiting for the adoption,

Verse 18. *For I reckon*—This verse gives the reason why he but now mentioned sufferings and glory. When that glory "shall be revealed in us," then the sons of God will be revealed also.

Verse 19. *For the earnest expectation*—The word denotes a lively hope of something drawing near, and a vehement longing after it. *Of the creation*—Of all visible creatures, believers excepted, who are spoken of apart; each kind, according as it is capable. All these have been sufferers through sin; and to all these (the finally impenitent excepted) shall refreshment redound from the glory of the children of God. Upright heathens are by no means to be excluded from this *earnest expectation*: nay, perhaps something of it may at some times be found even in the vainest of men; who (although in the hurry of life they mistake vanity for liberty, and partly stifle, partly dissemble, their groans, yet) in their sober, quiet, sleepless, afflicted hours, pour forth many sighs in the ear of God.

Verse 20 *The creation was made subject to vanity*—Abuse, misery, and corruption. *By him who subjected it*—Namely, God, Gen. iii. 17, v. 29. Adam only made it liable to the sentence which God pronounced; yet not without hope.

Verse 21. *The creation itself shall be delivered*—Destruction is not deliverance: therefore whatsoever is destroyed, or ceases to be, is not delivered at all. Will, then, any part of the creation be destroyed? *Into the glorious liberty*—The excellent state wherein they were created.

Verse 22. *For the whole creation groaneth together*—With joint groans, as it were with one voice. *And travaileth*—Literally, *is in the pains of childbirth,* to be delivered of the burden of the curse. *Until now*—To this very hour; and so on till the time of deliverance.

Verse 23. *And even we, who have the first-fruits of the Spirit*—That is, the Spirit, who is the first-fruits of our inheritance. *The adoption*—Persons who had been privately adopted among the Romans were often brought forth into the forum, and there publicly owned as their sons by those who adopted them. So at the general resurrection, when the body itself is redeemed from death, the sons of God shall be publicly owned

24 the redemption of our body. For we are saved by hope
but hope that is seen is not hope: for what a man seeth,
25 how doth he yet hope for? But if we hope for what we see
26 not, we patiently wait for it. Likewise the Spirit also helpeth our infirmities: for we know not what we should pray
for as we ought: but the Spirit itself maketh intercession
27 for us with groanings which cannot be uttered. But he who
searcheth the hearts knoweth what *is* the mind of the Spirit,
for he maketh intercession for the saints according to God.
28 And we know that all things work together for good to
them that love God, to them that are called according to

by him in the great assembly of men and angels. *The redemption of our body*—From corruption to glory and immortality.

Verse 24. *For we are saved by hope*—Our salvation is now only in hope. We do not yet possess this full salvation.

Verse 26. *Likewise the Spirit*—Nay, not only the universe, not only the children of God, but the Spirit of God also himself, as it were, groaneth, while he *helpeth our infirmities,* or weaknesses. Our understandings are weak, particularly in the things of God; our desires are weak; our prayers are weak. *We know not*—Many times. *What we should pray for*—Much less are we able to pray for it *as we ought: but the Spirit maketh intercession for us*—In our hearts, even as Christ does in heaven. *With groanings*—The matter of which is from ourselves, but the Spirit forms them; and they are frequently inexpressible, even by the faithful themselves.

Verse 27. *But he who searcheth the hearts*—Wherein the Spirit dwells and intercedes. *Knoweth*—Though man cannot utter it. *What is the mind of the Spirit, for he maketh intercession for the saints*—Who are near to God. *According to God*—According to his will, as is worthy of God and acceptable to him.

Verse 28. *And we know*—This in general; though we do not always know particularly what to pray for. *That all things*—Ease or pain, poverty or riches, and the ten thousand changes of life. *Work together for good*—Strongly and sweetly for spiritual and eternal good. *To them that are called according to his purpose*—His gracious design of saving a lost world by the death of his Son. This is a new proposition. St. Paul, being about to recapitulate the whole blessing contained in justification, (termed "glorification," verse 30,) first goes back to the *purpose* or decree of God, which is frequently mentioned in holy writ.

To explain this (nearly in the words of an eminent writer) a little more at large:—When a man has a work of time and importance before him, he pauses, consults, and contrives; and when he has laid a plan, resolves or decrees to proceed accordingly. Having observed this in ourselves, we are ready to apply it to God also; and he, in condescension to us, has applied it to himself

29 *his* purpose. For whom he foreknew, he also predestinated
conformable to the image of his Son, that he might be the
30 firstborn among many brethren. And whom he predestinated, them he also called: and whom he called, them he
also justified: and whom he justified, them he also glorified.

The works of providence and redemption are vast and stupendous, and therefore we are apt to conceive of God as deliberating and consulting on them, and then decreeing to act according to "the counsel of his own will;" as if, long before the world was made, he had been concerting measures both as to the making and governing of it, and had then writ down his decrees, which altered not, any more than the laws of the Medes and Persians. Whereas, to take this consulting and decreeing in a literal sense, would be the same absurdity as to ascribe a real human body and human passions to the ever-blessed God.

This is only a popular representation of his infallible knowledge and unchangeable wisdom; that is, he does all things as wisely as a man can possibly do, after the deepest consultation, and as steadily pursues the most proper method as one can do who has laid a scheme beforehand. But then, though the effects be such as would argue consultation and consequent decrees in man, yet what need of a moment's consultation in Him who sees all things at one view?

Nor had God any more occasion to pause and deliberate, and lay down rules for his own conduct from all eternity, than he has now. What! was there any fear of his mistaking afterwards, if he had not beforehand prepared decrees, to direct him what he was to do? Will any man say, he was wiser before the creation than since? or had he then more leisure, that he should take that opportunity to settle his affairs, and make rules for himself, from which he was never to vary?

He has doubtless the same wisdom and all other perfections at this day which he had from eternity; and is now as capable of making decrees, or rather has no more occasion for them now than formerly: his understanding being always equally clear and bright, his wisdom equally infallible.

Verse 29. *Whom he foreknew, he also predestinated conformable to the image of his Son*—Here the apostle declares who those are whom he foreknew and predestinated to glory; namely, those who are *conformable to the image of his Son*. This is the mark of those who are foreknown and will be glorified, 2 Tim. ii. 19; Phil. iii. 10, 21.

Verse 30. *Them he*—In due time. *Called*—By his gospel and his Spirit. *And whom he called*—When obedient to the heavenly calling, Acts xxvi. 19 *He also justified*—Forgave and accepted. *And whom he justified*—Provided they "continued in his goodness," Rom. xi. 22, *he* in the end *glorified*—St. Paul does not affirm, either here or in any other part of his writings, that precisely the same number of men are called, justified, and glorified He does not deny that a believer may fall away and be cut off between his special calling and his glorification, Rom. xi. 22. Neither does he deny that many are called who never are justified. He only affirms that this is the method whereby God leads us step by step toward heaven.

31 What shall we say then to these things? If God *be* for us,
32 who *can be* against us? He that spared not his own Son,
but delivered him up for us all, how shall he not with him
33 also freely give us all things? Who shall lay anything to

He glorified—He speaks as one looking back from the goal, upon the race of faith. Indeed grace, as it is glory begun, is both an earnest and a foretaste of eternal glory.

Verse 31. *What shall we say then to these things*—Related in the third, fifth, and eighth chapters? As if he had said, We cannot go, think, or wish anything farther. *If God be for us*—Here follow four periods, one general and three particular. Each begins with glorying in the grace of God, which is followed by a question suitable to it, challenging all opponents; to all which, "I am persuaded," &c., is a general answer. The general period is, *If God be for us, who can be against us?* The first particular period, relating to the past time, is, *He that spared not his own Son, how shall he not freely give us all things?* The second, relating to the present, is, *It is God that justifieth. Who is he that condemneth?* The third, relating to the future, is, *It is Christ that died—Who shall separate us from the love of Christ?*

Verse 32. *He that*—This period contains four sentences: He *spared not his own Son;* therefore he will *freely give us all things.* He *delivered him up for us all;* therefore, none can *lay anything to our charge. Freely*—For all that follows justification is a free gift also. *All things*—Needful or profitable for us.

Verse 33. *God's elect*—The above-cited author observes, that long before the coming of Christ the heathen world revolted from the true God, and were therefore reprobated, or rejected.

But the nation of the Jews were chosen to be the people of God, and were therefore styled, "the children" or "sons of God," Deut. xiv. 1; "holy people," Deut. vii. 6; xiv. 2; "a chosen seed," Deut. iv. 37; "the elect," Isaiah xli. 8, 9; xliii. 10; "the called of God," Isaiah xlviii. 12 And these titles were given to all the nation of Israel, including both good and bad.

Now the gospel having the most strict connexion with the Books of the Old Testament, where these phrases frequently occur; and our Lord and his apostles being native Jews, and beginning to preach in the land of Israel, the language in which they preached would of course abound with the phrases of the Jewish nation. And hence it is easy to see why such of them as would not receive him were styled *reprobated.* For they no longer continued to be *the people of God;* whereas this and those other honourable titles were continued to all such Jews as embraced Christianity And the same appellations which once belonged to the Jewish nation were now given to the gentile Christians also; together with which they were invested with all the privileges of "the chosen people of God;" and nothing could cut them off from these but their own wilful apostasy.

It does not appear that even good men were ever termed *God's elect* till

34 the charge of God's elect? *It is* God that justifieth. **Who**
is he that condemneth? *It is* Christ that died, yea rather,
that is risen again, who is also at the right hand of God, who
35 likewise maketh intercession for us. Who shall separate us
from the love of Christ? shall affliction, or distress, or perse
36 cution, or hunger, or nakedness, or peril, or sword? (As it is
written, * For thy sake we are killed all the day long; we
37 are accounted as sheep for the slaughter.) Nay, in all these
things we more than conquer through him who hath loved
38 us. For I am persuaded, that neither death, nor life, nor
angels, nor principalities, nor powers, nor things present, nor

* Psalm lxiv. 22.

above two thousand years from the creation. God's *electing* or *choosing* the nation of Israel, and separating them from the other nations, who were sunk in idolatry and all wickedness, gave the first occasion to this sort of language. And as the separating the Christians from the Jews was a like event, no wonder it was expressed in like words and phrases only with this difference, the term *elect* was of old applied to all the members of the visible church; whereas in the New Testament it is applied only to the members of the invisible.

Verse 34. *Yea rather, that is risen*—Our faith should not stop at his death, but be exercised farther on his resurrection, kingdom, second coming. *Who maketh intercession for us*—Presenting there his obedience, his sufferings, his prayers, and our prayers sanctified through him.

Verse 35. *Who shall separate us from the love of Christ*—Toward us? *Shall affliction or distress*—He proceeds in order, from less troubles to greater: can any of these separate us from his protection in it; and, if he sees good, deliverance from it?

Verse 36. *All the day*—That is, every day, continually. *We are accounted*—By our enemies; by ourselves.

Verse 37. *We more than conquer*—We are not only no losers, but abundant gainers, by all these trials. This period seems to describe the full assurance of hope.

Verse 38. *I am persuaded*—This is inferred from the thirty-fourth verse, in an admirable order:—

"Neither death" shall hurt us;	For "Christ is dead:"
"Nor life;"	"is risen:"
Nor angels, nor principalities, nor powers; nor things present, nor things to come;"	"is at the right hand of God:"
"Nor height, nor depth, nor any other creature;"	"maketh intercession for us."

Neither death—Terrible as it is to natural men; a violent death in particular, verse 36. *Nor life*—With all the affliction and distress it can bring, verse 35; or a long, easy life; or all living men. *Nor angels*—Whether

39 things to come, Nor height, nor depth, nor any other creature, shall be able to separate us from the love of God, which
is in Christ Jesus our Lord.

CHAP. IX. 1 I say the truth in Christ, I lie not, my
2 conscience also bearing me witness in the Holy Ghost. That
I have great sorrow and continual anguish in my heart.

good (if it were possible they should attempt it) or bad, with all their wisdom and strength. *Nor principalities, nor powers*—Not even those of the highest rank, or the most eminent power. *Nor things present*—Which may befal us during our pilgrimage; or the whole world, till it passeth away. *Nor things to come*—Which may occur either when our time on earth is past, or when time itself is at an end, as the final judgment, the general conflagration, the everlasting fire. *Nor height, nor depth*—The former sentence respected the differences of times; this, the differences of places. How many great and various things are contained in these words, we do not, need not, cannot know yet. *The height*—In St. Paul's sublime style, is put for heaven. *The depth*—For the great abyss: that is, neither the heights, I will not say of walls, mountains, seas, but, of heaven itself, can move us; nor the abyss itself, the very thought of which might astonish the boldest creature. *Nor any creature*—Nothing beneath the Almighty; visible enemies he does not even deign to name. *Shall be able*—Either by force, verse 35; or by any legal claim, verse 33, &c. *To separate us from the love of God in Christ*—Which will surely save, protect, deliver us who believe, in, and through, and from, them all.

CHAP. IX. In this chapter St. Paul, after strongly declaring his love and esteem for them, sets himself to answer the grand objection of his countrymen; namely, that the rejection of the Jews and reception of the gentiles was contrary to the word of God. That he had not here the least thought of personal election or reprobation is manifest, 1. Because it lay quite wide of his design, which was this, to show that God's rejecting the Jews and receiving the gentiles was consistent with his word; 2. Because such a doctrine would not only have had no tendency to convince, but would have evidently tended to harden, the Jews; 3. Because when he sums up his argument in the close of the chapter, he has not one word, or the least intimation, about it.

Verse 1. *In Christ*—This seems to imply an appeal to him. *In the Holy Ghost*—Through his grace.

Verse 2. *I have great sorrow*—A high degree of spiritual sorrow and of spiritual joy may consist together, Rom. viii. 39. By declaring his sorrow for the unbelieving Jews, who excluded themselves from all the blessings he had enumerated, he shows that what he was now about to speak, he did not speak from any prejudice to them.

CHAPTER IX.

3 For I could wish that I myself were accursed from Christ
4 for my brethren, my kinsmen after the flesh: Who are
Israelites; whose *is* the adoption, and the glory, and the
covenants, and the giving of the law, and the worship
5 *of God*, and the promises; Whose *are* the fathers, and from
whom according to the flesh Christ *came*, who is over all,
6 God blessed for ever. Not as if the word of God had

Verse 3. *I could wish*—Human words cannot fully describe the motions of souls that are full of God. As if he had said, I could wish to suffer in their stead; yea, to be an anathema from Christ in their place. In how high a sense he wished this, who can tell, unless himself had been asked and had resolved the question? Certainly he did not then consider himself at all, but only others and the glory of God. The thing could not be; yet the wish was pious and solid; though with a tacit condition, if it were right and possible.

Verse 4. *Whose is the adoption*, &c.—He enumerates six prerogatives, of which the first pair respect God the Father, the second Christ, the third the Holy Ghost. *The adoption and the glory*—That is, Israel is the first-born child of God, and the God of glory is their God, Deut. iv. 7; Psalm cvi. 20. These are relative to each other. At once God is the Father of Israel, and Israel are the people of God. He speaks not here of the ark, or any corporeal thing. God himself is "the glory of his people Israel." *And the covenants, and the giving of the law*—The covenant was given long before the law. It is termed *covenants*, in the plural, because it was so often and so variously repeated, and because there were two dispositions of it, Gal. iv. 24, frequently called two covenants; the one promising, the other exhibiting the promise. *And the worship, and the promises*—The true way of worshipping God; and all the promises made to the fathers.

Verse 5. To the preceding, St. Paul now adds two more prerogatives. Theirs *are the fathers*—The patriarchs and holy men of old, yea, the Messiah himself. *Who is over all, God blessed for ever*—The original words imply the self-existent, independent Being, who was, is, and is to come. *Over all*—The supreme; as being God, and consequently *blessed for ever*. No words can more clearly express his divine, supreme majesty, and his gracious sovereignty both over Jews and gentiles.

Verse 6. *Not as if*—The Jews imagined that the word of God must fail if all their nation were not saved. This St. Paul now refutes, and proves that the word itself had foretold their falling away. *The word of God*—The promises of God to Israel. *Had fallen to the ground*—This could not be. Even now, says the apostle, some enjoy the promises; and hereafter "all Israel shall be saved." This is the sum of the ninth, tenth, and eleventh chapters. *For*—Here he enters upon the proof of it. *All are not Israel, who are of Israel*—The Jews vehemently maintained the contrary; namely, that all who were born Israelites, and they only, were the people of God. The former part of this assertion is refuted

fallen to the ground. For all *are* not Israel, who are
7 of Israel: Neither, because they are the seed of Abraham,
are they all children: but, * In Isaac shall thy seed be
8 called. That is, Not the children of the flesh *are* the
children of God: but the children of promise are counted
9 for the seed. For this *is* the word of the promise, † At this
10 time I will come, and Sarah shall have a son. And not only
this; but when Rebecca also had conceived by one man,
11 our father Isaac, *The children* being not yet born, neither
having done any good or evil, (that the purpose of God
according to election might stand, not of works, but of him
12 that called,) It was said to her, ‡ The elder shall serve the

* Gen. xxi. 12. † Gen. xviii. 10. ‡ Gen. xxv. 23.

here, the latter, verse 24, &c. The sum is, God accepts all believers, and them only; and this is no way contrary to his word. Nay, he hath declared in his word, both by types and by express testimonies, that believers are accepted as the "children of the promise," while unbelievers are rejected, though they are "children after the flesh." *All are not Israel*—Not in the favour of God. *Who are* lineally descended *of Israel.*

Verse 7 *Neither because they are* lineally *the seed of Abraham,* will it follow that *they are all children of God*—This did not hold even in Abraham's own family; and much less in his remote descendants. *But* God then said, *In Isaac shall thy seed be called*—That is, Isaac, not Ishmael, shall be called thy seed; that seed to which the promise is made.

Verse 8. *That is, Not the children,* &c.—As if he had said, This is a clear type of things to come; showing us, that in all succeeding generations, *not the children of the flesh,* the lineal descendants of Abraham, *but the children of the promise,* they to whom the promise is made, that is, believers, *are the children of God.*

Verse 9. *For this is the word of the promise*—By the power of which Isaac was conceived, and not by the power of nature. Not, Whosoever is born of thee shall be blessed, but, *At this time*—Which I now appoint. *I will come, and Sarah shall have a son*—And he shall inherit the blessing.

Verse 10. *And* that God's blessing does not belong to all the descendants of Abraham, appears *not only* by *this* instance, but by that of Esau and Jacob, who was chosen to inherit the blessing, before either of them had done *good or evil.* The apostle mentions this to show, that neither were their ancestors accepted through any merit of their own. *That the purpose of God according to election might stand*—Whose purpose was, to elect or choose the promised seed. *Not of works*—Not for any preceding merit in him he chose. *But of him that called*—Of his own good pleasure, who called to that privilege whom he saw good.

Verse 12. *The elder*—Esau. *Shall serve the younger*—Not in person, for he never did; but in his posterity. Accordingly the Edomites were often brought into subjection by the Israelites.

13 younger. As it is written, * I have loved Jacob, and hated
Esau.
14 What shall we say then? *Is there* injustice with God?
15 God forbid. For he saith to Moses,† I will have mercy on
whom I will have mercy, and I will have compassion on
16 whom I will have compassion. *It is* not therefore of him
that willeth, nor of him that runneth, but of God that
17 showeth mercy. Moreover the scripture saith to Pharaoh,

* Mal. i. 2, 3. † Exod. xxxiii. 19.

Verse 13. *As it is written*—With which word in Genesis, spoken so long before, that of Malachi agrees. *I have loved Jacob*—With a peculiar love; that is, the Israelites, the posterity of Jacob. *And I have*, comparatively, *hated Esau*—That is, the Edomites, the posterity of Esau. But observe, 1. This does not relate to the person of Jacob or Esau: 2. Nor does it relate to the eternal state either of them or their posterity Thus far the apostle has been proving his proposition, namely, that the exclusion of a great part of the seed of Abraham, yea, and of Isaac, from the special promises of God, was so far from being impossible, that, according to the scriptures themselves, it had actually happened. He now introduces and refutes an objection.

Verse 14. *Is there injustice with God*—Is it unjust in God to give Jacob the blessing rather than Esau? or to accept believers, and them only? *God forbid*—In no wise. This is well consistent with justice; for he has a right to fix the terms on which he will show mercy, according to his declaration to Moses, petitioning for all the people, after they had committed idolatry with the golden calf. *I will have mercy on whom I will have mercy*—According to the terms I myself have fixed. *And I will have compassion on whom I will have compassion*—Namely, on those only who submit to my terms, who accept of it in the way that I have appointed.

Verse 16. *It*—The blessing. *Therefore is not of him that willeth, nor of him that runneth*—It is not the effect either of the will or the works of man, but of the grace and power of God. The will of man is here opposed to the grace of God, and man's running, to the divine operation. And this general declaration respects not only Isaac and Jacob, and the Israelites in the time of Moses, but likewise all the spiritual children of Abraham, even to the end of the world.

Verse 17. *Moreover*—God has an indisputable right to reject those who will not accept the blessings on his own terms. And this he exercised in the case of Pharaoh; to whom, after many instances of stubbornness and rebellion, he said, as it is recorded in scripture, *For this very thing have I raised thee up*—That is, Unless thou repent, this will surely be the consequence of my raising thee up, making thee a great and glorious king, that *my power* will be *shown upon thee*, (as indeed it was, by overwhelming him and his army in the sea,) *and my name declared through all the earth*—As it is at this day Perhaps this may have a still farther

* For this very thing have I raised thee up, that I may
show my power in thee, and that my name may be declared
18 through all the earth. So then he hath mercy on whom he
19 willeth, and whom he willeth he hardeneth. But thou wilt
say to me, Why doth he still find fault? For who hath
20 resisted his will? Nay, but who art thou, O man, that
repliest against God? Shall the thing formed say to him
21 that formed *it*, Why hast thou made me thus? † Hath
not the potter power over the clay, out of the same mass to

* Exod. ix. 16. † Jer. xviii. 6, 7

meaning. It seems that God was resolved to show his power over the river, the insects, other animals, (with the natural causes of their health, diseases, life, and death,) over the meteors, the air, the sun, (all of which were worshipped by the Egyptians, from whom other nations learned their idolatry,) and at once over all their gods, by that terrible stroke of slaying all their priests, and their choicest victims, the firstborn of man and beast; and all this with a design, not only to deliver his people Israel, (for which a single act of omnipotence would have sufficed,) but to convince the Egyptians, that the objects of their worship were but the creatures of Jehovah, and entirely in his power, and to draw them and the neighbouring nations, who should hear of all these wonders, from their idolatry, to worship the one God. For the execution of this design, (in order to the display of the divine power over the various objects of their worship, in variety of wonderful acts, which were at the same time just punishments for their cruel oppression of the Israelites,) God was pleased to raise to the throne of an absolute monarchy, a man, not whom he had made wicked on purpose, but whom he found so, the proudest, the most daring and obstinate of all the Egyptian princes; and who, being incorrigible, well deserved to be set up in that situation, where the divine judgments fell the heaviest.

Verse 18. *So then*—That is, accordingly he does show mercy on his own terms, namely, on them that believe. *And whom he willeth*—Namely, them that believe not. *He hardeneth*—Leaves to the hardness of their hearts.

Verse 19. *Why doth he still find fault*—The particle *still* is strongly expressive of the objector's sour, morose murmuring. *For who hath resisted his will*—The word *his* likewise expresses his surliness and aversion to God, whom he does not even deign to name.

Verse 20. *Nay, but who art thou, O man*—Little, impotent, ignorant man. *That repliest against God*—That accusest God of injustice, for himself fixing the terms on which he will show mercy? *Shall the thing formed say to him that formed it, Why hast thou made me thus*—Why hast thou made me capable of honour and immortality, only by believing?

Verse 21. *Hath not the potter power over the clay*—And much more

make one vessel to honour, and another to dishonour?
22 What if God, being willing to show *his* wrath, and to make
his power known, *yet* endured with much longsuffering the
23 vessels of wrath fitted for destruction: And that he might
make known the riches of his glory on the vessels of mercy,
24 whom he had before prepared for glory, Even us, whom he

hath not God power over his creatures, to appoint *one vessel,* namely, the believer, *to honour, and another,* the unbeliever, *to dishonour?*

If we survey the right which God has over us, in a more general way, with regard to his intelligent creatures, God may be considered in two different views, as Creator, Proprietor, and Lord of all; or, as their moral Governor, and Judge.,

God, as sovereign Lord and Proprietor of all, dispenses his gifts or favours to his creatures with perfect wisdom, but by no rules or methods of proceeding that we are acquainted with. The time when we shall exist, the country where we shall live, our parents, our constitution of body and turn of mind; these, and numberless other circumstances, are doubtless ordered with perfect wisdom, but by rules that lie quite out of our sight.

But God's methods of dealing with us, as our Governor and Judge, are clearly revealed and perfectly known; namely, that he will finally reward every man according to his works: "He that believeth shall be saved, and he that believeth not shall be damned."

Therefore, though "He hath mercy on whom he willeth, and whom he willeth he hardeneth," that is, suffers to be hardened in consequence of their obstinate wickedness; yet his is not the will of an arbitrary, capricious, or tyrannical being. He wills nothing but what is infinitely wise and good; and therefore his will is a most proper rule of judgment. He will show mercy, as he hath assured us, to none but true believers, nor harden any but such as obstinately refuse his mercy.

Verse 22. *What if God, being willing*—Referring to verses 18, 19. That is, although it was now his will, because of their obstinate unbelief. *To show his wrath*—Which necessarily presupposes sin. *And to make his power known*—This is repeated from the seventeenth verse. *Yet endured*—As he did Pharaoh. *With much longsuffering*—Which should have led them to repentance. *The vessels of wrath*—Those who had moved his wrath by still rejecting his mercy. *Fitted for destruction*—By their own wilful and final impenitence. Is there any injustice in this?

Verse 23. *That he might make known*—What if by showing such longsuffering even to "the vessels of wrath," he did the more abundantly show the greatness of his glorious goodness, wisdom, and power, *on the vessels of mercy;* on those *whom he had* himself, by his grace, *prepared for glory.* Is this any injustice?

Verse 24. *Even us*—Here the apostle comes to the other proposition, of grace free for all, whether Jew or gentile. *Of the Jews*—This he treats of, verse 25. *Of the gentiles*—Treated of in the same verse.

hath called, not only of the Jews, but also of the gentiles
25 As he saith also in Hosea, * I will call them my people, who
were not my people ; and her beloved, who was not beloved.
26 † And it shall come to pass, in the place where it was said
to them, Ye *are* not my people ; there shall they be called
27 the sons of the living God. But Isaiah crieth concerning
Israel, ‡ Though the number of the children of Israel be as
28 the sand of the sea, the remnant *only* shall be saved . For
he is finishing and cutting short *his* account in righteousness : for the Lord will make a short account upon earth
29 And as Isaiah had said before, Unless the Lord of Hosts
had left us a seed, we had been as Sodom, and had been made
30 like Gomorrah. What shall we say then? That the gentiles, who followed not after righteousness, have attained to
righteousness, even the righteousness which is by faith.

* Hosea ii. 23. † Hosea i. 10. ‡ Isaiah x. 22, 23

Verse 25. *Beloved*—As a spouse. *Who* once *was not beloved*—Consequently, not unconditionally elected. This relates directly to the final restoration of the Jews.

Verse 26. *There shall they be called the sons of God*—So that they need not leave their own country and come to Judea.

Verse 27. *But Isaiah* testifies, that (as many gentiles will be accepted, so) many Jews will be rejected ; that out of all the thousands of *Israel, a remnant only shall be saved.* This was spoken originally of the few that were saved from the ravage of Sennacherib's army.

Verse 28. *For he is finishing* or *cutting short his account*—In rigorous justice, will leave but a small remnant. There will be so general a destruction, that but a small number will escape.

Verse 29. *As Isaiah had said before*—Namely, Isaiah i. 9, concerning those who were besieged in Jerusalem by Rezin and Pekah. *Unless the Lord had left us a seed*—Which denotes, 1. The present paucity : 2. The future abundance. *We had been as Sodom*—So that it is no unexampled thing for the main body of the Jewish nation to revolt from God, and perish in their sin.

Verse 30. *What shall we say then*—What is to be concluded from all that has been said but this, *That the gentiles, who followed not after righteousness*—Who a while ago had no knowledge of, no care or thought about, it. *Have attained to righteousness*—Or justification. *Even the righteousness which is by faith.* This is the first conclusion we may draw from the preceding observations. The second is, that *Israel*—The Jews Although *following after the law of righteousness*—That law which, duly used, would have led them to faith, and thereby to righteousness. *Have not attained to the law of righteousness*—To that righteousness or justification which is one great end of the law

31 But Israel, following after the law of righteousness, hath not
32 attained to the law of righteousness. Wherefore? Because
they *sought it* not by faith, but as it were by works. For
33 they stumbled at the stumblingstone; As it is written,*
Behold, I lay in Sion a stone of stumbling, and a rock of
offence: and † every one that believeth on him shall not
be ashamed.

CHAP X. 1 Brethren, the desire of my heart, and my
2 prayer to God for them is, that they may be saved. For
I bear them record, that they have a zeal for God, but
3 not according to knowledge. For they being ignorant
of the righteousness of God, and seeking to establish their
own righteousness, have not submitted to the righteousness
4 of God. For Christ *is* the end of the law for righteousness

* Isaiah viii. 14. † Isaiah xxviii. 16

Verse 32. And *wherefore* have they not? Is it because God eternally decreed they should not? There is nothing like this to be met with; but agreeable to his argument the apostle gives us this good reason for it, *Because they sought it not by faith*—Whereby alone it could be attained. *But as it were*—In effect, if not professsedly, *by works. For they stumbled at that stumblingstone*—Christ crucified.

Verse 33. *As it is written*—Foretold by their own prophet. *Behold, I lay in Sion*—I exhibit in my church, what, though it is in truth the only sure foundation of happiness, yet will be in fact a *stumblingstone and rock of offence*—An occasion of ruin to many, through their obstinate unbelief.

Verse 1. *My prayer to God is, that they may be saved*—He would not have prayed for this, had they been absolutely reprobated.

Verse 2. *They have a zeal, but not according to knowledge*—They had zeal without knowledge; we have knowledge without zeal.

Verse 3. *For they being ignorant of the righteousness of God*—Of the method God has established for the justification of a sinner. *And seeking to establish their own righteousness*—Their own method of acceptance with God. *Have not submitted to the righteousness of God*—The way of justification which he hath fixed.

Verse 4. *For Christ is the end of the law*—The scope and aim of it. It is the very design of the law, to bring men to believe in Christ for justification and salvation. And he alone gives that pardon and life which the law shows the want of, but cannot give. *To every one*—Whether Jew or gentile, treated of, verse 11, &c. *That believeth*—Treated of, verse 5, &c.

5 to every one that believeth. For Moses describeth the
righteousness which is by the law, * The man who doeth
6 these things shall live by them. But the righteousness
which is by faith speaketh thus, † Say not in thy heart,
Who shall ascend into heaven? (that is, to bring Christ
7 down:) Or, Who shall descend into the abyss? (that is, to
8 bring Christ again from the dead.) But what saith he?
The word is nigh thee, *even* in thy mouth, and in thy heart:
9 that is, the word of faith which we preach; That if thou
confess with thy mouth the Lord Jesus, and believe in thy
heart that God raised him from the dead, thou shalt be
10 saved. For with the heart man believeth to righteousness,
and with the mouth confession is made to salvation.
11 For the scripture saith, ‡ Every one that believeth on
12 him shall not be ashamed. For there is no difference

* Lev. xviii. 5. † Deut. xxx. 14 ‡ Isaiah xxviii. 16.

Verse 5. *For Moses describeth the* only *righteousness* which is attainable *by the law,* when he saith, *The man who doeth these things shall live by them*—That is, he that perfectly keeps all these precepts in every point, he alone may claim life and salvation by them. But this way of justification is impossible to any who have ever transgressed any one law in any point.

Verse 6. *But the righteousness which is by faith*—The method of becoming righteous by believing. *Speaketh* a very different language, and may be considered as expressing itself thus: (to accommodate to our present subject the words which Moses spake, touching the plainness of his law:) *Say not in thy heart, Who shall ascend into heaven,* as if it were *to bring Christ down: or, Who shall descend into the grave,* as if it were *to bring him again from the dead*—Do not imagine that these things are to be done now, in order to procure thy pardon and salvation.

Verse 8. *But what saith he*—Moses. Even these words, so remarkably applicable to the subject before us. All is done ready to thy hand. *The word is nigh thee*—Within thy reach; easy to be understood, remembered, practised. This is eminently true of *the word of faith*—The gospel. *Which we preach*—The sum of which is, If thy heart believe in Christ, and thy life confess him, *thou shalt be saved.*

Verse 9. *If thou confess with thy mouth*—Even in time of persecution, when such a confession may send thee to the lions.

Verse 10. *For with the heart*—Not the understanding only. *Man believeth to righteousness*—So as to obtain justification. *And with the mouth confession is made*—So as to obtain final *salvation.* Confession here implies the whole of outward, as believing does the root of all inward, religion.

Verse 12. *The same Lord of all is rich*—So that his blessings are never

between the Jew and the Greek: for the same Lord of all
13 is rich to all that call upon him. For * whosoever shall call
14 upon the name of the Lord shall be saved. But how shall
they call on him in whom they have not believed? and how
shall they believe in him of whom they have not heard?
15 and how shall they hear without a preacher? But how
shall they preach, unless they be sent? as it is written,
† How beautiful *are* the feet of them who bring the good
tidings of peace, who bring the glad tidings of good things.
16 But all have not obeyed the gospel. For Isaiah saith
17 ‡ Lord, who hath believed our report? Faith then *cometh*
18 by hearing, and hearing by the word of God. But I say,
Have they not heard? Yes verily, || their voice is gone
into all the earth, and their words to the ends of the world.
19 But I say, Hath not Israel known? First Moses saith, § I
will provoke you to jealousy by *them that are* not a nation,
20 by a foolish nation I will anger you. But Isaiah is very
bold, and saith, ¶ I was found by them that sought me not:

* Joel ii. 32. † Isaiah lii. 7. ‡ Isaiah liii. 1. || Psalm xix. 4.
§ Deut. xxxii. 21. ¶ Isaiah lxv. 1, 2.

to be exhausted, nor is he ever constrained to hold his hand. The great truth proposed in the eleventh verse is so repeated here, and in the thirteenth, and farther confirmed, verses 14, 15, as not only to imply, that "whosoever calleth upon him shall be saved;" but also that the will of God is, that all should savingly call upon him.

Verse 15. *But how shall they preach, unless they be sent*—Thus by a chain of reasoning, from God's will that the gentiles also should "call upon him," St. Paul infers that the apostles were sent by God to preach to the gentiles also. *The feet*—Their very footsteps; their coming.

Verse 17. *Faith,* indeed, ordinarily *cometh by hearing;* even by hearing *the word of God.*

Verse 18. *But* their unbelief was not owing to the want of hearing For they *have heard. Yes verily*—So many nations have already heard the preachers of the gospel, that I may in some sense say of them as David did of the lights of heaven.

Verse 19. *But hath not Israel known*—They might have known, even from Moses and Isaiah, that many of the gentiles would be received, and many of the Jews rejected. *I will provoke you to jealousy by them that are not a nation*—As they followed gods that were not gods, so he accepted in their stead a nation that was not a nation; that is, a nation that was not in covenant with God. *A foolish nation*—Such are all which know not God.

Verse 20. *But Isaiah is very bold*—And speaks plainly what Moses but intimated.

I was made manifest to them that asked not after me.
21 Whereas with regard to Israel he saith, All the day have
I stretched forth my hands to an unbelieving and gainsaying people.

CHAP. XI. 1 I say then, Hath God rejected his people?
God forbid. For I also am an Israelite, of the seed of Abra-
2 ham, of the tribe of Benjamin. God hath not rejected his people whom he foreknew. Know ye not what the scripture saith
3 of Elijah? how he pleadeth with God against Israel, * Lord,
they have killed thy prophets, and digged down thy altars:
4 and I am left alone, and they seek my life. But what saith
the answer of God to him? I have reserved to myself seven
5 thousand men, who have not bowed the knee to Baal. And
so likewise at the present time there is a remnant according
6 to the election of grace. But if by grace, then *it is* no
more of works: else grace is no longer grace. And if *it be*
of works, then it is no more grace: else work is no longer

* 1 Kings xix. 10

Verse 21. *An unbelieving and gainsaying people*—Just opposite to those who believed with their hearts, and made confession with their mouths.

Verse 1. *Hath God rejected his* whole *people*—All Israel? In nowise. Now there is "a remnant" who believe, verse 5; and hereafter "all Israel will be saved," verse 26.

Verse 2. *God hath not rejected* that part of *his people whom he foreknew*—Speaking after the manner of men. For, in fact, knowing and foreknowing are the same thing with God, who knows or sees all things at once, from everlasting to everlasting. *Know ye not*—That in a parallel case, amidst a general apostasy, when Elijah thought the whole nation was fallen into idolatry, God "knew" there was "a remnant" of true worshippers.

Verse 4. *To Baal*—Nor to the golden calves.

Verse 5. *According to the election of grace*—According to that gracious purpose of God, "He that believeth shall be saved."

Verse 6. *And if by grace, then it is no more of works*—Whether ceremonial or moral. *Else grace is no longer grace*—The very nature of grace is lost. *And if it be of works, then it is no more grace: else work is no longer work*—But the very nature of it is destroyed. There is something so absolutely inconsistent between the being justified by grace, and the being justified by works, that, if you suppose either, you of necessity exclude the other. For what is given to works is the payment of a debt; whereas grace implies an unmerited favour. So that the same benefit cannot, in the very nature of things, be derived from both

7 work. What then? Israel hath not obtained that which
he seeketh; but the election hath obtained, and the rest
8 were blinded: According as it is written, * God hath given
them a spirit of slumber, eyes that they should not see, and
9 ears that they should not hear, unto this day And David
saith, † Let their table become a snare, and a trap, and a
10 stumblingblock, and a recompence to them: Let their eyes
be darkened, that they may not see, and bow down their
11 back alway. I say then, Have they stumbled so as to fall?
God forbid: but by their fall salvation *is come* to the gen-
12 tiles, to provoke them to jealousy. But if their fall *be* the
riches of the world, and their loss the riches of the gentiles;
13 how much more their fulness? For I speak to you gen-

* Isaiah xxix. 10. † Psalm lxix. 22, 23.

Verse 7. *What then*—What is the conclusion from the whole? It is this: that *Israel* in general *hath not obtained* justification; *but* those of them only who believe. *And the rest were blinded*—By their own wilful prejudice.

Verse 8. *God hath* at length withdrawn his Spirit, and so *given them* up to *a spirit of slumber;* which is fulfilled *unto this day*.

Verse 9. *And David saith*—In that prophetic imprecation, which is applicable to them, as well as to Judas. *A recompence*—Of their preceding wickedness. So sin is punished by sin; and thus the gospel, which should have fed and strengthened their souls, is become a means of destroying them.

Verse 11. *Have they stumbled so as to fall*—Totally and finally? No *But by their fall*—Or slip: it is a very soft word in the original *Salvation is come to the gentiles*—See an instance of this, Acts xiii. 46 *To provoke them*—The Jews themselves, *to jealousy*.

Verse 12. The first part of this verse is treated of, verses 13, &c.; the latter, *How much more their fulness,* (that is, their full conversion,) verses 23, &c.

So many prophecies refer to this grand event, that it is surprising any Christian can doubt of it. And these are greatly confirmed by the wonderful preservation of the Jews as a distinct people to this day. When it is accomplished, it will be so strong a demonstration, both of the Old and New Testament revelation, as will doubtless convince many thousand Deists, in countries nominally Christian; of whom there will, of course, be increasing multitudes among merely nominal Christians. And this will be a means of swiftly propagating the gospel among Mahometans and Pagans; who would probably have received it long ago, had they conversed only with real Christians.

Verse 13. *I magnify my office*—Far from being ashamed of ministering to the gentiles, I glory therein; the rather, as it may be a means of provoking my brethren to jealousy.

tiles as I am the apostle of the gentiles, I magnify my
14 office: If by any means I may provoke to jealousy *those*
15 *who are* my flesh, and save some of them. For if the casting away of them *be* the reconciling of the world, what *will*
16 the receiving *of them be*, but life from the dead? For
if the first-fruits *be* holy, so *is* the lump: and if the root
17 *be* holy, so *are* the branches. And if some of the branches
were broken off, and thou, being a wild olive tree, wert
grafted in among them, and with them partakest of the
18 root and fatness of the olive tree, Boast not against the
branches. But if thou boast, thou bearest not the root, but
19 the root thee. Wilt thou say then, The branches were
20 broken off, that I might be grafted in? Well; they were
broken off for unbelief, and thou standest by faith. Be not
21 highminded, but fear: For if God spared not the natural
22 branches, *take heed* lest he also spare not thee. Behold
therefore the goodness and severity of God: Toward them
that fell, severity; but toward thee, goodness, if thou con-
23 tinue in *his* goodness: else shalt thou also be cut off. And
they, if they do not continue in unbelief, shall be grafted in:

Verse 14. *My flesh*—My kinsmen.

Verse 15. *Life from the dead*—Overflowing life to the world, which was dead.

Verse 16. And this will surely come to pass. *For if the first-fruits be holy, so is the lump*—The consecration of them was esteemed the consecration of all; and so the conversion of a few Jews is an earnest of the conversion of all the rest. *And if the root be holy*—The patriarchs from whom they spring, surely God will at length make their descendants also holy.

Verse 17. *Thou*—O gentile. *Being a wild olive tree*—Had the graft been nobler than the stock, yet its dependance on it for life and nourishment would leave it no room to boast against it. How much less, when, contrary to what is practised among men, the wild olive tree is engrafted on the good!

Verse 18. *Boast not against the branches*—Do not they do this who despise the Jews? or deny their future conversion?

Verse 20. *They were broken off for unbelief, and thou standest by faith*—Both conditionally, not absolutely: if absolutely, there might have been room to boast. *By faith*—The free gift of God, which therefore ought to humble thee.

Verse 21. *Be not highminded, but fear*—We may observe, this *fear* is not opposed to trust, but to pride and security.

Verse 22. *Else shalt thou*—Also, who now "standest by faith," be both totally and finally *cut off*.

24 for God is able to graft them in again. For if thou wert
cut off from the natural wild olive tree, and grafted contrary
to nature into a good olive tree : how much more shall these,
who are natural *branches*, be grafted into their own olive
25 tree? Brethren, I would not that ye should be ignorant
of this mystery, lest ye should be wise in your own conceits;
that hardness is in part happened to Israel, till the fulness
26 of the gentiles be come in. And so all Israel shall be saved.
as it is written, * The deliverer shall come out of Sion, and
27 shall turn away iniquity from Jacob : And this *is* my cove-
28 nant with them, when I shall take away their sins. With
regard to the gospel, *they are* enemies for your sake : but as
for the election, *they are* beloved, for the sake of their
29 fathers. For the gifts and the calling of God *are* without
30 repentance. As then ye were once disobedient to God, but
31 have now obtained mercy through their disobedience: So
these also have now been disobedient, that through your
32 mercy they may likewise find mercy. For God hath shut
up all together in disobedience, that he might have mercy

* Isaiah lix. 20

Verse 24. *Contrary to nature*—For according to nature, we graft the fruitful branch into the wild stock; but here the wild branch is grafted into the fruitful stock.

Verse 25. St. Paul calls any truth known but to a few, a *mystery*. Such had been the calling of the gentiles: such was now the conversion of the Jews. *Lest ye should be wise in your own conceits*—Puffed up with your present advantages; dreaming that ye are the only church; or that the church of Rome cannot fail. *Hardness in part is happened to Israel, till*—Israel therefore is neither totally nor finally rejected. *The fulness of the gentiles be come in*—Till there be a vast harvest amongst the heathens.

Verse 26. *And so all Israel shall be saved*—Being convinced by the coming of the gentiles. But there will be a still larger harvest among the gentiles, when all Israel is come in. *The deliverer shall come*—Yea, the deliverer is come; but not the full fruit of his coming.

Verse 28. *They are* now *enemies*—To the gospel, to God, and to themselves, which God permits. *For your sake : but as for the election*—That part of them who believe, *they are beloved.*

Verse 29. *For the gifts and the calling of God are without repentance*—God does not repent of his *gifts* to the Jews, or his *calling* of the gentiles.

Verse 32. *For God hath shut up all together in disobedience*—Suffering each in their turn to revolt from him. First, God suffered the gentiles in the early age to revolt, and took the family of Abraham as a peculiar seed to himself. Afterwards he permitted them to fall through unbelief,

33 upon all. O the depth of the riches, and wisdom, and knowledge of God. How unsearchable *are* his judgments, and
34 his ways past tracing out! For * who hath known the
35 mind of the Lord? or who hath been his counsellor? Who
hath first given to him, and it shall be repaid him again?
36 For of him, and through him, and to him, *are* all things: to
him *be* glory for ever. Amen

CHAP. XII. 1 I exhort you therefore, brethren, by the tender mercies of God, to present your bodies unto God, a

* Isaiah xl. 13.

and took in the believing gentiles. And he did even this to provoke the Jews to jealousy, and so bring them also in the end to faith. This was truly a mystery in the divine conduct, which the apostle adores with such holy astonishment.

Verse 33. *O the depth of the riches, and wisdom, and knowledge of God*—In the ninth chapter, St. Paul had sailed but in a narrow sea: now he is in the ocean. The *depth of the riches* is described, verse 35; the *depth of wisdom,* verse 34; the *depth of knowledge,* in the latter part of this verse. *Wisdom* directs all things to the best end; *knowledge* sees that end. *How unsearchable are his judgments*—With regard to unbelievers. *His ways*—With regard to believers. *His ways* are more upon a level; *his judgments* "a great deep." But even his ways we cannot *trace.*

Verse 34. *Who hath known the mind of the Lord*—Before or any farther than he has revealed it.

Verse 35. *Given to him*—Either wisdom or power?

Verse 36. *Of him*—As the Creator. *Through him*—As the Preserver. *To him*—As the ultimate end, are all things. *To him be* the *glory* of his riches, wisdom, knowledge. *Amen*—A concluding word, in which the affection of the apostle, when it is come to the height, shuts up all.

Verse 1. *I exhort you*—St. Paul uses to suit his exhortations to the doctrines he has been delivering. So here the general use from the whole is contained in the first and second verses. The particular uses follow, from the third verse to the end of the Epistle. *By the tender mercies of God*—The whole sentiment is derived from Rom. i.—v. The expression itself is particularly opposed to "the wrath of God," Rom. i. 18. It has a reference here to the entire gospel, to the whole economy of grace or mercy, delivering us from "the wrath of God," and exciting us to all duty. *To present*—So Rom. vi. 13; xvi. 19; now actually to exhibit before God. *Your bodies*—That is, yourselves; a part is put for the whole; the rather, as in the ancient sacrifices of beasts, the body was the whole. These also are particularly named in opposition to that vile abuse of their bodies mentioned, Rom. i. 24. Several expressions follow, which have likewise a direct reference to other expressions in the same chapter. *A sacrifice*—Dead to sin and *living*—By that life which is

living sacrifice, holy, acceptable, *which is* your reasonable
2 service. And be not conformed to this world: but be ye
transformed by the renewing of your mind, that ye may
prove what *is* that good, and acceptable, and perfect will
3 of God. And I say through the grace which is given to me,
to every one that is among you, not to think *of himself* above
what he ought to think; but to think soberly, according as
4 God hath distributed to every one the measure of faith. For
as in one body we have many members, and all members have
5 not the same office: So we, being many, are one body in
6 Christ, and every one members of each other. Having then
gifts differing according to the grace that is given us, whether
it be prophecy, *let us prophesy* according to the analogy

mentioned, Rom. i. 17; vi. 4, &c. *Holy*—Such as the holy law requires, Rom. vii. 12. *Acceptable*—Rom. viii. 8. *Which is your reasonable service*—The worship of the heathens was utterly unreasonable, Rom. i. 18, &c; so was the glorying of the Jews, Rom. ii. 3, &c. But a Christian acts in all things by the highest reason, from the mercy of God inferring his own duty

Verse 2. *And be not conformed*—Neither in judgment, spirit, nor behaviour. *To this world*—Which, neglecting the will of God, entirely follows its own. *That ye may prove*—Know by sure trial; which is easily done by him who has thus presented himself to God. *What is that good, and acceptable, and perfect will of God—The will of God* is here to be understood of all the preceptive part of Christianity, which is in itself so excellently *good*, so *acceptable* to God, and so *perfective* of our natures.

Verse 3. *And I say*—He now proceeds to show what that will of God is. *Through the grace which is given to me*—He modestly adds this, lest he should seem to forget his own direction. *To every one that is among you*—Believers at Rome. Happy, had they always remembered this! *The measure of faith*—Treated of in the first and following chapters, from which all other gifts and graces flow.

Verse 5. *So we*—All believers. *Are one body*—Closely connected together *in Christ*, and consequently ought to be helpful to each other.

Verse 6. *Having then gifts differing according to the grace which is given us*—Gifts are various: grace is one. *Whether it be prophecy*—This, considered as an extraordinary gift, is that whereby heavenly mysteries are declared to men, or things to come foretold. But it seems here to mean the ordinary gift of expounding scripture. *Let us prophesy according to the analogy of faith*—St. Peter expresses it, "as the oracles of God;" according to the general tenor of them; according to that grand scheme of doctrine which is delivered therein, touching original sin, justification by faith, and present, inward salvation. There is a wonderful analogy between all these; and a close and intimate connexion between the chief heads of that faith "which was once delivered to the saints." Every article therefore concerning which there is any question should be deter-

7 of faith; Or ministry, *let us wait* on our ministering: or he
8 that teacheth, on teaching; Or he that exhorteth, on exhortation: he that imparteth, *let him do it* with simplicity; he
that presideth, with diligence; he that showeth mercy, with
cheerfulness.
9 *Let* love *be* without dissimulation. Abhor that which is
10 evil; cleave to that which is good. In brotherly love be
full of tender affection toward each other; in honour pre-
11 ferring one another; Not slothful in business; fervent in
12 spirit; serving the Lord; Rejoice in hope; be patient in
13 tribulation; continue instant in prayer; Communicate to
14 the necessities of the saints; pursue hospitality. Bless them
15 who persecute you: bless, and curse not. Rejoice with

mined by this rule; every doubtful scripture interpreted according to the grand truths which run through the whole.

Verse 7. *Ministering*—As deacons. *He that teacheth*—Catechumens; for whom particular instructers were appointed. *He that exhorteth*—Whose peculiar business it was to urge Christians to duty, and to comfort them in trials.

Verse 8. *He that presideth*—That hath the care of a flock. *He that showeth mercy*—In any instance. *With cheerfulness*—Rejoicing that he hath such an opportunity.

Verse 9. Having spoken of faith and its fruit, verses 3, &c., he comes now to *love*. The ninth, tenth, and eleventh verses refer to chapter the seventh; the twelfth verse to chapter the eighth; the thirteenth verse, of communicating to the saints, whether Jews or gentiles, to chapter the ninth, &c. Part of the sixteenth verse is repeated from chap. xi. 25. *Abhor that which is evil; cleave to that which is good*—Both inwardly and outwardly, whatever ill-will or danger may follow.

Verse 10. *In honour preferring one another*—Which you will do, if you habitually consider what is good in others, and what is evil in yourselves.

Verse 11. Whatsoever ye do, do it with your might. *In* every *business* diligently and fervently *serving the Lord*—Doing all to God, not to man.

Verse 12. *Rejoicing in hope*—Of perfect holiness and everlasting happiness. Hitherto of faith and love; now of hope also, see the fifth and eighth chapters; afterwards of duties toward others; saints, verse 13; persecutors, verse 14; friends, strangers, enemies, verses 15, &c.

Verse 13. *Communicate to the necessities of the saints*—Relieve all Christians that are in want. It is remarkable, that the apostle, treating expressly of the duties flowing from the communion of saints, yet never says one word about the dead. *Pursue hospitality*—Not only embracing those that offer, but seeking opportunities to exercise it.

Verse 14. *Curse not*—No, not in your heart.

Verse 15. *Rejoice*—The direct opposite to weeping is laughter; but this does not so well suit a Christian.

16 them that rejoice, and weep with them that weep. Agree
in the same affection toward each other. Mind not high,
but condescend to low, things. Be not wise in your own
17 conceit. Render to no man evil for evil. Provide things
18 honest in the sight of all men. If it be possible, as much
19 as lieth in you, live peaceably with all men. Dearly
beloved, revenge not yourselves, but rather give place unto
wrath: for it is written, * Vengeance *is* mine; I will repay,
20 saith the Lord. Therefore if † thy enemy hunger, feed
him; if he thirst, give him drink; for in so doing thou shalt
21 heap coals of fire upon his head. Be not overcome with
evil, but overcome evil with good.

CHAP. XIII. 1 Let every soul be subject to the
supreme powers. For there is no power but from God:

* Deut. xxxii. 35 † Prov. xxv. 21, &c.

Verse 16. *Mind not high things*—Desire not riches, honour, or the company of the great.

Verse 17. *Provide*—Think beforehand; contrive to give as little offence as may be to any.

Verse 19. *Dearly beloved*—So he softens the rugged spirit. *Revenge not yourselves, but* leave that to God. Perhaps it might more properly be rendered, *leave room for wrath;* that is, the wrath of God, to whom vengeance properly belongs.

Verse 20. *Feed him*—With your own hand: if it be needful, even put bread into his mouth. *Heap coals of fire upon his head*—That part which is most sensible.

> "So artists melt the sullen ore of lead,
> By heaping coals of fire upon its head;
> In the kind warmth the metal learns to glow,
> And pure from dross the silver runs below."

Verse 21. And if you see no present fruit, yet persevere. *Be not overcome with evil*—As all are who avenge themselves. *But overcome evil with good* Conquer your enemies by kindness and patience.

Verse 1. St. Paul, writing to the Romans, whose city was the seat of the empire, speaks largely of obedience to magistrates: and this was also, in effect, a public apology for the Christian religion. *Let every soul be subject to the supreme powers*—An admonition peculiarly needful for the Jews. *Power,* in the singular number, is the supreme authority; *powers* are they who are invested with it. That is more readily acknowledged to be from God than these. The apostle affirms it of both. They are all from God, who constituted all in general, and permits each in

2 the powers that be are appointed by God. Whosoever
therefore resisteth the power, resisteth the appointment of
God: and they that resist shall receive to themselves con-
3 demnation. For rulers are not a terror to good works,
but to evil. Wouldest thou then not be afraid of the power?
do that which is good, and thou shalt have praise from it:
4 for he is the servant of God to thee for good. But if thou
doest that which is evil, be afraid; for he beareth not the
sword in vain: for he is the servant of God, an avenger for
5 wrath against him that doeth evil. Wherefore *ye* must
needs be subject, not only for wrath, but also for conscience'
6 sake. For this cause ye pay tribute also: for they are the
ministers of God, attending continually on this very thing.
7 Render therefore to all their dues: tribute to whom tribute
is due; custom to whom custom; fear to whom fear;
8 honour to whom honour. Owe no man anything, but to
love one another: for he that loveth another hath fulfilled

particular by his providence. *The powers that be are appointed by God*—It might be rendered, *are subordinate to*, or, *orderly disposed under, God*; implying, that they are God's deputies or vicegerents; and consequently, their authority being, in effect, his, demands our conscientious obedience.

Verse 2. *Whosoever resisteth the power*—In any other manner than the laws of the community direct. *Shall receive condemnation*—Not only from the magistrate, but from God also.

Verse 3. *For rulers are*—In the general, notwithstanding some particular exceptions. *A terror to evil works*—Only. *Wouldest thou then not be afraid*—There is one fear which precedes evil actions, and deters from them: this should always remain. There is another fear which follows evil actions: they who *do* well are free from this.

Verse 4. *The sword*—The instrument of capital punishment, which God authorizes him to inflict.

Verse 5. *Not only for* fear of *wrath*—That is, punishment from man. *But for conscience' sake*—Out of obedience to God.

Verse 6. *For this cause*—Because *they are the ministers* (officers) *of God* for the public good. *This very thing*—The public good.

Verse 7. *To all*—Magistrates. *Tribute*—Taxes on your persons or estates. *Custom*—For goods exported or imported. *Fear*—Obedience. *Honour*—Reverence. All these are due to the supreme power.

Verse 8. From our duty to magistrates he passes on to general duties. *To love one another*—An eternal debt, which can never be sufficiently discharged; but yet if this be rightly performed, it discharges all the rest. *For he that loveth another*—As he ought *Hath fulfilled the* whole *law*—Toward his neighbour

9 the law. For this, Thou shalt not commit adultery,
Thou shalt not kill, Thou shalt not steal, Thou shalt
not bear false witness, Thou shalt not covet; and if *there
be* any other commandment, it is summed up in this saying,
10 Thou shalt love thy neighbour as thyself. Love worketh
no evil to *his* neighbour: therefore love *is* the fulfilling
of the law.
11 And *do* this, knowing the season, that *it is* high time now
to awake out of sleep; for salvation is nearer to us now
12 than when we *first* believed. The night is far spent, the
day is at hand: let us therefore put off the works of dark-
13 ness, and put on the armour of light. Let us walk decently,
as in the day; not in banqueting and drunken entertainments, not in uncleannesses and wantonness, not in strife and
14 envy. But put ye on the Lord Jesus Christ, and make not
provision for the flesh, *to fulfil* the desires *thereof*.

Verse 9. *If there be any other*—More particular. *Commandment*—Toward our neighbour; as there are many in the law. *It is summed up in this*—So that if you was not thinking of it, yet if your heart was full of love, you would fulfil it.

Verse 10. *Therefore love is the fulfilling of the law*—For the same love which restrains from all evil, incites us to all good.

Verse 11. *And do this*—Fulfil the law of love in all the instances above mentioned. *Knowing the season*—Full of grace, but hasting away. *That it is high time to awake out of sleep*—How beautifully is the metaphor carried on! This life, a night; the resurrection, the day; the gospel shining on the heart, the dawn of this day; we are to awake out of sleep; to rise up and throw away our night-clothes, fit only for darkness, and put on new; and, being soldiers, we are to arm, and prepare for fight, who are encompassed with so many enemies.

The day dawns when we receive faith, and then sleep gives place. Then it is time to rise, to arm, to walk, to work, lest sleep steal upon us again. Final *salvation*, glory, is *nearer* to us now, *than when we first believed*—It is continually advancing, flying forward upon the swiftest wings of time. And that which remains between the present hour and eternity is comparatively but a moment.

Verse 13. *Banqueting*—Luxurious, elegant feasts.

Verse 14. *But put ye on the Lord Jesus Christ*—Herein is contained the whole of our salvation. It is a strong and beautiful expression for the most intimate union with him, and being clothed with all the graces which were in him. The apostle does not say, Put on purity and sobriety, peacefulness and benevolence; but he says all this and a thousand times more at once, in saying, *Put on Christ*. And *make not provision*—To raise foolish desires, or, when they are raised already, to satisfy them.

CHAP. XIV. 1 Him that is weak in the faith, receive,
2 *but* not to doubtful disputations. For one believeth that
he may eat all things: another, who is weak, eateth herbs.
3 Let not him that eateth despise him that eateth not: and
let not him that eateth not judge him that eateth: for God
4 hath received him. Who art thou that judgest another's
servant? to his own master he standeth or falleth. Yea,
5 he shall be upheld for God is able to uphold him. One
man esteemeth one day above another. another esteemeth
every day *alike*. Let every man be fully persuaded in his
6 own mind. He that regardeth the day, regardeth *it* to the
Lord; and he that regardeth not the day, to the Lord he
doth not regard *it*. He that eateth, eateth to the Lord, for
he giveth God thanks; and he that eateth not, to the Lord
7 he eateth not, and giveth God thanks. For none of us
8 liveth to himself, and none dieth to himself. But if we
live, we live unto the Lord; and if we die, we die unto the
Lord: whether therefore we live, or die, we are the Lord's.
9 For to this end Christ both died, and lived, that he might
10 be the Lord both of the dead and of the living. But why
dost thou judge thy brother? or why dost thou despise thy
brother? for we shall all stand before the judgment seat
11 of Christ. For it is written, * As I live, saith the Lord

* Isaiah xlv. 23

Verse 1 *Him that is weak*—Through needless scruples. *Receive*—With all love and courtesy into Christian fellowship. *But not to doubtful disputations*—About questionable points.

Verse 2. *All things*—All sorts of food, though forbidden by the law.

Verse 3. *Despise him that eateth not*—As over-scrupulous or superstitious. *Judge him that eateth*—As profane, or taking undue liberties. *For God hath received him*—Into the number of his children, notwithstanding this.

Verse 5. *One day above another*—As new moons, and other Jewish festivals. *Let every man be fully persuaded*—That a thing is lawful, before he does it.

Verse 6. *Regardeth it to the Lord*—That is, out of a principle of conscience toward God. *To the Lord he doth not regard it*—He also acts from a principle of conscience. *He that eateth not*—Flesh. *Giveth God thanks*—For his herbs.

Verse 7. *None of us*—Christians, in the things we do. *Liveth to himself*—Is at his own disposal; doeth his own will.

Verse 10. *Or why dost thou despise thy brother*—Hitherto the apostle as addressed the weak brother: now he speaks to the stronger.

Verse 11. *As I live*—An oath proper to him, because he only possess-

every knee shall bow to me, and every tongue shall confess
12 to God. So then every one of us shall give an account
13 of himself to God. Let us therefore no longer judge one
another: but judge this rather, not to lay a stumblingblock
14 or a scandal before a brother. I know and am assured by
the Lord Jesus, that nothing *is* unclean of itself: but to
him that accounteth anything to be unclean, *it is* unclean.
15 But if thy brother is grieved by *thy* meat, thou no longer
walkest charitably. Destroy not him by thy meat, for whom
16 Christ died. Therefore let not your good be evil spoken
17 of: For the kingdom of God is not meat and drink; but
18 righteousness, and peace, and joy in the Holy Ghost. And
he that in these serveth Christ *is* acceptable to God, and
19 approved by men. Let us therefore pursue the things that

eth life infinite and independent. It is Christ who is here termed both Lord and God; as it is he to whom we live, and to whom we die. *Every tongue shall confess to God*—Shall own him as their rightful Lord; which shall then only be accomplished in its full extent. The Lord grant we may find mercy in that day; and may it also be imparted to those who have differed from us! yea, to those who have censured and condemned us for things which we have done from a desire to please him, or refused to do from a fear of offending him.

Verse 13. *But judge this rather*—Concerning ourselves. *Not to lay a stumblingblock*—By moving him to do as thou doest, though against his conscience. *Or a scandal*—Moving him to hate or judge thee.

Verse 14. *I am assured by the Lord Jesus*—Perhaps by a particular revelation. *That there is nothing*—Neither flesh nor herbs. *Unclean of itself*—Unlawful under the gospel.

Verse 15. *If thy brother is grieved*—That is, wounded, led into sin. *Destroy not him for whom Christ died*—So we see, he for whom Christ died may be destroyed. *With thy meat*—Do not value thy meat more than Christ valued his life.

Verse 16. *Let not then your good* and lawful liberty *be evil spoken of*—By being offensive to others.

Verse 17. *For the kingdom of God*—That is, true religion, does not consist in external observances. *But* in *righteousness*—The image of God stamped on the heart; the love of God and man, accompanied with the *peace* that passeth all understanding, *and joy in the Holy Ghost.*

Verse 18. *In these*—Righteousness, peace, and joy. *Men*—Wise and good men.

Verse 19. *Peace* and *edification* are closely joined. Practical divinity tends equally to peace and to edification. Controversial divinity less directly tends to edification, although sometimes, as they of old, we cannot build without it, Neh. iv. 17.

20 tend to peace, and to mutual edification. For meat destroy
not the work of God. All things indeed *are* pure; but *it is*
21 evil to that man who eateth with offence. *It is* good not to
eat flesh, neither to drink wine, nor *to do any* thing whereby
22 thy brother stumbleth, or is offended, or made weak. Hast
thou faith? have it to thyself before God. Happy *is* he
that condemneth not himself in that thing which he allow-
23 eth. But he that doubteth is condemned if he eat, because
it is not of faith: for whatsoever *is* not of faith is sin.

CHAP. XV. 1 Therefore we who are strong ought to
bear the infirmities of the weak, and not to please ourselves.
2 Let every one of us please *his* neighbour for *his* good to
3 edification. For Christ pleased not himself; but, as it is
written, * The reproaches of them that reproached thee fell
4 upon me. For whatsoever things were written aforetime
were written for our instruction, that we, through patience

* Psalm lxix. 9.

Verse 20. *The work of God*—Which he builds in the soul by faith, and in the church by concord. *It is evil to that man who eateth with offence*—So as to offend another thereby.

Verse 21. *Thy brother stumbleth*—By imitating thee against his conscience, contrary to righteousness. *Or is offended*—At what thou doest to the loss of his peace. *Or made weak*—Hesitating between imitation and abhorrence, to the loss of that joy in the Lord which was his strength.

Verse 22. *Hast thou faith*—That all things are pure? *Have it to thyself before God*—In circumstances like these, keep it to thyself, and do not offend others by it. *Happy is he that condemneth not himself*—By an improper use of even innocent things! and happy he who is free from a doubting conscience! He that has this may *allow* the thing, yet *condemn himself* for it.

Verse 23. *Because it is not of faith*—He does not believe it lawful; and, in all these cases, *whatsoever is not of faith is sin*—Whatever a man does without a full persuasion of its lawfulness, it is *sin* to him.

Verse 1. *We who are strong*—Of a clearer judgment, and free from these scruples. *And not to please ourselves*—Without any regard to others.

Verse 2. *For his good*—This is a general word: *edification* is one species of good.

Verse 3. *But* bore not only the infirmities, but *reproaches,* of his brethren; and so fulfilled that scripture.

Verse 4. *Aforetime*—In the Old Testament. *That we through patience and consolation of the scriptures may have hope*—That through the conso-

5 and consolation of the scriptures may have hope. Now the
God of patience and consolation give you to think the same
6 thing, *one with another*, according to Christ Jesus: That
ye may with one mind *and* one mouth glorify the God and
7 Father of our Lord Jesus Christ. Wherefore receive ye
one another, as Christ also hath received you to the glory
8 of God. Now I say Christ Jesus was a servant of the circumcision for the truth of God, to confirm the promises
9 *made* to the fathers: And that the gentiles might glorify
God for *his* mercy; as it is written, * For this cause I will
confess to thee among the gentiles, and sing unto thy name.
10 And again he saith, † Rejoice, ye gentiles, with his people.
11 And again, ‡ Praise the Lord, all ye gentiles; and laud him,
12 all ye people. And again, Isaiah saith, || There shall be the
root of Jesse, and he that ariseth to rule over the gentiles;
13 in him shall the gentiles hope. Now the God of hope fill
you with all joy and peace in believing, that ye may abound
in hope, by the power of the Holy Ghost.

* Psalm xviii. 49. † Deut. xxxii. 43. ‡ Psalm cxvii. 1. || Isaiah xi. 10.

lation which God gives us by these, we may have patience and a joyful hope.

Verse 5. *According to* the power of *Christ Jesus.*

Verse 6. *That ye*—Both Jews and gentiles, believing *with one mind,* and confessing *with one mouth.*

Verse 7. *Receive ye one another*—Weak and strong, with mutual love.

Verse 8. *Now I say*—The apostle here shows how Christ received us. *Christ Jesus—Jesus* is the name, *Christ* the surname. The latter was first known to the Jews; the former, to the gentiles. Therefore he is styled *Jesus Christ,* when the words stand in the common, natural order. When the order is inverted, as here, the office of Christ is more solemnly considered. *Was a servant*—Of his Father. *Of the circumcision*—For the salvation of the circumcised, the Jews. *For the truth of God*—To manifest the truth and fidelity of God.

Verse 9. *As it is written*—In the eighteenth psalm, where the gentiles and Jews are spoken of as joining in the worship of the God of Israel.

Verse 12. *There shall be the root of Jesse*—That kings and the Messiah should spring from his house, was promised to Jesse before it was to David. *In him shall the gentiles hope*—Who before had been "without hope," Eph. ii. 12.

Verse 13. *Now the God of hope*—A glorious title of God, but till now unknown to the heathens; for their goddess Hope, like their other idols, was nothing; whose temple at Rome was burned by lightning. It was, indeed, built again not long after, but was again burned to the ground

14 And I myself also am persuaded of you, my brethren, that
ye likewise are full of goodness, being filled with all know-
15 ledge, and able to admonish one another. Nevertheless,
brethren, I have written the more boldly to you, in some
respect, as putting you in mind, because of the grace which
16 is given to me of God, That I should be the servant of Jesus
Christ to the gentiles, ministering the gospel of God, that
the offering up of the gentiles may be acceptable, being
17 sanctified by the Holy Ghost. I have therefore whereof to
glory through Jesus Christ in the things pertaining to God.
18 For I will not dare to speak of anything which Christ hath
not wrought by me, to make the gentiles obedient, by word
19 and deed, Through mighty signs and wonders, by the power
of the Spirit of God; so that I have fully preached the gospel
of Christ, from Jerusalem round about, as far as Illyricum.
20 Striving so to preach the gospel, not where Christ had been
named, lest I should build upon another man's foundation:
21 But as it is written, * They to whom he was not spoken
of shall see: and they that have not heard shall understand.

* Isaiah lii. 15.

Verse 14. There are several conclusions of this Epistle The first begins at this verse; the second, Rom. xvi. 1; the third, verse 17; the fourth, verse 21; and the fifth, verse 25. *Ye are full of goodness*—By being created anew. *And filled with all knowledge*—By long experience of the things of God. *To admonish*—To instruct and confirm

Verse 15. *Because of the grace*—That is, because I am an apostle of the gentiles.

Verse 16. *The offering up of the gentiles*—As living sacrifices.

Verse 17. *I have whereof to glory through Jesus Christ*—All my glorying is in and through him.

Verse 18. *By word*—By the power of the Spirit. *By deed*—Namely, through "mighty signs and wonders."

Verse 20. *Not where Christ had been named*—These places he generally declined, though not altogether, having an holy *ambition* (so the Greek word means) to make the first proclamation of the gospel in places where it was quite unheard of, in spite of all the difficulty and dangers that attended it. *Lest I should* only *build upon another man's foundation*—The providence of God seemed in a special manner, generally, to prevent this, though not entirely, lest the enemies of the apostle, who sought every occasion to set light by him, should have had room to say that he was behind other apostles, not being sufficient for planting of churches himself, but only for preaching where others had been already; or that he declined the more difficult part of the ministry

22 Therefore I was also long hindered from coming to you.
23 But now having no longer place in these countries, and hav-
24 ing had a great desire for many years to come to you; Whenever I go into Spain, I hope to see you as I pass by, and to be brought forward by you in my way thither, if first I may be somewhat satisfied with your *company*.
25 But I am now going to Jerusalem serving the saints.
26 For it hath pleased them of Macedonia and Achaia to make a contribution for the poor of the saints that are in Jerusa-
27 lem. It hath pleased them; and they are their debtors. For if the gentiles have partook of their spiritual things, they
28 ought to minister to them in carnal things. When therefore I have performed this, and sealed to them this fruit, I will
29 go by you into Spain. And I know that, when I come to you, I shall come in the fulness of the blessing of the gospel
30 of Christ. Now I beseech you, brethren, by our Lord Jesus Christ, and by the love of the Spirit, to strive together with

Verse 22. *Therefore I have been long hindered from coming to you*--Among whom Christ had been named.

Verse 23. *Having no longer place in these parts*—Where Christ has now been preached in every city.

Verse 24. *Into Spain*—Where the gospel had not yet been preached. *If first I may be somewhat satisfied with your company*—How remarkable is the modesty with which he speaks! They might rather desire to be satisfied with his. *Somewhat satisfied*—Intimating the shortness of his stay; or, perhaps, that Christ alone can throughly satisfy the soul.

Verse 26. *The poor of the saints that are in Jerusalem*—It can by no means be inferred from this expression, that the community of goods among the Christians was then ceased. All that can be gathered from it is, that in this time of extreme dearth, Acts xi. 28, 29, some of the church in Jerusalem were in want; the rest being barely able to subsist themselves, but not to supply the necessities of their brethren.

Verse 27. *It hath pleased them; and they are their debtors*—That is, they are bound to it, in justice as well as mercy. *Spiritual things*—By the preaching of the gospel. *Carnal things*—Things needful for the body.

Verse 28. *When I have sealed to them this fruit*—When I have safely delivered to them, as under seal, this fruit of their brethren's love. *I will go by you into Spain*—Such was his design; but it does not appear that Paul went into Spain. There are often holy purposes in the minds of good men, which are overruled by the providence of God so as never to take effect. And yet they are precious in the sight of God.

Verse 30. *I beseech you by the love of the Spirit*—That is, by the love which is the genuine fruit of the Spirit. *To strive together with me in your prayers*—He must pray himself, who would have others strive together

31 me, in *your* prayers to God for me; That I may be delivered
from the unbelievers in Judea; and that my service at Jeru-
32 salem may be acceptable to the saints: That I may come to
you with joy by the will of God, and may be refreshed toge-
33 ther with you. Now the God of peace *be* with you all.

CHAP. XVI. 1 I commend unto you Phebe our sister,
2 who is a servant of the church in Cenchrea: That ye may
receive her in the Lord, as becometh saints, and help her in
whatsoever business she needeth you: for she hath been an
3 helper of many, and of myself *also*. Salute Priscilla and
4 Aquila my fellowlabourers in Christ Jesus: Who for my
life have laid down their own necks: to whom not I alone
owe my thanks, but likewise all the churches of the gentiles.
5 *Salute* also the church that is in their house. Salute my

with him in prayer. Of all the apostles, St. Paul alone is recorded to desire the prayers of the faithful for himself. And this he generally does in the conclusions of his Epistles; yet not without making a difference. For he speaks in one manner to them whom he treats as his children, with the gravity or even severity of a father, such as Timothy, Titus, the Corinthians, and Galatians; in another, to them whom he treats rather like equals, such as the Romans, Ephesians, Thessalonians, Colossians, Hebrews.

Verse 31. *That I may be delivered*—He is thus urgent from a sense of the importance of his life to the church. Otherwise he would have rejoiced "to depart, and to be with Christ." *And that my service may be acceptable*—In spite of all their prejudices; to the end the Jewish and gentile believers may be knit together in tender love.

Verse 32. *That I may come to you*—This refers to the former, *With joy*—To the latter, part of the preceding verse.

Verse 1. *I commend unto you Phebe*—The bearer of this letter. *A servant*—The Greek word is a *deaconness. Of the church in Cenchrea*—In the apostolic age, some grave and pious women were appointed deaconnesses in every church. It was their office, not to teach publicly, but to visit the sick, the women in particular, and to minister to them both in their temporal and spiritual necessities.

Verse 2. *In the Lord*—That is, for the Lord's sake, and in a Christian manner. St. Paul seems fond of this expression.

Verse 4. *Who have for my life*, as it were, *laid down their own necks*—That is, exposed themselves to the utmost danger. *But likewise all the churches of the gentiles*—Even that at Rome, for preserving so valuable a life.

Verse 5. *Salute the church that is in their house*—Aquila had been driven from Rome in the reign of Claudius, but was now returned, and performed

beloved Epenetus, who is the firstfruits of Asia unto Christ.
6 Salute Mary, who hath bestowed much labour on us. Salute
7 Andronicus and Junias, my kinsmen, and my fellowprisoners,
who are of note among the apostles, who also were in Christ
8 before me. Salute Amplias, my beloved in the Lord.
9 Salute Urbanus, our fellowlabourer in Christ, and my
10 beloved Stachys. Salute Apelles, approved in Christ.
11 Salute those *of the family* of Aristobulus. Salute my kinsman
man Herodion. Salute those *of the family* of Narcissus,
12 who are in the Lord. Salute Tryphena and Tryphosa, who
labour in the Lord. Salute the beloved Persis, who hath
13 laboured much in the Lord. Salute Rufus, chosen in the
14 Lord, and his mother and mine. Salute Asyncritus, Phlegon,
Hermes, Patrobas, Hermas, and the brethren who are with

the same part there which Caius did at Corinth, Rom. xvi. 23. Where any Christian had a large house, there they all assembled together; though as yet the Christians at Rome had neither bishops nor deacons So far were they from any shadow of papal power. Nay, there does not appear to have been then in the whole city any more than one of these domestic churches. Otherwise there can be no doubt but St. Paul would have saluted them also. *Epenetus*—Although the apostle had never been at Rome, yet had he many acquaintance there. But here is no mention of Linus or Clemens; whence it appears, they did not come to Rome till after this. *The firstfruits of Asia*—The first convert in the proconsular Asia.

Verse 7. *Who are of note among the apostles*—They seem to have been some of the most early converts. *Fellowprisoners*—For the gospel's sake.

Verse 9 *Our fellowlabourer*—Mine and Timothy's, verse 21.

Verse 11. *Those of the family of Aristobulus* and *Narcissus, who are in the Lord*—It seems only part of their families were converted. Probably, some of them were not known to St. Paul by face, but only by character. Faith does not create moroseness, but courtesy, which even the gravity of an apostle did not hinder.

Verse 12. *Salute Tryphena and Tryphosa*—Probably they were two sisters.

Verse 13. *Salute Rufus*—Perhaps the same that is mentioned, Mark xv. 21. *And his mother and mine*—This expression may only denote the tender care which Rufus's mother had taken of him.

Verse 14. *Salute Asyncritus, Phlegon, &c.*—He seems to join those together, who were joined by kindred, nearness of habitation, or any other circumstance. It could not but encourage the poor especially, to be saluted by name, who perhaps did not know that the apostle had ever heard of them. It is observable, that whilst the apostle forgets none who are worthy, yet he adjusts the nature of his salutation to the degrees of worth in those whom he salutes.

15 them. Salute Philologus, and Julias, Nereus, and his sister, and Olympas, and all the saints that are with them.
16 Salute one another with an holy kiss. The churches
of Christ salute you.
17 Now I beseech you, brethren, mark them who cause divisions and offences contrary to the doctrine which ye have
18 learned; and avoid them. For such serve not the Lord
Jesus Christ, but their own belly; and by good words and
19 fair speeches deceive the hearts of the harmless. For your
obedience is come abroad unto all men. I rejoice therefore
on your behalf: but I would have you wise with regard to
that which is good, and simple with regard to that which is
20 evil. And the God of peace shall bruise Satan under your
feet shortly. The grace of our Lord Jesus Christ *be* with you.
21 Timotheus my fellowlabourer, and Lucius, and Jason,
22 and Sosipater, my kinsmen, salute you. I Tertius, who

Verse 15. *Salute all the saints*—Had St. Peter been then at Rome, St. Paul would doubtless have saluted him by name; since no one in this numerous catalogue was of an eminence comparable to his. But if he was not then at Rome, the whole Roman tradition, with regard to the succession of their bishops, fails in the most fundamental article.

Verse 16. *Salute one another with an holy kiss*—Termed by St. Peter, "The kiss of love," 1 Peter v. 14. So the ancient Christians concluded all their solemn offices; the men saluting the men, and the women the women. And this apostolical custom seems to have continued for some ages in all Christian churches.

Verse 17. *Mark them who cause divisions*—Such there were, therefore, at Rome also. *Avoid them*—Avoid all unnecessary intercourse with them.

Verse 18. *By good words*—Concerning themselves, making great promises. *And fair speeches*—Concerning you, praising and flattering you. *The harmless*—Who, doing no ill themselves, are not upon their guard against them that do.

Verse 19. *But I would have you*—Not only obedient, but discreet also. *Wise with regard to that which is good*—As knowing in this as possible. *And simple with regard to that which is evil*—As ignorant of this as possible.

Verse 20. *And the God of peace*—The Author and Lover of it, giving a blessing to your discretion. *Shall bruise Satan under your feet*—Shall defeat all the artifices of that sower of tares, and unite you more and more together in love.

Verse 21. *Timotheus my fellowlabourer*—Here he is named even before St. Paul's kinsmen. But as he had never been at Rome, he is not named in the beginning of the epistle.

Verse 22 *I Tertius, who wrote this epistle, salute you*—Tertius, who

wrote this epistle, salute you in the Lord. Caius my host,
23 and of the whole church, saluteth you. Erastus the chamberlain of the city saluteth you, and Quartus a brother
24 The grace of our Lord Jesus Christ *be* with you all.
25 Now to him who is able to stablish you according to my
gospel, and the preaching of Jesus Christ, (according to the
revelation of the mystery, kept secret since the world began,
26 But now made manifest, and by the scriptures of the prophets, according to the commandment of the eternal God,
27 made known to all nations for the obedience of faith,) To
the only wise God, to him *be* glory through Jesus Christ
for ever. Amen.

wrote what the apostle dictated, inserted this, either by St. Paul's exhortation or ready permission. *Caius*—The Corinthian, 1 Cor. i. 14. *My host, and of the whole church*—Who probably met for some time in his house.

Verse 23. *The chamberlain of the city*—Of Corinth.

Verse 25. *Now to him who is able*—The last words of this epistle exactly answer the first, chapter i. 1—5 : in particular, concerning the power of God, the gospel, Jesus Christ, the scriptures, the obedience of faith, all nations. *To establish you*—Both Jews and gentiles. *According to my gospel, and the preaching of Jesus Christ*—That is, according to the tenor of the gospel of Jesus Christ, which I preach. *According to the revelation of the mystery*—Of the calling of the gentiles, which, as plainly as it was foretold in the Prophets, was still hid from many even of the believing Jews.

Verse 26. *According to the commandment*—The foundation of the apostolical office. *Of the eternal God*—A more proper epithet could not be. A new dispensation infers no change in God. Known unto him are all his works, and every variation of them, from eternity. *Made known to all nations*—Not barely that they might know, but enjoy it also, through obeying the faith.

Verse 27. *To the only wise God*—Whose manifold wisdom is known in the church through the gospel, Eph. iii. 10. "To him who is able," and, "to the wise God," are joined, as 1 Cor. i. 24, where Christ is styled "the wisdom of God," and "the power of God." *To him be glory through Christ Jesus for ever*—And let every believer say, *Amen!*

NOTES

ON

ST. PAUL'S FIRST EPISTLE TO THE CORINTHIANS

Corinth was a city of Achaia, situate on the isthmus which joins Peloponnesus, now called the Morea, to the rest of Greece. Being so advantageously situated for trade, the inhabitants of it abounded in riches, which, by too natural a consequence, led them into luxury, lewdness, and all manner of vice.

Yet even here St. Paul planted a numerous church, chiefly of heathen converts; to whom, about three years after he had left Corinth, he wrote this epistle from Ephesus; as well to correct various disorders of which they were guilty, as to answer some questions which they had proposed to him.

The Epistle consists of

I. The inscription,	C. i. 1—3
II. The treatise itself, in which is,	
1. An exhortation to concord, beating down all glorying in the flesh,	4—C. iv. 21
2 A reproof,	
1. For not excommunicating the incestuous person,	C. v. 1—13
2. For going to law before heathen judges,	C. vi. 1—11
3. A dissuasive from fornication,	12—20
4. An answer to the questions they had proposed concerning marriage,	C. vii. 1, 10, 25, 36, 39.
5 Concerning things sacrificed to idols,	C. viii. 1—C. ix. 1
6. Concerning the veiling of women,	2—16
7. Concerning the Lord's supper,	17—34
8. Concerning spiritual gifts,	C. xii. xiii. xiv
9. Concerning the resurrection,	C. xv. 1—58
10. Concerning the collection for the poor, the coming of himself, of Timothy, of Apollos, the sum of all,	C. xvi, 1, 5, 10, 12, 13, 14
III. The conclusion,	15, 17, 19—24

I. CORINTHIANS.

CHAPTER I. 1 PAUL, called to be an apostle of Jesus
Christ through the will of God, and Sosthenes the brother,
2 To the church of God which is in Corinth, to them that are
sanctified through Christ Jesus, called *and* holy, with all
that in every place call upon the name of our Lord Jesus
3 Christ, both theirs and ours: Grace *be* unto you, and peace,
from God our Father, and the Lord Jesus Christ.
4 I thank my God always on your behalf, for the grace
5 of God which is given you by Christ Jesus; That in every

Verse 1. *Paul, called to be an apostle*—There is great propriety in every clause of the salutation, particularly in this, as there were some in the church of Corinth who called the authority of his mission in question. *Through the will of God*—Called "the commandment of God," 1 Tim. i. 1. This was to the churches the ground of his authority; to Paul himself, of an humble and ready mind. By the mention of God, the authority of man is excluded, Gal. i. 1; by the mention of the will of God, the merit of Paul, 1 Cor. xv. 8, &c. *And Sosthenes*—A Corinthian, St. Paul's companion in travel. It was both humility and prudence in the apostle, thus to join his name with his own, in an epistle wherein he was to reprove so many irregularities. *Sosthenes the brother*—Probably this word is emphatical; as if he had said, Who, from a Jewish opposer of the gospel, became a faithful brother.

Verse 2. *To the church of God which is in Corinth*—St. Paul, writing in a familiar manner to the Corinthians, as also to the Thessalonians and Galatians, uses this plain appellation. To the other churches he uses a more solemn address. *Sanctified through Jesus Christ*—And so undoubtedly they were in general, notwithstanding some exceptions. *Called*—Of Jesus Christ, Rom. i. 6. *And*—As the fruit of that calling made *holy*. *With all that in every place*—Nothing could better suit that catholic love which St. Paul labours to promote in this epistle, than such a declaration of his good wishes for every true Christian upon earth. *Call upon the name of our Lord Jesus Christ*—This plainly implies that all Christians pray to Christ, as well as to the Father through him.

Verse 4. *Always*—Whenever I mention you to God in prayer.

Verse 5. *In all utterance and knowledge*—Of divine things. These gifts the Corinthians particularly admired. Therefore this congratulation naturally tended to soften their spirits, and make way for the reproofs which follow.

thing ye are enriched through him, in all utterance, and *in*
6 all knowledge; As the testimony of Christ was confirmed
7 among you: So that ye are wanting in no good gift; waiting
8 for the revelation of our Lord Jesus Christ: Who will also
confirm you to the end, *that ye may be* blameless in the day
9 of the Lord Jesus Christ. God *is* faithful, by whom ye
were called into the fellowship of his Son Jesus Christ our
Lord.
10 Now I exhort you, brethren, by the name of our Lord
Jesus Christ, that ye all speak the same thing, and *that*
there be no schisms among you; but *that* ye be perfectly
joined together in the same mind and in the same judgment.
11 For it hath been declared to me of you, my brethren, by
them *of the family* of Chloe, that there are contentions
12 among you. Now this I say, every one of you saith, I am

Verse 6. *The testimony of Christ*—The gospel. *Was confirmed among you*—By these gifts attending it. They knew they had received these by the hand of Paul: and this consideration was highly proper, to revive in them their former reverence and affection for their spiritual father.

Verse 7. *Waiting*—With earnest desire. *For the* glorious *revelation of our Lord Jesus Christ*—A sure mark of a true or false Christian, to long for, or dread, this revelation.

Verse 8. *Who will also*—If you faithfully apply to him. *Confirm you to the end. In the day of Christ*—Now it is our day, wherein we are to work out our salvation; then it will be eminently *the day of Christ,* and of his glory in the saints.

Verse 9. *God is faithful*—To all his promises; and therefore "to him that hath shall be given." *By whom ye are called*—A pledge of his willingness to save you unto the uttermost.

Verse 10. *Now I exhort you*—Ye have faith and hope; secure love also. *By the* endearing *name of our Lord Jesus Christ*—Infinitely preferable to all the human names in which ye glory. *That ye all speak the same thing*—They now spoke different things, verse 12. *And that there be no schisms among you*—No alienation of affection from each other. Is this word ever taken in any other sense in scripture? *But that ye be joined in the same mind*—Affections, desires. *And judgment*—Touching all the grand truths of the gospel.

Verse 11. *It hath been declared to me by them of the family of Chloe*—Whom some suppose to have been the wife of Stephanas, and the mother of Fortunatus and Achaicus. By these three the Corinthians had sent their letter to St. Paul, 1 Cor. xvi. 17. *That there are contentions*—A word equivalent with schisms in the preceding verse.

Verse 12. *Now this I say*—That is, what I mean is this: there are various parties among you, who set themselves, one against another, in

of Paul; and I of Apollos; and I of Cephas; and I
13 of Christ. Is Christ divided? was Paul crucified for you?
14 or were ye baptized into the name of Paul? I thank God,
15 that I baptized none of you, but Crispus and Caius; Lest
16 any should say that I had baptized in my own name. I
baptized also the family of Stephanas: I know not that I
baptized any other.
17 For Christ did not send me to baptize, but to preach the
gospel: *but* not with wisdom of speech, lest the cross
18 of Christ should be made of none effect. For the doctrine
of the cross is indeed to them that perish foolishness; but to
19 us who are saved it is the power of God. For it is written,*

* Isaiah xxix. 14.

behalf of the several teachers they admire. *And I of Christ*—They spoke well, if they had not on this pretence despised their teachers, 1 Cor. iv. 8. Perhaps they valued themselves on having heard Christ preach in his own person.

Verse 13. *Is Christ divided*—Are not all the members still under one head? Was not he alone crucified for you all; and were ye not all baptized in his name? The glory of Christ then is not to be divided between him and his servants; neither is the unity of the body to be torn asunder, seeing Christ is one still.

Verse 14. *I thank God*—(A pious phrase for the common one, "I rejoice,") that, in the course of his providence, *I baptized none of you, but Crispus*, once the ruler of the synagogue, *and Caius*.

Verse 15. *Lest any should say that I had baptized in my own name*—In order to attach them to myself.

Verse 16. *I know not*—That is, it does not at present occur to my memory, *that I baptized any other*.

Verse 17. *For God did not send me to baptize*—That was not my chief errand; those of inferior rank and abilities could do it: though all the apostles were sent to baptize also, Matt. xxviii. 19. *But to preach the gospel*—So the apostle slides into his general proposition: *but not with wisdom of speech*—With the artificial ornaments of discourse, invented by human wisdom. *Lest the cross of Christ should be made of none effect*—The whole effect of St. Paul's preaching was owing to the power of God accompanying the plain declaration of that great truth, "Christ bore our sins upon the cross." But this effect might have been imputed to another cause, had he come with that *wisdom of speech* which they admired.

Verse 18. *To them that perish*—By obstinately rejecting the only name whereby they can be saved. *But to us who are saved*—Now *saved* from our sins, and in the way to everlasting salvation, *it is* the great instrument of *the power of God*.

Verse 19. *For it is written*—And the words are remarkably applicable to this great event.

I will destroy the wisdom of the wise, and abolish the
20 understanding of the prudent. † Where *is* the wise?
where *is* the scribe? where *is* the disputer of this world?
21 hath not God made foolish the wisdom of this world? For
since, in the wisdom of God, the world by wisdom knew not
God, it pleased God by the foolishness of preaching to save
22 them that believe. For whereas the Jews demand signs,
23 and the Greeks seek wisdom: We preach Christ crucified,
to the Jews a stumblingblock, and to the Greeks foolishness;
24 But to them that are called, both Jews and Greeks, Christ
25 the power of God, and the wisdom of God. Because the
foolishness of God is wiser than men; and the weakness
26 of God is stronger than men. Behold your calling, brethren

* Isaiah xxxiii. 18.

Verse 20. *Where is the wise?* &c.—The deliverance of Judea from Sennacherib is what Isaiah refers to in these words; in a bold and beautiful allusion to which, the apostle in the clause that follows triumphs over all the opposition of human wisdom to the victorious gospel of Christ. What could the *wise* men of the gentiles do against this? or the Jewish *scribes?* or *the disputers of this world?*—Those among both, who, proud of their acuteness, were fond of controversy, and thought they could confute all opponents. *Hath not God made foolish the wisdom of this world*—That is, shown it to be very foolishness.

Verse 21. *For since in the wisdom of God*—According to his wise disposals, leaving them to make the trial. *The world*—Whether Jewish or gentile, *by* all its boasted *wisdom knew not God*—Though the whole creation declared its Creator, and though he declared himself by all the prophets; *it pleased God, by* a way which those who perish count mere *foolishness, to save them that believe.*

Verse 22. *For whereas the Jews demand* of the apostles, as they did of their Lord, more *signs* still, after all they have seen already; *and the Greeks,* or gentiles, *seek wisdom*—The depths of philosophy, and the charms of eloquence.

Verse 23. *We* go on to *preach,* in a plain and historical, not rhetorical or philosophical, manner, *Christ crucified, to the Jews a stumblingblock*—Just opposite to the "signs" they demand. *And to the Greeks foolishness*—A silly tale, just opposite to the *wisdom* they seek.

Verse 24. *But to them that are called*—And obey the heavenly calling. *Christ*—With his cross, his death, his life, his kingdom. And they experience, first, that he is *the power,* then, that he is *the wisdom, of God.*

Verse 25. *Because the foolishness of God*—The gospel scheme, which the world judge to be mere foolishness, *is wiser than* the wisdom of *men; and,* weak as they account it, *stronger than* all the strength of *men.*

Verse 26. *Behold your calling*—What manner of men they are whom

that not many wise men after the flesh, not many mighty,
27 not many noble, *are called:* But God hath chosen the foolish things of the world to shame the wise; and the weak
things of the world hath God chosen to shame the things
28 that are mighty; And the base things of the world, and
things that are despised, hath God chosen, yea, things that
29 are not, to bring to nought the things that are: That no
30 flesh may glory before God. But of him are ye in Christ
Jesus, who is made by God unto us wisdom, and righteous-
31 ness, and sanctification, and redemption: That, as it is writ-
II. 1 ten, * He that glorieth, let him glory in the Lord. And
I, brethren, when I came to you, came not with loftiness
of speech or of wisdom, declaring to you the testimony
2 of God. For I determined not to know anything among
3 you, save Jesus Christ, and him crucified. And I was with
4 you in weakness, and in fear, and in much trembling. And

* Jer ix. 23, 24.

God calls *That not many wise men after the flesh*—In the account of the world. *Not many mighty*—Men of power and authority.

Verse 28. *Things that are not*—The Jews frequently called the gentiles, "Them that are not," 2 Esdras vi. 56, 57. In so supreme contempt did they hold them. *The things that are*—In high esteem.

Verse 29. *That no flesh*—A fit appellation. Flesh is fair, but withering as grass. *May glory before God*—*In* God we ought to glory.

Verse 30. *Of him*—Out of his free grace and mercy. *Are ye*—Engrafted *into Christ Jesus, who is made unto us* that believe *wisdom,* who were before utterly foolish and ignorant. *Righteousness*—The sole ground of our justification, who were before under the wrath and curse of God. *Sanctification*—A principle of universal holiness, whereas before we were altogether dead in sin. *And redemption*—That is, complete deliverance from all evil, and eternal bliss both of soul and body.

Verse 31. *Let him glory in the Lord*—Not in himself, not in the flesh, not in the world.

Verse 1. *And I* accordingly *came to you, not with loftiness of speech or of wisdom*—I did not affect either deep wisdom or eloquence. *Declaring the testimony of God*—What God gave me to testify concerning his Son.

Verse 2. *I determined not to know anything*—To wave all my other knowledge, and not to preach anything, *save Jesus Christ, and him crucified*—That is, what he did, suffered, taught. A part is put for the whole.

Verse 3. *And I was with you*—At my first entrance. *In weakness*—Of body, 2 Cor. xii. 7. *And in fear*—Lest I should offend any. *And in much trembling*—The emotion of my mind affecting my very body.

Verse 4. *And my speech* in private, as well as *my* public *preaching, was*

my speech and my preaching *was* not with the persuasive
words of human wisdom, but with the demonstration of the
5 Spirit and of power: That your faith might not stand in the
wisdom of men, but in the power of God.
6 Yet we speak wisdom among the perfect. but not the
wisdom of this world, nor of the rulers of this world, that
7 come to nought: But we speak the hidden wisdom of God
in a mystery, which God ordained before the world for our
8 glory: Which none of the rulers of this world knew: for
had they known *it*, they would not have crucified the Lord
9 of glory. But as it is written, * Eye hath not seen, nor
hath ear heard, neither hath it entered into the heart of man,
what things God hath prepared for them that love him

* Isaiah lxiv. 4.

not with the persuasive words of human wisdom, such as the wise men of the world use; *but with the demonstration of the Spirit and of power*—With that powerful kind of demonstration, which flows from the Holy Spirit; which works on the conscience with the most convincing light, and the most persuasive evidence.

Verse 5. *That your faith might not* be built on *the wisdom* or power *of man, but on the* wisdom and *power of God.*

Verse 6. *Yet we speak wisdom*—Yea, the truest and most excellent wisdom. *Among the perfect*—Adult, experienced Christians. By *wisdom* here he seems to mean, not the whole Christian doctrine, but the most sublime and abstruse parts of it. *But not the wisdom* admired and taught by the men *of this world, nor of the rulers of this world,* Jewish or heathen, *that come to nought*—Both they and their wisdom, and the world itself.

Verse 7. *But we speak the* mysterious *wisdom of God,* which was *hidden* for many ages from all the world, and is still hidden even from "babes in Christ;" much more from all unbelievers. *Which God ordained before the world*—So far is this from *coming to nought,* like worldly wisdom. *For our glory*—Arising from the glory of our Lord, and then to be revealed when all worldly glory vanishes.

Verse 8. *Had they known it*—That wisdom. *They would not have crucified*—Punished as a slave. *The Lord of glory*—The giving Christ this august title, peculiar to the great Jehovah, plainly shows him to be the supreme God. In like manner the Father is styled, "the Father of glory," Eph. i. 17; and the Holy Ghost, "the Spirit of glory," 1 Peter iv. 14. The application of this title to all the three, shows that the Father, Son, and Holy Ghost are "the God of glory;" as the only true God is called, Psalm xxix. 3, and Acts vii. 2.

Verse 9. *But* this ignorance of theirs fulfils what *is written* concerning the blessings of the Messiah's kingdom. No natural man hath either *seen, heard,* or known, *the things which God hath prepared,* saith the prophet, *for them that love him*

10 But God hath revealed *them* to us by his Spirit: for the
Spirit searcheth all things, even the deep things of God.
11 For what man knoweth the things of a man, but the spirit
of a man which is in him? so the things of God also know-
12 eth no one, but the Spirit of God. Now we have received,
not the spirit of the world, but the spirit which is of God;
that we may know the things which are freely given to us
13 of God. Which also we speak, not in words taught by
human wisdom, but in those taught by the Spirit; explain-
14 ing spiritual things by spiritual *words*. But the natural
man receiveth not the things of the Spirit: for they are
foolishness to him: neither can he know them, because they
15 are spiritually discerned. But the spiritual man discerneth
indeed all things, yet he himself is discerned by no man.

Verse 10. *But God hath revealed*—Yea, and "freely given," verse 12. *Them to us*—Even inconceivable peace, and joy unspeakable. *By his Spirit*—Who intimately and fully knows them. *For the Spirit searcheth even the deep things of God*—Be they ever so hidden and mysterious; the depths both of his nature and his kingdom.

Verse 11. *For what man knoweth the things of a man*—All the inmost recesses of his mind; although men are all of one nature, and so may the more easily know one another. *So the things of God knoweth no one but the Spirit*—Who, consequently, is God.

Verse 12. *Now we have received, not the spirit of the world*—This spirit is not properly *received;* for the men of the world always had it. But Christians receive the Spirit of God, which before they had not.

Verse 13. *Which also we speak*—As well as know. *In words taught by the Holy Spirit*—Such are all the words of scripture. How high a regard ought we, then, to retain for them! *Explaining spiritual things by spiritual words;* or, *adapting spiritual words to spiritual things*—Being taught of the Spirit to express the things of the Spirit.

Verse 14. *But the natural man*—That is, every man who hath not the Spirit; who has no other way of obtaining knowledge, but by his senses and natural understanding. *Receiveth not*—Does not understand or conceive. *The things of the Spirit*—The things revealed by the Spirit of God, whether relating to his nature or his kingdom. *For they are foolishness to him*—He is so far from understanding, that he utterly despises, them *Neither can he know them*—As he has not the will, so neither has he the power. *Because they are spiritually discerned*—They can only be discerned by the aid of that Spirit, and by those spiritual senses, which he has not.

Verse 15. *But the spiritual man*—He that hath the Spirit. *Discerneth all* the *things* of God whereof we have been speaking. *Yet he himself is discerned by no man*—No natural men. They neither understand what he is, nor what he says.

16 * For who hath known the mind of the Lord, that he may
instruct him? But we have the mind of Christ.

CHAP. III. 1 And I, brethren, could not speak to you
as unto spiritual, but as unto carnal, as unto babes in Christ.
2 I fed you with milk, not with meat: for ye were not able *to*
3 *bear it*, nor are ye now able. For ye are still carnal for
while *there is* among you emulation, and strife, and divi-
4 sions, are ye not carnal, and walk according to man? For
while one saith, I am of Paul, and another, I *am* of Apollos; are ye not carnal?
5 Who then is Paul, and who *is* Apollos, but ministers by
whom ye believed, even as the Lord gave to every man?
6 I planted, Apollos watered; but God gave the increase.
7 So then, neither is he that planteth anything, nor he that
8 watereth; but God that giveth the increase. But he that
planteth and he that watereth are one: and every one shall

* Isaiah xl. 13.

Verse 16 *Who*—What natural man. *We*—Spiritual men; apostles in particular. *Have*—Know, understand. *The mind of Christ*—Concerning the whole plan of gospel salvation.

Verse 1. *And I, brethren*—He spoke before, 1 Cor. ii. 1, of his entrance, now of his progress, among them. *Could not speak to you as unto spiritual*—Adult, experienced Christians. *But as unto* men who were still in great measure *carnal, as unto babes in Christ*—Still weak in grace, though eminent in gifts, 1 Cor. i. 5.

Verse 2. *I fed you*, as babes, *with milk*—The first and plainest truths of the gospel. So should every preacher suit his doctrine to his hearers

Verse 3. *For while there is among you emulation* in your hearts, *strife* in your words, *and* actual *divisions, are ye not carnal, and walk according to man*—As mere men; not as Christians, according to God.

Verse 4. *I am of Apollos*—St. Paul named himself and Apollos, to show that he would condemn any division among them, even though it were in favour of himself, or the dearest friend he had in the world. *Are ye not carnal*—For the Spirit of God allows no party zeal.

Verse 5. *Ministers*—Or servants. *By whom ye believed, as the Lord*, the Master of those servants, *gave to every man*.

Verse 7. *God that giveth the increase*—Is all in all. without him neither planting nor watering avails.

Verse 8. *But he that planteth and he that watereth are one*—Which is another argument against division. Though their labours are different, they are all employed in one general work,—the saving souls. Hence he takes occasion to speak of the reward of them that labour faithfully,

9 receive his own reward according to his own labour. For
we are fellowlabourers of God: ye are God's husbandry, ye
10 are God's building. According to the grace of God given
to me, as a wise master builder, I have laid the foundation,
and another buildeth thereon. But let every one take heed
11 how he buildeth thereon. For other foundation can no man
12 lay than what is laid, which is Jesus Christ. And if any
one build on this foundation gold, silver, costly stones, wood,
13 hay, stubble; Every one's work shall be made manifest: for

and the awful account to be given by all. *Every man shall receive his own* peculiar *reward according to his own* peculiar *labour*—Not according to his success; but he who labours much, though with small success, shall have a great reward.

Has not all this reasoning the same force still? Ministers are still barely instruments in God's hand, and depend as entirely as ever on his blessing, to give the increase to their labours. Without this, they are nothing: with it, their part is so small, that they hardly deserve to be mentioned. May their hearts and hands be more united; and, retaining a due sense of the honour God doeth them in employing them, may they faithfully labour, not as for themselves, but for the great Proprietor of all, till the day come when he will reward them in full proportion to their fidelity and diligence!

Verse 9. *For we are all fellowlabourers*—God's labourers, and fellow-labourers with each other. *Ye are God's husbandry*—This is the sum of what went before: it is a comprehensive word, taking in both a field, a garden, and a vineyard. *Ye are God's building*—This is the sum of what follows.

Verse 10. *According to the grace of God given to me*—This he premises, lest he should seem to ascribe it to himself. *Let every one take heed how he buildeth thereon*—That all his doctrines may be consistent with the foundation.

Verse 11. *For other foundation*—On which the whole church, and all its doctrines, duties, and blessings may be built. *Can no man lay than what is laid*—In the counsels of divine wisdom, in the promises and prophecies of the Old Testament, in the preaching of the apostles, St. Paul in particular. *Which is Jesus Christ*—Who, in his person and offices, is the firm, immovable Rock of Ages, every way sufficient to bear all the weight that God himself, or the sinner, when he believes, can lay upon him.

Verse 12. *If any one build gold, silver, costly stones*—Three sorts of materials which will bear the fire; true and solid doctrines. *Wood, hay, stubble*—Three which will not bear the fire. Such are all doctrines, ceremonies, and forms of human invention; all but the substantial, vital truths of Christianity.

Verse 13. The time is coming when *every one's work shall be made manifest: for the day* of the Lord, that great and final day, *shall declare*

the day shall declare *it*, for it is revealed by fire; yea, the
14 fire shall try every one's work, of what sort it is. If any
one's work which he hath built thereon shall remain, he
15 shall receive a reward. If any one's work shall be burned,
he shall suffer loss: but himself shall be saved; yet so as
16 through the fire. Know ye not that ye are the temple
17 of God, and the Spirit of God dwelleth in you? If any
man destroy the temple of God, him shall God destroy;
18 for the temple of God is holy, which *temple* ye are. Let
none deceive himself. If any one among you thinketh himself to be wise, let him become a fool in this world, that he
19 may become wise. For the wisdom of this world is foolishness with God. As it is written, * He taketh the wise in

* Job v. 13.

it—To all the world. *For it is revealed*—What faith beholds as so certain and so near is spoken of as already present. *By fire; yea, the fire shall try every one's work, of what sort it is*—The strict process of that day will try every man's doctrines, whether they come up to the scripture standard or not. Here is a plain allusion to the flaming light and consuming heat of the general conflagration. But the expression, when applied to the trying of doctrines, and consuming those that are wrong, is evidently figurative; because no material fire can have such an effect on what is of a moral nature. And therefore it is added, he who builds *wood, hay,* or *stubble, shall be saved as through the fire*—Or, as narrowly as a man escapes through the fire, when his house is all in flames about him.

This text, then, is so far from establishing the Romish purgatory, that it utterly overthrows it. For the fire here mentioned does not exist till the day of judgment: therefore, if this be the fire of purgatory, it follows that purgatory does not exist before the day of judgment.

Verse 14. *He shall receive a reward*—A peculiar degree of glory. Some degree even the other will receive, seeing he held the foundation; though through ignorance he built thereon what would not abide the fire.

Verse 15. *He shall suffer loss*—The loss of that peculiar degree of glory.

Verse 16. *Ye*—All Christians. *Are the temple of God*—The most noble kind of building, verse 9.

Verse 17. *If any man destroy the temple of God*—Destroy a real Christian, by schisms, or doctrines fundamentally wrong. *Him shall God destroy*—He shall not be saved at all; not even as "through the fire."

Verse 18. *Let him become a fool in this world*—Such as the world accounts so. *That he may become wise*—In God's account.

Verse 19. *For* all *the* boasted *wisdom of the world is* mere *foolishness* in the sight of God. *He taketh the wise in their own craftiness*—Not only while they think they are acting wisely, but by their very wisdom, which itself is their snare, and the occasion of their destruction.

20 their own craftiness. And again, * The Lord knoweth the
21 reasonings of the wise, that they are vain. Therefore let
22 none glory in men. For all things are your's; whether
Paul, or Apollos, or Cephas, or the world, or life, or death,
23 or things present, or things to come; all are your's; And
IV. 1 ye *are* Christ's; and Christ *is* God's. Let a man so
account us, as servants of Christ, and stewards of the mys-
2 teries of God. Moreover it is required in stewards, that a
3 man be found faithful. But it is a very small thing with
me to be judged by you, or by any man's judgment: yea,
4 I judge not myself. For I am not conscious to myself
of anything; yet am I not hereby justified: but he that

* Psalm xciv. 11.

Verse 20. *That they are but vain*—Empty, foolish; they and all their thoughts.

Verse 21. *Therefore*—Upon the whole. *Let none glory in men*—So as to divide into parties on their account. *For all things are yours*—And we in particular. We are not your lords, but rather your servants.

Verse 22. *Whether Paul, or Apollos, or Cephas*—We are all equally yours, to serve you for Christ's sake. *Or the world*—This leap from Peter to *the world* greatly enlarges the thought, and argues a kind of impatience of enumerating the rest. Peter and every one in the whole world, however excellent in gifts, or grace, or office, are also your servants for Christ's sake. *Or life, or death*—These, with all their various circumstances, are disposed as will be most for your advantage. *Or things present*—On earth. *Or things to come*—In heaven. Contend, therefore, no more about these little things; but be ye united in love, as ye are in blessings.

Verse 23. *And ye are Christ's*—His property, his subjects, his members. *And Christ is God's*—As Mediator, he refers all his services to his Father's glory.

Verse 1. *Let a man account us, as servants of Christ*—The original word properly signifies such servants as laboured at the oar in rowing vessels; and, accordingly, intimates the pains which every faithful minister takes in his Lord's work. O God, where are these ministers to be found? Lord, thou knowest. *And stewards of the mysteries of God*—Dispensers of the mysterious truths of the gospel.

Verse 3. *Yea, I judge not myself*—My final state is not to be determined by my own judgment.

Verse 4. *I am not conscious to myself of anything* evil; *yet am I not hereby justified*—I depend not on this, as a sufficient justification of myself in God's account. *But he that judgeth me is the Lord*—By his sentence I am to stand or fall

5 judgeth me is the Lord. Therefore judge nothing before
the time, until the Lord come, who both will bring to light
the hidden things of darkness, and manifest the counsels
of the hearts: and then shall every one have praise from
God.
6 These things, brethren, I have by a figure transferred to
myself and Apollos for your sakes; that ye may learn by us
not to think *of men* above * what is *here* written, that ye
7 may not be puffed up for one against another. For who
maketh thee to differ *from another?* and what hast thou
which thou hast not received? but if thou hast received *it*,
8 why dost thou boast, as if thou hadst not received *it?* Now
ye are full, now ye are rich, ye have reigned as kings
without us and I would ye did reign, that we also might

* 1 Cor. iii. 7.

Verse 5. *Therefore judge nothing before the time*—Appointed for judging all men. *Until the Lord come, who,* in order to pass a righteous judgment, which otherwise would be impossible, *will both bring to light the things* which are now covered with impenetrable *darkness, and manifest* the most secret springs of action, the principles and intentions *of* every *heart. And then shall every one*—Every faithful steward, *have praise of God.*

Verse 6. *These things*—Mentioned, 1 Cor. i. 10, &c. *I have by a* very obvious *figure transferred to myself, and Apollos*—And Cephas, instead of naming those particular preachers at Corinth, to whom ye are so fondly attached. *That ye may learn by us*—From what has been said concerning us, who, however eminent we are, are mere instruments in God's hand. *Not to think of* any man *above what is here written*—Or above what scripture warrants.

Verse 7. *Who maketh thee to differ*—Either in gifts or graces. *As if thou hadst not received it*—As if thou hadst it originally from thyself.

Verse 8. *Now ye are full*—The Corinthians abounded with spiritual gifts; and so did the apostles: but the apostles, by continual want and sufferings, were kept from self-complacency. The Corinthians suffering nothing, and having plenty of all things, were pleased with and applauded themselves; and they were like children who, being raised in the world, disregard their poor parents. *Now ye are full,* says the apostle, in a beautiful gradation, *ye are rich, ye have reigned as kings*—A proverbial expression, denoting the most splendid and plentiful circumstances. *Without* any thought of *us. And I would ye did reign*—In the best sense: I would ye had attained the height of holiness. *That we might reign with you*—Having no more sorrow on your account, but sharing in your happiness.

Verse 9. *God hath set forth us last, as appointed to death*—Alluding to the Roman custom of bringing forth those persons last on the stage, either to fight with each other, or with wild beasts, who were devoted

9 reign with you. For I know assuredly God hath set forth
us the apostles last, as appointed to death: for we are made
10 a spectacle to the world, both to angels, and to men. We
are fools for Christ's sake, but ye *are* wise in Christ; we
are weak, but ye *are* strong; ye *are* honourable, but we
11 without honour. Even to this present hour we both hunger
and thirst, and are naked, and are buffeted, and have no
12 certain abode; And labour, working with our own hands.
being reviled, we bless; being persecuted, we suffer it
13 Being defamed, we intreat: we are made as the filth of the
14 world, and offscouring of all things to this day. I do not
write these things to shame you, but as my beloved children
15 I warn *you.* For if ye have ten thousand instructers in
Christ, yet *have ye* not many fathers: for I have begotten

to death; so that, if they escaped one day, they were brought out again and again, till they were killed.

Verse 10. *We are fools,* in the account of the world, *for Christ's sake, but ye are wise in Christ*—Though ye are Christians, ye think yourselves wise; and ye have found means to make the world think you so too. *We are weak*—In presence, in infirmities, in sufferings. *But ye are strong*—In just opposite circumstances.

Verse 11. *And are naked*—Who can imagine a more glorious triumph of the truth, than that which is gained in these circumstances; when St. Paul, with an impediment in his speech, and a person rather contemptible than graceful, appeared in a mean, perhaps tattered, dress before persons of the highest distinction, and yet commanded such attention, and made such deep impressions upon them!

Verse 12. *We bless—suffer it—intreat*—We do not return revilings, persecution, defamation; nothing but blessing.

Verse 13. *We are made as the filth of the world, and offscouring of all things*—Such were those poor wretches among the heathens, who were taken from the dregs of the people, to be offered as expiatory sacrifices to the infernal gods. They were loaded with curses, affronts, and injuries, all the way they went to the altars; and when the ashes of those unhappy men were thrown into the sea, these very names were given them in the ceremony.

Verse 14. *I do not write these things to shame you, but as my beloved children I warn you*—It is with admirable prudence and sweetness the apostle adds this, to prevent any unkind construction of his words.

Verse 15. *I have begotten you*—This excludes not only Apollos, his successor, but also Silas and Timothy, his companions; and the relation between a spiritual father and his children brings with it an inexpressible nearness and affection.

16 you in Christ Jesus through the gospel. I beseech you
17 therefore, be ye followers of me. For this cause I have
sent to you Timotheus, who is my beloved son, and faithful
in the Lord, who shall remind you of my ways in Christ,
18 as I teach everywhere in every church. Now some are
19 puffed up, as if I would not come to you. But I will come
to you shortly, if the Lord permit, and will know, not the
20 speech of them who are puffed up, but the power. For the
21 kingdom of God *is* not in speech, but in power. What will
ye? that I come to you with a rod, or in love, and the spirit of meekness?

CHAP. V. 1 It is commonly reported *that there* is fornication among you, and such fornication as *is* not even named
among the heathens, that one should have his father's wife.
2 And are ye puffed up? have ye not rather mourned, that
he who hath done this deed might be taken from among
3 you? For I verily, as absent in body, but present in spirit, have already, as if I were present, judged him who hath
4 so done this, In the name of our Lord Jesus Christ, when

Verse 16. *Be ye followers of me*—In that spirit and behaviour which I have so largely declared.

Verse 17. *My beloved son*—Elsewhere he styles him "brother," 2 Cor. i. 1; but here paternal affection takes place. *As I teach*—No less by example than precept.

Verse 18. *Now some are puffed up*—St. Paul saw, by a divine light, the thoughts which would arise in their hearts *As if I would not come*—Because I send Timothy.

Verse 19. *I will know*—He here shows his fatherly authority *Not the* big, empty *speech of* these vain boasters, *but* how much of *the power* of God attends them.

Verse 20. *For the kingdom of God*—Real religion, does *not* consist in words, *but in the power* of God ruling the heart.

Verse 21. *With a rod*—That is, with severity.

Verse 1. *Fornication*—The original word implies criminal conversation of any kind whatever. *His father's wife*—While his father was alive.

Verse 2. *Are ye puffed up?* Should *ye not rather have mourned*—Have solemnly humbled yourselves, and at that time of solemn mourning have expelled that notorious sinner from your communion?

Verse 3. *I verily, as present in spirit*—Having a full (it seems, a miraculous) view of the whole fact. *Have already, as if I were* actually *present, judged him who hath so* scandalously *done this.*

Verse 4. *And my spirit*—Present with you. *With the power of the Lord Jesus Christ*—To confirm my sentence.

ye are gathered together, and my spirit, with the power
5 of our Lord Jesus Christ, To deliver such an one to Satan
for the destruction of the flesh, that the spirit may be saved
6 in the day of the Lord Jesus. Your glorying *is* not good.
Know ye not that a little leaven leaveneth the whole lump?
7 Purge out the old leaven, that ye may be a new lump, as
ye are unleavened. For our passover is slain for us, *even*
8 Christ: Therefore let us keep the feast, not with the old
leaven, nor with the leaven of wickedness and malignity;
but with the unleavened bread of sincerity and truth.
9 I wrote to you an epistle not to converse with lewd per-
10 sons: But not altogether with the lewd persons of this
world, or the covetous, or the rapacious, or idolaters; for

Verse 5. *To deliver such an one*—This was the highest degree of punishment in the Christian church; and we may observe, the passing this sentence was the act of the apostle, not of the Corinthians. *To Satan*—Who was usually permitted, in such cases, to inflict pain or sickness on the offender. *For the destruction*—Though slowly and gradually *Of the flesh*—Unless prevented by speedy repentance.

Verse 6. *Your glorying*—Either in your gifts or prosperity, at such a time as this, *is not good. Know ye not that a little leaven*—One sin, or one sinner. *Leaveneth the whole lump*—Diffuses guilt and infection through the whole congregation.

Verse 7. *Purge out therefore the old leaven*—Both of sinners and of sin. *That ye may be a new lump, as ye are unleavened*—That is, that being *unleavened ye may be a new lump,* holy unto the Lord. *For our passover is slain for us*—The Jewish passover, about the time of which this epistle was wrote, 1 Cor. v. 11, was only a type of this. What exquisite skill both here and everywhere conducts the zeal of the inspired writer! How surprising a transition is here, and yet how perfectly natural! The apostle, speaking of the incestuous criminal, slides into his darling topic,—a crucified Saviour. Who would have expected it on such an occasion? Yet, when it is thus brought in, who does not see and admire both the propriety of the subject, and the delicacy of its introduction?

Verse 8. *Therefore let us keep the feast*—Let us feed on him by faith. Here is a plain allusion to the Lord's supper, which was instituted in the room of the passover. *Not with the old leaven*—Of heathenism or Judaism. *Malignity* is stubbornness in evil. *Sincerity and truth* seem to be put here for the whole of true, inward religion.

Verse 9. *I wrote to you* in a former *epistle*—And, doubtless, both St. Paul and the other apostles wrote many things which are not extant now. *Not to converse*—Familiarly; not to contract any intimacy or acquaintance with them, more than is absolutely necessary.

Verse 10. *But* I did *not* mean that you should *altogether* refrain from conversing with heathens, though they are guilty in some of these

11 then ye must go out of the world. But I have now written
unto you, if any who is named a brother be a lewd person,
or covetous, or an idolater, or a railer, or a drunkard, or rapacious; not to converse with such an one, no, not to eat with
12 him. For what have I to do to judge them that are with-
13 out? do not ye judge them that are within? (But them that
are without God will judge.) And ye will take away from
among yourselves that wicked person.

CHAP. VI. 1 Dare any of you, having a matter against
2 another, refer it to the unjust, and not to the saints? Know
ye not that the saints shall judge the world? and if the
world is judged by you, are ye unworthy to judge the small-
3 est matters? Know ye not that we shall judge angels? how
4 much more things pertaining to this life? If then ye have
any controversies of things pertaining to this life, do ye set
5 them to judge who are of no esteem in the church? I speak

respects. *Covetous, rapacious, idolaters*—Sinners against themselves, their neighbour, God. *For then ye must go out of the world*—Then all civil commerce must cease. So that going out of the world, which some account a perfection, St. Paul accounts an utter absurdity.

Verse 11. *Who is named a brother*—That is, a Christian; especially if a member of the same congregation. *Rapacious*—Guilty of oppression, extortion, or any open injustice. *No, not to eat with him*—Which is the lowest degree of familiarity.

Verse 12. I speak of Christians only. *For what have I to do to judge* heathens? But ye, as well as I, judge those of your own community.

Verse 13. *Them that are without God will judge*—The passing sentence on these he hath reserved to himself. *And ye will take away that wicked person*—This properly belongs to you.

Verse 1. *The unjust*—The heathens. A Christian could expect no justice from these. *The saints*—Who might easily decide these smaller differences in a private and friendly manner.

Verse 2. *Know ye not*—This expression occurs six times in this single chapter, and that with a peculiar force; for the Corinthians knew and gloried in it, but they did not practise. *That the saints*—After having been judged themselves. *Shall judge the world*—Shall be assessors with Christ in the judgment wherein he shall condemn all the wicked, as well angels as men, Matt. xix. 28; Rev. xx. 4.

Verse 4. *Them who are of no esteem in the church*—That is, heathens, who, as such, could be in no esteem with the Christians.

Verse 5. *Is there not one among you*, who are such admirers of wisdom, that is *wise* enough to decide such causes?

to your shame. What! is there not so much as one wise
man among you, that shall be able to judge between his
6 brethren? But brother goeth to law with brother, and this
7 before the infidels. Indeed there is altogether a fault among
you, that ye have contests with each other. Why do ye not
rather suffer wrong? why do ye not rather suffer yourselves
8 to be defrauded? Nay, ye do wrong, and defraud, even
9 *your* brethren. Know ye not that the unjust shall not inherit the kingdom of God? Be not deceived: neither forni-
cators, nor idolaters, nor adulterers, nor the effeminate, nor
10 sodomites, Nor thieves, nor the covetous, nor revilers, nor
11 the rapacious, shall inherit the kingdom of God. And such
were some of you: but ye are washed, but ye are sanctified,
but ye are justified in the name of the Lord Jesus, and by
the Spirit of our God.
12 All things are lawful for me, but all things are not expedient: all things are lawful for me, but I will not be brought

Verse 7. *Indeed there is a fault, that ye* quarrel with each other at all, whether ye go to law or no. *Why do ye not rather suffer wrong*—All men cannot or will not receive this saying. Many aim only at this, "I will neither do wrong, nor suffer it." These are honest heathens, but no Christians.

Verse 8. *Nay, ye do wrong*—Openly. *And defraud*—Privately. O how powerfully did the mystery of iniquity already work!

Verse 9. *Idolatry* is here placed between *fornication* and *adultery*, because they generally accompanied it. *Nor the effeminate*—Who live in an easy, indolent way; taking up no cross, enduring no hardship.

But how is this? These good-natured, harmless people are ranked with *idolaters* and *sodomites!* We may learn hence, that we are never secure from the greatest sins, till we guard against those which are thought the least; nor, indeed, till we think no sin is little, since every one is a step toward hell.

Verse 11. *And such were some of you: but ye are washed*—From those gross abominations; nay, and *ye are* inwardly *sanctified;* not before, but in consequence of, your being *justified in the name*—That is, by the merits, *of the Lord Jesus,* through which your sins are forgiven. *And by the Spirit of our God*—By whom ye are thus *washed* and *sanctified.*

Verse 12. *All things*—Which are lawful for you *Are lawful for me, but all things are not* always *expedient*—Particularly when anything would offend my weak brother; or when it would enslave my own soul. For though *all things are lawful for me,* yet *I will not be brought under the power of any*—So as to be uneasy when I abstain from it; for, if so, then I am under the power of it.

13 under the power of any. Meats *are* for the belly, and the
belly for meats: yet God will destroy both it and them.
But the body *is* not for fornication, but for the Lord; and
14 the Lord for the body. And God hath both raised up the
15 Lord, and will also raise us up by his power. Know ye not
that your bodies are members of Christ? shall I then take
the members of Christ, and make them the members of an
16 harlot? God forbid. Know ye not that he who is joined
to an harlot is one body? * for they two, saith he, shall be
17 one flesh. But he that is joined to the Lord is one spirit.
18 Flee fornication. Every sin that a man doeth is without the
body; but he that committeth fornication sinneth against his
19 own body. Know ye not that your body is the temple of the
Holy Ghost who is in you, whom ye have from God, and ye
20 are not your own? For ye are bought with a price: therefore glorify God with your body, and your spirit, which are
God's.

* Gen. ii. 24.

Verse 13. As if he had said, I speak this chiefly with regard to meats; (and would to God all Christians would consider it!) particularly with regard to those offered to idols, and those forbidden in the Mosaic law. These, I grant, are all indifferent, and have their use, though it is only for a time: then meats, and the organs which receive them, will together moulder into dust. But the case is quite otherwise with fornication. This is not indifferent, but at all times evil. *For the body is for the Lord*—Designed only for his service. *And the Lord,* in an important sense, *for the body*—Being the Saviour of this, as well as of the soul; in proof of which God hath already raised him from the dead.

Verse 17. *But he that is joined to the Lord*—By faith. *Is one spirit with him*—And shall he make himself one flesh with an harlot?

Verse 18. *Flee fornication*—All unlawful commerce with women, with speed, with abhorrence, with all your might. *Every sin that a man* commits against his neighbour terminates upon an object out of himself, and does not so immediately pollute his body, though it does his soul. *But he that committeth fornication, sinneth against his own body*—Pollutes, dishonours, and degrades it to a level with brute beasts.

Verse 19. And even your body is not, strictly speaking, your own even this *is the temple of the Holy Ghost*—Dedicated to him, and inhabited by him. What the apostle calls elsewhere "the temple of God," 1 Cor. iii. 16, 17, and "the temple of the living God," 2 Cor. vi. 16, he here styles *the temple of the Holy Ghost;* plainly showing that the Holy Ghost is the living God.

Verse 20. *Glorify God with your body, and your spirit*—Yield your bodies and all their members, as well as your souls and all their faculties, as instruments of righteousness to God. Devote and employ

CHAP. VII. 1 Now concerning the things whereof ye
wrote to me: *It is* good for a man not to touch a woman.
2 Yet, *to avoid* fornication, let every man have his own wife.
3 and let every woman have her own husband. Let the husband render the debt to the wife: and in like manner the
4 wife to the husband. The wife hath not power over her
own body, but the husband: and in like manner the husband also hath not power over his own body, but the wife.
5 Withdraw not from each other, unless *it be* by consent for
a time, that ye may give yourselves to prayer; and may
come together again, lest Satan tempt you through your
6 incontinence. But I say this by permission, not by way
7 of precept. For I would that all men were even as myself.
But every one hath his proper gift from God, one after this
manner, another after that.
8 But to the unmarried and the widows I say, It is good

all ye have, and all ye are, entirely, unreservedly, and for ever, to his glory.

Verse 1. *It is good for a man*—Who is master of himself. *Not to touch a woman*—That is, not to marry. So great and many are the advantages of a single life.

Verse 2. *Yet,* when it is needful, *in order to avoid fornication, let every man have his own wife. His own*—For Christianity allows no polygamy

Verse 3. *Let* not married persons fancy that there is any perfection in living with each other, as if they were unmarried. *The debt*—This ancient reading seems far more natural than the common one.

Verse 4. *The wife—the husband*—Let no one forget this, on pretence of greater purity.

Verse 5. *Unless it be by consent for a time*—That on those special and solemn occasions ye may entirely give yourselves up to the exercises of devotion. *Lest*—If ye should long remain separate. *Satan tempt you*—To unclean thoughts, if not actions too.

Verse 6. *But I say this*—Concerning your separating for a time and coming together again. Perhaps he refers also to verse 2.

Verse 7. *For I would that all men were* herein *even as I*—I would that all believers who are now unmarried would remain "eunuchs for the kingdom of heaven's sake" St. Paul, having tasted the sweetness of this liberty, wished others to enjoy it, as well as himself. *But every one hath his proper gift from God*—According to our Lord's declaration, "All men cannot receive this saying, save they," the happy few, "to whom it is given," Matt. xix. 11.

Verse 8. *It is good for them if they remain even as I*—That St. Paul was then single is certain; and from Acts vii. 58, compared with the following parts of the history, it seems probable that he always was so. It does

9 for them if they remain even as I. But if they have not
power over themselves, let them marry: for it is better to
marry than to burn.
10 The married I command, *yet* not I, but the Lord, * That
11 the wife depart not from her husband: But if she depart,
let her remain unmarried, or be reconciled to her husband:
12 and let not the husband put away his wife. To the rest
speak I, not the Lord: If any brother hath an unbelieving
wife, and she consent to dwell with him, let him not put
13 her away. And the wife who hath an unbelieving husband,
that consenteth to live with her, let her not put him away.
14 For the unbelieving husband hath been sanctified by the
wife, and the unbelieving wife hath been sanctified by the
husband: else were your children unclean; but now they
15 are holy. But if the unbeliever depart, let him depart. A brother or a sister is not enslaved in such *cases:* but God hath
16 called us to peace. For how knowest thou, O wife, but thou
mayest save thy husband? or knowest thou, O husband, but
17 thou mayest save thy wife? But as God hath distributed
to every one, as the Lord hath called every one, so let him

* Matt. v 32.

not appear that this declaration, any more than verse 1, hath any reference at all to a state of persecution.

Verse 10. *Not I*—Only. *But the Lord*—Christ; by his express command, Matt. v. 32.

Verse 11. *But if she depart*—Contrary to this express prohibition. *And let not the husband put away his wife*—Except for the cause of adultery.

Verse 12. *To the rest*—Who are married to unbelievers. *Speak I*—By revelation from God, though our Lord hath not left any commandment concerning it. *Let him not put her away*—The Jews, indeed, were obliged of old to put away their idolatrous wives, Ezra x. 3; but their case was quite different. They were absolutely forbid to marry idolatrous women; but the persons here spoken of were married while they were both in a state of heathenism.

Verse 14. *For the unbelieving husband hath,* in many instances, *been sanctified by the wife—Else your children* would have been brought up heathens; whereas *now they are* Christians. As if he had said, Ye see the proof of it before your eyes.

Verse 15. *A brother or a sister*—A Christian man or woman. *Is not enslaved*—Is at full liberty. *In such cases: but God hath called us to peace*—To live peaceably with them, if it be possible.

Verse 17. *But as God hath distributed*—The various stations of life, and various relations, *to every one,* let him take care to discharge his

18 walk. And thus I ordain in all the churches. Is any one
called being circumcised? let him not become uncircumcised. Is any one called in uncircumcision? let him not
19 be circumcised. Circumcision is nothing, and uncircumcision is nothing, but keeping the commandments of God.
20 Let every one in the calling wherein he is called therein
21 abide. Wast thou called *being* a bondman? care not for it:
22 but if thou canst be made free, use *it* rather. For he that
is called by the Lord, *being* a bondman, is the Lord's freeman: and in the like manner he that is called *being* free is
23 the bondman of Christ. Ye are bought with a price; do
24 not become the bondslaves of men. Brethren, let every
one, wherein he is called, therein abide with God.
25 Now concerning virgins I have no commandment from
the Lord: but I give my judgment, as one who hath

duty therein. The gospel disannuls none of these. *And thus I ordain in all the churches*—As a point of the highest concern.

Verse 19. *Circumcision is nothing, and uncircumcision is nothing*—Will neither promote nor obstruct our salvation. The one point is, *keeping the commandments of God;* "faith working by love."

Verse 20. *In the calling*—The outward state. *Wherein he is*—When God calls him. Let him not seek to change this, without a clear direction from Providence.

Verse 21. *Care not for it*—Do not anxiously seek liberty. *But if thou canst be free, use it rather*—Embrace the opportunity.

Verse 22. *Is the Lord's freeman*—Is free in this respect. The Greek word implies one that was a slave, but now is free. *Is the bondman of Christ*—Not free in this respect; not at liberty to do his own will.

Verse 23. *Ye are bought with a price*—Ye belong to God; therefore, where it can be avoided, *do not become the bondslaves of men*—Which may expose you to many temptations.

Verse 24. *Therein abide with God*—Doing all things as unto God, and as in his immediate presence. They who thus *abide with God* preserve an holy indifference with regard to outward things.

Verse 25. *Now concerning virgins*—Of either sex. *I have no commandment from the Lord*—By a particular revelation. Nor was it necessary he should; for the apostles wrote nothing which was not divinely inspired: but with this difference,—sometimes they had a particular revelation, and a special commandment; at other times they wrote from the divine light which abode with them, the standing treasure of the Spirit of God. And this, also, was not their private opinion, but a divine rule of faith and practice. *As one* whom God hath made *faithful* in my apostolic office; who therefore faithfully deliver what I receive from him.

26 obtained mercy of the Lord to be faithful. I apprehend
therefore that this is good for the present distress, that *it is*
27 good for a man to continue as he is. Art thou bound to
a wife? seek not to be loosed. Art thou loosed from a
28 wife? seek not a wife. Yet if thou dost marry, thou hast
not sinned; and if a virgin marry, she hath not sinned.
Nevertheless such will have trouble in the flesh: but I
29 spare you. But this I say, brethren, the time is short
it remaineth, that even they that have wives, be as if they
30 had none; And they that weep, as if they wept not;
and they that rejoice, as if they rejoiced not; and
31 they that buy, as if they possessed not; And they that
use this world, as not abusing it: for the fashion of this
32 world passeth away. Now I would have you without
carefulness. The unmarried man careth for the things of
33 the Lord, how he may please the Lord: But the married

Verses 26, 27. *This is good for the present distress*—While any church is under persecution. *For a man to continue as he is*—Whether married or unmarried. St. Paul does not here urge *the present distress* as a reason for celibacy, any more than for marriage; but for a man's not seeking to alter his state, whatever it be, but making the best of it.

Verse 28. *Such will have trouble in the flesh*—Many outward troubles. *But I spare you*—I speak as little and as tenderly as possible.

Verse 29. *But this I say, brethren*—With great confidence *The time* of our abode here *is short*. It plainly follows, *that even they who have wives* be as serious, zealous, active, dead to the world, as devoted to God, as holy in all manner of conversation, *as if they had none*—By so easy a transition does the apostle slide from every thing else to the one thing needful; and, forgetting whatever is temporal, is swallowed up in eternity

Verse 30. *And they that weep, as if they wept not*—"Though sorrowful, yet always rejoicing." *They that rejoice, as if they rejoiced not*—Tempering their joy with godly fear. *They that buy, as if they possessed not*—Knowing themselves to be only stewards, not proprietors.

Verse 31. *And they that use this world, as not abusing it*—Not seeking happiness in it, but in God: using every thing therein only in such a manner and degree as most tends to the knowledge and love of God. *For the* whole scheme and *fashion of this world*—This marrying, weeping, rejoicing, and all the rest, not only will pass, but now *passeth away*, is this moment flying off like a shadow.

Verse 32. *Now I would have you*—For this flying moment. *Without carefulness*—Without any incumbrance of your thoughts. *The unmarried man*—If he understand and use the advantage he enjoys—*Careth* only *for the things of the Lord, how he may please the Lord.*

Verse 33. *But the married careth for the things of the world*—And it is

careth for the things of the world, how he may please
34 his wife. There is a difference also between a wife and
a virgin. The unmarried woman careth for the things
of the Lord, that she may be holy both in body and spirit.
but the married careth for the things of the world, how
35 she may please her husband. And this I say for your own
profit, not that I may cast a snare upon you, but that ye
may decently wait upon the Lord, and without distraction.
36 But if any think that he acteth indecently toward his
virgin, if she be above age, and need so require, let him
37 do what he will, he sinneth not: let them marry. Nevertheless, he that standeth steadfast in his heart, having no
necessity, but having power over his own will, and hath
determined this in his heart, to keep his virgin, doeth well.
38 So then he also that giveth in marriage doeth well; but he
that giveth not in marriage doeth better.
39 The wife is bound as long as her husband liveth; but
if her husband be dead, she is at liberty to marry whom
40 she will, only in the Lord. But she is happier, if she con-

his duty so to do, so far as becomes a Christian. *How he may please his wife*—And provide all things needful for her and his family.

Verse 34. *There is a difference also between a wife and a virgin*—Whether the church be under persecution or not. *The unmarried woman*—If she know and use her privilege. *Careth* only *for the things of the Lord*—All her time, care, and thoughts centre in this, how *she may be holy both in body and spirit*. This is the standing advantage of a single life, in all ages and nations. But who makes a suitable use of it?

Verse 35. *Not that I may cast a snare upon you*—Who are not able to receive this saying. *But for your profit*—Who are able. *That ye may* resolutely and perseveringly *wait upon the Lord*—The word translated *wait* signifies *sitting close by* a person, in a *good* posture to hear. So Mary sat at the feet of Jesus, Luke x. 39. *Without distraction*—Without having the mind drawn any way from its centre; from its close attention to God; by any person, or thing, or care, or incumbrance whatsoever.

Verse 36. *But if any* parent *think he* should otherwise *act indecently*—Unbecoming his character. *Toward his virgin* daughter, *if she be above age*, (or of full age,) *and need so require*, verse 9, *let them marry*—Her suitor and she.

Verse 37. *Having no necessity*—Where there is no such need. *But having power over his own will*—Which would incline him to desire the increase of his family, and the strengthening it by new relations.

Verse 38. *Doeth better*—If there be no necessity.

Verse 39. *Only in the Lord*—That is, only let Christians marry Christians: a standing direction, and one of the utmost importance.

tinue as she is, in my judgment; and I think that I also
have the Spirit of God.

CHAP. VIII. 1 Now as to things sacrificed to idols,
we know; for all of us have knowledge. Knowledge
2 puffeth up, but love edifieth. And if any one think he
knoweth any thing, he knoweth nothing yet as he ought
3 to know. But if any one love God, he is known by him.
4 I say, as to the eating of things sacrificed to idols, we know
that an idol *is* nothing in the world, and that *there is* no
5 God but one. For though there be that are called gods,
whether in heaven or on earth, (as there are many gods and
6 many lords,) Yet to us *there is but* one God, the Father,
from whom are all things, and we for him; and one Lord
Jesus Christ, by whom *are* all things, and we by him

Verse 40. *I also*—As well as any of you. *Have the Spirit of God*—Teaching me all things This does not imply any doubt; but the strongest certainty of it, together with a reproof of them for calling it in question. Whoever, therefore, would conclude from hence, that St. Paul was not certain he had the Spirit of Christ, neither understands the true import of the words, nor considers how expressly he lays claim to the Spirit, both in this epistle, (ii. 16, xiv. 37,) and the other. (xiii. 3.) Indeed, it may be doubted whether the word here and elsewhere translated *think*, does not always imply the fullest and strongest assurance See 1 Cor. x. 12.

Verse 1. *Now concerning* the next question you proposed. *All of us have knowledge*—A gentle reproof of their self-conceit. *Knowledge* without love always *puffeth up*. *Love* alone *edifies*—Builds us up in holiness

Verse 2. *If any man think he knoweth any thing*—Aright, unless so far as he is taught by God. *He knoweth nothing yet as he ought to know*—Seeing there is no true knowledge without divine love.

Verse 3. *He is known*—That is, approved, *by him*. Psalm i. 6.

Verse 4. *We know that an idol is nothing*—A mere nominal god, having no divinity, virtue, or power.

Verse 5. *For though there be that are called gods*—By the heathens both celestial, (as they style them,) terrestrial, and infernal deities.

Verse 6. *Yet to us*—Christians. *There is but one God*—This is exclusive, not of the *One Lord*, as if he were an inferior deity; but only of the idols to which the *One God* is opposed. *From whom are all things*—By creation, providence, and grace. *And we for him*—The end of all we are, have, and do. *And one Lord*—Equally the object of divine worship. *By whom are all things*—Created, sustained, and governed. *And we by him*—Have access to the Father, and all spiritual blessings.

Verse 7. *Some eat, with consciousness of the idol*—That is, fancying it is

7 But *there is* not in all men this knowledge: for some do
even until now, with consciousness of the idol, eat *it* as
sacrificed to the idol; and their conscience, being weak, is
defiled.
8 But meat commendeth us not to God; for neither if we
eat are we the better, nor if we eat not are we the worse.
9 But take heed lest by any means this your liberty become a
10 stumblingblock to the weak. For if any one see thee, who
hast knowledge, sitting at meat in an idol-temple, will not
the conscience of him that is weak be encouraged to eat of
11 the things sacrificed to the idol? And through thy knowledge
12 shall the weak brother perish, for whom Christ died? But
when ye sin thus against your brethren, and wound their
13 weak conscience, ye sin against Christ. Wherefore if meat
make my brother to offend, I will eat no flesh while the
world standeth, lest I make my brother to offend.

CHAP. IX. 1 Am I not free? am I not an apostle?
have I not seen Jesus Christ our Lord? are not ye my work

something, and that it makes the meat unlawful to be eaten. *And their conscience, being weak*—Not rightly informed. *Is defiled*—contracts guilt by doing it.

Verse 8. *But meat commendeth us not to God*—Neither by eating, nor by refraining from it. Eating and not eating are in themselves things merely indifferent.

Verse 10. *For if any one see thee who hast knowledge*—Whom he believes to have more knowledge than himself, and who really hast this knowledge, that *an idol is nothing—sitting down* to an entertainment *in an idol-temple.* The heathens frequently made entertainments in their temples, on what had been sacrificed to their idols. *Will not the conscience of him that is weak*—Scrupulous. *Be encouraged*—By thy example. *To eat*—Though with a doubting conscience.

Verse 11. *And through thy knowledge shall the weak brother perish, for whom Christ died?*—And for whom thou wilt not lose a meal's meat, so far from dying for him! We see, Christ died even for them that perish.

Verse 12. *Ye sin against Christ*—Whose members they are.

Verse 13. *If meat*—Of any kind Who will follow this example? What preacher or private Christian will abstain from any thing lawful in itself, when it offends a weak brother?

Verse 1. *Am I not free? am I not an apostle?*—That is, Have not I the liberty of a common Christian? yea, that of an apostle? He vindicates his apostleship, verses 1—3: his apostolical liberty, verses 4—19.

2 in the Lord? If I am not an apostle to others, yet I am
3 to you: for ye are the seal of my apostleship. My answer
4 to them who examine me is this, Have we not power to eat
5 and to drink? Have we not power to lead about a sister, a
wife, as well as the other apostles, and the brethren of the Lord,
6 and Peter? Or I only and Barnabas, have we not power
7 to forbear working? Who ever serveth as a soldier at his
own charge? who planteth a vineyard, and doth not eat
its fruit? or who feedeth a flock, and doth not eat of the
8 milk of the flock? Do I speak these things as a man? doth
9 not the law also speak the same? For it is written in the
law of Moses, * Thou shalt not muzzle the ox that treadeth
10 out the corn. Doth God take care for oxen? Or speaketh he

* Deut. xxv. 4

Have I not seen Jesus Christ?—Without this he could not have been one of those first grand witnesses. *Are not ye my work in the Lord*—A full evidence that God hath sent me? And yet some, it seems, objected to his being an apostle, because he had not asserted his privilege in demanding and receiving such maintenance from the churches as was due to that office.

Verse 2. *Ye are the seal of my apostleship*—Who have received not only faith by my mouth, but all the gifts of the Spirit by my hands.

Verse 3. *My answer to them who examine me*—Concerning my apostleship. *Is this*—Which I have now given.

Verse 4. *Have we not power*—I and my fellow-labourers. *To eat and to drink*—At the expense of those among whom we labour.

Verse 5. *Have we not power to lead about with us a sister, a wife*—And to demand sustenance for her also? *As well as the other apostles*—Who therefore, it is plain, did this. *And Peter*—Hence we learn, 1. That St. Peter continued to live with his wife after he became an apostle: 2. That he had no rights as an apostle which were not common to St. Paul.

Verse 6. *To forbear working*—With our hands.

Verse 8. *Do I speak as a man*—Barely on the authority of human reason? Does not God also say, in effect, the same thing? *The ox that treadeth out the corn*—This was the custom in Judea, and many eastern nations. In several of them it is retained still. And at this day, horses tread out the corn in some parts of Germany.

Verse 9. *Doth God*—In this direction. *Take care for oxen*—Only? Hath he not a farther meaning? And so undoubtedly he hath in all the other Mosaic laws of this kind.

Verse 10. *He who ploweth ought to plow in hope*—Of reaping. This seems to be a proverbial expression. *And he that thresheth in hope*—Ought not to be disappointed, ought to eat the fruit of his labours. And ought they who labour in God's husbandry.

altogether for our sakes? For our sakes it was written: for
he who ploweth ought to plow in hope; and he that thresh-
11 eth in hope *ought* to be a partaker of his hope. If we have
sown unto you spiritual things, *is it* a great matter if we
12 shall reap your carnal things? If others partake of this
power over you, *do* not we rather? Yet we have not used
this power; but we suffer all things, lest we should give
13 any hinderance to the gospel of Christ. Know ye not that
they who are employed about holy things are fed out of the
temple? and they who wait at the altar are partakers with
14 the altar? So also hath the Lord * ordained that they who
15 preach the gospel should live of the gospel. But I have
used none of these things: nor have I written thus, that it
might be done so unto me: for *it were* better for me to die,
than that any man should make *this* my glorying void.
16 For if I preach the gospel, I have nothing to glory of;
for a necessity lieth upon me; and woe to me, if I preach not
17 the gospel! If indeed I do this willingly, I have a reward;
but if unwillingly, *yet* a dispensation is intrusted to me.
18 What then *is* my reward? That, when I preach the gospel, I may make the gospel without charge, that I abuse

* Matt. x. 10

Verse 11. *Is it a great matter if we shall reap* as much of *your carnal things*—As is needful for our sustenance? Do you give us things of greater value than those you receive from us?

Verse 12. *If others*—Whether true or false apostles. *Partake of this power*—Have a right to be maintained. *Do not we rather*—On account of our having laboured so much more? *Lest we should give any hinderance to the gospel*—By giving an occasion of cavil or reproach.

Verse 15. *It were better for me to die than*—To give occasion to them that seek occasion against me, 2 Cor. xi. 12.

Verse 17. *Willingly*—He seems to mean, without receiving anything. St. Paul here speaks in a manner peculiar to himself. Another might have preached willingly, and yet have received a maintenance from the Corinthians. But if he had received anything from them, he would have termed it preaching unwillingly. And so, in the next verse, another might have used that power without abusing it. But his own using it at all, he would have termed abusing it. *A dispensation is intrusted to me*—Therefore I dare not refrain.

Verse 18. *What then is my reward*—That circumstance in my conduct for which I expect a peculiar reward from my great Master? *That I abuse not*—Make not an unseasonable use of *my power* which I have *in* preaching *the gospel.*

19 not my power in the gospel. For though I am free from
all men, I made myself the servant of all, that I might gain
20 the more. To the Jews I became as a Jew, that I might
gain the Jews; to them that are under the law, as under
the law, that I might gain them that are under the law:
21 To them that are without the law, as without the law, (being
not without the law to God, but under the law to Christ,)
22 that I might gain them that are without the law. To the
weak I became as weak, that I might gain the weak: I
became all things to all men, that by all means I might save
23 some. And this I do for the gospel's sake, that I may be
24 partaker thereof with *you*. Know ye not, that they who
run in the race, all run, but one receiveth the prize? So
25 run that ye may obtain. And every one that contendeth is
temperate in all things. And they indeed to obtain a cor-

Verse 19. *I made myself the servant of all*—I acted with as self-denying a regard to their interest, and as much caution not to offend them, as if I had been literally their servant or slave. Where is the preacher of the gospel who treads in the same steps?

Verse 20. *To the Jews I became as a Jew*—Conforming myself in all things to their manner of thinking and living, so far as I could with innocence. *To them that are under the law*—Who apprehend themselves to be still bound by the Mosaic law. *As under the law*—Observing it myself, while I am among them. Not that he declared this to be necessary, or refused to converse with those who did not observe it. This was the very thing which he condemned in St. Peter, Gal. ii. 14.

Verse 21. *To them that are without the law*—The heathens. *As without the law*—Neglecting its ceremonies. *Being not without the law to God*—But as much as ever under its moral precepts. *Under the law to Christ*—And in this sense all Christians will be under the law for ever.

Verse 22. *I became as weak*—As if I had been scrupulous too. *I became all things to all men*—Accommodating myself to all, so far as I could consistent with truth and sincerity.

Verse 24. *Know ye not that*—In those famous games which are kept at the isthmus, near your city. *They who run in the* foot *race all run,* though *but one receiveth the prize*—How much greater encouragement have you to run; since ye may all receive the prize of your high calling!

Verse 25. *And every one that* there *contendeth is temperate in all things*—To an almost incredible degree; using the most rigorous self-denial in food, sleep, and every other sensual indulgence. *A corruptible crown*—A garland of leaves, which must soon wither. The moderns only have discovered that it is "legal" to do all this and more for an eternal crown than they did for a corruptible!

26 ruptible crown; but we an incorruptible. I therefore so
run, not as uncertainly; I so fight, not as one that beateth
27 the air: But I keep under my body, and bring *it* into subjection: lest by any means, after having preached to others, I myself should become a reprobate.

CHAP. X. 1 Now I would not have you ignorant, brethren, that our fathers were all * under the cloud, and all †
2 passed through the sea; And were all baptized unto Moses

* Exod. xiii. 21. † Exod. xiv. 22.

Verse 26. *I so run, not as uncertainly*—I look straight to the goal; I run straight toward it. I cast away every weight, regard not any that stand by. *I fight not as one that beateth the air*—This is a proverbial expression for a man's missing his blow, and spending his strength, not on his enemy, but on empty air.

Verse 27. *But I keep under my body*—By all kinds of self-denial. *And bring it into subjection*—To my spirit and to God. The words are strongly figurative, and signify the mortification of the "body of sin," by an allusion to the natural bodies of those who were bruised or subdued in combat. *Lest by any means after having preached*—The Greek word means, *after having discharged the office of an herald,* (still carrying on the allusion,) whose office it was to proclaim the conditions, and to display the prizes. *I myself should become a reprobate*—Disapproved by the Judge, and so falling short of the prize. This single text may give us a just notion of the scriptural doctrine of election and reprobation; and clearly shows us, that particular persons are not in holy writ represented as elected absolutely and unconditionally to eternal life, or predestinated absolutely and unconditionally to eternal death; but that believers in general are elected to enjoy the Christian privileges on earth; which if they abuse, those very elect persons will become reprobate. St. Paul was certainly an elect person, if ever there was one; and yet he declares it was possible he himself might *become a reprobate.* Nay, he actually would have become such, if he had not thus kept his body under, even though he had been so long an elect person, a Christian, and an apostle

Verse 1. *Now*—That ye may not become reprobates, consider how highly favoured your fathers were, who were God's elect and peculiar people, and nevertheless were rejected by him. They were *all under the cloud*—That eminent token of God's gracious presence, which screened them from the heat of the sun by day, and gave them light by night *And all passed through the sea*—God opening a way through the midst of the waters.

Verse 2. *And were all,* as it were, *baptized unto Moses*—Initiated into the religion which he taught them. *In the cloud and in the sea*—Perhaps sprinkled here and there with drops of water from the sea or the cloud, by which baptism might be the more evidently signified.

3 in the cloud and in the sea; And * all ate the same spiritual
4 meat; And † all drank the same spiritual drink: for they
drank out of the spiritual rock which followed them: and
5 that rock was Christ. Yet with the most of them God was
not well-pleased: for they were overthrown in the wilderness.
6 Now these things were our examples, that we might not
7 desire evil things, ‡ as they desired. Neither be ye idolaters, as *were* some of them; as it is written, ‖ The people
8 sat down to eat and drink, and rose up to play. Neither
let us commit fornication, as § some of them committed, and
9 fell in one day three and twenty thousand. Neither let us

* Exod. xvi. 15. † Exod. xvii. 6. ‡ Num. xi. 4. ‖ Exod. xxxii. 6. § Num. xxv. 1, 9.

Verse 3. *And all ate the same* manna, termed *spiritual meat,* as it was typical, 1. Of Christ and his spiritual benefits: 2. Of the sacred bread which we eat at his table.

Verse 4. *And all drank the same spiritual drink*—Typical of Christ, and of that cup which we drink. *For they drank out of the spiritual* or mysterious *rock,* the wonderful streams of *which followed them* in their several journeyings, for many years, through the wilderness. *And that rock was* a manifest type of *Christ*—The Rock of Eternity, from whom his people derive those streams of blessings which follow them through all this wilderness.

Verse 5. *Yet*—Although they had so many tokens of the divine presence. *They were overthrown*—With the most terrible marks of his displeasure.

Verse 6. *Now these things were our examples*—Showing what we are to expect if, enjoying the like benefits, we commit the like sins. The benefits are set down in the same order as by Moses in Exodus; the sins and punishments in a different order; evil desire first, as being the foundation of all; next, idolatry, verses 7, 14; then fornication, which usually accompanied it, verse 8; the tempting and murmuring against God, in the following verses. *As they desired*—Flesh, in contempt of manna.

Verse 7. *Neither be ye idolaters*—And so, "neither murmur ye," verse 10. The other cautions are given in the first person; but these in the second. And with what exquisite propriety does he vary the person! It would have been improper to say, Neither let *us* be idolaters; for he was himself in no danger of idolatry; nor probably of murmuring against Christ, or the divine providence. *To play*—That is, to dance, in honour of their idol.

Verse 8. *And fell in one day three and twenty thousand*—Beside the princes who were afterwards hanged, and those whom the judges slew so that there died in all four and twenty thousand.

Verse 9. *Neither let us tempt Christ*—By our unbelief. St. Paul enumerates five benefits, verses 1—4; of which the fourth and fifth were

tempt Christ, as * some of them also tempted, and were
10 destroyed by serpents. † Neither murmur ye, as some of
11 them murmured, and were destroyed by the destroyer. Now
all these things happened to them for examples: and they
are written for our admonition, on whom the ends of the
12 ages are come. Therefore let him that most assuredly
13 standeth take heed lest he fall. There hath no temptation
taken you but such as is common to man: and God *is* faithful, who will not suffer you to be tempted above your ability;
but will with the temptation make also a way to escape, that
14 ye may be able to bear *it*. Wherefore, my beloved, flee
from idolatry. I speak as to wise men; judge ye what I
15 say. The cup of blessing which we bless, is it not the com-
16 munion of the blood of Christ? The bread which we break,
17 is it not the communion of the body of Christ? For we
being many are one bread, and one body: for we are all par-

* Num. xxi. 4, &c † Num xiv. 1, 36.

closely connected together; and five sins, the fourth and fifth of which were likewise closely connected. In speaking of the fifth benefit, he expressly mentions Christ; and in speaking of the fourth sin, he shows it was committed against Christ. *As some of them tempted* him—This sin of the people was peculiarly against Christ; for when they had so long drank of that rock, yet they murmured for want of water.

Verse 10. *The destroyer*—The destroying angel.

Verse 11. *On whom the ends of the ages are come*—The expression has great force. All things meet together, and come to a crisis, under the last, the gospel, dispensation; both benefits and dangers, punishments and rewards. It remains, that Christ come as an avenger and judge. And even these *ends* include various periods, succeeding each other.

Verse 12. The common translation runs, *Let him that thinketh he standeth;* but the word translated *thinketh,* most certainly strengthens, rather than weakens, the sense.

Verse 13. *Common to man*—Or, as the Greek word imports, proportioned to human strength. *God is faithful*—In giving the help which he hath promised. *And he will with the temptation*—Provide for your deliverance.

Verse 14. *Flee from idolatry*—And from all approaches to it.

Verse 16. *The cup which we bless*—By setting it apart to a sacred use, and solemnly invoking the blessing of God upon it. *Is it not the communion of the blood of Christ*—The means of our partaking of those invaluable benefits, which are the purchase of *the blood of Christ. The communion of the body of Christ*—The means of our partaking of those benefits which were purchased by *the body of Christ*—offered for us.

Verse 17. *For* it is this communion which makes us all one. *We being*

18 takers of the one bread. Consider Israel after the flesh:
Are not they who eat of the sacrifices partakers of the altar?
19 What say I then? that a thing sacrificed to idols is anything,
20 or that an idol is anything? But that what the heathens
sacrifice, they sacrifice to devils, and not to God: now I
21 would not that ye should be partakers with devils. Ye cannot
drink the cup of the Lord, and the cup of devils: ye cannot
not be partakers of the table of the Lord, and the table
22 of devils. Do we provoke the Lord to jealousy? are we
23 stronger than he? All things are lawful for me, but all
things are not expedient: all things are lawful for me, but
24 all things edify not. Let no one seek his own, but every
25 one another's welfare. Whatever is sold in the shambles,
26 eat, asking no questions for conscience' sake: * For the earth
27 *is* the Lord's, and the fulness thereof. And if any of the
unbelievers invite you, and ye are disposed to go; eat whatever
is set before you, asking no questions for conscience' sake.
28 But if any one say to you, This hath been sacrificed to an

* Psalm xxiv 1

many are yet, as it were, but different parts of *one* and the same broken *bread,* which we receive to unite us in *one body.*

Verse 18. *Consider Israel after the flesh*—Christians are the spiritual "Israel of God." *Are not they who eat of the sacrifices partakers of the altar*—Is not this an act of communion with that God to whom they are offered? And is not the case the same with those who eat of the sacrifices which have been offered to idols?

Verse 19. *What say I then*—Do I in saying this allow *that an idol is anything* divine? I aver, on the contrary, *that what the heathens sacrifice, they sacrifice to devils.* Such in reality are the gods of the heathens; and with such only can you hold communion in those sacrifices.

Verse 21. *Ye cannot drink the cup of the Lord, and the cup of devils*—You cannot have communion with both.

Verse 22. *Do we provoke the Lord to jealousy*—By thus caressing his rivals? *Are we stronger than he*—Are we able to resist, or to bear his wrath?

Verse 23. Supposing this were *lawful* in itself, yet it is not *expedient,* it is not edifying to my neighbour.

Verse 24. *His own* only, *but another's welfare* also.

Verse 25. The apostle now applies this principle to the point in question. *Asking no questions*—Whether it has been sacrificed or not.

Verse 26. *For* God, who is the Creator, Proprietor, and Disposer of the earth and all that is therein, hath given the produce of it to the children of men, to be used without scruple.

Verse 28. *For his sake that showed thee, and for conscience' sake*—That is, for the sake of his weak conscience, lest it should be wounded

idol, eat not for his sake that showed thee, and for conscience
29 sake: Conscience I say, not thy own, but that of the other.
30 for why is my liberty judged by another's conscience? For
if I by grace am a partaker, why am I blamed for that for
31 which I give thanks? Therefore whether ye eat or drink, or
32 whatsoever ye do, do all to the glory of God. Give no offence,
either to the Jews, or to the gentiles, or to the church of God:
33 Even as I please all men in all things, not seeking my own
XI. 1 profit, but that of many, that they may be saved. Be ye
followers of me, as I also *am* of Christ.
2 Now I praise you, brethren, that ye remember me in all
3 things, and keep the orders, as I delivered *them* to you. But
I would have you know, that the head of every man is Christ;
and the head of the woman *is* the man; and the head
4 of Christ *is* God. Every man praying or prophesying, with

Verse 29. *Conscience I say, not thy own*—I speak of his conscience, not thine. *For why is my liberty judged by another's conscience*—Another's conscience is not the standard of mine, nor is another's persuasion the measure of *my liberty*.

Verse 30. *If I by grace am a partaker*—If I thankfully use the common blessings of God.

Verse 31 *Therefore*—To close the present point with a general rule, applicable not only in this, but in all cases, *Whatsoever ye do*—In all things whatsoever, whether of a religious or civil nature, in all the common, as well as sacred, actions of life, keep the glory of God in view, and steadily pursue in all this one end of your being, the planting or advancing the vital knowledge and love of God, first in your own soul, then in all mankind.

Verse 32. *Give no offence*—If, and as far as, it is possible.

Verse 33. *Even as I*, as much as lieth in me, *please all men.*

Verse 2. *I praise you*—The greater part of you.

Verse 3. *I would have you know*—He does not seem to have given them any order before concerning this. *The head of every man*—Particularly every believer. *Is Christ, and the head of Christ is God*—Christ, as he is Mediator, acts in all things subordinately to his Father. But we can no more infer that they are not of the same divine nature, because God is said to be *the head of Christ*, than that man and woman are not of the same human nature, because the man is said to be *the head of the woman.*

Verse 4. *Every man praying or prophesying*—Speaking by the immediate power of God. *With his head*—And face. *Covered*—Either with a veil or with long hair. *Dishonoureth his head*—St. Paul seems to mean, As in these eastern nations veiling the head is a badge of subjection, so a man who prays or prophesies with a veil on his head, reflects a dishonour on Christ, whose representative he is.

5 his head covered, dishonoureth his head. But every woman
praying or prophesying with *her* head uncovered dishonoureth her head: for it is the same as if she were shaved.
6 Therefore if a woman is not covered, let her also be shaved
but if it be shameful for a woman to have her hair shaved
7 off, or cut short, let her be covered. A man indeed ought
not to have *his* head covered, being the image and glory of
8 God. but the woman is the glory of the man. For the man
9 is not of the woman, but the woman of the man. Neither
was the man created for the sake of the woman; but the
10 woman for the sake of the man. For this cause *also* the
woman ought to have a veil upon *her* head because of the
11 angels. Nevertheless neither is the man without the woman,
12 nor the woman without the man, in the Lord. And as the
woman *was* of the man, so also the man *is* by the woman;
13 but all things *are* of God. Judge of yourselves · is it

Verse 5. *But every woman*—Who, under an immediate impulse of the Spirit, (for then only was a woman suffered *to speak in the church,*) prays or prophesies without a veil on her face, as it were disclaims subjection, and reflects dishonour on man, her head. *For it is the same,* in effect, as if she cut her hair short, and wore it in the distinguishing form of the men. In those ages, men wore their hair exceeding short, as appears from the ancient statues and pictures.

Verse 6. *Therefore if a woman is not covered*—If she will throw off the badge of subjection, let her appear with her hair cut like a man's. *But if it be shameful for a woman to* appear thus in public, especially in a religious assembly, let her, for the same reason, keep on her veil.

Verse 7. *A man indeed ought not to* veil his head, because he is *the image of God*—In the dominion he bears over the creation, representing the supreme dominion of God, which is his glory. *But the woman is* only matter of *glory* to the man, who has a becoming dominion over her. Therefore she ought not to appear, but with her head veiled, as a tacit acknowledgment of it.

Verse 8. *The man is not*—In the first production of nature.

Verse 10. *For this cause also a woman ought to* be veiled in the public assemblies, *because of the angels*—Who attend there, and before whom they should be careful not to do anything indecent or irregular.

Verse 11. *Nevertheless in the Lord* Jesus, *there is neither male nor female*—Neither is excluded; neither is preferred before the other in his kingdom.

Verse 12. *And as the woman was* at first taken out *of the man, so also the man is* now, in the ordinary course of nature, *by the woman; but all things are of God*—The man, the woman, and their dependence on each other.

Verse 13. *Judge of yourselves*—For what need of more arguments if

14 decent for a woman to pray to God uncovered? Doth not
nature itself teach you, that for a man to have long hair, is a
15 disgrace to him? Whereas for a woman to have long hair,
is a glory to her: for her hair was given her instead of a veil.
16 But if any one be resolved to be contentious, we have no
such custom, neither the churches of God.
17 But in this which I declare I praise *you* not, that ye come
18 together not for the better, but for the worse. For first,
when ye come together in the church, I hear there are

so plain a case? *Is it decent for a woman to pray to God*—The Most High, with that bold and undaunted air which she must have, when, contrary to universal custom, she appears in public with her head *uncovered?*

Verse 14. *For a man to have long hair,* carefully adjusted, is such a mark of effeminacy as *is a disgrace to him.*

Verse 15. *Given her*—Originally, before the arts of dress were in being.

Verse 16. *We have no such custom* here, nor any of the other *churches of God*—The several churches that were in the apostles' time had different customs in things that were not essential; and that under one and the same apostle, as circumstances, in different places, made it convenient. And in all things merely indifferent the custom of each place was of sufficient weight to determine prudent and peaceable men. Yet even this cannot overrule a scrupulous conscience, which really doubts whether the thing be indifferent or no. But those who are referred to here by the apostle were contentious, not conscientious, persons.

Verse 18. *In the church*—In the public assembly. *I hear there are schisms among you; and I partly believe it*—That is, I believe it of some of you. It is plain that by *schisms* is not meant any separation from the church, but uncharitable divisions in it; for the Corinthians continued to be one church; and, notwithstanding all their strife and contention, there was no separation of any one party from the rest, with regard to external communion. And it is in the same sense that the word is used, 1 Cor. i. 10; xii. 25; which are the only places in the New Testament, beside this, where church schisms are mentioned. Therefore, the indulging any temper contrary to this tender care of each other is the true scriptural schism. This is, therefore, a quite different thing from that orderly separation from corrupt churches which later ages have stigmatized as schisms; and have made a pretence for the vilest cruelties, oppressions, and murders, that have troubled the Christian world. Both heresies and schisms are here mentioned in very near the same sense; unless by schisms be meant, rather, those inward animosities which occasion heresies; that is, outward divisions or parties: so that whilst one said, "I am of Paul," another, "I am of Apollos," this implied both schism and heresy. So wonderfully have later ages distorted the words *heresy* and *schism* from their scriptural meaning *Heresy* is not, in all the Bible, taken for "an error in fundamentals," or in anything else; nor

19 schisms among you; (and I partly believe it. For there
must be heresies also among you, that the approved among
20 you may be manifest.) Therefore when ye come together into
21 one place, it is not eating the Lord's supper. For in eating every one taketh before *another* his own supper: and
22 one is hungry, another drinks largely. What? have ye
not houses to eat and drink in? or do ye despise the church
of God, and shame them that have not? What shall I say
23 to you? shall I praise you in this? I praise *you* not. For
I received from the Lord what I also delivered to you, that
the Lord Jesus, the night in which he was betrayed,
24 took bread: And when he had given thanks, he brake *it*,
and said, This is my body, which is broken for you: do this
25 in remembrance of me. In like manner also *he took* the
cup, after he had supped, saying, This cup is the new
covenant in my blood do this as often as ye drink *it*, in

schism, for any separation made from the outward communion of others. Therefore, both heresy and schism, in the modern sense of the words, are sins that the scripture knows nothing of; but were invented merely to deprive mankind of the benefit of private judgment, and liberty of conscience.

Verse 19. *There must be heresies*—Divisions. *Among you*—In the ordinary course of things; and God permits them, that it may appear who among you are, and who are not, upright of heart.

Verse 20. *Therefore*—That is, in consequence of those schisms. *It is not eating the Lord's supper*—That solemn memorial of his death; but quite another thing.

Verse 21. *For in eating* what ye call the Lord's supper, instead of all partaking of one bread, each person brings his own supper, and eats it without staying for the rest. And hereby the poor, who cannot provide for themselves, have nothing; while the rich eat and drink to the full: just as the heathens use to do at the feasts on their sacrifices

Verse 22. *Have ye not houses to eat and drink* your common meals *in? or do ye despise the church of God*—Of which the poor are both the larger and the better part. Do ye act thus in designed contempt of them?

Verse 23. *I received*—By an immediate revelation.

Verse 24. *This is my body, which is broken for you*—That is, this broken bread is the sign of my body, which is even now to be pierced and wounded for your iniquities. Take then, and eat of, this bread, in an humble, thankful, obediential remembrance of my dying love; of the extremity of my sufferings on your behalf, of the blessings I have thereby procured for you, and of the obligations to love and duty which I have by all this laid upon you

Verse 25. *After supper*—Therefore ye ought not to confound this with

26 remembrance of me. For as often as ye eat this bread, and
drink this cup, ye show forth the Lord's death, till he come.
27 So that whosoever eateth the bread, and drinketh the cup of
the Lord unworthily, shall be guilty of the body and blood
28 of the Lord. But let a man examine himself, and so let
29 him eat of the bread, and drink of the cup. For he that
eateth and drinketh unworthily, eateth and drinketh judg-
30 ment to himself, not distinguishing the Lord's body. For
this cause many *are* sick and weak among you, and many
31 sleep. For if we would judge ourselves, we should not be
32 judged. But when we are judged, we are chastened by the
Lord, that we may not be condemned with the world.
33 Wherefore, my brethren, when ye come together to eat,
34 wait one for another. And if any one be hungry, let him
eat at home; that ye come not together to condemnation
And the rest I will set in order when I come.

CHAP. XII. 1 Now concerning spiritual *gifts*, brethren,

a common meal. *Do this in remembrance of me*—The ancient sacrifices were in remembrance of sin: this sacrifice, once offered, is still represented in remembrance of the remission of sins.

Verse 26. *Ye show forth the Lord's death*—Ye proclaim, as it were, and openly avow it to God, and to all the world. *Till he come*—In glory.

Verse 27. *Whosoever shall eat this bread unworthily*—That is, in an unworthy, irreverent manner; without regarding either Him that appointed it, or the design of its appointment. *Shall be guilty of* profaning that which represents *the body and blood of the Lord.*

Verse 28. *But let a man examine himself*—Whether he know the nature and the design of the institution, and whether it be his own desire and purpose throughly to comply therewith.

Verse 29. *For he that eateth and drinketh* so *unworthily* as those Corinthians did, *eateth and drinketh judgment to himself*—Temporal judgments of various kinds, verse 30. *Not distinguishing* the sacred tokens of *the Lord's body*—From his common food.

Verse 30. *For this cause*—Which they had not observed. *Many sleep*—In death.

Verse 31. *If we would judge ourselves*—As to our knowledge, and the design with which we approach the Lord's table. *We should not be* thus *judged*—That is, punished by God.

Verse 32. *When we are* thus *judged*, it is with this merciful design, *that we may not be* finally *condemned with the world.*

Verse 33. *The rest*—The other circumstances relating to the Lord's supper.

Verse 1. *Now concerning spiritual gifts*—The abundance of these in the

2 I would not have you ignorant. Ye know that when ye
were heathens, ye were carried away after dumb idols, as ye
3 were led. Therefore I give you to know, that *as* no one
speaking by the Spirit of God calleth Jesus accursed; so
no one can say, Jesus *is* the Lord, but by the Holy Ghost.
4 Now there are diversities of gifts, but the same Spirit.
5 And there are diversities of administrations, but the same
6 Lord. And there are diversities of operations, but it is the
same God who worketh all in all.
7 But the manifestation of the Spirit is given to each to
8 profit withal. For to one is given by the Spirit the word

churches of Greece strongly refuted the idle learning of the Greek philosophers. But the Corinthians did not use them wisely, which occasioned St. Paul's writing concerning them. He describes, 1. The unity of the body, verses 1—27: 2. The ariety of members and offices, verses 27—30: 3. The way of exercising gifts rightly, namely, by love, verse 31, 1 Cor xiii. throughout: and adds, 4. A comparison of several gifts with each other, in the fourteenth chapter.

Verse 2. *Ye were heathens*—Therefore, whatever gifts ye have received, it is from the free grace of God. *Carried away*—By a blind credulity. *After dumb idols*—The blind to the dumb; idols of wood and stone, unable to speak themselves, and much more to open your mouths, as God has done *As ye were led*—By the subtlety of your priests.

Verse 3. *Therefore*—Since the heathen idols cannot speak themselves, much less give spiritual gifts to others, these must necessarily be among Christians only. *As no one speaking by the Spirit of God calleth Jesus accursed*—That is, as none who does this, (which all the Jews and heathens did,) *speaketh by the Spirit of God*—Is actuated by that Spirit, so as to speak with tongues, heal diseases, or cast out devils. *So no one can say, Jesus is the Lord*—None can receive him as such; for, in the scripture language, to say, or to believe, implies an experimental assurance. *But by the Holy Ghost*—The sum is, None have the Holy Spirit but Christians: all Christians have this Spirit.

Verse 4. *There are diversities of gifts, but the same Spirit*—Divers streams, but all from one fountain. This verse speaks of the Holy Ghost, the next of Christ, the sixth of God the Father. The apostle treats of the Spirit, verses 7, &c.; of Christ, verses 12, &c.; of God, verses 28, &c.

Verse 5. *Administrations*—Offices. *But the same Lord* appoints them all.

Verse 6. *Operations*—Effects produced. This word is of a larger extent than either of the former. *But it is the same God who worketh all* these effects *in all* the persons concerned.

Verse 7. *The manifestation*—The gift whereby the Spirit manifests itself. *Is given to each*—For the profit of the whole body.

Verse 8. *The word of wisdom*—A power of understanding and explain-

of wisdom: to another by the same Spirit the word of know-
9 ledge; To another faith by the same Spirit; to another the
10 gift of healing by the same Spirit; To another the working
of miracles; to another prophecy; to another the discerning of spirits; to another *divers* kinds of tongues; to ano-
11 ther the interpretation of tongues: But one and the same
Spirit worketh all these, dividing to every one severally as
he willeth.
12 For as the body is one, and yet hath many members, but
all the members of the body, many as they are, are one
13 body: so *is* Christ. For we are all baptized by one Spirit
into one body, whether *we are* Jews or gentiles, whether
14 slaves or freemen; and we have all drank of one Spirit. For
15 the body is not one member, but many. If the foot

ing the manifold wisdom of God in the grand scheme of gospel salvation *The word of knowledge*—Perhaps an extraordinary ability to understand and explain the Old Testament types and prophecies.

Verse 9. *Faith* may here mean an extraordinary trust in God under the most difficult or dangerous circumstances. *The gift of healing* need not be wholly confined to the healing diseases with a word or a touch. It may exert itself also, though in a lower degree, where natural remedies are applied; and it may often be this, not superior skill, which makes some physicians more successful than others. And thus it may be with regard to other gifts likewise. As, after the golden shields were lost, the king of Judah put brazen in their place, so, after the pure gifts were lost, the power of God exerts itself in a more covert manner, under human studies and helps; and that the more plentifully, according as there is the more room given for it.

Verse 10. *The working of* other *miracles. Prophecy*—Foretelling things to come *The discerning*—Whether men be of an upright spirit or no; whether they have natural or supernatural gifts for offices in the church; and whether they who profess to speak by inspiration speak from a divine, a natural, or a diabolical spirit

Verse 11. *As he willeth*—The Greek word does not so much imply arbitrary pleasure, as a determination founded on wise counsel.

Verse 12. *So is Christ*—That is, the body of Christ, the church.

Verse 13. *For by* that *one Spirit,* which we received in baptism, we are all united in one body. *Whether Jews or gentiles*—Who are at the greatest distance from each other by nature. *Whether slaves or freemen*—Who are at the greatest distance by law and custom. *We have all drank of one Spirit*—In that cup, received by faith, we all imbibed *one Spirit,* who first inspired, and still preserves, the life of God in our souls.

Verse 15. *The foot* is elegantly introduced as speaking of *the hand; the ear,* of *the eye;* each, of a part that has some resemblance to it. So among men each is apt to compare himself with those whose gifts some

should say, Because I am not the hand, I am not of the
16 body; is it therefore not of the body? And if the ear
should say, Because I am not the eye, I am not of the
17 body; is it therefore not of the body? If the whole body
were an eye, where *were* the hearing? If the whole *were*
18 hearing, where *were* the smelling? But now hath God set
the members every one in the body, as it hath pleased
19 him. And if all were one member, where *were* the body?
20 Whereas now there *are* indeed many members, yet but one
21 body. And the eye cannot say to the hand, I have no need
of thee: or again, the head to the feet, I have no need
22 of you. Yea, the members of the body, which appear to
23 be weaker, are much more necessary: And those which we
think to be the less honourable *parts* of the body, these we
surround with more abundant honour; and our uncomely
24 *parts* have more abundant comeliness. For our comely
parts have no need: but God hath tempered the body together, giving more abundant honour to that which lacked.
25 That there might be no schism in the body; but *that* the
26 members might have the same care for each other: And whether one member suffer, all the members might suffer with it;
or one member be honoured, all the members might rejoice
27 with it. Now ye are the body of Christ, and members in part

way resemble his own, rather than with those who are at a distance, either above or beneath him. *Is it therefore not of the body*—Is the inference good? Perhaps *the foot* may represent private Christians; *the hand,* officers in the church; *the eye,* teachers; *the ear,* hearers.

Verse 16. *The ear*—A less noble part. *The eye*—The most noble.

Verse 18. *As it hath pleased him*—With the most exquisite wisdom and goodness.

Verse 20. *But one body*—And it is a necessary consequence of this unity, that the several members need one another.

Verse 21. *Nor the head*—The highest part of all. *To the foot*—The very lowest.

Verse 22. *The members which appear to be weaker*—Being of a more delicate and tender structure; perhaps the brains and bowels, or the veins, arteries, and other minute channels in the body.

Verse 23. *We surround with more abundant honour*—By so carefully covering them. *More abundant comeliness*—By the help of dress.

Verse 24. *Giving more abundant honour to that which lacked*—As being cared for and served by the noblest parts.

Verse 27. *Now ye*—Corinthians. *Are the body and members of Christ*—Part of them, I mean, not the whole body.

28 And God hath set in the church, first apostles, secondly
prophets, thirdly teachers, afterward miracles, then gifts
of healing, helps, governments, *different* kinds of tongues.
29 *Are* all apostles? *are* all prophets? *are* all teachers? *have*
30 all miraculous powers? Have all the gifts of healing? do
31 all speak with tongues? do all interpret? Ye covet earnestly
the best gifts: but I show unto you a more excellent way.

CHAP. XIII. 1 Though I speak with the tongues of
men and of angels, and have not love, I am become *as*
2 sounding brass, or a tinkling cymbal. And though I have
the gift of prophecy, and understand all mysteries, and all
knowledge; and though I have all faith, so as to remove
3 mountains, and have not love, I am nothing. And though

Verse 28. *First apostles*—Who plant the gospel in the heathen nations. *Secondly prophets*—Who either foretel things to come, or speak by extraordinary inspiration, for the edification of the church. *Thirdly teachers*—Who precede even those that work miracles. Under *prophets* and *teachers* are comprised evangelists and pastors, Eph. iv. 11. *Helps, governments*—It does not appear that these mean distinct offices: rather, any persons might be called *helps*, from a peculiar dexterity in helping the distressed; and *governments*, from a peculiar talent for governing or presiding in assemblies

Verse 31. *Ye covet earnestly the best gifts*—And they are worth your pursuit, though but few of you can attain them. But there is a far more excellent gift than all these; and one which all may, yea, must. attain or perish.

CHAP. XIII. The necessity of love is shown, verses 1—3. The nature and properties, verses 4—7. The duration of it, verses 8—13.

Verse 1. *Though I speak with* all *the tongues*—Which are upon earth, and with the eloquence of an angel. *And have not love*—The love of God, and of all mankind for his sake, I am no better before God than the *sounding* instruments of *brass*, used in the worship of some of the heathen gods. *Or a tinkling cymbal*—This was made of two pieces of hollow brass, which, being struck together, made a tinkling, but very little variety of sound.

Verse 2. *And though I have the gift of prophecy*—Of foretelling future events. *And understand all* the *mysteries*—Both of God's word and providence. *And all knowledge*—Of things divine and human, that ever any mortal attained to. *And though I have* the highest degree of miracle-working *faith, and have not* this *love, I am nothing.*

Verse 3. *And though I*—Deliberately, piece by piece. *Give all my goods to feed the poor,* yea, though I *deliver up my body to be burned*—Rather than I would renounce my religion. *And have not* the *love*—Hereafter

I give all my goods to feed the poor, and deliver up my
body to be burned, and have not love, it profiteth me nothing.
4 Love suffereth long, *and* is kind; love envieth not; love
5 acteth not rashly, is not puffed up, Doth not behave indecently, seeketh not her own, is not provoked, thinketh no
6 evil; Rejoiceth not at iniquity, but rejoiceth in the truth;
7 Covereth all things, believeth all things, hopeth all things,

described *It profiteth me nothing*—Without this, whatever I speak, whatever I have, whatever I know, whatever I do, whatever I suffer, is nothing.

Verse 4. The love of God, and of our neighbour for God's sake, is patient toward all men. It suffers all the weakness, ignorance, errors, and infirmities of the children of God; all the malice and wickedness of the children of the world: and all this, not only for a time, but to the end. And in every step toward overcoming evil with good, it is kind, soft, mild, benign. It inspires the sufferer at once with the most amiable sweetness, and the most fervent and tender affection. *Love acteth not rashly*—Does not hastily condemn any one; never passes a severe sentence on a slight or sudden view of things. Nor does it ever act or behave in a violent, headstrong, or precipitate manner *Is not puffed up* --Yea, humbles the soul to the dust.

Verse 5. *It doth not behave indecently*—Is not rude, or willingly offensive, to any. It *renders to all their due*—Suitable to time, person, and all other circumstances. *Seeketh not her own*—Ease, pleasure, honour, or temporal advantage. Nay, sometimes the lover of mankind seeketh not, in some sense, even his own spiritual advantage; does not think of himself, so long as a zeal for the glory of God and the souls of men swallows him up. But, though he is all on fire for these ends, yet he *is not provoked* to sharpness or unkindness toward any one. Outward provocations indeed will frequently occur; but he triumphs over all. Love *thinketh no evil*—Indeed it cannot but see and hear evil things, and know that they are so; but it does not willingly think evil of any; neither infer evil where it does not appear. It tears up, root and branch, all imagining of what we have not proof. It casts out all jealousies, all evil surmises, all readiness to believe evil.

Verse 6. *Rejoiceth not in iniquity*—Yea, weeps at either the sin or folly of even an enemy; takes no pleasure in hearing or in repeating it, but desires it may be forgotten for ever. *But rejoiceth in the truth*—Bringing forth its proper fruit, holiness of heart and life. Good in general is its glory and joy, wherever diffused in all the world.

Verse 7. Love *covereth all things*—Whatever evil the lover of mankind sees, hears, or knows of any one, he mentions it to none; it never goes out of his lips, unless where absolute duty constrains to speak. *Believeth all things*—Puts the most favourable construction on everything, and is ever ready to believe whatever may tend to the advantage of any one' character And when it can no longer believe well, it *hopes* whatever

8 endureth all things. Love never faileth: but whether *there*
be prophecies, they shall fail; whether *there be* tongues, they
shall cease; whether *there be* knowledge, it shall vanish
9 away. For we know in part, and we prophesy in part. And
10 when that which is perfect is come, then that which is in
11 part shall vanish away. When I was a child, I talked as a
child, I understood as a child, I reasoned as a child: but
12 when I became a man, I put away childish things. And
now we see by means of a glass, obscurely; but then face

may excuse or extenuate the fault which cannot be denied. Where it cannot even excuse, it hopes God will at length give "repentance unto life." Meantime *it endureth all things*—Whatever the injustice, the malice, the cruelty of men can inflict. He can not only do, but likewise suffer, all things, through Christ who strengtheneth him.

Verse 8. *Love never faileth*—It accompanies to, and adorns us in, eternity; it prepares us for, and constitutes, heaven. *But whether there be prophecies, they shall fail*—When all things are fulfilled, and God is all in all. *Whether there be tongues, they shall cease*—One language shall prevail among all the inhabitants of heaven, and the low and imperfect languages of earth be forgotten. The *knowledge* likewise which we now so eagerly pursue, *shall* then *vanish away*—As starlight is lost in that of the midday sun, so our present knowledge in the light of eternity.

Verse 9. *For we know in part, and we prophesy in part*—The wisest of men have here but short, narrow, imperfect conceptions, even of the things round about them, and much more of the deep things of God. And even the prophecies which men deliver from God are far from taking in the whole of future events, or of that wisdom and knowledge of God which is treasured up in the scripture revelation.

Verse 10. *But when that which is perfect is come*—At death and in the last day. *That which is in part shall vanish away*—Both that poor, low, imperfect, glimmering light, which is all the knowledge we now can attain to; and these slow and unsatisfactory methods of attaining, as well as of imparting it to others.

Verse 11. In our present state we are mere infants in point of knowledge, compared to what we shall be hereafter. *I put away childish things*—Of my own accord, willingly, without trouble.

Verse 12. *Now we see*—Even the things that surround us. But *by means of a glass*—Or mirror, which reflects only their imperfect forms, in a dim, faint, obscure manner; so that our thoughts about them are puzzling and intricate, and everything is a kind of riddle to us. *But then*—We shall see, not a faint reflection, but the objects themselves. *Face to face*—Distinctly. *Now I know in part*—Even when God himself reveals things to me, great part of them is still kept under the veil. *But then I shall know even as also I am known*—In a clear, full, comprehensive manner; in some measure like God, who penetrates the centre of every object, and sees at one glance through my soul and all things.

to face: now I know in part; but then I shall know even
13 as also I am known. And now abide these three, faith,
hope, love; but the greatest of these *is* love.

CHAP. XIV. 1 Follow after love, and desire spiritual
2 *gifts*, but especially that ye may prophesy. For he that
speaketh in an *unknown* tongue speaketh not to men, but
to God: for no one understandeth *him;* though by the
3 Spirit he speaketh mysteries: Whereas he that prophesieth
speaketh to men to edification, and exhortation, and comfort.
4 He that speaketh in an *unknown* tongue edifieth himself;
5 but he that prophesieth edifieth the church: I would that ye
all spake with tongues, but rather that ye prophesied: for he
that prophesieth *is* greater than he that speaketh with tongues,
unless he interpret, that the church may receive edification.
6 Now, brethren, if I come to you speaking with tongues, what
shall I profit you, unless I speak to you either by revelation, or
7 by knowledge, or by prophecy, or by doctrine? So inanimate
things which give a sound, whether pipe or harp, unless they
give a distinction in the sounds, how shall it be known what
8 is piped or harped? And if the trumpet give an uncertain

Verse 13. *Faith, hope, love*—Are the sum of perfection on earth; love alone is the sum of perfection in heaven.

Verse 1. *Follow after love*—With zeal, vigour, courage, patience; else you can neither attain nor keep it. *And*—In their place, as subservient to this. *Desire spiritual gifts; but especially that ye may prophesy*—The word here does not mean foretelling things to come; but rather opening and applying the scripture.

Verse 2. *He that speaketh in an unknown tongue speaks,* in effect, *not to men, but to God*—Who alone understands him.

Verse 4. *Edifieth himself*—Only, on the most favourable supposition. *The church*—The whole congregation.

Verse 5. *Greater*—That is, more useful. By this alone are we to estimate all our gifts and talents

Verse 6. *Revelation*—Of some gospel mystery. *Knowledge*—Explaining the ancient types and prophecies. *Prophecy*—Foretelling some future event. *Doctrine*—To regulate your tempers and lives. Perhaps this may be the sense of these obscure words.

Verse 7. *How shall it be known what is piped or harped*—What music can be made, or what end answered?

Verse 8. *Who will prepare himself for the battle*—Unless he understand what the trumpet sounds? suppose a retreat or a march.

9 sound, who will prepare himself for the battle? So likewise
unless ye utter by the tongue words easy to be understood,
how shall it be known what is spoken? for ye will speak to
10 the air. Let there be ever so many kinds of languages in
11 the world, and none of them without signification: Yet if I
know not the meaning of the language, I shall be a barbarian to him that speaketh, and he that speaketh, a barbarian
12 to me. So ye also, seeing ye desire spiritual gifts, seek to
13 abound *in them* to the edifying of the church. Therefore
let him that speaketh in an *unknown* tongue pray that he
14 may interpret. For if I pray in an *unknown* tongue, my
15 spirit prayeth, but my understanding is unfruitful. What
then is *my duty?* I will pray with the spirit, but I will
pray with the understanding also. I will sing with the spirit,
16 but I will sing with the understanding also. Otherwise if
thou givest thanks with the spirit, how shall he that filleth
the place of a private person say Amen to thy thanksgiving,
17 seeing he understandeth not what thou sayest? For thou
18 verily givest thanks well, yet the other is not edified. I
thank God, that I speak with tongues more than you all.
19 Yet in the congregation I had rather speak five words with
my understanding, that I may teach others also, than ten
20 thousand words in an *unknown* tongue. Brethren, be not

Verse 9. *Unless ye utter by the tongue*—Which is miraculously given you. *Words easy to be understood*—By your hearers *Ye will speak to the air*—A proverbial expression. Will utterly lose your labour.

Verse 11. *I shall be a barbarian to him*—Shall seem to talk unintelligible gibberish.

Verse 13. *That he may* be able to *interpret*—Which was a distinct gift.

Verse 14. *If I pray in an unknown tongue*—The apostle, as he did at the sixth verse, transfers it to himself. *My spirit prayeth*—By the power of the Spirit I understand the words myself. *But my understanding is unfruitful*—The knowledge I have is no benefit to others.

Verse 15. *I will pray with the spirit, but I will pray with the understanding also*—I will use my own understanding, as well as the power of the Spirit. I will not act so absurdly, as to utter in a congregation what can edify none but myself.

Verse 16. *Otherwise how shall he that filleth the place of a private person*—That is, any private hearer. *Say Amen*—Assenting and confirming your words, as it was even then usual for the whole congregation to do.

Verse 19. *With my understanding*—In a rational manner; so as not only to understand myself, but to be understood by others.

Verse 20 *Be not children in understanding*—This is an admirable stroke

children in understanding: in wickedness be ye as infants,
21 but in understanding be ye grown men. It is written in the
law,* In foreign tongues and with foreign lips will I speak
to this people; and neither so will they hear me, saith the
22 Lord. So that tongues are for a sign, not to believers, but
to unbelievers: whereas prophecy *is* not for unbelievers, but
23 for believers. Yet if the whole church be met together, and
all speak with *unknown* tongues, and there come in ignorant persons, or unbelievers, will they not say that ye are
24 mad? Whereas if all prophesy, and there come in an unbeliever, or an ignorant person, he is convicted by all, he is
25 judged by all · The secrets of his heart are made manifest;

* Isaiah xxviii. 11.

of true oratory! to bring down the height of their spirits, by representing that wherein they prided themselves most, as mere folly and childishness. *In wickedness be ye infants*—Have all the innocence of that tender age. *But in understanding be ye grown men*—Knowing religion was not designed to destroy any of our natural faculties, but to exalt and improve them, our reason in particular.

Verse 21. *It is written in the law*—The word here, as frequently, means the Old Testament. *In foreign tongues will I speak to this people*—And so he did. He spake terribly to them by the Babylonians, when they had set at nought what he had spoken by the prophets, who used their own language. These words received a farther accomplishment on the day of pentecost.

Verse 22. *Tongues are* intended *for a sign to unbelievers*—To engage their attention, and convince them the message is of God. *Whereas prophecy is not* so much *for unbelievers*, as for the confirmation of them that already believe.

Verse 23. *Yet*—Sometimes prophecy is of more use, even to unbelievers, than speaking with tongues. For instance: *If the whole church be met together*—On some extraordinary occasion. It is probable, in so large a city, they ordinarily met in several places. *And there come in ignorant persons*—Men of learning might have understood the tongues in which they spoke. It is observable, St. Paul says here, *ignorant persons* or *unbelievers;* but in the next verse, *an unbeliever* or *an ignorant person.* Several bad men met together hinder each other by evil discourse. Single persons are more easily gained.

Verse 24. *He is convicted by all*—Who speak in their turns, and speak to the heart of the hearers. *He is judged by all*—Every one says something to which his conscience bears witness.

Verse 25. *The secrets of his heart are made manifest*—Laid open, clearly described; in a manner which to him is most astonishing and utterly unaccountable. How many instances of it are seen at this day! So does God still point his word.

and so falling down on *his* face he will worship God, and
declare that God is among you of a truth.
26 What a thing is it, brethren, that when ye come together,
every one of you hath a psalm, hath a doctrine, hath a
revelation, hath a tongue, hath an interpretation? Let all
27 things be done to edification. If any one speak in an
unknown tongue, *let it be* by two or three at most, and
28 that by course; let one interpret. But if there be no interpreter, let him be silent in the church; and let him speak to
29 himself, and to God. Let two or three of the prophets
30 speak, and let the rest judge. But if *anything* be revealed
31 to another that sitteth by, let the first be silent. For ye may
all prophesy one by one, that all may learn and all may be
32 comforted. For the spirits of the prophets are subject to

Verse 26. *What a thing is it, brethren*—This was another disorder among them. *Every one hath a psalm*—That is, at the same time one begins to sing a psalm; another to deliver *a doctrine;* another to speak in an unknown *tongue;* another to declare what has been *revealed* to him; another to *interpret* what the former is speaking; every one probably gathering a little company about him, just as they did in the schools of the philosophers. *Let all be done to edification*—So as to profit the hearers.

Verse 27. *By two or three at most*—Let not above two or three speak at one meeting. *And that by course*—That is, one after another. *And let one interpret*—Either himself, verse 13; or, if he have not the gift, some other, into the vulgar tongue. It seems, "the gift of tongues" was an instantaneous knowledge of a tongue till then unknown, which he that received it could afterwards speak when he thought fit, without any new miracle.

Verse 28. *Let him speak*—That tongue, if he find it profitable to himself in his private devotions.

Verse 29. *Let two or three of the prophets*—Not more, at one meeting. *Speak*—One after another, expounding the scripture.

Verse 31. *All*—Who have that gift. *That all may learn*—Both by speaking and by hearing.

Verse 32. *For the spirits of the prophets are subject to the prophets*—But what enthusiast considers this? The impulses of the Holy Spirit, even in men really inspired, so suit themselves to their rational faculties, as not to divest them of the government of themselves, like the heathen priests under their diabolical possession. Evil spirits threw their prophets into such ungovernable ecstasies, as forced them to speak and act like madmen But the Spirit of God left his prophets the clear use of their judgment, when, and how long, it was fit for them to speak, and never hurried them into any improprieties either as to the matter, manner, or time of their speaking.

33 the prophets. For God is not *the author* of confusion, but
34 of peace, as in all the churches of the saints. Let your
women be silent in the churches: for it is not permitted
them to speak; but to be in subjection, as * the law also
35 saith. And if they desire to learn anything, let them ask
their own husbands at home: for it is indecent for a woman
36 to speak in the assembly. Did the word of God come out
37 from you? or did it come to you alone? If any one think
himself to be a prophet, or spiritual, let him take knowledge
that the things which I write to you are the commandments
38 of the Lord. But if any one is ignorant, let him be ignorant.
39 Therefore, brethren, covet to prophesy, yet forbid not to
40 speak with tongues. Let all things be done decently and in
order.

CHAP XV. 1 Moreover, brethren, I declare to you the
gospel which I preached to you, which also ye received, and
2 wherein ye stand; By which also ye are saved, if ye hold
fast in what manner I preached to you, unless ye have
3 believed in vain. For I delivered to you first that which

* Gen. iii. 16.

Verse 34. *Let your women be silent in the churches*—Unless they are under an extraordinary impulse of the Spirit. *For*, in other cases, *it is not permitted them to speak*—By way of teaching in public assemblies. *But to be in subjection*—To the man whose proper office it is to lead and to instruct the congregation.

Verse 35. *And* even *if they desire to learn anything*—Still they are not to speak in public, but to *ask their own husbands at home*—That is the place, and those the persons to inquire of.

Verse 36. Are ye of Corinth either the first or the only Christians? If not, conform herein to the custom of all the churches.

Verse 37. *Or spiritual*—Endowed with any extraordinary gift of the Spirit. *Let him*—Prove it, by acknowledging that I now write by the Spirit.

Verse 38. *Let him be ignorant*—Be it at his own peril.

Verse 39. *Therefore*—To sum up the whole.

Verse 40. *Decently*—By every individual. *In order*—By the whole church

Verse 2. *Ye are saved, if ye hold fast*—Your salvation is begun, and will be perfected, if ye continue in the faith. *Unless ye have believed in vain*—Unless indeed your faith was only a delusion.

Verse 3. *I received*—From Christ himself. It was not a fiction of my own.

I also received, that Christ died for our sins * according to
4 the scriptures; And that he was buried, and that he was
5 raised the third day † according to the scriptures. And that
6 he was seen by Cephas, then by the twelve: Afterwards, he
was seen by above five hundred brethren at once, of whom
the greater part remain until now, but some are fallen
7 asleep. After this he was seen by James; then by all the
8 apostles. Last of all he was seen by me also, as an un-
9 timely birth. For I am the least of the apostles, who am
not worthy to be called an apostle, because I persecuted the
10 church of God. But by the grace of God I am what I
am: and his grace toward me was not in vain; but I laboured more abundantly than they all: yet not I, but the
11 grace of God that *was* with me. Whether therefore I or
12 they, so we preach, and so ye believed. But if Christ is
preached, that he rose from the dead, how say some among
13 you, that there is no resurrection of the dead? For if
there be no resurrection of the dead, neither is Christ raised.

* Isaiah liii. 8, 9. † Psalm xvi. 10.

Verse 4. *According to the scriptures*—He proves it first from scripture, then from the testimony of a cloud of witnesses.

Verse 5. *By the twelve*—This was their standing appellation; but their full number was not then present.

Verse 6. *Above five hundred*—Probably in Galilee. A glorious and incontestable proof! *The greater part remain*—Alive.

Verse 7. *Then by all the apostles*—The twelve were mentioned verse 5. This title here, therefore, seems to include the seventy; if not all those, likewise, whom God afterwards *sent* to plant the gospel in heathen nations.

Verse 8. *An untimely birth*—It was impossible to abase himself more than he does by this single appellation. As *an abortion* is not worthy the name of a man, so he affirms himself to be not worthy the name of an apostle.

Verse 9. *I persecuted the church*—True believers are humbled all their lives, even for the sins they committed before they believed.

Verse 10. *I laboured more than they all*—That is, more than any of them, from a deep sense of the peculiar love God had shown me. *Yet*, to speak more properly, it is *not I, but the grace of God that* is *with me.*—This it is which at first qualified me for the work, and still excites me to zeal and diligence in it.

Verse 11. *Whether I or they, so we preach*—All of us speak the same thing.

Verse 12 *How say some*—Who probably had been heathen philosophers.

14 And if Christ be not raised, then *is* our preaching vain, and
15 your faith *is* also vain. Yea, and we are found false witnesses of God; because we have testified from God, that
he raised up Christ, whom he did not raise, if the dead rise
16 not. For if the dead rise not, neither is Christ raised
17 And if Christ be not raised, your faith *is* vain; ye are still
18 in your sins. Then also they who sleep in Christ are pe-
19 rished. If in this life only we have hope in Christ, we are
20 more miserable than all men. But now is Christ risen
21 from the dead, the first fruit of them that slept. For since
by man *came* death, by man *came* also the resurrection of
22 the dead. For as through Adam all die, even so through

Verse 13. *If there be no resurrection*—If it be a thing flatly impossible.

Verse 14. *Then is our preaching*—From a commission supposed to be given after the resurrection. *Vain*—Without any real foundation.

Verse 15. *If the dead rise not*—If the very notion of a resurrection be, as they say, absurd and impossible.

Verse 17. *Ye are still in your sins*—That is, under the guilt of them. So that there needed something more than reformation, (which was plainly wrought,) in order to their being delivered from the guilt of sin · even that atonement, the sufficiency of which God attested by raising our great Surety from the grave.

Verse 18. *They who sleep in Christ*—Who have died for him, or believing in him *Are perished*—Have lost their life and being together

Verse 19. *If in this life only we have hope*—If we look for nothing beyond the grave. But if we have a divine evidence of things not seen, if we have "a hope full of immortality," if we now taste of "the powers of the world to come," and see "the crown that fadeth not away," then, notwithstanding all our present trials, we are more happy than all men

Verse 20. *But now*—St. Paul declares that Christians "have hope," not "in this life only." His proof of the resurrection lies in a narrow compass, verses 12—19. Almost all the rest of the chapter is taken up in illustrating, vindicating, and applying it. The proof is short, but solid and convincing, that which arose from Christ's resurrection. Now this not only proved a resurrection possible, but, as it proved him to be a divine teacher, proved the certainty of a general resurrection, which he so expressly taught. *The first fruit of them that slept*—The earnest, pledge, and insurance of their resurrection who slept in him : even of all the righteous. It is of the resurrection of these, and these only, that the apostle speaks throughout the chapter.

Verse 22. *As through Adam all*, even the righteous, *die, so through Christ all* these *shall be made alive*—He does not say, "shall revive," (as naturally as they die,) but *shall be made alive*, by a power not their own

23 Christ shall all be made alive. But every one in his own
order: Christ the first fruit; afterward they who are
24 Christ's, at his coming. Then *cometh* the end, when he
shall have delivered up the kingdom to God, even the Father: when he shall have abolished all rule and all authority
25 and power. For he must reign,* till he hath put all ene-
26 mies under his feet. The last enemy *that* is destroyed *is*
27 death. † For he hath put all things under his feet. But
when he saith, All things are put under *him*, *it is* manifest
28 that he who did put all things under him is excepted. But

* Psalm cx. 1. † Psalm viii. 7

Verse 23. *Afterward*—The whole harvest. At the same time the wicked shall rise also. But they are not here taken into the account.

Verse 24. *Then*—After the resurrection and the general judgment. *Cometh the end*—Of the world; the grand period of all those wonderful scenes that have appeared for so many succeeding generations. *When he shall have delivered up the kingdom to the Father, and he* (the Father) *shall have abolished all* adverse *rule, authority, and power*—Not that the Father will then begin to reign without the Son, nor will the Son then cease to reign. For the divine reign both of the Father and Son is from everlasting to everlasting. But this is spoken of the Son's mediatorial kingdom, which will then be delivered up, and of the immediate kingdom or reign of the Father, which will then commence. Till then the Son transacts the business which the Father hath given him, for those who are his, and by them as well as by the angels, with the Father, and against their enemies. So far as the Father gave the kingdom to the Son, the Son shall deliver it up to the Father, John xiii. 3. Nor does the Father cease to reign, when he gives it to the Son; neither the Son, when he delivers it to the Father: but the glory which he had before the world began (John xvii. 5; Heb. i. 8) will remain even after this is delivered up. Nor will he cease to be a king even in his human nature, Luke i. 33. If the citizens of the "new Jerusalem" shall "reign for ever," (Rev. xxii. 5,) how much more shall he?

Verse 25. *He must reign*—Because so it is written. *Till he*—the Father *hath put all* his *enemies under his feet.*

Verse 26. *The last enemy that is destroyed is death*—Namely, after Satan (Heb. ii. 14) and sin (1 Cor. xv. 56) are destroyed. In the same order they prevailed. Satan brought in sin, and sin brought forth death. And Christ, when he of old engaged with these enemies, first conquered Satan, then sin, in his death; and, lastly, death, in his resurrection. In the same order he delivers all the faithful from them, yea, and destroys these enemies themselves. Death he so destroys that it shall be no more; sin and Satan, so that they shall no more hurt his people

Verse 27. *Under him*—Under the Son.

when all things shall be put under him, then shall the Son
himself also be subject to him that put all things under him,
29 that God may be all in all. Else what shall they do who
are baptized for the dead, if the dead rise not at all? why
30 are they then baptized for them? Why are we also in
31 danger every hour? I protest by your rejoicing, brethren,
32 which I have in Christ Jesus our Lord, I die daily. If
after the manner of men, I have fought with wild beasts
at Ephesus, what advantageth it me, if the dead rise not?
33 Let us eat and drink; for to-morrow we die. Be not
deceived. Evil communications corrupt good manners:
34 Awake to righteousness, and sin not; for some have not the
knowledge of God. I speak *this* to your shame.

Verse 28. *The Son also shall be subject*—Shall deliver up the mediatorial kingdom. *That* the three-one *God may be all in all*—All things, (consequently all persons,) without any interruption, without the intervention of any creature, without the opposition of any enemy, shall be subordinate to God. All shall say, "My God, and my all." This is the end. Even an inspired apostle can see nothing beyond this.

Verse 29. *Who are baptized for the dead*—Perhaps baptized in hope of blessings to be received after they are numbered with the dead. Or, "baptized in the room of the dead"—Of them that are just fallen in the cause of Christ: like soldiers who advance in the room of their companio that fell just before their face.

Verse 30. *Why are we*—The apostles. *Also in danger every hour*—It is plain we can expect no amends in this life.

Verse 31. *I protest by your rejoicing, which I have*—Which love makes my own. *I die daily*—I am daily in the very jaws of death. Beside that I live, as it were, in a daily martyrdom.

Verse 32. *If* to speak *after the manner of men*—That is, to use a proverbial phrase, expressive of the most imminent danger *I have fought with wild beasts at Ephesus*—With the savage fury of a lawless multitude, Acts xix. 29, &c. This seems to have been but just before. *Let us eat*, &c.—We might, on that supposition, as well say, with the Epicureans, Let us make the best of this short life, seeing we have no other portion.

Verse 33. *Be not deceived*—By such pernicious counsels as this. *Evil communications corrupt good manners*—He opposes to the Epicurean saying, a well-known verse of the poet Menander. *Evil communications*—Discourse contrary to faith, hope, or love, naturally tends to destroy all holiness

Verse 34. *Awake*—An exclamation full of apostolical majesty. Shake off your lethargy! *To righteousness*—Which flows from the true knowledge of God, and implies that your whole soul be broad awake. *And sin not*—That is, and ye will not sin Sin supposes drowsiness of soul

35 But some one will say, How are the dead raised? and
36 with what kind of body do they come? Thou fool, that
37 which thou sowest is not quickened except it die: And that
which thou sowest, thou sowest not the body that shall be,
but a bare grain, perhaps of wheat, or of any other *corn:*
38 But God giveth it a body as it hath pleased him, and to
39 each of the seeds its own body. All flesh *is* not the same
flesh: but *there is* one *kind of* flesh of men, another of
40 beasts, another of birds, another of fishes. *There are* also
heavenly bodies, and *there are* earthly bodies: but the glory of the heavenly *is* one, and that of the earthly another.
41 *There is* one glory of the sun, and another glory of the

There is need to press this. *For some* among you *have not the knowledge of God*—With all their boasted knowledge, they are totally ignorant of what it most concerns them to know. *I speak this to your shame*—For nothing is more shameful, than sleepy ignorance of God, and of the word and works of God; in these especially, considering the advantages they had enjoyed

Verse 35. *But some one* possibly *will say, How are the dead raised up,* after their whole frame is dissolved? *And with what kind of bodies do they come* again, after these are mouldered into dust?

Verse 36. To the inquiry concerning the *manner* of rising, and the *quality* of the bodies that rise, the Apostle answers first by a similitude, verses 36—42, and then plainly and directly, verses 42, 43. *That which thou sowest,* is not quickened into new life and verdure, *except it die*—Undergo a dissolution of its parts, a change analogous to death. Thus St. Paul inverts the objection; as if he had said, Death is so far from hindering life, that it necessarily goes before it.

Verse 37. *Thou sowest not the body that shall be*—Produced from the seed committed to the ground, *but a bare,* naked *grain,* widely different from that which will afterward rise out of the earth.

Verse 38. *But God*—Not thou, O man, not the grain itself, *giveth it a body as it hath pleased him,* from the time he distinguished the various species of beings; *and to each of the seeds,* not only of the fruits, but animals also, (to which the Apostle rises in the following verse,) *its own body;* not only peculiar to that species, but proper to that individual, and arising out of the substance of that very grain.

Verse 39. *All flesh*—As if he had said, Even earthy bodies differ from earthy, and heavenly bodies from heavenly. What wonder then, if heavenly bodies differ from earthy? or the bodies which rise from those that lay in the grave?

Verse 40. *There are also heavenly bodies*—As the sun, moon, and stars; *and there are earthy*—as vegetables and animals. *But the* brightest lustre which the latter can have is widely different from that of the former

Verse 41. Yea, and the heavenly bodies themselves differ from each other.

moon, and another glory of the stars: and *one* star differeth
42 from *another* star in glory. So also *is* the resurrection of
the dead. It is sown in corruption, it is raised in incorrup-
43 tion. It is sown in dishonour; it is raised in glory: it is
44 sown in weakness; it is raised in power. It is sown an
animal body; it is raised a spiritual body. There is an
45 animal body, and there is a spiritual body. And so it is
written, * The first Adam was made a living soul; the last
46 Adam *is* a quickening Spirit. Yet the spiritual *body was*
47 not first, but the animal; afterward the spiritual. The
first man *was* from the earth, earthy. the second man *is*

* Gen. ii. 7

Verse 42. *So also is the resurrection of the dead*—So great is the difference between the body which fell, and that which rises. *It is sown*—A beautiful word; committed, as seed, to the ground. *In corruption*—Just ready to putrefy, and, by various degrees of corruption and decay, to return to the dust from whence it came. *It is raised in incorruption*—Utterly incapable of either dissolution or decay.

Verse 43. *It is sown in dishonour*—Shocking to those who loved it best. human nature in disgrace! *It is raised in glory*—Clothed with robes of light, fit for those whom the King of Heaven delights to honour. *It is sown in weakness*—Deprived even of that feeble strength which it once enjoyed. *It is raised in power*—Endued with vigour, strength, and activity, such as we cannot now conceive.

Verse 44. *It is sown* in this world *a* merely *animal body*—Maintained by food, sleep, and air, like the bodies of brutes: but *it is raised* of a more refined contexture, needing none of these animal refreshments, and endued with qualities of a spiritual nature, like the angels of God.

Verse 45. *The first Adam was made a living soul*—God gave him such life as other animals enjoy: but *the last Adam*, Christ, *is a quickening spirit*—As he "hath life in himself, so he quickeneth whom he will;" giving a more refined life to their very bodies at the resurrection.

Verse 47. *The first man* was *from the earth, earthy; the second man is the Lord from heaven*—*The first man*, being from the earth, is subject to corruption and dissolution, like the earth from which he came. *The second man*—St. Paul could not so well say, "Is from heaven, heavenly:" because, though man owes it to the earth that he is earthy, yet the Lord does not owe his glory to heaven. He himself made the heavens, and by descending from thence showed himself to us as the Lord. Christ was not *the second man* in order of time; but in this respect, that as Adam was a public person, who acted in the stead of all mankind, so was Christ. As Adam was the first general representative of men, Christ was the second and the last. And what they severally did, terminated not in themselves, but affected all whom they represented

48 the Lord from heaven. As *was* the earthy, such *are* they
also *that are* earthy: and as *was* the heavenly, such *are*
49 they also that are heavenly. And as we have borne the
image of the earthy, we shall also bear the image of the
heavenly.
50 But this I say, brethren, that flesh and blood cannot inherit the kingdom of God; neither doth corruption inherit
51 incorruption. Behold, I tell you a mystery; We shall not
52 all sleep, but we shall all be changed, In a moment, in the
twinkling of an eye, at the last trumpet: for the trumpet
shall sound, and the dead shall be raised incorruptible, and
53 we shall be changed. For this corruptible must put on in-
54 corruption, and this mortal put on immortality. So when
this corruptible shall have put on incorruption, and this
mortal shall have put on immortality, then shall be brought
to pass the saying that is written, * Death is swallowed up
55 in victory. † O death, where *is* thy sting? O hades, where
56 *is* thy victory? The sting of death *is* sin, and the strength

* Isaiah xxv. 8. † Hosea xiii. 14.

Verse 48. *They that are earthy*—Who continue without any higher principle. *They that are heavenly*—Who receive a divine principle from heaven.

Verse 49. *The image of the heavenly*—Holiness and glory.

Verse 50. *But* first we must be entirely changed; *for* such *flesh and blood* as we are clothed with now, *cannot* enter into that kingdom which is wholly spiritual: *neither doth* this corruptible body *inherit* that incorruptible kingdom.

Verse 51. *A mystery*—A truth hitherto unknown; and not yet fully known to any of the sons of men. *We*—Christians. The Apostle considers them all as one, in their succeeding generations. *Shall not all die*—Suffer a separation of soul and body. *But we shall all*—Who do not die, *be changed*—So that this animal body shall become spiritual

Verse 52. *In a moment*—Amazing work of omnipotence! And cannot the same power now change us into saints in a moment? *The trumpet shall sound*—To awaken all that sleep in the dust of the earth.

Verse 54. *Death is swallowed up in victory*—That is, totally conquered, abolished for ever.

Verse 55. *O death, where is thy sting?*—Which once was full of hellish poison. *O hades*, the receptacle of separate souls, *where is thy victory*—Thou art now robbed of all thy spoils; all thy captives are set at liberty. *Hades* literally means the invisible world, and relates to the soul; death, to the body. The Greek words are found in the Septuagint translation of Hosea xiii. 14.

Verse 56. *The sting of death is sin*—Without which it could have no

57 of sin *is* the law. But thanks *be* to God, who hath given
58 us the victory through our Lord Jesus Christ. Therefore,
my beloved brethren, be ye steadfast, unmovable, always
abounding in the work of the Lord, knowing that your labour is not in vain in the Lord.

CHAP. XVI. 1 Concerning the collection for the saints,
as I have ordered the churches of Galatia, so also do ye.
2 On the first *day* of the week let every one of you lay by him
in store, according as he hath been prospered, that there
3 may be no collections when I come. And when I am come,
whomsoever ye shall approve, them will I send with letters,
4 to carry your gift to Jerusalem. And if it be proper that I
5 also should go, they shall go with me. Now I will come to
you, when I have passed through Macedonia: for I pass
6 through Macedonia. And perhaps I may stay, yea, and
winter with you, that ye may bring me forward on my jour-

power. But this sting none can resist by his own strength. *And the strength of sin is the law*—As is largely declared, Rom. vii. 7, &c.

Verse 57. *But thanks be to God, who hath given us the victory*—Over sin, death, and hades.

Verse 58. *Be ye steadfast*—In yourselves. *Unmovable*—By others; continually increasing in the work of faith and labour of love. *Knowing your labour is not in vain in the Lord*—Whatever ye do for his sake shall have its full reward in that day.

Let us also endeavour, by cultivating holiness in all its branches, to maintain this hope in its full energy; longing for that glorious day, when, in the utmost extent of the expression, *death shall be swallowed up* for ever, and millions of voices, after the long silence of the grave, shall burst out at once into that triumphant song, *O death, where is thy sting? O hades, where is thy victory?*

Verse 1. *The saints*—A more solemn and a more affecting word, than if he had said, *the poor.*

Verse 2. *Let every one*—Not the rich only: let him also that hath little, gladly give of that little. *According as he hath been prospered*—Increasing his alms as God increases his substance. According to this lowest rule of Christian prudence, if a man when he has or gains one pound give a tenth to God, when he has or gains an hundred he will give the tenth of this also. And yet I show unto you a more excellent way. He that hath ears to hear, let him hear. Stint yourself to no proportion at all. But lend to God all you can.

Verse 4. *They shall go with me*—To remove any possible suspicion.

Verse 5. *I pass through Macedonia*—I purpose going that way.

7 ney whithersoever I go. For I will not see you now in my
way; but hope to stay some time with you, if the Lord per-
8 mit. But I will stay at Ephesus till Pentecost. For a great
9 and effectual door is opened to me, and there *are* many
adversaries.
10 But if Timotheus come, see that he be with you without
fear: for he worketh the work of the Lord, even as I.
11 Therefore let no man despise him: but conduct ye him forward on his journey in peace, that he may come to me.
12 for I look for him with the brethren. As to *our* brother
Apollos, I besought him much to come to you with the
brethren: yet he was by no means willing to come now; but
13 he will come when it shall be convenient. Watch ye, stand
14 fast in the faith, acquit yourselves like men, be strong. Let
all your affairs be done in love.
15 And I beseech you, brethren, *as* ye know the household
of Stephanas, that it is the first fruits of Achaia, and that
16 they have devoted themselves to serve the saints, That ye
also submit to such, and to every one that worketh with *us*,
17 and laboureth. I rejoice at the coming of Stephanas and

Verse 7. *I will not see you now*—Not till I have been in Macedonia.

Verse 8. *I will stay at Ephesus*—Where he was at this time.

Verse 9. *A great door*—As to the number of hearers. *And effectual*—As to the effects wrought upon them. *And there are many adversaries*—As there must always be where Satan's kingdom shakes. This was another reason for his staying there.

Verse 10. *Without fear*—Of any one's despising him for his youth. *For he worketh the work of the Lord*—The true ground of reverence to pastors. Those who do so, none ought to despise.

Verse 11. *I look for him with the brethren*—That accompany him.

Verse 12. *I besought him much*—To come to you. *With the brethren*—Who were then going to Corinth. *Yet he was by no means willing to come now*—Perhaps lest his coming should increase the divisions among them.

Verse 13. To conclude. *Watch ye*—Against all your seen and unseen enemies. *Stand fast in the faith*—Seeing and trusting him that is invisible. *Acquit yourselves like men*—With courage and patience. *Be strong*—To do and suffer all his will.

Verse 15. *The first fruits of Achaia*—The first converts in that province.

Verse 16. *That ye also*—In your turn. *Submit to such*—So repaying their free service. *And to every one that worketh with us and laboureth*—That labours in the gospel either with or without a fellow-labourer.

Verse 17. *I rejoice at the coming of Stephanas, and Fortunatus, and Achaiacus*—Who were now returned to Corinth: but the joy which their

Fortunatus and Achaiacus: for they have supplied what was
18 wanting on your part. For they have refreshed my spirit
19 and yours: such therefore acknowledge. The churches
of Asia salute you. Aquila and Priscilla, with the church
20 that is in their house, salute you much in the Lord. All the
brethren salute you. Salute one another with an holy kiss.
21 The salutation of *me* Paul with my own hand. If any
22 man love not the Lord Jesus Christ, let him be Anathema
23 Maran-atha. The grace of our Lord Jesus Christ *be* with
24 you. My love *be* with you all in Christ Jesus.

arrival had occasioned remained still in his heart. *They have supplied what was wanting on your part*—They have performed the offices of love, which you could not, by reason of your absence.

Verse 18. *For they have refreshed my spirit and yours*—Inasmuch as you share in my comfort. *Such therefore acknowledge*—With suitable love and respect.

Verse 19. *Aquila and Priscilla* had formerly made some abode at Corinth, and there St. Paul's acquaintance with them began, Acts xviii. 1, 2.

Verse 21. *With my own hand*—What precedes having been wrote by an amanuensis.

Verse 22. *If any man love not the Lord Jesus Christ*—If any be an enemy to his person, offices, doctrines, or commands. *Let him be Anathema Maran-atha*—*Anathema* signifies a thing devoted to destruction. It seems to have been customary with the Jews of that age, when they had pronounced any man an *Anathema*, to add the Syriac expression, *Maran-atha*, that is, "The Lord cometh;" namely, to execute vengeance upon him. This weighty sentence the apostle chose to write with his own hand; and to insert it between his salutation and solemn benediction, that it might be the more attentively regarded.

NOTES

ON

ST. PAUL'S SECOND EPISTLE TO THE CORINTHIANS.

In this epistle, written from Macedonia, within a year after the former, St. Paul beautifully displays his tender affection toward the Corinthians, who were greatly moved by the seasonable severity of the former, and repeats several of the admonitions he had there given them. In that he had written concerning the affairs of the Corinthians: in this he writes chiefly concerning his own; but in such a manner as to direct all he mentions of himself to their spiritual profit. The thread and connexion of the whole epistle is historical: other things are interwoven only by way of digression.

It contains,

I. The inscription, C. i. 1, 2

II. The treatise itself.

1. In Asia I was greatly pressed; but God comforted me; as I acted uprightly; even in this, that I have not yet come to you; who ought t obey me, 3 — C. ii. 11
2. From Troas I hastened to Macedonia, spreading the gospel everywhere, the glorious charge of which I execute, according to its importance, 12 — C. vii. 1
3. In Macedonia I received a joyful message concerning you, 2—16
4. In this journey I had a proof of the liberality of the Macedonians, whose example ye ought to follow, C. viii. 1—C. ix. 15
5. I am now on my way to you, armed with the power of Christ. Therefore obey, C. x 1—C. xiii. 10

The conclusion. 11—13

II. CORINTHIANS.

CHAPTER I. 1 PAUL, an apostle of Jesus Christ by
the will of God, and Timotheus *our* brother, to the church
of God that is in Corinth, with all the saints that are in all
2 Achaia: Grace and peace *be* to you from God our Father,
and *from* the Lord Jesus Christ.
3 Blessed *be* the God and Father of our Lord Jesus Christ,
4 the Father of mercies, and God of all comfort; Who comforteth us in all our affliction, that we may be able to comfort
them who are in any affliction, by the comfort wherewith we
5 ourselves are comforted of God. For as the sufferings
of Christ abound in us, so our comfort also aboundeth
6 through Christ. And whether we are afflicted, *it is* for your
comfort and salvation; or whether we are comforted, *it is* for
your comfort, which is effectual in the patient enduring the

Verse 1. *Timotheus our brother*—St. Paul writing to Timotheus styled him his *son;* writing of him, his *brother.*

Verse 3. *Blessed be the God and Father of our Lord Jesus Christ*—A solemn and beautiful introduction, highly suitable to the apostolical spirit. *The Father of mercies, and God of all comfort*—Mercies are the fountain of comfort; comfort is the outward expression of mercy. God shows mercy in the affliction itself. He gives comfort both in and after the affliction. Therefore is he termed, *the God of all comfort.* Blessed be this God!

Verse 4. *Who comforteth us in all our affliction, that we may be able to comfort them who are in any affliction*—He that has experienced one kind of affliction is able to comfort others in that affliction. He that has experienced all kinds of affliction is able to comfort them in all.

Verse 5. *For as the sufferings of Christ abound in us*—The sufferings endured on his account. *So our comfort also aboundeth through Christ*—The sufferings were many, the comfort one; and yet not only equal to, but overbalancing, them all.

Verse 6. *And whether we are afflicted, it is for your comfort and salvation*—For your present comfort, your present and future salvation. *Or whether we are comforted, it is for your comfort*—That we may be the better able to comfort you. *Which is effectual in the patient enduring the same sufferings which we also suffer*—Through the efficacy of which ye patiently endure the same kind of sufferings with us

7 same sufferings which we also suffer. And our hope concerning you is steadfast, knowing, that as ye are partakers of the
8 sufferings, so also of the comfort. For we would not have
you ignorant, brethren, of the trouble which befel us in Asia,
that we were exceedingly pressed, above *our* strength, so that
9 we despaired even of life: Yea, we had the sentence of death
in ourselves, that we might not trust in ourselves, but in God
10 who raiseth the dead: Who delivered us from so great a
death, and doth deliver: in whom we trust that he will still
11 deliver; You likewise helping together with us by prayer for
us, that for the gift *bestowed* upon us by means of many
persons thanks may be given by many on your behalf.
12 For this is our rejoicing, the testimony of our conscience,
that in simplicity and godly sincerity, not with carnal wisdom,
but by the grace of God, we have had our conversation in
13 the world, and more abundantly toward you. For we write
no other things to you, but what ye know and acknowledge;
14 and I trust will acknowledge even to the end; As also ye
have acknowledged us in part, that we are your rejoicing, as

Verse 7. *And our hope concerning you*—Grounded on your patience in suffering for Christ's sake, *is steadfast.*

Verse 8. *We would not have you ignorant, brethren, of the trouble which befel us in Asia*—Probably the same which is described in the nineteenth chapter of the Acts. The Corinthians knew before that he had been in trouble: he now declares the greatness and the fruit of it. *We were exceedingly pressed, above our strength*—Above the ordinary strength even of an apostle.

Verse 9. *Yea, we had the sentence of death in ourselves*—We ourselves expected nothing but death.

Verse 10. *We trust that he will still deliver*—That we may at length be able to come to you.

Verse 11. *You likewise*—As well as other churches. *Helping with us by prayer, that for the gift*—Namely, my deliverance. *Bestowed upon us by means of many persons*—Praying for it, *thanks may be given by many.*

Verse 12. *For* I am the more emboldened to look for this, because I am conscious of my integrity; seeing *this is our rejoicing*—Even in the deepest adversity. *The testimony of our conscience*—Whatever others think of us. *That in simplicity*—Having one end in view, aiming singly at the glory of God. *And godly sincerity*—Without any tincture of guile, dissimulation, or disguise. *Not with carnal wisdom, but by the grace of God*—Not by natural, but divine, wisdom. *We have had our conversation in the world*—In the whole world; in every circumstance.

Verse 14. *Ye have acknowledged us in part*—Though not so fully as ye will do. *That we are your rejoicing*—That ye rejoice in having known

15 ye also *are* ours in the day of the Lord Jesus. And in this
confidence I was minded to come to you before, that ye might
16 have had a second benefit: And to pass by you into Macedonia, and to come to you again from Macedonia, and to be
17 brought forward by you in my way toward Judea. Now
when I was thus minded, did I use levity? or the things
which I purpose, do I purpose according to the flesh, so
18 that there should be with me yea and nay? *As* God is faith-
19 ful, our word to you hath not been yea and nay. For Jesus
Christ, the Son of God, who was preached among you by us,
by me and Silvanus and Timotheus, was not yea and nay,
20 but was yea in him. For all the promises of God *are* yea
21 in him, and amen in him, to the glory of God by us. For
he that establisheth us with you in Christ, and that hath
22 anointed us, *is* God: Who hath also sealed us, and given us
the earnest of the Spirit in our hearts.

us *As ye also are ours*—As we also rejoice in the success of our labours among you; and we trust shall rejoice therein *in the day of the Lord Jesus.*

Verse 15. *In this confidence*—That is, being confident of this.

Verse 17. *Did I use levity*—Did I lightly change my purpose? *Do I purpose according to the flesh*—Are my purposes grounded on carnal or worldly considerations? *So that there should be with me yea and nay*—Sometimes one, sometimes the other; that is, variableness and inconstancy.

Verse 18. *Our word to you*—The whole tenor of our doctrine. *Hath not been yea and nay*—Wavering and uncertain.

Verse 19. *For Jesus Christ, who was preached by us*—That is, our preaching concerning him. *Was not yea and nay*—Was not variable and inconsistent with itself. *But was yea in him*—Always one and the same, centering in him.

Verse 20. *For all the promises of God are yea and amen in him*—Are surely established in and through him. They are *yea* with respect to God promising; *amen,* with respect to men believing; *yea,* with respect to the apostles; *amen,* with respect to their hearers.

Verse 21. I say, *to the glory of God*—For it is God alone that is able to fulfil these promises. *That establisheth us*—Apostles and teachers. *With you*—All true believers. *In* the faith of *Christ; and hath anointed us*—With the oil of gladness, with joy in the Holy Ghost, thereby giving us strength both to do and suffer his will.

Verse 22. *Who also hath sealed us*—Stamping his image on our hearts, thus marking and sealing us as his own property. *And given us the earnest of his Spirit*—There is a difference between an earnest and a pledge. A pledge is to be restored when the debt is paid; but an earnest is not taken away, but completed. Such an earnest is the Spirit. The first fruits of it we have Rom. viii. 23; and we wait for all the fulness.

23 But I call God for a record on my soul, that to spare you
24 I came not as yet to Corinth. Not that we have dominion
over your faith, but are helpers of your joy: for by faith ye
II. 1 have stood. But I determined this with myself, not to
2 come to you again in grief. For if I grieve you, who is he
3 that cheereth me, but he that is grieved by me? And I
wrote thus to you, that I might not when I come have
grief from those for whom I ought to rejoice; being persuaded concerning you all, that my joy is *the joy* of you all.
4 For from much affliction and anguish of heart I wrote to you
with many tears; not that ye might be grieved, but that ye
might know the abundant love which I have toward you.
5 And if any have caused grief, he hath grieved me but in
6 part, that I may not overburden you all. Sufficient for such

Verse 23. *I call God for a record upon my soul*—Was not St. Paul now speaking by the Spirit? And can a more solemn oath be conceived? Who then can imagine that Christ ever designed to forbid all swearing? *That to spare you I came not yet to Corinth*—Lest I should be obliged to use severity. He says elegantly *to Corinth*, not *to you*, when he is intimating his power to punish.

Verse 24. *Not that we have dominion over your faith*—This is the prerogative of God alone. *But are helpers of your joy*—And faith from which it springs. *For by faith ye have stood*—To this day.

We see the light in which ministers should always consider themselves, and in which they are to be considered by others. *Not as having dominion over the faith* of their people, and having a right to dictate by their own authority what they shall believe, or what they shall do; but as *helpers of their joy*, by helping them forward in faith and holiness. In this view, how amiable does their office appear! and how friendly to the happiness of mankind! How far, then, are they from true benevolence, who would expose it to ridicule and contempt!

Verse 1. *In grief*—Either on account of the particular offender, or of the church in general.

Verse 2. *For if I grieve you, who is he that cheereth me, but he that is grieved by me*—That is, I cannot be comforted myself till his grief is removed

Verse 3. *And I wrote thus to you*—I wrote to you before in this determination, *not to come to you in grief.*

Verse 4. *From much anguish I wrote to you, not* so much *that ye might be grieved, as that ye might know* by my faithful admonition my *abundant love toward you.*

Verse 5. *He hath grieved me but in part*—Who still rejoice over the greater part of you. Otherwise I might *burden you all.*

Verse 6. *Sufficient for such an one*—With what a remarkable tenderness

7 an one *is* this punishment, *inflicted* by many. So that on
the contrary *ye should* rather forgive and comfort *him*, lest
such an one should be swallowed up with over much sorrow.
8 I beseech you therefore to confirm *your* love toward him.
9 For to this end also did I write, that I might know the
10 proof of you, whether ye were obedient in all things. To
whom ye forgive anything, I *forgive* also: and what I have
forgiven, if I have forgiven anything, *it is* for your sakes in
11 the person of Christ; Lest Satan get an advantage over us:
for we are not ignorant of his devices.
12 Now when I came to Troas to *preach* the gospel of
13 Christ, and a door was opened to me by the Lord, I had
no rest in my spirit, because I did not find Titus my brother;
so taking leave of them I went forth into Macedonia.
14 Now thanks *be* to God, who causeth us always to triumph

does St. Paul treat this offender! He never once mentions his name. Nor does he here so much as mention his crime. *By many*—Not only by the rulers of the church: the whole congregation acquiesced in the sentence.

Verse 10. *To whom ye forgive*—He makes no question of their complying with his direction. *Anything*—So mildly does he speak even of that heinous sin, after it was repented of. *In the person of Christ*—By the authority wherewith he has invested me.

Verse 11. *Lest Satan*—To whom he had been delivered, and who sought to destroy not only his flesh, but his soul also. *Get an advantage over us*—For the loss of one soul is a common loss.

Verse 12. *Now when I came to Troas*—It seems, in that passage from Asia to Macedonia, of which a short account is given, Acts xx. 1, 2. Even though *a door was opened to me*—That is, there was free liberty to speak, and many were willing to hear: yet,

Verse 13. *I had no rest in my spirit*—From an earnest desire to know how my letter had been received. *Because I did not find Titus*—In his return from you. *So I went forth into Macedonia*—Where being much nearer, I might more easily be informed concerning you. The apostle resumes the thread of his discourse, 2 Cor. vii. 2, interposing an admirable digression concerning what he had done and suffered elsewhere, the profit of which he by this means derives to the Corinthians also; and this as a prelude to his apology against the false apostles.

Verse 14. *To triumph*, implies not only victory, but an open manifestation of it. And as in triumphal processions, especially in the east, incense and perfumes were burned near the conqueror, the apostle beautifully alludes to this circumstance in the following verse: as likewise to the different effects which strong perfumes have upon different persons; some of whom they revive, while they throw others into the most violent disorders.

through Christ, and manifesteth by us in every place the
15 odour of his knowledge. For we are to God a sweet odour
of Christ, in them that are saved, and in them that perish:
16 To these an odour of death unto death; but to those an
odour of life unto life. And who *is* sufficient for these
17 things? For we are not as many, who adulterate the word
of God: but as of sincerity, but as from God, in the sight
of God, speak we in Christ.

CHAP. III. 1 Do we again begin to recommend ourselves? unless we need, as some *do*, recommendatory letters
2 to you, or recommendatory *letters* from you? Ye are our
letter, written on our hearts, known and read by all men:
3 Manifestly declared to be the letter of Christ ministered by
us, written not with ink, but with the Spirit of the living

Verse 15. *For we*—The preachers of the gospel. *Are to God a sweet odour of Christ*—God is well-pleased with this perfume diffused by us, both *in them that* believe and *are saved,* treated of, 2 Cor iii. 1; iv. 2; *and in them that* obstinately disbelieve and, consequently, *perish,* treated of, 2 Cor. iv. 3—6.

Verse 16. *And who is sufficient for these things*—No man living, but by the power of God's Spirit.

Verse 17. *For we are not as many, who adulterate the word of God*—Like those vintners (so the Greek word implies) who mix their wines with baser liquors. *But as of sincerity*—Without any mixture. *But as from God*—This rises higher still; transmitting his pure word, not our own. *In the sight of God*—Whom we regard as always present, and noting every word of our tongue. *Speak we*—The tongue is ours, but the power is God's. *In Christ*—Words which he gives, approves, and blesses

Verse 1. *Do we begin again to recommend ourselves*—Is it needful? Have I nothing but my own word to recommend me? St. Paul chiefly here intends himself; though not excluding Timotheus, Titus, and Silvanus. *Unless we need*—As if he had said, Do I indeed want such recommendation?

Verse 2. *Ye are our* recommendatory *letter*—More convincing than bare words could be. *Written on our hearts*—Deeply engraven there, and plainly legible to all around us.

Verse 3. *Manifestly declared to be the letter of Christ*—Which he has formed and published to the world. *Ministered by us*—Whom he has used herein as his instruments · therefore ye are *our letter* also. *Written not in tables of stone*—Like the ten commandments. *But in the* tender, living *tables of their hearts*—God having taken away the hearts of stone, and given them hearts of flesh.

God; not in tables of stone, but in the fleshly tables of the
4 heart. Such trust have we in God through Christ: Not
5 that we are sufficient of ourselves to think anything as from
6 ourselves; but our sufficiency *is* from God; Who also hath
made us able ministers of the new covenant; not of the letter, but of the Spirit: for the letter killeth, but the Spirit
7 giveth life. And if the ministration of death engraven in
letters of stones was glorious, so that the children of Israel
could not look steadfastly on the face of Moses because
8 of the glory of his face; which is abolished: Shall not
9 rather the ministration of the Spirit be glorious? For if the
ministration of condemnation was glory, much more doth
10 the ministration of righteousness abound in glory. For
even that which was made glorious had no glory in this

Verse 4. *Such trust have we in God*—That is, we trust in God that this is so.

Verse 5. *Not that we are sufficient of ourselves*—So much as *to think* one good thought; much less, to convert sinners.

Verse 6. *Who also hath made us able ministers of the new covenant*—Of the new, evangelical dispensation. *Not of the* law, fitly called the *letter*, from God's literally writing it on the two tables. *But of the Spirit*—Of the gospel dispensation, which is written on the tables of our hearts by the Spirit. *For the letter*—The law, the Mosaic dispensation. *Killeth*—Seals in death those who still cleave to it. *But the Spirit*—The gospel, conveying the Spirit to those who receive it. *Giveth life*—Both spiritual and eternal: yea, if we adhere to the literal sense even of the moral law, if we regard only the precept and the sanction as they stand in themselves, not as they lead us to Christ, they are doubtless a killing ordinance, and bind us down under the sentence of death.

Verse 7. *And if the ministration of death*—That is, the Mosaic dispensation, which proves such to those who prefer it to the gospel, the most considerable part of which was *engraven* on those two *stones*, was attended with so great glory.

Verse 8. *The ministration of the Spirit*—That is, the Christian dispensation.

Verse 9. *The ministration of condemnation*—Such the Mosaic dispensation proved to all the Jews who rejected the gospel; whereas through the gospel (hence called *the ministration of righteousness)* God both imputed and imparted righteousness to all believers. But how can the moral law (which alone was engraven on stone) be the ministration of condemnation, if it requires no more than a sincere obedience, such as is proportioned to our infirm state? If this is sufficient to justify us, then the law ceases to be a *ministration of condemnation.* It becomes (flatly contrary to the apostle's doctrine) *the ministration of righteousness.*

Verse 10. *It hath no glory in this respect, because of the glory that excel-*

11 respect, because of the glory that excelleth. For if that
which is abolished *was* glorious, much more that which
12 remaineth *is* glorious. Having therefore such hope, we use
13 great plainness of speech: And not as Moses, *who* put a
veil over his face, so that the children of Israel could not
14 look steadfastly to the end of that which is abolished: But
their understandings were blinded: and until this day the
same veil remaineth unremoved on the reading of the old
15 testament; which is taken away in Christ. But the veil
lieth on their heart when Moses is read, until this day.
16 Nevertheless when it shall turn to the Lord, the veil shall
17 be taken away. Now the Lord is that Spirit: and where
18 the Spirit of the Lord *is*, there is liberty. And we all, with
unveiled face beholding as in a glass the glory of the Lord,

leth—That is, none in comparison of this more excellent glory. The greater light swallows up the less.

Verse 11. *That which remaineth*—That dispensation which remains to the end of the world; that spirit and life which remain for ever.

Verse 12. *Having therefore this hope*—Being fully persuaded of this.

Verse 13. *And* we do *not* act *as Moses* did, *who put a veil over his face*—Which is to be understood with regard to his writings also. *So that the children of Israel could not look steadfastly to the end of that* dispensation *which is* now *abolished*—The end of this was Christ. The whole Mosaic dispensation tended to, and terminated in, him; but the Israelites had only a dim, wavering sight of him, of whom Moses spake in an obscure, covert manner.

Verse 14. *The same veil remaineth* on their understanding *unremoved*—Not so much as *folded back*, (so the word implies,) so as to admit a little glimmering light. *On the* public *reading of the Old Testament*—The veil is not now on the face of Moses or of his writings, but *on the reading* of them, and *on the heart* of them that believe not. *Which is taken away in Christ*—That is, from the heart of them that truly believe on him.

Verse 16. *When it*—Their heart. *Shall turn to the Lord*—To Christ, by living faith. *The veil is taken away*—That very moment; and they see, with the utmost clearness, how all the types and prophecies of the law are fully accomplished in him.

Verse 17. *Now the Lord*—Christ *is that Spirit* of the law whereof I speak, to which *the letter* was intended to lead. *And where the Spirit of the Lord*, Christ, *is*, *there is liberty*—Not the veil, the emblem of slavery. There is liberty from servile fear, liberty from the guilt and from the power of sin, liberty to behold with open face the glory of the Lord.

Verse 18. *And*, accordingly, *all we* that believe in him, *beholding as in a glass*—In the mirror of the gospel. *The glory of the Lord*—His glorious love. *Are transformed into the same image*—Into the same love.

are transformed into the same image from glory to glory, as
by the Spirit of the Lord.

CHAP. IV. 1 Therefore having this ministry, as we
2 have received mercy, we faint not; But have renounced
the hidden things of shame, not walking in craftiness, nor
deceitfully corrupting the word of God; but by manifestation of the truth commending ourselves to every man's
3 conscience in the sight of God. But if our gospel also is
4 veiled, it is veiled to them that perish: Whose unbelieving
minds the god of this world hath blinded, lest the illumination of the glorious gospel of Christ, who is the image of
5 God, should shine upon them. For we preach not ourselves,
but Christ Jesus the Lord; and ourselves your servants for

From one degree of this *glory* to another, in a manner worthy of his almighty Spirit.

What a beautiful contrast is here! Moses saw the glory of the Lord, and it rendered his face so bright, that he covered it with a veil; Israel not being able to bear the reflected light. We behold his glory in the glass of his word, and our faces shine too; yet we veil them not, but diffuse the lustre which is continually increasing, as we fix the eye of our mind more and more steadfastly on his glory displayed in the gospel.

Verse 1. *Therefore having this ministry*—Spoken of, 2 Cor. iii. 6 *As we have received mercy*—Have been mercifully supported in all our trials. *We faint not*—We desist not in any degree from our glorious enterprise.

Verse 2. *But have renounced*—Set at open defiance. *The hidden things of shame*—All things which men need to hide, or to be ashamed of. *Not walking in craftiness*—Using no disguise, subtlety, guile. *Nor* privily *corrupting the* pure *word of God*—By any additions or alterations, or by attempting to accommodate it to the taste of the hearers.

Verse 3. *But if our gospel also*—As well as the law of Moses.

Verse 4. *The god of this world*—What a sublime and horrible description of Satan! He is indeed the god of all that believe not, and works in them with inconceivable energy. *Hath blinded*—Not only veiled, the eye of their understanding. *Illumination*—Is properly the reflection or propagation of light, from those who are already enlightened, to others. *Who is the image of God*—Hence also we may understand how great is the glory of Christ. He that sees the Son, sees the Father in the face of Christ. The Son exactly exhibits the Father to us.

Verse 5. *For*—The fault is not in us, neither in the doctrine they hear from us. *We preach not ourselves*—As able either to enlighten, or pardon, or sanctify you *But Jesus Christ*—As your only wisdom, righteousness, sanctification. *And ourselves your servants*—Ready to do the meanest offices *For Jesus' sake*—Not for honour, interest, or pleasure

6 Jesus' sake. For God, who commanded light to shine out
of darkness, hath shined in our hearts, to enlighten *us* with
the knowledge of the glory of God in the face of Jesus
Christ.
7 But we have this treasure in earthen vessels, that the
8 excellence of the power may be of God, and not of us. *W*
are troubled on every side, yet not crushed; perplexed, but
9 not in despair; Persecuted, but not forsaken; thrown down,
10 but not destroyed; Always bearing about in the body the
dying of the Lord Jesus, that the life also of Jesus may be
11 manifested in our body. We who live are always delivered
unto death for the sake of Jesus, that the life also of Jesus
may be manifested in our mortal body. So then death
12 worketh in us, but life in you. Yet having the same spirit

Verse 6. *For God hath shined in our hearts*—The hearts of all those whom the god of this world no longer blinds. God who is himself our light; not only the author of light, but also the fountain of it. *To enlighten us with the knowledge of the glory of God*—Of his glorious love, and of his glorious image. *In the face of Jesus Christ*—Which reflects his glory in another manner than the face of Moses did.

Verse 7. *But we*—Not only the apostles, but all true believers. *Have this treasure*—Of divine light, love, glory. *In earthen vessels*—In frail, feeble, perishing bodies. He proceeds to show, that afflictions, yea, death itself, are so far from hindering the ministration of the Spirit, that they even further it, sharpen the ministers, and increase the fruit. *That the excellence of the power,* which works these in us, *may* undeniably appear to *be of God.*

Verse 8. *We are troubled,* &c.—The four articles in this verse respec inward, the four in the next outward, afflictions. In each clause the former part shows the "earthen vessels;" the latter, "the excellence of the power." *Not crushed*—Not swallowed up in care and anxiety. *Perplexed*—What course to take, but never despairing of his power and love to carry us through.

Verse 10. *Always*—Wherever we go. *Bearing about in the body the dying of the Lord Jesus*—Continually expecting to lay down our lives like him. *That the life also of Jesus might be manifested in our body*—That we may also rise and be glorified like him.

Verse 11. *For we who* yet *live*—Who are not yet killed for the testimony of Jesus. *Are always delivered unto death*—Are perpetually in the very jaws of destruction; which we willingly submit to, that we may "obtain a better resurrection."

Verse 12. *So then death worketh in us, but life in you*—You live in peace; we die daily. *Yet*—Living or dying, so long as we believe, we cannot but speak

13 of faith, according to what is written, * I believed, and therefore have I spoken; we also believe, and therefore speak;
14 Knowing that he who raised up the Lord Jesus will
15 also raise us up by Jesus, and present *us* with you. For
all things *are* for your sakes, that the overflowing grace
might through the thanksgiving of many abound to the
16 glory of God. Therefore we faint not; but even though
the outward man perish, yet the inward man is renewed day
17 by day. For our light affliction, which is but for a moment,
worketh out for us a far more exceeding *and* eternal weight
18 of glory; While we aim not at the things that are seen,
but at the things that are not seen: for the things that are
seen *are* temporal; but the things that are not seen *are* eternal.
V. 1 For we know that if our earthly house of *this* tabernacle
be dissolved, we have a building from God, an house not
2 made with hands, eternal in the heavens. For in this we

* Psalm cxvi. 10.

Verse 13. *Having the same spirit of faith*—Which animated the saints of old; David, in particular, when he said, *I believed, and therefore have I spoken*—That is, I trusted in God, and therefore he hath put this song of praise in my mouth. *We also speak*—We preach the gospel, even in the midst of affliction and death, because we believe that God will *raise us up* from the dead, and will *present us,* ministers, *with you,* all his members, "faultless before his presence with exceeding joy."

Verse 15. *For all things*—Whether adverse or prosperous. *Are for your sakes*—For the profit of all that believe, as well as all that preach. *That the overflowing grace*—Which continues you alive both in soul and body. *Might abound* yet more *through the thanksgiving of many*—For thanksgiving invites more abundant grace.

Verse 16. *Therefore*—Because of this grace, *we faint not* *The outward man*—The body. *The inward man*—The soul.

Verse 17. *Our light affliction*—The beauty and sublimity of St. Paul's expressions here, as descriptive of heavenly glory, opposed to temporal afflictions, surpass all imagination, and cannot be preserved in any translation or paraphrase, which after all must sink infinitely below the astonishing original.

Verse 18. *The things that are seen*—Men, money, things of earth. *The things that are not seen*—God, grace, heaven.

Verse 1. *Our earthly house*—Which is only a tabernacle, or tent, not designed for a lasting habitation.

Verse 2. *Desiring to be clothed upon*—This body, which is now covered with flesh and blood, with the glorious house which is from heaven. Instead of flesh and blood, which cannot enter heaven, the rising body

groan, earnestly desiring to be clothed upon with our house
3 which is from heaven: If being clothed we shall not be
4 found naked. For we who are in *this* tabernacle groan,
being burdened: not that we would be unclothed, but clothed
5 upon, that what is mortal may be swallowed up of life. Now
he that hath wrought us to this very thing *is* God, who hath
6 also given us the earnest of the Spirit. Therefore *we* always
behave undauntedly, knowing that, while we are sojourning
7 in the body, we are absent from the Lord: (For we walk
8 by faith, not by sight:) We behave undauntedly, *I say*,
and are willing rather to be absent from the body, and present with the Lord.

9 Therefore we are ambitious, whether present or absent, to
10 be well-pleasing to him. For we must all appear before the

will be clothed or covered with what is analogous thereto, but incorruptible and immortal. Macarius speaks largely of this.

Verse 3. *If being clothed*—That is, with the image of God, while we are in the body. *We shall not be found naked*—Of the wedding garment.

Verse 4. *We groan being burdened*—The apostle speaks with exact propriety. A burden naturally expresses groans. And we are here burdened with numberless afflictions, infirmities, temptations. *Not that we would be unclothed*—Not that we desire to remain without a body. Faith does not understand that philosophical contempt of what the wise Creator has given. *But clothed upon*—With the glorious, immortal, incorruptible, spiritual body. *That what is mortal*—This present mortal body. *May be swallowed up of life*—Covered with that which lives for ever.

Verse 5. *Now he that hath wrought us to this very thing*—This longing for immortality. *Is God*—For none but God, none less than the Almighty, could have wrought this in us.

Verse 6. *Therefore we behave undauntedly*—But most of all when we have death in view; *knowing that* our greatest happiness lies beyond the grave.

Verse 7. *For* we cannot clearly see him in this life, wherein *we walk by faith* only: an evidence, indeed, that necessarily implies a kind of "seeing him who is invisible;" yet as far beneath what we shall have in eternity, as it is above that of bare, unassisted reason.

Verse 8. *Present with the Lord*—This demonstrates that the happiness of the saints is not deferred till the resurrection.

Verse 9. *Therefore we are ambitious*—The only ambition which has place in a Christian. *Whether present*—In the body. *Or absent*—From it.

Verse 10. *For we all*—Apostles as well as other men, whether now present in the body, or absent from it. *Must appear*—Openly, without covering, where all hidden things will be revealed; probably the sins

judgment seat of Christ; that every one may receive according to what he hath done in the body, whether good or evil.
11 Knowing therefore the terror of the Lord, we persuade men;
but we are made manifest to God; and I trust we are made
12 manifest in your consciences also. We do not again recommend ourselves to you, but we give you an occasion of glorying on our behalf, that ye may have something to *answer*
13 them who glory in appearance, and not in heart. For if
we are transported beyond ourselves, *it is* to God; if we
14 are sober, *it is* for your sakes. For the love of Christ constraineth us, while we thus judge, that if one died for all,
15 then were all dead: And *that* he died for all, that they who

even of the faithful, which were forgiven long before. For many of their good works, as their repentance, their revenge against sin, cannot otherwise appear. But this will be done at their own desire, without grief, and without shame. *According to what he hath done in the body, whether good or evil*—In the body he did either good or evil; in the body he is recompensed accordingly.

Verse 11. *Knowing therefore the terror of the Lord, we* the more earnestly *persuade men* to seek his favour; and as God knoweth this, so, *I trust,* ye know it *in your* own *consciences.*

Verse 12. *We do not* say this, as if we thought there was any need of *again recommending ourselves to you, but* to *give you an occasion* of rejoicing and praising God, and to furnish you with an *answer* to those false apostles *who glory in appearance,* but *not in heart,* being condemned by their own conscience.

Verse 13. *For if we are transported beyond ourselves*—Or at least, appear so to others, treated of, verse 15—21, speaking or writing with uncommon vehemence. *It is to God*—He understands (if men do not) the emotion which himself inspires. *If we be sober*—Treated of, chap. vi. 1—10. If I proceed in a more calm, sedate manner. *It is for your sakes*—Even good men bear this, rather than the other method, in their teachers. But these must obey God, whoever is offended by it.

Verse 14. *For the love of Christ*—To us, and our love to him. *Constraineth us*—Both to the one and the other; beareth us on with such a strong, steady, prevailing influence, as winds and tides exert when they waft the vessel to its destined harbour. *While we thus judge, that if* Christ *died for all, then are all,* even the best of men, naturally *dead*—In a state of spiritual death, and liable to death eternal. For had any man been otherwise, Christ had not needed to have died for him.

Verse 15. *And that he died for all*—That all might be saved. *That they who live*—That all who live upon the earth. *Should not henceforth*—From the moment they know him. *Live unto themselves*—Seek their own honour, profit, pleasure. *But unto him*—In all righteousness and true holiness.

live should not henceforth live to themselves, but to him
16 who died for them, and rose again. So that we from this
time know no one after the flesh ; yea, if we have known even
Christ after the flesh, yet now we know *him so* no more.
17 Therefore if any one *be* in Christ, *there is* a new creation :
the old things are passed away ; behold, all things are be-
18 come new. And all things *are* from God, who hath reconciled us to himself through Jesus Christ, and hath given to
19 us the ministry of reconciliation ; Namely, that God was in
Christ, reconciling the world to himself, not imputing their
trespasses to them ; and hath committed to us the word of
20 reconciliation. Therefore we are ambassadors for Christ,
as though God were intreating by us : we beseech *you*,

Verse 16. *So that we from this time*—That we knew the love of Christ. *Know no one*—Neither ourselves, nor you, neither the rest of the apostles, Gal. ii. 6, nor any other person. *After the flesh*—According to his former state, country, descent, nobility, riches, power, wisdom. We fear not the great. We regard not the rich or wise. We account not the least less than ourselves. We consider all, only in order to save all. Who is he that thus *knows no one after the flesh ?* In what land do these Christians live ? *Yea, if we have known even Christ after the flesh*—So as to love him barely with a natural love, so as to glory in having conversed with him on earth, so as to expect only temporal benefits from him.

Verse 17. *Therefore if any one be in Christ*—A true believer in him *There is a new creation*—Only the power that makes a world can make a Christian. And when he is so created, *the old things are passed away* —Of their own accord, even as snow in spring. *Behold*—The present, visible, undeniable change ! *All things are become new*—He has new life, new senses, new faculties, new affections, new appetites, new ideas and conceptions. His whole tenor of action and conversation is new, and he lives, as it were, in a new world. God, men, the whole creation, heaven, earth, and all therein, appear in a new light, and stand related to him in a new manner, since he was created anew in Christ Jesus.

Verse 18. *And all* these new *things are from God*, considered under this very notion, as *reconciling us*—The world, verse 19, *to himself*.

Verse 19. *Namely*—The sum of which is, *God*—The whole Godhead, but more eminently God the Father. *Was in Christ, reconciling the world*—Which was before at enmity with God. *To himself*—So taking away that enmity, which could no otherwise be removed than by the blood of the Son of God.

Verse 20. *Therefore we are ambassadors for Christ—we beseech you in Christ's stead*—Herein the apostle might appear to some "transported beyond himself." In general he uses a more calm, sedate kind of exhortation, as in the beginning of the next chapter. What unparalleled

21 in Christ's stead, be ye reconciled to God. For he hath
made him, who knew no sin, a sin offering for us; that we
might be made the righteousness of God through him.
VI. 1 We then, *as* fellowlabourers, do also exhort you, not
2 to receive the grace of God in vain. (For he saith, * I
have heard thee in an accepted time, and in a day of
salvation have I succoured thee: behold, now *is* the accept-
3 able time; behold, now *is* the day of salvation.) Giving
no offence in anything, that the ministry be not blamed:
4 But in all things approving ourselves as the ministers of
God in much patience, in afflictions, in necessities, in dis-

* Isaiah xlix. 8.

condescension and divinely tender mercies are displayed in this verse! Did the judge ever beseech a condemned criminal to accept of pardon? Does the creditor ever beseech a ruined debtor to receive an acquittance in full? Yet our almighty Lord, and our eternal Judge, not only vouchsafes to offer these blessings, but invites us, entreats us, and, with the most tender importunity, solicits us, not to reject them.

Verse 21. *He made him a sinoffering, who knew no sin*—A commendation peculiar to Christ. *For us*—Who knew no righteousness, who were inwardly and outwardly nothing but sin; who must have been consumed by the divine justice, had not this atonement been made for our sins. *That we might be made the righteousness of God through him*—Might *through him* be invested with that righteousness, first imputed to us, then implanted in us, which is in every sense *the righteousness of God.*

Verse 1. *We then* not only *beseech,* but *as fellow-labourers* with you, who are working out your own salvation, *do also exhort you, not* to *receive the grace of God*—Which we have been now describing. *In vain*—We *receive* it by faith; and *not in vain,* if we add to this, persevering holiness.

Verse 2. *For he saith*—The sense is, As of old there was a particular time wherein God was pleased to pour out his peculiar blessing, so there is now. And this is the particular time: this is a time of peculiar blessing.

Verse 3. *Giving,* as far as in us lies, *no offence, that the ministry be not blamed* on our account.

Verse 4. *But approving ourselves as the ministers of God*—Such as his ministers ought to be. *In much patience*—Shown, 1. *In afflictions, necessities, distresses*—All which are general terms. 2. *In stripes, imprisonments, tumults*—Which are particular sorts of affliction, necessity, distress 3. *In labours, watchings, fastings*—Voluntarily endured. All these are expressed in the plural number, to denote a variety of them In *afflictions,* several ways to escape may appear, though none without

5 tresses, In stripes, in imprisonments, in tumults, in labours,
6 in watchings, in fastings; By purity, by prudence, by
longsuffering, by kindness, by the Holy Ghost, by love
7 unfeigned, By the word of truth, by the power of God, by
the armour of righteousness on the right hand and the
8 left; Through honour and dishonour, through evil report
9 and good report: as deceivers, yet true; As unknown, yet
well known; as dying, yet behold we live; as chastened,
10 yet not killed; As sorrowing, yet always rejoicing; as poor,
yet making many rich; as having nothing, yet possessing
all things.
11 O ye Corinthians, our mouth is opened toward you, our
12 heart is enlarged. Ye are not straitened in us, but ye are

difficulty; in *necessities,* one only, and that a difficult one; in *distresses,* none at all appears.

Verse 5. *In tumults*—The Greek word implies such attacks as a man cannot stand against, but which bear him hither and thither by violence.

Verse 6 *By prudence*—Spiritual, divine; not what the world terms so. Worldly prudence is the practical use of worldly wisdom: divine prudence is the due exercise of grace, making spiritual understanding go as far as possible. *By love unfeigned*—The chief fruit of the Spirit.

Verse 7. *By the* convincing and converting *power of God*—Accompanying his word; and also attesting it by divers miracles. *By the armour of righteousness on the right hand and the left*—That is, on all sides; the panoply or whole armour of God

Verse 8. *By honour and dishonour*—When we are present. *By evil report and good report*—When we are absent. Who could bear honour and good report, were it not balanced by dishonour? *As deceivers*—Artful, designing men. So the world represents all true ministers of Christ. *Yet true*—Upright, sincere, in the sight of God.

Verse 9. *As unknown*—For the world knoweth us not, as it knew him not. *Yet well known*—To God, and to those who are the seals of our ministry. *As dying, yet behold*—Suddenly, unexpectedly, God interposes, and *we live.*

Verse 10. *As sorrowing*—For our own manifold imperfections, and for the sins and sufferings of our brethren. *Yet always rejoicing*—In present peace, love, power, and a sure hope of future glory. *As having nothing, yet possessing all things*—For all things are ours, if we are Christ's. What a magnificence of thought is this!

Verse 11. From the praise of the Christian ministry, which he began 2 Cor. ii. 14, he now draws his affectionate exhortation. *O ye Corinthians*—He seldom uses this appellation. But it has here a peculiar force. *Our mouth is opened toward you*—With uncommon freedom, because *our heart is enlarged*—In tenderness.

Verse 12. *Ye are not straitened in us*—Our heart is wide enough to

13 straitened in your own bowels Now for a recompence of
the same, (I speak as to *my* children,) be ye also enlarged.
14 Be not unequally yoked with unbelievers: for what fellowship hath righteousness with unrighteousness? or what
15 communion hath light with darkness? And what concord
hath Christ with Belial? or what part hath a believer with
16 an infidel? And what agreement hath the temple of God
with idols? now ye are the temple of the living God; as
God hath said, * I will dwell in them, and walk in *them*,
and I will be to them a God, and they shall be to me a
17 people. † Therefore come out from among them, and be
ye separate, and touch not the unclean person, saith the
18 Lord; and I will receive you, ‡ And will be to you a Father, and ye shall be to me sons and daughters, saith the

* Levit. xxvi. 11, &c. † Isaiah lii. 11; Zeph. iii. 19, 20. ‡ Isaiah xliii. 6.

receive you all. *But ye are straitened in your own bowels*—Your hearts are shut up, and so not capable of the blessings ye might enjoy.

Verse 13. *Now for a recompence of the same*—Of my parental tenderness. *I speak as to my children*—I ask nothing hard or grievous. *Be ye also enlarged*—Open your hearts, first to God, and then to us, (so 2 Cor. viii. 5,) that God may "dwell in you," 2 Cor. vi. 16; vii. 1; and that ye may "receive us," 2 Cor. vii. 2.

Verse 14. *Be not unequally yoked with unbelievers*—Christians with Jews or heathens. The apostle particularly speaks of marriage. But the reasons he urges equally hold against any needless intimacy with them. Of the five questions that follow, the three former contain the argument; the two latter, the conclusion.

Verse 15. *What concord hath Christ*—Whom ye serve. *With Belial*—To whom they belong.

Verse 16. *What agreement hath the temple of God with idols*—If God would not endure idols in any part of the land wherein he dwelt, how much less, under his own roof! He does not say, *with the temple of idols*, for idols do not dwell in their worshippers. *As God hath said*—To his ancient church, and in them to all the Israel of God. *I will dwell in them, and walk in them*—The former signifying his perpetual presence; the latter, his operation. *And I will be to them a God, and they shall be to me a people*—The sum of the whole gospel covenant.

Verse 17. *Touch not the unclean person*—Keep at the utmost distance from him. *And I will receive you*—Into my house and family.

Verse 18. *And ye shall be to me for sons and for daughters, saith the Lord Almighty*—The promise made to Solomon, 1 Chron. xxviii. 6, is here applied to all believers; as the promise made particularly to Joshua is applied to them, Heb. xiii. 5. Who can express the worth, who can conceive the dignity, of this divine adoption? Yet it belongs to all who

VII. 1 Lord Almighty. Having therefore, beloved, these promises, let us cleanse ourselves from all pollution of the flesh
and of the spirit, perfecting holiness in the fear of God.
2 Receive us; we have hurt no man, we have corrupted
3 no man, we have defrauded no man. I speak not to condemn *you*: for I have said before, that ye are in our hearts
4 to live and to die with *you*. Great *is* my freedom of speech
toward you, great *is* my glorying over you: I am filled
with comfort, I exceedingly abound with joy over all our
5 affliction. For when we were come into Macedonia, our
flesh had no rest, but we were troubled on every side; from
6 without *were* fightings, from within *were* fears. But God,
who comforteth them that are brought low, comforted us by
7 the coming of Titus; And not only by his coming, but
also by the comfort wherewith he was comforted over you,
when he told us your earnest desire, your grief, your zeal

believe the gospel, who have faith in Christ. They have access to the Almighty; such free and welcome access, as a beloved child to an indulgent father. To him they may fly for aid in every difficulty, and from him obtain a supply in all their wants.

Verse 1. *Let us cleanse ourselves*—This is the latter part of the exhortation, which was proposed, 2 Cor. vi. 1, and resumed, verse 14. *From all pollution of the flesh*—All outward sin. *And of the spirit*—All inward. Yet let us not rest in negative religion, but *perfect holiness*—Carrying it to the height in all its branches, and enduring to the end *in the* loving *fear of God*, the sure foundation of all holiness.

Verse 2. *Receive us*—The sum of what is said in this, as well as in the tenth and following chapters. *We have hurt no man*—In his person. *We have corrupted no man*—In his principles. *We have defrauded no man*—Of his property. In this he intimates likewise the good he had done them, but with the utmost modesty, as it were not looking upon it.

Verse 3. *I speak not to condemn you*—Not as if I accused you of laying this to my charge. I am so far from thinking so unkindly of you, that *ye are in our hearts, to live and die with you*—That is, I could rejoice to spend all my days with you.

Verse 4. *I am filled with comfort*—Of this he treats, verse 6, &c.; of his joy, verse 7, &c.; of both, verse 13.

Verse 5. *Our flesh*—That is, we ourselves. *Had no rest: from without*—From the heathens. *Were fightings*—Furious and cruel oppositions *From within*—From our brethren. *Were fears*—Lest they should be seduced.

Verse 7. *Your earnest desire*—To rectify what had been amiss. *Your grief*—For what had offended God, and troubled me.

8 for me, so that I rejoiced the more. For I do not repent
that I grieved you by the letter, though I did repent: (for
I see that letter grieved you, though but for a season.)
9 Now I rejoice, not that ye were grieved, but that ye
grieved to repentance: for ye grieved in a godly manner, so
10 that ye received damage by us in nothing. For godly sorrow worketh repentance unto salvation not to be repented
11 of: whereas the sorrow of the world worketh death. For
behold this very thing, that ye sorrowed after a godly manner, how great diligence it wrought in you, yea, clearing of
yourselves, yea, indignation, yea, fear, yea, vehement desire,
yea, zeal, yea, revenge! In all things ye have approved
12 yourselves to be pure in this matter. And though I wrote
to you, *it was* not for his sake who had done the wrong, nor
for his sake who had suffered it, but for the sake of manifesting to you in the sight of God our diligent care over you.
13 Therefore we were comforted in your comfort: and we
rejoiced the more exceedingly in the joy of Titus, because
14 his spirit was refreshed by you all. So that if I had boasted
anything of you to him, I am not ashamed; but as we
speak all things to you in truth, so also our boasting to
15 Titus is found a truth. And his tender affection is more
abundant toward you, calling to mind the obedience of you

Verse 8. *I did repent*--That is, I felt a tender sorrow for having grieved you, till I saw the happy effect of it.

Verse 10. *The sorrow of the world*—Sorrow that arises from worldly considerations. *Worketh death*—Naturally tends to work or occasion death, temporal, spiritual, and eternal.

Verse 11. *How great diligence it wrought in you*—Shown in all the following particulars. *Yea, clearing of yourselves*—Some had been more, some less, faulty; whence arose these various affections. Hence their *apologizing* and *indignation,* with respect to themselves; their *fear* and *desire,* with respect to the apostle; their *zeal* and *revenge,* with respect to the offender, yea, and themselves also. *Clearing of yourselves*—From either sharing in, or approving of, his sin. *Indignation*—That ye had not immediately corrected the offender. *Fear*—Of God's displeasure, or lest I should come with a rod. *Vehement desire*—To see me again. *Zeal*—For the glory of God, and the soul of that sinner. *Yea, revenge*—Ye took a kind of holy revenge upon yourselves, being scarce able to forgive yourselves. *In all things ye*—As a church. *Have approved yourselves to be pure*—That is, free from blame, since ye received my letter.

Verse 12. *It was not* only, or chiefly, *for the sake of* the incestuous person, or of his father; but to show my *care over you.*

16 all, how ye received him with fear and trembling. I rejoice
therefore that I have confidence in you in all things.

CHAP. VIII. 1 Moreover, brethren, we declare to you
the grace of God, bestowed on the churches in Macedonia;
2 That in a great trial of affliction their overflowing joy and
their deep poverty abounded to the riches of their liberality:
3 That to *their* power, I testify, and beyond *their* power *they*
4 were willing of themselves; Praying us with much intreaty
to receive the gift, and take a part in ministering *it* to the
5 saints. And *this they did*, not as we hoped, but first gave
6 themselves to the Lord, and to us by the will of God. So
that we desired Titus, that as he had begun before, so he
7 would also complete this gift among you. Therefore, as ye
abound in everything, in faith, and utterance, and knowledge, and all diligence, and in your love to us, *see* that ye
8 abound in this grace also. I speak not by way of command,
but that by the diligence of others I may prove the sincerity
9 of your love. For ye know the grace of our Lord Jesus
Christ, that, though he was rich, yet for your sakes he
became poor, that ye through his poverty might be rich.
10 And herein I give *my* advice: for this is expedient for you,
who have begun a year ago, not only to do, but also to do
11 it willingly. Now therefore complete the work: that as
there was a ready will, so *there may* be also a performance
12 in proportion to what ye have. For if there be first a ready

Verse 1. *We declare to you the grace of God*—Which evidently appeared by this happy effect.

Verse 2. *In a great trial of affliction*—Being continually persecuted, harassed, and plundered.

Verse 4. *Praying us with much entreaty*—Probably St. Paul had lovingly admonished them not to do beyond their power.

Verse 5. *And not as we hoped*—That is, beyond all we could hope *They gave themselves to us, by the will of God*—In obedience to his will, to be wholly directed by us.

Verse 6. *As he had begun*—When he was with you before.

Verse 9. *For ye know*—And this knowledge is the true source of love. *The grace*—The most sincere, most free, and most abundant love. *He became poor*—In becoming man, in all his life; in his death. *Rich*—In the favour and image of God.

Verse 12. *A man*—Every believer. *Is accepted*—With God. *According to what he hath*—And the same rule holds universally. Whoever acknowledges himself to be a vile, guilty sinner, and, in consequence of this

mind, a man is accepted according to what he hath, not
13 according to what he hath not. For *I do* not *mean* that
14 others should be eased, and you burdened: But by an
equality, *let* your abundance *be* at this time *a supply* to
their want, that their abundance also may be *a supply* to
15 your want: that there may be an equality: As it is written,
* He that *had gathered* the most had nothing over; and
he that *had gathered* the least did not lack.
16 But thanks be to God, who putteth the same diligent
17 care for you in the heart of Titus. For he accepted indeed
the exhortation; but being more forward, he went to you
18 of his own accord. And we have sent with him the brother,
19 whose praise in the gospel is through all the churches; (And
not only *so*, but he was also appointed by the churches *to be*
a fellowtraveller with us with this gift, which is adminis-
tered by us to the glory of the Lord himself, and for *the*
20 *declaration* of our ready mind;) Avoiding this, lest any
one should blame us in this abundance which is adminis-
21 tered by us: For we provide things honest, not only before

* Exod. xvi. 18.

acknowledgment, flies for refuge to the wounds of a crucified Saviour, and relies on his merits alone for salvation, may in every circumstance of life apply this indulgent declaration to himself.

Verse 14. *That their abundance*—If need should so require. *May be*—At another time. *A supply to your want: that there may be an equality*—No want on one side, no superfluity on the other. It may likewise have a further meaning:—that as the temporal bounty of the Corinthians did now supply the temporal wants of their poor brethren in Judea, so the prayers of these might be a means of bringing down many spiritual blessings on their benefactors: so that all the spiritual wants of the one might be amply supplied; all the temporal of the other.

Verse 15. *As it is written, He that had gathered the most had nothing over; and he that had gathered the least did not lack*—That is, in which that scripture is in another sense fulfilled.

Verse 17. *Being more forward*—Than to need it, though he received it well.

Verse 18. *We*—I and Timothy. *The brother*—The ancients generally supposed this was St. Luke. *Whose praise*—For faithfully dispensing *the gospel, is through all the churches.*

Verse 19. *He was appointed by the churches*—Of Macedonia. *With this gift*—Which they were carrying from Macedonia to Jerusalem. *For the declaration of our ready mind*—That of Paul and his fellow-traveller, ready to be the servants of all.

22 the Lord, but also before men. And we have sent with
them our brother, whom we have often proved diligent in
many things, but now much more diligent, through his
23 great confidence in you. If *any inquire* concerning Titus,
he is my partner and fellowlabourer with respect to you:
or *concerning* our brethren, *they are* the messengers of the
24 churches, the glory of Christ. Show therefore to them
before the churches the proof of your love and of our boast-
IX. 1 ing on your behalf. For concerning the ministering to
2 the saints, it is superfluous for me to write to you: For I
know your readiness, which I boast concerning you to the
Macedonians, that Achaia was ready a year ago; and your
3 zeal hath provoked very many. Yet I have sent the brethren, lest our boasting of you on this head should be made
4 vain; that, as I said, ye may be ready: Lest if any of the
Macedonians come up with me, and find ye unprepared,
we (not to say, you) be ashamed of this confident boasting.
5 Therefore I thought it necessary to desire the brethren to
go before to you, and complete this your bounty, which had
been spoken of before, that it may be ready, as a bounty,
6 and not as *a matter* of covetousness. And this *I say*, He
that soweth sparingly shall reap also sparingly; and he that
7 soweth bountifully shall reap also bountifully: *Let* every
man *do* as he chooseth in his heart; not grudgingly, or
8 of necessity: for * God loveth a cheerful giver. And God

* Prov. xxii. 9.

Verse 22. *With them*—With Titus and Luke. *Our brother*—Perhaps Apollos.

Verse 23. *My partner*—In my cares and labours. *The glory of Christ*—Signal instruments of advancing his glory.

Verse 24. *Before the churches*—Present by their messengers.

Verse 1. *To write to you*—Largely.

Verse 2. *I boast to them of Macedonia*—With whom he then was.

Verse 3. *I have sent the* above mentioned *brethren* before me.

Verse 5. *Spoken of before*—By me, to the Macedonians. *Not as a matter of covetousness*—As wrung by importunity from covetous persons.

Verse 6. *He that soweth sparingly shall reap sparingly; he that soweth bountifully shall reap bountifully*—A general rule. God will proportion the reward to the work, and the temper whence it proceeds.

Verse 7. *Of necessity*—Because he cannot tell how to refuse.

Verse 8. How remarkable are these words! Each is loaded with matter and increases all the way it goes. *All grace*—Every kind of blessing.

is able to make all grace abound toward you; that having
always all sufficiency in all things, ye may abound to every
9 good work; (As it is written, * He hath scattered abroad;
he hath given to the poor: his righteousness remaineth for
10 ever. † And he who supplieth seed to the sower, and bread
for *your* food, will supply and multiply your seed sown, and
11 increase the fruits of your righteousness;) Being enriched
in everything to all bountifulness, which worketh by us
12 thanksgiving to God. For the administration of this service doth not only supply the necessities of the saints, but
13 likewise aboundeth by many thanksgivings to God; (Who,
by experiment of this administration, glorify God for your
avowed subjection to the gospel of Christ, and for your
14 liberal communication to them and to all men;) And by
their prayer for you, who long after you for the exceeding
15 grace of God which is in you. Thanks *be* to God for his
unspeakable gift.

CHAP. X. 1 Now I Paul myself, who when present
am base among you, but being absent am bold toward you,

* Psalm cxii. 9. † Isai. lv. 10.

That ye may abound to every good work—God gives us everything, that we may do good therewith, and so receive more blessings. All things in this life, even rewards, are, to the faithful, seeds in order to a future harvest.

Verse 9. *He hath scattered abroad*—(A generous word.) With a full hand, without any anxious thought which way each grain falls. *His righteousness*—His beneficence, with the blessed effects of it. *Remaineth for ever*—Unexhausted, God still renewing his store

Verse 10. *And he who supplieth seed*—Opportunity and ability to help others. *And bread*—All things needful for your own souls and bodies. *Will* continually *supply* you with that *seed*, yea, *multiply* it to you more and more. *And increase the fruits of your righteousness*—The happy effects of your love to God and man.

Verse 11. *Which worketh by us thanksgiving to God*—Both from us who distribute, and them who receive, your bounty.

Verse 13. *Your avowed subjection*—Openly testified by your actions. *To all men*—Who stand in need of it.

Verse 15. *His unspeakable gift*—His outward and inward blessings, the number and excellence of which cannot be uttered.

Verse 1. *Now I Paul myself*—A strongly emphatical expression. *Who when present am base among you*—So, probably, some of the false teachers

entreat you, by the meekness and gentleness of Christ,
2 I beseech, that I may not when I am present be bold with
that confidence wherewith I think to be bold toward some,
3 who think of us as walking after the flesh. For though we
4 walk in the flesh, we do not war after the flesh: (For the
weapons of our warfare *are* not carnal, but mighty through
5 God to the throwing down of strong holds:) Destroying
reasonings, and every high thing which exalteth itself against
the knowledge of God, and bringing every thought into cap-
6 tivity to the obedience of Christ; And being in readiness to
avenge all disobedience, when your obedience is fulfilled.
7 Do ye look at the outward appearance of things? If any

affirmed. Copying after *the meekness and gentleness of Christ, entreat*—Though I might command *you.*

Verse 2. Do not constrain me *when present to be bold*—To exert my apostolical authority. *Who think of us as walking after the flesh*—As acting in a cowardly or crafty manner.

Verse 3. *Though we walk in the flesh*—In mortal bodies, and, consequently, are not free from human weakness. Yet *we do not war*—Against the world and the devil. *After the flesh*—By any carnal or worldly methods. Though the apostle here, and in several other parts of this epistle, speaks in the plural number, for the sake of modesty and decency, yet he principally means himself. On him were these reflections thrown, and it is his own authority which he is vindicating.

Verse 4. *For the weapons of our warfare*—Those we use in this war *Are not carnal*—But spiritual, and therefore *mighty to the throwing down of strong holds*—Of all the difficulties which men or devils can raise in our way. Though faith and prayer belong also to the Christian armour, Ephes. vi. 15, &c., yet the word of God seems to be here chiefly intended.

Verse 5. *Destroying* all vain *reasonings, and every high thing which exalteth itself*—As a wall or rampart. *Against the knowledge of God, and bringing every thought*—Or, rather, faculty of the mind. *Into captivity to the obedience of Christ*—Those evil reasonings are destroyed. The mind itself, being overcome and taken captive, lays down all authority of its own, and entirely gives itself up to perform, for the time to come, to Christ its conqueror *the obedience of* faith.

Verse 6. *Being in readiness to avenge all disobedience*—Not only by spiritual censure, but miraculous punishments. *When your obedience is fulfilled*—When the sound part of you have given proof of your obedience, so that I am in no danger of punishing the innocent with the guilty.

Verse 7. *Do ye look at the outward appearance of things*—Does any of you judge of a minister of Christ by his person, or any outward circumstance? *Let him again think this of himself*—Let him learn it from his own reflection, before I convince him by a severer method.

man be confident that he is Christ's, let him again think this
8 of himself, that, as he *is* Christ's, so *are* we also. Yea, if I
should boast something more also of the authority which the
Lord hath given us for edification, and not for your destruc-
9 tion, I should not be ashamed: That I may not seem as it
10 were to terrify you by letters. For *his* letters, indeed, say
they, *are* weighty and strong; but *his* bodily presence *is*
11 weak, and *his* speech contemptible. Let such an one think
this, that, such as we are in word by letters when we are
absent, such *are* we also in deed when we are present.
12 For we presume not to equal, or to compare ourselves
with some of those who recommend themselves: but they
among themselves limiting themselves, and comparing them-
13 selves with themselves, are not wise. But we will not boastingly extend ourselves beyond *our* measure, but according
to the measure of the province which God hath allotted us,
14 a measure to reach even unto you. For we do not extend
ourselves excessively, as not reaching to you: for we are
15 come even to you in the gospel of Christ: Not boastingly
extending ourselves beyond *our* measure, in the labours of
others; but having hope, now your faith is increased, to be
enlarged by you *yet still* within our province abundantly,

Verse 8. *I should not be ashamed*—As having said more than I could make good.

Verse 9. I say this, *that I may not seem to terrify you by letters*—Threatening more than I can perform.

Verse 10. *His bodily presence is weak*—His stature, says St. Chrysostom, was low, his body crooked, and his head bald.

Verse 12. *For we presume not*—A strong irony. *To equal ourselves*—As partners of the same office. *Or to compare ourselves*—As partakers of the same labour. *They among themselves limiting themselves*—Choosing and limiting their provinces according to their own fancy.

Verse 13. *But we will not*, like them, *boastingly extend ourselves beyond our measure, but according to the measure of the province which God hath allotted us*—To me, in particular, as the apostle of the gentiles. *A measure* which *reaches even unto you*—God allotted to each apostle his province, and the measure or bounds thereof.

Verse 14. *We are come even to you*—By a gradual, regular process, having taken the intermediate places in our way, *in* preaching *the gospel of Christ*.

Verse 15. *Having hope, now your faith is increased*—So that you can the better spare us. *To be enlarged by you abundantly*—That is, enabled by you to go still further

16 So as to preach the gospel in the regions beyond you, not to
boast in another's province of things made ready to our
17 hand. But he that glorieth, let him glory in the Lord.
18 For not he that commendeth himself is approved, but whom
the Lord commendeth.

CHAP. XI. 1 I wish ye would bear a little with my folly
2 yea, bear with me. For I am jealous over you with a godly
jealousy: for I have espoused you to one husband, that I
3 may present *you as* a chaste virgin to Christ. But I fear,
lest, as the serpent deceived Eve, through his subtilty, so
your minds should be corrupted from the simplicity that is
4 in Christ. If indeed he that cometh preach another Jesus,
whom we have not preached, or *if* ye receive another Spirit,
which ye have not received, or another gospel, which ye
5 have not accepted, ye might well bear with *him*. But I
suppose that I fall nothing short of the very chief apostles.
6 For if *I am* unskilful in speech, yet not in knowledge; but
we have been thoroughly made manifest to you in all things.
7 Have I committed an offence in humbling myself that ye

Verse 16. *In the regions beyond you*—To the west and south, where the gospel had not yet been preached.

Verse 1. *I wish ye would bear*—So does he pave the way for what might otherwise have given offence. *With my folly*—Of commending myself; which to many may appear folly; and really would be so, were it not on this occasion absolutely necessary.

Verse 2. *For*—The cause of his seeming folly is expressed in this and the following verse; the cause why they should bear with him, verse 4.

Verse 3. *But I fear*—Love is full of these fears. *Lest as the serpent*—A most apposite comparison. *Deceived Eve*—Simple, ignorant of evil. *By his subtilty*—Which is in the highest degree dangerous to such a disposition. *So your minds*—We might therefore be tempted, even if there were no sin in us. *Might be corrupted*—Losing their virginal purity. *From the simplicity that is in Christ*—That simplicity which is lovingly intent on him alone, seeking no other person or thing.

Verse 4. *If indeed*—Any could show you another Saviour, a more powerful Spirit, a better gospel. *Ye might well bear with him*—But this is impossible.

Verse 6. *If I am unskilful in speech*—If I speak in a plain, unadorned way, like an unlearned person. So the Greek word properly signifies.

Verse 7. *Have I committed an offence*—Will any turn this into an objection? *In humbling myself*—To work at my trade. *That ye might be exalted*—To be children of God.

might be exalted, because I have preached the gospel of
8 God to you at free cost? I spoiled other churches, taking
9 wages *of them*, to serve you. And when I was present with
you, and wanted, I was chargeable to no man. For the
brethren who came from Macedonia supplied my want: and
I have in all things kept myself from being burdensome,
10 and will keep *myself*. As the truth of Christ is in me, this
my boasting shall not be stopped in the regions of Achaia.
11 Wherefore? because I love you not? God knoweth. But
12 what I do, I will do, that I may cut off the occasion from them
who desire occasion; that wherein they boast, they may be
13 found even as we. For such *are* false apostles, deceitful workers,
14 transforming themselves into apostles of Christ. And no marvel; for Satan himself is transformed into an angel of light.
15 Therefore *it is* no great thing if his ministers also be transformed as the ministers of righteousness; whose end shall be
16 according to their works. I say again, Let no man think me a
fool; but if otherwise, yet as a fool receive me, that I also may
17 boast a little. What I speak, I speak not after the Lord, but

Verse 8. *I spoiled other churches*—I, as it were, took the spoils of them: it is a military term. *Taking wages* (or *pay*, another military word) *of them*—When I came to you at first. *And when I was present with you, and wanted*—My work not quite supplying my necessities. *I was chargeable to no man*—Of Corinth.

Verse 9. *For*—I choose to receive help from the poor Macedonians, rather than the rich Corinthians! Were the poor in all ages more generous than the rich?

Verse 10. *This my boasting shall not be stopped*—For I will receive nothing from you.

Verse 11. Do I refuse to receive anything of you, *because I love you not? God knoweth* that is not the case.

Verse 12. *Who desire* any *occasion*—To censure me. *That wherein they boast, they may be found even as we*—They boasted of being "burdensome to no man." But it was a vain boast in them, though not in the apostle.

Verse 14. *Satan himself is transformed*—Uses to transform himself; to put on the fairest appearances.

Verse 15. *Therefore it is no great*, no strange, *thing; whose end*, notwithstanding all their disguises, *shall be according to their works.*

Verse 16. *I say again*—He premises a new apology to this new commendation of himself. *Let no man think me a fool*—Let none think I do this without the utmost necessity. But if any do think me foolish herein, yet bear with my folly.

Verse 17. *I speak not after the Lord*—Not by an express command

18 as it were foolishly, in this confidence of boasting. Seeing
19 many glory after the flesh, I will glory also. For ye, being
20 wise, suffer fools willingly. For ye suffer, if a man enslave
you, if he devour *you*, if he take *from you*, if he exalt him-
21 self, if he smite you on the face. I speak with regard to
reproach, as though we had been weak. Whereas in whatever any is confident, (I speak as a fool,) I am confident
22 also. Are they Hebrews? so *am* I. Are they Israelites?
23 so *am* I. Are they the seed of Abraham? so *am* I. Are
they ministers of Christ? (I speak foolishly) I more; in
labours more abundantly, in stripes more exceedingly, in
24 prisons more abundantly, in deaths often. Five times I
25 received from the Jews forty *stripes* save one. Thrice I
was beaten with rods, once I was stoned, thrice I have been
26 shipwrecked, a day and a night I passed in the deep; In
journeyings often, in dangers from rivers, in dangers from
robbers, in dangers from my own countrymen, in dangers
from the heathen, in dangers in the city, in dangers in the
wilderness, in dangers in the sea, in dangers among false

from him; though still under the direction of his Spirit. *But as it were foolishly*—In such a manner as many may think foolish.

Verse 18. *After the flesh*—That is, in external things.

Verse 19. *Being wise*—A beautiful irony.

Verse 20. *For ye suffer*—Not only the folly, but the gross abuses, of those false apostles. *If a man enslave you*—Lord it over you in the most arbitrary manner. *If he devour you*—By his exorbitant demands; notwithstanding his boast of not being burdensome. *If he take from you*—By open violence. *If he exalt himself*—By the most unbounded self-commendation. *If he smite you on the face*—(A very possible case,) under pretence of divine zeal.

Verse 21. *I speak with regard to reproach, as though we had been weak*—I say, "Bear with me," even on supposition that the weakness be real which they reproach me with.

Verse 22. *Are they Hebrews, Israelites, the seed of Abraham*—These were the heads on which they boasted.

Verse 23. I am *more* so than they. *In deaths often*—Surrounding me in the most dreadful forms

Verse 24. *Five times I received from the Jews forty stripes save one*—Which was the utmost that the law allowed. With the Romans he sometimes pleaded his privilege as a Roman; but from the Jews he suffered all things.

Verse 25. *Thrice I have been shipwrecked*—Before his voyage to Rome. *In the deep*—Probably floating on some part of the vessel.

27 brethren; In labour and toil, in watchings often, in hunger
28 and thirst, in fastings often, in cold and nakedness. Beside
the things which are from without, that which rusheth upon
29 me daily, the care of all the churches. Who is weak, and I
30 am not weak? who is offended, and I burn not? Since I
must glory, I will glory of the things that concern my infirm-
31 ities. The God and Father of the Lord Jesus Christ, who
32 is blessed for ever, knoweth that I lie not. In Damascus
the governor under king Aretas kept the city of the Damas-
33 cenes with a guard, being determined to apprehend me: But
I was let down through a window in a basket by the wall,
XII. 1 and escaped from his hands. Surely it is not expedient
for me to boast: yet I will come to visions and revelations
2 of the Lord. I knew a man in Christ above fourteen years
ago; (whether in the body, I know not; or out of the body,

Verse 27. *In cold and nakedness*—Having no place where to lay my head; no convenient raiment to cover me; yet appearing before noblemen, governors, kings; and not being ashamed.

Verse 28. *Beside the things which are from without*—Which I suffer on the account of others; namely, *the care of all the churches*—A more modest expression than if he had said, *the care of the whole church. All*—Even those I have not seen in the flesh. St. Peter himself could not have said this in so strong a sense.

Verse 29. *Who*—So he had not only the care of the churches, but of every person therein. *Is weak, and I am not weak*—By sympathy, as well as by condescension. *Who is offended*—Hindered in, or turned out of, the good way. *And I burn not*—Being pained as though I had fire in my bosom.

Verse 30. *I will glory of the things that concern my infirmities*—Of what shows my weakness, rather than my strength.

Verse 32. *The governor under Aretas*—King of Arabia and Syria, of which Damascus was a chief city, willing to oblige the Jews, *kept the city*—Setting guards at all the gates day and night.

Verse 33. *Through a window*—Of an house which stood on the city wall.

Verse 1. *It is not expedient*—Unless on so pressing occasion. *Visions* are seen; *revelations,* heard.

Verse 2. *I knew a man in Christ*—That is, a Christian. It is plain from verses 6, 7, that he means himself, though in modesty he speaks as of a third person. *Whether in the body or out of the body I know not*—It is equally possible with God to present distant things to the imagination in the body, as if the soul were absent from it, and present with them; or to transport both soul and body for what time he pleases to heaven; or to transport the soul only thither for a season, and in the mean time to preserve the body fit for its re-entrance. But since the

I know not: God knoweth;) such an one caught up to the
3 third heaven. Yea, I knew such a man, (whether in the
4 body, or out of the body, I know not: God knoweth,) That
he was caught up into paradise, and heard unspeakable things,
5 which it is not possible for man to utter. Of such an one I
will glory: but I will not glory of myself, unless in my
6 infirmities. For if I should resolve to boast, I should not
be a fool; for I speak the truth: but I forbear, lest any one
should think of me above what he seeth me, or heareth from
me.
7 And lest I should be lifted up with the abundance of the
revelations, there was given me a thorn in the flesh, a mes-

apostle himself did not know whether his soul was in the body, or whether one or both were actually in heaven, it would be vain curiosity for us to attempt determining it. *The third heaven*—Where God is; far above the aerial and the starry heaven. Some suppose it was here the apostle was let into the mystery of the future state of the church; and eceived his orders to turn from the Jews and go to the gentiles.

Verse 3. *Yea, I knew such a man*—That at another time.

Verse 4. *He was caught up into paradise*—The seat of happy spirits in their separate state, between death and the resurrection. *Things which it is not possible for man to utter*—Human language being incapable of expressing them. Here he anticipated the joyous rest of the righteous that die in the Lord. But this rapture did not precede, but follow after, his being caught up to the third heaven: a strong intimation that he must first discharge his mission, and then enter into glory. And beyond all doubt, such a foretaste of it served to strengthen him in all his after trials, when he could call to mind the very joy that was prepared for him.

Verse 5. *Of such an one I will*—I might, *glory; but I will not glory of myself*—As considered in myself.

Verse 6. *For if I should resolve to glory*—Referring to, *I might glory* of such a glorious revelation. *I should not be a fool*—That is, it could not justly be accounted folly to relate the naked truth. *But I forbear*—I speak sparingly of these things, for fear *any one should think* too highly *of me*—O where is this fear now to be found? Who is afraid of this?

Verse 7. *There was given me*—By the wise and gracious providence of God. *A thorn in the flesh*—A visitation more painful than any thorn sticking in the flesh. *A messenger* or angel *of Satan to buffet me*—Perhaps both visibly and invisibly; and the word in the original expresses the present, as well as the past, time. All kinds of affliction had befallen the apostle. Yet none of those did he deprecate. But here he speaks of one, as above all the rest, one that macerated him with weakness, and by the pain and ignominy of it prevented his being lifted up more, or, at least, not less, than the most vehement head ache could have done; which many of the ancients say he laboured under. St. Paul seems to

8 senger of Satan to buffet me, lest I should be lifted up. Concerning this I besought the Lord thrice, that it might depart
9 from me. But he said to me, My grace is sufficient for
thee: for my strength is made perfect in weakness. Most
gladly therefore will I rather glory in my weaknesses, that
10 the strength of Christ may rest upon me. Therefore I am
well pleased in weaknesses, in reproaches, in necessities, in
persecutions, in distresses for Christ's sake: for when I am
11 weak, then I am strong. I am become a fool in boasting;
but ye have compelled me: for I ought to have been com-
mended by you: for in nothing have I fallen short of the
very chief apostles, though I am nothing.
12 Truly the signs of an apostle were wrought among you in
13 all patience, in signs, and wonders, and mighty deeds. For
wherein were ye inferior to the other churches, unless that I
myself was not burdensome to you? forgive me this wrong.
14 Behold, the third time I am ready to come to you; yet I
will not be burdensome to you: for I seek not yours, but
you: for the children ought not to lay up treasure for the
15 parents, but the parents for the children. And I will most
gladly spend and be spent for your souls; though the more
16 abundantly I love you, the less I am loved. But be it so,

have had a fresh fear of these *buffetings* every moment, when he so frequently represses himself in his boasting, though it was extorted from him by the utmost necessity.

Verse 8. *Concerning this*—He had now forgot his being lifted up. *I besought the Lord thrice*—As our Lord besought his Father.

Verse 9. *But he said to me*—In answer to my third request. *My grace is sufficient for thee*—How tender a repulse! We see there may be grace where there is the quickest sense of pain. *My strength is* more illustriously displayed by the *weakness* of the instrument. *Therefore I will glory in my weaknesses rather* than my revelations, *that the strength of Christ may rest upon me*—The Greek word properly means, may *cover me all over like a tent.* We ought most willingly to accept whatever tends to this end, however contrary to flesh and blood.

Verse 10. *Weaknesses*—Whether proceeding from Satan or men. *For when I am weak*—Deeply conscious of my weakness, *then* does the strength of Christ rest upon me.

Verse 11. *Though I am nothing*—Of myself.

Verse 14. *The third time*—Having been disappointed twice. *I seek not yours*—Your goods. *But you*—Your souls.

Verse 15. *I will gladly spend*—All I have. *And be spent*—Myself.

Verse 16. *But* some may object, though *I did not burden you,* though

I did not burden you: but, being crafty, I caught you with
17 guile. Did I make a gain of you by any of them whom I
18 sent to you? I desired Titus, and with him I sent a brother. Did Titus make a gain of you? did we not walk in
the same spirit? in the same steps?
19 Think ye that we again excuse ourselves to you? we
speak before God in Christ: and all things, beloved, for
20 your edification. For I fear, lest, when I come, I should
not find you such as I would, and *lest* I should be found by
you such as ye would not: lest *there should be* contentions,
envyings, wraths, strifes, backbitings, whisperings, swellings,
21 tumults: Lest my God should humble me when I come to
you again, and I should mourn over many of them who had
sinned before, and have not repented of the uncleanness, and
fornication, and lasciviousness, which they have committed.

CHAP. XIII. 1 I am coming to you this third time.
Every word shall be established by the mouth of two or
2 three witnesses I told *you* before, and do tell beforehand
(though now absent, as if I were present the second time)
those who had sinned before, and all the rest, that, if I come
3 again, I will not spare: Since ye seek a proof of Christ
speaking in me, who is not weak toward you, but powerful

I did not take anything of you myself, yet *being crafty I caught you with guile*—I did secretly by my messengers what I would not do openly, or in person.

Verse 17. I answer this lying accusation by appealing to plain fact *Did I make a gain of you by Titus*—Or any other of my messengers? You know the contrary.

It should be carefully observed, that St. Paul does not allow, but absolutely denies, that *he had caught them with guile;* so that the common plea for guile, which has been often drawn from this text, is utterly without foundation.

Verse 18. *I desired Titus*—To go to you.

Verse 19. *Think ye that we again excuse ourselves*—That I speak this for my own sake? No. I speak all this for your sakes.

Verse 21. *Who had sinned before*—My last coming to Corinth. *Uncleanness*—Of married persons. *Lasciviousness*—Against nature.

Verse 1. *I am coming this third time*—He had been coming twice before, though he did not actually come.

Verse 2. *All the rest*—Who have since then sinned in any of these kinds. *I will not spare*—I will severely punish them.

4 among you. For though he was crucified through weakness, yet he liveth by the power of God. And we also are
weak with him, but we shall live with him by the power
5 of God in you. Examine yourselves, whether ye are in the
faith; prove yourselves. Do ye not know yourselves, that
6 Jesus Christ is in you, unless ye are reprobates? And I
7 trust ye shall know that we are not reprobates. Now I
pray God that ye may do no evil; not that we may appear
approved, but that ye may do that which is good, though
8 we should be as reprobates. For we can do nothing against
9 the truth, but for the truth. For we rejoice, when we are
weak, and ye are strong: and this also we wish, *even* your
10 perfection. Therefore I write these things being absent,
lest being present I should use severity, according to the
power which the Lord hath given me for edification, and
not for destruction.

11 Finally, brethren, farewell. Be perfect, be of good comfort, be of one mind, live in peace; and the God of love

Verse 4. *He was crucified through weakness*—Through the impotence of human nature. *We also are weak with him*—We appear weak and despicable by partaking of the same sufferings for his sake. *But we shall live with him*—Being raised from the dead. *By the power of God in you*—By that divine energy which is now in every believer, verse 5.

Verse 5. *Prove yourselves*—Whether ye are such as can, or *such as cannot, bear the test*—This is the proper meaning of the word which we translate, *reprobates. Know ye not yourselves, that Jesus Christ is in you*—All Christian believers know this, by the witness and by the fruit of his Spirit. Some translate the words, *Jesus Christ is among you;* that is, in the church of Corinth; and understand them of the miraculous gifts and the power of Christ which attended the censures of the apostle.

Verse 6. *And I trust ye shall know*—By proving yourselves, not by putting my authority to the proof.

Verse 7. *I pray God that ye may do no evil*—To give me occasion of showing my apostolical power. I do not desire to *appear approved*—By miraculously punishing you. *But that ye may do that which is good, though we should be as reprobates*—Having no occasion to give that proof of our apostleship.

Verse 8. *For we can do nothing against the truth*—Neither against that which is just and right, nor against those who walk according to the truth of the gospel.

Verse 9. *For we rejoice when we are weak*—When we appear so, having no occasion to show our apostolic power. *And this we wish, even your perfection*—In the faith that worketh by love.

Verse 11. *Be perfect*—Aspire to the highest degree of holiness. *Be*

and peace shall be with you. Salute one another with an
12 holy kiss. All the saints salute you. The grace of the
Lord Jesus Christ, and the love of God, and the communion of the Holy Ghost, *be* with you all.

of good comfort—Filled with divine consolation. *Be of one mind*—Desire, labour, pray for it, to the utmost degree that is possible.

Verse 13. *The grace*—Or favour. *Of our Lord Jesus Christ*—By which alone we can come to the Father. *And the love of God*—Manifested to you, and abiding in you. *And the communion*—Or fellowship. *Of the Holy Ghost*—In all his gifts and graces.

It is with great reason that this comprehensive and instructive blessing is pronounced at the close of our solemn assemblies; and it is a very indecent thing to see so many quitting them, or getting into postures of remove, before this short sentence can be ended.

How often have we heard this awful benediction pronounced! Let us study it more and more, that we may value it proportionably; that we may either deliver or receive it with a becoming reverence, with eyes and hearts lifted up to God, "who giveth the blessing out of Sion, and life for evermore."

NOTES

ON

ST. PAUL'S EPISTLE TO THE GALATIANS.

This epistle is not written, as most of St. Paul's are, to the Christians of a particular city, but to those of a whole country in Asia Minor, the metropolis of which was Ancyra. These readily embraced the gospel; but, after St. Paul had left them, certain men came among them, who (like those mentioned, Acts xv.) taught that it was necessary to be circumcised, and to keep the Mosaic law. They affirmed, that all the other apostles taught thus; that St. Paul was inferior to them; and that even he sometimes practised and recommended the law, though at other times he opposed it.

The first part, therefore, of this epistle is spent in vindicating himself and his doctrine; proving, 1. That he had it immediately from Christ himself; and that he was not inferior to the other apostles. 2. That it was the very same which the other apostles preached. And, 3. That his practice was consistent with his doctrine.

The second contains proofs, drawn from the Old Testament, that the law and all its ceremonies were abolished by Christ.

The third contains practical inferences, closed with his usual benediction.

To be a little more distinct —

This epistle contains,

I. The inscription, C. i. 1—5

II. The calling the Galatians back to the true gospel; wherein he,

1. Reproves them for leaving it, 6—10
2. Asserts the authority of the gospel he had preached, who,
   1. Of a persecutor was made an apostle, by an immediate call from heaven, 11—17
   2 Was no way inferior to Peter himself, 18— C. ii. 21
   3. Defends justification by faith, and again reproves the Galatians, C. iii. 1— iv. 11
   4. Explains the same thing by an allegory taken out of the law itself, 12—31
   5. Exhorts them to maintain their liberty, C. v. 1—12
   Warns them not to abuse it, and admonishes them to walk not after the flesh, but after the Spirit, 13— C. vi. 10

III The conclusion, 11—18

GALATIANS.

CHAPTER I. 1 Paul, an apostle, (not of men, neither
by man, but by Jesus Christ, and God the Father, who
2 raised him from the dead,) And all the brethren who are
3 with me, to the churches of Galatia: Grace *be* to you and
peace from God the Father, and the Lord Jesus Christ,
4 Who gave himself for our sins, that he might deliver us
from the present evil world, according to the will of our
5 God and Father: To him be glory for ever and ever.
Amen.
6 I marvel that ye are so soon removed from him who
7 called you by the grace of Christ to another gospel: Which

Verse 1. *Paul, an apostle*—Here it was necessary for St. Paul to assert his authority; otherwise he is very modest in the use of this title. He seldom mentions it when he mentions others in the salutations with himself, as in the Epistles to the Philippians and Thessalonians; or when he writes about secular affairs, as in that to Philemon; nor yet in writing to the Hebrews; because he was not properly their apostle. *Not of men*—Not commissioned from them, but from God the Father. *Neither by man*—Neither by any man as an instrument, but by Jesus Christ. *Who raised him from the dead*—Of which it was the peculiar business of an apostle to bear witness.

Verse 2. *And all the brethren*—Who agree with me in what I now write.

Verse 4. *That he might deliver us from the present evil world*—From the guilt, wickedness, and misery wherein it is involved, and from its vain and foolish customs and pleasures. *According to the will of God*—Without any merit of ours. St. Paul begins most of his epistles with thanksgiving; but, writing to the Galatians, he alters his style, and first sets down his main proposition, That by the merits of Christ alone, *giving himself for our sins*, we are justified: neither does he term them, as he does others, either "saints," "elect," or "churches of God."

Verse 5. *To whom be glory*—For this his gracious will.

Verse 6. *I marvel that ye are removed so soon*—After my leaving you *From him who called you by the grace of Christ*—His gracious gospel, and his gracious power.

Verse 7. *Which*, indeed, *is not* properly *another* gospel. For what ye have now received is no gospel at all: it is not glad, but heavy, tidings, as setting your acceptance with God upon terms impossible to

is not another; but there are some that trouble you, and
8 would subvert the gospel of Christ. But if we, or an angel
from heaven, preach to you another gospel than we have
9 preached to you, let him be accursed. As we have said
before, so I say now again, If any one preach to you another
10 gospel than that ye received, let him be accursed. For do
I now satisfy men or God? or do I seek to please men?
for if I still pleased men, I should not be the servant of
Christ.

11 But I certify you, brethren, that the gospel which was
12 preached by me is not according to man. For neither did
I receive it from man, neither was I taught *it*, but by the
13 revelation of Jesus Christ. For ye have heard of my behaviour in time past in the Jewish religion, that above measure

be performed. *But there are some that trouble you*—The same word occurs, Acts xv. 24. *And would*—If they were able. *Subvert* or overthrow *the gospel of Christ*—The better to effect which, they suggest, that the other apostles, yea, and I myself, insist upon the observance of the law.

Verse 8. *But if we*—I and all the apostles. *Or an angel from heaven*—If it were possible. *Preach another gospel, let him be accursed*—Cut off from Christ and God.

Verse 9. *As*—He speaks upon mature deliberation; after pausing, it seems, between the two verses. *We*—I and the brethren who are with me. *Have said before*—Many times, in effect, if not in terms. *So I say*—All those brethren knew the truth of the gospel. St. Paul knew the Galatians had received the true gospel.

Verse 10. *For*—He adds the reason why he speaks so confidently. *Do I now satisfy men*—Is this what I aim at in preaching or writing? *If I still*—Since I was an apostle. *Pleased men*—Studied to please them; if this were my motive of action; nay, if I did in fact please the men who know not God. *I should not be the servant of Christ*—Hear this, all ye who vainly hope to keep in favour both with God and with the world!

Verse 11. *But I certify you, brethren*—He does not till now give them even this appellation. *That the gospel which was preached by me* among you *is not according to man*—Not from man, not by man, not suited to the taste of man.

Verse 12. *For neither did I receive it*—At once. *Nor was I taught it*—Slowly and gradually, by any man. *But by the revelation of Jesus Christ*—Our Lord revealed to him at first, his resurrection, ascension, and the calling of the gentiles, and his own apostleship; and told him then, there were other things for which he would appear to him.

Verse 13. *I persecuted the church of God*—That is, the believers in Christ.

14 I persecuted the church of God, and wasted it. And I profited in the Jewish religion above many of my years among
my countrymen, being more abundantly zealous for the tra-
15 ditions of my fathers. But when it pleased God, who
separated me from my mother's womb, and called *me* by his
16 grace, To reveal his Son in me, that I might preach him
among the gentiles; I did not confer with flesh and blood
17 Neither did I go up to Jerusalem, to them that were apostles
before me; but I immediately went into Arabia, and returned
18 again to Damascus. Then after three years I went up to
Jerusalem to visit Peter, and abode with him fifteen days.
19 But other of the apostles I saw none, save James the
20 brother of the Lord. Now the things which I write to you,
21 behold, before God, I lie not. Afterwards I came into the
22 regions of Syria and Cilicia; And I was unknown by face to
23 the churches of Judea which were in Christ: But only they
had heard, He that persecuted us in time past now preacheth

Verse 14. *Being zealous of the* unwritten *traditions*—Over and above those written in the law

Verse 15. *But when it pleased God*—He ascribes nothing to his own merits, endeavours, or sincerity. *Who separated me from my mother's womb*—Set me apart for an apostle, as he did Jeremiah for a prophet, Jer. i. 5. Such an unconditional predestination as this may consist both with God's justice and mercy. *And called me by his grace*—By his free and almighty love, to be both a Christian and an apostle.

Verse 16. *To reveal his Son in me*—By the powerful operation of his Spirit, 2. Cor. iv. 6; as well as to me, by the heavenly vision. *That I might preach him to others*—Which I should have been ill qualified to do, had I not first known him myself. *I did not confer with flesh and blood*—Being fully satisfied of the divine will, and determined to obey, I took no counsel with any man, neither with my own reason or inclinations, which might have raised numberless objections.

Verse 17. *Neither did I go up to Jerusalem*—The residence of the apostles. *But I immediately went again into Arabia, and returned again to Damascus*—He presupposes the journey to Damascus, in which he was converted, as being known to them all.

Verse 18. *Then after three years*—Wherein I had given full proof of my apostleship. *I went to visit Peter*—To converse with him.

Verse 19. *But other of the apostles I saw none, save James the brother* (that is, the kinsman) *of the Lord*—Therefore when Barnabas is said to have "brought him into the apostles," Acts ix. 27, only St. Peter and St James are meant.

Verse 22. *I was unknown by face to the churches of Judea*—Except to that of Jerusalem.

24 the faith which once he destroyed. And they glorified God
II 1 in me. Then fourteen years after, I went up again to
2 Jerusalem with Barnabas, taking Titus also with me. But
I went up by revelation, and laid before them the gospel
which I preach among the gentiles, but severally to those
of eminence, lest by any means I should run, or should have
3 run, in vain. (But neither was Titus, who was with me,
4 being a Greek, compelled to be circumcised: Because of
false brethren introduced unawares, who had slipped in to
spy out our liberty which we have through Christ Jesus,
5 that they might bring us into bondage: To whom we did
not yield by submission, no, not an hour; that the truth of

Verse 24. *In me*—That is, on my account

Verse 1 *Then fourteen years after*—My first journey thither. *I went up again to Jerusalem*—This seems to be the journey mentioned Acts xv.; several passages here referring to that great council, wherein all the apostles showed that they were of the same judgment with him.

Verse 2. *I went up*—Not by any command from them, but *by* an express *revelation* from God. *And laid before them*—The chief of the church in Jerusalem. *The gospel which I preach among the gentiles*—Acts xv. 4, touching justification by faith alone; not that they might confirm me therein, but that I might remove prejudice from them. Yet not publicly at first, *but severally to those of eminence*—Speaking to them one by one. *Lest I should run, or should have run, in vain*—Lest I should lose the fruit either of my present or past labours. For they might have greatly hindered this, had they not been fully satisfied both of his mission and doctrine. The word *run* beautifully expresses the swift progress of the gospel.

Verse 3. *But neither was Titus who was with me*—When I conversed with them. *Compelled to be circumcised*—A clear proof that none of the apostles insisted on the circumcising gentile believers. The sense is, And it is true, some of those false brethren would fain have compelled Titus to be circumcised; but I utterly refused it.

Verse 4. *Because of false brethren*– Who seem to have urged it. *Introduced unawares*—Into some of those private conferences at Jerusalem. *Who had slipped in to spy out our liberty*—From the ceremonial law. *That they might*, if possible, *bring us into* that *bondage* again.

Verse 5. *To whom we did not yield by submission*—Although in love he would have yielded to any. With such wonderful prudence did the apostle use his Christian liberty! circumcising Timothy, Acts xvi. 3, because of weak brethren, but not Titus, because of false brethren. *That the truth of the gospel*—That is, the true genuine gospel. *Might continue with you*—With you gentiles. So we defend, for your sakes, the privilege which you would give up.

6 the gospel might continue with you.) And they who undoubtedly were something; (*but* whatsoever they were, it is no
difference to me: God accepteth no man's person;) they who
7 undoubtedly were something, added nothing to me: But on
the contrary, when they saw that I was intrusted with the
gospel of the uncircumcision, as Peter *with that* of the cir-
8 cumcision; (For he that wrought effectually in Peter for the
apostleship of the circumcision, wrought likewise effectuall
9 in me toward the gentiles;) And when James, and Cephas,
and John, who undoubtedly were pillars, knew the grace
that was given to me, they gave the right hands of fellowship
to me and Barnabas, that we *should go* to the gentiles, and
10 they to the circumcision: Only *they desired* that we would
be mindful of the poor; which very thing I also was forward
11 to do. But when Cephas came to Antioch, I withstood him

Verse 6. *And they who undoubtedly were something*—Above all others. *What they were*—How eminent soever. *It is no difference to me*—So that I should alter either my doctrine or my practice. *God accepteth no man's person*—For any eminence in gifts or outward prerogatives In that conference *added nothing to me*—Neither as to doctrine nor mission.

Verse 7. *But when they saw*—By the effects which I laid before them, verse 8; Acts xv. 12. *That I was intrusted with the gospel of the uncircumcision*—That is, with the charge of preaching it to the uncircumcised heathens.

Verse 8. *For he that wrought effectually in Peter for the apostleship of the circumcision*—To qualify him for, and support him in, the discharge of that office to the Jews. *Wrought likewise effectually in* and by *me*—For and in the discharge of my office *toward the gentiles.*

Verse 9. *And when James*—Probably named first because he was bishop of the church in Jerusalem. *And Cephas*—Speaking of him at Jerusalem he calls him by his Hebrew name. *And John*—Hence it appears that he also was at the council, though he is not particularly named in the Acts. *Who undoubtedly were pillars*—The principal supporters and defenders of the gospel. *Knew*—After they had heard the account I gave them. *The grace*—Of apostleship. *Which was given me, they*—In the name of all *Gave to me and Barnabas*—My fellow-labourer. *The right hands of fellowship*—They gave us their hands in token of receiving us as their fellow-labourers, mutually agreeing *that we*—I and those in union with me. *Should go to the gentiles*—Chiefly. *And they*—With those that were in union with them, chiefly *to the circumcision*—The Jews.

Verse 10. *Of the poor*—The poor Christians in Judea, who had lost all they had for Christ's sake

Verse 11. *But*—The argument here comes to the height. Paul reproves Peter himself. So far was he from receiving his doctrine from man, or from being inferior to the chief of the apostles. *When Peter*—Afterwards.

12 to the face, because he was to be blamed. For before some
came from James, he ate with the Gentiles: but when they
were come, he withdrew and separated himself, fearing those
13 of the circumcision. And the other Jews also dissembled
with him; so that even Barnabas was carried away with
14 their dissimulation. But when I saw that they did not walk
uprightly according to the truth of the gospel, I said to
Peter before *them* all, If thou, being a Jew, livest after the
manner of the gentiles, and not of the Jews, why compellest
15 thou the gentiles to judaize? We *who are* Jews by nature,
16 and not sinners of the gentiles, Even we (knowing that a
man is not justified by the works of the law, but by the faith
of Jesus Christ) have believed in Christ Jesus, that we might
be justified by the faith of Christ, and not by the works of
the law: because by the works of the law no flesh shall be

Came to Antioch—Then the chief of all the gentile churches. *I withstood him to the face, because he was to be blamed*—For fear of man, verse 12; for dissimulation, verse 13; and for not walking uprightly, verse 14.

Verse 13. *And the other* believing *Jews*—Who were at Antioch. *Dissembled with him, so that even Barnabas was carried away with their dissimulation*—Was borne away, as with a torrent, into the same ill practice.

Verse 14. *I said to Cephas before them all*—See Paul single against Peter and all the Jews! *If thou being a Jew,* yet *livest,* in thy ordinary conversation, *after the manner of the gentiles*—Not observing the ceremonial law, which thou knowest to be now abolished. *Why compellest thou the gentiles*—By withdrawing thyself and all the ministers from them; either *to judaize,* to keep the ceremonial law, or to be excluded from church communion.

Verse 15. *We*—St. Paul, to spare St. Peter, drops the first person singular, and speaks in the plural number. Verse 18, he speaks in the first person singular again by a figure; and without a figure, verse 19, &c *Who are Jews by nature*—By birth, not proselytes only. *And not sinners of the gentiles*—That is, not sinful gentiles; not such gross, enormous, abandoned sinners, as the heathens generally were.

Verse 16. *Knowing that a man is not justified by the works of the law*—Not even of the moral, much less the ceremonial, law. *But by the faith of Jesus Christ*—That is, by faith in him. The name Jesus was first known by the gentiles; the name Christ by the Jews. And they are not always placed promiscuously; but generally in a more solemn way of speaking, the Apostle says, Christ Jesus; in a more familiar, Jesus Christ. *Even we*—And how much more must the gentiles, who have still less pretence to depend on their own works! *Have believed*—Knowing there is no other way. *Because*—Considering the demands of the law, and the state of human nature, it is evident, that *by the works of the law*—By such an obedience as it requires. *Shall no flesh living*—No human creature, Jew

17 justified But if, while we seek to be justified by Christ, we
ourselves also are found sinners, *is* Christ therefore the
18 minister of sin? God forbid. For if I build again the things
19 which I destroyed, I make myself a transgressor. For I
through the law am dead to the law, that I may live to God.
20 I am crucified with Christ: and I live no longer, but Christ
liveth in me: and the life that I now live in the flesh I live
by faith in the Son of God, who loved me and delivered up
21 himself for me. I do not make void the grace of God: for
if righteousness *is* by the law, then Christ died in vain.

or gentile, *be justified.* Hitherto St. Paul had been considering that single question, "Are Christians obliged to observe the ceremonial law?" But he here insensibly goes farther, and, by citing this scripture, shows that what he spoke directly of the ceremonial, included also the moral, law. For David undoubtedly did so, when he said, Psalm cxliii. 2, the place here referred to, "In thy sight shall no man living be justified;" which the Apostle likewise explains, Rom. iii. 19, 20, in such a manner as can agree to none but the moral law.

Verse 17. *But if while we seek to be justified by Christ, we ourselves are* still *found sinners*—If we continue in sin, will it therefore follow, that *Christ* is *the minister* or countenancer *of sin?*

Verse 18. By no means. *For if I build again*—By my sinful practice. *The things which I destroyed*—By my preaching, *I* only *make myself*—Or show myself, not Christ, to be a *transgressor;* the whole blame lies on me, not him or his gospel. As if he had said, The objection were just, if the gospel promised justification to men continuing in sin. But it does not. Therefore if any who profess the gospel do not live according to it, they are sinners, it is certain, but not justified, and so the gospel is clear.

Verse 19. *For I through the law*—Applied by the Spirit to my heart, and deeply convincing me of my utter sinfulness and helplessness. *Am dead to the law*—To all hope of justification from it. *That I may live to God*—Not continue in sin. For this very end am I, in this sense, freed from the law, that I may be freed from sin.

Verse 20. The Apostle goes on to describe how he is freed from sin; how far he is from continuing therein. *I am crucified with Christ*—Made conformable to his death; "the body of sin is destroyed." Rom. vi. 6. *And I*—As to my corrupt nature. *Live no longer*—Being *dead to sin. But Christ liveth in me*—Is a fountain of life in my inmost soul, from which all my tempers, words, and actions flow. *And the life that I now live in the flesh*—Even in this mortal body, *I live by faith in the Son of God*—I derive every moment from that supernatural principle; from a divine evidence and conviction, that "he loved me, and delivered up himself for me."

Verse 21. Meantime *I do not make void*—In seeking to be justified by

CHAP. III 1 O thoughtless Galatians, who hatn
bewitched you, before whose eyes Jesus Christ hath been
2 evidently set forth, crucified among you? This only would
I learn of you, Did ye receive the Spirit by the works of the
3 law, or by the hearing of faith? Are ye so thoughtless?
having begun in the Spirit, are ye now made perfect by the
4 flesh? Have ye suffered so many things in vain? if *it be*
5 yet in vain. Doth he that ministereth the Spirit to you, and
worketh miracles among you, *do it* by the works of the law,
6 or by the hearing of faith? As Abraham* believed God, and

* Gen. xv. 6.

my own works. *The grace of God*—The free love of God in Christ Jesus. But they do, who seek justification by the law. *For if righteousness is by the law*—If men might be justified by their obedience to the law, moral or ceremonial. *Then Christ died in vain*—Without any necessity for it, since men might have been saved without his death; might by their own obedience have been both discharged from condemnation, and entitled to eternal life.

Verse 1. *O thoughtless Galatians*—He breaks in upon them with a beautiful abruptness. *Who hath bewitched you*—Thus to contradict both your own reason and experience. *Before whose eyes Jesus Christ hath been* as *evidently set forth*—By our preaching, as if he had been *crucified among you.*

Verse 2. *This only would I learn of you*—That is, this one argument might convince you. *Did ye receive* the witness and the fruit of *the Spirit by* performing *the works of the law, or by hearing of* and receiving *faith?*

Verse 3. *Are ye so thoughtless*—As not to consider what you have yourselves experienced? *Having begun in the Spirit*—Having set out under the light and power of the Spirit by faith, do ye now, when ye ought to be more spiritual, and more acquainted with the power of faith, expect to be *made perfect by the flesh?* Do you think to complete either your justification or sanctification, by giving up that faith, and depending on the law, which is a gross and carnal thing when opposed to the gospel?

Verse 4. *Have ye suffered*—Both from the zealous Jews and from the heathens. *So many things*—For adhering to the gospel. *In vain*—So as to lose all the blessings which ye might have obtained, by enduring to the end. *If it be yet in vain*—As if he had said, I hope better things, even that ye will endure to the end.

Verse 5. And, at the present time, *Doth he that ministereth* the gift of *the Spirit to you, and worketh miracles among you, do it by the works of the law*—That is, in confirmation of his preaching justification by works, or of his preaching justification by faith?

Verse 6. Doubtless in confirmation of that grand doctrine, that we are

7 it was imputed to him for righteousness. Know then that
8 they who are of faith, these are the sons of Abraham. And
the scripture, foreseeing that God would justify the gentiles
by faith, declared before the glad tidings to Abraham, * In
9 thee shall all the nations be blessed. So then they who are
10 of faith are blessed with faithful Abraham. For as many as
are of the works of the law are under a curse: for it is written, † Cursed *is* every one who continueth not in all the
11 things which are written in the book of the law to do them
But that none is justified by the law in the sight of God, *is*
12 evident: for, ‡ The just shall live by faith. Now the law is
not of faith: but, || He that doeth them shall live by them.

* Gen. xii. 3. † Deut. xxvii. 26. ‡ Hab. ii. 4.
|| Levit. xviii. 5.

justified by faith, even *as Abraham* was. The Apostle, both in this and in the epistle to the Romans, makes great use of the instance of Abraham: the rather, because from Abraham the Jews drew their great argument, as they do this day, both for their own continuance in Judaism, and for denying the gentiles to be the church of God.

Verse 7. *Know then that they who are partakers of* his *faith, these,* and these only, *are the sons of Abraham,* and therefore heirs of the promises made to him.

Verse 8. *And the scripture*—That is, the Holy Spirit, who gave the scripture. *Foreseeing that God would justify the gentiles* also *by faith, declared before*—So great is the excellency and fulness of the scripture, that all the things which can ever be controverted are therein both foreseen and determined. *In* or *through thee*—As the father of the Messiah, *shall all the nations be blessed.*

Verse 9. *So then* all *they,* and they only, *who are of faith*—Who truly believe. *Are blessed with faithful Abraham*—Receive the blessing as he did, namely, by faith.

Verse 10. They only receive it. *For as many as are of the works of the law*—As God deals with on that footing, only on the terms the law proposes, *are under a curse; for it is written, Cursed is every one who continueth not in all the things which are written in the law. Who continueth not in all the things*—So it requires what no man can perform, namely, perfect, uninterrupted, and perpetual obedience.

Verse 11. *But that none is justified by* his obedience to *the law in the sight of God*—Whatever may be done in the sight of man, is farther *evident* from the words of Habakkuk, *The just shall live by faith*—That is, the man who is accounted just or righteous before God, shall continue in a state of acceptance, life, and salvation, *by faith.* This is the way God hath chosen.

Verse 12. *And the law is not of faith*—But quite opposite to it: it does not say, *Believe;* but, *Do*

13 Christ hath redeemed us from the curse of the law, being
made a curse for us: (for it is written, * Cursed *is* every one
14 that hangeth on a tree:) That the blessing of Abraham might
come on the gentiles through Christ Jesus; that we might
15 receive the promise of the Spirit through faith. I speak
after the manner of men; Though it be but a man's covenant, yet if it be confirmed, none disannulleth, or addeth
16 thereto. Now the promises were made to Abraham and his
seed. He saith not, And to seeds, as of many; but as
17 of one, † And to thy seed, which is Christ. And this I say,
the covenant which was before confirmed of God through
Christ, the law, which was four hundred and thirty years

* Deut. xxi. 23. † Gen. xxii. 18.

Verse 13. *Christ*—Christ alone. The abruptness of the sentence shows an holy indignation at those who reject so great a blessing. *Hath redeemed us*—Whether Jews or gentiles, at an high price. *From the curse of the law*—The curse of God, which the law denounces against all transgressors of it. *Being made a curse for us*—Taking the curse upon himself, that we might be delivered from it, willingly submitting to that death which the law pronounces peculiarly accursed.

Verse 14. *That the blessing of Abraham*—The blessing promised to him. *Might come on the gentiles*—Also. *That we*—Who believe, whether Jews or gentiles. *Might receive the promise of the Spirit*—Which includes all the other promises. *Through faith*—Not by works; for faith looks wholly to the promise.

Verse 15. *I speak after the manner of men*—I illustrate this by a familiar instance, taken from the practice of men. *Though it be but a man's covenant, yet, if it be* once legally *confirmed, none*—No, not the covenanter himself, unless something unforeseen occur, which cannot be the case with God. *Disannulleth, or addeth thereto*—Any new conditions.

Verse 16. *Now the promises were made to Abraham and his seed*—Several promises were made to Abraham; but the chief of all, and which was several times repeated, was that of the blessing through Christ. *He*—That is, God. *Saith not, And to seeds, as of many*—As if the promise were made to several kinds of seed. *But as of one*—That is, one kind of seed, one posterity, one kind of sons. And to all these the blessing belonged by promise. *Which is Christ*—Including all that believe in him.

Verse 17. *And this I say*—What I mean is this. *The covenant which was before confirmed of God*—By the promise itself, by the repetition of it, and by a solemn oath, concerning the blessing all nations. *Through Christ, the law which was four hundred and thirty years after*—Counting from the time when the promise was first made to Abraham, Gen. xii. 2, 3. *Doth not disannul, so as to make the promise of no effect*—With regard to all nations, if only the Jewish were to receive it; yea, with regard to

after, doth not disannul, so as to make the promise of no
18 effect. And again, if the inheritance *be* by the law, *it is* no
more by promise: but God gave *it* to Abraham by promise.
19 Wherefore then *was* the law? It was added because
of transgressions, till the seed should come to whom the promise was made; *and it was* ordained by angels in the hand
20 of a mediator. Now the mediator is not a *mediator* of one,
21 but God is one. *Is* then the law against the promises
of God? God forbid: but if there had been a law given
which could have given life, verily righteousness would have
22 been by the law. But the scripture hath concluded all under

them also, if it was by works, so as to supersede it, and introduce another way of obtaining the blessing.

Verse 18. *And again*—This is a new argument. The former was drawn from the time, this from the nature, of the transaction. *If the* eternal *inheritance be* obtained *by* keeping *the law, it is no more by* virtue of the free *promise*—These being just opposite to each other. But it is by promise. Therefore it is not by the law.

Verse 19. *It*—The ceremonial law. *Was added*—To the promise. *Because of transgressions*—Probably, the yoke of the ceremonial law was inflicted as a punishment for the national sin of idolatry, Exod. xxxii. 1, at least the more grievous parts of it; and the whole of it was a prophetic type of Christ. The moral law was added to the promise to discover and restrain transgressions, to convince men of their guilt, and need of the promise, and give some check to sin. And this law passeth not away; but the ceremonial law was only introduced *till* Christ, *the seed to* or through *whom the promise was made, should come. And it was ordained by angels in the hand of a mediator*—It was not given to Israel, like the promise to Abraham, immediately from God himself; but was conveyed by the ministry of angels to Moses, and delivered into his hand as a mediator between God and them, to remind them of the great Mediator.

Verse 20. *Now the mediator is not a mediator of one*—There must be two parties, or there can be no mediator between them; *but God* who made the free promise to Abraham *is* only *one* of the parties. The other, Abraham, was not present at the time of Moses. Therefore in the promise Moses had nothing to do. The law, wherein he was concerned, was a transaction of quite another nature.

Verse 21. Will it follow from hence that *the law is against,* opposite *to, the promises of God?* By no means. They are well consistent. But yet the law cannot give life, as the promise doth. *If there had been a law which could have given life*—Which could have entitled a sinner to life, God would have spared his own Son, and *righteousness,* or justification, with all the blessings consequent upon it, *would have been by* that *law.*

Verse 22. *But,* on the contrary, *the scripture* wherein that law is written, *hath concluded all under sin*—Hath shut them up together, (as the

sin, that the promise by faith of Jesus Christ might be given
23 to them that believe. But before faith came, we were kept
under the law, shut up together unto the faith which was to
24 be revealed. Wherefore the law was our schoolmaster unto
25 Christ, that we might be justified by faith. But faith being
26 come, we are no longer under a schoolmaster. For ye are
27 all sons of God by faith in Jesus Christ For as many
of you as have been baptized into Christ have put on Christ.
28 There is neither Jew nor Greek, there is neither bond nor
free, there is neither male nor female: for ye are all one in
29 Christ Jesus. And if ye *are* Christ's, then are ye the seed
IV. 1 of Abraham, and heirs according to the promise. Now I
say, the heir, as long as he is a child, differeth nothing from
2 a servant, though he be lord of all; But is under tutors and

word properly signifies,) as in a prison, under sentence of death, to the end *that* all being cut off from expecting justification by the law, *the promise might be* freely *given to them that believe.*

Verse 23. *But before faith*—That is, the gospel dispensation, *Came, we were kept*—As in close custody. *Under the law*—The Mosaic dispensation. *Shut up unto the faith which was to be revealed*—Reserved and prepared for the gospel dispensation.

Verse 24. *Wherefore the law was our schoolmaster unto Christ*—It was designed to train us up for Christ. And this it did both by its commands, which showed the need we had of his atonement; and its ceremonies, which all pointed us to him.

Verse 25. *But faith*—That is, the gospel dispensation. *Being come, we are no longer under* that *schoolmaster*—The Mosaic dispensation.

Verse 26. *For ye*—Christians. *Are all* adult *sons of God*—And so need a schoolmaster no longer.

Verse 27. *For as many of you as have* testified your faith by being *baptized* in the name of Christ, have *put on Christ*—Have received him as your righteousness, and are therefore sons of God through him.

Verse 28. *There is neither Jew nor Greek*—That is, there is no difference between them; they are equally accepted through faith. *There is neither male nor female*—Circumcision being laid aside, which was peculiar to males, and was designed to put a difference, during that dispensation, between Jews and gentiles.

Verse 29. *If ye are Christ's*—That is, believers in him.

Verse 1. *Now*—To illustrate by a plain similitude the pre-eminence of the Christian, over the legal, dispensation. *The heir, as long as he is a child*—As he is under age. *Differeth nothing from a servant*—Not being at liberty either to use or enjoy his estate. *Though he be lord*—Proprietor *of* it *all.*

Verse 2. *But is under tutors*—As to his person. *And stewards*—As to his substance.

3 stewards till the time appointed by the father. So we also,
when we were children, were in bondage under the elements
4 of the world: But when the fulness of the time was come,
God sent forth his Son, made of a woman, made under the
5 law, To redeem those under the law, that we might receive
6 the adoption of sons. And because ye are sons, God hath
sent forth the Spirit of his Son into your hearts, crying,
7 Abba, Father. Wherefore thou art no more a servant, but
a son; and if a son, then an heir of God through Christ.
8 Indeed then when ye knew not God, ye served them
9 that by nature are not gods. But now having known God,
or rather being known of God, how turn ye back to the

Verse 3. *So we*—The church of God. *When we were children*—In our minority, under the legal dispensation. *Were in bondage*—In a kind of servile state. *Under the elements of the world*—Under the typical observances of the law, which were like the first elements of grammar, the A B C of children; and were of so gross a nature, as hardly to carry our thoughts beyond this world.

Verse 4. *But when the fulness of the time*—Appointed by the Father, verse 2. *Was come, God sent forth*—From his own bosom. *His Son,* miraculously *made* of the substance *of a woman*—A virgin, without the concurrence of a man. *Made under the law*—Both under the precept, and under the curse, of it.

Verse 5. *To redeem those under the law*—From the curse of it, and from that low, servile state. *That we*—Jews who believe. *Might receive the adoption*—All the privileges *of* adult *sons.*

Verse 6. *And because ye*—Gentiles who believe, *are* also thus made his adult *sons, God hath sent forth the Spirit of his Son into your hearts* likewise, *crying, Abba, Father*—Enabling you to call upon God both with the confidence, and the tempers, of dutiful children. The Hebrew and Greek word are joined together, to express the joint cry of the Jews and gentiles.

Verse 7. *Wherefore thou*—Who believest in Christ. *Art no more a servant*—Like those who are under the law. *But a son*—Of mature age. *And if a son, then an heir of* all the promises, and of the all-sufficient God himself.

Verse 8. *Indeed then when ye knew not God, ye served them that by nature*—That is, in reality. *Are no gods*—And so were under a far worse bondage than even that of the Jews. For they did serve the true God, though in a low, slavish manner

Verse 9. *But now being known of God*—As his beloved children. *How turn ye back to the weak and poor elements*—*Weak,* utterly unable to purge your conscience from guilt, or to give that filial confidence in God. *Poor*—incapable of enriching the soul with such holiness and happiness as ye are heirs to *Ye desire to be again in bondage*—Though of another kind; now to these elements, as before to those idols

weak and poor elements, to which ye desire to be in bondage
10 again? Ye observe days, and months, and times, and
11 years. I am afraid for you, lest I have laboured among
you in vain.
12 Brethren, I beseech you, be ye as I *am*; for I also *am*
13 as ye *were*: ye have not injured me at all. Ye know
that notwithstanding infirmity of the flesh, I preached the
14 gospel to you at first. And ye did not slight or disdain my
temptation which was in the flesh; but received me as an
15 angel of God, as Christ Jesus. What was then the blessedness ye spake of? for I bear you witness, that, if possible,
ye would have plucked out your eyes, and have given them
16 to me. Am I become your enemy, because I tell you the
17 truth? They zealously affect you, but not well; yea, they
18 would exclude you, that ye might affect them. Now *it is*
good to be zealous in a good thing always, and not only
19 while I am present with you. My little children, of whom

Verse 10. *Ye observe days*—Jewish sabbaths. *And months*—New moons. *And times*—As that of the passover, pentecost, and the feast of tabernacles. *And years*—Annual solemnities. It does not mean sabbatic years. These were not to be observed out of the land of Canaan.

Verse 11. The apostle here, dropping the argument, applies to the affections, verses 11—20, and humbles himself to the Galatians, with an inexpressible tenderness.

Verse 12. *Brethren, I beseech you, be as I am*—Meet me in mutual love. *For I am as ye were*—I still love you as affectionately as ye once loved me. Why should I not? *Ye have not injured me at all*—I have received no personal injury from you.

Verse 13. *I preached to you, notwithstanding infirmity of the flesh*—That is, notwithstanding bodily weakness, and under great disadvantage from the despicableness of my outward appearance.

Verse 14. *And ye did not slight my temptation*—That is, ye did not slight or disdain me for my temptation, my "thorn in the flesh."

Verse 15. *What was then the blessedness ye spake of*—On which ye so congratulated one another.

Verse 17. *They*—The judaizing teachers who are come among you. *Zealously affect you*—Express an extraordinary regard for you. *But not well*—Their zeal is not according to knowledge; neither have they a single eye to your spiritual advantage. *Yea, they would exclude you*—From me and from the blessings of the gospel. *That ye might affect*—Love and esteem *them*.

Verse 18. *In a good thing*—In what is really worthy our zeal. True zeal is only fervent love.

Verse 19. *My little children*—He speaks as a parent, both with au-

20 I travail in birth again, till Christ be formed in you, I could
wish to be present with you now, and to change my voice;
for I stand in doubt of you.
21 Tell me, ye that would be under the law, do ye not hear
22 the law? For it is written, * Abraham had two sons, one
23 by the bondwoman, another by the freewoman. And he of
the bondwoman was born after the flesh; but he of the free-
24 woman by promise. Which things are an allegory; for
these are the two covenants; one from mount Sinai, bearing
25 children to bondage, which is Agar. For this is mount
Sinai in Arabia, and answereth to Jerusalem that now is,
26 and is in bondage with her children. But Jerusalem that
27 is above is free, which is the mother of us all. (For it is
written, † Rejoice, thou barren, that bearest not; break forth

* Gen. xxi. 2, 9. † Isaiah liv. 1.

thority, and the most tender sympathy, toward weak and sickly children. *Of whom I travail in birth again*—As I did before, verse 13, in vehement pain, sorrow, desire, prayer. *Till Christ be formed in you*—Till there be in you all the mind that was in him.

Verse 20. *I could wish to be present with you now*—Particularly in this exigence. *And to change*—Variously to attemper. *My voice*—He writes with much softness; but he would speak with more. The voice may more easily be varied according to the occasion than a letter can. *For I stand in doubt of you*—So that I am at a loss how to speak at this distance.

Verse 21. *Do ye not hear the law*—Regard what it says.

Verse 23. *Was born after the flesh*—In a natural way. *By promise*—Through that supernatural strength which was given Abraham in consequence of the promise.

Verse 24. *Which things are an allegory*—An allegory is a figurative speech, wherein one thing is expressed, and another intended. *For those* two sons *are* types of *the two covenants*. One covenant is that given *from mount Sinai, which beareth children to bondage*—That is, all who are under this, the Jewish covenant, are in bondage. *Which* covenant *is* typified by *Agar*.

Verse 25. *For this is mount Sinai in Arabia*—That is, the type of mount *Sinai*. *And answereth to*—Resembles *Jerusalem that now is, and is in bondage*—Like Agar, both to the law and to the Romans.

Verse 26. *But* the other covenant is derived from *Jerusalem that is above*, which *is free*—Like Sarah, from all inward and outward bondage, and *is the mother of us all*—That is, all who believe in Christ, are free citizens of the New Jerusalem.

Verse 27. *For it is written*—Those words in the primary sense promise a flourishing state to Judea, after its desolation by the Chaldeans. *Rejoice, thou barren, that bearest not*—Ye heathen nations, who, like a

and cry, thou that travailest not; for the desolate hath
28 many more children than she that hath an husband.) Now
29 we, brethren, like Isaac, are children of promise. But as
then, he that was born after the flesh persecuted him *that*
30 *was born* after the Spirit, so *it is* now also. But what
saith the scripture? * Cast out the bondwoman and her
son: for the son of the bondwoman shall not be heir with
31 the son of the freewoman. So then, brethren, we are not
children of the bondwoman, but of the free.

CHAP. V. 1 Stand fast therefore in the liberty wherewith Christ hath made us free, and be not entangled again
2 with the yoke of bondage. Behold, I Paul say unto you,
3 If ye be circumcised, Christ will profit you nothing. For I

* Gen. xxi. 10.

barren woman, were destitute, for many ages, of a seed to serve the Lord. *Break forth and cry aloud for joy, thou that,* in former time, *travailedst not: for the desolate hath many more children than she that hath an husband*—For ye that were so long utterly desolate shall at length bear more children than the Jewish church, which was of old espoused to God.

Verse 28. *Now we*—Who believe, whether Jews or Gentiles. *Are children of the promise*—Not born in a natural way, but by the supernatural power of God. And as such we are heirs of the promise made to believing Abraham.

Verse 29. *But as then, he that was born after the flesh persecuted him that was born after the Spirit, so it is now also*—And so it will be in all ages and nations to the end of the world.

Verse 30. *But what saith the scripture*—Showing the consequence of this. *Cast out the bondwoman and her son*—Who mocked Isaac. In like manner will God cast out all who seek to be justified by the law; especially if they persecute them who are his children by faith.

Verse 31. *So then*—To sum up all. *We*—Who believe. *Are not children of the bondwoman*—Have nothing to do with the servile Mosaic dispensation. *But of the free*—Being free from the curse and the bond of that law, and from the power of sin and Satan.

Verse 1. *Stand fast therefore in the liberty*—From the ceremonial law *Wherewith Christ hath made us*—And all believers, *free; and be not entangled again with the yoke of* legal *bondage.*

Verse 2. *If ye be circumcised*—And seek to be justified thereby. *Christ*—The Christian institution. *Will profit you nothing*—For you hereby disclaim Christ, and all the blessings which are through faith in him.

Verse 3. *I testify to every man*—Every gentile *That is circumcised*

testify again to every man that is circumcised, he is a debtor
4 to do the whole law. Christ is become of no effect to you,
whosoever of you are justified by the law; ye are fallen from
5 grace. For we through the Spirit wait for the hope of
6 righteousness by faith. For in Christ Jesus neither circumcision availeth anything, nor uncircumcision; but faith
7 which worketh by love. Ye did run well; who hath hin-
8 dered you from obeying the truth? This persuasion *cometh*
9 not from him that called you. A little leaven leaveneth the
10 whole lump. I have confidence in you through the Lord,
that ye will be no otherwise minded; but he that troubleth
11 you shall bear *his* judgment, whosoever he be. But if I,
brethren, still preach circumcision, why do I still suffer per-

—He thereby makes himself *a debtor*—Obliges himself, at the peril of his salvation, *to do the whole law.*

Verse 4. Therefore *Christ is become of no effect to you*—Who seek to be *justified by the law. Ye are fallen from grace*—Ye renounce the new covenant. Ye disclaim the benefit of this gracious dispensation.

Verse 5. *For we*—Who believe in Christ, who are under the gospel dispensation. *Through the Spirit*—Without any of those carnal ordinances. *Wait for*—In sure confidence of attaining. *The hope of righteousness*—The righteousness we hope for, and full reward of it. This righteousness we receive of God through faith; and *by faith* we shall obtain the reward.

Verse 6. *For in Christ Jesus*—According to the institution which he hath established, according to the tenor of the Christian covenant. *Neither circumcision*—With the most punctual observance of the law *Nor uncircumcision*—With the most exact heathen morality. *Availeth anything*—Toward present justification or eternal salvation. *But faith*—Alone; even that faith *which worketh by love*—All inward and outward holiness.

Verse 7. *Ye did run well*—In the race of faith. *Who hath hindered you* in your course, *that ye should not* still *obey the truth?*

Verse 8. *This* your present *persuasion cometh not from God, who called you*—To his kingdom and glory.

Verse 9. *A little leaven leaveneth the whole lump*—One troubler, verse 10, troubles all.

Verse 10. Yet *I have confidence that*—After ye have read this. *Ye will be no otherwise minded*—Than I am, and ye were. *But he that troubleth you*—It seems to have been one person chiefly who endeavoured to seduce them. *Shall bear his judgment*—A heavy burden, already hanging over his head.

Verse 11. *But if I still preach circumcision*—As that troubler seems to have affirmed, probably taking occasion from his having circumcised Timothy. *Why do I still suffer persecution? then is the offence of the*

12 secution? then is the offence of the cross ceased. I wish it;
and they shall be cut off that trouble you.
13 Brethren, ye have been called to liberty; only *use* not
this liberty for an occasion to the flesh, but by love serve
14 one another. For all the law is fulfilled in one word, in
15 this; * Thou shalt love thy neighbour as thyself. But if
ye bite and devour one another, take heed ye be not consumed one of another.
16 I say then, Walk by the Spirit, and fulfil not the desire
17 of the flesh. For the flesh desireth against the Spirit, but
the Spirit *desireth* against the flesh: (these are contrary
to each other:) that ye may not do the things which ye

* Levit. xix. 18.

cross ceased—The grand reason why the Jews were so offended at his preaching Christ crucified, and so bitterly persecuted him for it, was, that it implied the abolition of the law. Yet St. Paul did not condemn the conforming, out of condescension to the weakness of any one, even to the ceremonial law; but he did absolutely condemn those who taught it as necessary to justification.

Verse 12. *I would they were even cut off*—From your communion; cast out of your church, *that* thus *trouble you.*

Verse 13. *Ye have been called to liberty*—From sin and misery, as well as from the ceremonial law. *Only use not liberty for an occasion to the flesh*—Take not occasion from hence to gratify corrupt nature. *But by love serve one another*—And hereby show that Christ has made you free.

Verse 14. *For all the law is fulfilled in this, Thou shalt love thy neighbour as thyself*—Inasmuch as none can do this without loving God, 1 John iv. 12; and the love of God and man includes all perfection.

Verse 15. *But if*—On the contrary, in consequence of the divisions which those troublers have occasioned among you, *ye bite* one another by evil speaking. *And devour one another*—By railing and clamour. *Take heed ye be not consumed one of another*—By bitterness, strife, and contention, our health and strength, both of body and soul, are consumed, as well as our substance and reputation.

Verse 16. *I say then*—He now explains what he proposed, verse 13. *Walk by the Spirit*—Follow his guidance in all things. *And fulfil not*—In anything. *The desire of the flesh*—Of corrupt nature.

Verse 17. *For the flesh desireth against the Spirit*—Nature desires what is quite contrary to the Spirit of God. *But the Spirit against the flesh*—But the Holy Spirit on his part opposes your evil nature. *These are contrary to each other*—The flesh and the Spirit; there can be no agreement between them. *That ye may not do the things which ye would*—That, being thus strengthened by the Spirit, ye may not fulfil the desire of the flesh, as otherwise ye would do

18 would. But if ye are led by the Spirit, ye are not under
19 the law. Now the works of the flesh are manifest, which are
these ; adultery, fornication, uncleanness, lasciviousness,
20 Idolatry, witchcraft, enmities, contentions, emulations,
21 wraths, strifes, divisions, heresies, Envyings, murders, drunk-
enness, revellings, and such like: of which I tell you before,
(as I have also told you in time past,) that they who practise
22 such things shall not inherit the kingdom of God. But the
fruit of the Spirit is love, joy, peace, longsuffering, gentle-
23 ness, goodness, fidelity, Meekness, temperance: against such
24 there is no law. And they that are Christ's have crucified

Verse 18. *But if ye are led by the Spirit*—Of liberty and love, into all holiness. *Ye are not under the law*—Not under the curse or bondage of it; not under the guilt or the power of sin.

Verse 19. *Now the works of the flesh*—By which that inward principle is discovered. *Are manifest*—Plain and undeniable. *Works* are mentioned in the plural because they are distinct from, and often inconsistent with, each other. But "the fruit of the Spirit" is mentioned in the singular, verse 22, as being all consistent and connected together. *Which are these*—He enumerates those "works of the flesh" to which the Galatians were most inclined; and those parts of "the fruit of the Spirit" of which they stood in the greatest need. *Lasciviousness*—The Greek word means anything inward or outward that is contrary to chastity, and yet short of actual uncleanness.

Verse 20. *Idolatry, witchcraft*—That this means witchcraft, strictly speaking, (not poisoning,) appears from its being joined with the worship of devil-gods, and not with murder. This is frequently and solemnly forbidden in the Old Testament. To deny therefore that there is, or ever was, any such thing, is, by plain consequence, to deny the authority both of the Old and New Testament. *Divisions*—In domestic or civil matters *Heresies* are divisions in religious communities.

Verse 21. *Revellings*—Luxurious entertainments. Some of the works here mentioned are wrought principally, if not entirely, in the mind; and yet they are called "works of the flesh." Hence it is clear, the apostle does not by "the flesh" mean the body, or sensual appetites and inclinations only, but the corruption of human nature, as it spreads through all the powers of the soul, as well as all the members of the body. *Of which I tell you before*—Before the event, I forewarn you.

Verse 22. *Love*—The root of all the rest. *Gentleness*—Toward all men; ignorant and wicked men in particular. *Goodness*—The Greek word means all that is benign, soft, winning, tender, either in temper or behaviour.

Verse 23. *Meekness*—Holding all the affections and passions in even balance.

Verse 24. *And they that are Christ's*—True believers in him. *Have*

25 the flesh with its affections and desires. If we live by the
26 Spirit, let us also walk by the Spirit. Be not desirous of
vain glory, provoking one another, envying one another
VI 1 Brethren, if a man be overtaken in any fault, ye who
are spiritual, restore such an one in the spirit of meekness;
2 considering thyself, lest thou also be tempted. Bear ye one
3 another's burdens, and so fulfil the law of Christ. For if
any one think himself to be something, when he is nothing,
4 he deceiveth himself. But let every one try his own work,
and then shall he have rejoicing in himself alone, and not in

thus *crucified the flesh*—Nailed it, as it were, to a cross, whence it has no power to break loose, but is continually weaker and weaker. *With its affections and desires*—All its evil passions, appetites, and inclinations.

Verse 25. *If we live by the Spirit*—If we are indeed raised from the dead, and are alive to God, by the operation of his Spirit. *Let us walk by the Spirit*—Let us follow his guidance, in all our tempers, thoughts, words, and actions.

Verse 26 *Be not desirous of vain glory*—Of the praise or esteem of men. They who do not carefully and closely follow the Spirit, easily slide into this: the natural effects of which are, *provoking* to envy them that are beneath us, and *envying* them that are above us.

Verse 1. *Brethren, if a man be overtaken in any fault*—By surprise, ignorance, or stress of temptation. *Ye who are spiritual*—Who continue to live and walk by the Spirit. *Restore such an one*—By reproof, instruction, or exhortation. Every one who can, ought to help herein; only *in the spirit of meekness*—This is essential to a spiritual man; and in this lies the whole force of the cure. *Considering thyself*—The plural is beautifully changed into the singular. Let each take heed to himself *Lest thou also be tempted*—Temptation easily and swiftly passes from one to another; especially if a man endeavours to cure another without preserving his own meekness.

Verse 2. *Bear ye one another's burdens*—Sympathize with, and assist, each other, in all your weaknesses, grievances, trials. *And so fulfil the law of Christ*—*The law of Christ* (an uncommon expression) is the law of love: this our Lord peculiarly recommends; this he makes the distinguishing mark of his disciples.

Verse 3. *If any one think himself to be something*—Above his brethren, or by any strength of his own. *When he is nothing, he deceiveth himself*—He alone will bear their burdens, who knows himself to be *nothing*.

Verse 4. *But let every man try his own work*—Narrowly examine all he is, and all he doeth. *And then he shall have rejoicing in himself*—He will find in himself matter of rejoicing, if his works are right before God. *And not in another*—Not in glorying over others.

5 another. For every one shall bear his own burden. Let
6 him that is taught in the word impart to him that teacheth
7 in all good things. Be not deceived; God is not mocked;
8 for whatsoever a man soweth, that also shall he reap. For
he that soweth to his flesh shall of the flesh reap corruption;
but he that soweth to the Spirit shall of the Spirit reap life
9 everlasting. But let us not be weary in well doing: for in
10 due season we shall reap, if we faint not. Therefore, as
we have opportunity, let us do good unto all men; but
especially to them who are of the household of faith.
11 Ye see how large a letter I have written to you with my
12 own hand. As many as desire to make a fair appearance in
the flesh, these constrain you to be circumcised; only lest

Verse 5. *For every one shall bear his own burden*—In that day · shall give an account of himself to God.

Verse 6. *Let him that is taught impart to him that teacheth all* such temporal *good things* as he stands in need of.

Verse 7. *God is not mocked*—Although they attempt to mock him, who think to reap otherwise than they sow.

Verse 8. *For he that* now *soweth to the flesh*—That follows the desires of corrupt nature. *Shall* hereafter *of the flesh*—Out of this very seed. *Reap corruption*—Death everlasting. *But he that soweth to the Spirit*—That follows his guidance in all his tempers and conversation *Shall of the Spirit*—By the free grace and power of God, *reap life everlasting*.

Verse 9. *But let us not be weary in well doing*—Let us persevere in sowing to the Spirit. *For in due season*—When the harvest is come, *we shall reap, if we faint not*.

Verse 10. *Therefore as we have opportunity*—At whatever time or place, and in whatever manner we can. The opportunity in general is our lifetime; but there are also many particular opportunities. Satan is quickened in doing hurt, by the shortness of the time, Rev. xii. 12. By the same consideration let us be quickened in doing good. *Let us do good*—In every possible kind, and in every possible degree. *Unto all men*—Neighbours or strangers, good or evil, friends or enemies. *But especially to them who are of the household of faith* For all believers are but one family.

Verse 11. *Ye see how large a letter*—St. Paul had not yet wrote a larger to any church. *I have written with my own hand*—He generally wrote by an amanuensis.

Verse 12. *As many as desire to make a fair appearance in the flesh*—To preserve a fair character. *These constrain you*—Both by their example and importunity. *To be circumcised*—Not so much from a principle of conscience, as *lest they should suffer persecution*—From the unbelieving Jews. *For the cross of Christ*—For maintaining that faith in a crucified Saviour is alone sufficient for justification.

13 they should suffer persecution for the cross of Christ. For
neither they themselves who are circumcised keep the law;
but they desire to have you circumcised, that they may
14 glory in your flesh. But God forbid that I should glory, save
in the cross of our Lord Jesus Christ, by which the world
15 is crucified to me, and I unto the world. For neither circumcision is anything, nor uncircumcision, but a new crea-
16 tion. And as many as shall walk by this rule, peace and
mercy *be* upon them, and upon the Israel of God.
17 From henceforth let none trouble me: for I bear in my
18 body the marks of the Lord Jesus. Brethren, the grace
of the Lord Jesus Christ *be* with your spirit. Amen.

Verse 13. *For neither they themselves keep the* whole *law*—So far are they from a real zeal for it. *But* yet *they desire to have you circumcised, that they may glory in your flesh*—That they may boast of you as their proselytes, and make a merit of this with the other Jews.

Verse 14. *But God forbid that I should glory*—Should boast of anything I have, am, or do; or rely on anything for my acceptance with God, but what Christ hath done and suffered for me. *By* means of *which the world is crucified to me*—All the things and persons in it are to me as nothing. *And I unto the world*—I am dead to all worldly pursuits, cares, desires, and enjoyments.

Verse 15 *For neither circumcision is anything, nor uncircumcision*—Neither of these is of any account. *But a new creation*—Whereby all things in us become new.

Verse 16. *And as many as walk according to this rule*—1. Glorying only in the cross of Christ. 2. Being crucified to the world. And, 3. Created anew. *Peace and mercy be upon them, and upon the Israel,* that is, the church, *of God*—Which consists of all those, and those only, of every nation and kindred, who walk by this rule

Verse 17. *From henceforth let none trouble me*—By quarrels and disputes. *For I bear*—And afflictions should not be added to the afflicted. *In my body the marks of the Lord Jesus*—The scars, marks, and brands of my sufferings for him.

NOTES

ON

ST. PAUL'S EPISTLE TO THE EPHESIANS.

Ephesus was the chief city of that part of Asia, which was a Roman province. Here St. Paul preached for three years, Acts xx. 31; and from hence the gospel was spread throughout the whole province, Acts xix. 10. At his taking leave of the church there, he forewarned them both of great persecutions from without, and of divers heresies and schisms which would arise among themselves. And accordingly he writes this epistle, nearly resembling that to the Colossians, written about the same time, to establish them in the doctrine he had delivered, to arm them against false teachers, and to build them up in love and holiness, both of heart and conversation.

He begins this, as most of his epistles, with thanksgiving to God for their embracing and adhering to the gospel. He shows the inestimable blessings and advantages they received thereby, as far above all the Jewish privileges, as all the wisdom and philosophy of the heathens. He proves that our Lord is the Head of the whole church; of angels and spirits, the church triumphant, and of Jews and gentiles, now equally members of the church militant. In the three last chapters he exhorts them to various duties, civil and religious, personal and relative, suitable to their Christian character, privileges, assistances, and obligations.

In this epistle we may observe,

I. The inscription, — C. i. 1, 2

II. The doctrine pathetically explained, which contains,

1. Praise to God for the whole gospel blessing, — 3—14
   With thanksgiving and prayer for the saints, — 15—C. ii. 10
2. A more particular admonition concerning their once miserable, but now happy, condition, — 11—12
   A prayer for their establishment, — C. iii. 1—19
   A doxology, — 20, 21

III. The exhortation,

1. General: to walk worthy of their calling, agreeably to,
   1. The unity of the Spirit, and the diversity of his gifts, — C. iv. 1—16
   2. The difference between their former and their present state, — 17—24

EPHESIANS.

CHAPTER I. 1 PAUL an apostle of Jesus Christ by
the will of God, to the saints who are at Ephesus, even to
2 the faithful in Christ Jesus, Grace *be* to you, and peace from
God our Father, and the Lord Jesus Christ.
3 Blessed *be* the God and Father of our Lord Jesus Christ,
who hath blessed us with all spiritual blessings in heavenly
4 *things* through Christ: As he hath chosen us through him

Verse 1. *By the will of God*—Not by any merit of my own. *To the saints who are at Ephesus*—And in all the adjacent places. For this epistle is not directed to the Ephesians only, but likewise to all the other churches of Asia.

Verse 3. *Blessed be the God and Father of our Lord Jesus Christ, who hath blessed us*—God's blessing us is his bestowing all spiritual and heavenly blessings upon us. Our blessing God is the paying him our solemn and grateful acknowledgments, both on account of his own essential blessedness, and of the blessings which he bestows upon us. He is *the God of our Lord Jesus Christ,* as man and Mediator: he is his *Father,* primarily, with respect to his divine nature, as his only-begotten Son; and, secondarily, with respect to his human nature, as that is personally united to the divine. *With all spiritual blessings in heavenly things*—With all manner of spiritual blessings, which are heavenly in their nature, original, and tendency, and shall be completed in heaven: far different from the external privileges of the Jews, and the earthly blessings they expected from the Messiah.

Verse 4. *As he hath chosen us*—Both Jews and gentiles, whom he foreknew as believing in Christ, 1 Peter i. 2

before the foundation of the world, that we might be holy
5 and blameless before him in love: Having predestinated us
by Jesus Christ to the adoption of sons unto himself, accord-
6 ing to the good pleasure of his will, To the praise of the
glory of his grace, by which he hath freely accepted us
7 through the Beloved. By whom we have redemption
through his blood, the forgiveness of *our* sins, according
8 to the riches of his grace; Wherein he hath abounded
9 toward us in all wisdom and prudence; Having made known
unto us the mystery of his will, according to his good plea-
10 sure which he had before purposed in himself: That in the
dispensation of the fulness of the times he might gather
together into one in Christ all things which are in heaven,
11 and which are on earth; In him through whom we also

Verse 5. *Having predestinated us to the adoption of sons*—Having fore-ordained that all who afterwards believed should enjoy the dignity of being sons of God, and joint-heirs with Christ. *According to the good pleasure of his will*—According to his free, fixed, unalterable purpose to confer this blessing on all those who should believe in Christ, and those only.

Verse 6. *To the praise of the glory of his grace*—His glorious, free love, without any desert on our part.

Verse 7. *By whom we*—Who believe. *Have*—From the moment we believe. *Redemption*—From the guilt and power of sin. *Through his blood*—Through what he hath done and suffered for us. *According to the riches of his grace*—According to the abundant overflowings of his free mercy and favour.

Verse 8. *In all wisdom*—Manifested by God in the whole scheme of our salvation. *And prudence*—Which he hath wrought in us, that we may know and do all his acceptable and perfect will.

Verse 9. *Having made known to us*—By his word and by his Spirit. *The mystery of his will*—The gracious scheme of salvation by faith, which depends on his own sovereign will alone. This was but darkly discovered under the law; is now totally hid from unbelievers; and has heights and depths which surpass all the knowledge even of true believers.

Verse 10. *That in the dispensation of the fulness of the times*—In this last administration of God's fullest grace, which took place when the time appointed was fully come. *He might gather together into one in Christ*—Might recapitulate, re-unite, and place in order again under Christ, their common Head. *All things which are in heaven, and on earth*—All angels and men, whether living or dead, in the Lord.

Verse 11. *Through whom we*—Jews. *Also have obtained an inheritance*—The glorious inheritance of the heavenly Canaan, to which, when believers, we were *predestinated according to the purpose of him that work-*

have obtained an inheritance, being predestinated according
to the purpose of him that worketh all things after the
12 counsel of his own will. That we who first believed in
13 Christ might be to the praise of his glory. In whom ye
likewise *believed*, after ye had heard the word of truth, the
gospel of your salvation: in whom after ye had believed,
14 ye were also sealed by that Holy Spirit of promise, Who is
an earnest of our inheritance till the redemption of the purchased possession, to the praise of his glory.
15 Wherefore I also, since I heard of your faith in the Lord
16 Jesus, and love to all saints, Cease not to give thanks for
17 you, making mention of you in my prayers; That the God
of our Lord Jesus Christ, the Father of glory, may give

eth all things after the counsel of his own will—The unalterable decree, "He that believeth shall be delivered;" which *will* is not an arbitrary will, but flowing from the rectitude of his nature. else, what security would there be that it would be his *will* to keep his word even with the elect?

Verse 12. *That we*—Jews. *Who first believed*—Before the gentiles. So did some of them in every place. Here is another branch of the true gospel predestination: he that believes is not only elected to salvation, (if he endures to the end,) but is fore-appointed of God to walk in holiness, *to the praise of his glory.*

Verse 13. *In whom ye*—Gentiles. *Likewise believed, after ye had heard the gospel*—Which God made the means *of your salvation; in whom after ye had believed*—Probably some time after their first believing. *Ye were sealed by that Holy Spirit of promise*—Holy both in his nature and in his operations, and promised to all the children of God. The sealing seems to imply, 1. A full impression of the image of God on their souls. 2. A full assurance of receiving all the promises, whether relating to time or eternity

Verse 14. *Who*, thus sealing us, *is an earnest*—Both a pledge and a foretaste of our inheritance. *Till the redemption of the purchased possession*—Till the church, which he has purchased with his own blood, shall be fully delivered from all sin and sorrow, and advanced to everlasting glory. *To the praise of his glory*—Of his glorious wisdom, power, and mercy.

Verse 15. *Since I heard of your faith and love*—That is, of their perseverance and increase therein.

Verse 16. *I cease not*—In all my solemn addresses to God. *To give thanks for you, making mention of you in my prayers*—So he did of all the churches, Col. i. 9.

Verse 17 *That the Father of* that infinite *glory* which shines in the face of *Christ*, from whom also we receive the glorious inheritance, verse 18, *may give you the Spirit of wisdom and revelation*—The same who is the

you the spirit of wisdom and revelation through the know-
18 ledge of him: The eyes of your understanding being
enlightened; that ye may know what is the hope of his
calling, and what the riches of the glory of his inheritance
19 in the saints, And what the exceeding greatness of his power
toward us who believe, according to the energy of his mighty
20 power, Which he exerted in Christ, raising him from the
dead; and he hath seated him at his own right hand in
21 heavenly *places*, Far above all principality, and power, and
might, and dominion, and every name that is named, not
22 only in this world, but also in that which is to come: And
he hath put all things under his feet, and hath given him

Spirit of promise is also, in the progress of the faithful, *the Spirit of wisdom and revelation;* making them wise unto salvation, and revealing to them the deep things of God. He is here speaking of that wisdom and revelation which are common to all real Christians.

Verse 18. *The eyes of your understanding*—It is with these alone that we discern the things of God. *Being* first opened, and then *enlightened*—By his Spirit. *That ye may know what is the hope of his calling*—That ye may experimentally and delightfully know what are the blessings which God has called you to hope for by his word and his Spirit. *And what is the riches of the glory of his inheritance in the saints*—What an immense treasure of blessedness he hath provided as an inheritance for holy souls.

Verse 19. *And what the exceeding greatness of his power toward us who believe*—Both in quickening our dead souls, and preserving them in spiritual life. *According to the power which he exerted in Christ, raising him from the dead*—By the very same almighty power whereby he raised Christ; for no less would suffice.

Verse 20. *And he hath seated him at his own right hand*—That is, he hath exalted him in his human nature, as a recompence for his sufferings, to a quiet, everlasting possession of all possible blessedness, majesty, and glory.

Verse 21. *Far above all principality, and power, and might, and dominion*—That is, God hath invested him with uncontrollable authority over all demons in hell, all angels in heaven, and all the princes and potentates on earth. *And every name that is named*—We know the king is above all, though we cannot name all the officers of his court. So we know that Christ is above all, though we are not able to name all his subjects. *Not only in this world, but also in that which is to come*—The *world to come* is so styled, not because it does not yet exist, but because it is not yet visible. Principalities and powers are *named* now; but those also who are not even *named in this world,* but shall be revealed *in the world to come,* are all subject to Christ.

Verse 22. *And he hath given him to be head over all things to the church*—An head both of guidance and government, and likewise of life and

23 *to be* head over all things to the church. Which is his
body, *who is* the fulness of him that filleth all in all.
II. 1 And *he hath quickened* you, who were dead in trespasses
2 and sins; Wherein ye formerly walked according to the
course of this world, according to the prince of the power
of the air, the spirit that now worketh in the sons of disobe-
3 dience: Among whom also we all formerly had our conversation in the desires of the flesh, doing the will of the flesh
and the mind; and were by nature children of wrath, even

influence, to the whole and every member of it. All these stand in the nearest union with him, and have as continual and effectual a communication of activity, growth, and strength from him, as the natural body from its head.

Verse 23. *The fulness of him that filleth all in all*—It is hard to say in what sense this can be spoken of the church; but the sense is easy and natural, if we refer it to Christ, *who is the fulness of* the Father.

Verse 1. *And he hath quickened you*—In the nineteenth and twentieth verses of the preceding chapter, St. Paul spoke of God's working in them by the same almighty power whereby he raised Christ from the dead. On the mention of this he, in the fulness of his heart, runs into a flow of thought concerning the glory of Christ's exaltation in the three following verses. He here resumes the thread of his discourse. *Who were dead*—Not only diseased, but dead; absolutely void of all spiritual life; and as incapable of quickening yourselves, as persons literally dead. *In trespasses and sins*—*Sins* seem to be spoken chiefly of the gentiles, who knew not God; *trespasses,* of the Jews, who had his law, and yet regarded it not, verse 5. The latter herein obeyed the flesh; the former, the prince of the power of the air.

Verse 2. *According to the course of this world*—The word translated *course* properly means *a long series of times,* wherein one corrupt age follows another. *According to the prince of the power of the air*—The effect of which power all may perceive, though all do not understand the cause of it: a power unspeakably penetrating and widely diffused; but yet, as to its baneful influences, beneath the orb of believers. The evil spirits are united under one head, the seat of whose dominion is in the air. Here he sometimes raises storms, sometimes makes visionary representations, and is continually roving to and fro. *The spirit that now worketh*—With mighty power; and so he did, and doth in all ages. *In the sons of disobedience*—In all who do not believe and obey the gospel.

Verse 3. *Among whom we*—Jews. *Also formerly had our conversation: doing the will of the flesh*—In gross, brutal sins. *And of the mind*—By spiritual, diabolical wickedness. In the former clause, *flesh* denotes the whole evil nature; in the latter, the body opposed to the soul. *And were by nature*—That is, in our natural state. *Children of wrath*—Having the wrath of God abiding on us, *even as the gentiles.* This expression, *by*

4 as the others. But God, being rich in mercy, through his
5 great love wherewith he loved us, Hath quickened **even us**
together with Christ, who were dead in trespasses, (by grace
6 ye are saved,) And hath raised *us* up together, and made
us sit together in heavenly *places* through Christ Jesus:
7 That he might show in the ages to come the exceeding
riches of his grace in *his* kindness toward us through Christ
8 Jesus. For by grace ye are saved through faith; and this
9 not of yourselves; *it is* the gift of God: Not by works,
10 lest any man should boast. For we are his workmanship,
created through Christ Jesus unto good works, which God
had before prepared that we might walk in them.

nature, occurs also, Gal. iv. 8; Rom. ii. 14; and thrice in the eleventh chapter. But in none of these places does it signify, *by custom*, or *practice*, or *customary practice*, as a late writer affirms Nor can it mean so here. For this would make the apostle guilty of gross tautology, their customary sinning having been expressed already, in the former part of the verse. But all these passages agree in expressing what belongs to the *nature* of the persons spoken of.

Verse 4. *Mercy* removes misery: *love* confers salvation.

Verse 5. *He hath quickened us together with Christ*—In conformity to him, and by virtue of our union with him. *By grace ye are saved*—Grace is both the beginning and end. The apostle speaks indifferently either in the first or second person; the Jews and gentiles being in the same circumstance, both by nature and by grace. This text lays the axe to the very root of spiritual pride, and all glorying in ourselves. Therefore St. Paul, foreseeing the backwardness of mankind to receive it, yet knowing the absolute necessity of its being received, again asserts the very same truth, verse 8, in the very same words.

Verse 6. *And hath raised us up together*—Both Jews and gentiles already in spirit; and ere long our bodies too will be raised. *And made us* all *sit together in heavenly places*—This is spoken by way of anticipation. Believers are not yet possessed of their seats in heaven; but each of them has a place prepared for him.

Verse 7. *The ages to come*—That is, all succeeding ages.

Verse 8. *By grace ye are saved through faith*—Grace, without any respect to human worthiness, confers the glorious gift. Faith, with an empty hand, and without any pretence to personal desert, receives the heavenly blessing. *And this* is *not of yourselves*—*This* refers to the whole preceding clause, That *ye are saved through faith*, is *the gift of God.*

Verse 9. *Not by works*—Neither this faith nor this salvation is owing to any works you ever did, will, or can do.

Verse 10. *For we are his workmanship*—Which proves both that salvation is by faith, and that faith is the gift of God. *Created unto good works*—That afterwards we might give ourselves to them. *Which God*

11 Wherefore remember, that ye *being* formerly gentiles in
the flesh, (who were called the uncircumcision by that which
is called the circumcision performed with hands in the flesh,)
12 Were at that time without Christ, being aliens from the
commonwealth of Israel, and strangers to the covenants of
promise, having no hope, and without God in the world:
13 But now through Christ Jesus ye who were formerly far off
14 are brought nigh by the blood of Christ. For he is our
peace, he who hath made both one, having broken down the
15 middle wall of partition; Having abolished by his flesh the
enmity, the law of commandments, through *his* decrees, that

had before prepared—The occasions of them: so we must still ascribe the whole to God. *That we might walk in them*—Though not be justified by them.

Verse 11. *Wherefore remember*—Such a remembrance strengthens faith, and increases gratitude. *That ye being formerly gentiles in the flesh*—Neither circumcised in body nor in spirit. *Who were* accordingly *called the uncircumcision*—By way of reproach. *By that which is called the circumcision*—By those who call themselves the circumcised, and think this a proof that they are the people of God; and who indeed have that outward circumcision which is *performed by hands in the flesh.*

Verse 12. *Were at that time without Christ*—Having no faith in, or knowledge of, him. *Being aliens from the commonwealth of Israel*—Both as to their temporal privileges and spiritual blessings. *And strangers to the covenants of promise*—The great promise in both the Jewish and Christian covenant was the Messiah. *Having no hope*—Because they had no promise whereon to ground their hope. *And* being *without God*—Wholly ignorant of the true God, and so in effect atheists. Such in truth are, more or less, all men, in all ages, till they know God by the teaching of his own Spirit. *In the world*—The wide, vain world, wherein ye wandered up and down, unholy and unhappy.

Verse 13. *Far off*—From God and his people. *Nigh*—Intimately united to both.

Verse 14. *For he is our peace*—Not only as he purchased it, but as he is the very bond and centre of union. *He who hath made both*—Jews and gentiles, *one* church. The apostle describes, 1. The conjunction of the gentiles with Israel, verses 14, 15. And, 2. The conjunction of both with God, verses 15—18. Each description is subdivided into two parts. And the former part of the one, concerning *abolishing the enmity*, answers the former part of the other; the latter part of the one, concerning the evangelical *decrees*, the latter part of the other. *And hath broken down the middle wall of partition*—Alluding to that wall of old, which separated the court of Israel from the court of the gentiles. Such a wall was the ceremonial law, which Christ had now taken away.

Verse 15. *Having abolished by his* suffering in the *flesh the* cause of

he might form the two into one new man in himself, *so*
16 making peace; And might reconcile both in one body to
God through the cross, having slain the enmity thereby.
17 And he came and preached peace to you that were afar off, and
18 to them that were nigh. For through him we both have access
19 by one Spirit to the Father. Therefore ye are no longer
strangers and foreigners, but fellowcitizens with the saints,
20 and of the household of God; Built upon the foundation
of the apostles and prophets, Jesus Christ himself being the
21 chief corner stone; On whom all the building fitly framed
22 together groweth into an holy temple in the Lord: On whom
ye also are built together for an habitation of God through
the Spirit.

CHAP. III. 1 For this cause I Paul *am* the prisoner

enmity between the Jews and gentiles, *even the law of* ceremonial *commandments, through his decrees*—Which offer mercy to all; see Col. ii. 14. *That he might form the two*—Jew and gentile. *Into one new man*—One mystical body.

Verse 16. *In one body*—One church. *Having slain*—By his own death on the cross. *The enmity*—Which had been between sinners and God.

Verse 17. *And he came*—After his resurrection. *And preached peace*—By his ministers and his Spirit. *To you*—Gentiles. *That were afar off*—At the utmost distance from God. *And to them that were nigh*—To the Jews, who were comparatively nigh, being his visible church.

Verse 18. *For through him, we both*—Jews and gentiles. *Have access*—Liberty of approaching, *by* the guidance and aid of *one Spirit to* God as our *Father*. Christ, the Spirit, and the Father, the three-one God, stand frequently in the same order.

Verse 19. *Therefore ye are no longer strangers, but citizens* of the heavenly Jerusalem; no longer *foreigners,* but received into the very *family of God.*

Verse 20. *And are built upon the foundation of the apostles and prophets*—As the foundation sustaing the building, so the word of God, declared by the apostles and prophets, sustains the faith of all believers. God laid the foundation by them; but *Christ himself is the chief corner-stone* of the foundation. Elsewhere he is termed the foundation itself, 1 Cor. iii. 11.

Verse 21. *On whom all the building fitly framed together*—The whole fabric of the universal church rises up like a great pile of living materials. *Into an holy temple in the Lord*—Dedicated to Christ, and inhabited by him, in which he displays his presence, and is worshipped and glorified. What is the temple of Diana of the Ephesians, whom ye formerly worshipped, to this?

Verse 1. *For this cause*—That ye may be so "built together," *I am a*

2 of Jesus Christ for you gentiles, (Seeing ye have heard the
dispensation of the grace of God, given me in your behalf,)
3 That by revelation he made known to me the mystery; as
4 I wrote before in few words, By reading which, ye may
5 understand my knowledge in the mystery of Christ; Which
in other ages was not made known to the sons of men, as it
hath now been revealed to his holy apostles and prophets by
6 the Spirit; That the gentiles are joint-heirs, and of the
same body, and joint-partakers of his promise by Christ
7 through the gospel: Of which I have been made a minister,
according to the gift of the grace of God given to me by
8 the effectual working of his power. Unto me who am less
than the least of all saints, hath this grace been given, to
preach among the gentiles the unsearchable riches of Christ;
9 And to make all men see what *is* the fellowship of the
mystery, which was hidden from eternity by God, who
10 created all things by Jesus Christ: That the manifold

prisoner for you gentiles—For your advantage, and for asserting your right to these blessings. This it was which so enraged the Jews against him.

Verse 2. *The dispensation of the grace of God given me in your behalf*—That is, the commission to dispense the gracious gospel; to you gentiles in particular. This they had *heard* from his own mouth.

Verse 3. *The mystery*—Of salvation by Christ alone, and that both to Jews and gentiles. *As I wrote before*—Namely, Eph. i. 9, 10; the very words of which passage he here repeats.

Verse 5. *Which in other*—In former, *ages was not* so clearly or fully *made known to the sons of men*—To any man, no, not to Ezekiel, so often styled, "son of man;" nor to any of the ancient prophets. Those here spoken of are New Testament prophets.

Verse 6. *That the gentiles are joint-heirs*—Of God. *And of the same body*—Under Christ the head. *And joint-partakers of his promise*—The communion of the Holy Ghost.

Verse 7. *According to the gift of the grace of God*—That is, the apostleship which he hath graciously given me, and which he hath qualified me for. *By the effectual working of his power*—In me and by me.

Verse 8. *Unto me, who am less than the least of all saints, is this grace given*—Here are the noblest strains of eloquence to paint the exceeding low opinion the apostle had of himself, and the fulness of unfathomable blessings which are treasured up in Christ.

Verse 9. *What is the fellowship of the mystery*—What those mysterious blessings are whereof all believers jointly partake. *Which was*, in a great measure, *hidden from eternity by God, who*, to make way for the free exercise of his love, *created all things*—This is the foundation of all his dispensations.

Verse 10. *That the manifold wisdom of God might be made known by the*

wisdom of God might now be made known by the church
11 to the principalities and powers in heavenly *places*, According to the eternal purpose which he purposed in Christ
12 Jesus our Lord: By whom we have boldness and access
13 with confidence through faith in him. Wherefore I entreat
you not to faint at my afflictions for you, which is your
14 glory. For this cause I bend my knees to the Father of
15 our Lord Jesus Christ, (Of whom the whole family in heaven
16 and earth is named,) That he would give you, according to
the riches of his glory, to be strengthened with might by his
17 Spirit in the inner man; That Christ may dwell in your
hearts by faith; that being rooted and grounded in love,
18 Ye may be able to comprehend with all the saints, what is the
19 breadth, and length, and depth, and height; And to know
the love of Christ, which surpasseth knowledge, that ye may
20 be filled with all the fulness of God. Now to him that is

church—By what is done in the church, which is the theatre of the divine wisdom.

Verse 12. *By whom we have* free *access*—Such as those petitioners have, who are introduced to the royal presence by some distinguished favourite. *And boldness*—Unrestrained liberty of speech, such as children use in addressing an indulgent father, when, without fear of offending, they disclose all their wants, and make known all their requests.

Verse 13. The not fainting *is your glory.*

Verse 15. *Of whom*—The Father. *The whole family* of angels *in heaven,* saints in paradise, *and* believers on *earth is named.* Being the "children of God," (a more honourable title than "children of Abraham,") and depending on him as the Father of the family.

Verse 16. *The riches of his glory*—The immense fulness of his glorious wisdom, power, and mercy. *The inner man*—The soul.

Verse 17. *Dwell*—That is, constantly and sensibly abide.

Verse 18. *That being rooted and grounded*—That is, deeply fixed and firmly established, *in love. Ye may comprehend*—So far as an human mind is capable. *What is the breadth of the love of Christ*—Embracing all mankind. *And length*—From everlasting to everlasting. *And depth*—Not to be fathomed by any creature. *And height*—Not to be reached by any enemy.

Verse 19. *And to know*—But the apostle corrects himself, and immediately observes, it cannot be fully known. This only we know, that the love of Christ *surpasses* all *knowledge. That ye may be filled*—Which is the sum of all. *With all the fulness of God*—With all his light, love, wisdom, holiness, power, and glory. A perfection far beyond a bare freedom from sin.

Verse 20. *Now to him*—This doxology is admirably adapted to

able to do exceeding abundantly above all that we ask or
21 think, according to the power that worketh in us, To him *be*
glory in the church by Christ Jesus, throughout all ages,
world without end. Amen.

CHAP. IV. 1 I therefore, the prisoner of the Lord, beseech you to walk worthy of the calling wherewith ye are
2 called, With all lowliness and meekness; with longsuffering
3 forbear one another in love, Endeavouring to keep the
4 unity of the Spirit, by the bond of peace. *There is* one
body and Spirit as ye are also called in one hope of your
5 calling; One Lord, one faith, one baptism, One God and
6 Father of all, who *is* above all, and through all, and in us
7 all. But to every one of us is given grace according to the
8 measure of the gift of Christ. Wherefore he saith, * Having

* Psalm lxviii. 18.

strengthen our faith, that we may not stagger at the great things the apostle has been praying for, as if they were too much for God to give, or for us to expect from him. *That is able*—Here is a most beautiful gradation. When he has given us *exceeding*, yea, *abundant* blessings, still we may *ask for* more. And he *is able to do* it. But we may *think* of more than we have asked. He is able to do this also. Yea, and above all this. *Above all we ask*—Above all we can *think*. Nay, exceedingly, abundantly above all that we can either ask or think

Verse 21. *In the church*—On earth and in heaven

Verse 1. *I therefore, the prisoner of the Lord*—Imprisoned for his sake and for your sakes; for the sake of the gospel which he had preached amongst them. This was therefore a powerful motive to them to comfort him under it by their obedience.

Verse 3. *Endeavouring to keep the unity of the Spirit*—That mutual union and harmony, which is a fruit of the Spirit. *The bond of peace* is love.

Verse 4. *There is one body*—The universal church, all believers throughout the world. *One Spirit, one Lord, one God and Father*—The ever-blessed Trinity. *One hope*—Of heaven.

Verse 5. *One* outward *baptism.*

Verse 6. *One God and Father of all*—That believe. *Who is above all*—Presiding over all his children, operating *through* them *all* by Christ, *and* dwelling *in all* by his Spirit.

Verse 7. *According to the measure of the gift of Christ*—According as Christ is pleased to give to each.

Verse 8. *Wherefore he saith*—That is, in reference to which God saith by David, *Having ascended on high, he led captivity captive*—He triumphed over all his enemies, Satan, sin, and death, which had before enslaved

ascended on high, he led captivity captive, and gave gifts
9 to men. (Now this *expression*, He ascended, what is it,
but that he also descended first to the lower parts of the
10 earth? He that descended is the same that ascended also,
far above all the heavens, that he might fill all things.)
11 And he gave some apostles, and some prophets, and some
12 evangelists, and some pastors and teachers; For the perfecting of the saints to the work of the ministry, to the
13 edifying the body of Christ: Till we all come to the

all the world: alluding to the custom of ancient conquerors, who led those they had conquered in chains after them. *And*, as they also used to give donatives to the people, at their return from victory, so he *gave gifts to men*—Both the ordinary and extraordinary gifts of the Spirit.

Verse 9. *Now this expression, He ascended, what is it, but that he descended*—That is, does it not imply, that he descended first? Certainly it does, on the supposition of his being God. Otherwise it would not: since all the saints will ascend to heaven, though none of them descended thence. *Into the lower parts of the earth*—So the womb is called, Psalm cxxxix. 15; the grave, Psalm lxiii. 9.

Verse 10. *He that descended*—That thus amazingly humbled himself. *Is the same that ascended*—That was so highly exalted. *That he might fill all things*—The whole church, with his Spirit, presence, and operations.

Verse 11. *And*, among other his free gifts, *he gave some apostles*—His chief ministers and special witnesses, as having seen him after his resurrection, and received their commission immediately from him. *And some prophets, and some evangelists*—A prophet testifies of things to come; an evangelist of things past: and that chiefly by preaching the gospel before or after any of the apostles. All these were extraordinary officers. The ordinary were *Some pastors*—Watching over their several flocks. *And* some *teachers*—Whether of the same or a lower order, to assist them, as occasion might require.

Verse 12 In this verse is noted the office of ministers; in the next, the aim of the saints; in the 14th, 15th, 16th, the way of growing in grace. And each of these has three parts, standing in the same order. *For the perfecting the saints*—The completing them both in number and their various gifts and graces. *To the work of the ministry*—The serving God and his church in their various ministrations. *To the edifying of the body of Christ*—The building up this his mystical body in faith, love, holiness

Verse 13. *Till we all*—And every one of us. *Come to the unity of the faith, and knowledge of the Son of God*—To both an exact agreement in the Christian doctrine, and an experimental knowledge of Christ as the Son of God. *To a perfect man*—To a state of spiritual manhood both in understanding and strength. *To the measure of the stature of the fulness*

unity of the faith and knowledge of the Son of God,
to a perfect man, to the measure of the stature of the
14 fulness of Christ: That we may be no longer children,
fluctuating to and fro, and carried about with every wind
of doctrine, by the sleight of men, by cunning craftiness,
15 whereby they lie in wait to deceive; But speaking the
truth in love, may grow up into him in all things, who is the
16 head, *even* Christ: From whom the whole body fitly joined
together and compacted by that which every joint supplieth,
according to the effectual working in the measure of every
member, maketh an increase of the body to the edifying of
itself in love.
17 This therefore I say, and testify in the Lord, that ye no
longer walk as the rest of the gentiles walk, in the vanity
18 of your mind, Having the understanding darkened, being
alienated from the life of God by the ignorance that is in

of Christ—To that maturity of age and spiritual stature wherein we shall be filled with Christ, so that he will be all in all.

Verse 14. *Fluctuating to and fro*—From within, even when there is no wind. *And carried about with every wind*—From without; when we are assaulted by others, who are unstable as the wind *By the sleight of men*—By their "cogging the dice;" so the original word implies.

Verse 15. *Into him*—Into his image and Spirit, and into a full union with him.

Verse 16. *From whom the whole* mystical *body fitly joined together*—All the parts being fitted for and adapted to each other, and most exactly harmonizing with the whole. *And compacted*—Knit and cemented together with the utmost firmness. *Maketh increase by that which every joint supplieth*—Or by the mutual help of every joint. *According to the effectual working in the measure of every member*—According as every member in its measure effectually works for the support and growth of the whole. A beautiful allusion to the human body, composed of different joints and members, knit together by various ligaments, and furnished with vessels of communication from the head to every part.

Verse 17. *This therefore I say*—He returns thither where he begun, verse 1. *And testify in the Lord*—In the name and by the authority of the Lord Jesus. *In the vanity of their mind*—Having lost the knowledge of the true God, Rom. i. 21. This is the root of all evil walking.

Verse 18. *Having their understanding darkened, through the ignorance that is in them*—So that they are totally void of the light of God, neither have they any knowledge of his will. *Being alienated from the life of God*—Utter strangers to the divine, the spiritual life. *Through the hardness of their hearts*—Callous and senseless And where there is no sense, there can be no life.

19 them, through the hardness of their hearts. Who being
past feeling have given themselves up to lasciviousness, to
20 work all uncleanness with greediness But ye have not so
21 learned Christ; Seeing ye have heard him, and been taught
22 by him, as the truth is in Jesus: To put off, with respect to
the former conversation, the old man, which is corrupt
23 according to the deceitful desires; But to be renewed in the
24 spirit of your mind; And to put on the new man, which is
created after God in righteousness and true holiness.
25 Wherefore putting away lying, speak ye every man truth
with his neighbour; for we are members one of another.
26 Be ye angry, and sin not: let not the sun go down upon
27 your wrath; Neither give place to the devil. Let him that
28 stole steal no more; but rather let him labour, working with
his hands the thing which is good, that he may have to give

Verse 19. *Who being past feeling*—The original word is peculiarly significant. It properly means, *past feeling pain*. Pain urges the sick to seek a remedy, which, where there is no pain, is little thought of. *Have given themselves up*—Freely, of their own accord. *Lasciviousness* is but one branch of *uncleanness*, which implies impurity of every kind.

Verse 20. *But ye have not so learned Christ*—That is, ye cannot act thus, now ye know him, since you know the Christian dispensation allows of no sin.

Verse 21. *Seeing ye have heard him*—Teaching you inwardly by his Spirit. *As the truth is in Jesus*—According to his own gospel.

Verse 22. *The old man*—That is, the whole body of sin. All sinful *desires* are *deceitful*; promising the happiness which they cannot give.

Verse 23. *The spirit of your mind*—The very ground of your heart.

Verse 24. *The new man*—Universal holiness. *After*—In the very image of God.

Verse 25. *Wherefore*—Seeing ye are thus created anew, walk accordingly, in every particular. *For we are members one of another*—To which intimate union all deceit is quite repugnant.

Verse 26. *Be ye angry, and sin not*—That is, if ye are angry, take heed ye sin not. Anger at sin is not evil; but we should feel only pity to the sinner. If we are angry at the person, as well as the fault, we sin. And how hardly do we avoid it! *Let not the sun go down upon your wrath*—Reprove your brother, and be reconciled immediately. Lose not one day. A clear, express command. Reader, do you keep it?

Verse 27. *Neither give place to the devil*—By any delay.

Verse 28. *But rather let him labour*—Lest idleness lead him to steal again. And whoever has sinned in any kind ought the more zealously to practise the opposite virtue. *That he may have to give*—And so be no longer a burden and nuisance, but a blessing, to his neighbours.

29 to him that needeth. Let no corrupt discourse proceed out
of your mouth, but that which is good to the use of edifying,
30 that it may minister grace to the hearers. And grieve not
the Holy Spirit of God, whereby ye have been sealed unto
31 the day of redemption. Let all bitterness, and wrath, and
anger, and clamour, and evil speaking, be put away from
32 you, with all malice: But be ye kind one to another, tenderhearted, forgiving one another, as God also for Christ's sake
V. 1 hath forgiven you. Be ye therefore followers of God,
2 as beloved children; And walk in love, as Christ also hath
loved us, and given himself up for us an offering and a
3 sacrifice to God of a sweet-smelling savour. But let not
fornication, or any uncleanness, or covetousness, be even
4 named among you, as becometh saints; Neither obscenity,
nor foolish talking, or jesting, which are not convenient:

Verse 29. *But that which is good*—Profitable to the speaker and hearers. *To the use of edifying*—To forward them in repentance, faith, or holiness. *That it may minister grace*—Be a means of conveying more grace into their hearts. Hence we learn, what *discourse* is *corrupt*, as it were stinking in the nostrils of God; namely, all that is not *profitable*, not *edifying*, not apt to *minister grace to the hearers*.

Verse 30. *Grieve not the Holy Spirit*—By any disobedience. Particularly by corrupt discourse; or by any of the following sins. Do not force him to withdraw from you, as a friend does whom you grieve by unkind behaviour. *The day of redemption*—That is, the day of judgment, in which our redemption will be completed.

Verse 31. *Let all bitterness*—The height of settled anger, opposite to *kindness*, verse 32. *And wrath*—Lasting displeasure toward the ignorant, and them that are out of the way, opposite to *tenderheartedness*. *And anger*—The very first risings of disgust at those that injure you, opposite to *forgiving one another*. *And clamour*—Or bawling. "I am not angry," says one; "but it is my way to speak so." Then unlearn that way: it is the way to hell. *And evil speaking*—Be it in ever so mild and soft a tone, or with ever such professions of kindness. Here is a beautiful retrogradation, beginning with the highest, and descending to the lowest, degree of the want of love.

Verse 32. *As God*, showing himself *kind* and *tenderhearted* in the highest degree, *hath forgiven you*.

Verse 1. *Be ye therefore followers*—Imitators. *Of God*—In forgiving and loving. O how much more honourable and more happy, to be an imitator of God, than of Homer, Virgil, or Alexander the Great!

Verse 3. *But let not* any impure love *be even named* or heard of *among you*—Keep at the utmost distance from it, *as becometh saints*.

Verse 4 *Nor foolish talking*—Tittle tattle, talking of nothing, the

5 but rather thanksgiving. For this ye know, that no whore-
monger, or unclean person, or covetous man, who is an
idolater, hath any inheritance in the kingdom of Christ and
6 of God. Let no one deceive you with vain words: for
because of these things the wrath of God cometh upon the
7 sons of disobedience. Be ye not therefore partakers with
8 them. For ye were once darkness, but now *ye are* light in
9 the Lord: walk as children of light: (The fruit of the light
10 *is* in all goodness and righteousness and truth:) Proving
11 what is acceptable to the Lord. And have no fellowship
with the unfruitful works of darkness, but rather reprove
12 them. For it is a shame even to speak the things which are
13 done by them in secret. But all things which are reproved
are made manifest by the light: for whatsoever doth make
14 manifest is light. Wherefore he saith, Awake thou that
sleepest, and arise from the dead, and Christ shall give thee
15 light. See then that ye walk circumspectly, not as fools,

weather, fashions, meat and drink. *Or jesting*—The word properly means, *wittiness, facetiousness,* esteemed by the heathens an half-virtue. But how frequently even this quenches the Spirit, those who are tender of conscience know. *Which are not convenient*—For a Christian; as neither increasing his faith nor holiness

Verse 6. *Because of these things*—As innocent as the heathens esteem them, and as those dealers in *vain words* would persuade you to think them.

Verse 8. *Ye were once darkness*—Total blindness and ignorance. *Walk as children of light*—Suitably to your present knowledge.

Verse 9. *The fruit of the light*—Opposite to "the unfruitful works of darkness," verse 11. *Is in*—That is, consists in. *Goodness and righteousness and truth*—Opposite to the sins spoken of, Ephesians iv. 25, &c.

Verse 11 *Reprove them*—To avoid them is not enough.

Verse 12 *In secret*—As flying the light.

Verse 13. *But all things which are reproved, are* thereby dragged out into the light, and *made manifest*—Shown in their proper colours, *by the light. For whatsoever doth make manifest is light*--That is, for nothing but light, yea, light from heaven, can make anything manifest.

Verse 14. *Wherefore he*—God. *Saith*—In the general tenor of his word, to all who are still in darkness. *Awake thou that sleepest*—In ignorance of God and thyself; in stupid insensibility. *And arise from the dead*—From the death of sin. *And Christ shall give thee light*—Knowledge, holiness, happiness.

Verse 15. *Circumspectly*—Exactly, with the utmost accuracy, getting to the highest pitch of every point of holiness. *Not as fools*—Who think not where they are going, or do not make the best of their way.

but as wise men, Redeeming the time, because the days are
17 evil. Wherefore be ye not unwise, but understanding what
18 *is* the will of the Lord. And be not drunken with wine,
19 wherein is excess; but be ye filled with the Spirit; Speaking to each other in psalms and hymns and spiritual songs,
singing and making melody with your hearts unto the Lord;
20 Giving thanks always for all things to God even the Father
21 in the name of our Lord Jesus Christ; Submitting yourselves one to another in the fear of God.
22 Wives, submit yourselves to your own husbands, as unto
23 the Lord. For the husband is head of the wife, as Christ
also is head of the church· (and he is the Saviour of the

Verse 16. With all possible care *redeeming the time*—Saving all you can for the best purposes; buying every possible moment out of the hands of sin and Satan; out of the hands of sloth, ease, pleasure, worldly business; the more diligently, because *the* present *are evil days*, days of the grossest ignorance, immorality, and profaneness.

Verse 17. *What the will of the Lord is*—In every time, place, and circumstance.

Verse 18. *Wherein is excess*—That is, which leads to debauchery of every kind. *But be ye filled with the Spirit*—In all his graces, who gives a more noble pleasure than wine can do.

Verse 19. *Speaking to each other*—By the Spirit. *In* the *Psalms*—Of David. *And hymns*—Of praise. *And spiritual songs*—On any divine subject. By there being no inspired songs, peculiarly adapted to the Christian dispensation, as there were to the Jewish, it is evident that the promise of the Holy Ghost to believers, in the last days, was by his larger effusion to supply the lack of it. *Singing with your hearts*—As well as your voice. *To the Lord*—Jesus, who searcheth the heart.

Verse 20. *Giving thanks*—At all times and places. And *for all things*—Prosperous or adverse, since all work together for good. *In the name of*, or through, *our Lord Jesus Christ*—By whom we receive all good things.

Verse 22. In the following directions concerning relative duties, the inferiors are all along placed before the superiors, because the general proposition is concerning submission; and inferiors ought to do their duty, whatever their superiors do. *Wives, submit yourselves to your own husbands*—Unless where God forbids. Otherwise, in all indifferent things, the will of the husband is a law to the wife. *As unto the Lord*—The obedience a wife pays to her husband is at the same time paid to Christ himself; he being *head of the wife, as Christ is head of the church.*

Verse 23. *The head*—The governor, guide, and guardian of the wife. *And he is the Saviour of the body*—The church, from all sin and misery

24 body.) Therefore as the church is subject to Christ, so also
25 *let* the wives *be* to their own husbands in everything. Husbands, love your wives, even as Christ loved the church,
26 and gave up himself for it; That he might sanctify it
(having cleansed *it* by the washing of water) through the
27 word, That he might present it to himself a glorious church,
not having spot, or wrinkle, or any such thing; that it may
28 be holy and unblamable. Men ought so to love their wives
as their own bodies. He that loveth his wife loveth him-
29 self. Now no one ever hated his own flesh; but nourisheth
30 and cherisheth it, as also the Lord the church: For we are
31 members of his body, of his flesh, and of his bones. * For
this cause shall a man leave his father and mother, and
shall be joined to his wife, and they two shall be one flesh.
32 This is a great mystery: I mean concerning Christ and the
33 church. But let every one of you in particular so love his
wife as himself; and let the wife reverence her husband.

* Gen. ii. 24.

Verse 24. *In everything*—Which is not contrary to any command of God.

Verse 25. *Even as Christ loved the church*—Here is the true model of conjugal affection. With this kind of affection, with this degree of it, and to this end, should husbands love their wives.

Verse 26. *That he might sanctify it through the word*—The ordinary channel of all blessings. *Having cleansed it*—From the guilt and power of sin. *By the washing of water*—In baptism; if, with "the outward and visible sign," we receive the "inward and spiritual grace."

Verse 27. *That he might present it*—Even in this world. *To himself*—As his spouse. *A glorious church*—All glorious within. *Not having spot*—Of impurity from any sin. *Or wrinkle*—Of deformity from any decay.

Verse 28. *As their own bodies*—That is, as themselves. *He that loveth his wife loveth himself*—Which is not a sin, but an indisputable duty.

Verse 29. *His own flesh*—That is, himself *Nourisheth and cherisheth*—That is, feeds and clothes *it*.

Verse 30. *For we*—The reason why Christ nourishes and cherishes the church is, that close connexion between them which is here expressed in the words of Moses, originally spoken concerning Eve. *Are members*—Are as intimately united to Christ, in a spiritual sense, as if we were literally "flesh of his flesh, and bone of his bone."

Verse 31. *For this cause*—Because of this intimate union.

CHAP. VI. 1 Children, obey your parents in the Lord:
2 for this is right. * Honour thy father and mother; (which
3 is the first commandment with a promise;) That it may be
well with thee, and thou mayest live long upon the earth.
4 And, ye fathers, provoke not your children to wrath: but
bring them up in the instruction and discipline of the Lord.
5 Servants, obey *your* masters according to the flesh, with
fear and trembling, in singleness of your heart, as unto the
6 Lord; Not with eye-service, as menpleasers; but as ser-
7 vants of Christ, doing the will of God from the soul; With
good will doing service, as unto the Lord, and not to men:

* Exod. xx. 12.

Verse 1. *Children, obey your parents*—In all things lawful the will of the parent is a law to the child. *In the Lord*—For his sake. *For this is right*—Manifestly just and reasonable.

Verse 2. *Honour*—That is, love, reverence, obey, assist, in all things. The mother is particularly mentioned, as being more liable to be slighted than the father. *Which is the first commandment with a promise*—For the promise implied in the second commandment does not belong to the keeping that command in particular, but the whole law.

Verse 3. *That thou mayest live long upon the earth*—This is usually fulfilled to eminently dutiful children; and he who lives long and well has a long seed-time for the eternal harvest. But this promise, in the Christian dispensation, is to be understood chiefly in a more exalted and spiritual sense.

Verse 4. *And, ye fathers*—Mothers are included; but fathers are named, as being more apt to be stern and severe. *Provoke not your children to wrath*—Do not needlessly fret or exasperate them. *But bring them up*—With all tenderness and mildness. *In the instruction and discipline of the Lord*—Both in Christian knowledge and practice.

Verse 5. *Your masters according to the flesh*—According to the present state of things: afterward the servant is free from his master. *With fear and trembling*—A proverbial expression, implying the utmost care and diligence. *In singleness of heart*—With a single eye to the providence and will of God.

Verse 6. *Not with eye-service*—Serving them better when under their eye than at other times. *But doing the will of God from the heart*—Doing whatever you do, as the will of God, and with your might.

Verse 7. *Unto the Lord, and not to men*—That is, rather than to men; and by making every action of common life a sacrifice to God; having an eye to him in all things, even as if there were no other master

CHAPTER VI.

8 Knowing that whatsoever good each man doeth, the same
shall he receive from the Lord, whether *he be* a servant or
9 free. And, ye masters, do the same things to them, forbearing threatening: knowing that your own master is in heaven; and there is no respect of persons with him.
10 Finally, brethren, be strong through the Lord, and
11 through the power of his might. Put on the whole armour
of God, that ye may be able to stand against the wiles
12 of the devil. For our wrestling is not against flesh and
blood, but against principalities, against powers, against the
rulers of the world, of the darkness of this age, against
13 wicked spirits in heavenly places. Wherefore take to you

Verse 8 *He shall receive the same*—That is, a full and adequate recompence for it.

Verse 9. *Do the same things to them*—That is, act toward them from the same principle. *Forbearing threatening*—Behaving with gentleness and humanity, not in a harsh or domineering way.

Verse 10. *Brethren*—This is the only place in this epistle where he uses this compellation. Soldiers frequently use it to each other in the field. *Be strong*—Nothing less will suffice for such a fight: to be weak, and remain so, is the way to perish. *In the power of his might*—A very uncommon expression, plainly denoting what great assistance we need. as if *his might* would not do, it must be the *powerful exertion* of his might.

Verse 11. *Put on the whole armour of God*—The Greek word means a complete suit of armour. Believers are said to *put on* the girdle, breastplate, shoes; to *take* the shield of faith, and sword of the Spirit. *The whole armour*—As if the *armour* would scarce do, it must be the *whole* armour. This is repeated, verse 13, because of the strength and subtilty of our adversaries, and because of an "evil day" of sore trial being at hand.

Verse 12. *For our wrestling is not* only, not chiefly, *against flesh and blood*—Weak men, or fleshly appetites. *But against principalities, against powers*—The mighty princes of all the infernal legions. And great is their power, and that likewise of those legions whom they command *Against the rulers of the world*—Perhaps these *principalities* and *powers* remain mostly in the citadel of their kingdom of darkness. But there are other evil spirits who range abroad, to whom the provinces of the world are committed. *Of the darkness*—This is chiefly spiritual darkness. *Of this age*—Which prevails during the present state of things. *Against wicked spirits*—Who continually oppose faith, love, holiness, either by force or fraud; and labour to infuse unbelief, pride, idolatry malice, envy, anger, hatred. *In heavenly places*—Which were once their abode, and which they still aspire to, as far as they are permitted.

Verse 13. *In the evil day*—The war is perpetual; but the fight is one

the whole armour of God, that ye may be able to withstand
14 in the evil day, and having done all, to stand. Stand therefore, having your loins girt about with truth, and having
15 put on the breastplate of righteousness; And having your
feet shod with the preparation of the gospel of peace;
16 Above all, taking the shield of faith, whereby ye shall be
17 able to quench all the fiery darts of the wicked one. And
take the helmet of salvation, and the sword of the Spirit,

day less, another more, violent *The evil day* is either at the approach of death, or in life; may be longer or shorter; and admits of numberless varieties. *And having done all, to stand*—That ye may still keep on your armour, still *stand* upon your guard, still watch and pray; and thus ye will be enabled to endure unto the end, and *stand* with joy before the face of the Son of Man.

Verse 14. *Having your loins girt about*—That ye may be ready for every motion. *With truth*—Not only with the truths of the gospel, but with "truth in the inward parts;" for without this all our knowledge of divine truth will prove but a poor girdle "in the evil day." So our Lord is described, Isaiah xi. 5. And as a girded man is always ready to go on, so this seems to intimate an obedient heart, a ready will. Our Lord adds to the loins girded, the lights burning, Luke xii. 35; showing that watching and ready obedience are the inseparable companions of faith and love. *And having on the breastplate of righteousness*—The righteousness of a spotless purity, in which Christ will present us faultless before God, through the merit of his own blood. With this *breastplate* our Lord is described, Isaiah lix. 17. In the breast is the seat of conscience, which is guarded by righteousness. No armour for the back is mentioned. We are always to face our enemies.

Verse 15. *And your feet shod with the preparation of the gospel*—Let this be always ready to direct and confirm you in every step. This part of the armour, for the feet, is needful, considering what a journey we have to go; what a race to run. Our feet must be so shod, that our footsteps slip not. To order our life and conversation aright, we are *prepared* by the gospel blessing, the peace and love of God ruling in the heart, Col. iii. 14, 15. By this only can we tread the rough ways, surmount our difficulties, and hold out to the end.

Verse 16. *Above* or over *all*—As a sort of universal covering to every other part of the armour itself, continually exercise a strong and lively *faith.* This you may use as a *shield,* which will *quench all the fiery darts,* the furious temptations, violent and sudden injections *of the devil.*

Verse 17. *And take for an helmet* the hope *of salvation*—1 Thess. v. 8. The head is that part which is most carefully to be defended. One stroke here may prove fatal. The armour for this is *the hope of salvation.* The lowest degree of this hope is a confidence that God will work the whole

18 which is the word of God: Praying alway by the Spirit
with all prayer and supplication, and watching thereunto
with all perseverance and supplication for all the saints;
19 And for me, that utterance may be given me, by the opening
my mouth to make known boldly the mystery of the gospel,
20 For which I am an ambassador in bonds: that I may speak
boldly therein, as I ought to speak.

work of faith in us the highest is a full assurance of future glory, added to the experimental knowledge of pardoning love. Armed with this *helmet*, the hope of the joy set before him, Christ "endured the cross, and despised the shame," Heb. xii. 2. *And the sword of the Spirit, the word of God*—This Satan cannot withstand, when it is edged and wielded by faith. Till now our armour has been only defensive. But we are to attack Satan, as well as secure ourselves; the shield in one hand, and the sword in the other Whoever fights with the powers of hell will need both. He that is covered with armour from head to foot, and neglects this, will be foiled after all. This whole description shows us how great a thing it is to be a Christian. The want of any one thing makes him incomplete. Though he has his loins girt with truth, righteousness for a breastplate, his feet shod with the preparation of the gospel, the shield of faith, the helmet of salvation, and the sword of the Spirit; yet one thing he wants after all. What is that? It follows,

Verse 18. *Praying always*—At all times, and on every occasion, in the midst of all employments, inwardly *praying without ceasing*. *By the Spirit*—Through the influence of the Holy Spirit. *With all prayer*—With all sort of prayer, public, private, mental, vocal. Some are careful in respect of one kind of prayer, and negligent in others. If we would have the petitions we ask, let us use all. Some there are who use only mental prayer or ejaculations, and think they are in a state of grace, and use a way of worship, far superior to any other: but such only fancy themselves to be above what is really above them; it requiring far more grace to be enabled to pour out a fervent and continued prayer, than to offer up mental aspirations. *And supplication*—Repeating and urging our prayer, as Christ did in the garden. *And watching*—Inwardly attending on God, to know his will, to gain power to do it, and to attain to the blessings we desire. *With all perseverance*—Continuing to the end in this holy exercise. *And supplication for all the saints*—Wrestling in fervent, continued intercession for others, especially for the faithful, that they may do all the will of God, and be steadfast to the end. Perhaps we receive few answers to prayer, because we do not intercede enough for others.

Verse 19. *By the opening my mouth*—Removing every inward and every outward hinderance.

Verse 20. *An ambassador in bonds*—The ambassadors of men usually appear in great pomp How differently does the ambassador of Christ appear!

21 But that ye also may know my affairs, how I do, Tychicus,
a beloved brother and faithful minister in the Lord, will
22 make known to you all things: Whom I have sent to you
for this very thing, that ye might know our affairs, and that
23 he might comfort your hearts. Peace *be* to the brethren,
and love with faith, from God the Father and the Lord
24 Jesus Christ. Grace *be* with all that love our Lord Jesus
Christ in sincerity. Amen.

Verse 21. *Ye also*—As well as others.

Verse 22 *That he might comfort your hearts*—By relating the supports I find from God, and the success of the gospel.

Verse 23. *Peace*—This verse recapitulates the whole epistle.

Verse 24. *In sincerity*—Or in incorruption; without corrupting his genuine gospel, without any mixture of corrupt affections. And that with continuance, till grace issue in glory.

NOTES

ON

ST PAUL'S EPISTLE TO THE PHILIPPIANS.

Philippi was so called from Philip, king of Macedonia, who much enlarged and beautified it. Afterwards it became a Roman colony, and the chief city of that part of Macedonia. Hither St. Paul was sent by a vision to preach; and here, not long after his coming, he was shamefully entreated. Nevertheless many were converted by him, during the short time of his abode there; by whose liberality he was more assisted than by any other church of his planting. And they had now sent large assistance to him by Epaphroditus; by whom he returns them this epistle.

It contains six parts :—

I. The inscription,	C. i.	1, 2
II. Thanksgiving and prayers for them,		3—11
III. He relates his present state and good hope:		12—24
Whence he exhorts them,		
1. While he remains with them to walk worthy of the gospel,		25—30
	C. ii.	1—16
2. Though he should be killed, to rejoice with him,		17, 18
And promises,		
1. To certify them of all things by Timotheus,		19—24
2. In the mean time to send Epaphroditus,		25—30
IV. He exhorts them to rejoice,	C. iii.	1—3
admonishing them to beware of false teachers, and to imitate the true,		2—21
commending concord,	C. iv.	1—3
He again exhorts them to joy and meekness		4—7
and to whatsoever things are excellent,		8—9
V. He accepts of their liberality,		10—20
VI. The conclusion,		21—23

PHILIPPIANS.

CHAP. I. 1 PAUL and Timotheus, servants of Jesus
Christ, to all the saints in Christ Jesus who are at Philippi,
2 with the bishops and deacons: Grace *be* unto you, and
peace from God our Father, and the Lord Jesus Christ.
3 I thank my God upon every mention of you, Always in all
4 my prayers making supplication for you all with joy, For
5 your fellowship in the gospel from the first day until now;
6 Being persuaded of this very thing, that he who hath begun
a good work in you will perfect *it* until the day of Jesus
7 Christ: As it is right for me to think this of you all, because
I have you in my heart, who were all partakers of my grace,
both in my bonds, and in the defence and confirmation of

Verse 1. *Servants*—St. Paul, writing familiarly to the Philippians, does not style himself an apostle. And under the common title of *servants*, he tenderly and modestly joins with himself his son *Timotheus*, who had come to Philippi not long after St. Paul had received him, Acts xvi. 3, 12. *To all the saints*—The apostolic epistles were sent more directly to the churches, than to the pastors of them. *With the bishops and deacons*—The former properly took care of the internal state, the latter, of the externals, of the church, 1 Tim. iii. 2—8; although these were not wholly confined to the one, neither those to the other. The word *bishops* here includes all the presbyters at Philippi, as well as the ruling presbyters: the names bishop and presbyter, or elder, being promiscuously used in the first ages.

Verse 4. *With joy*—After the epistle to the Ephesians, wherein love reigns, follows this, wherein there is perpetual mention of joy. "The fruit of the Spirit is love, joy." And joy peculiarly enlivens prayer. The sum of the whole epistle is, I rejoice. Rejoice ye.

Verse 5. The sense is, *I thank God for your fellowship* with us *in* all the blessings of *the gospel*, which I have done *from the first day* of your receiving it *until now*.

Verse 6. *Being persuaded*—The grounds of which persuasion are set down in the following verse. *That he who hath begun a good work in you, will perfect it until the day of Christ*—That he who having justified, hath begun to sanctify you, will carry on this work, till it issue in glory.

Verse 7. *As it is right for me tc think this of you all*—Why? He does not say, "Because of an eternal decree;" or, "Because a saint must persevere;" but, *because I have you in my heart, who were all partakers*

8 the gospel. For God is my witness, how I long for you all
9 with the bowels of Jesus Christ. And this I pray, that your
love may abound yet more and more in all knowledge and
10 *in* all *spiritual* sense; That ye may try the things that are
excellent; that ye may be sincere and without offence unto
11 the day of Christ; Being filled with the fruits of righteousness, which are through Christ Jesus, to the glory and
praise of God.
12 Now I would have you know, brethren, that the things
concerning me have fallen out rather to the furtherance
13 of the gospel; So that my bonds in Christ have been made

of my grace—That is, because *ye were all (for which I have you in my heart,* I bear you the most grateful and tender affection) *partakers of my grace*—That is, sharers in the afflictions which God vouchsafed me as a *grace* or favour, verses 29, 30; *both in my bonds, and* when I was called forth to answer for myself, and to *confirm the gospel.* It is not improbable that, after they had endured that *great trial of affliction,* God had sealed them unto full victory, of which the apostle had a prophetic sight

Verse 8. *I long for you with the bowels of Jesus Christ*—In Paul, not Paul lives, but Jesus Christ. Therefore he longs for them *with the bowels,* the tenderness, not of Paul, but of Jesus Christ.

Verse 9. *And this I pray, that your love*—Which they had already shown. *May abound yet more and more*—The fire which burned in the apostle never says, It is enough. *In knowledge and in all spiritual sense*—Which is the ground of all spiritual knowledge. We must be inwardly *sensible* of divine peace, joy, love; otherwise, we cannot *know* what they are.

Verse 10. *That ye may try*—By that spiritual sense. *The things that are excellent*—Not only good, but the very best; the superior excellence of which is hardly discerned, but by the adult Christian. *That ye may be* inwardly *sincere*—Having a single eye to the very best things, and a pure heart. *And* outwardly *without offence*—Holy, unblamable in all things.

Verse 11. *Being filled with the fruits of righteousness, which are through Jesus Christ, to the glory and praise of God*—Here are three properties of that sincerity which is acceptable to God: 1. It must bear fruits, *the fruits of righteousness,* all inward and outward holiness, all good tempers, words, and works; and that so abundantly, that we may be *filled* with them. 2. The branch and the fruits must derive both their virtue and their very being from the all-supporting, all-supplying root, *Jesus Christ.* 3. As all these flow from the grace of Christ, so they must issue in *the glory and praise of God.*

Verse 12. *The things concerning me*—My sufferings. *Have fallen out rather to the furtherance,* than, as you feared, the hinderance, *of the gospel*

Verse 13. *My bonds in Christ*—Endured for his sake *Have been made*

14 manifest in the whole palace, and to all others; And many
of the brethren, trusting in the Lord through my bonds, are
more abundantly bold to speak the word without fear.
15 Some indeed preach Christ even through envy and strife;
16 but some through good will: The one preach Christ out
of contention, not sincerely, supposing to add affliction to my
17 bonds: But the others out of love, knowing that I am set
18 for the defence of the gospel. What then? still, every way,
whether in pretence, or in truth, Christ is preached; and in
19 this I rejoice, yea, and will rejoice. For I know that this
shall turn to my salvation, through your prayer, and the sup-
20 ply of the Spirit of Jesus Christ, According to my earnest
expectation and hope, that I shall be ashamed in nothing,
but that with all boldness, as always, *so* now also, Christ
shall be magnified in my body, whether by life, or by death.
21 For to me to live *is* Christ, and to die *is* gain. But if *I*
22 *am* to live in the flesh, this *is* the fruit of my labour: and

manifest—Much taken notice of. *In the whole palace*—Of the Roman emperor.

Verse 14. *And many*—Who were before afraid. *Trusting in the Lord through my bonds*—When they observed my constancy, and safety notwithstanding, are more bold.

Verses 15, 16. *Some indeed preach Christ out of contention*—Envying St. Paul's success, and striving to hurt him thereby. *Not sincerely*—From a real desire to glorify God. *But supposing*—Though they were disappointed. *To add* more *affliction to my bonds*—By enraging the Romans against me.

Verse 17. *But the others out of love*—To Christ and me. *Knowing*—Not barely, supposing. *That I am set*—Literally, *I lie;* yet still going forward in his work. He remained at Rome as an ambassador in a place where he is employed on an important embassy.

Verse 18. *In pretence*—Under colour of propagating the gospel. *In truth*—With a real design so to do.

Verse 19. *This shall turn to my salvation*—Shall procure me an higher degree of glory. *Through your prayer*—Obtaining for me a larger *supply of the Spirit.*

Verse 20. *As always*—Since my call to the apostleship *In my body*—However it may be disposed of. How that might be, he did not yet know. For the apostles did not know all things; particularly in things pertaining to themselves, they had room to exercise faith and patience.

Verse 21. *To me to live is Christ*—To know, to love, to follow Christ, is my life, my glory, my joy.

Verse 22. Here he begins to treat of the former clause of the preceding verse. Of the latter he treats, Philip. ii. 17. *But if I am to live in*

23 what I should choose I know not. For I am in a strait
between two, having a desire to depart, and to be with
24 Christ; *which is* far better: But to remain in the flesh *is*
25 more needful for you. And being persuaded of this, I know
that I shall remain and continue with you all for your fur-
26 therance and joy of faith; That your rejoicing for me may
abound through Christ Jesus by my presence with you again.
27 Only let your behaviour be worthy of the gospel of Christ
that whether I come and see you, or be absent, I may hear
concerning you, that ye stand fast in one spirit, with one soul
28 striving together for the faith of the gospel; And in nothing
terrified by your adversaries: which is to them an evident
token of perdition, but to you of salvation. This also *is*
29 of God. For to you it is given with regard to Christ, not
30 only to believe on him, but also to suffer for him; Having
the same conflict which ye saw in me, and now hear *to be* in
II. 1 me. If *there be* then any consolation in Christ, if any
comfort of love, if any fellowship of the Spirit, if any bowels

the flesh, this is the fruit of my labour—This is the fruit of my living longer, that I can labour more Glorious labour! desirable fruit! In this view, long life is indeed a blessing. *And what I should choose I know not*—That is, if it were left to my choice.

Verse 23. *To depart*—Out of bonds, flesh, the world. *And to be with Christ*—In a nearer and fuller union It is better *to depart;* it is far better *to be with Christ*

Verse 25. *I know*—By a prophetic notice given him while he was writing this. *That I shall continue* some time longer *with you*—And doubtless he did see them after this confinement.

Verse 27. *Only*—Be careful for this, and nothing else. *Stand fast in one spirit*—With the most perfect unanimity. *Striving together*—With united strength and endeavours. *For the faith of the gospel*—For all the blessings revealed and promised therein.

Verse 28. *Which*—Namely, their being adversaries to the word of God, and to you the messengers of God. *Is an evident token*—That they are in the high road to *perdition;* and you, in the way of *salvation.*

Verse 29. *For to you it is given*—As a special token of God's love, and of your being in the way of salvation.

Verse 30. *Having the same* kind of *conflict* with your adversaries, *which ye saw in me*—When I was with you, Acts xvi. 12, 19, &c.

Verse 1. *If there be therefore any consolation*—In the grace of Christ. *If any comfort*—In the love of God. *If any fellowship of the* Holy Ghost; *if any bowels of mercies*—Resulting therefrom; any tender affection towards each other

2 of mercies, Fulfil ye my joy, that ye think the same thing,
3 having the same love, being of one soul, of one mind. Do
nothing through strife or vainglory; but in lowliness of mind
4 esteem each the others better than themselves. Aim not
every one at his own things, but every one also at the things
5 of others. Let this mind be in you, which was also in Christ
6 Jesus: Who, being in the form of God, counted it no act
7 of robbery to be equal with God: Yet emptied himself,

Verse 2. *Think the same thing*—Seeing Christ is your common Head *Having the same love*—To God, your common Father. *Being of one soul*—Animated with the same affections and tempers, as ye have all drank into one spirit. *Of one mind*—Tenderly rejoicing and grieving together

Verse 3. *Do nothing through contention*—Which is inconsistent with your thinking the same thing. *Or vainglory*—Desire of praise, which is directly opposite to the love of God. *But esteem each the others better than themselves*—(For every one knows more evil of himself than he can of another :) Which is a glorious fruit of the Spirit, and an admirable help to your continuing "of one soul."

Verse 4. *Aim not every one at his own things*—Only. If so, ye have not bowels of mercies.

Verse 6. *Who being in the* essential *form*—The incommunicable nature. *Of God*—From eternity, as he was afterward in the form of man; real God, as real man. *Counted it no act of robbery*—That is the precise meaning of the words,—no invasion of another's prerogative, but his own strict and unquestionable right. *To be equal with God*—The word here translated *equal,* occurs in the adjective form five or six times in the New Testament, Matt. xx. 12; Luke vi. 34; John v. 18; Acts xi. 17; Rev. xxi. 16. In all which places it expresses not a bare resemblance, but a real and proper *equality*. It here implies both the fulness and the supreme height of the Godhead; to which are opposed, he *emptied* and he *humbled himself*.

Verse 7 *Yet*—He was so far from tenaciously insisting upon, that he willingly relinquished, his claim. He was content to forego the glories of the Creator, and to appear in the form of a creature; nay, to be made in the likeness of the fallen creatures; and not only to share the disgrace, but to suffer the punishment, due to the meanest and vilest among them all. *He emptied himself*—Of that divine fulness, which he received again at his exaltation. Though he remained *full,* John i. 14, yet he appeared as if he had been *empty;* for he veiled his fulness from the sight of men and angels. Yea, he not only veiled, but, in some sense, renounced, the glory which he had before the world began. *Taking*—And by that very act emptying himself. *The form of a servant*—The *form*, the *likeness*, the *fashion,* though not exactly the same, are yet nearly related to each other. *The form* expresses something absolute; *the likeness* refers to other things of the same kind; *the fashion* respects what appears to sight

taking the form of a servant, being made in the likeness of
8 men: And being found in fashion as a man, he humbled
himself, becoming obedient even unto death, yea, the death
9 of the cross. Wherefore God also hath highly exalted him,
and hath given him a name which is above every name:
10 That at the name of Jesus every knee might bow, of those
in heaven, and those on earth, and those under the earth;
11 And every tongue might confess that Jesus Christ is Lord
12 in the glory of God the Father. Wherefore, my beloved,
as you have always obeyed, not as in my presence only, but
much more now in my absence, work out your own salvation
13 with fear and trembling. For it is God that worketh in

and sense. *Being made in the likeness of men*—A real man, like other men. Hereby he took *the form of a servant.*

Verse 8. *And being found in fashion as a man*—A common man, without any peculiar excellence or comeliness. *He humbled himself*—To a still greater depth. *Becoming obedient*—To God, though equal with him. *Even unto death*—The greatest instance both of humiliation and obedience *Yea, the death of the cross*—Inflicted on few but servants or slaves.

Verse 9 *Wherefore*—Because of his voluntary humiliation and obedience. He humbled himself; but *God hath exalted him*—So recompensing his humiliation. *And hath given him*—So recompensing his emptying himself. *A name which is above every name*—Dignity and majesty superior to every creature.

Verse 10. *That every knee*—That divine honour might be paid in every possible manner by every creature. *Might bow*—Either with love or trembling. *Of those in heaven, earth, under the earth*—That is, through the whole universe.

Verse 11. *And every tongue*—Even of his enemies. *Confess that Jesus Christ is Lord*—Jehovah; not now "in the form of a servant," but enthroned *in the glory of God the Father.*

Verse 12. *Wherefore*—Having proposed Christ's example, he exhorts them to secure the salvation which Christ has purchased. *As ye have always*—Hitherto. *Obeyed*—Both God, and me his minister. *Now in my absence*—When ye have not me to instruct, assist, and direct you. *Work out your own salvation*—Herein let every man aim at his own things. *With fear and trembling*—With the utmost care and diligence.

Verse 13. *For it is God*—God alone, who is with you, though I am not. *That worketh in you according to his good pleasure*—Not for any merit of yours. Yet his influences are not to supersede, but to encourage, our own efforts. *Work out your own salvation*—Here is our duty. *For it is God that worketh in you*—Here is our encouragement. And O, what a glorious encouragement, to have the arm of Omnipotence stretched out for our support and our succour!

you according to his good pleasure both to will and to do.
14 Do all things without murmurings and disputings: That ye
15 may be blameless and simple; the sons of God, unrebukable,
in the midst of a crooked and perverse generation, among
16 whom ye shine as lights in the world; Holding fast the
word of life, that I may glory in the day of Christ, that I
have not run in vain, neither laboured in vain.
17 Yea, and if I be offered up on the sacrifice and service
18 of your faith, I rejoice, and congratulate you all. For the
19 same cause rejoice ye likewise, and congratulate me. Now
I trust in the Lord Jesus to send Timotheus to you shortly,
that I also may be encouraged, when I know your state.
20 For I have none likeminded, who will naturally care for
21 what concerneth you. For all seek their own, not the
22 things of Jesus Christ. But ye know the proof of him, that,
as a son with his father, he hath served with me in the gos-

Verse 14. *Do all things*—Not only without contention, verse 3, but even *without murmurings and disputings*—Which are real, though smaller, hinderances of love.

Verse 15. *That ye may be blameless*—Before men. *And simple*—Before God, aiming at him alone. *As the sons of God*—The God of love; acting up to your high character. *Unrebukable in the midst of a crooked*—Guileful, serpentine, *and perverse generation*—Such as the bulk of mankind always were. *Crooked*—By a corrupt nature, and yet more *perverse* by custom and practice.

Verse 17. Here he begins to treat of the latter clause of chap. i. 22. *Yea, and if I be offered*—Literally, *If I be poured out. Upon the sacrifice of your faith*—The Philippians, as the other converted heathens, were a sacrifice to God through St. Paul's ministry, Rom. xv. 16. And as in sacrificing, wine was poured at the foot of the altar, so he was willing that his blood should be poured out. The expression well agrees with that kind of martyrdom by which he was afterwards offered up to God.

Verse 18. *Congratulate me*—When I am offered up.

Verse 19. *When I know*—Upon my return, that ye stand steadfast.

Verse 20. *I have none*—Of those who are now with me.

Verse 21. *For all*—But Timotheus. *Seek their own*—Ease, safety, pleasure, or profit. Amazing! In that golden age of the church, could St. Paul throughly approve of one only, among all the labourers that were with him? Phil. i. 14, 17. And how many do we think can now approve themselves to God? *Not the things of Jesus Christ*—They who seek these alone, will sadly experience this. They will find few helpers likeminded with themselves, willing naked to follow a naked Master!

Verse 22. *As a son with his father*—He uses an elegant peculiarity of phrase, speaking partly as of a son, partly as of a fellowlabourer.

23 pel. Him therefore I hope to send, as soon as ever I know
24 how it will go with me. But I trust in the Lord that I also
25 myself shall come shortly. Yet I thought it necessary to
send to you Epaphroditus, my brother and companion in
labour, and fellowsoldier, but your messenger, and him that
26 ministered to my need. For he longed after you all, and
was full of heaviness, because ye had heard that he was sick
27 He was indeed sick nigh unto death; but God had compassion on him; and not on him only, but on me likewise,
28 lest I should have sorrow upon sorrow. I have sent him therefore the more willingly, that ye seeing him again may rejoice,
29 and that I also may be the less sorrowful. Receive him
therefore in the Lord with all gladness; and honour such:
30 Because for the work of Christ he was nigh unto death, not
regarding his own life, to supply your deficiency of service
toward me.

CHAP. III. 1 Finally, my brethren, rejoice in the Lord.
To write the same things to you, *is* not tedious to me, and
2 *it is* safe for you. Beware of dogs, beware of evil workers,
3 beware of the concision. For we are the circumcision, who
worship God in spirit, and glory in Christ Jesus, and have

Verse 25. *To send Epaphroditus*—Back immediately. *Your messenger*—The Philippians had sent him to St. Paul with their liberal contribution

Verse 26. *He was full of heaviness*—Because he supposed you would be afflicted at hearing that *he was sick*.

Verse 27. *God had compassion on him*—Restoring him to health.

Verse 28. *That I may be the less sorrowful*—When I know you are rejoicing.

Verse 30. *To supply your deficiency of service*—To do what you could not do in person.

Verse 1. *The same things*—Which you have heard before.

Verse 2. *Beware of dogs*—Unclean, unholy, rapacious men. The title which the Jews usually gave the gentiles, he returns upon themselves. *The concision*—Circumcision being now ceased, the apostle will not call them the circumcision, but coins a term on purpose, taken from a Greek word used by the LXX, Lev. xxi. 5, for such a cutting as God had forbidden.

Verse 3. *For we*—Christians. *Are the* only true *circumcision*—The people now in covenant with God *Who worship God in spirit*—Not barely in the letter, but with the spiritual worship of inward holiness *And glory in Christ Jesus*—As the only cause of all our blessings. *And have no confidence in the flesh*—In any outward advantage or prerogative.

4 no confidence in the flesh. Though I might have confidence
even in the flesh. If any other man be fully persuaded that
5 he may have confidence in the flesh, I more: Circumcised
the eighth day, of the stock of Israel, of the tribe of Benjamin, an Hebrew of Hebrews; touching the law, a pharisee;
6 Touching zeal, persecuting the church; touching the righ-
7 teousness which is by the law, blameless. But whatsoever
things were gain to me, those I have accounted loss for
8 Christ. Yea, doubtless, and I account all things to be loss
for the excellency of the knowledge of Christ Jesus my Lord;
for whom I have suffered the loss of all things, and do
9 account them but dung, that I may gain Christ, And be

Verse 4. *Though I*—He subjoins this in the singular number, because the Philippians could not say thus.

Verse 5. *Circumcised the eighth day*—Not at ripe age, as a proselyte. *Of the tribe of Benjamin*—Sprung from the wife, not the handmaid. *An Hebrew of Hebrews*—By both my parents; in everything, nation, religion, language. *Touching the law, a pharisee*—One of that sect who most accurately observe it.

Verse 6. Having such a *zeal* for it as to *persecute* to the death those who did not observe it. *Touching the righteousness which is* described and enjoined *by the law*—That is, external observances, *blameless.*

Verse 7. *But* all these *things, which* I then accounted *gain,* which were once my confidence, my glory, and joy, *those,* ever since I have believed, *I have accounted loss,* nothing worth in comparison of Christ.

Verse 8. *Yea, I* still *account* both all these and *all things* else *to be* mere *loss,* compared to the inward, experimental *knowledge of Christ,* as *my Lord,* as my prophet, priest, and king, as teaching me wisdom, atoning for my sins, and reigning in my heart. To refer this to justification only, is miserably to pervert the whole scope of the words. They manifestly relate to sanctification also; yea, to that chiefly. *For whom I have* actually *suffered the loss of all things*—Which the world loves, esteems, or admires; of which I am so far from repenting, that I still *account them but dung*—The discourse rises. *Loss* is sustained with patience, but *dung* is cast away with abhorrence. The Greek word signifies any, the vilest refuse of things, the dross of metals, the dregs of liquors, the excrements of animals, the most worthless scraps of meat, the basest offals, fit only for dogs. *That I may gain Christ*—He that loses all things, not excepting himself, gains Christ, and is gained by Christ. And still there is more; which even St. Paul speaks of his having not yet gained.

Verse 9. *And be found* by God ingrafted *in him, not having my own righteousness, which is of the law*—That merely outward righteousness prescribed by the law, and performed by my own strength. *But that* inward righteousness *which is through faith*—Which can flow from no other

found in him, not having my own righteousness, which is
of the law, but that which is through faith in Christ, the
10 righteousness which is from God by faith: That I may
know him, and the power of his resurrection, and the fellowship of his sufferings, being made conformable to his death;
11 If by any means I may attain unto the resurrection of the
12 dead. Not that I have already attained, or am already perfected: but I pursue, if I may apprehend that for which I
13 was also apprehended by Christ Jesus. Brethren, I do not
account myself to have apprehended: but one thing I *do*,
forgetting the things that are behind, and reaching forth
14 unto the things which are before, I press toward the goal,
for the prize of the high calling of God in Christ Jesus.
15 Let us therefore, as many as are perfect, be thus minded;
and if in anything ye be otherwise minded, God shall reveal

fountain. *The righteousness which is from God*—From his almighty Spirit, not by my own strength, but *by faith* alone. Here also the apostle is far from speaking of justification only.

Verse 10. The knowledge of Christ, mentioned in the eighth verse, is here more largely explained. *That I may know him*—As my complete Saviour. *And the power of his resurrection*—Raising me from the death of sin, into all the life of love. *And the fellowship of his sufferings*—Being crucified with him. *And made conformable to his death*—So as to be dead to all things here below.

Verse 11. *The resurrection of the dead*—That is, the resurrection to glory.

Verse 12. *Not that I have already attained*—The prize. He here enters on a new set of metaphors, taken from a race. But observe how, in the utmost fervour, he retains his sobriety of spirit. *Or am already perfected*—There is a difference between one that is perfect, and one that is *perfected*. The one is fitted for the race, verse 15; the other, ready to receive the prize. *But I pursue, if I may apprehend that*—Perfect holiness, preparatory to glory. *For*, in order to *which I was apprehended by Christ Jesus*—Appearing to me in the way, Acts xxvi. 14. The speaking conditionally both here and in the preceding verse, implies no uncertainty, but only the difficulty of attaining.

Verse 13. *I do not account myself to have apprehended* this already; to be already possessed of perfect holiness.

Verse 14. *Forgetting the things that are behind*—Even that part of the race which is already run. *And reaching forth unto*—Literally, *stretched out over the things that are before*—Pursuing with the whole bent and vigour of my soul, perfect holiness and eternal glory. *In Christ Jesus*—The author and finisher of every good thing.

Verse 15 *Let us, as many as are perfect*—Fit for the race, strong in faith; so it means here *Be thus minded*—Apply wholly to this one thing.

16 even this unto you. But whereunto we have already attained,
let us walk by the same rule, let us mind the same thing.
17 Brethren, be ye followers together of me, and mark them
18 who walk as ye have us for an example. (For many walk,
of whom I have told you often, and now tell you even weep-
19 ing, *that they are* enemies of the cross of Christ: Whose
end *is* destruction, whose god *is* their belly, and *whose* glory
20 *is* in their shame, who mind earthly things.) For our conversation is in heaven; from whence also we look for the
21 Saviour, the Lord Jesus Christ: Who will transform our
vile body, that it may be fashioned like unto his glorious
body, according to the mighty working whereby he is able
even to subject all things to himself.

CHAP. IV. 1 Therefore, my brethren beloved and longed
for, my joy and crown, so stand fast in the Lord, *my* beloved.
2 I beseech Euodias, and I beseech Syntyche, to be of one
3 mind in the Lord. And I entreat thee also, true yoke-

And if in anything ye—Who are not perfect, who are weak in faith. *Be otherwise minded*—Pursuing other things. God, if ye desire it, *shall reveal even this unto you*—Will convince you of it.

Verse 16. *But* let us take care not to lose the ground we have already gained. *Let us walk by the same rule* we have done hitherto.

Verse 17. *Mark them*—For your imitation.

Verse 18. *Weeping*—As he wrote. *Enemies of the cross of Christ*—Such are all cowardly, all shamefaced, all delicate Christians.

Verse 19. *Whose end is destruction*—This is placed in the front, that what follows may be read with the greater horror. *Whose god is their belly*—Whose supreme happiness lies in gratifying their sensual appetites. *Who mind*—Relish, desire, seek, *earthly things.*

Verse 20. *Our conversation*—The Greek word is of a very extensive meaning: our citizenship, our thoughts, our affections, are already *in heaven.*

Verse 21. *Who will transform our vile body*—Into the most perfect state, and the most beauteous form. It will then be purer than the unspotted firmament, brighter than the lustre of the stars; and, which exceeds all parallel, which comprehends all perfection, *like unto his glorious body*—Like that wonderfully glorious body which he wears in his heavenly kingdom, and on his triumphant throne.

Verse 1. *So stand*—As ye have done hitherto

Verse 2. *I beseech*—He repeats this twice, as if speaking to each face to face, and that with the utmost tenderness

Verse 3 *And I entreat thee also, true yokefellow*—St. Paul had many

fellow, help those women who laboured together with me in
the gospel, with both Clement, and my other fellowlabourers,
whose names *are* in the book of life.
4 Rejoice in the Lord always: again I say, Rejoice. Let
5 your gentleness be known to all men. The Lord *is* at hand.
6 Be careful for nothing; but in everything by prayer and
supplication with thanksgiving let your requests be made
7 known to God. And the peace of God, which surpasseth
all understanding, shall keep your hearts and your minds
through Christ Jesus.

fellowlabourers, but not many yokefellows. In this number was Barnabas first, and then Silas, whom he probably addresses here; for Silas had been his yokefellow at the very place, Acts xvi. 19. *Help those women who laboured together with me*—Literally, *who wrestled.* The Greek word doth not imply preaching, or anything of that kind; but danger and toil endured for the sake of the gospel, which was also endured at the same time, probably at Philippi, by *Clement and my other fellowlabourers*—This is a different word from the former, and does properly imply fellowpreachers. *Whose names,* although not set down here, *are in the book of life*—As are those of all believers. An allusion to the wrestlers in the Olympic games, whose names were all enrolled in a book. Reader, is thy name there? Then walk circumspectly, lest the Lord blot thee out of his book!

Verse 5. *Let your gentleness*—Yieldingness, sweetness of temper, the result of joy in the Lord. *Be known*—By your whole behaviour. *To all men*—Good and bad, gentle and froward. Those of the roughest tempers are good-natured to some, from natural sympathy and various motives; a Christian, to all. *The Lord*—The judge, the rewarder, the avenger *Is at hand*—Standeth at the door.

Verse 6. *Be* anxiously *careful for nothing*—If men are not gentle towards you, yet neither on this, nor any other account, be careful, but pray. Carefulness and prayer cannot stand together. *In everything*—Great and small. *Let your requests be made known*—They who by a preposterous shame or distrustful modesty, cover, stifle, or keep in their desires, as if they were either too small or too great, must be racked with care; from which they are entirely delivered, who pour them out with a free and filial confidence. *To God*—It is not always proper to disclose them to men. *By supplication*—Which is the enlarging upon and pressing our petition. *With thanksgiving*—The surest mark of a soul free from care, and of prayer joined with true resignation. This is always followed by peace. Peace and thanksgiving are both coupled together, Col. iii. 15.

Verse 7. *And the peace of God*—That calm, heavenly repose, that tranquillity of spirit, which God only can give. *Which surpasseth all understanding*—Which none can comprehend, save he that receiveth it. *Shall keep*—Shall guard, as a garrison does a city. *Your hearts*—Your affections

8 Finally, brethren, whatsoever things are true, whatsoever
things *are* honest, whatsoever things *are* just, whatsoever
things *are* pure, whatsoever things *are* lovely, whatsoever
things *are* of good report; if *there be* any virtue, and if *there*
9 *be* any praise, think on these things. The things which ye
have both learned, and received, and heard, and seen in me
these do: and the God of peace shall be with you
10 I rejoiced in the Lord greatly, that now at last your care
of me hath flourished again; wherein ye were also careful,
11 but ye wanted opportunity. Not that I speak in respect
of want; for I have learned, in whatsoever state I am, to
12 be content. I know how to be abased, and I know how to
abound: everywhere and in everything I am instructed
both to be full and to be hungry, both to abound and to

Your minds—Your understandings, and all the various workings of them; *through* the Spirit and power of *Christ Jesus,* in the knowledge and love of God. Without a guard set on these likewise, the purity and vigour of our affections cannot long be preserved.

Verse 8. *Finally*—To sum up all. *Whatsoever things are true*—Here are eight particulars placed in two fourfold rows; the former containing their duty; the latter, the commendation of it. The first word in the former row answers the first in the latter; the second word, the second; and so on. *True*—In speech. *Honest*—In action. *Just*—With regard to others. *Pure*—With regard to yourselves. *Lovely*—And what more lovely than truth? *Of good report*—As is honesty, even where it is not practised. *If there be any virtue*—And all virtues are contained in justice *If there be any praise*—In those things which relate rather to ourselves than to our neighbour. *Think on these things*—That ye may both practise them yourselves, and recommend them to others.

Verse 9. *The things which ye have learned*—As catechumens. *And received*—By continual instructions. *And heard and seen*—In my life and conversation. *These do, and the God of peace shall be with you*—Not only the peace of God, but God himself, the fountain of peace.

Verse 10. *I rejoiced greatly*—St. Paul was no Stoic: he had strong passions, but all devoted to God. *That your care of me hath flourished again*—As a tree blossoms after the winter. *Ye wanted opportunity*—Either ye had not plenty yourselves, or you wanted a proper messenger

Verse 11. *I have learned*—From God. He only can teach this. *In everything, therewith to be content*—Joyfully and thankfully patient. Nothing less is Christian content. We may observe a beautiful gradation in the expressions, *I have learned; I know; I am instructed; I can.*

Verse 12. *I know how to be abased*—Having scarce what is needful for my body. *And to abound*—Having wherewith to relieve others also Presently after, the order of the words is inverted, to intimate his frequent transition from scarcity to plenty, and from plenty to scarcity.

13 want. I can do all things through Christ strengthening
14 me. Nevertheless ye have done well, that ye did commu-
15 nicate to me in my affliction. And ye know likewise, O
Philippians, that in the beginning of the gospel, when I
departed from Macedonia, no church communicated with
16 me in respect of giving and receiving, but you only. For
even in Thessalonica ye sent once and again to my neces-
17 sities. Not that I desire a gift, but I desire fruit that may
18 abound to your account. But I have all things, and
abound: I am filled, having received of Epaphroditus the
things *which came* from you, an odour of a sweet smell, an
19 acceptable sacrifice, wellpleasing to God. And my God
shall supply all your need according to his riches in glory
20 through Christ Jesus. Now unto our God and Father *be*
glory for ever and ever. Amen.
21 Salute every saint in Christ Jesus. The brethren who
22 are with me salute you. All the saints salute you, chiefly
23 they that are of Cæsar's household. The grace of the Lord
Jesus Christ *be* with you all.

I am instructed—Literally, *I am initiated* in that mystery, unknown to all but Christians. *Both to be full and to be hungry*—For one day *Both to abound and to want*—For a longer season.

Verse 13. *I can do all things*—Even fulfil all the will of God.

Verse 15. *In the beginning of the gospel*—When it was first preached at Philippi. *In respect of giving*—On your part. *And receiving*—On mine.

Verse 17. *Not that I desire*—For my own sake, the very *gift* which I receive of you.

Verse 18. *An odour of a sweet smell*—More pleasing to God than the sweetest perfumes to men.

Verse 19. *All your need*—As ye have mine. *According to his riches in glory*—In his abundant, eternal glory.

NOTES

ON

ST. PAUL'S EPISTLE TO THE COLOSSIANS.

Colosse was a city of the Greater Phrygia, not far from Laodicea and Hierapolis. Though St. Paul preached in many parts of Phrygia, yet he never had been at this city. It had received the gospel by the preaching of Epaphras, who was with St. Paul when he wrote this epistle.

It seems the Colossians were now in danger of being seduced by those who strove to blend Judaism, or heathen superstitions, with Christianity; pretending that God, because of his great majesty, was not to be approached but by the mediation of angels; and that there were certain rites and observances, chiefly borrowed from the law, whereby these angels might be made our friends.

In opposition to them, the apostle, 1. Commends the knowledge of Christ, as more excellent than all other, and so entire and perfect that no other knowledge was necessary for a Christian. He shows, 2. That Christ is above all angels, who are only his servants; and that, being reconciled to God through him, we have free access to him in all our necessities

This epistle contains,

I. The inscription, C. i. 1, 2
II. The doctrine, wherein the apostle pathetically explains the mystery of Christ,
  By thanksgiving for the Colossians, 3—8
  By prayers for them, 9—23
  With a declaration of his affection for them, 24—29
  C. ii. 1—3
III. The exhortation,
  1. General, wherein he excites them to perseverance, and warns them not to be deceived, 4—8
  Describes again the mystery of Christ in order, 9—15
  And in the same order, draws his admonitions,
    1. From Christ the head, 16—19
    2. From his death, 20—23
    3. From his exaltation, C. iii. 1—4
  2. Particular,
    1. To avoid several vices, 5—9

2.	To practise several virtues,	10, 11
	Especially to love one another,	12—15
	And study the scriptures,	16, 17
3.	To the relative duties of wives and husbands,	18, 19
	Children and parents,	20, 21
	Servants and masters,	22—25
	C. iv.	1
3.	Final, to prayer,	2—4
	to spiritual wisdom,	5, 6
V.	The conclusion,	7—16

COLOSSIANS.

CHAPTER I. 1 Paul, an apostle of Jesus Christ by the
2 will of God, and Timotheus a brother, To the saints and
faithful brethren in Christ at Colosse: Grace *be* unto you, and
peace, from God our Father and the Lord Jesus Christ.
3 We give thanks to the God and Father of our Lord
4 Jesus Christ, (praying always for you, Hearing of your faith
5 in Christ Jesus, and of your love to all the saints,) For the
hope which is laid up for you in heaven, of which ye
6 heard before in the word of truth, of the gospel, Which is
come to you, as also *it is* in all the world; and bringeth
forth fruit, as *it hath done* likewise among you, from the day
7 ye heard *it*, and knew the grace of God in truth: As ye
likewise learned of Epaphras our beloved fellowservant,
8 who is a faithful minister of Christ for you; Who also
9 declared to us your love in the Spirit. For this cause, from

Verse 2. *The saints*—This word expresses their union with God. *And brethren*—This, their union with their fellow-Christians.

Verse 3. *We give thanks*—There is a near resemblance between this epistle, and those to the Ephesians and Philippians.

Verse 5. *Ye heard before*—I wrote to you. *In the word of truth, of the gospel*—The true gospel preached to you.

Verse 6. *It bringeth forth fruit in all the world*—That is, in every place where it is preached. *Ye knew the grace of God in truth*—Truly experienced the gracious power of God.

Verse 7. *The fellowservant*—Of Paul and Timotheus.

Verse 8. *Your love in the Spirit*—Your love wrought in you by the Spirit.

Verse 9. *We pray for you*—This was mentioned in general, verse 3; but now more particularly. *That ye may be filled with the knowledge*

the day we heard *it*, we do not cease to pray also for you,
and to desire that ye may be filled with the knowledge
10 of his will in all wisdom and spiritual understanding; That
ye may walk worthy of the Lord unto all pleasing, being
fruitful in every good work, and increasing in the knowledge
11 of God; Strengthened with all might, according to his glorious power, unto all patience and longsuffering with joyful-
12 ness; Giving thanks unto the Father, who hath made us
meet to partake of the inheritance of the saints in light
13 Who hath delivered us from the power of darkness, and
hath translated *us* into the kingdom of his beloved Son
14 In whom we have redemption through his blood, the for-
15 giveness of sins: Who is the image of the invisible God,
16 the first begotten of every creature: For through him were

of his will—Of his revealed will. *In all wisdom*—With all the wisdom from above. *And spiritual understanding*—To discern by that light whatever agrees with, or differs from, his will.

Verse 10 *That,* knowing his whole will, *ye may walk worthy of the Lord, unto all pleasing*—So as actually to please him in all things; daily *increasing in the* living, experimental *knowledge of God,* our Father, Saviour, Sanctifier.

Verse 11 *Strengthened unto all patience and longsuffering with joyfulness*—This is the highest point: not only to know, to do, to suffer, the whole will of God; but to suffer it to the end, not barely with *patience,* but with thankful joy.

Verse 12. *Who,* by justifying and sanctifying us, *hath made us meet* for glory.

Verse 13. *Power* detains reluctant captives . a *kingdom* cherishes willing subjects. *His beloved Son*—This is treated of in the fifteenth and following verses.

Verse 14. *In whom we have redemption*—This is treated of from the middle of the eighteenth verse. The voluntary passion of our Lord appeased the Father's wrath, obtained pardon and acceptance for us, and, consequently, dissolved the dominion and power which Satan had over us through our sins. So that *forgiveness* is the beginning of redemtion, as the resurrection is the completion of it.

Verse 15. *Who is*—By describing the glory of Christ, and his preeminence over the highest angels, the apostle here lays a foundation for the reproof of all worshippers of angels. *The image of the invisible God*—Whom none can represent, but his only begotten Son; in his divine nature the invisible image, in his human the visible image, of the Father. *The first begotten of every creature*—That is, begotten before every creature; subsisting before all worlds, before all time, from all eternity.

Verse 16. *For*—This explains the latter part of the preceding verse. *Through* implies something prior to the particles *by* and *for;* so denot-

created all things that are in heaven, and that are on earth,
visible and invisible, whether *they be* thrones, or dominions.
or principalities, or powers: all things were created by him,
17 and for him: And he is before all things, and by him all
18 things consist. And he is the head of his body, the church.
who is the beginning, the first begotten from the dead;
19 that in all things he might have the pre-eminence. For it
pleased *the Father* that all fulness should dwell in him;
20 And by him to reconcile all things to himself; (having
made peace by him, through the blood of the cross;)
21 whether things on earth, or things in heaven. And you
that were once alienated, and enemies in your mind by

ing the beginning, the progress, and the end. *Him*—This word, frequently repeated, signifies his supreme majesty, and excludes every creature. *Were created all things that are in heaven*—And heaven itself. But the inhabitants are named, because more noble than the house. *Invisible*—The several species of which are subjoined. *Thrones* are superior to *dominions; principalities,* to *powers.* Perhaps the two latter may express their office with regard to other creatures: the two former may refer to God, who maketh them his chariots, and, as it were, rideth upon their wings.

Verse 17. *And he is before all things*—It is not said, he *was:* he *is* from everlasting to everlasting. *And by him all things consist*—The original expression not only implies, that he sustains all things in being, but more directly, *All things were and are compacted in him into one system.* He is the cement, as well as support, of the universe. And is he less than the supreme God?

Verse 18. *And*—From the whole he now descends to the most eminent part, the church. *He is the head of the church*—Universal; the supreme and only head both of influence and of government to the whole body of believers. *Who is*—The repetition of the expression (see verse 15) points out the entrance on a new paragraph. *The beginning*—Absolutely, the Eternal. *The first begotten from the dead*—From whose resurrection flows all the life, spiritual and eternal, of all his brethren. *That in all things*—Whether of nature or grace. *He might have the pre-eminence*—Who can sound this depth?

Verse 19. *For it pleased the Father that all fulness*—All the fulness of God. *Should dwell in him*—Constantly, as in a temple; and always ready for our approach to him.

Verse 20. *Through the blood of the cross*—The blood shed thereon. *Whether things on earth*—Here the enmity began: therefore this is mentioned first. *Or things in heaven*—Those who are now in paradise; the saints who died before Christ came.

Verse 21. *And you that were alienated, and enemies*—Actual alienation of affection makes habitual enmity. *In your mind*—Both your under-

22 wicked works, he hath now reconciled By the body of his
flesh through death, to present you holy and spotless and unre-
23 provable in his sight: If ye continue in the faith grounded
and settled, and are not removed from the hope of the
gospel, which ye have heard, which is preached to every
creature that is under heaven; whereof I Paul am made a
24 minister. Now I rejoice in my sufferings for you, and fill up
in my flesh that which is behind of the sufferings of Christ
25 for his body, which is the church: Of which I am made a
minister, according to the dispensation of God which is
26 given to me for you, fully to preach the word of God; The
mystery which hath been hid from ages and generations,
27 but now is manifested to his saints: To whom among the
gentiles it was the will of God to make known what is the
riches of this glorious mystery; which is Christ in you, the

standing and your affections. *By wicked works*—Which continually feed and increase inward alienation from, and enmity to, God. *He hath now reconciled*—From the moment ye believed.

Verse 22. *By the body of his flesh*—So distinguished from his body, the church. The body here denotes his entire manhood. *Through death*—Whereby he purchased the reconciliation which we receive by faith. *To present you*—The very end of that reconciliation. *Holy*—Toward God. *Spotless*—In yourselves. *Unreprovable*—As to your neighbour.

Verse 23. *If ye continue in the faith*—Otherwise, ye will lose all the blessings which ye have already begun to enjoy. *And be not removed from the hope of the gospel*—The glorious hope of perfect love. *Which is preached*—Is already begun to be preached *to every creature under heaven.*

Verse 24. *Now I rejoice in my sufferings for you, and fill up*—That is, whereby I fill up. *That which is behind of the sufferings of Christ*—That which remains to be suffered by his members. These are termed the sufferings of Christ, 1. Because the suffering of any member is the suffering of the whole; and of the head especially, which supplies strength, spirits, sense, and motion to all. 2. Because they are for his sake, for the testimony of his truth. And these also are necessary for the church; not to reconcile it to God, or satisfy for sin, (for that Christ did perfectly,) but for example to others, perfecting of the saints, and increasing their reward.

Verse 25. *According to the dispensation of God which is given me*—Or, the stewardship with which I am intrusted.

Verse 26. *The mystery*—Namely, Christ both justifying and sanctifying gentiles, as well as Jews. *Which hath been* comparatively *hid from* former *ages and* past *generations* of men.

Verse 27. *Christ* dwelling and reigning *in you, the hope of glory*—The ground of your hope.

28 hope of glory: Whom we preach, admonishing every man,
and teaching every man with all wisdom; that we may pre-
29 sent every man perfect through Christ Jesus: For which
also I labour, striving according to his mighty working, who
worketh in me mightily.

CHAP. II. 1 For I would have you know how great a
conflict I have for you, and *for* them at Laodicea, and *for*
2 as many as have not seen my face in the flesh; That their
hearts may be comforted, being knit together in love, even
unto all riches of the full assurance of understanding, unto
the acknowledgment of the mystery of God, both the Father
3 and Christ; In whom are hid all the treasures of wisdom
4 and knowledge. And this I say, that no man may beguile
5 you with enticing words. For though I am absent from
you in the flesh, yet I am present with you in spirit, rejoicing to behold your order, and the steadfastness of your
6 faith in Christ As ye have therefore received Christ Jesus
7 the Lord, *so* walk in him: Rooted and built up in him, and
established in the faith, as ye have been taught, abounding
therein with thanksgiving.
8 Beware lest any man make a prey of you through philosophy and empty deceit, after the tradition of men, after the
9 rudiments of the world, and not after Christ. For in him

Verse 28. We *teach* the ignorant, and *admonish* them that are already taught.

Verse 1. *How great a conflict*—Of care, desire, prayer. *As many as have not seen my face*—Therefore, in writing to the Colossians, he refrains from those familiar appellations, "Brethren," "Beloved."

Verse 2. *Unto all riches of the full assurance of understanding, unto the acknowledgment of the mystery of God*—That is, unto the fullest and clearest understanding and knowledge of the gospel.

Verse 6. *So walk in him*—In the same faith, love, holiness.

Verse 7. *Rooted in him*—As the vine. *Built*—On the sure foundation.

Verse 8. *Through philosophy and empty deceit*—That is, through the empty deceit of philosophy blended with Christianity. This the apostle condemns, 1. Because it was *empty* and *deceitful*, promising happiness, but giving none 2. Because it was grounded, not on solid reason, but *the traditions of men*, Zeno, Epicurus, and the rest. And, 3. Because it was so shallow and superficial, not advancing beyond the knowledge of sensible things; no, not beyond the first *rudiments* of them.

Verse 9. *For in him dwelleth*—Inhabiteth, continually abideth, *all the ful-*

10 dwelleth all the fulness of the Godhead bodily. And ye are
filled by him, who is the head of all principality and power.:
11 By whom also ye have been circumcised with a circumcision
not performed with hands, in putting off the body of the sins
12 of the flesh by the circumcision of Christ: Buried with him
in baptism, by which ye are also risen with *him* through the
faith of the operation of God, who raised him from the dead.
13 And you, who were dead in trespasses and the uncircumcision of your flesh, hath he quickened together with him,

ness of the Godhead. Believers are "filled with all the fulness of God," Eph iii. 19. But in Christ *dwelleth all the fulness of the Godhead;* the most full Godhead; not only divine powers, but divine nature, Col. i. 19. *Bodily*—Personally, really, substantially. The very substance of God, if one might so speak, dwells in Christ in the most full sense.

Verse 10. *And ye*—Who believe. *Are filled with him*—John i. 16. Christ is filled with God, and ye are filled with Christ. And *ye* are filled *by him.* The fulness of Christ overflows his church, Psalm cxxxiii. 3. He is originally full. We *are filled by him* with wisdom and holiness. *Who is the head of all principality and power*—Of angels as well as men Not from angels therefore, but from their head, are we to ask whatever we stand in need of.

Verse 11. *By whom also ye have been circumcised*—Ye have received the spiritual blessings typified of old by circumcision. *With a circumcision not performed with hands*—By an inward, spiritual operation. *In putting off,* not a little skin, but *the* whole *body of the sins of the flesh*—All the sins of your evil nature. *By the circumcision of Christ*—By that spiritual circumcision which Christ works in your heart.

Verse 12. Which he wrought in you, when ye were as it were *buriea with him in baptism*—The ancient manner of baptizing by immersion is as manifestly alluded to here, as the other manner of baptizing by sprinkling or pouring of water is, Heb. x. 22. But no stress is laid on the age of the baptized, or the manner of performing it, in one or the other; but only on our being risen with Christ, through the powerful operation of God in the soul; which we cannot but know assuredly, if it really is so: and if we do not experience this, our baptism has not answered the end of its institution. *By which ye are also risen with him*—From the death of sin to the life of holiness. It does not appear, that in all this St. Paul speaks of justification at all, but of sanctification altogether.

Verse 13, *And you who were dead*—Doubly dead to God, not only wallowing in *trespasses,* outward sins, but also in *the uncircumcision of your flesh*—A beautiful expression for original sin, the inbred corruption of your nature, your uncircumcised heart and affections. *Hath he*—God the Father. *Quickened together with him*—Making you partakers of the power of his resurrection. It is evident the apostle thus far speaks, not of justification, but of sanctification only.

14 having forgiven you all trespasses; Having blotted out by
his decrees the handwriting against us, which was contrary
to us, and having nailed it to his cross, he took it out of the
15 way; *And* having spoiled the principalities and powers, he
exposed them openly, triumphing over them in him.
16 Let none therefore judge you in meat, or drink, or in
respect of a feast day, or of the new moon, or of sabbath
17 days: Which are a shadow of things to come; but the body
18 *is* of Christ. Let none defraud you of your reward by a
voluntary humility and worship of angels, intruding into the
things which he hath not seen, vainly puffed up by his
19 fleshly mind, And not holding the head, from which all the
body being nourished and knit together, by the joints and
20 ligaments, increaseth with the increase of God. Therefore
if ye are dead with Christ from the rudiments of the world,

Verse 14. *Having blotted out*—In consequence of his gracious *decrees*, that Christ should come into the world to save sinners, and that whosoever believeth on him should have everlasting life. *The handwriting against us*—Where a debt is contracted, it is usually testified by some handwriting; and when the debt is forgiven, the handwriting is destroyed, either by blotting it out, by taking it away, or by tearing it. The apostle expresses in all these three ways, God's destroying the handwriting *which was contrary to us*, or at enmity with us. This was not properly our sins themselves, (they were the debt,) but their guilt and cry before God.

Verse 15. *And having spoiled the principalities and powers*—The evil angels, of their usurped dominion. *He*—God the Father. *Exposed them openly*—Before all the hosts of hell and heaven. *Triumphing over them in* or *by him*—By Christ. Thus the paragraph begins with Christ, goes on with him, and ends with him.

Verse 16. *Therefore*—Seeing these things are so. *Let none judge you*—That is, regard none who judge you. *In meat or drink*—For not observing the ceremonial law in these or any other particulars. *Or in respect of a* yearly *feast, the new moon*, or the weekly Jewish *sabbaths*.

Verse 17. *Which are* but *a* lifeless *shadow; but the body*, the substance, *is of Christ*.

Verse 18. Out of pretended *humility*, they *worshipped angels*, as not daring to apply immediately to God. Yet this really sprung from their being *puffed up*: (the constant forerunner of a fall, Prov. xvi. 18:) so far was it from being an instance of true humility.

Verse 19. *And not holding the head*—He does not hold Christ, who does not trust in him alone. All the members are *nourished* by faith, and *knit together* by love and mutual sympathy.

Verse 20. *Therefore*—The inference begun, verse 16, is continued. A new inference follows, Col. iii. 1. *If ye are dead with Christ from the rudiments of the world*—That is, *If ye are dead with Christ*, and so

21 why, as living in the world, receive ye ordinances, (Touch
22 not; taste not; handle not; All which are to perish in the
using,) after the commandments and doctrines of men?
23 Which things (though they have indeed a show of wisdom
in voluntary worship, and humility, and not sparing the
body;) *yet are* not of any value, *but* are to the satisfying
III. 1 of the flesh. If ye then are risen with Christ, seek the
things above, where Christ sitteth at the right hand of God.
2 Set your affections on the things above, not the things on the
3 earth. For ye are dead, and your life is hid with Christ in
4 God. When Christ, our life, shall appear, then shall ye also
appear with him in glory.
5 Mortify therefore your members which are upon the
earth; fornication, uncleanness, inordinate affection, evil

freed *from* them, *why receive ye ordinances*—Which Christ hath not enjoined, from which he hath made you free.

Verse 21. *Touch not*—An unclean thing. *Taste not*—Any forbidden meat. *Handle not*—Any consecrated vessel.

Verse 22. *Perish in the using*—Have no farther use, no influence on the mind.

Verse 23. *Not sparing the body*—Denying it many gratifications, and putting it to many inconveniences. Yet they are *not of any* real *value* before God, nor do they, upon the whole, mortify, but *satisfy, the flesh.* They indulge our corrupt nature, our self-will, pride, and desire of being distinguished from others.

Verse 1. *If ye are risen, seek the things above*—As Christ being risen, immediately went to heaven

Verse 3 *For ye are dead*—To the things on earth. *And your* real, spiritual *life is hid* from the world, and laid up *in God, with Christ*—Who hath merited, promised, prepared it for us, and gives us the earnest and foretaste of it in our hearts.

Verse 4. *When Christ*—The abruptness of the sentence surrounds us with sudden light. *Our life*—The fountain of holiness and glory. *Shall appear*—In the clouds of heaven.

Verse 5. *Mortify therefore*—Put to death, slay with a continued stroke. *Your members*—Which together make up the body of sin. *Which are upon the earth*—Where they find their nourishment. *Uncleanness*—In act, word, or thought. *Inordinate affection*—Every passion which does not flow from and lead to the love of God. *Evil desire*—The desire of the flesh, the desire of the eye, and the pride of life. *Covetousness*—According to the derivation of the word, means the desire of having more, or of any thing independent on God. *Which is idolatry*—Properly and directly; for it is giving the heart to a creature.

6 desire, and covetousness, which is idolatry. For which the
7 wrath of God cometh on the children of disobedience: In
8 which ye also once walked, when ye lived in them. But now
put ye likewise all these things off; anger, wrath, ill-nature,
9 evil-speaking, filthy discourse out of your mouth. Lie not
one to another, seeing ye have put off the old man with his
10 deeds; And have put on the new *man*, which is renewed in
11 knowledge, after the image of him that created him: Where
there is neither Greek nor Jew, circumcision nor uncircumcision, barbarian, Scythian, slave *nor* free: but Christ is all,
12 and in all. Put on therefore as the elect of God, holy and
beloved, bowels of mercies, kindness, humbleness of mind,
13 meekness, longsuffering; Forbearing one another, and forgiving one another, if any have a complaint against any:
14 even as Christ forgave you, so also *do* ye. And above all
15 these *put on* love, which is the bond of perfection: And
the peace of God shall rule in your hearts, to which also ye
16 have been called in one body; and be ye thankful. Let
the word of Christ dwell in you richly in all wisdom; teach-

Verse 6. *For which*—Though the heathens lightly regarded them.

Verse 7. *Living* denotes the inward principle; *walking*, the outward acts.

Verse 8. *Wrath*—Is lasting anger. *Filthy discourse*—And was there need to warn even these saints of God against so gross and palpable a sin as this? O what is man, till perfect love casts out both fear and sin!

Verse 10. *In knowledge*—The knowledge of God, his will, his word.

Verse 11. *Where*—In which case, it matters not what a man is externally, whether *Jew* or gentile, *circumcised*, or *uncircumcised*, *barbarian*, void of all the advantages of education, yea, *Scythian*, of all barbarians most barbarous. *But Christ is in all* that are thus renewed, *and* is *all* things in them and to them.

Verse 12. All who are thus renewed are *elected of God, holy, and* therefore the more *beloved* of him. Holiness is the consequence of their *election*, and God's superior love, of their holiness.

Verse 13. *Forbearing one another*—If anything is now wrong. *And forgiving one another*—What is past.

Verse 14. The *love* of God contains the whole of Christian perfection, and connects all the parts of it together.

Verse 15. *And* then *the peace of God shall rule in your hearts*—Shall sway every temper, affection, thought, as the *reward* (so the Greek word implies) of your preceding love and obedience.

Verse 16. *Let the word of Christ*—So the apostle calls the whole scripture, and thereby asserts the divinity of his Master *Dwell*—Not make a short stay, or an occasional visit, but take up its stated residence.

ing and admonishing one another in psalms and hymns and
spiritual songs, singing with grace in your heart unto the
17 Lord. And whatsoever ye do in word or deed, *do* all in the
name of the Lord Jesus, giving thanks unto God and the
Father through him.
18 * Wives, submit yourselves to your own husbands (as is fit)
19 in the Lord. Husbands, love your wives, and be not bitter
20 against them. Children, obey your parents in all things:
21 for this is wellpleasing to the Lord. Fathers, provoke not
22 your children to anger, lest they be discouraged. Servants,
obey in all things your masters according to the flesh: not
with eyeservice, as menpleasers; but in singleness of heart,
23 fearing God. And whatsoever ye do, do it heartily, as to
24 the Lord, and not to men; Knowing that of the Lord ye
shall receive the reward of the inheritance: for ye serve the
25 Lord Christ. But he that doeth wrong shall receive for the
wrong he hath done: and there is no respect of persons.
IV. 1 Masters, render unto your servants that which is just and
equitable; knowing that ye also have a master in heaven.
2 Continue in prayer, and watch therein with thanksgiving;

* Eph. v. 22, &c.

Richly—In the largest measure, and with the greatest efficacy; so as to fill and govern the whole soul.

Verse 17. *In the name*—In the power and Spirit *of the Lord Jesus Giving thanks unto God*—The Holy Ghost. *And the Father through him*—Christ.

Verse 18. *Wives, submit*—Or be subject *to.* It is properly a military term, alluding to that entire submission that soldiers pay to their general

Verse 19. *Be not bitter*—(Which may be without any appearance of anger) either in word or spirit.

Verse 21. *Lest they be discouraged*—Which may occasion their turning either desperate or stupid

Verse 22. *Eyeservice*—Being more diligent under their eye than at other times. *Singleness of heart*—A simple intention of *doing right,* without looking any farther. *Fearing God*—That is, acting from this principle.

Verse 23. *Heartily*—Cheerfully, diligently. *Menpleasers* are soon dejected and made angry: the *single-hearted* are never displeased or disappointed; because they have another aim, which the good or evil treatment of those they serve cannot disappoint.

Verse 1. *Just*—According to your contract *Equitable*—Even beyond the letter of your contract.

3 Withal praying likewise for us, that God would open to us
a door of utterance, to speak the mystery of Christ, for
4 which I am also in bonds: That I may make it manifest,
5 as I ought to speak. Walk in wisdom toward them that
6 are without, redeeming the time. Let your speech *be*
always with grace, seasoned with salt, that ye may know
how ye ought to answer every one.
7 All my concerns will Tychicus declare to you, a beloved
brother, and a faithful minister and fellowservant in the
8 Lord: Whom I have sent to you for this very thing, that
9 he might know your state, and comfort your hearts; With
Onesimus, a faithful and beloved brother, who is one of you.
They will make known to you all things that *are done* here.
10 Aristarchus my fellowprisoner saluteth you, and Marcus,
sister's son to Barnabas, (touching whom ye have received
11 directions: if he come to you, receive him,) And Jesus,
called Justus, who are of the circumcision. These *are* the
only fellowworkers unto the kingdom of God, who have
12 been a comfort to me. Epaphras, who is one of you, a servant of Christ, saluteth you, always labouring fervently for
you in prayers, that ye may stand perfect and filled with all
13 the will of God. For I bear him witness, that he hath a
great zeal for you, and for them in Laodicea, and for them

Verse 3. *That God would open to us a door of utterance*—That is, give us utterance, that we "may open our mouth boldly," Eph. vi. 19, and give us an opportunity of speaking, so that none may be able to hinder

Verse 6. *Let your speech be always with grace*—*Seasoned* with the grace of God, as flesh is *with salt*.

Verse 10. *Aristarchus my fellowprisoner*—Such was Epaphras likewise for a time, Philemon 23 *Ye have received directions*—Namely, by Tychicus, bringing this letter. The ancients adapted their language to the time of reading the letter; not, as we do, to the time when it was written. It is not improbable, they might have scrupled to *receive him*, without this fresh direction, after he had left St. Paul, and "departed from the work."

Verse 11. *These*—Three, *Aristarchus, Marcus,* and *Justus*. *Of* all *the circumcision*—That is, of all my Jewish fellowlabourers. *Are the only fellowworkers unto the kingdom of God*—That is, in preaching the gospel. *Who have been a comfort to me*—What, then, can *we* expect? that all our fellowworkers should be a comfort to us?

Verse 12. *Perfect*—Endued with every Christian grace. *Filled*—As no longer being babes, but grown up to the measure of the stature of Christ; being full of his light, grace, wisdom, holiness

14 in Hierapolis. Luke, the beloved physician, and Demas,
15 salute you. Salute the brethren at Laodicea, and Nym-
16 phas, and the church in his house. And when this epistle
hath been read among you, cause that it be read also in the
church of the Laodiceans; and that ye likewise read the
17 epistle from Laodicea. And say to Archippus, Take heed
that thou fulfil the ministry which thou hast received in the
18 Lord. The salutation of Paul by my own hand. Be mindful of my bonds. Grace *be* with you.

Verse 14. *Luke, the physician*—Such he had been, at least, if he was not then.

Verse 15. *Nymphas*—Probably an eminent Christian at *Laodicea.*

Verse 16. *The epistle from Laodicea*—Not to Laodicea. Perhaps some letter had been written to St. Paul from thence.

Verse 17. *And say to Archippus*—One of the pastors of that church. *Take heed*—It is the duty of the flock to try them that say they are apostles; to reject the false, and to warn, as well as to receive, the real. *The ministry*—Not a lordship, but a service; a laborious and painful work; an obligation to do and suffer all things; to be the least, and the servant, of all. *In the Lord*—Christ; by whom, and for whose sake, we receive the various gifts of the Holy Spirit.

NOTES

ON

ST. PAUL'S FIRST EPISTLE TO THE THESSALONIANS.

This is the first of all the epistles which St. Paul wrote. Thessalonica was one of the chief cities of Macedonia. Hither St. Paul went after the persecution at Philippi: but he had not preached here long before the unbelieving Jews raised a tumult against him and Silvanus and Timotheus. On this the brethren sent them away to Berea. Thence St. Paul went by sea to Athens, and sent for Silvanus and Timotheus to come speedily to him. But being in fear, lest the Thessalonian converts should be moved from their steadfastness, after a short time he sends Timotheus to them, to know the state of their church. Timotheus returning found the apostle at Corinth; from whence he sent them this epistle, about a year after he had been at Thessalonica.

The parts of it are these:—

I. The inscription,	C. i.	1
II. He celebrates the grace of God towards them,		2—10
Mentions the sincerity of himself and his fellow-labourers,	C. ii.	1—12
And the teachableness of the Thessalonians,		13—16
III. He declares,		
1. His desire,		17—20
2. His care,	C. iii.	1—5
3. His joy and prayer for them,		6—13
IV. He exhorts them to grow,		
1. In holiness,	C. iv.	1—8
2. In brotherly love with industry,		9—12
V. He teaches and exhorts,		
1. Concerning them that sleep,		13—18
2. Concerning the times,	C. v	1—11
VI. He adds miscellaneous exhortations,		12—24
VII. The conclusion,		25—28

I. THESSALONIANS.

CHAPTER I. 1 Paul, and Silvanus, and Timotheus,
to the church of the Thessalonians in God the Father and
the Lord Jesus Christ: Grace *be* unto you, and peace,
from God our Father, and the Lord Jesus Christ.
2 We give thanks to God always for you all, (making men-
3 tion of you in our prayers; Remembering without ceasing
your work of faith, and labour of love, and patience of hope
in our Lord Jesus Christ, in the sight of our God and
4 Father;) Knowing, beloved brethren, your election of God.
5 For our gospel came not to you in word only, but also with
power, and with the Holy Ghost, and with much assurance;
as ye know what manner of men we were among you, for

Verse 1. *Paul*—In this epistle St. Paul neither uses the title of an apostle, nor any other, as writing to pious and simple-hearted men, with the utmost familiarity. There is a peculiar sweetness in this epistle, unmixed with any sharpness or reproof: those evils which the apostles afterward reproved having not yet crept into the church.

Verse 3. *Remembering in the sight of God*—That is, praising him for it. *Your work of faith*—Your active, ever-working faith. *And labour of love*—Love continually labouring for the bodies or souls of men. They who do not thus labour, do not love. *Faith* works, *love* labours, *hope* patiently suffers all things.

Verse 4. *Knowing your election*—Which is through faith, by these plain proofs.

Verse 5. *With power*—Piercing the very heart with a sense of sin; and deeply convincing you of your want of a Saviour from guilt, misery, and eternal ruin. *With the Holy Ghost*—Bearing an outward testimony, by miracles, to the truth of what we preached, and you felt: also by his descent through laying on of hands. *With much assurance*—Literally, with *full assurance,* and *much* of it: the Spirit bearing witness by shedding the love of God abroad in your hearts, which is the highest testimony that can be given. And these signs, if not the miraculous gifts, always attend the preaching of the gospel, unless it be in vain: neither are the extraordinary operations of the Holy Ghost ever wholly withheld, where the gospel is preached with power, and men are alive to God. *For your sake*—Seeking your advantage, not our own

6 your sake. And ye became imitators of us, and of the **Lord**,
having received the word in much affliction, with joy of the
7 Holy Ghost: So that ye became examples to all that
8 believed in Macedonia and Achaia. For from you the word
of the Lord sounded forth not only in Macedonia and
Achaia, but your faith toward God went abroad in every
9 place also; so that we need not speak anything. For they
themselves declare concerning us what manner of entrance
to you we had, and how ye turned from idols to God to serve
10 the living and true God; And to wait for his Son from
heaven, whom he hath raised from the dead, *even* Jesus,
who delivereth us from the wrath to come.

CHAP. II. 1 For yourselves, brethren, know our entrance
2 to you, that it was not in vain: But even after we had
suffered before, and had been shamefully treated at Philippi,
as ye know, we were bold through our God to speak to you
3 the gospel of God with much contention. For our exhorta
4 tion *is* not of deceit, nor of uncleanness, nor in guile: But
as we have been approved of God to be intrusted with the

Verse 6. Though *in much affliction*, yet *with* much *joy*.

Verse 8. *For from you the word sounded forth*—(Thessalonica being a city of great commerce.) Being echoed, as it were, from you. And your conversion was divulged far beyond *Macedonia* and *Achaia*. *So that we need not speak anything*—Concerning it.

Verse 9. *For they themselves*—The people wherever we come

Verse 10. *Whom he hath raised from the dead*—In proof of his future coming to judgment. *Who delivereth us*—He redeemed us once; he delivers us continually; and will deliver all that believe *from the wrath*, the eternal vengeance, which will then *come* upon the ungodly

Verse 1. What was proposed, 1 Thess. i. 5, 6, is now more largely treated of: concerning Paul and his fellowlabourers, verses 1—12; concerning the Thessalonians, verses 13—16.

Verse 2. *We had suffered*—In several places. *We are bold*—Notwithstanding. *With much contention*— Notwithstanding both inward and outward conflicts of all kinds.

Verse 3. *For our exhortation*—That is, our preaching. A part is put for the whole. *Is not*, at any time, *of deceit*—We preach not a lie, but the truth of God. *Nor of uncleanness*—With any unholy or selfish view This expression is not always appropriated to lust, although it is sometimes emphatically applied thereto *Nor in guile*—But with great plainness of speech.

gospel, so we speak; not as pleasing men, but God who
5 trieth our hearts. For neither at any time used we flattering words, as ye know, nor a cloak of covetousness; God is
6 witness: Nor sought we glory of men, neither from you
nor from others, when we might have been burdensome, as
7 the apostles of Christ. But we were gentle in the midst
8 of you, even as a nurse cherisheth her own children; So
loving you tenderly, we were ready to impart to you, not
only the gospel of God, but our own souls also, because ye
9 were dear to us. For ye remember, brethren, our labour
and toil: working night and day, that we might not burden
10 any of you, we preached to you the gospel of God. Ye *are*
witnesses, and God, how holily and justly and unblamably
11 we behaved among you that believe: As ye know how we
exhorted and comforted every one of you, as a father his
12 own children, And charged you to walk worthy of God, who
13 hath called you to his kingdom and glory. For this cause
also thank we God without ceasing, *even* because, when ye
received the word of God which ye heard from us, ye received
it not *as* the word of men, but (as it is in truth) the word
of God, who likewise effectually worketh in you that believe.
14 For ye, brethren, became followers of the churches of God
in Christ Jesus, which are in Judea: for ye also suffered the

Verse 5. *Flattering words*—This *ye know. Nor a cloak of covetousness*—Of this *God is witness.* He calls men to witness an open fact; God, the secret intentions of the heart. In a point of a mixed nature, verse 10, he appeals both to God and man.

Verse 6. *Nor from others*—Who would have honoured us more, if we had *been burdensome*—That is, taken state upon ourselves.

Verse 7. *But we were gentle*—Mild, tender. *In the midst of you*—Like a hen surrounded with her young. *Even as a nurse cherisheth her own children*—The offspring of her own womb.

Verse 8. *To impart our own souls*—To lay down our lives for your sake.

Verse 10. *Holily*—In the things of God. *Justly*—With regard to men. *Unblamable*—In respect of ourselves. *Among you that believe*—Who were e constant observers of our behaviour.

Verse 11. By *exhorting*, we are moved to do a thing willingly; by *comforting*, to do it joyfully; by *charging*, to do it carefully

Verse 12. *To his kingdom* here, *and glory* hereafter.

Verse 14. *Ye suffered the same things*—The same fruit, the same afflictions, and the same experience, at all times, and in all places, are an excellent criterion of evangelical truth. *As they from the Jews*—Their countrymen.

same things from your own countrymen, as they likewise
15 from the Jews: Who both killed the Lord Jesus, and their
own prophets, and have persecuted us; and they please not
16 God, and are contrary to all men: Forbidding us to speak
to the gentiles that they may be saved, to fill up their sins
always: but wrath is come upon them to the uttermost.
17 But we, brethren, being taken from you for a short time,
in presence, not in heart, laboured with great desire the more
18 abundantly to see your face. Wherefore we would have
come to you (even I Paul) once and again; but Satan
19 hindered us. For what is our hope, or joy, or crown of
20 rejoicing? Are not ye also before our Lord Jesus at his
III. 1 appearing? For ye are our glory and joy. Therefore
when we could bear no longer, we thought good to be left
2 at Athens alone; And sent Timotheus, our brother, and
a minister of God, and our fellowworker in the gospel
of Christ, to establish you, and to comfort you concerning
3 your faith; That no one might be moved by these afflic-

Verse 15. *Us*—Apostles and preachers of the gospel. *They please not God*—Nor are they even careful to please him, notwithstanding their fair professions. *And are contrary to all men*—Are common enemies of mankind; not only by their continual seditions and insurrections, and by their utter contempt of all other nations; but in particular, by their endeavouring to hinder their hearing or receiving the gospel.

Verse 16. *To fill up*—The measure of *their sins always*, as they have ever done. *But* the vengeance of God *is come upon them*—Hath overtaken them unawares, whilst they were seeking to destroy others, and will speedily complete their destruction.

Verse 17. In this verse we have a remarkable instance, not so much of the transient affections of holy grief, desire, or joy, as of that abiding tenderness, that loving temper, which is so apparent in all St. Paul's writings, towards those he styles his children in the faith. This is the more carefully to be observed, because the passions occasionally exercising themselves, and flowing like a torrent, in the apostle, are observable to every reader; whereas it requires a nicer attention to discern those calm standing tempers, that fixed posture of his soul, from whence the others only flow out, and which more peculiarly distinguish his character.

Verse 18. *Satan*—By those persecuting Jews, Acts xvii. 13

Verse 19. *Ye also*—As well as our other children.

Verse 1. *We*—Paul and Silvanus. *Could bear no longer*—Our desire and fear for you.

Verse 3. *We are appointed hereto*—Are in every respect laid in a fit posture for it, by the very design and contrivance of God himself for the

tions: for ye yourselves know that we are appointed hereto.
4 For when we were with you, we told you before, we should
5 be afflicted; as it came to pass, and ye know. Therefore
when I could bear no longer, I sent to know your faith, lest
by any means the tempter should have tempted you, and
6 our labour be in vain. But now when Timotheus was come
to us from you, and had brought us the good tidings of your
faith and love, and that ye have a good remembrance of us
7 always, longing to see us, as we also *to see* you: Therefore,
brethren, we were comforted over you in all our affliction
8 and distress by your faith: For now we live, if ye stand
9 fast in the Lord. For what thanks can we render to God
for you, for all the joy wherewith we rejoice for your sake
10 before our God; Night and day praying exceedingly that
we may see your face, and perfect that which is wanting in
11 your faith? Now our God and Father himself, and our
12 Lord Jesus, direct our way unto you. And the Lord make
you to increase and abound in love towards one another,
13 and towards all men, as we also *do* towards you: That he
may establish your hearts unblamable in holiness (before
our God and Father, at the appearing of our Lord Jesus
Christ) with all his saints.

CHAP. IV. 1 It remaineth then, brethren, that we
beseech and exhort you by the Lord Jesus, as ye have
received of us how ye ought to walk and to please God,
2 that ye abound *therein* more and more. For ye know what

trial and increase of our faith and all other graces. He gives riches to the world; but stores up his treasure of wholesome afflictions for his children

Verse 6. *But now when Timotheus was come to us from you*—Immediately after his return, St. Paul wrote; while his joy was fresh, and his tenderness at the height.

Verse 8. *Now we live*—Indeed; we enjoy life: so great is our affection for you.

Verse 10. *And perfect that which is wanting in your faith*—So St. Paul did not know that "they who are once upon the rock no longer need to be taught by man."

Verse 11. *Direct our way*—This prayer is addressed to Christ, as well as to the Father.

Verse 13. *With all his*, Christ's, *saints*—Both angels and men.

Verse 1. *More and more*—It is not enough to have faith, even so as to please God, unless we *abound more and more therein.*

3 commandments we gave you by the Lord Jesus. For this
is the will of God, *even* your sanctification, that ye abstain
4 from fornication: That every one of you know *how* to pos-
5 sess his vessel in sanctification and honour; Not in passion-
6 ate desire, as the gentiles who know not God: That *none*
circumvent or defraud his brother in this matter: because
the Lord is an avenger of all these things, as we have also
7 told you before and testified. For God hath not called us
8 to uncleanness, but to holiness. He therefore that despiseth, despiseth not man, but God, who hath also given you
his Holy Spirit.
9 Touching brotherly love we need not write to you: for ye
10 yourselves are taught of God to love one another. And
indeed ye do it toward all the brethren that are in all Macedonia: but we exhort you, brethren, that ye increase more
11 and more; And that ye study to be quiet, and to do your

Verse 3. *Sanctification*—Entire holiness of heart and life: particular branches of it are subjoined. *That ye abstain from fornication*—A beautiful transition from sanctification to a single branch of the contrary; and this shows that nothing is so seemingly distant, or below our thoughts, but we have need to guard against it.

Verse 4. *That every one know*—For this requires knowledge, as well as chastity. *To possess his vessel*—His wife. *In sanctification and honour*—So as neither to dishonour God or himself, nor to obstruct, but further, holiness; remembering, marriage is not designed to inflame, but to conquer, natural desires.

Verse 5. *Not in passionate desire*—Which had no place in man when in a state of innocence. *Who know not God*—And so may naturally seek happiness in a creature. What seemingly accidental words slide in; and yet how fine, and how vastly important!

Verse 6. *In this matter*—By violating his bed. The things forbidden here are three: *fornication*, verse 3; the passion of *desire*, or inordinate affection in the married state, verse 5; and the breach of the marriage contract.

Verse 8. *He that despiseth*—The commandments we gave. *Despiseth God*—Himself. *Who hath also given you his Holy Spirit*—To convince you of the truth, and enable you to be holy. What naked majesty of words! How oratorical, and yet with what great simplicity!—a simplicity that does not impair, but improve, the understanding to the utmost; that, like the rays of heat through a glass, collects all the powers of reason into one orderly point, from being scattered abroad in utter confusion.

Verse 9. *We need not write*—Largely. *For ye are taught of God*—By his Spirit

Verse 11. *That ye study*—Literally, *that ye be ambitious:* an ambition

own business, and to work with your hands, as we com-
12 manded you; That ye may walk decently toward them that
are without, and may want nothing.
13 Now we would not have you ignorant, brethren, concerning them that are asleep, that ye sorrow not, even as others
14 who have no hope. For if we believe that Jesus died and
rose again, so will God bring with him those also that sleep
15 in Jesus. For this we say unto you by the word of the
Lord, that we who are alive who are left to the appearing
16 of the Lord shall not prevent them that are asleep. For
the Lord himself shall descend from heaven with a shout,
with the voice of an archangel, and with the trumpet
17 of God: and the dead in Christ shall rise first: Then we
who are alive who are left shall be caught up together with
them in clouds, to meet the Lord in the air: and so shall
18 we be ever with the Lord. Wherefore comfort one another
with these words.

worthy a Christian. *To work with your hands*—Not a needless caution; for temporal concerns are often a cross to them who are newly filled with the love of God.

Verse 12. *Decently*—That they may have no pretence to say, (but they will say it still,) "This religion makes men idle, and brings them to beggary" *And may want nothing*—Needful for life and godliness. What Christian desires more?

Verse 13. *Now*—Herein the efficacy of Christianity greatly appears,—that it neither takes away nor embitters, but sweetly tempers, that most refined of all affections, our desire of or love to the dead.

Verse 14. *So*—As God raised him. *With him*—With their living head.

Verse 15. *By the word of the Lord*—By a particular revelation. *We who are left*—This intimates the fewness of those who will be then alive, compared to the multitude of the dead. Believers of all ages and nations make up, as it were, one body; in consideration of which, the believers of that age might put themselves in the place, and speak in the person, of them who were to live till the coming of the Lord. Not that St. Paul hereby asserted (though some seem to have imagined so) that the day of the Lord was at hand.

Verse 16. *With a shout*—Properly, a proclamation made to a great multitude. Above this is, *the voice of the archangel;* above both, *the trumpet of God;* the voice of God, somewhat analogous to the sound of a trumpet.

Verse 17. *Together*—In the same moment. *In the air*—The wicked will remain beneath, while the righteous, being absolved, shall be assessors with their Lord in the judgment *With the Lord*—In heaven.

CHAPTER V.

CHAP. V. 1 But of the times and seasons, brethren, ye
2 have no need that I write to you. For ye yourselves know
perfectly that the day of the Lord so cometh as a thief in
3 the night. When they say, Peace and safety; then sudden
destruction cometh upon them, as travail upon a woman
4 with child; and they shall not escape. But ye, brethren,
are not in darkness, that that day should overtake you as a
5 thief. Ye are all children of the light, and children of the
day: we are not *children* of the night, nor of darkness
6 Therefore let us not sleep, as the others; but let us awake,
7 and keep awake. For they that sleep sleep in the night;
8 and they that are drunken are drunken in the night. But
let us, who are of the day, keep awake, having put on the
breastplate of faith and love; and for an helmet, the hope
9 of salvation. For God hath not appointed us to wrath, but
10 to obtain salvation by our Lord Jesus Christ. Who died
for us, that, whether we wake or sleep, we may live together
11 with him. Wherefore comfort one another, and edify one
another, as also ye do.

12 Now we beseech you, brethren, to know them that labour
among you, and are over you in the Lord, and admonish

Verse 1. *But of the* precise *times* when this shall be.

Verse 2 *For* this in general *ye* do *know;* and ye can and need know no more.

Verse 3. *When they*—The men of the world *say.*

Verse 4. *Ye are not in darkness*—Sleeping secure in sin.

Verse 6. *Awake, and keep awake*—Being awakened, let us have all our spiritual senses about us.

Verse 7. *They* usually *sleep and are drunken in the night*—These things do not love the light

Verse 9. *God hath not appointed us to wrath*—As he hath the obstinately impenitent

Verse 10. *Whether we wake or sleep*—Be alive or dead at his coming.

Verse 12. *Know them that,* 1. *Labour among you:* 2. *Are over you in the Lord:* 3. *Admonish you. Know*—See, mark, take knowledge of them and their work. Sometimes the same person may both *labour,* that is, preach; *be over,* or govern; and *admonish* the flock by particular application to each: sometimes two or more different persons, according as God variously dispenses his gifts. But O, what a misery is it when a man undertakes this whole work without either gifts or graces for any part of it! Why, then, will he undertake it? for pay? What! will he sell both his own soul and all the souls of the flock? What words can describe such a wretch as this? And yet even this may be "an honourable man!"

13 you; And to esteem them very highly in love for their
14 work's sake. *And* be at peace among yourselves. And we
exhort you, brethren, warn the disorderly, comfort the feeble-
minded, support the weak, be longsuffering toward all men.
15 See that none render to any man evil for evil; but ever follow that which is good, both to one another and to all men.
16, 17 Rejoice evermore: Pray without ceasing: In everything
18 give thanks; for this is the will of God in Christ Jesus con-
19, 20 cerning you. Quench not the Spirit. Despise not pro-

Verse 13. *Esteem them very highly*—Literally, *more than abundantly, in love*—The inexpressible sympathy that is between true pastors and their flock is intimated, not only here, but also in divers other places of this epistle. See 1 Thess. ii. 7, 8. *For their work's sake*—The principal ground of their vast regard for them. But how are we to esteem them who do not work at all?

Verse 14. *Warn the disorderly*—Them that stand, as it were, out of their rank in the spiritual warfare. Some such were even in that church. *The feeble-minded*—Literally, *them of little soul;* such as have no spiritual courage.

Verse 15. *See that none*—Watch over both yourselves and each other *Follow that which is good*—Do it resolutely and perseveringly.

Verse 16. *Rejoice evermore*—In uninterrupted happiness in God. *Pray without ceasing*—Which is the fruit of *always rejoicing* in the Lord. *In everything give thanks*—Which is the fruit of both the former. This is Christian perfection. Farther than this we cannot go; and we need not stop short of it. Our Lord has purchased joy, as well as righteousness, for us. It is the very design of the gospel that, being saved from guilt, we should be happy in the love of Christ. Prayer may be said to be the breath of our spiritual life. He that lives cannot possibly cease breathing. So much as we really enjoy of the presence of God, so much prayer and praise do we offer up *without ceasing;* else our rejoicing is but delusion. Thanksgiving is inseparable from true prayer: it is almost essentially connected with it. He that always prays is ever giving praise, whether in ease or pain, both for prosperity and for the greatest adversity. He blesses God for all things, looks on them as coming from him, and receives them only for his sake; not choosing nor refusing, liking nor disliking, anything, but only as it is agreeable or disagreeable to his perfect will.

Verse 18. *For this*—That you should thus rejoice, pray, give thanks. *Is the will of God*—Always good, always pointing at our salvation.

Verse 19. *Quench not the Spirit*—Wherever it is, it burns; it flames in holy love, in joy, prayer, thanksgiving. O quench it not, damp it not in yourself or others, either by neglecting to do good, or by doing evil!

Verse 20. *Despise not prophesyings*—That is, preaching; for the apostle is not here speaking of extraordinary gifts. It seems, one means of

21 phesyings. Prove all things; hold fast that which is good.
22, 23 Abstain from all appearance of evil. And the God of peace
himself sanctify you wholly; and may the whole of you, the
spirit and the soul and the body, be preserved blameless
24 unto the appearing of our Lord Jesus Christ. Faithful is
25 he that calleth you, who also will do *it*. Brethren, pray for
26, 27 us. Salute all the brethren with an holy kiss. I adjure
you by the Lord, that this epistle be read to all the holy
28 brethren. The grace of our Lord Jesus Christ *be* with you.
Amen.

grace is put for all; and whoever despises any of these, under whatever pretence, will surely (though perhaps gradually and almost insensibly) *quench the Spirit*.

Verse 21. Meantime, *prove all things*—Which any preacher recommends. (He speaks of practice, not of doctrines.) Try every advice by the touchstone of scripture, and *hold fast that which is good*—Zealously, resolutely, diligently practise it, in spite of all opposition.

Verse 22. And be equally zealous and careful to *abstain from all appearance of evil*—Observe, those who "heap to themselves teachers, having itching ears," under pretence of proving all things, have no countenance or excuse from this scripture.

Verse 23. *And may the God of peace sanctify you*—By the peace ne works in you, which is a great means of sanctification. *Wholly*—The word signifies *wholly and perfectly;* every part and all that concerns you; all that is of or about you. *And may the whole of you, the spirit and the soul and the body*—Just before he said *you;* now he denominates them from their spiritual state. *The spirit*—Gal. vi. 8; wishing that it may be preserved *whole and entire:* then from their natural state, *the soul and the body;* (for these two make up the whole nature of man, Matt. x. 28;) wishing it *may be preserved blameless till the coming of Christ.* To explain this a little further: of the three here mentioned, only the two last are the natural constituent parts of man. The first is adventitious, and the supernatural gift of God, to be found in Christians only. That man cannot possibly consist of three parts, appears hence: The soul is either matter or not matter: there is no medium. But if it is matter, it is part of the body: if not matter, it coincides with the spirit.

Verse 24. *Who also will do it*—Unless you quench the Spirit.

Verse 27. *I charge you by the Lord*—Christ, to whom proper divine worship is here paid. *That this epistle*—The first he wrote. *Be read to all the brethren*—That is, in all the churches. They might have concealed it out of modesty, had not this been so solemnly enjoined: but what Paul commands under so strong an adjuration, Rome forbids under pain of excommunication.

NOTES

ON

ST. PAUL'S SECOND EPISTLE TO THE THESSALONIANS.

This epistle seems to have been written soon after the former, chiefly on occasion of some things therein which had been misunderstood. Herein he, 1. Congratulates their constancy in the faith, and exhorts them to advance daily in grace and wisdom. 2. Reforms their mistake concerning the coming of our Lord. And, 3. Recommends several Christian duties.

The parts of it are five :—

I. The inscription,	C. i.	1, 2
II. Thanksgiving and prayer for them,		3—12
III. The doctrine concerning the man of sin,	C. ii.	1—12
Whence he comforts them against this trial,		13, 14
Adding exhortation and prayer,		15—17
IV. An exhortation to prayer, with a prayer for them,	C. iii.	1— 5
to correct the disorderly,		6—16
V The conclusion,		17, 18

II. THESSALONIANS.

CHAPTER I. 1 Paul, and Silvanus, and Timotheus,
to the church of the Thessalonians in God our Father and
2 the Lord Jesus Christ: Grace *be* unto you, and peace, from
God our Father and from our Lord Jesus Christ.
3 We are bound to thank God always for you, brethren, as
it is meet, because your faith groweth exceedingly, and the
4 love of every one of you toward each other aboundeth; So

Verse 3. It is highly observable, that the apostle wraps up his praise of men in praise to God; giving him the glory. *Your faith groweth*—Probably he had heard from them since his sending the former letter. *Aboundeth*—Like water that overflows its banks, and yet increaseth still.

Verse 4. *Which ye endure*—"That ye may be accounted worthy of the kingdom"

that we ourselves glory of you in the churches of God for
your patience and faith in all your persecutions and suffer-
5 ings which ye endure: A manifest token of the righteous
judgment of God, that ye may be accounted worthy of the
6 kingdom of God, for which also ye suffer: Seeing *it is* a
righteous thing with God to recompense affliction to them
7 that afflict you; And to you that are afflicted rest with us,
at the revelation of the Lord Jesus from heaven with his
8 mighty angels, In flaming fire taking vengeance on them
who know not God, and who obey not the gospel of our
9 Lord Jesus. Who shall be punished with everlasting
destruction from the presence of the Lord, and from the
10 glory of his power, When he shall come to be glorified in
his saints, and to be admired in all that believe (for our tes-
11 timony was believed among you) in that day. To this end
we pray always for you, that our God would make you worthy of *this* calling, and fulfil *in you* all the good pleasure

Verse 5. *A manifest token*—This is treated of in the sixth and following verses.

Verse 6. *It is a righteous thing with God*—(However men may judge) to transfer the pressure from you to them. And it is remarkable tha about this time, at the passover, the Jews raising a tumult, a great number (some say thirty thousand) of them were slain. St. Paul seems to allude to this beginning of sorrows, 1 Thess. ii. 16, which did not end but with their destruction.

Verse 8. *Taking vengeance*—Does God barely permit this, or (as "the Lord" once "rained brimstone and fire from the Lord out of heaven," Gen. xix. 24) does a fiery stream go forth from him for ever? *Who know not God*—(The root of all wickedness and misery) who remain in heathen ignorance. *And who obey not*—This refers chiefly to the Jews, who had heard *the gospel.*

Verse 9. *From the glory of his power*—Tremble, ye stout-hearted *Everlasting destruction*—As there can be no end of their sins, (the same enmity against God continuing,) so neither of their punishment; sin and its punishment running parallel throughout eternity itself. They must of necessity, therefore, be cut off from all good, and all possibility of it. *From the presence of the Lord*—Wherein chiefly consists the salvation of the righteous. What unspeakable punishment is implied even in falling short of this, supposing that nothing more were implied in his *taking vengeance!*

Verse 10. *To be glorified in his saints*—For the wonderful glory of Christ shall shine in them.

Verse 11. *All the good pleasure of his goodness*—Which is no less than perfect holiness.

12 of *his* goodness, and the work of faith with power: That
the name of our Lord Jesus may be glorified in you, and
ye in him, according to the grace of our God and the Lord
Jesus Christ.

CHAP. II. 1 Now I beseech you, brethren, concerning
the appearing of our Lord Jesus Christ, and our gathering
2 together unto him, That ye be not soon shaken in mind, or
terrified, neither by spirit, nor by word, nor by letter as from
3 us, as if the day of the Lord were at hand. Let no man
deceive you by any means, for *that day shall not come*,
unless the falling away come first, and the man of sin be
4 revealed, the son of perdition; Who opposeth and exalteth
himself above all that is called God, or that is worshipped;
so that he sitteth in the temple of God as God, declaring
5 himself that he is God. Remember ye not, that I told you
6 these things, when I was yet with you? And now ye know

Verse 12. *That the name*—The love and power *of our Lord may be glorified*—Gloriously displayed in you.

Verse 1. *Our gathering together to him*—In the clouds.

Verse 2. *Be not shaken in mind*—In judgment *Or terrified*—As those easily are who are immoderately fond of knowing future things. *Neither by* any pretended revelation from the *Spirit, nor by* pretence of any *word* spoken by me.

Verse 3. *Unless the falling away*—From the pure faith of the gospel, *come first.* This began even in the apostolic age But *the man of sin, the son of perdition*—Eminently so called, is not come yet. However, in many respects, the Pope has an indisputable claim to those titles. He is, in an emphatical sense, *the man of sin,* as he increases all manner of sin above measure. And he is, too, properly styled, *the son of perdition,* as he has caused the death of numberless multitudes, both of his opposers and followers, destroyed innumerable souls, and will himself perish everlastingly. He it is that *opposeth* himself to the emperor, once his rightful sovereign; and that *exalteth himself above all that is called God, or that is worshipped*—Commanding angels, and putting kings under his feet, both of whom are *called gods* in scripture; claiming the highest power, the highest honour; suffering himself, not once only, to be styled God or vice-god. Indeed no less is implied in his ordinary title, "Most Holy Lord," or, "Most Holy Father." *So that he sitteth*—Enthroned. *In the temple of God*—Mentioned Rev. xi. 1. *Declaring himself that he is God*—Claiming the prerogatives which belong to God alone.

Verse 6. *And now ye know*—By what I told you when I was with you *That which restraineth*—The power of the Roman emperors When

that which restraineth that he may be revealed in his time.
7 For the mystery of iniquity already worketh: only he that
restraineth *will restrain*, till he be taken out of the way.
8 And then will that wicked one be revealed, whom the Lord
will consume with the Spirit of his mouth, and destroy with
9 the brightness of his appearing: Whose appearing is after
the mighty working of Satan with all power and signs and
10 lying wonders, And with all deceivableness of unrighteousness in them that perish; because they received not the love
11 of the truth, that they might be saved. And therefore God
shall send them strong delusion, so that they shall believe the
12 lie: That they all may be condemned who believed not the
13 truth, but had pleasure in unrighteousness. But we ought
to give thanks to God always for you, brethren beloved

this is *taken away, the wicked one will be revealed* *In his time*—His appointed season, and not before

Verse 7. He will surely be revealed; *for the mystery*—The deep, secret power *of iniquity*, just opposite to the power of godliness, already worketh. It began with the love of honour, and the desire of power; and is completed in the entire subversion of the gospel of Christ. This *mystery of iniquity* is not wholly confined to the Romish church, but extends itself to others also. It seems to consist of, 1. Human inventions added to the written word. 2. Mere outside performances put in the room of faith and love. 3. Other mediators besides the man Christ Jesus. The two last branches, together with idolatry and bloodshed, are the direct consequences of the former; namely, the adding to the word of God. *Already worketh*—In the church. *Only he that restraineth*—That is, the potentate who successively has Rome in his power. The emperors, heathen or Christian; the kings, Goths or Lombards; the Carolingian or German emperors.

Verse 8. *And then*—When every prince and power that restrains is taken away. *Will that wicked one*—Emphatically so called, *be revealed. Whom the Lord will* soon *consume with the spirit of his mouth*—His immediate power. *And destroy*—With the very first appearance of his glory.

Verse 10. *Because they received not the love of the truth*—Therefore God suffered them to fall into that "strong delusion."

Verse 11. *Therefore God shall send them*—That is, judicially permit to come upon them, *strong delusion.*

Verse 12. *That they all may be condemned*—That is, the consequence of which will be, that they *all* will *be condemned who believed not the truth, but had pleasure in unrighteousness*—That is, who believed not the truth, because they loved sin.

Verse 13. *God hath from the beginning*—Of your hearing the gospel. *Chosen you to salvation*—Taken you out of the world, and placed you in the way to glory.

of the Lord, because God hath from the beginning chosen
you to salvation through sanctification of the Spirit and
14 belief of the truth. To which he hath called you by our
gospel, to the obtaining of the glory of our Lord Jesus
15 Christ. Therefore, brethren, stand fast and hold the traditions which ye have been taught, whether by word, or by our
16 epistle. Now our Lord Jesus Christ himself, and God, even
our Father, who hath loved us, and given us everlasting
17 consolation and good hope through grace, Comfort your
hearts, and stablish you in every good word and work.

CHAP. III. 1 Finally, brethren, pray for us, that the
word of the Lord may run and be glorified, even as among
2 you: And that we may be delivered from unreasonable and
3 wicked men: for all men have not faith. But the Lord is
faithful, who will stablish, and guard you from the evil one.
4 And we trust in the Lord concerning you, that ye both do
5 and will do the things which we command you. And the
Lord direct your hearts into the love of God, and into the
patience of Christ.
6 Now we command you, brethren, in the name of our Lord
Jesus Christ, to withdraw yourselves from every brother

Verse 14 *To which*—Faith and holiness. *He hath called you by our gospel*—That which we preached, accompanied with the power of his Spirit.

Verse 15. *Hold*—Without adding to, or diminishing from, *the traditions which ye have been taught*—The truths which I have delivered to you. *Whether by word or by our epistle*—He preached before he wrote. And he had written concerning this in his former epistle.

Verse 1. *May run*—Go on swiftly, without any interruption. *And be glorified*—Acknowledged as divine, and bring forth much fruit.

Verse 2. *All men have not faith*—And all men who have not are more or less *unreasonable and wicked men*.

Verse 3. *Who will stablish you*—That cleave to him by faith. *And guard you from the evil one*—And all his instruments.

Verse 4. *We trust in the Lord concerning you*—Thus only should we trust in any man.

Verse 5. *Now the Lord*—The Spirit, whose proper work this is. *Direct*—Lead you straight forward. *Into the patience of Christ*—Of which he set you a pattern.

Verse 6. *That walketh disorderly*—Particularly by not working. *Not according to the tradition he received of us*—The admonition we gave, both by word of mouth, and in our former epistle.

that walketh disorderly, and not according to the tradition
7 which he received of us. For yourselves know how ye ought
to imitate us: we behaved not disorderly among you;
8 Neither did we eat any man's bread for nothing; but wrought
with labour and toil night and day, that we might not bur-
9 den any of you: Not because we have not authority, but
that we might make ourselves an example to you that ye
10 might imitate us. For when we were with you, this we
commanded you, If any will not work, neither let him eat.
11 For we hear there are some among you who walk disorderly,
12 doing nothing, but being busybodies. Now such we command and exhort by our Lord Jesus Christ, to work quietly,
13 and eat their own bread. But ye, brethren, be not weary in
14 well doing. And if any man obey not our word by this
epistle, note that man, and have no company with him, that
15 he may be ashamed. Yet count *him* not as an enemy, but
16 admonish *him* as a brother Now the Lord of peace himself give you peace always by all means. The Lord *be* with
you all.
17 The salutation of Paul with my own hand, which is the
18 token in every epistle: so I write. The grace of our Lord
Jesus Christ *be* with you all. Amen.

Verse 10. *Neither let him eat*—Do not maintain him in idleness.

Verse 11. *Doing nothing, but being busybodies*—To which idleness naturally disposes.

Verse 12. *Work quietly*—Letting the concerns of other people alone.

Verse 14. *Have no company with him*—No intimacy, no familiarity, no needless correspondence.

Verse 15. *Admonish him as a brother*—Tell him lovingly of the reason why you shun him.

Verse 16. *The Lord of peace*—Christ. *Give you peace by all means*—In every way and manner.

NOTES

ON

ST. PAUL'S FIRST EPISTLE TO TIMOTHY.

The mother of Timothy was a Jewess, but his father was a gentile He was converted to Christianity very early; and while he was yet but a youth, was taken by St. Paul to assist him in the work of the gospel, chiefly in watering the churches which he had planted.

He was therefore properly, as was Titus, an itinerant evangelist, a kind of secondary apostle, whose office was, to regulate all things in the churches to which he was sent; and to inspect and reform whatsoever was amiss either in the bishops, deacons, or people.

St. Paul had doubtless largely instructed him in private conversation for the due execution of so weighty an office. Yet to fix things more upon his mind, and to give him an opportunity of having recourse to them afterward, and of communicating them to others, as there might be occasion, as also to leave divine directions in writing, for the use of the church and its ministers in all ages; he sent him this excellent pastoral letter, which contains a great variety of important sentiments for their regulation.

Though St. Paul styles him his "own son in the faith," yet he does not appear to have been converted by the apostle; but only to have been exceeding dear to him, who had established him therein; and whom he had diligently and faithfully served, like a son with his father in the gospel. Phil. ii. 22.

The epistle contains three parts:—

I. The inscription, C. i. 1, 2.

II. The instruction of Timothy how to behave at Ephesus, wherein,

1. In general, he gives him an injunction to deliver to them that taught the law in a wrong manner, and confirms at the same time the sum of the gospel as exemplified in himself, 3—20

2. In particular,

1. He prescribes to men, a method of prayer, C. ii. 1— 8

To women, good works and modesty, 9—15

2. He recounts the requisites of a bishop, C. iii. 1— 7

CHAPTER I

	The duties of deacons,	8—10
	of women,	11—13
3	He shows what Timothy should teach	14—C. iv 1— 6
	What he should avoid,	7—11
	What follow after,	12—16
	How he should treat men and women,	C. v. 1, 2
	Widows,	3—16
	Elders,	17—19
	Offenders,	20, 21
	Himself,	22, 23
	Those he doubts of,	24, 25
	Servants,	C. vi. 1, 2
4	False teachers are reproved,	3—10
	Timothy is admonished,	
	quickened,	11, 12
	and charged,	13—16
	Precepts are prescribed to be enforced on the rich,	17—19
III.	The conclusion,	20, 21

I. TIMOTHY.

CHAPTER I. 1 Paul, an apostle of Jesus Christ
according to the commandment of God our Saviour, and
2 Christ Jesus, our hope ; To Timotheus, my own son in the
faith. Grace, mercy, peace, from God our Father and
Christ Jesus our Lord.
3 As I exhorted thee when I was going into Macedonia,
abide at Ephesus, that thou mayest charge some to teach no
4 other doctrine, Neither to give heed to fables and endless

Verse 1. *Paul an apostle*—Familiarity is to be set aside where the things of God are concerned. *According to the commandment of God*—The authoritative appointment of God the Father. *Our Saviour*—So styled in many other places likewise, as being the grand orderer of the whole scheme of our salvation. *And Christ our hope*—That is, the author, object, and ground, of all our hope.

Verse 2. *Grace, mercy, peace*—St. Paul wishes *grace* and *peace* in his epistles to the churches. To Timotheus he adds *mercy*, the most tender grace towards those who stand in need of it. The experience of this prepares a man to be a minister of the gospel.

Verse 3. *Charge some to teach no other doctrine*—Than I have taught. Let them put nothing in the place of it, add nothing to it.

Verse 4. *Neither give heed*—So as either to teach or regard them. *To fables*—Fabulous Jewish traditions. *And endless genealogies*—Not

genealogies, that afford questions, and not godly edifying,
5 which is through faith. Whereas the end of the commandment is love out of a pure heart, and a good conscience, and
6 faith unfeigned: From which some having missed the mark,
7 are turned aside to vain jangling; Desiring to be teachers
of the law; understanding neither the things they say, nor
those concerning which they confidently affirm. We know
9 the law *is* good, if a man use it lawfully; Knowing this,
that the law doth not lie against a righteous man, but against
the lawless and disobedient, against the ungodly and sinners,
the unholy and profane, against killers of their fathers or
10 their mothers, against murderers, Against whoremongers,
sodomites, manstealers, liars, perjured persons, and if there
be any other thing that is contrary to wholesome doctrine;

those delivered in scripture, but the long intricate pedigrees whereby they strove to prove their descent from such or such a person. *Which afford questions*—Which lead only to useless and endless controversies.

Verse 5. *Whereas the end of the commandment*—Of the whole Christian institution. *Is love*—And this was particularly the end of the commandment which Timotheus was to enforce at Ephesus, verses 3, 18. The foundation is faith; the end, love. But this can only subsist in *an heart purified* by faith, and is always attended with a *good conscience.*

Verse 6. *From which*—Love and a good conscience. *Some are turned aside*—An affectation of high and extensive knowledge sets a man at the greatest distance from faith, and all sense of divine things. *To vain jangling*—And of all vanities, none are more vain than dry, empty disputes on the things of God.

Verse 7. *Understanding neither the* very *things they speak,* nor the subject they speak of.

Verse 8. *We* grant *the* whole Mosaic *law is good,* answers excellent purposes, *if a man use it* in a proper manner. Even the ceremonial is good, as it points to Christ; and the moral law *is holy, just, and good,* in its own nature; and of admirable use both to convince unbelievers, and to guide believers in all holiness.

Verse 9. *The law doth not lie against a righteous man*—Doth not strike or condemn him. *But against the lawless and disobedient*—They who despise the authority of the lawgiver violate the first commandment, which is the foundation of the law, and the ground of all obedience. *Against the ungodly and sinners*—Who break the second commandment, worshipping idols, or not worshipping the true God. *The unholy and profane*—Who break the third commandment by taking his name in vain.

Verse 10. *Manstealers*—The worst of all thieves, in comparison of whom, highwaymen and housebreakers are innocent. What then are most traders in negroes, procurers of servants for America, and all who list soldiers by lies, tricks, or enticements?

11 According to the glorious gospel of the blessed God, with
12 which I am intrusted. And I thank Christ Jesus our Lord,
who hath enabled me, in that he accounted me faithful,
13 having put me into the ministry; Who was before a blasphemer, and a persecutor, and an oppressor: but I obtained
14 mercy, because I did *it* ignorantly in unbelief. And the
grace of our Lord was exceeding abundant with faith and
15 love which is in Christ Jesus. This is a faithful saying, and
worthy of all acceptation, that Christ Jesus came into the
16 world to save sinners; of whom I am chief. Yet for this
cause I obtained mercy, that on me the chief, Jesus Christ
might show all longsuffering, for a pattern to them who
17 should hereafter believe in him to life everlasting. Now to
the King of eternity, immortal, invisible, the only God, *be*
honour and glory for ever and ever. Amen.
18 This charge I commit to thee, son Timotheus, according

Verse 11. *According to the glorious gospel*—Which, far from "making void," does effectually "establish, the law."

Verse 12. *I thank Christ, who hath enabled me, in that he accounted me faithful, having put me into the ministry*—The meaning is, I thank him for putting me into the ministry, and enabling me to be faithful therein.

Verse 13. *A blasphemer*—Of Christ. *A persecutor*—Of his church. *A reviler*—Of his doctrine and people. *But I obtained mercy*—He does not say, because I was unconditionally elected; but *because I did it in ignorance.* Not that his ignorance took away his sin; but it left him capable of mercy; which he would hardly have been, had he acted thus contrary to his own conviction.

Verse 14. *And the grace*—Whereby I obtained mercy. *Was exceeding abundant with faith*—Opposite to my preceding *unbelief. And love*—Opposite to my *blasphemy, persecution,* and *oppression.*

Verse 15. *This is a faithful saying*—A most solemn preface. *And worthy of all acceptation*—Well deserving to be accepted, received, embraced, with all the faculties of our whole soul. *That Christ*—Promised. *Jesus*—Exhibited. *Came into the world to save sinners*—All sinners, without exception.

Verse 16. *For this cause* God showed me *mercy,* that *all* his *longsuffering* might be shown, and that none might hereafter despair.

Verse 17. *The King of eternity*—A phrase frequent with the Hebrews. How unspeakably sweet is the thought of eternity to believers!

Verse 18. *This charge I commit to thee*—That thou mayest deliver it to the church. *According to the prophecies concerning thee*—Uttered when thou wast received as an evangelist, 1 Tim. iv. 14; probably by many persons, 1 Tim. vi. 12; *that,* being encouraged *by them, thou mightest war the good warfare.*

to the prophecies which went before concerning thee, that
19 thou mightest by them war the good warfare; Holding fast
faith and a good conscience; which some having thrust away
20 have made shipwreck of their faith: Of whom are Hymeneus and Alexander; whom I have delivered to Satan, that
they may learn not to blaspheme.

CHAP. II. 1 I exhort therefore, that, first of all, supplications, prayers, intercessions, thanksgivings, be made for
2 all men; For kings, and all that are in authority; that we
may lead a quiet and peaceable life in all godliness and
3 honesty. For this *is* good and acceptable in the sight

Verse 19. *Holding fast faith*—Which is as a most precious liquor *And a good conscience*—Which is as a clean glass *Which*—Namely, a good conscience. *Some having thrust away*—It goes away unwillingly it always says, "Do not hurt me." And they who retain this do not *make shipwreck of their faith*. Indeed, none can make shipwreck of faith who never had it. These, therefore, were once true believers: yet they fell not only foully, but finally; for ships once wrecked cannot be afterwards saved.

Verse 20. *Whom*—Though absent. *I have delivered to Satan, that they may learn not to blaspheme*—That by what they suffer they may be in some measure restrained, if they will not repent.

Verse 1. *I exhort therefore*—Seeing God is so gracious In this chapter he gives directions, 1. With regard to public prayers: 2. With regard to doctrine. *Supplication* is here the imploring help in time of need: *prayer* is any kind of offering up our desires to God. But true prayer is the vehemency of holy zeal, the ardour of divine love, arising from a calm, undisturbed soul, moved upon by the Spirit of God. *Intercession* is prayer for others. We may likewise *give thanks for all men*, in the full sense of the word, for that God "willeth all men to be saved," and Christ is the Mediator of all.

Verse 2. *For all that are in authority*—Seeing even the lowest country magistrates frequently do much good or much harm. God supports the power of magistracy for the sake of his own people, when, in the present state of men, it could not otherwise be kept up in any nation whatever. *Godliness*—Inward religion; the true worship of God. *Honesty*—A comprehensive word taking in the whole duty we owe to our neighbour.

Verse 3. *For this*—That we pray for all men. Do you ask, "Why are not more converted?" We do not pray enough. *Is acceptable in the sight of God our Saviour*—Who has actually saved us that believe, and *willeth all men to be saved*. It is strange that any whom he has actually saved should doubt the universality of his grace!

4 of God our Saviour; Who willeth all men to be saved, and
5 to come to the knowledge of the truth. For *there is* one
God, one mediator also between God and men, the man
6 Christ Jesus; Who gave himself a ransom for all, to be
7 testified of in due season. Whereunto I am ordained a
preacher, and an apostle, (I speak the truth, I lie not,) a
8 teacher of the gentiles in faith and truth. I will therefore
that men pray in every place, lifting up holy hands, without
9 wrath and doubting. Likewise, that women adorn themselves in decent apparel, with modesty and sobriety; not

Verse 4. *Who willeth* seriously *all men*—Not a part only, much less the smallest part. *To be saved*—Eternally. This is treated of, verses 5, 6. *And,* in order thereto, *to come*—They are not compelled. *To the knowledge of the truth*—Which brings salvation. This is treated of, verses 6, 7.

Verse 5. *For*—The fourth verse is proved by the fifth; the first, by the fourth. *There is one God*—And they who have not him, through the one Mediator, have no God. *One mediator also*—We could not rejoice that there is a God, were there not a mediator also; one who stands between God and men, to reconcile man to God, and to transact the whole affair of our salvation. This excludes all other mediators, as saints and angels, whom the Papists set up and idolatrously worship as such: just as the heathens of old set up many mediators, to pacify their superior gods. *The man*—Therefore all men are to apply to this mediator, "who gave himself for all."

Verse 6. *Who gave himself a ransom for all*—Such a ransom, the word signifies, wherein a like or equal is given; as an eye for an eye, or life for life: and this ransom, from the dignity of the person redeeming, was more than equivalent to all mankind. *To be testified of in due season*—Literally, *in his own seasons;* those chosen by his own wisdom.

Verse 8. *I will*—A word strongly expressing his apostolical authority. *Therefore*—This particle connects the eighth with the first verse. *That men pray in every place*—Public and private. Wherever men are, there prayer should be. *Lifting up holy hands*—Pure from all known sin. *Without wrath*—In any kind, against any creature. And every temper or motion of our soul that is not according to love is *wrath. And doubting*—Which is contrary to faith. And wrath, or unholy actions, or want of faith in him we call upon, are the three grand hinderances of God's hearing our petitions. Christianity consists of faith and love, embracing truth and grace: therefore the sum of our wishes should be, to pray, and live, and die, without any wrath or doubt.

Verse 9. *With sobriety*—Which, in St. Paul's sense, is the virtue which governs our whole life according to true wisdom. *Not with curled hair, not with gold*—Worn by way of ornament. *Not with pearls*—Jewels of any kind: a part is put for the whole. *Not with costly raiment*—These ur are expressly forbidden by name to all *women* (here is no excep-

10 with curled hair, or gold, or pearls, or costly raiment; But
(which becometh women professing godliness) with good
11 works. Let a woman learn in silence with all subjection.
12 For I suffer not a woman to teach, nor to usurp authority
13 over the man, but to be in silence. For Adam was first
14 formed, then Eve. And Adam was not deceived, but the
15 woman being deceived transgressed. Yet she shall be saved
in childbearing, if they continue in faith and love and holiness with sobriety.

CHAP. III. 1 This *is* a faithful saying, If a man desire
2 the office of a bishop, he desireth a good work. A bishop
therefore must be blameless, the husband of one wife, vigilant, prudent, of good behaviour, hospitable, apt to teach;
3 Not given to wine, no striker, not desirous of filthy gain;

tion) *professing godliness*, and no art of man can reconcile with the Christian profession the wilful violation of an express command.

Verse 12. *To usurp authority over the man*—By public teaching.

Verse 13. *First*—So that woman was originally the inferior.

Verse 14. *And Adam was not deceived*—The serpent deceived Eve: Eve did not deceive Adam, but persuaded him. "Thou hast hearkened unto the voice of thy wife," Gen. iii. 17. The preceding verse showed why a woman should not "usurp authority over the man." this shows why she ought not "to teach." She is more easily deceived, and more easily deceives *The woman being deceived transgressed*—"The serpent deceived" her, Gen. iii. 13, and she transgressed.

Verse 15. *Yet she*—That is, women in general, who were all involved with Eve in the sentence pronounced, Gen. iii. 16. *Shall be saved in childbearing*—Carried safe through the pain and danger which that sentence entails upon them for the transgression; yea, and finally saved, *if they continue in* loving *faith* and holy wisdom.

Verse 1. *He desireth a good work*—An excellent, but laborious, employment.

Verse 2. *Therefore*—That he may be capable of it. *A bishop*—Or pastor of a congregation. *Must be blameless*—Without fault or just suspicion. *The husband of one wife*—This neither means that a bishop *must* be married, nor that he *may not* marry a second wife; which it is just as lawful for him to do as to marry a first, and may in some cases be his bounden duty. But whereas polygamy and divorce on slight occasions were common both among the Jews and heathens, it teaches us that ministers, of all others, ought to stand clear of those sins. *Vigilant, prudent*—Lively and zealous, yet calm and wise. *Of good behaviour*—Naturally flowing from that vigilance and prudence.

4 but gentle, patient, not loving money, Ruling his own
house well, having his children in subjection with all seri-
5 ousness; (For if a man know not how to rule his own
6 house, how shall he take care of the church of God?) Not
a new convert, lest being puffed up he fall into the condem-
7 nation of the devil He ought also to have a good report
from them that are without; lest he fall into reproach and
8 the snare of the devil. Likewise the deacons *must be*
serious, not doubletongued, not given to much wine, not
9 desirous of filthy gain; Holding fast the mystery of the
10 faith in a pure conscience. And let these be proved first;
11 then let them minister, being blameless. In like manner
their wives *must be* serious, not slanderers, vigilant, faithful
12 in all things. Let the deacons be husbands of one wife,
13 ruling their children and their own houses well. For they
that have discharged the office of a deacon well purchase
to themselves a good degree, and much boldness in the faith
14 which is in Christ Jesus. These things I write to thee,

Verse 4. *Having his children in subjection with all seriousness*—For levity undermines all domestic authority; and this direction, by a parity of reason, belongs to all parents.

Verse 6. *Lest being puffed up*—With this new honour, or with the applause which frequently follows it. *He fall into the condemnation of the devil*—The same into which the devil fell.

Verse 7. *He ought also to have a good report*—To have had a fair character in time past *From them that are without*—That are not Christians *Lest he fall into reproach*—By their rehearsing his former life, which might discourage and prove a snare to him.

Verse 8. *Likewise the deacons must be serious*—Men of a grave, decent, venerable behaviour. But where are presbyters? Were this order essentially distinct from that of bishops, could the apostle have passed it over in silence? *Not desirous of filthy gain*—With what abhorrence does he everywhere speak of this! All that is gained (above food and raiment) by ministering in holy things is *filthy gain* indeed; far more filthy than what is honestly gained by raking kennels, or emptying common sewers.

Verse 9. *Holding fast the faith in a pure conscience*—Steadfast in faith, holy in heart and life.

Verse 10. *Let these be proved first*—Let a trial be made how they behave. *Then let them minister*—Let them be fixed in that office.

Verse 11. *Faithful in all things*—Both to God, their husbands, and the poor.

Verse. 13. *They purchase a good degree*—Or step, toward some higher office. *And much boldness*—From the testimony of a good conscience.

15 hoping to come to thee shortly: But if I tarry, that thou
mayest know how thou oughtest to behave in the house of
God, which is the church of the living God.
16 The mystery of godliness is the pillar and ground of the
truth, and without controversy a great thing: God was
manifested in the flesh, was justified by the Spirit, seen by
angels, preached among the gentiles, believed on in the
IV. 1 world, taken up into glory. But the Spirit saith expressly,
that in the latter times some will depart from the faith, giving
2 heed to seducing spirits, and doctrines of devils; By the
hypocrisy of them that speak lies, having their own con-
3 sciences seared as with an hot iron; Forbidding to marry,
and *commanding* to abstain from meats which God hath

Verse 15. *That thou mayest know how to behave*—This is the scope of the epistle. *In the house of God*—Who is the master of the family. *Which is*—As if he had said, By the house of God, I mean *the church.*

Verse 16. *The mystery of godliness*—Afterwards specified in six articles, which sum up the whole economy of Christ upon earth. *Is the pillar and ground*—The foundation and support *of* all *the truth* taught in his church. *God was manifest in the flesh*—In the form of a servant, the fashion of a man, for three and thirty years. *Justified by the Spirit*—Publicly "declared to be the Son of God," by his resurrection from the dead. *Seen*—Chiefly after his resurrection. *By angels*—Both good and bad. *Preached among the gentiles*—This elegantly follows. The angels were the least, the gentiles the farthest, removed from him; and the foundation both of this preaching and of their faith was laid before his assumption. *Was believed on in the world*—Opposed to heaven, into which he was *taken up*. The first point is, *He was manifested in the flesh;* the last, *He was taken up into glory.*

Verse 1. *But the Spirit saith*—By St. Paul himself to the Thessalonians, and probably by other contemporary prophets. *Expressly*—As concerning a thing of great moment, and soon to be fulfilled. *That in the latter times*—These extend from our Lord's ascension till his coming to judgment. *Some*—Yea, many, and by degrees the far greater part. *Will depart from the faith*—The doctrine once delivered to the saints. *Giving heed to seducing spirits*—Who inspire false prophets

Verse 2. These *will depart from the faith, by the hypocrisy of them that speak lies, having their own consciences* as senseless and unfeeling as flesh that is *seared with an hot iron.*

Verse 3. *Forbidding* priests, monks, and nuns *to marry, and commanding* all men *to abstain from* such and such *meats* at such and such times. *Which God hath created to be received by them that know the truth*—That all meats are now clean *With thanksgiving*—Which supposes a pure conscience.

created to be received with thanksgiving by them that
4 believe and know the truth. For every creature of God
is good, and nothing to be rejected, being received with
5 thanksgiving: For it is sanctified by the word of God and
6 prayer: If thou remind the brethren of these things, thou
wilt be a good minister of Jesus Christ, nourishing *them*
with the words of faith and of the good doctrine, which thou
7 hast accurately traced out. But avoid profane and old
8 wives' fables, and exercise thyself unto godliness. For
bodily exercise profiteth a little: but godliness is profitable for
all things, having the promise of the present life, and of that
9 which is to come. This *is* a faithful saying, and worthy of
10 all acceptation. For therefore we both labour and suffer
reproach, because we trust in the living God, who is the
11 Saviour of all men, especially of them that believe. These
12 things command and teach. Let no one despise thy youth:
but be a pattern to them that believe, in word, in behaviour,
13 in love, in spirit, in faith, in purity. Till I come, give
14 thyself to reading, to exhortation, to teaching. Neglect

Verse 5. *It is sanctified by the word of God*—Creating all, and giving it to man for food. *And by prayer*—The children of God are to pray for the sanctification of all the creatures which they use. And not only the Christians, but even the Jews, yea, the very heathens used to consecrate their table by prayer.

Verse 7. Like those who were to contend in the Grecian games, *exercise thyself unto godliness*—Train thyself up in holiness of heart and life, with the utmost labour, vigour, and diligence.

Verse 8. *Bodily exercise profiteth a little*—Increases the health and strength of the body.

Verse 10. *Therefore*—Animated by this promise. *We both labour and suffer reproach*—We regard neither pleasure, ease, nor honour. *Because we trust*—For this very thing the world will hate us. *In the living God*—Who will give us the life he has promised. *Who is the Saviour of all men*—Preserving them in this life, and willing to save them eternally *But especially*—In a more eminent manner *Of them that believe*—And so are saved everlastingly.

Verse 12. *Let no one* have reason to *despise* thee for *thy youth.* To prevent this, *Be a pattern in word*—Public and private. *In spirit*—In your whole temper. *In faith*—When this is placed in the midst of several other Christian graces, it generally means a particular branch of it; fidelity or faithfulness.

Verse 13. *Give thyself to reading*—Both publicly and privately. Enthusiasts, observe this! Expect no end without the means.

Verse 14. *Neglect not*—They neglect it who do not exercise it to the full.

not the gift that is in thee, which was given thee by
prophecy, with the laying on of the hands of the pres-
15 bytery. Meditate on these things; be wholly in them;
16 that thy profiting may appear in all things. Take heed
to thyself and to *thy* teaching: continue in them, for in
so doing thou shalt save both thyself and them that hear
thee.

CHAP. V. 1 Rebuke not an aged man, but exhort *him*
2 as a father; the younger men as brethren; The aged
women as mothers, the younger as sisters, with all purity.
3 Honour widows that are widows indeed. But if any
4 widow have children or grandchildren, let these learn first to
show piety at home, and to requite their parents: for this is
5 good and acceptable before God. Now she that is a widow
indeed, and desolate, trusteth in God, and continueth in
6 supplications and prayers night and day. But she that
7 liveth in pleasure is dead while she liveth. And enjoin

The gift—Of feeding the flock, of power, and love, and sobriety. *Which was given thee by prophecy*—By immediate direction from God. *By the laying on of my hands*—2 Tim i. 6; while the elders joined also in the solemnity. This *presbytery* probably consisted of some others, together with Paul and Silas.

Verse 15. *Meditate*—The Bible makes no distinction between this and to contemplate, whatever others do. True meditation is no other than faith, hope, love, joy, melted down together, as it were, by the fire of God's Holy Spirit; and offered up to God in secret. He that is *wholly in these,* will be little in worldly company, in other studies, in collecting books, medals, or butterflies: wherein many pastors drone away so considerable a part of their lives.

Verse 16. *Continue in them*—In all the preceding advices.

Verse 1. *Rebuke not*—Considering your own youth, with such a severity as would otherwise be proper.

Verse 3. *Honour*—That is, maintain out of the public stock.

Verse 4. *Let these learn to requite their parents*—For all their former care, trouble, and expense.

Verse 5. *Widows indeed*—Who have no near relations to provide for them; and who are wholly devoted to God. *Desolate*—Having neither children, nor grandchildren to relieve her.

Verse 6. *She that liveth in pleasure*—Delicately, voluptuously, in elegant, regular sensuality, though not in the use of any such pleasures as are unlawful in themselves.

Verse 7. *That they*—That is, the widows.

8 these things, that they may be blameless. But if any provide not for his own, and especially for those of his own
family, he hath denied the faith, and is worse than an infidel.
9 Let not a widow be chosen under threescore years old,
10 having been the wife of one husband, Well reported of for
good works; if she hath brought up children, if she hath
lodged strangers, if she hath washed the feet of the saints, if
she hath relieved the afflicted, if she hath diligently followed
11 every good work. But the younger widows refuse; for
when they are waxed wanton against Christ, they want to
12 marry; Having condemnation, because they have rejected
13 their first faith. And withal they learn *to be* idle, going
about from house to house; and not only idle, but triflers
14 and busybodies, speaking what they ought not. I counsel

Verse 8. *If any provide not*—Food and raiment *For his own*—Mother and grandmother, being desolate widows. *He hath*—Virtually. *Denied the faith*—Which does not destroy, but perfect, natural duties. What has this to do with heaping up money for our children, for which it is often so impertinently alleged? But all men have their reasons for laying up money. One will go to hell for fear of want; another acts like a heathen, lest he should be *worse than an infidel.*

Verse 9. *Let not a widow be chosen*—Into the number of deaconesses, who attended sick women or travelling preachers. *Under threescore*—Afterwards they were admitted at forty, if they were eminent for holiness *Having been the wife of one husband*—That is, having lived in lawful marriage, whether with one or more persons successively.

Verse 10. *If she hath washed the feet of the saints*—Has been ready to do the meanest offices for them.

Verse 11. *Refuse*—Do not choose. *For when they are waxed wanton against Christ*—To whose more immediate service they had addicted themselves. *They want to marry*—And not with a single eye to the glory of God; and so withdraw themselves from that entire service of the church to which they were before engaged.

Verse 12. *They have rejected their first faith*—Have deserted their trust in God, and have acted contrary to the first conviction, namely, that wholly to devote themselves to his service was the most excellent way. When we first receive power to believe, does not the Spirit of God generally point out what are the most excellent things; and at the same time, give us an holy resolution to walk in the highest degree of Christian severity? And how unwise are we ever to sink into anything below it!

Verse 14. *I counsel therefore the younger women*—Widows or virgins, such as are not disposed to live single. *To marry, to bear children, to guide the family*—Then will they have sufficient employment of their own. *And give no occasion of reproach to the adversary*—Whether Jew or heathen.

therefore the younger women to marry, bear children, guide
the family, give no occasion of reproach to the adversary.
15 For some are already turned aside after Satan. If any
16 believing man or woman hath widows, let them relieve them,
and let not the church be burdened; that it may relieve
them that are widows indeed.
17 Let the elders who rule well be counted worthy of double
honour, especially those who labour in the word and teach-
18 ing. For the scripture saith, * Thou shalt not muzzle the
ox that treadeth out the corn. And, The labourer *is* wor-
19 thy of his reward. Against an elder receive not an accusa-
20 tion, unless by two or three witnesses. Those that sin
21 rebuke before all, that the rest also may fear. I charge
thee before God, and the Lord Jesus Christ, and the elect
angels, that thou observe these things without prejudging,
22 doing nothing by partiality. Lay hands suddenly on no

* Deut xxv. 4

Verse 15 *Some*—Widows. *Have turned aside after Satan*—Who has drawn them from Christ.

Verse 17. *Let the elders that rule well*—Who approve themselves faithful stewards of all that is committed to their charge. *Be counted worthy of double honour*—A more abundant provision, seeing that such will employ it all to the glory of God As it was the most laborious and disinterested men who were put into these offices, so whatever any one had to bestow, in his life or death, was generally lodged in their hands for the poor. By this means the churchmen became very rich in after ages; but as the design of the donors was something else, there is the highest reason why it should be disposed of according to their pious intent. *Especially those*—Of them. *Who labour*—Diligently and painfully. *In the word and teaching*—In teaching the word.

Verse 19. *Against an elder*—Or presbyter. Do not even *receive an accusation, unless by two or three witnesses*—By the Mosaic law, a private person might be cited (though not condemned) on the testimony of one witness; but St. Paul forbids an elder to be even cited on such evidence, his reputation being of more importance than that of others.

Verse 20. *Those*—Elders. *That sin*—Scandalously, and are duly convicted. *Rebuke before all*—The church.

Verse 21. *I charge thee before God*—Referring to the last judgment, in which we shall stand *before God and Christ,* with his *elect,* that is, holy, *angels,* who are the witnesses of our conversation. The apostle looks through his own labours, and even through time itself, and seems to stand as one already in eternity. *That thou observe these things without prejudging*—Passing no sentence till the cause is fully heard. Or *partiality*—For or against any one.

Verse 22. *Lay hands suddenly on no man*—That is, appoint no man to

man, neither partake of other men's sins: keep thyself pure.
23 Drink water no longer, but use a little wine for thy sto-
24 mach's sake and thy frequent infirmities. Some men's sins
are manifest beforehand, going before to judgment; and
25 some they follow after. In like manner the good works
also *of some* are manifest; and they that are otherwise cannot be hid.

CHAP. VI. 1 Let as many servants as are under the
yoke account their own masters worthy of all honour, lest
2 the name of God and *his* doctrine be blasphemed. And
they that have believing masters, let them not despise *them*,
because they are brethren; but rather do *them* service,
because they are faithful and beloved, partakers of the bene-
3 fit. These things teach and exhort. If any teach other-

church offices without full trial and examination; else thou wilt be accessary to, and accountable for, his misbehaviour in his office. *Keep thyself pure*—From the blood of all men.

Verse 24. *Some men's sins are manifest beforehand*—Before any strict inquiry be made. *Going before to judgment*—So that you may immediately judge them unworthy of any spiritual office. *And some they*—Their sins. *Follow after*—More covertly.

Verse 25. *They that are otherwise*—Not so manifest. *Cannot be* long *hid*—From thy knowledge. On this account, also, be not hasty in laying on of hands.

Verse 1. *Let servants under the yoke*—Of heathen masters. *Account* them *worthy of all honour*—All the honour due from a servant to a master. *Lest the name of God and his doctrine be blasphemed*—As it surely will, if they do otherwise.

Verse 2. *Let them not despise them*—Pay them the less honour or obedience. *Because they are brethren*—And in that respect on a level with them. They that live in a religious community know the danger of this; and that greater grace is requisite to bear with the faults of a brother, than of an infidel, or man of the world. *But rather do them service*—Serve them so much the more diligently. *Because they are* joint *partakers of the* great *benefit*—Salvation. *These things*—Paul, the aged, gives young Timotheus a charge to dwell upon practical holiness. Less experienced teachers are apt to neglect the superstructure, whilst they lay the foundation; but of so great importance did St. Paul see it to enforce obedience to Christ, as well as to preach faith in his blood, that, after strongly urging the life of faith on professors, he even adds another charge for the strict observance of it.

Verse 3. *If any teach otherwise*—Than strict practical holiness in all its branches. *And consent not to sound words*—Literally, *healthful words;*

wise, and consent not to sound words, those of our Lord
Jesus Christ, and to the doctrine which is after godliness;
4 He is puffed up, knowing nothing, but being sick of questions and strifes of words, whereof cometh envy, contention,
5 evil speakings, evil surmisings, Perverse disputings of men
of corrupt minds, and destitute of the truth, supposing that
6 gain is godliness. from such withdraw thyself. But godli-
7 ness with content is great gain. For we brought nothing
into the world: *it is* manifest that neither can we carry
8 anything out. Having then food and covering, with these
9 let us be content. But they that desire to be rich fall into
temptation and a snare, and *into* many foolish and hurtful
desires, which plunge men into destruction and perdition.

words that have no taint of falsehood, or tendency to encourage sin. *And the doctrine which is after godliness*—Exquisitely contrived to answer all the ends, and secure every interest, of real piety.

Verse 4. *He is puffed up*—Which is the cause of his not consenting to the doctrine which is after inward, practical religion. By this mark we may know them. *Knowing nothing*—As he ought to know. *Sick of questions*—Doatingly fond of dispute; an evil, but common, disease; especially where practice is forgotten. Such, indeed, contend earnestly for singular phrases, and favourite points of their own. Everything else, however, like the preaching of Christ and his apostles, is all "law," and "bondage," and "carnal reasoning." *Strifes of words*—Merely verbal controversies. *Whereof cometh envy*—Of the gifts and success of others. *Contention*—For the pre-eminence. Such disputants seldom like the prosperity of others, or to be less esteemed themselves. *Evil surmisings*—It not being their way to think well of those that differ from themselves in opinion.

Verse 5. *Supposing that gain is godliness*—Thinking the best religion is the getting of money: a far more common case than is usually supposed.

Verse 6. *But godliness with content*—The inseparable companion of true, vital religion. *Is great gain*—Brings unspeakable profit in time, as well as eternity.

Verse 7. *Neither can we carry anything out*—To what purpose, then, do we heap together so many things? O, give me one thing,—a safe and ready passage to my own country!

Verse 8. *Covering*—That is, raiment and an house to cover us. This is all that a Christian needs, and all that his religion allows him to desire.

Verse 9. *They that desire to be rich*—To have more than these; for then they would be so far rich; and the very desire banishes content, and exposes them to ruin. *Fall—plunge*—A sad gradation! *Into temptation*—Miserable food for the soul! *And a snare*—Or trap. Dreadful

10 **For the love of money is the root of all evils: which some
coveting have erred from the faith, and pierced themselves
11 through with many sorrows. But thou, O man of God, flee
these things; and follow after righteousness, godliness, faith,
12 love, patience, meekness. Fight the good fight of faith, lay
hold on eternal life, to which thou hast been called, and
hast confessed the good confession before many witnesses.
13 I charge thee before God, who quickeneth all things, and
Christ Jesus, who witnessed the good confession before
14 Pontius Pilate, That thou keep the commandment without
spot, unrebukable, until the appearing of our Lord Jesus
15 Christ: Which in his own times the blessed and only Poten-**

"covering!" *And into many foolish and hurtful desires*—Which are sown and fed by having more than we need. Then farewell all hope of content! What then remains, but *destruction* for the body, and *perdition* for the soul?

Verse 10. *Love of money*—Commonly called "prudent care" of what a man has. *Is the root*—The parent *of all* manner of *evils. Which some coveting have erred*—Literally, *missed the mark.* They aimed not at *faith,* but at something else. *And pierced themselves with many sorrows*—From a guilty conscience, tormenting passions, desires contrary to reason, religion, and one another. How cruel are worldly men to themselves!

Verse 11. *But thou, O man of God*—Whatever all the world else do A *man of God* is either a prophet, a messenger of God, or a man devoted to God; a man of another world. *Flee*—As from a serpent, instead of coveting *these things. Follow after righteousness*—The whole image of God; though sometimes this word is used, not in the general, but in the particular, acceptation, meaning only that single branch of it which is termed *justice. Faith*—Which is also taken here in the general and full sense; namely, a divine, supernatural sight of God, chiefly in respect of his mercy in Christ. This *faith* is the foundation of *righteousness,* the support of *godliness,* the root of every grace of the Spirit. *Love*—This St. Paul intermixes with everything that is good: he, as it were, penetrates whatever he treats of with *love,* the glorious spring of all inward and outward holiness.

Verse 12. *Fight the good fight of faith*—Not about words. *Lay hold on eternal life*—Just before thee. *Thou hast confessed the good confession*—Perhaps at his baptism: so likewise, verse 13; but with a remarkable variation of the expression. *Thou hast confessed the good confession before many witnesses*—To which they all assented. He *witnessed the good confession;* but Pilate did not assent to it.

Verse 13. *I charge thee before God, who quickeneth all things*—Who hath quickened thee, and will quicken thee at the great day.

Verse 15. *Which*—Appearing. *In his own times*—The power, the knowledge, and the revelation of which, remain in his eternal mind.

16 tate will show, the King of kings, and Lord of lords; Who
only hath immortality, dwelling in light unapproachable;
whom no man hath seen, neither can see: to whom *be*
honour and power everlasting. Amen.
17 Charge the rich in this world, not to be highminded,
neither to trust in uncertain riches, but in the living God,
18 who giveth us richly all things to enjoy; To do good, to be
rich in good works, ready to distribute, willing to communi-
19 cate; Treasuring up for themselves a good foundation
against the time to come, that they may lay hold on eternal
life.
20 O Timotheus, keep that which is committed to thy trust,
avoiding profane empty babblings, and oppositions of know-
21 ledge falsely so called: Which some professing have erred
from the faith. Grace *be* with thee.

Verse 16. *Who only hath* underived, independent *immortality. Dwelling in light unapproachable*—To the highest angel. *Whom no man hath seen, or can see*—With bodily eyes. Yet "we *shall* see him as he is."

Verse 17. What follows seems to be a kind of a postscript. *Charge the rich in this world*—Rich in such beggarly riches as *this world* affords. *Not to be highminded*—O who regards this! Not to think better of themselves for their money, or anything it can purchase. *Neither to trust in uncertain riches*—Which they may lose in an hour; either for happiness or defence. *But in the living God*—All the rest is dead clay. *Who giveth us*—As it were holding them out to us in his hand. *All things*—Which we have. *Richly*—Freely, abundantly. *To enjoy*—As his gift, in him and for him. When we use them thus, we do indeed *enjoy* all things Where else is there any notice taken of the *rich*, in all the apostolic writings, save to denounce woes and vengeance upon them?

Verse 18. *To do good*—To make this their daily employ, that they may *be rich*—May abound *in* all *good works. Ready to distribute*—Singly to particular persons. *Willing to communicate*—To join in all public works of charity.

Verse 19. *Treasuring up for themselves a good foundation*—Of an abundant reward, by the free mercy of God. *That they may lay hold on eternal life*—This cannot be done by alms-deeds; yet they "come up for a memorial before God," Acts x. 4. And the lack even of this may be the cause why God will withhold grace and salvation from us.

Verse 20. *Keep that which is committed to thy trust*—The charge I have given thee, 1 Tim. i. 18. *Avoid profane empty babblings*—How weary of controversy was this acute disputant! *And knowledge falsely so called*—Most of the ancient heretics were great pretenders to knowledge.

NOTES

ON

ST. PAUL'S SECOND EPISTLE TO TIMOTHY.

This epistle was probably wrote by St. Paul, during his second confinement at Rome, not long before his martyrdom. It is, as it were, the swan's dying song. But though it was wrote many years after the former, yet they are both of the same kind, and nearly resemble each other.

It has three parts :—

I. The inscription,	C. i. 1, 2
II. An invitation, "Come to me," variously expressed,	
1. Having declared his love to Timothy,	3— 5
He exhorts him, "Be not ashamed of me,"	6—14
And subjoins various examples,	15—18
2. He adds the twofold proposition,	
1. "Be strong,"	
2. "Commit the ministry" to faithful men,	C. ii. 1, 2
The former is treated of,	3—13
The latter,	14
With farther directions concerning his own behaviour,	15—C. iv. 8
3. "Come quickly." Here St. Paul,	9
1. Mentions his being left alone,	10—12
2. Directs to bring his books,	13
3. Gives a caution concerning Alexander,	14, 15
4. Observes the inconstancy of men, and the faithfulness of God,	16—18
4. "Come before winter." Salutations,	19—21
III. The concluding blessing,	22

II. TIMOTHY.

CHAPTER I. 1 Paul, an apostle of Jesus Christ by
the will of God, according to the promise of life which is by
2 Christ Jesus, To Timotheus, my beloved son: Grace,
mercy, peace, from God the Father and Christ Jesus our
Lord.
3 I thank God, whom I serve from *my* forefathers with a
pure conscience, that I have remembrance of thee in my
4 prayers without ceasing night and day; Longing to see
thee, being mindful of thy tears, that I may be filled with
5 joy; Remembering the unfeigned faith that is in thee,
which dwelt first in thy grandmother Lois, and thy mother
6 Eunice; I am persuaded in thee also. Wherefore I remind
thee of stirring up the gift of God, which is in thee by the
7 laying on of my hands. For God hath not given us the spirit
8 of fear, but of power, and love, and sobriety. Therefore be

Verse 3. *Whom I serve from my forefathers*—That is, whom both I and my ancestors served. *With a pure conscience*—He always worshipped God according to his conscience, both before and after his conversion One who stands on the verge of life is much refreshed by the remembrance of his predecessors, to whom he is going.

Verse 4. *Being mindful of thy tears*—Perhaps frequently shed, as well as at the apostle's last parting with him.

Verse 5. *Which dwelt*—A word not applied to a transient guest, but only to a settled inhabitant. *First*—Probably this was before Timothy was born, yet not beyond St. Paul's memory.

Verse 6. *Wherefore*—Because I remember this. *I remind thee of stirring up*—Literally, blowing up the coals into a flame. *The gift of God*—All the spiritual gifts, which the grace of God has given thee.

Verse 7. And let nothing discourage thee, *for God hath not given us*—That is, the spirit which God hath given us Christians, is *not the spirit of fear*—Or cowardice. *But of power*—Banishing fear. *And love and sobriety*—These animate us in our duties to God, our brethren, and our selves. *Power* and *sobriety* are two good extremes. *Love* is between, the tie and temperament of both; preventing the two bad extremes of fearfulness and rashness. More is said concerning power, verse 8; concerning love, 2 Tim. ii. 14, &c.; concerning sobriety, 2 Tim. iii. 1, &c.

Verse 8. *Therefore be not thou ashamed*—When fear is banished, evil

not thou ashamed of the testimony of our Lord, nor of me
his prisoner: but be thou partaker of the afflictions of the
9 gospel according to the power of God; Who hath saved
and called us with an holy calling, not according to our
works, but according to his own purpose and grace, which
10 was given us in Christ Jesus before the world began; But
is now made manifest by the appearing of our Saviour Jesus
Christ, who hath abolished death, and hath brought life and
11 immortality to light through the gospel: Whereunto I am
appointed a preacher, and an apostle, and a teacher of the
12 gentiles. For which cause also I suffer these things: yet I
am not ashamed; for I know whom I have trusted, and am
persuaded that he is able to keep that which I have com-
13 mitted to him until that day. Hold fast the pattern of sound
words, which thou hast heard from me, in faith and love
14 which is in Christ Jesus. The good thing which is committed to thee keep through the Holy Spirit who dwelleth
15 in us. This thou knowest, that all who are in Asia are
turned away from me; of whom are Phygellus and Hermo-

shame also flees away. *Of the testimony of our Lord*—The gospel, and of testifying the truth of it to all men. *Nor of me*—The cause of the servants of God doing his work, cannot be separated from the cause of God himself. *But be thou partaker of the afflictions*—Which I endure for the gospel's sake. *According to the power of God*—This which overcomes all things is nervously described in the two next verses.

Verse 9. *Who hath saved us*—By faith. The love of the Father, the grace of our Saviour, and the whole economy of salvation, are here admirably described. *Having called us with an holy calling*—Which is all from God, and claims us all for God. *According to his own purpose and grace*—That is, his own gracious purpose. *Which was given us*—Fixed for our advantage, *before the world began.*

Verse 10. *By the appearing of our Saviour*—This implies his whole abode upon earth. *Who hath abolished death*—Taken away its sting, and turned it into a blessing. *And hath brought life and immortality to light*—Hath clearly revealed by *the gospel* that immortal life which he hath purchased for us.

Verse 12. *That which I have committed to him*—My soul. *Until that day*—Of his final appearing.

Verse 13. *The pattern of sound words*—The model of pure, wholesome doctrine.

Verse 14. *The good thing*—This wholesome doctrine.

Verse 15. *All who are in Asia*—Who had attended me at Rome for a while. *Are turned away from me*—What, from Paul the aged, the faithful soldier, and now prisoner of Christ! This was a glorious trial, and

16 genes. The Lord give mercy to the family of Onesiphorus;
for he hath often refreshed me, and hath not been ashamed
17 of my chain: But, when he was at Rome, he sought me
18 out very diligently, and found *me*. The Lord grant him to
find mercy from the Lord in that day: and in how many
things he served me at Ephesus, thou knowest very well.

CHAP. II. 1 Thou therefore, my son, be strong through
2 the grace which is by Christ Jesus. And the things which
thou hast heard from me before many witnesses, these commit to faithful men, who will be able to teach others also.
3 Thou therefore endure affliction, as a good soldier of Jesus
4 Christ. No man that warreth entangleth himself in the
affairs of *this* life; that he may please him who hath enlisted
5 *him*. And if a man strive, he is not crowned, unless he strive
6 lawfully. The husbandman that laboureth first must be
7 partaker of the fruits. Consider what I say; and the Lord
8 give thee understanding in all things. Remember Jesus
Christ of the seed of David raised from the dead according
9 to my gospel; For which I endure affliction, even unto
bonds, as an evildoer; but the word of God is not bound.
10 Therefore I suffer all things for the elect's sake, that they

wisely reserved for that time, when he was on the borders of immortality. Perhaps a little measure of the same spirit might remain with him under whose picture are those affecting words, "The true effigy of Francis Xavier, apostle of the Indies, forsaken of all men, dying in a cottage."

Verse 16. *The family of Onesiphorus*—As well as himself *Hath often refreshed me*—Both at Ephesus and Rome.

Verse 2. *The things*—The wholesome doctrine, 2 Timothy i. 13. *Commit*—Before thou leavest Ephesus. *To faithful men, who will be able,* after thou art gone, *to teach others*.

Verse 4. *No man that warreth entangleth himself*—Any more than is unavoidable. *In the affairs of this life*—With worldly business or cares. *That*—Minding war only, *he may please* his captain. In this and the next verse there is a plain allusion to the Roman law of arms, and to that of the Grecian games. According to the former, no soldier was to engage in any civil employment; according to the latter, none could be crowned as conqueror, who did not keep strictly to the rules of the game.

Verse 6. Unless he *labour first*, he will reap no fruit.

Verse 8. *Of the seed of David*—This one genealogy attend to.

Verse 9. *Is not bound*—Not hindered in its course.

Verse 10. *Therefore*—Encouraged by this, that "the word of God is not bound." *I endure all things*—See the spirit of a real Christian!

also may obtain the salvation which is through Christ Jesus
11 with eternal glory. *It is* a faithful saying: If we are dead
12 with *him*, we shall also live with *him:* If we suffer, we shall
also reign with *him:* if we deny *him*, he will also deny us:
13 If we believe not, he remaineth faithful: he cannot deny
himself.
14 Remind *them* of these things, charging *them* before the
Lord not to strive about words to no profit, *but* to the sub-
15 verting of the hearers. Be diligent to present thyself unto
God approved, a workman that needeth not to be ashamed,
16 rightly dividing the word of truth. But avoid profane empty
17 babblings: for they will increase to more ungodliness. And
their word will eat as a gangrene: of whom are Hymeneus
18 and Philetus; Who have erred concerning the truth, saying the resurrection is already past, and overthrow the faith
19 of some. But the foundation of God standeth firm, having
this seal, The Lord knoweth those that are his. And, Let

Who would not wish to be likeminded? *Salvation* is deliverance from all evil; *glory*, the enjoyment of all good.

Verse 11. *Dead with him*—Dead to sin, and ready to die for him.

Verse 12. *If we deny him*—To escape suffering for him.

Verse 13. *If we believe not*—That is, though some believe not, God will make good all his promises to them that do believe. *He cannot deny himself*—His word cannot fail.

Verse 14. *Remind them*—Who are under thy charge. O how many unnecessary things are thus unprofitably, nay hurtfully, contended for.

Verse 15. *A workman that needeth not to be ashamed*—Either of unfaithfulness or unskilfulness. *Rightly dividing the word of truth*—Duly explaining and applying the whole scripture, so as to give each hearer his due portion. But they that give one part of the gospel to all (the promises and comforts to unawakened, hardened, scoffing men) have real need to be ashamed.

Verse 16. *They*—Who babble thus will grow worse and worse.

Verse 17. *And their word*—If they go on, will be mischievous as well as vain, and *will eat as a gangrene.*

Verse 18. *Saying the resurrection is already past*—Perhaps asserting that it is only the spiritual passing from death unto life.

Verse 19. *But the foundation of God*—His truth and faithfulness. *Standeth fast*—Can never be overthrown; being as it were sealed with a seal, which has an inscription on each side: on the one, *The Lord knoweth those that are his;* on the other, *Let every one who nameth the name of the Lord*, as his Lord, *depart from iniquity.* Indeed, they only are his who depart from iniquity. To all others he will say, "I know you not." Matt. vii. 22, 23

every one who nameth the name of the Lord depart from
20 iniquity. But in a great house there are not only vessels
of gold and silver, but also of wood and of earth; and some
21 to honour, some to dishonour. If a man therefore purge
himself from these, he shall be a vessel unto honour, consecrated, and fit for the master's use, prepared for every good
22 work. Flee also youthful desires: but follow after righteousness, faith, love, peace, with them that call upon the
23 Lord, out of a pure heart. But avoid foolish and unlearned
24 questions, knowing that they beget strifes. And a servant
of the Lord must not strive; but be gentle toward all men,
25 apt to teach, patient of evil, In meekness instructing those
that oppose themselves; if haply God may give them
26 repentance to the acknowledging of the truth; And they
may awake out of the snare of the devil, who are taken captive by him at his will.

CHAP. III. 1 But know this, that in the last days
2 grievous times will come. For men will be lovers of them-

Verse 20. *But in a great house*—Such as the church, it is not strange that *there are not only vessels of gold and silver,* designed for honourable uses, *but also of wood and of earth*—For less honourable purposes. Yet a vessel even of gold may be put to the vilest use, though it was not the design of him that made it.

Verse 21. *If a man purge himself from these*—Vessels of dishonour, so as to have no fellowship with them.

Verse 22. *Flee youthful desires*—Those peculiarly incident to youth *Follow peace with them*—Unity with all true believers. *Out of a pure heart*—*Youthful desires,* destroy this purity: *righteousness, faith, love, peace,* accompany it.

Verse 24. *A servant of the Lord must not*—Eagerly or passionately *Strive*—As do the vain wranglers spoken of, verse 23 *But be apt to teach*—Chiefly by patience and unwearied assiduity.

Verse 25. *In meekness*—He has often need of zeal, always of meekness. *If haply God*—For it is wholly his work. *May give them repentance*—*The acknowledging of the truth* would then quickly follow.

Verse 26. *Who*—At present *are* not only *captives,* but asleep; utterly insensible of their captivity.

Verse 1. *In the last days*—The time of the gospel dispensation, commencing at the time of our Lord's death, is peculiarly styled the *last days. Grievous*—Troublesome and dangerous.

Verse 2. *For men*—Even in the church. *Will be*—In great numbers,

selves, lovers of money, arrogant, proud, evilspeakers,
3 disobedient to parents, ungrateful, unholy, Without natural
affection, implacable, slanderers, intemperate, fierce, des-
4 pisers of good men, Traitors, rash, puffed up, lovers of
5 pleasure more than lovers of God; Having a form of godliness, but denying the power of it: from these also turn away.
6 For of these are they who creep into houses, and captivate
silly women laden with sins, led away by various desires,
7 Ever learning, but never able to come to the knowledge of
8 the truth. Now as Jannes and Jambres withstood Moses,
so do these also withstand the truth: men of corrupt minds,
9 void of judgment as to the faith. But they shall proceed no
farther: for their folly shall be manifest to all men, as theirs
10 also was. But thou hast accurately traced my doctrine,
manner of life, intention, faith, longsuffering, love, patience,
11 Persecutions, afflictions, which befel me at Antioch, at
Iconium, at Lystra; what persecutions I endured; but the
12 Lord delivered me out of all. Yea, and all that are resolved
13 to live godly in Christ Jesus shall suffer persecution. But
evil men and impostors will grow worse and worse, deceiving

and to an higher degree than ever. *Lovers of themselves*—Only, not their neighbours, the first root of evil. *Lovers of money*—The second.

Verse 3. *Without natural affection*—To their own children. *Intemperate, fierce*—Both too soft, and too hard.

Verse 4. *Lovers of* sensual *pleasure*—Which naturally extinguishes all love and sense of God.

Verse 5. *Having a form*—An appearance of godliness, but not regarding, nay, even *denying* and blaspheming, the inward power and reality of it. Is not this eminently fulfilled at this day?

Verse 6. *Of these*—That is, mere formalists.

Verse 7. *Ever learning*—New things. But not *the truth of* God.

Verse 8. Several ancient writers speak of *Jannes* and *Jambres,* as the chief of the Egyptian magicians. *Men of corrupt minds*—Impure notions and wicked inclinations. *Void of judgment*—Quite ignorant, as well as careless, of true, spiritual religion.

Verse 9. *They shall proceed no farther*—In gaining proselytes.

Verse 12. *All that are resolved to live godly*—Therefore count the cost Art thou resolved? *In Christ*—Out of Christ there is no godliness. *Shall suffer persecution*—More or less. There is no exception. Either the truth of scripture fails, or those that think they are religious, and are not persecuted, in some shape or other, on that very account, deceive themselves.

Verse 13. *Deceiving and being deceived*—He who has once begun to

14 and being deceived. But continue thou in the things which
thou hast learned and been fully assured of, knowing of
15 whom thou hast learned *them* ; And that from an infant
thou hast known the holy scriptures, which are able to make
thee wise unto salvation through faith which is in Christ
16 Jesus. All scripture *is* inspired of God, and is profitable
for doctrine, for reproof, for correction, for instruction in
17 righteousness ; That the man of God may be perfect·
IV 1 throughly furnished unto every good work. I charge
thee therefore before God, and the Lord Jesus Christ, who
who will judge the living and the dead at his appearing and
2 his kingdom ; Preach the word ; be instant in season, out
of season ; convince, rebuke, exhort with all longsuffering
3 and teaching. For the time will come when they will not
endure wholesome doctrine ; but will heap up to themselves
teachers, according to their own desires, having itching ears

deceive others is both the less likely to recover from his own error, and the more ready to embrace the errors of other men.

Verse 14. *From whom*—Even from me a teacher approved of God.

Verse 15. *From an infant thou hast known the holy scriptures*—Of the Old Testament. These only were extant when Timothy was an infant. *Which are able to make thee wise unto salvation, through faith in* the Messiah that was to come. How much more are the Old and New Testament together able, in God's hand, to make us more abundantly wise unto salvation ! Even such a measure of present salvation as was not known before Jesus was glorified.

Verse 16. *All scripture is inspired of God*—The Spirit of God not only once inspired those who wrote it, but continually inspires, supernaturally assists, those that read it with earnest prayer. Hence *it is* so *profitable for doctrine*, for instruction of the ignorant, *for* the *reproof* or conviction of them that are in error or sin, *for* the *correction* or amendment of whatever is amiss, and for instructing or training up the children of God *in* all *righteousness.*

Verse 17. *That the man of God*—He that is united to and approved of God. *May be perfect*—Blameless himself, and *throughly furnished*—By the scripture, either to teach, reprove, correct, or train up others.

Verse 1. *I charge thee therefore*—This is deduced from the whole preceding chapter. *At his appearing and his kingdom*—That is, at his appearing in the kingdom of glory.

Verse 2. *Be instant*—Insist on, urge these things *in season, out of season*—That is, continually, at all times and places. It might be translated, *with and without opportunity*—Not only when a fair occasion is given : even when there is none, one must be made.

Verse 3. *For they will heap up teachers*—Therefore thou hast need of " all

4 And they will turn away *their* ears from the truth, and turn
5 aside to fables. But watch thou in all things, endure
affliction, do the work of an evangelist, fulfil thy ministry.
6 For I am now ready to be offered up, and the time of
7 my departure is at hand. I have fought the good fight, I
8 have finished the course, I have kept the faith; Henceforth there is laid up for me the crown of righteousness,
which the Lord, the righteous judge, will render me in that
day: and not to me only, but to all them likewise that have
loved his appearing.
9 10 Do thy diligence to come to me shortly. For Demas

longsuffering." *According to their own desires*—Smooth as they can wish *Having itching ears*—Fond of novelty and variety, which the number of new teachers, as well as their empty, soft, or philosophical discourses, pleased. Such teachers, and such hearers, seldom are much concerned with what is strict or to the purpose. *Heap to themselves*—Not enduring *sound doctrine,* they will reject the sound preachers, and gather together all that suit their own taste. Probably they send out one another as teachers, and so are never at a loss for numbers.

Verse 5. *Watch*—An earnest, constant, persevering exercise. The scripture watching, or waiting, implies steadfast faith, patient hope, labouring love, unceasing prayer; yea, the mighty exertion of all the affections of the soul that a man is capable of. *In all things*—Whatever you are doing, yet in that, and *in all things, watch. Do the work of an evangelist*—Which was next to that of an apostle.

Verse 6. *The time of my departure is at hand*—So undoubtedly God had shown him. *I am ready to be offered up*—Literally, *to be poured out,* as the wine and oil were on the ancient sacrifices.

Verse 8. *The crown of* that *righteousness*—Which God has imputed to me and wrought in me. *Will render to all*—This increases the joy of Paul, and encourages Timotheus. Many of these St. Paul himself had gained. *That have loved his appearing*—Which only a real Christian can do. I say a real Christian, to comply with the mode of the times: else they would not understand, although the word Christian necessarily implies whatsoever is holy, as God is holy. Strictly speaking, to join real or sincere to a word of so complete an import, is grievously to debase its noble signification, and is like adding long to eternity or wide to immensity.

Verse 9. *Come to me*—Both that he might comfort him, and be strengthened by him. Timotheus himself is said to have suffered at Ephesus.

Verse 10. *Demas*—Once my fellowlabourer, Philemon 24. *Hath forsaken me. Crescens,* probably a preacher also, *is gone,* with my consent, *to Galatia, Titus to Dalmatia,* having now left *Crete.* These either went with him to *Rome,* or visited him there.

hath forsaken me, loving the present world, and is gone to
Thessalonica; Crescens to Galatia, Titus to Dalmatia. Only
11 Luke is with me. Take Mark, and bring him with thee: for
12 he is profitable to me for *my* ministry. Tychicus I have sent
13 to Ephesus. When thou comest, bring the cloak which I
left at Troas with Carpus, and the books, especially the
14 parchments. Alexander the coppersmith did me much evil.
15 the Lord will reward him according to his works. Of whom
be thou also aware; for he hath greatly withstood our words.
16 At my first defence no man appeared with me, but all forsook
17 me: may it not be laid to their charge. But the Lord
stood by me, and strengthened me: that through me the
preaching might be fully known, even that all nations
might hear: and I was delivered out of the mouth of the lion.
18 And the Lord will deliver me from every evil work, and
preserve *me* unto his heavenly kingdom: to whom *be* the
19 glory for ever and ever. Amen. Salute Priscilla and Aquila,
20 and the family of Onesiphorus. Erastus abode at Corinth:
21 but Trophimus I have left at Miletus sick. Do thy diligence
to come before winter. Eubulus saluteth thee, and Pudens,
22 and Linus, and Claudia, and all the brethren. The Lord
Jesus Christ *be* with thy spirit. Grace *be* with you.

Verse 11. *Only Luke*—Of my fellowlabourers, *is with me*—But God is with me; and it is enough. *Take Mark*—Who, though he once "departed from the work," *is* now again *profitable to me.*

Verse 13. *The cloak*—Either the *toga,* which belonged to him as a Roman citizen, or an upper garment, which might be needful as winter came on. *Which I left at Troas with Carpus*—Who was probably his host there. *Especially the parchments*—The books written on parchment.

Verse 14. *The Lord will reward him*—This he spoke prophetically.

Verse 16. *All*—My friends and companions. *Forsook me*—And do we expect to find such as will not forsake us? *My first defence*—Before the savage emperor Nero.

Verse 17. *The preaching*—The gospel which we preach.

Verse 18. *And the Lord will deliver me from every evil work*—Which is far more than delivering me from death. Yea, *and,* over and above, *preserve me unto his heavenly kingdom*—Far better than that of Nero.

Verse 20. When I came on, *Erastus abode at Corinth*—Being chamberlain of the city, Rom. xvi. 23 But *Trophimus I have left sick*—Not having power (as neither had any of the apostles) to work miracles when he pleased, but only when God pleased

NOTES

ON

ST. PAUL'S EPISTLE TO TITUS.

Titus was converted from heathenism by St. Paul, Gal. ii. 3; and, as it seems, very early; since the apostle accounted him as his brother at his first going into Macedonia: and he managed and settled the churches there, when St. Paul thought not good to go thither himself. He had now left him at Crete, to regulate the churches; to assist him wherein, he wrote this epistle, as is generally believed, after the First, and before the Second, to Timothy. The tenor and style are much alike in this and in those; and they cast much light on each other, and are worthy the serious attention of all Christian ministers and churches in all ages.

This epistle has four parts :—

I. The inscription,	C. i.	1— 4
II. The instruction of Titus to this effect:		
1. Ordain good presbyters,		5— 9
2. Such are especially needful at Crete,		10—12
3. Reprove and admonish the Cretans,		13—16
4. Teach aged men and women,	C. ii.	1— 5
And young men, being a pattern to them,		6— 8
And servants, urging them by a glorious motive,		9—15
5. Press obedience to magistrates, and gentleness to all men,	C. iii.	1— 2
Enforcing it by the same motive,		3— 7
6. Good works are to be done, foolish questions avoided, heretics shunned,		8—11
III. An invitation of Titus to Nicopolis, with some admonitions,		12—14
IV. The conclusion,		15

TITUS.

CHAPTER I. 1 Paul, a servant of God, and an apostle of Jesus Christ, according to the faith of the elect of God,
and the knowledge of the truth which is after godliness;
2 In hope of eternal life, which God, who cannot lie, promised
3 before the world began; And he hath in his own times manifested his word, through the preaching wherewith I am
intrusted according to the commandment of God our Savi-
4 our: To Titus, my own son after the common faith: Grace,
mercy, peace, from God the Father and the Lord Jesus
Christ our Saviour.
5 For this cause I left thee in Crete, that thou mightest

Verse 1. *Paul, a servant of God, and an apostle of Jesus Christ*—Titles suitable to the person of Paul, and the office he was assigning to Titus *According to the faith*—The propagating of which is the proper business of an apostle. *A servant of God*—According to the faith of the elect. *An apostle of Jesus Christ*—According to the knowledge of the truth. We serve God according to the measure of our faith: we fulfil our public office according to the measure of our knowledge. *The truth that is after godliness*—Which in every point runs parallel with and supports the vital, spiritual worship of God; and, indeed, has no other end or scope. These two verses contain the sum of Christianity, which Titus was always to have in his eye. *Of the elect of God*—Of all real Christians

Verse 2. *In hope of eternal life*—The grand motive and encouragement of every apostle and every servant of God. *Which God promised before the world began*—To Christ, our Head.

Verse 3 *And he hath in his own times*—At sundry times; and *his own times* are fittest for his own work. What creature dares ask, "Why no sooner?" *Manifested his word*—Containing that promise, and the whole "truth which is after godliness." *Through the preaching wherewith I am intrusted according to the commandment of God our Saviour*—And who dares exercise this office on any less authority?

Verse 4. *My own son*—Begot in the same image of God, and repaying a paternal with a filial affection. *The common faith*—Common to me and all my spiritual children.

Verse 5. *The things which are wanting*—Which I had not time to settle myself. *Ordain elders*—Appoint the most faithful, zealous men to watch over the rest. Their character follows, verses 6—9. These were the

set in order the things which are wanting, and ordain elders
6 in every city, as I appointed thee: If a man is blameless,
the husband of one wife, having believing children, not
7 accused of luxury, or unruly. For a bishop must be blameless, as the steward of God; not selfwilled, not passionate,
not given to wine, not a striker, not desirous of filthy gain;
8 But hospitable, a lover of good men, prudent, just, holy,
9 temperate; Holding fast the faithful word as he hath been
taught, that he may be mighty by sound doctrine both to
10 exhort and to convince the gainsayers. For there are many
and unruly vain talkers and deceivers, especially they of the
11 circumcision: Whose mouths must be stopped, who over-
turn whole families, teaching things which they ought not,
12 for the sake of filthy gain. One of themselves, a prophet
of their own, hath said, The Cretans *are* always liars, evil
13 wild beasts, lazy gluttons. This witness is true. Therefore
rebuke them sharply, that they may be sound in the faith;
14 Not giving heed to Jewish fables, and commandments
15 of men, that turn from the truth. To the pure all things
are pure: but to the defiled and unbelieving nothing *is*
pure; but both their understanding and conscience are

elders, or bishops, that Paul approved of;—men that had living faith, a pure conscience, a blameless life

Verse 6. *The husband of one wife*—Surely the Holy Ghost, by repeating this so often, designed to leave the Romanists without excuse.

Verse 7. *As the steward of God*—To whom he intrusts immortal souls. *Not selfwilled*—Literally, *pleasing himself;* but all men "for their good to edification." *Not passionate*—But mild, yielding, tender.

Verse 9. *As he hath been taught*—Perhaps it might be more literally rendered, *according to the teaching,* or doctrine, of the apostles; alluding to Acts ii. 42.

Verse 10. *They of the circumcision*—The Jewish converts.

Verse 11. *Stopped*—The word properly means, to *put a bit into the mouth* of an unruly horse.

Verse 12. *A prophet*—So all poets were anciently called; but, besides, Diogenes Laertius says that Epimenides, the Cretan poet, foretold many things. *Evil wild beasts*—Fierce and savage.

Verse 14. *Commandments of men*—The Jewish or other teachers, whoever they were that *turned from the truth.*

Verse 15. *To the pure*—Those whose hearts are purified by faith: this we allow. *All things are pure*—All kinds of meat; the Mosaic distinction between clean and unclean meats being now taken away. *But to the defiled and unbelieving nothing is pure*—The apostle joins *defiled* and *unbelieving,* to intimate that nothing can be clean without a true faith: for

16 defiled. They profess to know God; but by *their* works
they deny *him*, being abominable, and disobedient, and void
of judgment as to every good work.

CHAP. II. 1 But speak thou the things which become
2 wholesome doctrine: That the aged men be vigilant, seri-
3 ous, prudent, sound in faith, love, patience. That the aged
women in like manner *be* in behaviour as becometh holiness,
not slanderers, not given to much wine, teachers of that
4 which is good; That they instruct the young women to be
5 wise, to love their husbands, to love their children, Discreet,
chaste, keepers at home, good, obedient to their own hus-
6 bands, that the word of God be not blasphemed. The
7 young men likewise exhort to be discreet. In all things
showing thyself a pattern of good works: in doctrine, uncor-
8 ruptness, seriousness, Wholesome speech, that cannot be

both the understanding and conscience, those leading powers of the soul, are polluted; consequently, so is the man and all he does.

Verse 1. *Wholesome*—Restoring and preserving spiritual health.

Verse 2. *Vigilant*—As veteran soldiers, not easily to be surprised *Patience*—A virtue particularly needful for and becoming them. *Serious*—Not drolling or diverting on the brink of eternity.

Verse 3. *In behaviour*—The particulars whereof follow. *As becometh holiness*—Literally, *observing an holy decorum. Not slanderers*—Or evil-speakers. *Not given to much wine*—If they use a little for their often infirmities. *Teachers*—Age and experience call them so to be. Let them teach *good* only.

Verse 4. *That they instruct the young women*—These Timothy was to instruct himself; Titus, by the elder women. *To love their husbands, their children*—With a tender, temperate, holy, wise affection. O how hard a lesson!

Verse 5. *Discreet*—Particularly in the love of their children. *Chaste*—Particularly in the love of their husbands. *Keepers at home*—Whenever they are not called out by works of necessity, piety, and mercy. *Good*—Well tempered, sweet, soft, obliging. *Obedient to their husbands*—Whose will, in all things lawful, is a rule to the wife. *That the word of God be not blasphemed*—Or evil spoken of; particularly by unbelieving husbands, who lay all the blame on the religion of their wives.

Verse 6. *To be discreet*—A virtue rarely found in youth.

Verse 7. *Showing thyself a pattern*—Titus himself was then young. *In* the *doctrine* which thou teachest in public: as to matter, *uncorruptness;* as to the manner of delivering it, *seriousness*—Weightiness, solemnity.

Verse 8. *Wholesome speech*—In private conversation.

reproved; that he who is on the contrary part may be
9 ashamed, having no evil thing to say of us. *Exhort* servants to be subject to their own masters, to please *them* in
10 all things; not answering again; Not stealing, but showing
all good fidelity; that they may in all things adorn the
gospel of God our Saviour.
11 For the saving grace of God hath appeared to all men,
12 Instructing us that, having renounced ungodliness and all
worldly desires, we should live soberly, and righteously, and
13 godly in the present world; Looking for the blessed hope,
and the glorious appearing of the great God, even our Savi-
14 our Jesus Christ; Who gave himself for us, that he might
redeem us from all iniquity, and purify to himself a peculiar
15 people, zealous of good works. These things speak, and

Verse 9. *Please them in all things*—Wherein it can be done without sin. *Not answering again*—Though blamed unjustly. This honest servants are most apt to do. *Not stealing*—Not taking or giving any thing without their master's leave this fair-spoken servants are apt to do.

Verse 10. *Showing all good fidelity*—Soft, obliging faithfulness *That they may adorn the doctrine of God our Saviour*—More than St. Paul says of kings. How he raises the lowness of his subject! So may they, the lowness of their condition.

Verse 11. *The saving grace of God*—So it is in its nature, tendency, and design. *Hath appeared to all men*—High and low.

Verse 12. *Instructing us*—All who do not reject it. *That, having renounced ungodliness*—Whatever is contrary to the fear and love of God. *And worldly desires*—Which are opposite to sobriety and righteousness. *We should live soberly*—In all purity and holiness. *Sobriety*, in the scripture sense, is rather the whole temper of a man, than a single virtue in him. It comprehends all that is opposite to the drowsiness of sin, the folly of ignorance, the unholiness of disorderly passions. Sobriety is no less than all the powers of the soul being consistently and constantly awake, duly governed by heavenly prudence, and entirely conformable to holy affections. *And righteously*—Doing to all as we would they should do to us. *And godly*—As those who are consecrated to God both in heart and life.

Verse 13 *Looking*—With eager desire. *For* that *glorious appearing*—Which we *hope* for. *Of the great God, even our Saviour Jesus Christ*—So that, if there be (according to the Arian scheme) a great God and a little God, Christ is not the little God, but the great one.

Verse 14. *Who gave himself for us*—To die in our stead. *That he might redeem us*—Miserable bondslaves, as well from the power and the very being, as from the guilt, of all our sins.

Verse 15 *Let no man despise thee*—That is, let none have any just

exhort, and rebuke with all authority Let no man
despise thee.

CHAP. III. 1 Remind them to be subject to principalities and powers, to obey *magistrates*, to be ready for every
2 good work, To speak evil of no man, not to be quarrelsome,
3 *to be* gentle, showing all meekness toward all men. For
we also were formerly without understanding, disobedient,
deceived, enslaved to various desires and pleasures, living in
4 wickedness and envy, hateful, hating one another. But
when the kindness and love of God our Saviour toward
5 man appeared, Not by works of righteousness which we
have done, but according to his own mercy he saved us, by
the laver of regeneration, and renewing of the Holy Ghost;
6 Which he poured forth richly upon us through Jesus Christ
7 our Saviour; That, being justified by his grace, we might

cause to despise thee. Yet they surely will. Men who know not God will despise a true minister of his word.

Verse 1. *Remind them*—All the Cretan Christians. *To be subject*—Passively, not resisting. *To principalities*—Supreme. *And powers*—Subordinate governors. And *to obey*—Them actively, so far as conscience permits

Verse 2. *To speak evil*—Neither of them nor any man. *Not to be quarrelsome*—To assault none. *To be gentle*—When assaulted. *Toward all men*—Even those who are such as we were.

Verse 3. *For we*—And as God hath dealt with us, so ought we to d with our neighbour. *Were without understanding*—Wholly ignorant of God. *And disobedient*—When he was declared to us.

Verse 4. *When the love of God appeared*—By the light of his Spirit to our inmost soul.

Verse 5. *Not by works*—In this important passage the apostle presents us with a delightful view of our redemption. Herein we have, 1. The cause of it; not our *works* or *righteousness*, but "the kindness and love of God our Saviour." 2. The effects; which are, (1.) Justification; "being justified," pardoned and accepted through the alone merits of Christ, not from any desert in us, *but according to his own mercy*, "by his grace," his free, unmerited goodness. (2.) Sanctification, expressed by *the laver of regeneration*, (that is, baptism, the thing signified, as well as the outward sign,) *and the renewal of the Holy Ghost;* which purifies the soul, as water cleanses the body, and renews it in the whole image of God. 3. The consummation of all;—*that we might become heirs of eternal life*, and live now in the joyful hope of it.

8 become heirs according to the hope of eternal life. *This is*
a faithful saying, and these things I will that thou affirm
constantly, that they who have believed in God be careful
to excel in good works. These things are good and profit-
9 able to men. But avoid foolish questions, and genealogies,
and contentions, and strivings about the law; for they are
10 unprofitable and vain. An heretic (after a first and second
11 admonition) reject; Knowing that such an one is perverted,
and sinneth, being self-condemned.
12 When I shall send Artemas or Tychicus to thee, be dili-

Verse 8. *Be careful to excel in good works*—Though the apostle does not lay these for the foundation, yet he brings them in at their proper place, and then mentions them, not slightly, but as affairs of great importance. He desires that all believers should be *careful*—Have their thoughts upon them: use their best contrivance, their utmost endeavours, not barely to practise, but *to excel*, to be eminent and distinguished in them: because, though they are not the ground of our reconciliation with God, yet they are amiable and honourable to the Christian profession. *And profitable to men*—Means of increasing the everlasting happiness both of ourselves and others.

Verse 10. *An heretic (after a first and second admonition) reject*—Avoid, leave to himself. This is the only place, in the whole scripture, where this word *heretic* occurs; and here it evidently means, a man that obstinately persists in contending about "foolish questions," and thereby occasions strife and animosities, schisms and parties in the church. This, and this alone, is an heretic in the scripture sense; and his punishment likewise is here fixed:—Shun, avoid him, leave him to himself. As for the Popish sense, "A man that errs in fundamentals," although it crept, with many other things, early into the church, yet it has no shadow of foundation either in the Old or New Testament.

Verse 11. *Such an one is perverted*—In his heart, at least. *And sinneth, being self-condemned*—Being convinced in his own conscience that he acts wrong.

Verse 12. *When I shall send Artemas or Tychicus*—To succeed thee in thy office. Titus was properly an evangelist, who, according to the nature of that office, had no fixed residence;, but presided over other elders, wherever he travelled from place to place, assisting each of the apostles according to the measure of his abilities. *Come to me to Nicopolis*—Very probably not the Nicopolis in Macedonia, as the vulgar subscription asserts: (indeed, none of those subscriptions at the end of St. Paul's epistles are of any authority:) rather it was a town of the same name which lay upon the sea-coast of Epirus. *For I have determined to winter there*—Hence it appears, he was not there yet if so, he would have said, to winter *here*. Consequently, this letter was not written from thence.

gent to come to me to Nicopolis: for I have determined to
13 winter there. Send forward with diligence Zenas the lawyer
14 and Apollos, that they may want nothing. And let ours also
learn to excel in good works for necessary uses, that they be
not unfruitful. All that are with me salute thee. Salute
them that love us in the faith. Grace *be* with you all.

Verse 13 *Send forward Zenas the lawyer*—Either a Roman lawyer or an expounder of the Jewish law.

Verse 14. *And let ours*—All our brethren at Crete. *Learn*—Both by thy admonition and example. Perhaps they had not before assisted Zenas and Apollos as they ought to have done.

NOTES

ON

ST. PAUL'S EPISTLE TO PHILEMON.

Onesimus, a servant to Philemon, an eminent person in Colosse, ran away from his master to Rome. Here he was converted to Christianity by St. Paul, who sent him back to his master with this letter. It seems, Philemon not only pardoned, but gave him his liberty; seeing Ignatius makes mention of him, as succeeding Timotheus at Ephesus.

The letter has three parts:—

I. The inscription,	1— 3
II. After commending Philemon's faith and love,	4— 7
He desires him to receive Onesimus again,	8—21
And to prepare a lodging for himself,	22
III. The conclusion,	23—25

PHILEMON.

CHAPTER I. 1 Paul, a prisoner of Jesus Christ, and
Timotheus a brother, to Philemon the beloved, and our fel-
2 lowlabourer, And to the beloved Apphia, and Archippus our
3 fellowsoldier, and the church which is in thy house: Grace
be unto you, and peace, from God our Father, and the Lord
Jesus Christ.

4 I thank my God, making mention of thee always in my
5 prayers, (Hearing of thy faith which thou hast toward the

Verse 1. This single epistle infinitely transcends all the wisdom of the world. And it gives us a specimen how Christians ought to treat of secular affairs from higher principles. *Paul, a prisoner of Christ*—To whom, as such, Philemon could deny nothing. *And Timotheus*—This was written before the second epistle to Timothy, verse 22.

Verse 2. *To Apphia*—His wife, to whom also the business in part belonged. *And the church in thy house*—The Christians who meet there.

Verse 5. *Hearing*—Probably from Onesimus.

6 Lord Jesus, and love toward all saints,) That the communication of thy faith may become effectual by the acknowledgment of every good thing which is in you towards Christ
7 Jesus. For we have great joy and consolation in thy love,
because the bowels of the saints are refreshed by thee, bro-
8 ther. Wherefore, though I might be very bold in Christ to
9 enjoin thee what is convenient, Yet out of love I rather
entreat *thee*, being such an one as Paul the aged, and now
10 also a prisoner of Jesus Christ. I entreat thee for my son,
1 whom I have begotten in my bonds, Onesimus: Who was
formerly unprofitable to thee, but now profitable to thee and
12 me: Whom I have sent again: thou therefore receive him,
13 that is, my own bowels. Whom I was desirous to have
retained with me, to serve me in thy stead in the bonds
14 of the gospel. But I would do nothing without thy consent;
that thy benefit might not be as it were by constraint, but
15 willingly. And perhaps for this end was he separated for a

Verse 6. I pray *that the communication of thy faith may become effectual*—That is, that thy faith may be effectually communicated to others, who see and acknowledge thy piety and charity

Verse 7 *The saints*—To whom Philemon's house was open, verse 2.

Verse 8 *I might be bold in Christ*—Through the authority he hath given me

Verse 9. *Yet out of love I rather entreat thee*—In how handsome a manner does the apostle just hint, and immediately drop, the consideration of his power to command, and tenderly *entreat* Philemon to hearken to his friend, his aged friend, and now prisoner for Christ! With what endearment, in the next verse, does he call Onesimus his son, before he names his name! And as soon as he had mentioned it, with what fine address does he just touch on his former faults, and instantly pass on to the happy change that was now made upon him! So disposing Philemon to attend to his request, and the motives wherewith he was going to enforce it.

Verse 10. *Whom I have begotten in my bonds*—The son of my age.

Verse 11. *Now profitable*—None should be expected to be a good servant before he is a good man. He manifestly alludes to his name, Onesimus, which signifies *profitable*

Verse 12. *Receive him, that is, my own bowels*—Whom I love as my own soul. Such is the natural affection of a father in Christ toward his spiritual children.

Verse 13. *To serve me in thy stead*—To do those services for me which thou, if present, wouldest gladly have done thyself.

Verse 14. *That thy benefit might not be by constraint*—For Philemon could not have refused it

Verse 15. God might permit him to be *separated* (a soft word) *for a*

16 season, that thou mightest have him for ever, No longer as
a servant, but above a servant, a brother beloved, especially
to me, and how much more to thee, both in the flesh, and in
17 the Lord? If therefore thou accountest me a partner
18 receive him as myself. If he hath wronged thee, or oweth
19 *thee* any thing, put that to my account; I Paul have written with my own hand, I will repay *it:* not to say unto
20 thee, that thou owest also thyself to me besides. Yea,
brother, let me have joy of thee in the Lord: refresh my
21 bowels in Christ. Having confidence of thy obedience I have
written to thee, knowing that thou wilt do even more than
22 I say. Withal prepare me also a lodging: for I trust I shall
23 be given to you through your prayers. Epaphras my fellow-
24 prisoner in Christ Jesus saluteth you, Mark, Aristarchus,
25 Demas, Luke, my fellowlabourers. The grace of our Lord
Jesus Christ *be* with your spirit.

season, that thou mightest have him for ever—Both on earth and in heaven.

Verse 16. *In the flesh*—As a dutiful servant. *In the Lord*—As a fellow-Christian.

Verse 17. *If thou accountest me a partner*—So that thy things are mine, and mine are thine.

Verse 19. *I will repay it*—If thou requirest it. *Not to say, that thou owest me thyself*—It cannot be expressed, how great our obligation is to those who have gained our souls to Christ. *Beside*—Receiving Onesimus.

Verse 20. *Refresh my bowels in Christ*—Give me the most exquisite and Christian pleasure.

Verse 22. *Given to you*—Restored to liberty.

NOTES

ON

THE EPISTLE TO THE HEBREWS

It is agreed by the general tenor of antiquity that this epistle was written by St. Paul, whose other epistles were sent to the gentile converts; this only to the Hebrews. But this improper inscription was added by some later hand. It was sent to the Jewish Hellenist Christians, dispersed through various countries. St. Paul's method and style are easily observed therein. He places, as usual, the proposition and division before the treatise, Heb. ii. 17; he subjoins the exhortatory to the doctrinal part, quotes the same scriptures, Heb. ii. 8; x. 30, 38; . 6; and uses the same expressions as elsewhere. But why does he not prefix his name, which, it is plain from Heb. iii. 19, was dear to them to whom he wrote? Because he prefixes no inscription, in which, if at all, the name would have been mentioned. The ardour of his spirit carries him directly upon his subject, (just like St. John in his First Epistle,) and throws back his usual salutation and thanksgiving to the conclusion.

This epistle of St Paul, and both those of St. Peter, (one may add, that of St. James and of St. Jude also,) were written both to the same persons, dispersed through Pontus, Galatia, and other countries, and nearly at the same time. St. Paul suffered at Rome, three years before the destruction of Jerusalem. Therefore this epistle, likewise, was written while the temple was standing. St. Peter wrote a little before his martyrdom, and refers to the epistles of St. Paul; this in particular.

The scope of it is, to confirm their faith in Christ; and this he does by demonstrating his glory. All the parts of it are full of the most earnest and pointed admonitions and exhortations; and they go on in one tenor, the particle *therefore* everywhere connecting the doctrine and the use.

The sum is, The glory of Christ appears,

I. From comparing with him the prophets and angels,	C. i.	1—14
Therefore we ought to give heed to him,	C. ii	1— 4
II From his passion and consummation.		
Here we may observe,		
1 The proposition and sum,		5— 9
2. The treatise itself. We have a perfect author of salvation, who suffered for our sake, that he might be, (1.) a merciful, and, (2.) a faithful, (3.) high priest,		10—18
These three are particularly explained, his passion and consummation being continually interwoven.		

1. He has the virtues of an high priest		
a. He is faithful,	C. iii.	1—
Therefore be ye not unfaithful ·	C. iv.	13
b. He is merciful,		15—
Therefore come to him with confidence	C. v.	3
2. He is called of God an high priest. Here,		
a. The sum is proposed,		4—10
With a summary exhortation	11—C. vi	20
b. The point is copiously,		
1. Explained. We have a great high priest,		
1 Such as is described in the hundred and tenth Psalm:—		
After the order of Melchisedec,	C. vii.	1—19
Established by an oath,		20—22
For ever,		23—28
2. Therefore peculiarly excellent —		
Heavenly,	C. viii.	1— 6
Of the new covenant,		7—13
By whom we have an entrance into the sanctuary ·	C. ix.	1
	C. x.	18
2 Applied. Therefore,		
1 Believe, hope, love		19—25
These three are farther inculcated,		
a. Faith, with patience,		26—39
Which, after the example of the ancients,	C. xi.	
	C. xii.	1
And of Christ himself,		2, 3
Is to be exercised,		4—11
Cheerfully, peaceably, holily,		12—17
b Hope,		18—20
c. Love,	C. xiii.	1— 6
2 In order to grow in these graces, make use of		
The remembrance of your former,		7—16
The vigilance of your present, pastors,		17—19
To this period, and to the whole epistle, answers		
The prayer, the doxology, and the mild conclusion,		20—25

There are many comparisons in this epistle, which may be nearly reduced to two heads: 1. The prophets, the angels, Moses, Joshua, Aaron, are great; but Jesus Christ is infinitely greater 2. The ancient believers enjoyed high privileges; but Christian believers enjoy far higher. To illustrate this, examples both of happiness and misery are everywhere interspersed: so that in this epistle there is a kind of recapitulation of the whole Old Testament. In this also Judaism is abrogated, and Christianity carried to its height

HEBREWS.

CHAPTER I. 1 God, who at sundry times and in
divers manners spake of old to the fathers by the prophets,
2 Hath in these last days spoken to us by *his* Son, whom he
hath appointed heir of all things, by whom he also made
3 the worlds; Who, being the brightness of his glory, and

Verse 1. *God, who at sundry times*—The creation was revealed in the time of Adam; the last judgment, in the time of Enoch: and so at various times, and in various degrees, more explicit knowledge was given. *In divers manners*—In visions, in dreams, and by revelations of various kinds. Both these are opposed to the one entire and perfect revelation which he has made to us by Jesus Christ. The very number of the prophets showed that they prophesied only "in part." *Of old*—There were no prophets for a large tract of time before Christ came, that the great Prophet might be the more earnestly expected. *Spake*—A part is put for the whole; implying every kind of divine communication. *By the prophets*—The mention of whom is a virtual declaration that the apostle received the whole Old Testament, and was not about to advance any doctrine in contradiction to it. *Hath in these last times*—Intimating that no other revelation is to be expected. *Spoken*—All things, and in the most perfect manner. *By his Son*—Alone. The Son spake by the apostles. The majesty of the Son of God is proposed, 1. Absolutely, by the very name of *Son*, verse 1, and by three glorious predicates,—"whom he hath appointed," "by whom he made," who "sat down;" whereby he is described from the beginning to the consummation of all things, verses 2, 3. 2. Comparatively to angels, verse 4. The proof of this proposition immediately follows: the name of *Son* being proved, verse 5; his being "heir of all things," verses 6—9; his making the worlds, verses 10—12; his sitting at God's right hand, verses 13, &c.

Verse 2. *Whom he hath appointed heir of all things*—After the name of Son, his inheritance is mentioned. God *appointed* him the *heir* long before he made the worlds, Eph. ii. 11; Prov. viii. 22, &c. The Son is the firstborn, born before all things: the *heir* is a term relating to the creation which followed, verse 6. *By whom he also made the worlds*—Therefore the Son was before all worlds. His glory reaches from everlasting to everlasting, though God spake by him to us only "in these last days."

Verse 3. *Who sat down*—The third of these glorious predicates, with which three other particulars are interwoven, which are mentioned like-

the express image of his person, and sustaining all things
by the word of his power, when he had by himself purged
our sins, sat down on the right hand of the Majesty on
4 high; Being so much higher than the angels, as he hath
5 by inheritance a more excellent name than they. For to

wise, and in the same order, Col. i. 15, 17, 20. *Who, being*—The glory which he received in his exaltation at the right hand of the Father no angel was capable of; but the Son alone, who likewise enjoyed it long before. *The brightness of his glory*—Glory is the nature of God revealed in its brightness. *The express image*—Or stamp. Whatever the Father is, is exhibited in the Son, as a seal in the stamp on wax. *Of his person*—Or substance. The word denotes the unchangeable perpetuity of divine life and power. *And sustaining all things*—Visible and invisible, in being. *By the word of his power*—That is, by his powerful word. *When he had by himself*—Without any Mosaic rites or ceremonies. *Purged our sins*—In order to which it was necessary he should for a time divest himself of his glory. In this chapter St. Paul describes his glory chiefly as he is the Son of God; afterwards, Heb. ii. 6, &c., the glory of the man Christ Jesus. He speaks, indeed, briefly of the former before his humiliation, but copiously after his exaltation; as from hence the glory he had from eternity began to be evidently seen. Both his purging our sins, and sitting on the right hand of God, are largely treated of in the seven following chapters. *Sat down*—The priests stood while they ministered: sitting, therefore, denotes the consummation of his sacrifice. This word, *sat down*, contains the scope, the theme, and the sum, of the epistle.

Verse 4. This verse has two clauses, the latter of which is treated of, verse 5; the former, verse 13. Such transpositions are also found in the other epistles of St. Paul, but in none so frequently as in this. The Jewish doctors were peculiarly fond of this figure, and used it much in all their writings. The apostle therefore, becoming all things to all men, here follows the same method. All the inspired writers were readier in all the figures of speech than the most experienced orators. *Being*—By his exaltation, after he had been lower than them, Heb. ii. 9. *So much higher than the angels*—It was extremely proper to observe this, because the Jews gloried in their law, as it was delivered by the ministration of angels. How much more may we glory in the gospel, which was given, not by the ministry of angels, but of the very Son of God! *As he hath by inheritance a more excellent name*—Because he is the Son of God, he inherits that name, in right whereof he inherits all things His inheriting that name is more ancient than all worlds; his inheriting all things, as ancient as all things. *Than they*—This denotes an immense pre-eminence. The angels do not inherit all things, but are themselves a portion of the Son's inheritance, whom they worship as their Lord.

Verse 5. *Thou art my Son*—God of God, Light of Light *This day have I begotten thee*—I have begotten thee from eternity, which, by its unalter-

which of the angels did he ever say, * Thou art my Son, this
day have I begotten thee? And again, † I will be to him a
6 Father, and he shall be to me a Son? And again, ‡ when he
bringeth in the first begotten into the world, he saith, And
7 let all the angels of God worship him. And of the angels
he saith, || Who maketh his angels spirits, and his ministers
8 a flame of fire. But unto the Son, § Thy throne, O God, *is*
for ever and ever: the sceptre of thy kingdom *is* a sceptre
9 of righteousness. Thou hast loved righteousness, and hated
iniquity; therefore God, *even* thy God, hath anointed thee
10 with the oil of gladness above thy fellows. And, ¶ Thou,
Lord, hast in the beginning laid the foundation of the earth;

* Psalm ii. 7. † 2 Sam. vii. 14. ‡ Psalm xcvii. 7. || Psalm civ 4. § Psalm xlv. 6, 7 ¶ Psalm cii. 25, 26.

able permanency of duration, is one continued, unsuccessive day. *I will be to him a Father, and he shall be to me a Son*—I will own myself to be his Father, and him to be my Son, by eminent tokens of my peculiar love The former clause relates to his natural Sonship, by an eternal, inconceivable generation; the other, to his Father's acknowledgment and treatment of him as his incarnate Son. Indeed this promise related immediately to Solomon, but in a far higher sense to the Messiah.

Verse 6. *And again*—That is, in another scripture. *He*—God. *Saith, when he bringeth in his first-begotten*—This appellation includes that of Son, together with the rights of primogeniture, which the first-begotten Son of God enjoys, in a manner not communicable to any creature. *Into the world*—Namely, at his incarnation. *He saith, Let all the angels of God worship him*—So much higher was he, when in his lowest estate, than the highest angel.

Verse 7. *Who maketh his angels*—This implies, they are only creatures, whereas the Son is eternal, verse 8; and the Creator himself, verse 10. *Spirits and a flame of fire*—Which intimates not only their office, but also their nature; which is excellent indeed, the metaphor being taken from the most swift, subtle, and efficacious things on earth; but nevertheless infinitely below the majesty of the Son.

Verse 8. *O God*—God, in the singular number, is never in scripture used absolutely of any but the supreme God. *Thy* reign, of which the *sceptre* is the ensign, is full of justice and equity.

Verse 9. *Thou hast loved righteousness and hated iniquity*—Thou art infinitely pure and holy. *Therefore God*—Who, as thou art Mediator, is *thy God. Hath anointed thee with the oil of gladness*—With the Holy Ghost, the fountain of joy. *Above thy fellows*—Above all the children of men.

Verse 10. *Thou*—The same to whom the discourse is addressed in the preceding verse.

11 and the heavens are the works of thy hands: They shall
perish; but thou endurest; yea, they all shall grow old as a
12 garment; And as a mantle shalt thou change them, and they
shall be changed: but thou art the same, and thy years shall
13 not fail. But to which of the angels did he ever say, * Sit
at my right hand, till I make thine enemies thy footstool?
14 Are they not all ministering spirits, sent forth to attend on
II. 1 them who shall inherit salvation? Therefore we ought
to give the more earnest heed to the things which we have
2 heard, lest at any time we should let *them* slip. For if the
word spoken by angels was steadfast, and every transgression
3 and disobedience received a just recompence; How shall we
escape, if we neglect so great a salvation; which having at
its beginning been spoken by the Lord, was confirmed to us
4 by them that had heard *him*; God also bearing witness,
both by signs and wonders, and various miracles, and distributions of the Holy Ghost, according to his own will?
5 For he hath not subjected to the angels the world to come,

* Psalm cx 1

Verse 12. *As a mantle*—With all ease. *They shall be changed*—Into new heavens and a new earth. *But thou art* eternally *the same.*

Verse 14. *Are they not all*—Though of various orders. *Ministering spirits, sent forth*—Ministering before God, sent forth to men *To attend on them*—In numerous offices of protection, care, and kindness. *Who*—Having patiently continued in welldoing, *shall inherit* everlasting *salvation.*

CHAP. II. In this and the two following chapters the apostle subjoins an exhortation, answering each head of the preceding chapter.

Verse 1 *Lest we should let them slip*—As water out of a leaky vessel. So the Greek word properly signifies.

Verse 2. In giving the law, God *spoke by angels;* but in proclaiming the gospel, by his Son. *Steadfast*—Firm and valid. *Every transgression*—Commission of sin. *Every disobedience*—Omission of duty.

Verse 3. *So great a salvation*—A deliverance from so great wickedness and misery, into so great holiness and happiness. This was first *spoken of* (before he came it was not known) *by* Him who is *the Lord*—Of angels as well as men. *And was confirmed to us*—Of this age, even every article of it. *By them that had heard him*—And had been themselves also both eye-witnesses and ministers of the word.

Verse 4. *By signs and wonders*—While he lived. *And various miracles and distributions of the Holy Ghost*—Miraculous gifts, distributed after his exaltation *According to his will*—Not theirs who received them.

Verse 5. This verse contains a proof of the third; the greater the sal-

6 whereof we speak. But one in a certain place testified, saying, * What is man, that thou art mindful of him? or the
7 son of man, that thou visitest him? Thou hast made him a
little lower than the angels; thou hast crowned him with
glory and honour, and hast set him over the works of thy
8 hands: Thou hast put all things in subjection under his
feet. Now in putting all things in subjection under him, he
left nothing *that is* not put under him. But now we do not
9 yet see all things put under him. But we see Jesus crowned
with glory and honour, for the suffering of death, who was
made a little lower than the angels, that by the grace of God

* Psalm viii. 4.

vation is, and the more glorious the Lord whom we despise, the greater will be our punishment. *God hath not subjected the world to come*—That is, the dispensation of the Messiah; which being to succeed the Mosaic was usually styled by the Jews, *the world to come*, although it is still in great measure to come *Whereof we now speak*—Of which I am now speaking. In this last great dispensation the Son alone presides.

Verse 6. *What is man*—To the vast expanse of heaven, to *the moon and the stars which thou hast ordained!* This psalm seems to have been composed by David, in a clear, moonshiny, and starlight night, while he was contemplating the wonderful fabric of heaven; because in his magnificent description of its luminaries, he takes no notice of the sun, the most glorious of them all. The words here cited concerning dominion were doubtless in some sense applicable to Adam; although in their complete and highest sense, they belong to none but the second Adam. *Or the son of man, that thou visitest him*—The sense rises: we are *mindful* of him that is absent; but to *visit*, denotes the care of a present God.

Verse 7. *Thou hast made him*—Adam. *A little lower than the angels*—The Hebrew is, *a little lower than* (that is, next to) *God*. Such was man as he came out of the hands of his Creator: it seems, the highest of all created beings. But these words are also, in a farther sense, as the apostle here shows, applicable to the Son of God. It should be remembered that the apostles constantly cited the Septuagint translation, very frequently without any variation. It was not their business, in writing to the Jews, who at that time had it in high esteem, to amend or alter this, which would of consequence have occasioned disputes without end.

Verse 8. *Now* this *putting all things under him,* implies that there is *nothing that is not put under him.* But it is plain, this is not done now, with regard to man in general.

Verse 9. It is done only with regard to Jesus, God-Man, who is now *crowned with glory and honour*—As a reward for his having suffered death. *He was made a little lower than the angels*—Who cannot either suffer or die. *That by the grace of God, he might taste death*—An expression

10 he might taste death for every man. For it became him, fo
whom *are* all things, and by whom *are* all things, in bringing many sons to glory, to perfect the captain of their salva-
11 tion by sufferings. For both he that sanctifieth, and all
they that are sanctified, *are* of one· for which cause he is
12 not ashamed to call them brethren, Saying, * I will declare
thy name to my brethren, † in the midst of the church will

* Psalm xxii. 22. † Psalm xxii. 22

denoting both the reality of his death, and the shortness of its continuance. *For every man*—That ever was or will be born into the world

Verse 10. In this verse the apostle expresses, in his own words, what he expressed before in those of the Psalmist. *It became him*—It was suitable to all his attributes, both to his justice, goodness, and wisdom. *For whom*—As their ultimate end. *And by whom*—As their first cause. *Are all things, in bringing many* adopted *sons to glory*—To this very thing, that they are sons, and are treated as such *To perfect the captain*—Prince, leader, and author *of their salvation, by* his atoning *sufferings* for them To *perfect* or consummate implies the bringing him to a full and glorious end of all his troubles, Heb. v. 9. This consummation by sufferings intimates, 1. The glory of Christ, to whom, being consummated, all things are made subject. 2. The preceding sufferings. Of these he treats expressly, verses 11—18; having before spoken of his glory, both to give an edge to his exhortation, and to remove the scandal of sufferings and death. A fuller consideration of both these points he interweaves with the following discourse on his priesthood. But what is here said of our Lord's being *made perfect through sufferings,* has no relation to our being saved or sanctified by sufferings. Even he himself was perfect, as God and as man, before ever he suffered. By his sufferings, in his life and death, he was made a perfect or complete sin-offering. But unless we were to be made the same sacrifice, and to atone for sin, what is said of him in this respect is as much out of our sphere as his ascension into heaven. It is his atonement, and his Spirit carrying on "the work of faith with power" in our hearts, that alone can sanctify us. Various afflictions indeed may be made subservient to this; and so far as they are blessed to the weaning us from sin, and causing our affections to be set on things above, so far they do indirectly help on our sanctification.

Verse 11. *For*—They are nearly related to each other. *He that sanctifieth*—Christ, Heb. xiii. 12. *And all they that are sanctified*—That are brought to God; that draw near or come to him, which are synonymous terms. *Are all of one*—Partakers of one nature, from one parent, Adam.

Verse 12. *I will declare thy name to my brethren*—Christ declares the name of God, gracious and merciful, plenteous in goodness and truth, to all who believe, that they also may praise him. *In the midst of the church will I sing praise unto thee*—As the precentor of the choir. This he did literally, in the midst of his apostles, on the night before his pas

13 I sing praise unto thee. And again, * I will put my trust
in him. And again, Behold I and the children whom God
14 hath given me. Since then the children partake of flesh
and blood, he also himself in like manner took part of the
same; that through death he might destroy him that had
15 the power of death, that is, the devil; And deliver them, as
many as through fear of death were all their lifetime subject
16 to bondage. For verily he taketh not hold of angels; but
17 he taketh hold of the seed of Abraham. Wherefore it

* Isaiah viii. 17, 18.

sion. And as it means, in a more general sense, setting forth the praise of God, he has done it in the church by his word and his Spirit; he still does, and will do it throughout all generations.

Verse 13. *And again*—As one that has communion with his brethren in sufferings, as well as in nature, he says, *I will put my trust in him*—To carry me through them all. *And again*—With a like acknowledgment of his near relation to them, as younger brethren, who were yet but in their childhood, he presents all believers to God, saying, *Behold I and the children whom thou hast given me.*

Verse 14. *Since then these children partake of flesh and blood*—Of human nature with all its infirmities. *He also in like manner took part of the same; that through* his own *death he might destroy* the tyranny of *him that had,* by God's permission, *the power of death* with regard to the ungodly. Death is the devil's servant and serjeant, delivering to him those whom he seizes in sin. *That is, the devil*—The power was manifest to all; but who exerted it, they saw not.

Verse 15. *And deliver them, as many as through fear of death were all their lifetime,* till then, *subject to bondage*—Every man who fears death is subject to bondage; is in a slavish, uncomfortable state. And every man fears death, more or less, who knows not Christ: death is unwelcome to him, if he knows what death is. But he delivers all true believers from this bondage.

Verse 16. *For verily he taketh not hold of angels*—He does not take their nature upon him. *But he taketh hold of the seed of Abraham*—He takes human nature upon him. St. Paul says *the seed of Abraham,* rather than the seed of Adam, because to Abraham was the promise made.

Verse 17. *Wherefore it behoved him*—It was highly fit and proper, yea, necessary, in order to his design of redeeming them. *To be made in all things*—That essentially pertain to human nature, and in all sufferings and temptations. *Like his brethren*—This is a recapitulation of all that goes before: the sum of all that follows is added immediately. *That he might be a merciful and faithful High Priest*—*Merciful* toward sinners; *faithful* toward God. A priest or high priest is one who has a right of approaching God, and of bringing others to him. *Faithful* is treated of, Heb iii. 2, &c., with its use; *merciful,* Heb. iv. 14, &c., with

behoved him to be made in all things like his brethren,
that he might be a merciful and faithful high priest in
things pertaining to God, to expiate the sins of the people.
18 For in that he hath suffered being tempted himself, he is
able to succour them that are tempted.

CHAP. III. 1 Wherefore, holy brethren, partakers
of the heavenly calling, consider the Apostle and High
2 Priest of our profession, Jesus; Who was faithful to him
that appointed him, as *was* also * Moses in all his house.
3 For this person was counted worthy of more glory than
Moses, inasmuch as he that hath builded it hath more
4 honour than the house. Now every house is builded by
5 some one; but he that built all things *is* God. And Moses
verily was faithful in all his house, as a servant, for a testimony of the things which were to be afterwards spoken;
6 But Christ as a Son over his own house; whose house we

* Numbers xii. 7.

the use also; *High Priest,* Heb. v. 4, &c.; vii. 1, &c. The use is added from Heb. x. 19. *In things pertaining to God, to expiate the sins of the people*—Offering up their sacrifices and prayers to God; deriving God's grace, peace, and blessings upon them.

Verse 18. *For in that he hath suffered being tempted himself, he is able to succour them that are tempted*—That is, he has given a manifest, demonstrative proof that he is able so to do.

Verse 1. *The heavenly calling*—God calls from heaven, and to heaven, by the gospel. *Consider the Apostle*—The messenger of God, who pleads the cause of God with us. *And High Priest*—Who pleads our cause with God. Both are contained in the one word *Mediator.* He compares Christ, as an Apostle, with Moses; as a Priest, with Aaron. Both these offices, which Moses and Aaron severally bore, he bears together, and far more eminently. *Of our profession*—The religion we profess.

Verse 2. *His house*—The church of Israel, then the peculiar family of God.

Verse 3. *He that hath builded it hath more glory than the house*—Than the family itself, or any member of it

Verse 4. *Now* Christ, *he that built* not only this house, but *all things, is God*—And so infinitely greater than Moses or any creature.

Verse 5. *And Moses verily*—Another proof of the pre-eminence of Christ above Moses. *Was faithful in all his house, as a servant, for a testimony of the things which were afterwards to be spoken*—That is, which was a full confirmation of the things which he afterward spake concerning Christ.

Verse 6. *But Christ* was faithful *as a Son; whose house we are,* while

are, if we hold fast the confidence and the glorying of hope
7 firm to the end. Wherefore (as the Holy Ghost saith)
8 * To-day, if ye will hear his voice, harden not your hearts,
as in the provocation, † in the day of temptation in the
9 wilderness: Where your fathers tempted me, proved me,
10 and saw my works forty years. Therefore I was grieved
with that generation, and said, They always err in their
11 hearts; and they have not known my ways. So I sware in
12 my wrath, They shall not enter into my rest. Take heed,
brethren, lest there be in any of you an evil heart of unbe-
13 lief, in departing from the living God. But exhort one
another daily, while it is called To-day; lest any of you be
14 hardened through the deceitfulness of sin. (For we are made
partakers of Christ, if we hold fast the beginning of our

* Psalm xcv. 7, &c. † Exod. xvii. 7.

we hold fast, and shall be unto the end, *if we hold fast our confidence* in God, *and glorying* in his promises; our faith and hope.

Verse 7. *Wherefore*—Seeing he is faithful, be not ye unfaithful.

Verse 8. *As in the provocation*—When Israel provoked me by their strife and murmurings. *In the day of temptation*—When at the same time they tempted me, by distrusting my power and goodness.

Verse 9. *Where your fathers*—That hard-hearted and stiff-necked generation. So little cause had their descendants to glory in them. *Tempted me*—Whether I could and would help them *Proved me*—Put my patience to the proof, even while they *saw my* glorious *works* both of judgment and mercy, and that for *forty years*.

Verse 10. *Wherefore*—To speak after the manner of men. *I was grieved*—Displeased, offended *with that generation, and said, They always err in their hearts*—They are led astray by their stubborn will and vile affections. *And*—For this reason, because wickedness has blinded their understanding. *They have not known my ways*—By which I would have led them like a flock. *Into my rest*—In the promised land.

Verse 12. *Take heed, lest there be in any of you*—As there was in them. *An evil heart of unbelief*—Unbelief is the parent of all evil, and the very essence of unbelief lies in *departing from God*, as *the living God*—The fountain of all our life, holiness, happiness.

Verse 13. *But*, to prevent it, *exhort one another, while it is called To-day*—This *to-day* will not last for ever. The day of life will end soon, and perhaps the day of grace yet sooner.

Verse 14. *For we are made partakers of Christ*—And we shall still partake of him and all his benefits, *if we hold fast our* faith *unto the end*. *If*—But not else; and a supposition made by the Holy Ghost is equal to the strongest assertion. Both the sentiment and the manner of expression are the same as verse 6.

15 confidence firm to the end.) While it is said, To-day if ye
will hear his voice, harden not your hearts, as in the provo-
16 cation. For who, when they had heard, provoked *God?*
17 *were* they not all that came out of Egypt by Moses? And
with whom was he grieved forty years? *was it* not with
them who had sinned, whose carcases fell in the wilderness?
18 And to whom sware he that they should not enter into his
19 rest, but to them that believed not? So we see they could
IV. 1 not enter in because of unbelief. Let us therefore fear,
lest, a promise being left *us* of entering into his rest, any
2 of us should altogether come short *of it.* For unto us have
the good tidings been declared, as well as unto them: but
the word heard did not profit them, not being mixed with
3 faith in those that heard *it.* For we that have believed do
enter into the rest, as he said, I have sworn in my wrath, They
shall not enter into my rest: though the works were finished
4 from the foundation of the world. For he said thus in a
certain place of the seventh day, * And God rested on the
5 seventh day from all his works. And in this again, They
shall not enter into my rest. Seeing then it remaineth that

* Gen. ii. 2.

Verse 16. *Were they not all that came out of Egypt*—An awful consideration! The whole elect people of God (a very few excepted) *provoked God* presently after their great deliverance, continued to grieve his Spirit for forty years, and perished in their sin!

Verse 19. *So we see they could not enter in*—Though afterward they desired it.

Verse 2. *But the word* which they heard *did not profit them*—So far from it, that it increased their damnation. It is then only when *it is mixed with faith,* that it exerts its saving power.

Verse 3. *For we* only *that have believed enter into the rest*—The proposition is, There remains a rest for us. This is proved, verses 3—11, thus: That psalm mentions a rest: yet it does not mean, 1. God's rest from creating; for this was long before the time of Moses. Therefore in his time another rest was expected, of which they who then heard fell short Nor is it, 2 The rest which Israel obtained through Joshua; for the Psalmist wrote after him. Therefore it is, 3. The eternal rest in heaven. *As he said*—Clearly showing that there is a farther rest than that which followed the finishing of the creation. *Though the works were finished*—Before: whence it is plain, God did not speak of resting from them.

Verse 4. *For,* long after he had *rested from his works,* he speaks again.

Verse 5. *In this* psalm, of a rest yet to come.

some enter into it, and they to whom the good tidings were
7 declared before entered not in because of unbelief: He
again, after so long a time, fixeth a certain day, saying by
David, To-day; as it was said before, To-day if ye will hear
8 his voice, harden not your hearts. For if Joshua had given
them the rest, he would not have afterward spoken of ano-
9 ther day. There remaineth therefore a rest for the people
10 of God. For he that hath entered into his rest hath him-
11 self also ceased from his works, as God *did* from his. Let
us labour therefore to enter into that rest, lest any one
12 should fall after the same example of unbelief. For the
word of God *is* living and powerful, and sharper than any
two-edged sword, piercing even to the dividing asunder both
of the soul and spirit, both of the joints and marrow, and *is*
a discerner of the thoughts and intentions of the heart.
13 Neither is there any creature that is not manifest in his
sight: but all things *are* naked and opened to the eyes
of him with whom we have to do.
14 Having therefore a great high priest, that is passed

Verse 7. *After so long a time*—It was above four hundred years from the time of Moses and Joshua to David. *As it was said before*—St. Paul here refers to the text he had just cited.

Verse 8. *The rest*—All th rest which God had promised.

Verse 9. *Therefore*—Since he still speaks of another day, *there* must *remain a* farther, even an eternal, *rest for the people of God.*

Verse 10. For they do not yet so rest. Therefore a fuller rest remains for them.

Verse 11. *Lest any one should fall*—Into perdition.

Verse 12. *For the word of God*—Preached, verse 2, and armed with threatenings, verse 3. *Is living and powerful*—Attended with the power of the living God, and conveying either life or death to the hearers. *Sharper than any two-edged sword*—Penetrating the heart more than this does the body. *Piercing*—Quite through, and laying open. *The soul and spirit, joints and marrow*—The inmost recesses of the mind, which the apostle beautifully and strongly expresses by this heap of figurative words *And is a discerner*—Not only *of the thoughts,* but also of the *intentions.*

Verse 13. *In his sight*—It is God whose word is thus "powerful:" it is God in whose sight every *creature* is *manifest;* and of this his word, working on the conscience, gives the fullest conviction. *But all things are naked and opened*—Plainly alluding to the sacrifices under the law which were first flayed, and then (as the Greek word literally means) *cleft asunder through the neck* and backbone; so that everything both without and within was exposed to open view.

Verse 14. *Having therefore a great high priest*—Great indeed, being *the*

through the heavens, Jesus the Son of God, let us hold fast
15 *our* profession. For we have not an high priest who cannot
sympathize with our infirmities; but one who was in all
16 points tempted like as *we are, yet* without sin. Let us
therefore come boldly to the throne of grace, that we may
receive mercy, and find grace to help in time of need.
V. 1 For every high priest being taken from among men is
appointed for men in things pertaining to God, that he may
2 offer both gifts and sacrifices for sins: Who can have compassion on the ignorant, and the wandering; seeing he him-
3 self also is compassed with infirmity. And because hereof it
behoveth him, as for the people, so also for himself, to offer
4 for sins. And no one taketh this honour to himself, but he

eternal *Son of God, that is passed through the heavens*—As the Jewish high priest passed through the veil into the holy of holies, carrying with him the blood of the sacrifices, on the yearly day of atonement; so our great high priest went once for all through the visible heavens, with the virtue of his own blood, into the immediate presence of God.

Verse 15. He *sympathizes with* us even in *our* innocent *infirmities*, wants, weaknesses, miseries, dangers. *Yet without sin*—And, therefore, is indisputably able to preserve us from it in all our temptations.

Verse 16. *Let us therefore come boldly*—Without any doubt or fear. *Unto the throne of* God, our reconciled Father, even his throne of *grace*—Grace erected it, and reigns there, and dispenses all blessings in a way of mere, unmerited favour.

Verse 1. *For every high priest being taken from among men*—Is, till he is taken, of the same rank with them. *And is appointed*—That is, is wont to be appointed. *In things pertaining to God*—To bring God near to men, and men to God. *That he may offer both gifts*—Out of things inanimate, and animal *sacrifices*.

Verse 2. *Who can have compassion*—In proportion to the offence: so the Greek word signifies. *On the ignorant*—Them that are in error. *And the wandering*—Them that are in sin. *Seeing himself also is compassed with infirmity*—Even with sinful infirmity; and so needs the compassion which he shows to others.

Verse 4. The apostle begins here to treat of the priesthood of Christ. The sum of what he observes concerning it is, Whatever is excellent in the Levitical priesthood is in Christ, and in a more eminent manner; and whatever is wanting in those priests is in him. *And no one taketh this honour*—The priesthood. *To himself, but he that is called of God, as was Aaron*—And his posterity, who were all of them called at one and the same time. But it is observable, Aaron did not preach at all; preaching being no part of the priestly office.

5 that is called of God, as *was* Aaron. So also Christ glorified not himself to be made an high priest; but he that said
to him, * Thou art my Son, this day have I begotten thee.
6 As he saith also in another *place*, † Thou *art* a priest for
7 ever after the order of Melchisedec: Who in the days
of his flesh, having offered up prayers and supplications
with strong crying and tears unto him that was able to save
8 him from death, and being heard in that he feared; Though

* Psalm ii. 7. † Psalm cx 4.

Verse 5. *So also Christ glorified not himself to be an high priest*—That is, did not take this honour to himself, but received it from him *who said, Thou art my Son, this day have I begotten thee*—Not, indeed, at the same time; for his generation was from eternity.

Verse 7. The sum of the things treated of in the seventh and following chapters is contained, verses 7—10; and in this sum is admirably comprised the process of his passion, with its inmost causes, in the very terms used by the evangelists. *Who in the days of his flesh*—Those two days, in particular, wherein his sufferings were at the height. *Having offered up prayers and supplications*—Thrice. *With strong crying and tears*—In the garden. *To him that was able to save him from death*—Which yet he endured, in obedience to the will of his Father. *And being heard in that* which *he* particularly *feared*—When the cup was offered him first, there was set before him that horrible image of a painful, shameful, accursed death, which moved him to pray conditionally against it: for, if he had desired it, his heavenly Father would have sent him more than twelve legions of angels to have delivered him. But what he most exceedingly feared was the weight of infinite justice; the being "bruised" and "put to grief" by the hand of God himself. Compared with this, everything else was a mere nothing; and yet, so greatly did he even thirst to be obedient to the righteous will of his Father, and to "lay down" even "his life for the sheep," that he vehemently longed to be baptized with this baptism, Luke xii. 50. Indeed, his human nature needed the support of Omnipotence; and for this he sent up *strong crying and tears:* but, throughout his whole life, he showed that it was not the sufferings he was to undergo, but the dishonour that sin had done to so holy a God, that grieved his spotless soul. The consideration of its being the will of God tempered his fear, and afterwards swallowed it up; and he was *heard,* not so that the cup should pass away, but so that he drank it without any fear.

Verse 8. *Though he were a Son*—This is interposed, lest any should be offended at all these instances of human weakness. In the garden, how frequently did he call God his Father! Matt. xxvi. 39, &c. And hence it most evidently appears that his being the Son of God did not arise merely from his resurrection. *Yet learned he*—The word *learned,* premised to the word *suffered,* elegantly shows how willingly he learned.

he was a Son, yet he learned obedience by the things which he
9 suffered; And being perfected, became the author of eternal
10 salvation to all that obey him; Called of God an high priest
after the order of Melchisedec.
11 Concerning whom we have many things to say, and hard
12 to be explained, seeing ye are become dull of hearing. For
whereas for the time ye ought to be teachers, ye have need
that one teach you again which *are* the first principles of the
oracles of God; and are become such as have need of milk,
13 and not of strong meat. For every one that useth milk *is* unexperienced in the word of righteousness; for he is a babe.
14 But strong meat belongeth to them of full age, to them who
have senses exercised by habit to discern both good and evil.

He *learned obedience,* when he began to suffer; when he applied himself to drink that cup: obedience in suffering and dying.

Verse 9. *And being perfected*—By sufferings, Heb. ii. 10; brought through all to glory. *He became the author*—The procuring and efficient cause. *Of eternal salvation to all that obey him*—By doing and suffering his whole will.

Verse 10. *Called*—The Greek word here properly signifies *surnamed.* His name is, "the Son of God." The Holy Ghost seems to have concealed who *Melchisedec* was, on purpose that he might be the more eminent type of Christ. This only we know,—that he was a priest, and king of Salem, or Jerusalem.

Verse 11. *Concerning whom*—The apostle here begins an important digression, wherein he reproves, admonishes, and exhorts the Hebrews *We*—Preachers of the gospel. *Have many things to say, and hard to be explained*—Though not so much from the subject-matter, as from your slothfulness in considering, and dulness in apprehending, the things of God.

Verse 12. *Ye have need that one teach you again which are the first principles of* religion. Accordingly these are enumerated in the first verse of the ensuing chapter *And have need of milk*—The first and plainest doctrines.

Verse 13. *Every one that useth milk*—That neither desires, nor can digest, anything else: otherwise strong men use milk; but not milk chiefly, and much less that only. *Is unexperienced in the word of righteousness*—The sublimer truths of the gospel. Such are all who desire and can digest nothing but the doctrine of justification and imputed righteousness.

Verse 14. *But strong meat*—These sublimer truths relating to "perfection," Heb. vi. 1. *Belong to them of full age, who by habit*—Habit here signifies strength of spiritual understanding, arising from maturity of spiritual age. *By,* or in consequence of, this habit they exercise themselves in these things with ease, readiness, cheerfulness, and profit.

CHAP. VI. 1 Therefore leaving the principles of the
doctrine of Christ, let us go on to perfection; not laying
again the foundation of repentance from dead works, and
2 of faith in God, Of the doctrine of baptisms, and laying
on of hands, and the resurrection of the dead, and eternal
3 judgment. And this we will do, if God permit. For *it is*
4 impossible for those who were once enlightened, and have
tasted the heavenly gift, and been made partakers of the
5 Holy Ghost, And have tasted the good word of God, and
6 the powers of the world to come, And have fallen away, to
renew *them* again unto repentance; seeing they crucify to
themselves the Son of God afresh, and put *him* to an open

Verse 1. *Therefore leaving the principles of the doctrine of Christ*—That is, saying no more of them for the present. *Let us go on to perfection; not laying again the foundation of repentance from dead works*—From open sins, the very first thing to be insisted on. *And faith in God*—The very next point. So St. Paul in his very first sermon at Lystra, Acts xiv. 15, "Turn from those vanities unto the living God." And when they believed, they were to be baptized with the baptism, not of the Jews, or of John, but of Christ. The next thing was, to lay hands upon them, that they might receive the Holy Ghost: after which they were more fully instructed, touching the resurrection, and the general judgment; called eternal, because the sentence then pronounced is irreversible, and the effects of it remain for ever.

Verse 3. *And this we will do*—We will go on to perfection; and so much the more diligently, because,

Verse 4. *It is impossible for those who were once enlightened*—With the light of the glorious love of God in Christ. *And have tasted the heavenly gift*—Remission of sins, sweeter than honey and the honeycomb. *And been made partakers of the Holy Ghost*—Of the witness and the fruit of the Spirit.

Verse 5. *And have tasted the good word of God*—Have had a relish for, and a delight in it. *And the powers of the world to come*—Which every one tastes, who has an hope full of immortality. Every child that is naturally born, first sees the light, then receives and tastes proper nourishment, and partakes of the things of this world. In like manner, the apostle, comparing spiritual with natural things, speaks of one born of the Spirit, as seeing the light, tasting the sweetness, and partaking of the things "of the world to come."

Verse 6. *And have fallen away*—Here is not a supposition, but a plain relation of fact. The apostle here describes the case of those who have cast away both the power and the form of godliness; who have lost both their faith, hope, and love, verse 10, &c., and that wilfully, Heb. x. 26 Of these wilful total apostates he declares, *it is impossible to renew them again to repentance*, (though they were renewed once,) either to the foun-

7 shame. For the earth which drinketh in the rain that
cometh often upon it, and bringeth forth herbage meet for
them for whom it is tilled, receiveth blessing from God
8 But that which beareth thorns and briers *is* rejected, and
9 nigh unto a curse; whose end *is* to be burned. But,
beloved, we are persuaded better things of you, and things
10 that accompany salvation, though we thus speak. For God
is not unrighteous to forget your work and labour of love,
which ye have showed toward his name, in that ye have
11 ministered to the saints, and do minister. But we desire
that every one of you may show unto the end the same dili-
12 gence to the full assurance of hope: That ye be not slothful, but followers of them who through faith and longsuffer-
13 ing inherited the promises. For when God made the promise

dation, or anything built thereon. *Seeing they crucify the Son of God afresh*—They use him with the utmost indignity. *And put him to an open shame*—Causing his glorious name to be blasphemed.

Verse 8. *That which beareth thorns and briers*—Only or chiefly. *Is rejected*—No more labour is bestowed upon it. *Whose end is to be burned*—As Jerusalem was shortly after

Verse 9. *But, beloved*—In this one place he calls them so. He never uses this appellation, but in exhorting. *We are persuaded of you things that accompany salvation*—We are persuaded you are now saved from your sins; and that ye have that faith, love, and holiness, which lead to final salvation. *Though we thus speak*—To warn you, lest you should fall from your present steadfastness.

Verse 10. *For*—Ye give plain proof of your faith and love, which the righteous God will surely reward.

Verse 11. *But we desire you may show the same diligence unto the end*—And therefore we thus speak *To the full assurance of hope*—Which you cannot expect, if you abate your diligence. The full assurance of faith relates to present pardon; the full assurance of hope, to future glory. The former is the highest degree of divine evidence that God is reconciled to *me* in the Son of his love; the latter is the same degree of divine evidence (wrought in the soul by the same immediate inspiration of the Holy Ghost) of persevering grace, and of eternal glory. So much, and no more, as faith every moment "beholds with open face," so much does hope see to all eternity But this assurance of faith and hope is not an opinion, not a bare construction of scripture, but is given immediately by the power of the Holy Ghost; and what none can have for another, but for himself only.

Verse 12. *Inherited the promises*—The promised rest; paradise.

Verse 13. *For*—Ye have abundant encouragement, seeing no stronger promise could be made than that great promise which God made to Abraham, and in him to us

to Abraham, because he could swear by no greater, he swore
14 by himself, Saying, * Surely blessing I will bless thee, and
15 multiplying I will multiply thee. And so, after he had
16 patiently waited, he obtained the promise. For men verily
swear by the greater, and an oath for confirmation *is* to them
17 an end of all contradiction. Wherefore God, being willing
to show more abundantly to the heirs of the promise the
unchangeableness of his counsel, interposed by an oath:
18 That by two unchangeable things, in which *it was* impossible for God to lie, we might have strong consolation, who
19 have fled to lay hold on the hope set before us: Which *hope*
we have as an anchor of the soul, both sure and steadfast,
20 and which entereth into the place within the veil; Whither
Jesus *our* forerunner is entered for us, who is made an high
priest for ever after the order of Melchisedec.

CHAP. VII. 1 For this Melchisedec, king of Salem,

* Gen. xxii. 17.

Verse 15. *After he had waited*—Thirty years. *He obtained the promise*—Isaac, the pledge of all the promises.

Verse 16. *Men* generally *swear* by him who is infinitely *greater* than themselves, *and an oath for confirmation,* to confirm what is promised or asserted, usually puts *an end to all contradiction.* This shows that an oath taken in a religious manner is lawful even under the gospel: otherwise the apostle would never have mentioned it with so much honour, as a proper means to confirm the truth

Verse 17. *God interposed by an oath*—Amazing condescension! He who is greatest of all acts as if he were a middle person; as if while he swears, he were less than himself, by whom he swears! Thou that hearest the promise, dost thou not yet believe?

Verse 18. *That by two unchangeable things*—His promise and his oath, *in* either, much more in both of *which, it was impossible for God to lie, we might have strong consolation*—Swallowing up all doubt and fear. *Who have fled*—After having been tossed by many storms. *To lay hold on the hope set before us*—On Christ, the object of our hope, and the glory we hope for through him.

Verse 19. *Which hope* in Christ *we have as an anchor of the soul*—Entering into heaven itself, and fixed there *Within the veil*—Thus he slides back to the priesthood of Christ.

Verse 20. A *forerunner* uses to be less in dignity than those that are to follow him. But it is not so here; for Christ who is gone before us is infinitely superior to us. What an honour is it to believers, to have so glorious a forerunner, now appearing in the presence of God for them!

Verse 1. The sum of this chapter is, Christ, as appears from his type,

priest of the most high God, * who met Abraham returning
2 from the slaughter of the kings, and blessed him ; To whom
also Abraham divided a tenth part of all the *spoils ;* being
by interpretation, first, king of righteousness, and then king
3 of Salem also, which is king of peace ; Without father,
without mother, without pedigree, having neither beginning
of days, nor end of life ; but being made like the Son of God ;
4 remaineth a priest continually. Now consider how great this
man *was,* to whom even the patriarch Abraham gave the
5 tenth of the spoils. And verily they of the sons of Levi,
who receive the priesthood, have a commandment according
to the law to take tithes of the people, that is, of their
brethren, though they come out of the loins of Abraham.
6 But he whose pedigree is not from them took tithes of Abra-
7 ham, and blessed him who had the promises. And without

* Gen. xiv 18, &c.

Melchisedec, who was greater than Abraham himself, from whom Levi descended, has a priesthood altogether excellent, new, firm, perpetual.

Verse 2. *Being first*—According to the meaning of his own name. *King of righteousness, then*—According to the name of his city. *King of peace*—So in him, as in Christ, righteousness and peace were joined. And so they are in all that believe in him.

Verse 3. *Without father, without mother, without pedigree*—Recorded, without any account of his descent from any ancestors of the priestly order. *Having neither beginning of days, nor end of life*—Mentioned by Moses. *But being*—In all these respects *Made like the Son of God*—Who is really *without father,* as to his human nature ; *without mother,* as to his divine ; and in this also, *without pedigree*—Neither descended from any ancestors of the priestly order. *Remaineth a priest continually*—Nothing is recorded of the death or successor of Melchisedec. But Christ alone does really remain without death, and without successor.

Verse 4. The greatness of Melchisedec is described in all the preceding and following particulars. But the most manifest proof of it was, that Abraham gave him tithes as to a priest of God and a superior ; though he was himself a patriarch, greater than a king, and a progenitor of many kings.

Verse 5. *The sons of Levi take tithes of their brethren*—Sprung from Abraham as well as themselves. The Levites therefore are greater than they ; but the priests are greater than the Levites, the patriarch Abraham than the priests, and Melchisedec than him.

Verse 6. *He who is not from them*—The Levites *Blessed*—Another proof of his superiority. *Even him that had the promises*—That was so highly favoured of God. When St. Paul speaks of Christ, he says, " the promise ; " *promises* refer to other blessings also.

Verse 7. *The less is blessed*—Authoritatively, *of the greater.*

8 all contradiction the less is blessed of the greater. And here
men that die receive tithes; but there, he of whom it is tes-
9 tified that he liveth. And even Levi, who received tithes,
10 paid tithes (so to speak) through Abraham. For he was yet
11 in the loins of his father, when Melchisedec met him. Now
if perfection had been by the Levitical priesthood, (for under
it the people received the law,) what farther need *was there*
that another priest should rise after the order of Melchisedec,
12 and not be called after the order of Aaron? For the priesthood
being changed, there is also necessarily a change of the law.
13 For he of whom these things are spoken pertaineth to another
14 tribe, of which no man attended on the altar. For *it is* evident
that our Lord sprang out of Judah; of which tribe Moses spake
15 nothing concerning the priesthood. And it is still far more evident, that another priest is raised up after the likeness of Mel-

Verse 8. *And here*—In the Levitical priesthood. *But there*—In the case of Melchisedec. *He of whom it is testified that he liveth*—Who is not spoken of as one that died for another to succeed him; but is represented only as living, no mention being made either of his birth or death.

Verse 9. *And even Levi, who received tithes*—Not in person, but in his successors, as it were, *paid tithes*—In the person of Abraham.

Verse 11. The apostle now demonstrates that the Levitical priesthood must yield to the priesthood of Christ, because Melchisedec, after whose order he is a priest, 1. Is opposed to Aaron, verses 11—14. 2. Hath no end of life, verses 15—19, but "remaineth a priest continually." *If now perfection were by the Levitical priesthood*—If this perfectly answered all God's designs and man's wants *For under it the people received the law*—Whence some might infer, that perfection was by that priesthood. *What farther need was there, that another priest*—Of a new order, should be set up? From this single consideration it is plain, that both the priesthood and the law, which were inseparably connected, were now to give way to a better priesthood and more excellent dispensation

Verse 12. *For*—One of these cannot be changed without the other.

Verse 13. But the priesthood is manifestly changed from one order to another, and from one tribe to another. *For he of whom these things are spoken*—Namely, Jesus *Pertaineth to another tribe*—That of Judah *Of which no man* was suffered by the law to *attend on*, or minister at, *the altar*.

Verse 14. *For it is evident that our Lord sprang out of Judah*—Whatever difficulties have arisen since, during so long a tract of time, it was then clear beyond dispute.

Verse 15 *And it is still far more evident, that*—Both the priesthood and the law are changed, because the priest now raised up is not only of another tribe, but of a quite different order.

16 chisedec, Who was made, not after the law of a carnal com-
17 mandment, but after the power of an endless life. For it is
testified, Thou *art* a priest for ever after the order of Mel-
18 chisedec. For verily there is a disannulling of the preceding
commandment for the weakness and unprofitableness thereof.
19 For the law made nothing perfect, but the bringing in of a
20 better hope *did ;* by which we draw nigh to God. And inas-
21 much as *he was not made a priest* without an oath : (For
those *priests* were made without an oath ; but this with an
oath by him that said unto him, The Lord sware and will
not repent, Thou *art* a priest for ever after the order of Mel-
22 chisedec :) Of so much better a covenant was Jesus made
23 a surety. And they truly were many priests, because they
24 were hindered by death from continuing : But this, because
he continueth for ever, hath a priesthood that passeth not
25 away Wherefore he is able also to save them to the utter-

Verse 16. *Who is made*—A priest. *Not after the law of a carnal commandment*—Not according to the Mosaic law, which consisted chiefly of *commandments* that were *carnal,* compared to the spirituality of the gospel. *But after the power of an endless life*—Which he has in himself, as the eternal Son of God.

Verse 18. *For there is* implied in this new and everlasting priesthood, and in the new dispensation connected therewith, *a disannulling of the preceding commandment*—An abrogation of the Mosaic law. *For the weakness and unprofitableness thereof*—For its insufficiency either to justify or to sanctify.

Verse 19. *For the law*—Taken by itself, separate from the gospel. *Made nothing perfect*—Could not perfect its votaries, either in faith or love, in happiness or holiness. *But the bringing in of a better hope*—Of the gospel dispensation, which gives us a better ground of confidence, does. *By which we draw nigh to God*—Yea, so nigh as to be one spirit with him. And this is true perfection.

Verse 20. *And*—The greater solemnity wherewith he was made priest, farther proves the superior excellency of his priesthood.

Verse 21. *The Lord sware and will not repent*—Hence also it appears, that his is an unchangeable priesthood.

Verse 22. *Of so much better a covenant*—Unchangeable, eternal. *Was Jesus made a surety*—Or mediator. The word *covenant* frequently occurs in the remaining part of this epistle. The original word means either a covenant or a last will and testament. St. Paul takes it sometimes in the former, sometimes in the latter, sense ; sometimes he includes both.

Verse 23. *They were many priests*—One after another.

Verse 24. *He continueth for ever*—In life and in his priesthood. *That passeth not away*—To any successor.

Verse 25. *Wherefore he is able to save to the uttermost*—From all the

most who come to God through him, seeing he ever liveth to
26 make intercession for them. For such an high priest suited
us, holy, harmless, undefiled, separated from sinners, and
27 made higher than the heavens; Who needeth not daily, as
those high priests, to offer up sacrifices, first for his own sins,
then for those of the people: for this he did once for all,
28 when he offered up himself. For the law maketh men high
priests that have infirmity; but the word of the oath, which
was since the law, *maketh* the son, who is consecrated for
evermore.

CHAP. VIII. 1 The sum of what hath been spoken *is*.
We have such an high priest, who is set down at the right
2 hand of the throne of the Majesty in the heavens; A
minister of the sanctuary and of the true tabernacle, which

guilt, power, root, and consequence of sin. *Them who come*—By faith. *To God through him*—As their priest. *Seeing he ever liveth to make intercession*—That is, he ever lives and intercedes. He died once; he intercedes perpetually.

Verse 26. *For such an high priest suited us*—Unholy, mischievous, defiled sinners: a blessed paradox! *Holy*—With respect to God. *Harmless*—With respect to men. *Undefiled*—With any sin in himself. *Separated from sinners*—As well as free from sin. And so he was when he left the world. *And made*—Even in his human nature. *Higher than the heavens*—And all their inhabitants.

Verse 27. *Who needeth not to offer up sacrifices daily*—That is, on every yearly day of expiation; for he offered *once for all:* not *for his own sins,* for he then offered up himself "without spot to God."

Verse 28. *The law maketh men high priests that have infirmity*—That are both weak, mortal, and sinful. *But the oath which was since the law*—Namely, in the time of David. *Maketh the son, who is consecrated for ever*—Who being now free, both from sin and death, from natural and moral infirmity, *remaineth a priest for ever.*

Verse 1. *We have such an high priest*—Having finished his description of the type in Melchisedec, the apostle begins to treat directly of the excellency of Christ's priesthood, beyond the Levitical. *Who is set down*—Having finished his oblation. *At the right hand of the Majesty*—Of God.

Verse 2. *A minister*—Who represents his own sacrifice, as the high priest did the blood of those sacrifices once a year. *Of the sanctuary*—Heaven, typified by the holy of holies. *And of the true tabernacle*—Perhaps his human nature, of which the old tabernacle was a type. *Which the Lord hath fixed*—For ever. *Not man*—As Moses fixed the tabernacle.

3 the Lord hath fixed, and not man. For *every* high priest
is ordained to offer up gifts and sacrifices: whence *it was*
4 necessary that this also should have somewhat to offer. But
if he were on earth, he could not be a priest, there being
5 priests that offer gifts according to the law. Who serve
after the pattern and shadow of heavenly things, as Moses
was admonished of God when he was about to finish the
tabernacle: for, saith he, * See thou make all things accord-
6 ing to the model which was showed thee in the mount. But
he hath now obtained a more excellent ministry, by how
much better a covenant he is a mediator of, which is estab-
7 lished upon better promises. For if the first had been fault-
8 less, no place would have been sought for a second. For
finding fault with them, he saith, † Behold, the days come,

* Exod. xxv 40. † Jer. xxxi. 31, &c.

Verse 4 *But if he were on earth*—If his priesthood terminated here *He could not be a priest*—At all, consistently with the Jewish institutions. *There being* other *priests*—To whom alone this office is allotted.

Verse 5 *Who serve*—The temple, which was not yet destroyed. *After the pattern and shadow of heavenly things*—Of spiritual, evangelical worship, and of everlasting glory. *The pattern*—Somewhat like the strokes pencilled out upon a piece of fine linen, which exhibit the figures of leaves and flowers, but have not yet received their splendid colours and curious shades. *And shadow*—Or shadowy representation, which gives you some dim and imperfect idea of the body, but not the fine features, not the distinguishing air; none of those living graces which adorn the real person. Yet both the pattern and shadow lead our minds to something nobler than themselves: the *pattern*, to that holiness and glory which complete it; the *shadow*, to that which occasions it

Verse 6. *And now he hath obtained a more excellent ministry*—His priesthood as much excels theirs, as the promises of the gospel (whereof he is a surety) excels those of the law. These *better promises* are specified, verses 10, 11: those in the law were mostly temporal promises.

Verse 7. *For if the first had been faultless*—If that dispensation had answered all God's designs and man's wants, if it had not been weak and unprofitable, unable to make anything perfect, *no place would have been for a second.*

Verse 8. But there is; *for finding fault with them*—Who were under the old covenant *He saith, I make a new covenant with the house of Israel*—With all the Israel of God, in all ages and nations. It is new in many respects, though not as to the substance of it: 1. Being ratified by the death of Christ. 2. Freed from those burdensome rites and ceremonies. 3. Containing a more full and clear account of spiritual religion. 4. Attended with larger influences of the Spirit 5. Extended to all men. And, 6. Never to be abolished.

saith the Lord, when I will make a new covenant with the
9 house of Israel and with the house of Judah: Not according to the covenant which I made with their fathers in the
day when I took them by the hand, to lead them out of the
land of Egypt; because they continued not in my covenant,
10 and I regarded them not, saith the Lord. For this is the
covenant which I will make with the house of Israel after
those days, saith the Lord; I will put my laws in their
minds, and write them on their hearts: and I will be to
11 them a God, and they shall be to me a people: And they
shall not teach every one his neighbour, and every one his
brother, saying, Know the Lord: for they shall all know
12 me, from the least even to the greatest. For I will be
merciful to their unrighteousness, and their sins and their
13 iniquities will I remember no more. In saying, A new *cove-*

Verse 9. *When I took them by the hand*—With the care and tenderness of a parent. And just while this was fresh in their memory, they obeyed; but presently after they shook off the yoke. *They continued not in my covenant, and I regarded them not*—So that covenant was soon broken in pieces.

Verse 10. *This is the covenant I will make after those days*—After the Mosaic dispensation is abolished. *I will put my laws in their minds*—I will open their eyes, and enlighten their understanding, to see the true, full, spiritual meaning thereof. *And write them on their hearts*—So that they shall inwardly experience whatever I have commanded. *And I will be to them a God*—Their all-sufficient portion, and exceeding great reward. *And they shall be to me a people*—My treasure, my beloved, loving, and obedient children.

Verse 11. *And they* who are under this covenant (though in other respects they will have need to teach each other to their lives' end, yet) *shall not* need to *teach every one his brother, saying, Know the Lord; for they shall all know me*—All real Christians. *From the least to the greatest*—In this order the saving knowledge of God ever did and ever will proceed; not first to the greatest, and then to the least. But "the Lord shall save the tents," the poorest, "of Judah first, that the glory of the house of David," the royal seed, "and the glory of the inhabitants of Jerusalem," the nobles and the rich citizens, "do not magnify themselves," Zech. xii. 7.

Verse 12. *For I will* justify them, which is the root of all true knowledge of God. This, therefore, is God's method. First, a sinner is pardoned: then he knows God, as gracious and merciful: then God's laws are written on his heart: he is God's, and God is his

Verse 13. *In saying, A new covenant, he hath antiquated the first*—Hath shown that it is disannulled, and out of date *Now that which is anti-*

nant, he hath antiquated the first. Now that which is antiquated and decayed is ready to vanish away.

CHAP. IX. 1 And verily the first *covenant* also had
2 ordinances of worship, and a worldly sanctuary. For the
first tabernacle was prepared, in which *was* the candlestick,
and the table, and the shewbread; which is called the holy
3 *place*. And beyond the second veil, the tabernacle which
4 is called the holy of holies, Having the golden censer, and
the ark of the covenant overlaid round about with gold,
wherein *was* a golden pot having the manna, and Aaron's
5 rod that blossomed, and the tables of the covenant; And
over it *were* the cherubim of glory shadowing the mercy-
6 seat; of which we cannot now speak particularly. Now
these things being thus prepared, the priests go always into

quated is ready to vanish away—As it did quickly after, when the temple was destroyed.

Verse 1. *The first covenant had ordinances of* outward *worship, and a worldly*, a visible, material *sanctuary*, or tabernacle. Of this *sanctuary* he treats, verses 2—5; of those *ordinances*, verses 6—10.

Verse 2. *The first*—The outward tabernacle. *In which was the candlestick, and the table—The shewbread*, shown continually before God and all the people, consisting of twelve loaves, according to the number of the tribes, was placed on this table in two rows, six upon one another in each row. This candlestick and bread seem to have typified the light and life which are more largely dispensed under the gospel by Him who is the Light of the world, and the Bread of life.

Verse 3. *The second veil* divided the holy place from the most holy, as the first veil did the holy place from the courts

Verse 4. *Having the golden censer*—Used by the high priest only, on the great day of atonement. *And the ark*, or chest, *of the covenant*—So called from *the tables of the covenant* contained therein. *Wherein was the manna*—The monument of God's care over Israel. *And Aaron's rod*—The monument of the regular priesthood. *And the tables of the covenant*—The two tables of stone, on which the ten commandments were written by the finger of God; the most venerable monument of all.

Verse 5. *And over it were the cherubim of glory*—Over which the glory of God used to appear. Some suppose each of these had four faces, and so represented the Three-One God, with the manhood assumed by the Second Person. With out-spread wings *shadowing the mercy-seat*—Which was a lid or plate of gold, covering the ark.

Verse 6. *Always*—Every day. *Accomplishing their services*—Lighting the lamps, changing the shewbread, burning incense, and sprinkling the blood of the sin-offerings.

7 the first tabernacle, accomplishing their services. But into
the second, only the high priest once a year, not without
blood, which he offereth for himself, and the errors of the
8 people: The Holy Ghost evidently showing this, that the
way into the holiest was not yet made manifest, while the
9 first tabernacle was still subsisting: Which *is* a figure for
the time present, in which are offered both gifts and sacrifices, which cannot perfect the worshipper, as to *his* consci-
10 ence; Only with meats and drinks, and divers washings,
and carnal ordinances, imposed till the time of reformation.
11 But Christ being come an high priest of good things to
come, through a greater and more perfect tabernacle, not
12 made with hands, that is, not of this creation; And not by
the blood of goats and calves, but by his own blood, entered
in once for all into the holy place, having obtained eternal
13 redemption *for us.* For if the blood of bulls and goats, and
the * ashes of an heifer sprinkling the unclean, sanctifieth to
14 the purifying of the flesh: How much more shall the blood
of Christ, who through the eternal Spirit offered himself with-

* Numb. xix. 17, 18, 19.

Verse 7. *Errors*—That is, sins of ignorance, to which only those atonements extended.

Verse 8. *The Holy Ghost evidently showing*—By this token. *That the way into the holiest*—Into heaven. *Was not made manifest*—Not so clearly revealed. *While the first tabernacle,* and its service, *were still subsisting*—And remaining in force.

Verse 9. *Which*—Tabernacle, with all its furniture and services. *Is a figure*—Or type, of good things to come *Which cannot perfect the worshipper*—Neither the priest nor him who brought the offering. *As to his conscience*—So that he should be no longer conscious of the guilt or power of sin. Observe, the temple was as yet standing.

Verse 10. They could not so perfect him, *with* all their train of precepts relating to *meats and drinks, and carnal,* gross, external *ordinances;* and were therefore *imposed* only *till the time of reformation*—Till Christ came.

Verse 11. *An high priest of good things to come*—Described, verse 15. *Entered through a greater,* that is, a more noble, *and perfect tabernacle*—Namely, his own body. *Not of this creation*—Not framed by man, as that tabernacle was.

Verse 12. *The holy place*—Heaven. *For us*—All that believe.

Verse 13. *If the ashes of an heifer*—Consumed by fire as a sin-offering, being sprinkled on them who were legally *unclean. Purified the flesh*—Removed that legal uncleanness, and re-admitted them to the temple and the congregation.

Verse 14. *How much more shall the blood of Christ*—The merit of all his

out spot to God, purge our conscience from dead works to serve
15 the living God? And for this end he is the Mediator of the new
covenant, that by means of death, for the redemption of the
transgressions that *were* under the first covenant, they who
are called might receive the promise of the eternal inherit-
16 ance. For where *such* a covenant *is*, there must also necessarily be the death of him by whom the covenant is confirmed.
17 For the covenant is of force after he is dead: whereas it is
of no strength while he by whom it is confirmed liveth.
18 Whence neither was the first *covenant* originally transacted
19 without blood. For when Moses had spoken all the commandment according to the law to all the people, * he took

* Exod. xxiv. 7, 8.

sufferings. *Who through the eternal Spirit*—The work of redemption being the work of the whole Trinity. Neither is the Second Person alone concerned even in the amazing condescension that was needful to complete it. The Father delivers up the kingdom to the Son; and the Holy Ghost becomes the gift of the Messiah, being, as it were, sent according to his good pleasure. *Offered himself*—Infinitely more precious than any created victim, and that *without spot to God. Purge our conscience*—Our inmost soul. *From dead works*—From all the inward and outward works of the devil, which spring from spiritual death in the soul, and lead to death everlasting. *To serve the living God*—In the life of faith, in perfect love and spotless holiness.

Verse 15. *And for this end he is the Mediator of a new covenant, that they who are called*—To the engagements and benefits thereof. *Might receive the eternal inheritance* promised to Abraham: not *by means* of legal sacrifices, but *of* his meritorious *death. For the redemption of the transgressions that were under the first covenant*—That is, for the redemption of transgressors from the guilt and punishment of those sins which were committed in the time of the old covenant. The article of his death properly divides the old covenant from the new.

Verse 16. I say by means of death; *for where such a covenant is, there must be the death of him by whom it is confirmed*—Seeing it is by his death that the benefits of it are purchased. It seems beneath the dignity of the apostle to play upon the ambiguity of the Greek word, as the common translation supposes him to do.

Verse 17. *After he is dead*—Neither this, nor *after men are dead* is a literal translation of the words. It is a very perplexed passage.

Verse 18. *Whence neither was the first*—The Jewish covenant, *originally transacted without the blood* of an appointed sacrifice.

Verse 19. *He took the blood of calves*—Or heifers. *And of goats, with water, and scarlet wool, and hyssop*—All these circumstances are not particularly mentioned in that chapter of Exodus, but are supposed to be already known from other passages of Moses *And the book itself*—Which

the blood of calves and of goats, with water, and scarlet wool,
and hyssop, and the book itself, and sprinkled all the people,
20 Saying, * This *is* the blood of the covenant which God hath
21 enjoined unto you. And in like manner he sprinkled with
blood both the tabernacle, and all the vessels of the service
22 And almost all things are according to the law purified with
blood; and without shedding of blood there is no forgive-
23 ness. *It was* therefore necessary that the patterns of things
in heaven should be purified by these; but the heavenly
24 things themselves by better sacrifices than these. For Christ
did not enter into the holy place made with hands, the figure
of the true; but into heaven itself, now to appear in the
25 presence of God for us: Nor *did he enter* that he might
offer himself often, (as the high priest entered into the holy
26 place every year with the blood of others;) For then he

* Exod. xxiv. 8.

contained all he had said. *And sprinkled all the people*—Who were near him. The blood was mixed with water to prevent its growing too stiff for sprinkling; perhaps also to typify that blood and water, John xix. 34.

Verse 20. *Saying, This is the blood of the covenant which God hath enjoined* me to deliver *unto you*—By this it is established.

Verse 21. *And in like manner he* ordered *the tabernacle*—When it was made, and all its vessels, to be sprinkled with blood once a year.

Verse 22. *And almost all things*—For some were purified by water or fire. *Are according to the law purified with blood*—Offered or sprinkled. *And* according to the law, *there is no forgiveness* of sins *without shedding of blood*—All this pointed to the blood of Christ effectually cleansing from all sin, and intimated, there can be no purification from it by any other means.

Verse 23. *Therefore*—That is, it plainly appears from what has been said. *It was necessary*—According to the appointment of God. *That the* tabernacle and all its utensils, which were *patterns,* shadowy representations, *of things in heaven, should be purified by these*—Sacrifices and sprinklings. *But the heavenly things themselves*—Our heaven-born spirits: what more this may mean we know not yet. *By better sacrifices than these*—That is, by a better sacrifice, which is here opposed to all the legal sacrifices, and is expressed plurally, because it includes the signification of them all, and is of so much more eminent virtue.

Verse 24. *For Christ did not enter into the holy place made with hands*—He never went into the holy of holies at Jerusalem, *the figure of the true* tabernacle in heaven, Heb. viii. 2. *But into heaven itself, to appear in the presence of God for us*—As our glorious high priest and powerful intercessor.

Verse 26. *For then he must often have suffered from the foundation of the*

must often have suffered since the foundation of the world
but now once at the consummation of the ages hath he been
27 manifested to abolish sin by the sacrifice of himself. And as
it is appointed for men once to die, and after this the judg-
28 ment: So Christ also, having been once offered to bear the
sins of many, will appear the second time without sin to them
that look for him, unto salvation.

CHAP. X. 1 For the law having a shadow of good things
to come, not the very image of the things, can never with the
same sacrifices which they offer year by year continually
2 make the comers thereunto perfect. Otherwise would they
not have ceased to be offered? because the worshippers having been once purged would have had no more consciousness
3 of sins. But in those *sacrifices, there is* a commemoration

world—This supposes, 1. That by suffering once he atoned for all the sins which had been committed from the foundation of the world. 2. That he could not have atoned for them without suffering. *At the consummation of the ages*—The sacrifice of Christ divides the whole age or duration of the world into two parts, and extends its virtue backward and forward, from this middle point wherein they meet to *abolish* both the guilt and power of *sin*.

Verse 27. *After this, the judgment*—Of the great day. At the moment of death every man's final state is determined. But there is not a word in scripture of a particular judgment immediately after death.

Verse 28. *Christ having once* died *to bear the sins*—The punishment due to them. *Of many*—Even as many as are born into the world. *Will appear the second time*—When he comes to judgment. *Without sin*—Not as he did before, bearing on himself the sins of many, but to bestow everlasting salvation.

Verse 1. From all that has been said it appears, that the law, the Mosaic dispensation, being a bare, unsubstantial *shadow of good things to come*, of the gospel blessings, *and not the* substantial, solid *image of them, can never with the same* kind of *sacrifices*, though continually repeated, *make the comers thereunto perfect*, either as to justification or sanctification How is it possible, that any who consider this should suppose the attainments of David, or any who were under that dispensation, to be the proper measure of gospel holiness; and that Christian experience is to rise no higher than Jewish?

Verse 2. They who had *been once* perfectly *purged, would have* been no longer *conscious* either of the guilt or power *of* their *sins*.

Verse 3. *There is a* public *commemoration of* the *sins* both of the last and of all the preceding years; a clear proof that the guilt thereof is not perfectly purged away.

4 of sins every year. For *it is* impossible that the blood
5 of bulls and of goats should take away sins. Therefore when
he cometh into the world, he saith, * Sacrifice and offering
thou hast not chosen, but a body hast thou prepared for me:
6 Burnt offerings and *sacrifices* for sin thou hast not delighted
7 in. Then I said, Lo, I come (in the volume of the book it
8 is written of me) to do thy will, O God. Above when he
said, Sacrifice and offering and burnt offerings and *offering*
for sin thou hast not chosen, neither delighted in; which are
9 offered according to the law; Then said he, Lo, I come to
do thy will. He taketh away the first, that he may estab-
10 lish the second. By which will we are sanctified through the
11 offering of the body of Jesus Christ once for all. And indeed
every priest standeth daily ministering and offering often the
12 same sacrifices, which can never take away sins: But he,
having offered one sacrifice for sins, for ever sat down at the
13 right hand of God; From thenceforth waiting till his † ene-
14 mies be made his footstool. For by one offering he hath
15 perfected for ever them that are sanctified. And *this* the

* Psalm xl. 6, &c. † Psalm cx. 1.

Verse 4. *It is impossible the blood of goats should take away sins*—Either the guilt or the power of them.

Verse 5. *When he cometh into the world*—In the fortieth psalm the Messiah's coming into the world is represented. It is said, *into the world*, not into the tabernacle, Heb. ix. 1; because all the world is interested in his sacrifice. *A body hast thou prepared for me*—That I may offer up myself.

Verse 7. *In the volume of the book*—In this very psalm *it is written of me.* Accordingly *I come to do thy will*—By the sacrifice of myself.

Verse 8. *Above when he said, Sacrifice thou hast not chosen*—That is, when the Psalmist pronounced those words in his name.

Verse 9. *Then said he*—In that very instant he subjoined. *Lo, I come to do thy will*—To offer a more acceptable sacrifice; and by this very act *he taketh away the* legal, *that he may establish the* evangelical, dispensation.

Verse 10. *By which will*—Of God, done and suffered by Christ. *We are sanctified*—Cleansed from guilt, and consecrated to God.

Verse 11. *Every priest standeth*—As a servant in an humble posture.

Verse 12. *But he*—The virtue of whose *one sacrifice* remains *for ever. Sat down*—As a son, in majesty and honour.

Verse 14. *He hath perfected them for ever*—That is, has done all that was needful in order to their full reconciliation with God

Verse 15. In this and the three following verses, the apostle winds up his argument concerning the excellency and perfection of the priesthood

Holy Ghost also testifieth to us after he had said before,
16 * This *is* the covenant which I will make with them after
those days, saith the Lord, I will put my laws into their
17 hearts, and write them on their minds; And their sins, and
18 their iniquities will I remember no more. Now where remission of these *is*, *there is* no more offering for sin.
19 Having therefore, brethren, free liberty to enter into the
20 holiest by the blood of Jesus, By a new and living way,
which he hath consecrated for us, through the veil, that is,
21 his flesh; And *having* a great high priest over the house
22 of God; Let us draw near with a true heart in full assurance of faith, having our hearts sprinkled from an evil con-
23 science, and our bodies washed with pure water. Let us
hold fast the profession of our hope without wavering; (for
24 he *is* faithful that hath promised;) And let us consider one
another to provoke *one another* to love and to good works.
25 Not forsaking the assembling ourselves together, as the
manner of some *is;* but exhorting *one another:* and so

* Jer. xxxi. 33, &c

and sacrifice of Christ. He had proved this before by a quotation from Jeremiah; which he here repeats, describing the new covenant as now completely ratified, and all the blessings of it secured to us by the one offering of Christ, which renders all other expiatory sacrifices, and any repetition of his own, utterly needless.

Verse 19. Having finished the doctrinal part of his epistle, the apostle now proceeds to exhortation deduced from what has been treated of from Heb. v. 4, which he begins by a brief recapitulation. *Having therefore liberty to enter,—*

Verse 20. *By a living way*—The way of faith, whereby we live indeed. *Which he hath consecrated*—Prepared, dedicated, and established *for us. Through the veil, that is, his flesh*—As by rending the veil in the temple, the holy of holies became visible and accessible; so by wounding the body of Christ, the God of heaven was manifested, and the way to heaven opened.

Verse 22. *Let us draw near*—To God. *With a true heart*—In godly sincerity. *Having our hearts sprinkled from an evil conscience*—So as to condemn us no longer *And our bodies washed with pure water*—All our conversation spotless and holy, which is far more acceptable to God than all the legal sprinklings and washings.

Verse 23. *The profession of our hope*—The hope which we professed at our baptism.

Verse 25. *Not forsaking the assembling ourselves*—In public or private worship. *As the manner of some is*—Either through fear of persecution, or from a vain imagination that they were above external ordinances. *But*

26 much the more, as ye see the day approaching. For when
we sin wilfully after having received the knowledge of the
27 truth, there remaineth no more sacrifice for sins, But a
certain fearful looking for of judgment and fiery indignation,
28 which is ready to devour the adversaries. He that despised
the law of Moses died without mercy under two or three
29 witnesses: Of how much sorer punishment, suppose ye,
shall he be thought worthy, who hath trodden under foot the
Son of God, and counted the blood of the covenant, by which
he hath been sanctified, an unholy thing, and done despite to
30 the Spirit of grace? For we know him that hath said,
* Vengeance *is* mine, I will recompense. And again, The
31 Lord will judge his people. *It is* a fearful thing to fall into
32 the hands of the living God. But call ye to mind the former days, in which, after ye were enlightened, ye endured so
33 great a conflict of sufferings; Partly, being made a gazing-
stock both by reproaches and afflictions; partly, being par-
34 takers with them who were so treated. For ye sympathized
with my bonds, and received with joy the spoiling of your

* Deut. xxxii. 35, &c.

exhorting one another—To faith, love, and good works. *And so much the more, as ye see the day approaching*—The great day is ever in your eye.

Verse 26. *For when we*—Any of us Christians. *Sin wilfully*—By total apostasy from God, termed "drawing back," verse 38. *After having received the* experimental *knowledge of the* gospel *truth, there remaineth no more sacrifice for sins*—None but that which we obstinately reject.

Verse 28. *He that*, in capital cases, *despised* (presumptuously transgressed) *the law of Moses died without mercy*—Without any delay or mitigation of his punishment.

Verse 29. *Of how much sorer punishment is he worthy, who*—By wilful, total apostasy. It does not appear that this passage refers to any other sin. *Hath*, as it were, *trodden under foot the Son of God*—A lawgiver far more honourable than Moses. *And counted the blood* wherewith *the* better *covenant* was established, *an unholy*, a common, worthless *thing. By which he hath been sanctified*—Therefore Christ died for him also, and he was at least justified once. *And done despite to the Spirit of grace*—By rejecting all his motions.

Verse 30. *The Lord will judge his people*—Yea, far more rigorously than the heathens, if they rebel against him

Verse 31. *To fall into the hands*—Of his avenging justice.

Verse 32. *Enlightened*—With the knowledge of God and of his truth

Verse 34. *For ye sympathized with* all your suffering brethren, and *with me* in particular; *and received joyfully the* loss of your own goods.

goods, knowing that ye have for yourselves in heaven a better
35 and an enduring substance. Cast not away therefore your
36 confidence, which hath great recompence of reward. For ye
have need of patience, that, having done the will of God, ye
37 may receive the promise. For yet a very little while, and he
38 that cometh will come, and will not tarry. * Now the just
shall live by faith: but if he draw back, my soul hath no
39 pleasure in him. But we are not of them who draw back to
perdition; but of them that believe to the saving of the
soul.

CHAP. XI. 1 Now faith is the subsistence of things
2 hoped for, the evidence of things not seen. And by it the

* Hab. ii. 3, &c.

Verse 35. *Cast not away therefore* this *your confidence*—Your faith and hope; which none can deprive you of but yourselves.

Verse 36. *The promise*—Perfect love; eternal life.

Verse 37. *He that cometh*—To reward every man according to his works

Verse 38. *Now the just*—The justified person. *Shall live*—In God's favour, a spiritual and holy life. *By faith*—As long as he retains that gift of God. *But if he draw back*—If he make shipwreck of his faith *My soul hath no pleasure in him*—That is, I abhor him; I cast him off.

Verse 39. *We are not of them who draw back to perdition*—Like him mentioned verse 38. *But of them that believe*—To the end, so as to attain eternal life.

Verse 1. The definition of faith given in this verse, and exemplified in the various instances following, undoubtedly includes justifying faith, but not directly as justifying. For faith justifies only as it refers to, and depends on, Christ. But here is no mention of him as the object of faith; and in several of the instances that follow, no notice is taken of him or his salvation, but only of temporal blessings obtained by faith. And yet they may all be considered as evidences of the power of justifying faith in Christ, and of its extensive exercise in a course of steady obedience amidst difficulties and dangers of every kind. *Now faith is the subsistence of things hoped for, the evidence* or conviction *of things not seen*—Things hoped for are not so extensive as things not seen. The former are only things future and joyful to us; the latter are either future, past, or present, and those either good or evil, whether to us or others. *The subsistence of things hoped for*—Giving a kind of present subsistence to the good things which God has promised: the divine supernatural *evidence* exhibited to, the conviction hereby produced in, a believer *of things not seen*, whether past, future, or spiritual; particularly of God and the things of God.

Verse 2 *By it the elders*—Our forefathers. This chapter is a kind of summary of the Old Testament, in which the apostle comprises the

3 elders obtained a *good* testimony. Through faith we understand that the worlds were framed by the word of God, so
that the things which are seen were made of things which
4 do not appear. By faith Abel offered unto God a more
excellent sacrifice than Cain, by which he obtained a testimony that he was righteous, God testifying of his gifts: and
5 by it being dead, he yet speaketh. By faith Enoch was
translated so as not to see death; and was not found, because
God had translated him: for before his translation he had a
6 testimony that he pleased God. But without faith *it is*
impossible to please *him:* for he that cometh to God must
believe that he is, and *that* he is a rewarder of them that

designs, labours, sojournings, expectations, temptations, martyrdoms of the ancients. The former of them had a long exercise of their patience; the latter suffered shorter but sharper trials. *Obtained a good testimony*—A most comprehensive word. God gave a *testimony*, not only *of* them but *to* them: and they received his testimony as if it had been the things themselves of which he testified, verses 4, 5, 39. Hence they also gave testimony to others, and others testified of them.

Verse 3. *By faith we understand that the worlds*—Heaven and earth and all things in them, visible and invisible. *Were made*—Formed, fashioned, and finished. *By the word*—The sole command *of God*, without any instrument or preceding matter. And as creation is the foundation and specimen of the whole divine economy, so faith in the creation is the foundation and specimen of all faith. *So that things which are seen*—As the sun, earth, stars. *Were made of things which do not appear*—Out of the dark, unapparent chaos, Gen. i. 2. And this very chaos was created by the divine power; for before it was thus created it had no existence in nature

Verse 4. *By faith*—In the future Redeemer. *Abel offered a more excellent sacrifice*—The firstlings of his flock, implying both a confession of what his own sins deserved, and a desire of sharing in the great atonement. *Than Cain*—Whose offering testified no such faith, but a bare acknowledgment of God the Creator. *By which* faith *he obtained* both righteousness and *a testimony* of it: *God testifying*—Visibly that his gifts were accepted; probably by sending fire from heaven to consume his sacrifice, a token that justice seized on the sacrifice instead of the sinner who offered it. *And by it*—By this faith. *Being dead, he yet speaketh*—That a sinner is accepted only through faith in the great sacrifice.

Verse 5. *Enoch was not* any longer *found* among men, though perhaps they sought for him as they did for Elijah, 2 Kings ii. 17. *He had this testimony*—From God in his own conscience.

Verse 6. *But without faith*—Even some divine faith in God, *it is impossible to please him. For he that cometh to God*—In prayer, or any other act of worship, *must believe that he is.*

7 diligently seek him. By faith Noah, being warned of God
of things not seen as yet, moved with fear, prepared an ark
for the saving of his household; by which he condemned the
world, and became heir of the righteousness which is by
8 faith. * By faith Abraham, being called to go out into the
place which he was to receive for an inheritance, obeyed;
9 and went out, though he knew not whither he went. † By
faith he sojourned in the land of promise, as *in* a strange
country, dwelling in tents with Isaac and Jacob, the joint-
10 heirs of the same promise. For he looked for the city which
11 hath foundations, whose builder and former *is* God. By
faith ‡ Sarah also herself received power to conceive seed,
even when she was past age, because she accounted him
12 faithful who had promised. Therefore there sprang even
from one, and him as it were dead, *a posterity* as the stars in
heaven for multitude, and as the sand which is on the sea
13 shore innumerable. All these died in faith, not having
received the promises, but having seen them afar off, and
embraced *them*, and confessed that they were strangers and
14 sojourners on the earth. For they who speak thus show

* Gen. xii. 1, 4, 5 † Gen. xvii. 8 ‡ Gen. xxi. 2.

Verse 7. *Noah being warned of things not seen as yet*—Of the future deluge. *Moved with fear, prepared an ark, by which* open testimony *he condemned the world*—Who neither believed nor feared.

Verse 9. *By faith he sojourned in the land of promise*—The promise was made before, Gen. xii. 7. *Dwelling in tents*—As a sojourner *With Isaac and Jacob*—Who by the same manner of living showed the same faith Jacob was born fifteen years before the death of Abraham. *The joint heirs of the same promise*—Having all the same interest therein. Isaac did not receive this inheritance from Abraham, nor Jacob from Isaac, but all of them from God.

Verse 10. *He looked for a city which hath foundations*—Whereas a tent has none. *Whose builder and former is God*—Of which God is the sole contriver, former, and finisher.

Verse 11. *Sarah also herself*—Though at first she laughed at the promise, Gen. xviii. 12.

Verse 12. *As it were dead*—Till his strength was supernaturally restored. which continued for many years after

Verse 13. *All these*—Mentioned verses 7—11. *Died in faith*—In death faith acts most vigorously. *Not having received the promises*—The promised blessings. *Embraced*—As one does a dear friend when he meets him.

Verse 14. *They who speak thus show plainly that they seek their own country*—That they keep in view, and long for, their native home.

15 plainly that they seek their own country. And truly, if they
had been mindful of that from which they came out, they
16 might have had opportunity to return. But now they desire
a better *country*, that is, an heavenly: therefore God is not
ashamed to be called their God: for he hath prepared a city
17 for them. By faith * Abraham, being tried, offered up
Isaac; yea, he that had received the promises, offered up
18 his only begotten *son*, Of whom it had been said, † In
19 Isaac shall thy seed be called: Accounting that God was
able even to raise *him* from the dead; from whence also he did
20 receive him in a figure. By faith Isaac blessed Jacob and
21 Esau concerning things to come. By faith Jacob, when
dying, ‡ blessed each of the sons of Joseph; and || worshipped,
22 *bowing down* on the top of his staff. By faith Joseph, when
dying, made mention of the children of Israel; and gave
23 charge concerning his bones. By faith Moses, when he was
born, was hid three months by his parents, because they saw

* Gen xxii. 1, &c. † Gen. xxi. 12. ‡ Gen. xlviii. 16. || Gen. xlvii. 31.

Verse 15. *If they had been mindful of*—Their earthly country, Ur of the Chaldeans, they might have easily returned.

Verse 16 *But they desire a better country, that is, an heavenly*—This is a full convincing proof that the patriarchs had a revelation and a promise of eternal glory in heaven. *Therefore God is not ashamed to be called their God:* seeing *he hath prepared for them a city*—Worthy of God to give.

Verse 17. *By faith Abraham*—When God made that glorious trial of him. *Offered up Isaac*—The will being accepted as if he had actually done it. *Yea, he that had received the promises*—Particularly that grand promise, "In Isaac shall thy seed be called." *Offered up*—This very son; the only one he had by Sarah.

Verse 18. *In Isaac shall thy seed be called*—From him shall the blessed seed spring.

Verse 19. *Accounting that God was able even to raise him from the dead*—Though there had not been any instance of this in the world. *From whence also*—To speak in a figurative way. *He did receive him*—Afterwards, snatched from the jaws of death.

Verse 20. *Blessed*—Gen. xxvii. 27, 39; prophetically foretold the particular blessings they should partake of. *Jacob and Esau*—Preferring the elder before the younger.

Verse 21. *Jacob when dying*—That is, when near death. *Bowing down on the top of his staff*—As he sat on the side of his bed.

Verse 22. *Concerning his bones*—To be carried into the land of promise.

Verse 23. *They saw*—Doubtless with a divine presage of things to come.

he was a beautiful child; and they were not afraid of the
24 king's commandment. By faith Moses, when he was grown up,
25 refused to be called the son of Pharaoh's daughter; Choosing
rather to suffer affliction with the people of God, than to enjoy
26 the pleasures of sin for a season; Esteeming the reproach
of Christ greater riches than the treasures in Egypt: for he
27 looked off unto the recompence of reward. * By faith he left
Egypt, not fearing the wrath of the king: for he endured,
28 as seeing him that is invisible. By faith he † celebrated the
passover, and the pouring out of the blood, that he who
29 destroyed the firstborn might not touch them. By faith they
passed through the Red Sea as by dry land: which the
30 Egyptians trying to do were drowned. By faith the walls of
31 Jericho, having been compassed seven days, fell down. By
faith Rahab the harlot did not perish with them that believed
32 not, having received the spies with peace. And what shall
I say more? for the time would fail me to discourse of Gideon,
and Barak, and Samson, and Jephthah, and David, and

* Exod. xiv. 15, &c. † Exod. xii. 12—18.

Verse 24. *Refused to be called*—Any longer.

Verse 26. *The reproach of Christ*—That which he bore for believing in the Messiah to come, and acting accordingly. *For he looked off*—From all those perishing treasures, and beyond all those temporal hardships *Unto the recompence of reward*—Not to an inheritance in Canaan; he had no warrant from God to look for this, nor did he ever attain it; but what his believing ancestors looked for,—a future state of happiness in heaven.

Verse 27. *By faith he left Egypt*—Taking all the Israelites with him. *Not* then *fearing the wrath of the king*—As he did many years before, Exod. ii. 14

Verse 28. *The pouring out of the blood*—Of the paschal lamb, which was sprinkled on the door-posts, lest the destroying angel should touch the Israelites.

Verse 29. *They*—Moses, Aaron, and the Israelites. *Passed the Rea Sea*—It washed the borders of Edom, which signifies red. Thus far the examples are cited from Genesis and Exodus; those that follow are from the former and the latter Prophets.

Verse 30. By the faith of Joshua.

Verse 31. *Rahab*—Though formerly one not of the fairest character.

Verse 32. After Samuel, the prophets are properly mentioned. David also was a prophet; but he was a king too. *The prophets*—Elijah, Elisha, &c., including likewise the believers who lived with them.

33 Samuel, and the prophets: Who by faith * subdued kingdoms, † wrought righteousness, obtained promises, ‡ stopped
34 the mouths of lions, ∥ Quenched the violence of fire, § escaped
the edge of the sword, ¶ out of weakness was made strong,
** became valiant in fight, †† put to flight armies of the ali-
35 ens. ‡‡ Women received their dead raised to life again: others
were tortured, not accepting deliverance; that they might
36 obtain a better resurrection: And others had trial of mockings
and scourging, yea, moreover of bonds and imprisonment:
37 They were stoned, were sawn asunder, were tempted, were
slain with the sword: they wandered about in sheepskins, in
38 goatskins; destitute, afflicted, tormented: (Of whom the
world was not worthy:) they wandered in deserts, and

* 2 Sam. viii. 1, &c. † 1 Sam. viii. 9, &c.; xiii. 3, &c ‡ Dan. vi. 22. ∥ Dan. iii. 27. § Judges xii. 3. ¶ Judges xv. 19, &c.; xvi. 28, &c. ** Judges iv. 14, &c. †† Judges vii. 21. ‡‡ 1 Kings xvii. 22; 2 Kings iv. 35.

Verses 33, 34. David, in particular, *subdued kingdoms.* Samuel (not excluding the rest) *wrought righteousness.* The prophets, in general, *obtained promises,* both for themselves, and to deliver to others. Prophets also *stopped the mouths of lions,* as Daniel; and *quenched the violence of fire,* as Shadrach, Meshach, and Abednego. To these examples, whence the nature of faith clearly appears, those more ancient ones are subjoined, (by a transposition, and in an inverted order,) which receive light from these. Jephthah *escaped the edge of the sword;* Samson *out of weakness was made strong;* Barak *became valiant in fight;* Gideon *put to flight armies of the aliens.* Faith animates to the most heroic enterprises, both civil and military. Faith overcomes all impediments; effects the greatest things; attains to the very best; and inverts, by its miraculous power, the very course of nature.

Verse 35. *Women*—Naturally weak. *Received their dead*—Children. *Others were tortured*—From those who acted great things the apostle rises higher, to those who showed the power of faith by suffering. *Not accepting deliverance*—On sinful terms. *That they might obtain a better resurrection*—An higher reward, seeing the greater their sufferings the greater would be their glory.

Verse 36. *And others*—The apostle seems here to pass on to recent examples.

Verse 37 *They were sawn asunder*—As, according to the tradition of the Jews, Isaiah was by Manasseh. *Were tempted*—Torments and death are mentioned alternately. Every way; by threatenings, reproaches, tortures, the variety of which cannot be expressed; and again by promises and allurements.

Verse 38. *Of whom the world was not worthy*—It did not deserve so great a blessing. *They wandered*—Being driven out from men.

39 mountains, and dens, and caves of the earth. And all these
having obtained a good testimony through faith, did not
40 receive the promise: God having provided some better thing
for us, that they might not be perfected without us.

CHAP. XII. 1 Wherefore, let us also, being encompassed with so great a cloud of witnesses, lay aside every
weight, and the sin which easily besetteth *us*, and run with
2 patience the race that is set before us, Looking to Jesus, the
author and finisher of *our* faith; who for the joy that was
set before him endured the cross, despising the shame, and
3 is set down at the right hand of the throne of God. For
consider him that endured such contradiction from sinners
against himself, lest ye be weary and faint in your minds.
4 Ye have not yet resisted unto blood, striving against sin.
5 And yet ye have forgotten the exhortation which speaketh

Verse 39. *And all these*—Though they *obtained a good testimony*, verse 2, yet did not receive the great promise, the heavenly inheritance.

Verse 40. *God having provided some better thing for us*—Namely, everlasting glory. *That they might not be perfected without us*—That is, that we might all be perfected together in heaven.

Verse 1. *Wherefore, being encompassed with a cloud*—A great multitude, tending upward with a holy swiftness. *Of witnesses*—Of the power of faith. *Let us lay aside every weight*—As all who run a race take care to do. Let us throw off whatever weighs us down, or damps the vigour of our soul. *And the sin which easily besetteth us*—As doth the sin of our constitution, the sin of our education, the sin of our profession.

Verse 2. *Looking*—From all other things. *To Jesus*—As the wounded Israelites to the brazen serpent. Our crucified Lord was prefigured by the lifting up of this; our guilt, by the stings of the fiery serpents; and our faith, by their looking up to the miraculous remedy. *The author and finisher of our faith*—Who begins it in us, carries it on, and perfects it. *Who for the joy that was set before him*—Patiently and willingly *endured the cross*, with all the pains annexed thereto. *And is set down*—Where there is fulness of joy.

Verse 3. *Consider*—Draw the comparison and think. The Lord bore all this; and shall his servants bear nothing? *Him that endured such contradiction from sinners*—Such enmity and opposition of every kind. *Lest ye be weary*—Dull and languid, *and* so actually *faint* in your course.

Verse 4. *Unto blood*—Unto wounds and death.

Verse 5. *And yet ye* seem already to *have forgotten the exhortation*—Wherein God speaketh to you with the utmost tenderness. *Despise not thou the chastening of the Lord*—Do not slight or make little of it; do

to you as to sons, * My son, despise not thou the chastening
6 of the Lord, nor faint when thou art rebuked of him: For
whom the Lord loveth he chasteneth, and scourgeth every
7 son whom he receiveth. If ye endure chastening, God deal-
eth with you as with sons; for what son is there whom his
8 father chasteneth not? But if ye are without chastening,
of which all are partakers, then are ye bastards, and not sons.
9 Now if we have had fathers of our flesh who corrected us,
and we reverenced *them:* shall we not much rather be in
10 subjection to the Father of spirits, and live? For they
verily for a few days chastened *us* as they thought good;
but he for our profit, that we may be partakers of his holi-
11 ness. Now all chastening for the present is assuredly not
joyous, but grievous: yet afterwards it yieldeth the peaceable fruit of righteousness to them that are exercised thereby
12 Wherefore * lift up the hands that hang down, and the

* Prov. iii. 11, &c. † Isaiah xxxv. 3.

not impute any affliction to chance or second causes; but see and revere the hand of God in it. *Neither faint when thou art rebuked of him*—But endure it patiently and fruitfully

Verse 6. *For*—All springs from love; therefore neither despise nor faint.

Verse 7 *Whom his father chasteneth not*—When he offends

Verse 8 *Of which all* sons *are partakers*—More or less.

Verse 9. *And we reverenced them*—We neither despised nor fainted under their correction. *Shall we not much rather*—Submit with reverence and meekness *To the Father of spirits*—That we may *live* with him for ever. Perhaps these expressions, *fathers of our flesh,* and *Father of spirits,* intimate that our earthly fathers are only the parents of our bodies, our souls not being originally derived from them, but all created by the immediate power of God; perhaps, at the beginning of the world.

Verse 10. *For they verily for a few days*—How few are even all our days on earth! *Chastened us as they thought good*—Though frequently they erred therein, by too much either of indulgence or severity. *But he* always, unquestionably, *for our profit, that we may be partakers of his holiness*—That is, of himself and his glorious image.

Verse 11. *Now all chastening*—Whether from our earthly or heavenly Father *Is for the present grievous, yet it yieldeth the peaceable fruit of righteousness*--Holiness and happiness. *To them that are exercised thereby*—That receive this exercise as from God, and improve it according to his will

Verse 12. *Wherefore lift up the hands*—Whether your own or your brethren's. *That hang down*—Unable to continue the combat. *And the feeble knees*—Unable to continue the race.

13 feeble knees; And make straight paths for your feet, that
the lame be not turned out of the way; but rather healed.
14 Follow peace with all men, and holiness, without which no
15 man shall see the Lord: Looking diligently lest any one
fall from the grace of God; lest any root of bitterness spring-
16 ing up trouble *you*, and thereby many be defiled: Lest *there*
be any fornicator, or profane person, as Esau, who for one
17 meal gave away his birth-right. For ye know that afterward,
even when he desired to inherit the blessing, he was rejected.
for he found no place for repentance, though he sought it
diligently with tears.
18 For ye are not come to the mountain that could be
touched, and the burning fire, and the thick cloud, and dark-
19 ness, and tempest, And the sound of a trumpet, and the
voice of words; which they that heard entreated that no

Verse 13. *And make straight paths* both *for your* own and for their *feet*—Remove every hinderance, every offence. *That the lame*—They who are weak, scarce able to walk. *Be not turned out of the way*—Of faith and holiness.

Verse 14. *Follow peace with all men*—This second branch of the exhortation concerns our neighbours; the third, God. *And holiness*—The not following after *all* holiness, is the direct way to fall into sin of every kind.

Verse 15. *Looking diligently, lest any one*—If he do not lift up the hands that hang down. *Fall from the grace of God: lest any root of bitterness*—Of envy, anger, suspicion. *Springing up*—Destroy the sweet peace; lest any, not following after holiness, fall into fornication or profaneness. In general, any corruption, either in doctrine or practice, is a *root of bitterness,* and may pollute many.

Verse 16. *Esau* was *profane* for so slighting the *blessing* which went along with the *birth-right.*

Verse 17. *He was rejected*—He could not obtain it. *For he found no place for repentance*—There was no room for any such repentance as would regain what he had lost. *Though he sought it*—The blessing of the *birth-right. Diligently with tears*—He sought too late. Let us use the present time.

Verse 18. *For*—A strong reason this why they ought the more to regard the whole exhortation drawn from the priesthood of Christ: because both salvation and vengeance are now nearer at hand. *Ye are not come to the mountain that could be touched*—That was of an earthy, material nature.

Verse 19. *The sound of a trumpet*—Formed, without doubt, by the ministry of angels, and preparatory to *the words,* that is, the Ten Commandments, which were uttered with a loud *voice,* Deut. v. 22.

20 more might be spoken to them: (For they could not bear
that which was commanded, * If even a beast touch the
21 mountain, let it be stoned. And so terrible was the appearance, *that* Moses said, I exceedingly fear and tremble:)
22 But ye are come to mount Sion, and to the city of the living
God, the heavenly Jerusalem, and to an innumerable com-
23 pany, To the general assembly of angels, and to the church
of the first-born, who are enrolled in heaven, and to God the
Judge of all, and to the spirits of just men made perfect,
24 And to Jesus the mediator of the new covenant, and to the

Exod. xix. 12, &c

Verse 20 *For they could not bear*—The terror which seized them, when they heard those words proclaimed, *If even a beast*, &c

Verse 21. Even *Moses*—Though admitted to so near an intercourse with God, who "spake to him as a man speaketh to his friend." At other times he acted as a mediator between God and the people. But while the ten words were pronounced, he stood as one of the hearers, Exod. xix. 25; xx. 19

Verse 22. *But ye*—Who believe in Christ. *Are come*—The apostle does not here speak of their coming to the church militant, but of that glorious privilege of New Testament believers, their communion with the church triumphant. But this is far more apparent to the eyes of celestial spirits than to ours which are yet veiled. St. Paul here shows an excellent knowledge of the heavenly economy, worthy of him who had been caught up into the third heaven. *To mount Sion*—A spiritual mountain. *To the city of the living God, the heavenly Jerusalem*—All these glorious titles belong to the New Testament church. *And to an innumerable company*—Including all that are afterwards mentioned.

Verse 23. *To the general assembly*—The word properly signifies a stated convention on some festival occasion. *And church*—The whole body of true believers, whether on earth or in paradise. *Of the first-born*—*The first-born* of Israel were enrolled by Moses; but these are *enrolled in heaven*, as citizens there. It is observable, that in this beautiful gradation, these first-born are placed nearer to God than the angels. See James i. 18. *And to God the Judge of all*—Propitious to you, adverse to your enemies. *And to the spirits*—The separate souls. *Of just men*—It seems to mean, of New Testament believers. The number of these, being not yet large, is mentioned distinct from the *innumerable company of just men* whom their Judge hath acquitted. These are now *made perfect* in an higher sense than any who are still alive. Accordingly, St. Paul, while yet on earth, denies that he was thus *made perfect*, Phil. iii. 12.

Verse 24. *To Jesus, the mediator*—Through whom they had been perfected. *And to the blood of sprinkling*—To all the virtue of his precious

blood of sprinkling, which speaketh better things than *that*
25 *of* Abel. See that ye refuse not him that speaketh. For
if they escaped not who refused him that delivered the oracle
on earth, much more *shall not* we, who turn away from him
26 *that speaketh* from heaven. Whose voice then shook the
earth: but now he has promised, saying,* Yet once more I
27 will shake, not only the earth, but also the heaven. And
this *word*, Yet once more, showeth the removal of the things
which are shaken, as being made, that the things which are
28 not shaken may remain. Therefore let us, receiving a kingdom which cannot be shaken, hold fast the grace, whereby
we may serve God acceptably, with reverence and godly
29 fear: For our God *is* a consuming fire.

* Hag. ii. 6.

blood shed for you, whereby ye are sprinkled from an evil conscience. This blood of sprinkling was the foundation of our Lord's mediatorial office. Here the gradation is at the highest point. *Which speaketh better things than that of Abel*—Which cried for vengeance.

Verse 25. *Refuse not*—By unbelief. *Him that speaketh*—And whose speaking even now is a prelude to the final scene. The same voice which spake both by the law and in the gospel, when heard from heaven, will shake heaven and earth. *For if they escaped not*—His vengeance. *Much more shall not we*—Those of us who *turn from him that speaketh from heaven*—That is, who came from heaven to speak to us

Verse 26. *Whose voice then shook the earth*—When he spoke from mount Sinai. *But now*—With regard to his next speaking. *He hath promised*—It is a joyful promise to the saints, though dreadful to the wicked. *Yet once more I will shake, not only the earth, but also the heaven*—These words may refer in a lower sense to the dissolution of the Jewish church and state; but in their full sense they undoubtedly look much farther, even to the end of all things. This universal shaking began at the first coming of Christ. It will be consummated at his second coming.

Verse 27. *The things which are shaken*—Namely, heaven and earth. *As being made*—And consequently liable to change. *That the things which are not shaken may remain*—Even "the new heavens and the new earth," Rev. xxi. 1.

Verse 28. *Therefore let us, receiving*—By willing and joyful faith. *A kingdom*—More glorious than the present heaven and earth. *Hold fast the grace, whereby we may serve God*—In every thought, word, and work. *With reverence*—Literally, *with shame.* Arising from a deep consciousness of our own unworthiness. *And godly fear*—A tender, jealous fear of offending, arising from a sense of the gracious majesty of God.

Verse 29. *For our God is a consuming fire*—In the strictness of his justice, and purity of his holiness.

CHAP. XIII. 1 Let brotherly love continue. Forget
2 not hospitality: for hereby* some have entertained angels
3 unawares. Remember them that are in bonds, as being bound
with them; *and* them that suffer adversity, as being your-
4 selves also in the body. Marriage *is* honourable in all
men, and the bed undefiled: but whoremongers and adul-
5 terers God will judge. *Let your* disposition *be* without
covetousness; *be* content with the things that are present:
for he hath said, † No, I will not leave thee; verily I will
6 not forsake thee. So that we may boldly say, ‡ The Lord
is my helper, I will not fear what man can do unto me.
7 Remember them that had the rule over you, who spake to
you the word of God: whose faith follow, considering the
end of their conversation.
8 Jesus Christ *is* the same yesterday, and to-day, and for
9 ever. Be not carried about with various and strange doctrines. For *it is* good that the heart be stablished with grace;
not with meats, in which they that have walked have not been

* Gen. xviii. 2; xix.1. † Gen. xxviii. 15; Jos. i. 5; 1 Chron. xxviii. 20. ‡ Psalm cxviii. 6.

Verse 1. *Brotherly love* is explained in the following verses.

Verse 2. *Some*—Abraham and Lot. *Have entertained angels unawares*—So may an unknown guest, even now, be of more worth than he appears, and may have angels attending him, though unseen.

Verse 3. *Remember*—In your prayers, and by your help. *Them that are in bonds, as being bound with them*—Seeing ye are members one of another. *And them that suffer, as being yourselves in the body*—And consequently liable to the same.

Verse 4. *Marriage is honourable in,* or for *all* sorts of *men,* clergy as well as laity: though the Romanists teach otherwise. *And the bed undefiled*—Consistent with the highest purity; though many spiritual writers, so called, say it is only licensed whoredom. *But whoremongers and adulterers God will judge*—Though they frequently escape the sentence of men.

Verse 5. *He*—God. *Hath said*—To all believers, in saying it to Jacob, Joshua, and Solomon.

Verse 7. *Remember them*—Who are now with God, *considering the* happy *end of their conversation* on earth.

Verse 8. Men may die; but *Jesus Christ,* yea, and his gospel, *is the same* from everlasting to everlasting.

Verse 9. *Be not carried about with various doctrines*—Which differ from that one faith in our one unchangeable Lord. *Strange*—To the ears and hearts of all that abide in him. *For it is good*—It is both honourable before God, and pleasant and profitable *That the heart be stablished*

10 profited. We have an altar, whereof they have no right to
11 eat who serve the tabernacle. For the bodies of those
animals, whose blood is brought into the holy place by the
12 high priest for sin, are burned without the camp. Wherefore
Jesus also, that he might sanctify the people by his own
13 blood, suffered without the gate. Let us then go forth to
14 him without the camp, bearing his reproach. For we have
15 here no continuing city, but we seek one to come. By him
therefore let us offer the sacrifice of praise continually to
God, that is, the fruit of *our* lips giving thanks to his name.
16 But to do good, and to distribute, forget not. for with such
sacrifices God is well pleased.

17 Obey them that have the rule over you, and submit yourselves: for they watch over your souls, as they that shall
give account, that they may do this with joy, and not with

with grace—Springing from faith in Christ. *Not with meats*—Jewish ceremonies, which indeed can never stablish the heart.

Verse 10. On the former part of this verse, the fifteenth and sixteenth depend; on the latter, the intermediate verses. *We have an altar*—The cross of Christ. *Whereof they have no right to eat*—To partake of the benefits which we receive therefrom. *Who serve the tabernacle*—Who adhere to the Mosaic law.

Verse 11. *For*—According to their own law, the sin-offerings were wholly consumed, and no Jew ever ate thereof. But Christ was a sin-offering. Therefore they cannot feed upon him, as we do, who are freed from the Mosaic law.

Verse 12. *Wherefore Jesus also*—Exactly answering those typical sin-offerings. *Suffered without the gate*—Of Jerusalem, which answered to the old camp of Israel. *That he might sanctify*—Reconcile and consecrate to God. *The people*—Who believe in him. *By his own blood*—Not those shadowy sacrifices, which are now of no farther use.

Verse 13. *Let us then go forth without the camp*—Out of the Jewish dispensation. *Bearing his reproach*—All manner of shame, obloquy, and contempt for his sake.

Verse 14. *For we have here*—On earth *No continuing city*—All things here are but for a moment; and Jerusalem itself was just then on the point of being destroyed.

Verse 15. *The sacrifice*—The altar is mentioned, verse 10; now the sacrifices: 1. Praise; 2. Beneficence; with both of which *God is well pleased.*

Verse 17. *Obey them that have the rule over you*—The word implies also, that lead or guide you; namely, in truth and holiness. *And submit yourselves*—Give up (not your conscience or judgment, but) your own will, in all things purely indifferent. *For they watch over your souls*—With all

18 groans: for that *is* unprofitable for you. Pray for us: for
we trust we have a good conscience, desiring to behave our-
19 selves well in all things. And I beseech you to do this the
more earnestly, that I may be restored to you the sooner.
20 Now the God of peace, who brought again from the dead
the great shepherd of the sheep, our Lord Jesus, by the
21 blood of the everlasting covenant, Make you perfect in every
good work to do his will, working in you that which is well
pleasing in his sight, through Christ Jesus; to whom *be* the
glory for ever and ever. Amen.
22 I beseech you, brethren, suffer the word of exhortation:
23 for I have written a letter to you in few words. Know that
our brother Timotheus is set at liberty; with whom, if he
come soon, I will see you.
24 Salute all them that have the rule over you, and all the
25 saints. They of Italy salute you. Grace *be* with you all.

zeal and diligence, they guard and caution you against all danger. *As they that must give account*—To the great Shepherd, for every part of their behaviour toward you. How vigilant then ought every pastor to be! How careful of every soul committed to his charge! *That they may do this*—Watch over you. *With joy and not with groans*—He is not a good shepherd, who does not either rejoice over them, or groan for them. The groans of other creatures are heard: how much more shall these come up in the ears of God! Whoever answers this character of a Christian pastor may undoubtedly demand this obedience.

Verse 20. *The everlasting covenant*—The Christian covenant, which is not temporary, like the Jewish, but designed to remain for ever. By the application of that *blood*, by which this covenant was established, may he make you, in every respect, inwardly and outwardly holy!

Verse 22 *Suffer the word of exhortation*—Addressed to you in this letter, which, though longer than my usual letters, is yet contained *in few words*, considering the copiousness of the subject.

Verse 23. *If he come*—To me.

Verse 25.—*Grace be with you all*—St. Paul's usual benediction. **God apply it to our hearts!**

NOTES

ON

THE GENERAL EPISTLE OF ST. JAMES.

This is supposed to have been written by James the son of Alpheus, the brother (or kinsman) of our Lord. It is called a General Epistle, because written not to a particular person or church, but to all the converted Israelites. Herein the apostle reproves that antinomian spirit, which had even then infected many, who had perverted the glorious doctrine of justification by faith into an occasion of licentiousness. He likewise comforts the true believers under their sufferings, and reminds them of the judgments that were approaching.

It has three parts:—

I. The inscription, C. i 1

II The exhortation,

1. To patience, enduring outward, conquering inward, temptations, 2—15
2. Considering the goodness of God, 16—18
   to be swift to hear, slow to speak, slow to wrath
   And these three are,
   1. Proposed, 19—21
   2. Treated of at large.
      a. Let hearing be joined with practice, 22—26
         Particularly with bridling the tongue, 26
         With mercy and purity, 27
         Without respect of persons, C. ii. 1—13
         And so faith universally with works, 14—26
      b. Let the speech be modest, C. iii 1—12
      c. Let anger, with all the other passions, be restrained, 13—C. iv. 1—17
3. To patience again.
   a. Confirmed by the coming of the judge, in which draws near
      The calamity of the wicked, C. v 1— 6
      The deliverance of the righteous, 7—12
   b. Nourished by prayer, 13—18

III The conclusion, 19, 20

JAMES.

CHAPTER I. 1 James, a servant of God and of the
Lord Jesus Christ, to the twelve tribes which are scattered
abroad, greeting.
2 My brethren, count it all joy when ye fall into divers
3 temptations; Knowing, that the trying of your faith worketh
4 patience. But let patience have *its* perfect work, that ye may
5 be perfect and entire, wanting nothing. If any of you want
wisdom, let him ask of God, who giveth to all men liberally,
6 and upbraideth not; and it shall be given him. But let him

Verse 1. *A servant of Jesus Christ*—Whose name the apostle mentions but once more in the whole epistle, James ii. 1. And not at all in his whole discourse, Acts xv. 14, &c.; or xxi. 20—25. It might have seemed, if he mentioned him often, that he did it out of vanity, as being the brother of the Lord. *To the twelve tribes*—Of Israel; that is, those of them that believe. *Which are scattered abroad*—In various countries. Ten of the tribes were scattered ever since the reign of Hosea; and great part of the rest were now dispersed through the Roman empire: as was foretold, Deut. xxviii 25, &c.; xxx. 4. *Greeting*—That is, all blessings, temporal and eternal.

Verse 2. *My brethren, count it all joy*—Which is the highest degree of patience, and contains all the rest. *When ye fall into divers temptations*—That is, trials.

Verse 4. *Let patience have its perfect work*—Give it full scope, under whatever trials befal you. *That ye may be perfect and entire*—Adorned with every Christian grace *And wanting nothing*—Which God requires in you.

Verse 5. *If any want*—The connexion between the first and following verses, both here and in the fourth chapter, will be easily discerned by him who reads them, while he is suffering wrongfully. He will then readily perceive, why the apostle mentions all those various affections of the mind. *Wisdom*—To understand, whence and why temptations come, and how they are to be improved. Patience is in every pious man already. Let him exercise this, and ask for wisdom. The sum of wisdom, both in the temptation of poverty and of riches, is described in the ninth and tenth verses. *Who giveth to all*—That ask aright. *And upbraideth not*—Either with their past wickedness, or present unworthiness.

Verse 6. *But let him ask in faith*—A firm confidence in God. St. James also both begins and ends with faith, James v. 15; the hinderances of which he removes in the middle part of his epistle. *He that doubteth is*

ask in faith, nothing doubting. For he that doubteth is like
7 a wave of the sea driven with the wind and tossed. For let
not that man think that he shall receive anything from the
8 Lord. A doubleminded man is unstable in all his ways.
9 Let the brother of low degree rejoice in that he is exalted:
10 But the rich, in that he is made low: because as the flower
11 of the grass he shall pass away. For the sun arose with a
scorching heat, and withered the grass, and the flower fell
off, and the beauty of its form perished: so also shall the
12 rich man fade away in his ways. Happy *is* the man that
endureth temptation: for when he hath been proved, he shall
receive the crown of life, which the Lord hath promised to
13 them that love him. Let no man who is tempted say, I am
tempted of God: for God cannot be tempted with evil,
14 neither tempteth he any man. But every man is tempted,

like a wave of the sea—Yea, such are all who have not asked and obtained wisdom. *Driven with the wind*—From without. *And tossed*—From within, by his own unstableness.

Verse 8. *A doubleminded man*—Who has, as it were, two souls; whose heart is not simply given up to God. *Is unstable*—Being without the true wisdom; perpetually disagrees both with himself and others, James iii. 16.

Verse 9. *Let the brother*—St James does not give this appellation to the rich. *Of low degree*—Poor and tempted. *Rejoice*—The most effectual remedy against doublemindedness. *In that he is exalted*—To be a child of God, and an heir of glory.

Verse 10. *But the rich, in that he is made low*—Is humbled by a deep sense of his true condition. *Because as the flower*—Beautiful, but transient. *He shall pass away*—Into eternity.

Verse 11. *For the sun arose and withered the grass*—There is an unspeakable beauty and elegance, both in the comparison itself, and in the very manner of expressing it, intimating both the certainty and the suddenness of the event. *So shall the rich fade away in his ways*—In the midst of his various pleasures and employments

Verse 12. *Happy is the man that endureth temptation*—Trials of various kinds. *He shall receive the crown*—That fadeth not away. *Which the Lord hath promised to them that love him*—And his enduring proves his love. For it is love only that "endureth all things."

Verse 13. But *let no man who is tempted*—To sin. *Say, I am tempted of God*—God thus *tempteth no man.*

Verse 14. *Every man is tempted, when*—In the beginning of the temptation. *He is drawn away*—Drawn out of God, his strong refuge. *By his own desire*—We are therefore to look for the cause of every sin, *in*, not *out of*, ourselves. Even the injections of the devil cannot hurt before we

when he is drawn away by his own desire, and enticed.
15 Then desire, having conceived, bringeth forth sin: and sin,
being perfected, bringeth forth death.
16 Do not err, my beloved brethren. Every good gift and
17 every perfect gift is from above, descending from the Father
of lights, with whom is no variableness, neither shadow
18 of turning. Of his own will begat he us by the word of truth,
that we might be a kind of first-fruits of his creatures.
19 Wherefore, my beloved brethren, let every man be swift
20 to hear, slow to speak, slow to wrath: For the wrath of man

make them our own. And every one has desires arising from his own constitution, tempers, habits, and way of life. *And enticed*—In the progress of the temptation, catching at the bait: so the original word signifies

Verse 15. *Then desire having conceived*—By our own will joining therewith. *Bringeth forth* actual *sin*—It doth not follow that the desire itself is not sin. He that begets a man is himself a man. *And sin being perfected*—Grown up to maturity, which it quickly does. *Bringeth forth death*—Sin is born big with death.

Verse 16. *Do not err*—It is a grievous error to ascribe the evil and not the good which we receive to God.

Verse 17. No evil, but *every good gift*—Whatever tends to holiness *And every perfect gift*—Whatever tends to glory. *Descendeth from the Father of lights*—The appellation of Father is here used with peculiar propriety. It follows, "he begat us." He is the Father of all light, material or spiritual, in the kingdom of grace and of glory. *With whom is no variableness*—No change in his understanding. *Or shadow of turning*—In his will. He infallibly discerns all good and evil; and invariably loves one, and hates the other. There is, in both the Greek words, a metaphor taken from the stars, particularly proper where the *Father of lights* is mentioned. Both are applicable to any celestial body, which has a daily vicissitude of day and night, and sometimes longer days, sometimes longer nights. In God is nothing of this kind. He is mere light. If there is any such vicissitude, it is in ourselves, not in him.

Verse 18. *Of his own will*—Most loving, most free, most pure, just opposite to our evil desire, verse 15. *Begat he us*—Who believe. *By the word of truth*—The true word, emphatically so termed; the gospel. *That we might be a kind of first-fruits of his creatures*—Christians are the chief and most excellent of his visible creatures; and sanctify the rest. Yet he says, *A kind of*—For Christ alone is absolutely *the first-fruits*.

Verse 19. *Let every man be swift to hear*—This is treated of from verse 21 to the end of the next chapter. *Slow to speak*—Which is treated of in the third chapter. *Slow to wrath*—Neither murmuring at God, nor angry at his neighbour. This is treated of in the third, and throughout the fourth and fifth chapters.

Verse 20. *The righteousness of God* here includes all duties prescribed by him, and pleasing to him.

21 worketh not the righteousness of God. Therefore laying
aside all the filthiness and superfluity of wickedness, receive
with meekness the ingrafted word, which is able to save your
22 souls. But be ye doers of the word, and not hearers only,
23 deceiving yourselves. For if any one be an hearer of the
word, and not a doer, he is like a man beholding his natural
24 face in a glass: For he beheld himself, and went away, and
25 immediately forgot what manner of man he was. But he
that looketh diligently into the perfect law, *the law* of liberty,
and continueth *therein*, this man being not a forgetful hearer,
but a doer of the work, this man shall be happy in his doing.
26 If any one be ever so religious, and bridleth not his tongue,
but deceiveth his own heart, this man's religion is vain.
27 Pure religion and undefiled before God even the Father is

Verse 21 *Therefore laying aside*—As a dirty garment. *All the filthiness and superfluity of wickedness*—For however specious or necessary it may appear to worldly wisdom, all wickedness is both vile, hateful, contemptible, and really superfluous. Every reasonable end may be effectually answered without any kind or degree of it. Lay this, every known sin, aside, or all your hearing is vain. *With meekness*—Constant evenness and serenity of mind. *Receive*—Into your ears, your heart, your life. *The word*—Of the gospel. *Ingrafted*—In believers, by regeneration, verse 18; and by habit, Heb. v. 14. *Which is able to save your souls*—The hope of salvation nourishes meekness.

Verse 23. *Beholding his face in a glass*—How exactly does the scripture glass show a man the face of his soul!

Verse 24. *He beheld himself, and went away*—To other business *And forgot*—But such forgetting does not excuse.

Verse 25. *But he that looketh diligently*—Not with a transient glance, but *bending down*, fixing his eyes, and searching all to the bottom. *Into the perfect law*—Of love as established by faith. St. James here guards us against misunderstanding what St. Paul says concerning the "yoke and bondage of the law." He who keeps the law of love is free, John viii. 31, &c. He that does not, is not free, but a slave to sin, and a criminal before God, James ii. 10. *And continueth therein*—Not like him who forgot it, and went away. *This man*—There is a peculiar force in the repetition of the word. *Shall be happy*—Not barely in hearing, but *doing* the will of God

Verse 26. *If any one be ever so religious*—Exact in the outward offices of religion. *And bridleth not his tongue*—From backbiting, talebearing, evilspeaking, he only *deceiveth his own heart*, if he fancies he has any true religion at all.

Verse 27. The only true *religion* in the sight of God, *is this, to visit*—With counsel, comfort, and relief. *The fatherless and widows*—Those who need it most. *In their affliction*—In their most helpless and hopeless

this, To visit the fatherless and widows in their affliction,
and to keep himself unspotted from the world.

CHAP. II. 1 My brethren, hold not the faith of our
Lord Jesus Christ, *the Lord* of glory, with respect of persons.
2 For if there come unto your assembly a man with gold
rings, in fine apparel, and there come in also a poor man in
3 dirty raiment; And ye look upon him that weareth the fine
apparel, and say to him, Sit thou here in a good place; and
say to the poor man, Stand thou there, or sit thou here
4 under my footstool: Ye distinguish not in yourselves, but
5 are become evil-reasoning judges. Hearken, my beloved
brethren, Hath not God chosen the poor of this world rich
in faith, and heirs of the kingdom which he hath promised
6 to them that love him? But ye have disgraced the poor.
Do not the rich oppress you, and drag you to the judgment-
7 seats? Do they not blaspheme that worthy name by which

state. *And to keep himself unspotted from the world*—From the maxims, tempers, and customs of it. But this cannot be done, till we have given our hearts to God, and love our neighbour as ourselves.

Verse 1. *My brethren*—The equality of Christians, intimated by this name, is the ground of the admonition. *Hold not the faith of our* common *Lord, the Lord of glory*—Of which glory all who believe in him partake. *With respect of persons*—That is, honour none merely for being rich; despise none merely for being poor.

Verse 2. *With gold rings*—Which were not then so common as now.

Verse 3. *Ye look upon him*—With respect.

Verse 4. *Ye distinguish not*—To which the most respect is due, to the poor or to the rich. *But are become evil-reasoning judges*—You reason ill, and so judge wrong: for fine apparel is no proof of worth in him that wears it.

Verse 5. *Hearken*—As if he had said, Stay, consider, ye that judge thus. Does not the presumption lie rather in favour of the poor man? *Hath not God chosen the poor*—That is, are not they whom God hath chosen, generally speaking, *poor in this world?* who yet are *rich in faith, and heirs of the kingdom*—Consequently, the most honourable of men: and those whom God so highly honours, ought not ye to honour likewise?

Verse 6. *Do not the rich* often *oppress you*—By open violence; often *drag you*—Under colour of law.

Verse 7. *Do not they blaspheme that worthy name*—Of God and of Christ. The apostle speaks chiefly of rich heathens: but are Christians, so called, a whit behind them?

8 ye are called? If ye fulfil the royal law, (according to the
scripture,) * Thou shalt love thy neighbour as thyself, ye
9 do well: But if ye have respect of persons, ye commit sin,
10 being convicted by the law † as transgressors. For whosoever shall keep the whole law, but offend in one point, is
11 become guilty of all. For he that said, Do not commit
adultery, said also, Do not commit murder. If then thou
commit no adultery, yet if thou commit murder, thou art
12 become a transgressor of the law. So speak ye, and so act,
13 as they that shall be judged by the law of liberty. For
judgment without mercy *shall be* to him that hath showed
no mercy; but mercy glorieth over judgment.
14 What doth it profit, my brethren, though a man say he
hath faith, and have not works? can *that* faith save him?

* Lev. xix. 18. † Exod. xxiii. 3.

Verse 8. *If ye fulfil the royal law*—The supreme law of the great King which is love; and that to every man, poor as well as rich, *ye do well.*

Verse 9. *Being convicted*—By that very law.

Verse 10. *Whosoever keepeth the whole law,* except *in one point, he is guilty of all*—Is as liable to condemnation as if he had offended in every point.

Verse 11. *For* it is the same authority which establishes every commandment.

Verse 12. *So speak and act*—In all things. *As they that shall be judged*—Without respect of persons. *By the law of liberty*—The gospel; the law of universal love, which alone is perfect freedom. For their transgressions of this, both in word and deed, the wicked shall be condemned; and according to their works, done in obedience to this, the righteous will be rewarded.

Verse 13. *Judgment without mercy shall be to him*—In that day. *Who hath showed no mercy*—To his poor brethren. But the *mercy* of God to believers, answering to that which they have shown, will then *glory over judgment.*

Verse 14. From James i. 22, the apostle has been enforcing Christian practice. He now applies to those who neglect this, under the pretence of faith St. Paul had taught that "a man is justified by faith without the works of the law." This some began already to wrest to their own destruction. Wherefore St. James, purposely repeating (verses 21, 23, 25) the same phrases, testimonies, and examples, which St. Paul had used, Rom. iv. 3, Heb. xi. 17, 31, refutes not the doctrine of St. Paul, but the error of those who abused it. There is, therefore, no contradiction between the apostles: they both delivered the truth of God, but in a different manner, as having to do with different kinds of men. On another occasion St. James himself pleaded the cause of faith, Acts xv.

15 If a brother or a sister be naked, and want daily food, And
16 one of you say to them, Depart in peace, be ye warmed and
filled; but give them not the things needful for the body;
17 what doth it profit? So likewise faith, if it hath not works,
18 is dead in itself. But one will say, Thou hast faith, and I
have works: show me thy faith without thy works, and I
19 will show thee my faith by my works. Thou believest there
is one God; thou doest well: the devils also believe, and
20 tremble. But art thou willing to know, O empty man, that
21 the faith *which is* without works is dead? Was not Abra-

13—21; and St. Paul himself strenuously pleads for works, particularly in his latter epistles. This verse is a summary of what follows. *What profiteth it?* is enlarged on, verses 15—17; *though a man say,* verses 18, 19; *can that faith save him?* verse 20. It is not, *though he have faith;* but, *though he say he have faith.* Here, therefore, true, living faith is meant: but in other parts of the argument the apostle speaks of a dead, imaginary faith. He does not, therefore, teach that true faith *can,* but that it *cannot,* subsist without works: nor does he oppose faith to works; but that empty name of faith, to real faith working by love. *Can that faith* "which is without works" *save him?* No more than it can profit his neighbour.

Verse 17. *So likewise* that *faith* which *hath not works is* a mere *dead,* empty notion; of no more profit to him that hath it, than the bidding the naked be clothed is to him.

Verse 18 *But one*—Who judges better. *Will say*—To such a vain talker. *Show me,* if thou canst, *thy faith without thy works.*

Verse 19. *Thou believest there is one God*—I allow this: but this proves only that thou hast the same faith with the devils. Nay, they not only believe, but *tremble*—At the dreadful expectation of eternal torments. So far is that faith from either justifying or saving them that have it.

Verse 20 *But art thou willing to know*—Indeed thou art not: thou wouldest fain be ignorant of it. *O empty man*—Empty of all goodness. *That* the *faith* which is *without works is dead*—And so is not properly faith, as a dead carcase is not a man.

Verse 21. *Was not Abraham justified by works*—St. Paul says he was justified by faith, Rom. iv. 2, &c.: yet St. James does not contradict him; for he does not speak of the same justification. St. Paul speaks of that which Abraham received many years before Isaac was born, Gen. xv. 6; St. James, of that which he did not receive till *he had offered up Isaac on the altar.* He was justified, therefore, in St. Paul's sense, (that is, accounted righteous,) by faith, antecedent to his works. He was justified in St. James's sense, (that is, made righteous,) by works, consequent to his faith. So that St. James's justification by works is the fruit of St Paul's justification by faith.

ham our father justified by works, when he had offered up
22 Isaac his son upon the altar? Thou seest that faith
wrought together with his works, and by works was faith
23 made perfect. And the scripture was fulfilled which saith,
* Abraham believed God, and it was imputed to him for
24 righteousness: and he was called the Friend of God. Ye
25 see then that a man is justified by works, and not by faith
only. In like manner was not Rahab the harlot also justified by works, having received the messengers, and sent
26 them out another way? Therefore as the body without
the spirit is dead, so the faith *which is* without works is
dead also.

* Gen. xv. 6; 2 Chron. xx. 7

Verse 22. *Thou seest that faith*—For by faith Abraham offered him, Heb. xi. 17. *Wrought together with his works*—Therefore faith has one energy and operation; works, another: and the energy and operation of faith are before works, and *together with* them. Works do not give life to faith, but faith begets works, and then is perfected by them *And by works was faith made perfect*—Here St. James fixes the sense wherein he uses the word *justified;* so that no shadow of contradiction remains between his assertion and St. Paul's. Abraham returned from that sacrifice perfected in faith, and far higher in the favour of God. Faith hath not its being from works, (for it is before them,) but its perfection. That vigour of faith which begets works is then excited and increased thereby, as the natural heat of the body begets motion, whereby itself is then excited and increased. See 1 John iii. 22.

Verse 23. *And the scripture*—Which was afterwards written. *Was* hereby eminently *fulfilled, Abraham believed God, and it was imputed to him for righteousness*—This was twice fulfilled,—when Abraham first believed, and when he offered up Isaac. St. Paul speaks of the former fulfilling; St. James, of the latter. *And he was called the Friend of God*—Both by his posterity, 2 Chron. xx. 7; and by God himself, Isai. xli. 8. so pleasing to God were the works he wrought in faith.

Verse 24. *Ye see then that a man is justified by works, and not by faith only*—St. Paul, on the other hand, declares, "A man is justified by faith," and not by works, Rom. iii. 28. And yet there is no contradiction between the apostles: because, 1. They do not speak of the same faith: St. Paul speaking of *living* faith; St. James here, of *dead* faith. 2. They do not speak of the same works: St. Paul speaking of works antecedent to faith; St. James, of works subsequent to it.

Verse 25. After Abraham, the father of the Jews, the apostle cites Rahab, a woman, and a sinner of the gentiles; to show, that in every nation and sex true faith produces works, and is perfected by them; that is, by the grace of God working in the believer, while he is showing his faith by his works.

CHAP. III. 1 My brethren, be not many teachers,
2 knowing that we shall receive greater condemnation. For
in many things we all offend. If any one offend not in word,
the same *is* a perfect man, able also to bridle the whole body.
3 Behold, we put bridles into the mouths of horses, that they
4 may obey us; and we turn about their whole body. Behold
also the ships, though they are so large, and driven by fierce
winds, yet are turned about by a very small helm, whither-
5 soever the steersman listeth. So the tongue also is a little
member, yet boasteth great things. Behold, how much
6 matter a little fire kindleth! (And the tongue *is* a fire, a
world of iniquity:) so is the tongue among the members,
which defileth the whole body, and setteth on fire the course
7 of nature; and is set on fire of hell. Every kind both
of wild beasts and of birds, both of reptiles and things in the
8 sea, is tamed, and hath been tamed by mankind: But the
tongue can no man tame; *it is* an unruly evil, full of deadly
9 poison. Therewith bless we God, even the Father; and
therewith curse we men, made after the likeness of God.
10 Out of the same mouth proceedeth blessing and cursing.

Verse 1. *Be not many teachers*—Let no more of you take this upon you than God thrusts out; seeing it is so hard not to offend in speaking much. *Knowing that we*—That all who thrust themselves into the office. *Shall receive greater condemnation*—For more offences. St. James here, as in several of the following verses, by a common figure of speech, includes himself: *we shall receive,—we offend,—we put bits,—we curse—* None of which, as common sense shows, are to be interpreted either of him or of the other apostles.

Verse 2. *The same is able to bridle the whole body*—That is, the whole man. And doubtless some are able to do this, and so are in this sense *perfect.*

Verse 3. *We*—That is, men.

Verse 5. *Boasteth great things*—Hath great influence.

Verse 6. *A world of iniquity*—Containing an immense quantity of all manner of wickedness. *It defileth*—As fire by its smoke. *The whole body*—The whole man. *And setteth on fire the course of nature*—All the passions, every wheel of his soul.

Verse 7. *Every kind*—The expression perhaps is not to be taken strictly. *Reptiles*—That is, creeping things.

Verse 8. *But no man can tame the tongue*—Of another; no, nor his own, without peculiar help from God.

Verse 9. *Men made after the likeness of God*—Indeed we have now lost this likeness; yet there remains from thence an indelible nobleness, which we ought to reverence both in ourselves and others.

11 My brethren, these things ought not so to be. Doth a fountain send out of the same opening sweet *water* and bitter?
12 Can a fig-tree, my brethren, bear olives? or a vine, figs?
neither *can* a fountain yield salt water and fresh.
13 Who *is* a wise and knowing man among you? let him
show by a good conversation his works with meekness of
14 wisdom. But if ye have bitter zeal and strife in your hearts,
15 do not glory and lie against the truth. This is not the wisdom which descendeth from above, but *is* earthly, animal,
16 devilish. For where bitter zeal and strife *is*, there is unquiet-
17 ness and every evil work. But the wisdom that is from
above is first pure, then peaceable, gentle, easy to be entreated,
full of mercy and good fruits, without partiality, and without
18 dissimulation. And the fruit of righteousness is sown in
peace for them that make peace.

CHAP. IV. 1 From whence *come* wars and fightings
among you? *is it* not hence, from your pleasures that war

Verse 13. *Let him show* his wisdom as well as his faith *by his works;* not by words only.

Verse 14. *If ye have bitter zeal*—True Christian zeal is only the flame of love. Even *in your hearts*—Though it went no farther. *Do not lie against the truth*—As if such zeal could consist with heavenly wisdom.

Verse 15. *This wisdom*—Which is consistent with such zeal. *Is earthly*—Not heavenly; not from the Father of Lights *Animal*—Not spiritual; not from the Spirit of God. *Devilish*—Not the gift of Christ, but such as Satan breathes into the soul.

Verse 17. *But the wisdom from above is first pure*—From all that is earthly, natural, devilish. *Then peaceable*—True peace attending purity, it is quiet, inoffensive. *Gentle*—Soft, mild, yielding, not rigid. *Easy to be entreated*—To be persuaded, or convinced; not stubborn, sour, or morose. *Full of good fruits*—Both in the heart and in the life, two of which are immediately specified. *Without partiality*—Loving all, without respect of persons; embracing all good things, rejecting all evil. *And without dissimulation*—Frank, open.

Verse 18. *And the* principle productive of this *righteousness is sown,* like good seed, *in* the *peace* of a believer's mind, and brings forth a plentiful harvest of happiness, (which is the proper *fruit of righteousness,*) *for them that make peace*—That labour to promote this pure and holy peace among all men.

Verse 1. *From whence come wars and fightings*—Quarrels and jars *among you,* quite opposite to this peace? *Is it not from your pleasures*—Your desires of earthly pleasures *Which war*—Against your souls. *In your*

2 in your members? Ye desire, and have not: ye kill, and
envy, and cannot obtain: ye fight and war, yet ye have not,
3 because ye ask not. Ye ask, and receive not, because ye
4 ask amiss, that ye may expend it on your pleasures. Ye
adulterers and adulteresses, know ye not that the friendship
of the world is enmity against God? whosoever therefore
5 desireth to be a friend of the world is an enemy of God. Do
ye think, that the scripture saith in vain, The spirit that
6 dwelleth in us lusteth against envy? But he giveth greater
grace. Therefore it saith, * God resisteth the proud, but
7 giveth grace to the humble. Submit yourselves therefore to
8 God. Resist the devil, and he will flee from you. Draw
nigh to God, and he will draw nigh to you. Cleanse *your*

* Prov. iii. 34

members—Here is the first seat of the war. Hence proceeds the war of man with man, king with king, nation with nation.

Verse 2. *Ye kill*—In your heart, for "he that hateth his brother is a murderer." *Ye fight and war*—That is, furiously strive and contend. *Ye ask not*—And no marvel; for a man full of evil desire, of envy or hatred, cannot pray.

Verse 3. But *if ye* do *ask, ye receive not, because ye ask amiss*—That is, from a wrong motive.

Verse 4. *Ye adulterers and adulteresses*—Who have broken your faith with God, your rightful spouse. *Know ye not that the friendship* or love *of the world*—The desire of the flesh, the desire of the eye, and the pride of life, or courting the favour of worldly men, *is enmity against God? Whosoever desireth to be a friend of the world*—Whosoever seeks either the happiness or favour of it, does thereby constitute himself *an enemy of God;* and can he expect to obtain anything of him?

Verse 5. *Do you think that the scripture saith in vain*—Without good ground. St. James seems to refer to many, not any one particular scripture. *The spirit* of love *that dwelleth in* all believers *lusteth against envy*—Gal. v. 17; is directly opposite to all those unloving tempers which necessarily flow from the friendship of the world.

Verse 6. *But he giveth greater grace*—To all who shun those tempers. *Therefore it*—The scripture. *Saith, God resisteth the proud*—And pride is the great root of all unkind affections.

Verse 7. Therefore by humbly *submitting yourselves to God, resist the devil*—The father of pride and envy.

Verse 8. Then *draw nigh to God* in prayer, *and he will draw nigh unto you,* will hear you; which that nothing may hinder, *cleanse your hands*—Cease from doing evil. *And purify your hearts*—From all spiritual adultery. Be no more *double minded,* vainly endeavouring to serve both God and mammon

hands, ye sinners ; and purify *your* hearts, ye double minded.
9 Be afflicted, and mourn, and weep : let your laughter be
10 turned into mourning, and *your* joy into heaviness. Humble
yourselves before the Lord, and he will lift you up.
11 Speak not evil one of another, brethren. He that speaketh evil of his brother, and judgeth his brother, speaketh
evil of the law, and judgeth the law : but if thou judgest the
12 law, thou art not a doer of the law, but a judge. There is
one lawgiver, that is able to save and to destroy : who art
thou that judgest another ?
13 Come now, ye that say, To-day or to-morrow we will go
to such a city, and continue there a year, and traffick, and
14 get gain · Who know not what *shall be* on the morrow. For
what *is* your life ? It is a vapour that appeareth for a little
15 time, and then vanisheth away : Instead of your saying, If
16 the Lord will, we shall both live, and do this, or that. But
now ye glory in your boastings : all such glorying is evil.
17 Therefore to him that knoweth to do good, and doeth it not,
to him it is sin

CHAP. V. 1 Come now, ye rich, weep and howl for your

Verse 9. *Be afflicted*—For your past unfaithfulness to God.

Verse 11. *Speak not evil one of another*—This is a grand hinderance of peace. O who is sufficiently aware of it ! *He that speaketh evil of another* does in effect *speak evil of the law,* which so strongly prohibits it. *Thou art not a doer of the law, but a judge*—Of it ; thou settest thyself above, and as it were condemnest, it.

Verse 12. *There is one lawgiver that is able*—To execute the sentence he denounces. But *who art thou*—A poor, weak, dying worm.

Verse 13. *Come now, ye that say*—As peremptorily as if your life were in your own hands.

Verse 15. *Instead of your saying*—That is, whereas ye ought to say.

Verse 17. *Therefore to him that knoweth to do good and doeth it not*—That knows what is right, and does not practise it. *To him it is sin*—His knowledge does not prevent, but increase, his condemnation.

Verse 1. *Come now, ye rich*—The apostle does not speak this so much for the sake of the rich themselves, as of the poor children of God, who were then groaning under their cruel oppression. *Weep and howl for your miseries which are coming upon you*—Quickly and unexpectedly. This was written not long before the siege of Jerusalem ; during which, as well as after it, huge calamities came on the Jewish nation, not only in Judea, but through distant countries. And as these were an awful

2 miseries that are coming *upon you* Your riches are cor-
3 rupted, and your garments are become motheaten. Your
gold and silver is cankered; and the canker of them will be
a testimony against you, and will eat your flesh as fire. Ye
4 have laid up treasure in the last days. Behold, the hire
of your labourers who have reaped your fields, which is
kept back by you, crieth: and the cries of them who have
gathered in your harvest are entered into the ears of the
5 Lord of sabaoth. Ye have lived delicately and luxuriously
on earth; ye have cherished your hearts, as in a day of sacri-
6 fice. Ye have condemned, ye have killed the just: he doth
7 not resist you. Be patient, therefore, brethren, till the coming of the Lord. Behold, the husbandman waiteth for the
precious fruit of the earth, and hath patience for it, till he
8 receives the former and the latter rain. Be ye also patient;

prelude of that wrath which was to fall upon them in the world to come, so this may likewise refer to the final vengeance which will then be executed on the impenitent.

Verse 2. The *riches* of the ancients consisted much in large stores of corn, and of costly apparel.

Verse 3. *The canker of them*—Your perishing stores and motheaten garments. *Will be a testimony against you*—Of your having buried those talents in the earth, instead of improving them according to your Lord's will. *And will eat your flesh as fire*—Will occasion you as great torment as if fire were consuming your flesh. *Ye have laid up treasure in the last days*—When it is too late; when you have no time to enjoy them.

Verse 4. *The hire of your labourers crieth*—Those sins chiefly cry to God concerning which human laws are silent. Such are luxury, unchastity, and various kinds of injustice. The *labourers* themselves also cry to God, who is just coming to avenge their cause. *Of sabaoth*—Of hosts, or armies

Verse 5. *Ye have cherished your hearts*—Have indulged yourselves to the uttermost. *As in a day of sacrifice*—Which were solemn feast-days among the Jews.

Verse 6. *Ye have killed the just*—Many just men; in particular, "that Just One," Acts iii. 14. They afterwards killed James, surnamed the Just, the writer of this epistle. *He doth not resist you*—And therefore you are secure. But the Lord cometh quickly, verse 8.

Verse 7. *The husbandman waiteth for the precious fruit*—Which will recompense his labour and patience. *Till he receives the former rain*—Immediately after sowing. *And the latter*—Before the harvest.

Verse 8. *Stablish your hearts*—In faith and patience. *For the coming of the Lord*—To destroy Jerusalem. *Is nigh*—And so is his last coming to the eye of a believer.

stablish your hearts: for the coming of the Lord is nigh.
9 Murmur not one against another, brethren, lest ye be con-
10 demned: behold, the judge standeth before the door. Take,
my brethren, the prophets, who spoke in the name of the
Lord, for an example of suffering affliction, and of patience.
11 Behold, we count them happy that endured. Ye have
heard of the patience of Job, and have seen the end of the
Lord; for the Lord is full of compassion and of tender
12 mercy. But above all things, my brethren, swear not, neither by heaven, nor by the earth, nor by any other oath:
but let your yea be yea; and your nay, nay; lest ye fall
under condemnation.
13 Is any among you afflicted? let him pray. Is any cheer-
14 ful? let him sing psalms. Is any among you sick? let him
call for the elders of the church, and let them pray over
him, having anointed him with oil in the name of the Lord:

Verse 9. *Murmur not one against another*—Have patience also with each other *The judge standeth before the door*—Hearing every word, marking every thought.

Verse 10. *Take the prophets for an example*—Once persecuted like you, even for *speaking in the name of the Lord.* The very men that gloried in having prophets yet could not bear their message: nor did either their holiness or their high commission screen them from suffering.

Verse 11. *We count them happy that endured*—That suffered patiently. The more they once suffered, the greater is their present happiness. *Ye have seen the end of the Lord*—The end which the Lord gave him.

Verse 12. *Swear not*—However provoked. The Jews were notoriously guilty of common swearing, though not so much by God himself as by some of his creatures. The apostle here particularly forbids these oaths, as well as all swearing in common conversation. It is very observable, how solemnly the apostle introduces this command. *above all things, swear not*—As if he had said, Whatever you forget, do not forget this. This abundantly demonstrates the horrible iniquity of the crime. But he does not forbid the taking a solemn oath before a magistrate. *Let your yea be yea; and your nay, nay*—Use no higher asseverations in common discourse; and let your word stand firm. Whatever ye say, take care to make it good.

Verse 14. *Having anointed him with oil*—This single conspicuous gift, which Christ committed to his apostles, Mark vi. 13, remained in the church long after the other miraculous gifts were withdrawn. Indeed, it seems to have been designed to remain always; and St. James directs the elders, who were the most, if not the only, gifted men, to administer it. This was the whole process of physic in the Christian church, till it was lost through unbelief. That novel invention among the Romanists,

15 And the prayer of faith shall save the sick, and the Lord
shall raise him up; and if he have committed sins, they
16 shall be forgiven him. Confess *your* faults one to another,
brethren, and pray one for another, that ye may be healed.
The fervent prayer of a righteous man availeth much.
17 Elijah was a man of like passions with us, and he prayed
earnestly that it might not rain: and it rained not on the
18 land for three years and six months. And he prayed again,
and the heaven gave rain, and the land brought forth her
fruit.
19 Brethren, if any one among you err from the truth, and
20 one convert him; Let him know, that he who converteth a
sinner from the error of his way shall save a soul from death,
and hide a multitude of sins.

extreme unction, practised not for cure, but where life is despaired of, bears no manner of resemblance to this.

Verse 15. *And the prayer* offered in *faith shall save the sick*—From his sickness; *and if* any sin be the occasion of his sickness, *it shall be forgiven him.*

Verse 16. *Confess your faults*—Whether ye are sick or in health. *To one another*—He does not say, to the elders: this may, or may not, be done; for it is nowhere commanded. We may confess them to any who can pray in faith: he will then know how to pray for us, and be more stirred up so to do. *And pray one for another, that ye may be healed*—Of all your spiritual diseases.

Verse 17. *Elijah was a man of like passions*—Naturally as weak and sinful as we are *And he prayed*—When idolatry covered the land.

Verse 18. *He prayed again*—When idolatry was abolished.

Verse 19. As if he had said, I have now warned you of those sins to which you are most liable; and, in all these respects, watch not only over yourselves, but every one over his brother also. Labour, in particular, to recover those that are fallen *If any one err from the truth*—Practically, by sin.

Verse 20. *He shall save a soul*—Of how much more value than the body! verse 14. *And hide a multitude of sins*—Which shall no more, how many soever they are, be remembered to his condemnation.

NOTES

ON

THE FIRST EPISTLE GENERAL OF ST. PETER.

There is a wonderful weightiness, and yet liveliness and sweetness, in the epistles of St. Peter. His design in both is, to stir up the minds of those to whom he writes, by way of remembrance, 2 Peter iii. 1, and to guard them, not only against error, but also against doubting, v. 12. This he does by reminding them of that glorious grace which God had vouchsafed them through the gospel, by which believers are inflamed to bring forth the fruits of faith, hope, love, and patience.

The parts of this epistle are three :—

I. The inscription, — C. i. 1, 2

II. The stirring up of them to whom he writes :

1. As born of God. Here he recites and interweaves alternately both the benefits of God toward believers, and the duties of believers toward God :

 1 God hath regenerated us to a living hope, to an eternal inheritance, — 3—12

 Therefore hope to the end, — 13

 2. As obedient children bring forth the fruit of faith to your heavenly Father, — 14—21

 3 Being purified by the Spirit, love with a pure heart, — 22—C. ii. 10

2. As strangers in the world, abstain from fleshly desires, — 11

 And show your faith by,

 1 A good conversation, — 12

  a. In particular,

   Subjects, — 13—17

   Servants, after the example of Christ, — 18—25

   Wives, — C. iii. 1—6

   Husbands, — 7

  b. In general, all, — 8—15

 2. A good profession,

  a. By readiness to give an answer to every one, — 15—22

  b By shunning evil company, — C. iv. 1—6

  (This part is enforced by what Christ both did and suffered, from his passion to his coming to judgment.)

c. By the exercise of Christian virtues, and by a due use of miraculous gifts, 7—1·
3. As fellow-heirs of glory, sustain adversity · let each do this,
1. In general, as a Christian, 12—19
2. In his own particular state, C. v. 1—11
The title *beloved* divides the second part from the first, ii. 11, and the third from the second, iv. 12.
III. The conclusion, 12—14

I. ST. PETER.

CHAPTER I. 1 Peter, an apostle of Jesus Christ, to
the sojourners scattered through Pontus, Galatia, Cappa-
2 docia, Asia, and Bithynia, Elect according to the foreknowledge of God the Father, through sanctification of the
Spirit, unto obedience and sprinkling of the blood of Jesus
Christ: grace and peace be multiplied to you.

Verse 1. *To the sojourners*—Upon earth, the Christians, chiefly those of Jewish extraction. *Scattered*—Long ago driven out of their own land. Those scattered by the persecution mentioned Acts viii. 1, were scattered only through Judea and Samaria, though afterwards some of them travelled to Phenice, Cyprus, and Antioch. *Through Pontus, Galatia, Cappadocia, Asia, and Bithynia*—He names these five provinces in the order wherein they occurred to him, writing from the east. All these countries lie in the Lesser Asia. The Asia here distinguished from the other provinces is that which was usually called the Proconsular Asia being a Roman province.

Verse 2. *According to the foreknowledge of God*—Speaking after the manner of men Strictly speaking, there is no foreknowledge, no more than afterknowledge, with God: but all things are known to him as present from eternity to eternity. This is therefore no other than an instance of the divine condescension to our low capacities. *Elect*—By the free love and almighty power of God taken out of, separated from, the world. Election, in the scripture sense, is God's doing anything that our merit or power have nc part in. The true predestination, or fore-appointment of God is, 1. He that believeth shall be saved from the guilt and power of sin. 2. He that endureth to the end shall be saved eternally. 3. They who receive the precious gift of faith, thereby become the sons of God; and, being sons, they shall receive the Spirit of holiness to walk as Christ also walked. Throughout every part of this appointment of God, promise and duty go hand in hand. All is free gift; and yet such is the gift, that the final issue depends on our future obedience

3 Blessed *be* the God and Father of our Lord Jesus Christ,
who according to his abundant mercy hath regenerated us to a
living hope by the resurrection of Jesus Christ from the dead,
4 To an inheritance incorruptible, and undefiled, and that fadeth

to the heavenly call. But other predestination than this, either to life or death eternal, the scripture knows not of. Moreover, it is, 1. Cruel respect of persons; an unjust regard of one, and an unjust disregard of another. It is mere creature partiality, and not infinite justice. 2. It is not plain scripture doctrine, if true; but rather, inconsistent with the express written word, that speaks of God's universal offers of grace; his invitations, promises, threatenings, being all general. 3. We are bid to choose life, and reprehended for not doing it 4. It is inconsistent with a state of probation in those that must be saved or must be lost. 5. It is of fatal consequence; all men being ready, on very slight grounds, to fancy themselves of the elect number. But the doctrine of predestination is entirely changed from what it formerly was. Now it implies neither faith, peace, nor purity. It is something that will do without them all. Faith is no longer, according to the modern predestinarian scheme, a divine "evidence of things not seen," wrought in the soul by the immediate power of the Holy Ghost; not an evidence at all; but a mere notion. Neither is faith made any longer a means of holiness; but something that will do without it. Christ is no more a Saviour from sin; but a defence, a countenancer of it. He is no more a fountain of spiritual life in the soul of believers, but leaves his elect inwardly dry, and outwardly unfruitful; and is made little more than a refuge from the image of the heavenly; even from righteousness, peace, and joy in the Holy Ghost. *Through sanctification of the Spirit*—Through the renewing and purifying influences of his Spirit on their souls. *Unto obedience*—To engage and enable them to yield themselves up to all holy obedience, the foundation of all which is, the *sprinkling of the blood of Jesus Christ*—The atoning blood of Christ, which was typified by the sprinkling of the blood of sacrifices under the law; in allusion to which it is called "the blood of sprinkling."

Verse 3. *Blessed be the God and Father of our Lord Jesus Christ*—His Father, with respect to his divine nature; his God, with respect to his human. *Who hath regenerated us to a living hope*—An hope which implies true spiritual life, which revives the heart, and makes the soul lively and vigorous. *By the resurrection of Christ*—Which is not only a pledge of ours, but a part of the purchase-price. It has also a close connexion with our rising from spiritual death, that as he liveth, so shall we live with him He was acknowledged to be the Christ, but usually called Jesus till his resurrection; then he was also called Christ.

Verse 4. *To an inheritance*—For if we are sons, then heirs. *Incorruptible*—Not like earthly treasures. *Undefiled*—Pure and holy, incapable of being itself defiled, or of being enjoyed by any polluted soul. *And that fadeth not away*—That never decays in its value, sweetness, or beauty, like all the enjoyments of this world, like the garlands of leaves

5 not away, reserved in heaven for you, Who are kept by the
power of God through faith unto salvation ready to be
6 revealed in the last time. Wherein ye greatly rejoice,
though now for a little while, if need be, ye are in heaviness
7 through manifold temptations: That the trial of your faith,
which is much more precious than gold, (that perisheth,
though it be tried with fire,) may be found unto praise and
8 honour and glory at the revelation of Jesus Christ: Whom
having not seen, ye love; in whom, though ye see *him* not,
yet believing, ye now rejoice with joy unspeakable and full
9 of glory: Receiving the end of your faith, the salvation of
10 your souls. Of which salvation the prophets, who prophesied of the grace *of God* toward you, inquired and searched

or flowers, with which the ancient conquerors were wont to be crowned. *Reserved in heaven for you*—Who "by patient continuance in welldoing, seek for glory and honour and immortality."

Verse 5. *Who are kept*—The inheritance is reserved; the heirs are kept for it. *By the power of God*—Which worketh all in all, which guards us against all our enemies. *Through faith*—Through which alone salvation is both received and retained. *Ready to be revealed*—That revelation is made in the last day. It was more and more ready to be revealed, ever since Christ came.

Verse 6. *Wherein*—That is, in being so kept *Ye* even now *greatly rejoice, though now for a little while*—Such is our whole life, compared to eternity. *If need be*—For it is not always needful. If God sees it to be the best means for your spiritual profit. *Ye are in heaviness*—Or sorrow; but not in darkness; for they still retained both faith, verse 5, hope, and love; yea, at this very time were rejoicing with joy unspeakable, verse 8.

Verse 7 *That the trial of your faith*—That is, your faith which is tried. *Which is much more precious than gold*—For gold, though it bear the fire, yet will perish with the world. *May be found*—Though it doth not yet appear. *Unto praise*—From God himself. *And honour*—From men and angels. *And glory*—Assigned by the great Judge.

Verse 8. *Having not seen*—In the flesh.

Verse 9. *Receiving*—Now already. *Salvation*—From all sin into all holiness, which is the qualification for, the forerunner and pledge of, eternal salvation.

Verse 10. *Of which salvation*—So far beyond all that was experienced under the Jewish dispensation. The very *prophets who prophesied* long ago *of the grace of God toward you*—Of his abundant, overflowing grace to be bestowed on believers under the Christian dispensation. *Inquired*—Were earnestly inquisitive. *And searched diligently*—Like miners searching after precious ore, after the meaning of the prophecies which they delivered

11 diligently: Searching what, and what manner of time the
Spirit of Christ which was in them signified, when he testified beforehand the sufferings of Christ, and the glories that
12 were to follow. To whom it was revealed, that not for
themselves, but for us they ministered the things which
have been now declared to you by them that have preached
the gospel to you with the Holy Ghost sent down from
13 heaven; which things angels desire to look into. Wherefore gird up the loins of your mind, be watchful, and hope
perfectly for the grace that shall be brought to you at the
14 revelation of Jesus Christ; As obedient children, conform
not yourselves to your former desires in your ignorance
15 But as he who hath called you is holy, so be ye yourselves
16 also holy in all manner of conversation; For it is written,*
17 Be ye holy; for I am holy And if ye call on the Father,

* Lev xi. 44.

Verse 11. *Searching what time*—What particular period. *And what manner of time*—By what marks to be distinguished. *The glories that were to follow*—His sufferings; namely, the glory of his resurrection, ascension, exaltation, and the effusion of his Spirit; the glory of the last judgment, and of his eternal kingdom; and also the glories of his grace in the hearts and lives of Christians.

Verse 12. *To whom*—So searching *It was revealed, that not for themselves, but for us they ministered*—They did not so much by those predictions serve themselves, or that generation, as they did us, who now enjoy what they saw afar off. *With the Holy Ghost sent down from heaven*—Confirmed by the inward, powerful testimony of the Holy Ghost, as well as the mighty effusion of his miraculous gifts. *Which things angels desire to look into*—A beautiful gradation; prophets, righteous men, kings, desired to see and hear what Christ did and taught. What the Holy Ghost taught concerning Christ the very angels long to know.

Verse 13. *Wherefore*—Having such encouragement. *Gird up the loins of your mind*—As persons in the eastern countries were wont, in travelling or running, to gird up their long garments, so gather ye up all your thoughts and affections, and keep your mind always disencumbered and prepared to run the race which is set before you. *Be watchful*—As servants that wait for their Lord. *And hope to the end*—Maintain a full expectation of all *the grace*—The blessings flowing from the free favour of God. *Which shall be brought to you at the* final *revelation of Jesus Christ*—And which are now brought to you by the revelation of Christ in you.

Verse 14. *Your desires*—Which ye had while ye were ignorant of God.

Verse 17. *Who judgeth according to every man's work*—According to the tenor of his life and conversation. *Pass the time of your sojourning*—

who without respect of persons judgeth according to every
man's work, pass the time of your sojourning in fear:
18 Seeing ye know ye were not redeemed with corruptible
things, *as* silver and gold, from your vain conversation
19 delivered by tradition from your fathers; but with the precious blood of Christ, as of a lamb without blemish and
20 without spot: Who verily was foreknown before the foundation of the world, but was manifested in the last times for
21 you, Who through him believe in God, that raised him from
the dead, and gave him glory; that your faith and hope
might be in God.
22 Having purified your souls by obeying the truth through
the Spirit unto unfeigned love of the brethren, love one
23 another with a pure heart fervently: Being born again, not
by corruptible seed, but incorruptible, through the word of
24 God, which liveth and abideth for ever. For * all flesh *is*
grass, and all the glory of it as the flower of grass. The
25 grass is withered, and the flower is fallen off. But the word
of the Lord endureth for ever. And this is the word which
is preached to you in the gospel.

* Isaiah xl. 6, &c.

Your short abode on earth. *In* humble, loving *fear*—The proper companion and guard of hope.

Verse 18. *Your vain conversation*—Your foolish, sinful way of life.

Verse 19. *Without blemish*—In himself. *Without spot*—From the world.

Verse 21. *Who through him believe*—For all our faith and hope proceed from the power of his resurrection. *In God that raised* Jesus, *and gave him glory*—At his ascension. Without Christ we should only dread God; whereas through him we believe, hope, and love.

Verse 22. *Having purified your souls by obeying the truth through the Spirit,* who bestows upon you freely, both obedience and purity of heart, and *unfeigned love of the brethren,* go on to still higher degrees of love *Love one another fervently*—With the most strong and tender affection; and yet *with a pure heart*—Pure from any spot of unholy desire or inordinate passion.

Verse 23. *Which liveth*—Is full of divine virtue. *And abideth* the same *for ever.*

Verse 24. *All flesh*—Every human creature is transient and withering as *grass. And all the glory of it*—His wisdom, strength, wealth, righteousness. *As the flower*—The most short-lived part of it. *The grass*—That is, man. *The flower*—That is, his glory. *Is fallen off*—As it were, while we are speaking.

CHAPTER II.

CHAP. II. 1 Wherefore laying aside all wickedness, and
all guile, and dissimulation, and envies, and all evilspeakings,
2 As new born babes, desire the sincere milk of the word, that
3 ye may grow hereby: Since ye have tasted that the Lord
4 is gracious. To whom coming *as unto* a living stone,
rejected indeed by men, but chosen of God, *and* precious,
5 Ye also, as living stones, are built up a spiritual house, an
holy priesthood, to offer up spiritual sacrifices, acceptable to
6 God through Jesus Christ. Wherefore also it is contained
in the scripture, * Behold, I lay in Sion a chief corner stone,
elect, precious; and he that believeth on him shall not be
7 confounded. Therefore to you who believe *he is* precious.
but as to them who believe not, † The stone which the

* Isaiah xxviii. 16. † Psalm cxviii. 22.

Verse 1. *Wherefore laying aside*—As inconsistent with that pure love. *All dissimulation*—Which is the outward expression of guile in the heart.

Verse 2. *Desire*—Always, as earnestly *as new born babes* do, 1 Pet. i. 3. *The milk of the word*—That word of God which nourishes the soul as milk does the body, and which is *sincere*, pure from all guile, so that none are deceived who cleave to it. *That you may grow thereby*—In faith, love, holiness, unto the full stature of Christ.

Verse 3. *Since ye have tasted*—Sweetly and experimentally known.

Verse 4. *To whom coming*—By faith. *As unto a living stone*—Living from eternity; alive from the dead. There is a wonderful beauty and energy in these expressions, which describe Christ as a spiritual foundation, solid, firm, durable; and believers as a building erected upon it, in preference to that temple which the Jews accounted their highest glory. And St. Peter speaking of him thus, shows he did not judge himself, but Christ, to be the rock on which the church was built. *Rejected indeed by men*—Even at this day, not only by Jews, Turks, heathens, infidels; but by all Christians, so called, who live in sin, or who hope to be saved by their own works. *But chosen of God*—From all eternity, to be the foundation of his church. *And precious*—In himself, in the sight of God, and in the eyes of all believers.

Verse 5. *Ye*—Believers. *As living stones*—Alive to God through him. *Are built up*—In union with each other. *A spiritual house*—Being spiritual yourselves, and an habitation of God through the Spirit. *An holy priesthood*—Consecrated to God, and "holy as he is holy." *To offer up*—Your souls and bodies, with all your thoughts, words, and actions, *as spiritual sacrifices to God.*

Verse 6. *He that believeth shall not be confounded*—In time or in eternity.

Verse 7. *To them who believe, he is become the head of the corner*—The chief corner stone, on which the whole building rests. Unbelievers too will at length find him such to their sorrow, Matt. xxi. 44.

8 builders rejected is become the head of the corner, And
stone of stumbling, and a rock of offence, *to them* who
stumble, not believing the word, whereunto also they were
9 appointed. But ye *are* a chosen race, a royal priesthood, an
holy nation, a purchased people; that ye may show forth the
virtues of him who hath called you out of darkness into his
10 marvellous light: Who in time past *were* not a people, but
now *are* the people of God: who had not obtained mercy,
but now have obtained mercy.
11 Beloved, I beseech *you* as sojourners and pilgrims, abstain
12 from fleshly desires, which war against the soul; Having
your conversation honest among the gentiles: that, wherein
they speak against you as evildoers, they may by your good
works, which they shall behold, glorify God in the day
13 of visitation. Be subject to every ordinance of man for the

Verse 8. *Who stumble, whereunto also they were appointed*—They who believe not, *stumble,* and fall, and perish for ever; God having *appointed* from all eternity, "he that believeth not shall be damned."

Verse 9. *But ye*—Who believe in Christ *Are*—In a higher sense than ever the Jews were. *A chosen* or *elect race, a royal priesthood*—"Kings and priests unto God," Rev. i. 6. As princes, ye have power with God, and victory over sin, the world, and the devil as priests, ye are consecrated to God, for offering spiritual sacrifices. Ye Christians are as one *holy nation,* under Christ your King. *A purchased people*—Who are his peculiar property. *That ye may show forth*—By your whole behaviour, to all mankind. *The virtues*—The excellent glory, the mercy, wisdom, and power of *him,* Christ, *who hath called you out of* the *darkness* of ignorance, error, sin, and misery.

Verse 10. *Who in time past were not a people*—Much less the people of God; but scattered individuals of many nations The former part of the verse particularly respects the gentiles; the latter, the Jews.

Verse 11. Here begins the exhortation drawn from the second motive. *Sojourners: pilgrims*—The first word properly means, those who are in a strange house; the second, those who are in a strange country. You *sojourn* in the body; you are *pilgrims* in this world. *Abstain from desires* of anything in this house, or in this country.

Verse 12. *Honest*—Not barely unblamable, but virtuous in every respect But our language sinks under the force, beauty, and copiousness of the original expressions. *That they by your good works which they shall behold*—See with their own eyes. *May glorify God*—By owning his grace in you, and following your example. *In the day of visitation*—The time when he shall give them fresh offers of his mercy.

Verse 13. *Submit yourselves to every ordinance of man*—To every secular power. Instrumentally these are *ordained* by men; but originally all their power is from God.

14 Lord's sake: whether it be to the king, as supreme; Or to
governors, as sent by him for the punishment of evildoers,
15 and the praise of them that do well. For so is the will
of God, that by welldoing ye put to silence the ignorance
16 of foolish men: As free, yet not having your liberty for a
17 cloak of wickedness, but as the servants of God. Honour
all men. Love the brotherhood. Fear God. Honour the
18 king. Servants, be subject to *your* masters with all fear; not
19 only to the good and gentle, but also to the froward. For
this *is* thankworthy, if a man for conscience toward God
20 endure grief, though he suffer wrongfully. For what glory
is it, if, when ye commit faults and are buffeted, ye take it
patiently? But if, when ye do well, and yet suffer, ye take
21 it patiently, this *is* acceptable with God. For even hereunto
are ye called: for Christ also suffered for us, leaving you an
22 example, that ye might follow his steps: * Who did no sin,
23 neither was guile found in his mouth: Who, when he was
reviled, reviled not again; when he suffered, he threatened
not; but committed *himself* to him that judgeth righteously
24 Who himself bore our sins in his own body on the tree, that

* Isaiah liii. 4, 6, 7, 9.

Verse 14. *Or to* subordinate *governors*, or magistrates.

Verse 15. *The ignorance*—Of them who blame you, because they do not know you: a strong motive to pity them.

Verse 16. *As free*—Yet obeying governors, for God's sake.

Verse 17. *Honour all men*—As being made in the image of God, bought by his Son, and designed for his kingdom. *Honour the king*—Pay him all that regard both in affection and action which the laws of God and man require.

Verse 18. *Servants*—Literally, *household servants. With all fear*—Of offending them or God. *Not only to the good*—Tender, kind. *And gentle*—Mild, easily forgiving.

Verse 19. *For conscience toward God*—From a pure desire of pleasing him. *Grief*—Severe treatment.

Verse 21. *Hereunto are ye*—Christians. *Called*—To suffer wrongfully *Leaving you an example*—When he went to God. *That ye might follow his steps*—Of innocence and patience.

Verses 22, 23. In all these instances the example of Christ is peculiarly adapted to the state of servants, who easily slide either into *sin* or *guile*, *reviling* their fellowservants, or *threatening* them, the natural result of anger without power. *He committed himself to him that judgeth righteously*—The only solid ground of patience in affliction.

Verse 24. *Who himself bore our sins*—That is, the punishment due to them. *In his* afflicted, torn, dying *body on the tree*—The cross, whereon

we, being dead to sin, might live to righteousness: by whose
25 stripes ye were healed. For ye were as sheep going astray,
but are now returned to the shepherd and bishop of your
souls.

CHAP. III. 1 In like manner, ye wives, be subject to
your own husbands; that, if any obey not the word, they
also may without the word be won by the deportment of the
2 wives; Beholding your chaste deportment *joined* with fear
3 Whose adorning let it not be the outward *adorning* of curling the hair, and of wearing gold, or of putting on apparel;
4 But the hidden man of the heart, in the incorruptible *ornament* of a meek and quiet spirit, which in the sight of God
5 is of great price. For thus the holy women also of old time,
who trusted in God, adorned themselves, being subject to

chiefly slaves or servants were wont to suffer. *That we being dead to sin*—Wholly delivered both from the guilt and power of it: indeed, without an atonement first made for the guilt, we could never have been delivered from the power. *Might live to righteousness*—Which is one only. The sins we had committed, and he bore, were manifold.

Verse 25. *The bishop*—The kind observer, inspector, or overseer *of your souls.*

Verse 1. *If any*—He speaks tenderly. *Won*—Gained over to Christ.

Verse 2. *Joined with* a loving fear of displeasing them.

Verse 3. Three things are here expressly forbidden: *curling the hair, wearing gold,* (by way of ornament,) and *putting on* costly or gay *apparel.* These, therefore, ought never to be allowed, much less defended, by Christians.

Verse 4. *The hidden man of the heart*—Complete inward holiness, which implies *a meek and quiet spirit.* A meek spirit gives no trouble willingly to any: a quiet spirit bears all wrongs without being troubled. *In the sight of God*—Who looks at the heart. All superfluity of dress contributes more to pride and anger than is generally supposed. The apostle seems to have his eye to this by substituting meekness and quietness in the room of the ornaments he forbids. "I do not *regard* these things," is often said by those whose hearts are wrapped up in them: but offer to take them away, and you touch the very idol of their soul. Some, indeed, only dress elegantly that they may be looked on; that is, they squander away their Lord's talent to gain applause: thus making sin to beget sin, and then plead one in excuse of the other.

Verse 5. The adorning of those *holy women, who trusted in God,* and therefore did not act thus from servile fear, was, 1. Their meek *subjection to their husbands:* 2. Their quiet spirit, "not afraid," or amazed: and 3. Their unblamable behaviour, "doing" all things "well."

6 their own husbands; As * Sarah obeyed Abraham, calling
him lord: whose children ye are, while ye do well, and are
7 not afraid with any amazement. In like manner, ye husbands, dwell according to knowledge with *the woman*, as
the weaker vessel, giving them honour, as being also joint-
heirs of the grace of life; that your prayers be not hindered.
8 Finally, *be* ye all of one mind, sympathizing with each
9 other, love as brethren, *be* pitiful, *be* courteous: Not render-
ing evil for evil, or railing for railing: but contrariwise blessing; knowing that ye are called to this, to inherit a blessing.
10 For † let him that desireth to love life, and to see good days,
refrain his tongue from evil, and his lips that they speak no
11 guile: Let him turn from evil, and do good; let him seek
12 peace, and pursue it. For the eyes of the Lord *are* over
the righteous, and his ears *are open* to their prayer: but
13 the face of the Lord *is* against them that do evil. And who

* Gen xviii. 12. † Psalm xxxiv. 12, &c.

Verse 6. *Whose children ye are*—In a spiritual as well as natural sense, and entitled to the same inheritance, *while ye* discharge your conjugal duties, not out of fear, but for conscience' sake.

Verse 7. *Dwell with the woman according to knowledge*—Knowing they are weak, and therefore to be used with all tenderness. Yet do not despise them for this, but *give them honour*—Both in heart, in word, and in action; *as* those who are called to be *joint-heirs of* that eternal *life* which ye and they hope to receive by the free *grace of* God. *That your prayers be not hindered*—On the one part or the other. All sin hinders prayer; particularly anger. Anything at which we are angry is never more apt to come into our mind than when we are at prayer; and those who do not forgive will find no forgiveness from God.

Verse 8. *Finally*—This part of the epistle reaches to chapter iv. 11. The apostle seems to have added the rest afterwards. *Sympathizing*—Rejoicing and sorrowing together. *Love* all believers *as brethren. Be pitiful*—Toward the afflicted. *Be courteous*—To all men. Courtesy is such a behaviour toward equals and inferiors as shows respect mixed with love.

Verse 9. *Ye are called to inherit a blessing*—Therefore their railing cannot hurt you; and, by *blessing* them, you imitate God, who blesses you.

Verse 10. *For he that desireth to love life, and to see good days*—That would make life amiable and desirable.

Verse 11. *Let him seek*—To live peaceably with all men. *And pursue it*—Even when it seems to flee from him.

Verse 12. *The eyes of the Lord are over the righteous*—For good. Anger appears in the whole face; love, chiefly in the eyes.

Verse 13. *Who is he that will harm you*—None can.

is he that will harm you, if ye be followers of that which is
14 good? But even if ye do suffer for righteousness' sake,
happy *are* ye: and fear ye not their fear, neither be ye
15 troubled; But sanctify the Lord God in your hearts: and
be always ready to give an answer to every one that asketh
you a reason of the hope that is in you with meekness and
16 fear: Having a good conscience; that, wherein they speak
against you, as evildoers, they may be ashamed who falsely
17 accuse your good conversation in Christ. For *it is* better,
if the will of God be so, to suffer for well doing than for evil
18 doing. For Christ also once suffered for sins, the just for
the unjust, that he might bring us to God, being put to
19 death in the flesh, but raised up to life by the Spirit: By
which likewise he went and preached to the spirits in prison;

Verse 14. *But if ye* should *suffer*—This is no harm to you, but a good. *Fear ye not their fear*—The very words of the Septuagint, Isaiah viii. 12, 13. Let not that fear be in you which the wicked feel.

Verse 15. *But sanctify the Lord God in your hearts*—Have an holy fear, and a full trust in his wise providence. *The hope*—Of eternal life. *With meekness*—For anger would hurt your cause as well as your soul. *And fear*—A filial fear of offending God, and a jealousy over yourselves, lest ye speak amiss.

Verse 16 *Having a good conscience*—So much the more beware of anger, to which the very consciousness of your innocence may betray you Join with a good conscience meekness and fear, and you obtain a complete victory. *Your good conversation in Christ*—That is, which flows from faith in him.

Verse 17. *It is* infinitely *better, if it be the will of God,* ye should suffer. His permissive will appears from his providence.

Verse 18. *For*—This is undoubtedly best, whereby we are most conformed to Christ. Now *Christ suffered once*—To suffer no more *For sins*—Not his own, but ours. *The just for the unjust*—The word signifies, not only them who have wronged their neighbours, but those who have transgressed any of the commands of God; as the preceding word, *just,* denotes a person who has fulfilled, not barely social duties, but all kind of righteousness. *That he might bring us to God*—Now to his gracious favour, hereafter to his blissful presence, by the same steps of suffering and of glory. *Being put to death in the flesh*—As man. *But raised to life by the Spirit*—Both by his own divine power, and by the power of the Holy Ghost.

Verse 19. *By which* Spirit *he preached*—Through the ministry of Noah. *To the spirits in prison*—The unholy men before the flood, who were then reserved by the justice of God, as in a prison, till he executed the sentence upon them all; and are now also reserved to the judgment of the great day.

CHAPTER IV.

20 Who were disobedient of old, when the longsuffering of God
waited in the days of Noah, while the ark was preparing,
wherein few, that is, eight persons were carried safely
21 through the water. The antitype whereof, baptism, now
saveth us, (not the putting away the filth of the flesh, but
the answer of a good conscience toward God,) by the resur-
22 rection of Jesus Christ: Who being gone into heaven, is
on the right hand of God; angels and authorities and
IV. 1 powers being subjected to him. Seeing then Christ
hath suffered for us in the flesh, arm yourselves also with
the same mind: (for he that hath suffered in the flesh hath
2 ceased from sin:) That *ye* may no longer live the rest
of *your* time in the flesh to the desire of men, but to the
3 will of God. For the time of life that is past sufficeth to
have wrought the will of the gentiles, when ye walked in
lasciviousness, evil desires, excess of wine, banquetings,
4 revellings, and abominable idolatries: Wherein they think

Verse 20. *When the longsuffering of God waited*—For an hundred and twenty years; all the time *the ark was preparing:* during which *Noah* warned them all to flee from the wrath to come.

Verse 21. *The antitype whereof*—The thing typified by the ark, even *baptism, now saveth us*—That is, through the water of baptism we are saved from the sin which overwhelms the world as a flood: *not,* indeed, the bare outward sign, but the inward grace; a divine consciousness that both our persons and our actions are accepted through him who died and rose again for us.

Verse 22. *Angels and authorities and powers*—That is, all orders both of angels and men.

Verse 1. *Arm yourselves with the same mind*—Which will be armour of proof against all your enemies. *For he that hath suffered in the flesh*—That hath so suffered as to be thereby made inwardly and truly conformable to the sufferings of Christ. *Hath ceased from sin*—Is delivered from it.

Verse 2. *That ye may no longer live in the flesh*—Even in this mortal body. *To the desires of men*—Either your own or those of others. These are various; but *the will of God* is one.

Verse 3. *Revellings, banquetings*—Have these words any meaning now? They had, seventeen hundred years ago. Then the former meant, meetings to eat; meetings, the direct end of which was, to please the taste: the latter, meetings to drink: both of which Christians then ranked with *abominable idolatries.*

Verse 4. *The same*—As ye did once. *Speaking evil of you*—As proud, singular, silly, wicked, and the like.

it strange that ye run not with them to the same profusion
5 of riot, speaking evil of *you:* Who shall give account to
6 him that is ready to judge the living and the dead. For to
this end was the gospel preached to them that are dead also,
that they might be judged according to men in the flesh, but
7 live according to God in the spirit. But the end of all
things is at hand: be ye therefore sober, and watch unto
8 prayer. And above all things have fervent love to each
9 other: for love covereth a multitude of sins.* Use hospi-
10 tality one to another without murmuring. As every one
hath received a gift, *so* minister it one to another, as good
11 stewards of the manifold grace of God. If any man speak,
let him speak as the oracles of God; if any man minister,

* Prov. x. 12.

Verse 5. *Who shall give account*—Of this, as well as all their other ways. *To him who is ready*—So faith represents him now.

Verse 6. *For to this end was the gospel preached*—Ever since it was given to Adam. *To them that are* now *dead*—In their several generations. *That they might be judged*—That though they were judged. *In the flesh according to* the manner of *men*—With rash, unrighteous judgment. *They might live according to* the will and word of *God, in the Spirit;* the soul renewed after his image.

Verse 7. *But the end of all things*—And so of their wrongs, and your sufferings. *Is at hand: be ye therefore sober, and watch unto prayer*—Temperance helps watchfulness, and both of them help prayer Watch, that ye may pray; and pray, that ye may watch.

Verse 8. *Love covereth a multitude of sins*—Yea, "love covereth all things." He that loves another, covers his faults, how many soever they be. He turns away his own eyes from them; and, as far as is possible, hides them from others. And he continually prays that all the sinner's iniquities may be forgiven and his sins covered. Meantime the God of love measures to him with the same measure into his bosom.

Verse 9. *One to another*—Ye that are of different towns or countries. *Without murmuring*—With all cheerfulness.

Verse 10. *As every one hath received a gift*—Spiritual or temporal, ordinary or extraordinary, although the latter seems primarily intended. *So minister it one to another*—Employ it for the common good. *As good stewards of the manifold grace of God*—The talents wherewith his free love has intrusted you.

Verse 11. *If any man speak, let him*—In his whole conversation, public and private. *Speak as the oracles of God*—Let all his words be according to this pattern, both as to matter and manner, more especially in public. By this mark we may always know who are, so far, the true or false prophets *The oracles of God* teach that men should repent, believe, obey.

let him minister as of the ability which God supplieth: that
God in all things may be glorified through Jesus Christ,
whose is the glory and the might for ever and ever. Amen.
12 Beloved, wonder not at the burning which is among you,
13 which is for your trial, as if a strange thing befel you: But
as ye partake of the sufferings of Christ, rejoice; that, when
his glory shall be revealed, ye may likewise rejoice with
14 exceeding great joy. If ye are reproached for the name
of Christ, happy *are ye;* for the spirit of glory and of God
resteth upon you: on their part he is blasphemed, but on
15 your part he is glorified. But let none of you suffer as a
murderer, or a thief, or an evildoer, or as a meddler in other
16 men's matters. Yet if *any suffer* as a Christian, let him not
17 *be* ashamed; but let him glorify God on this behalf. For
the time *is come* for judgment to begin at the house of God:

He that treats of faith and leaves out repentance, or does not enjoin practical holiness to believers, does not speak as the oracles of God: he does not preach Christ, let him think as highly of himself as he will. *If any man minister*—Serve his brother in love, whether in spirituals or temporals. *Let him minister as of the ability which God giveth*—That is, humbly and diligently, ascribing all his power to God, and using it with his might. *Whose is the glory*—Of his wisdom, which teaches us to speak. *And the might*—Which enables us to act.

Verse 12. *Wonder not at the burning which is among you*—This is the literal meaning of the expression. It seems to include both martyrdom itself, which so frequently was by fire, and all the other sufferings joined with, or previous to, it; *which is* permitted by the wisdom of God *for your trial.* Be not surprised at this.

Verse 13. *But as ye partake of the sufferings of Christ*—Verse 1, while ye suffer for his sake, *rejoice* in hope of more abundant glory. For the measure of glory answers the measure of suffering; and much more abundantly.

Verse 14. *If ye are reproached for Christ*—Reproaches and cruel mockings were always one part of their sufferings. *The Spirit of glory and of God resteth upon you*—The same Spirit which was upon Christ, Luke iv 18. He is here termed, *the Spirit of glory,* conquering all reproach and shame, and *the Spirit of God,* whose Son, Jesus Christ is. *On their part he is blasphemed, but on your part he is glorified*—That is, while they are blaspheming Christ, you glorify him in the midst of your sufferings, verse 16.

Verse 15. *Let none of you* deservedly *suffer, as an evildoer*—In any kind.

Verse 16. *Let him glorify God*—Who giveth him the honour so to suffer, and so great a reward for suffering.

Verse 17. *The time is come for judgment to begin at the house of God*—

but if it begin at us, what *shall* the end *be* of them that obey
18 not the gospel of God? And if the * righteous scarcely be
saved, where shall the ungodly and the sinner appear?
19 Wherefore let them also that suffer according to the will
of God commit their souls *to him* in well doing, as unto a
faithful Creator.

CHAP. V. 1 The elders that are among you I exhort,
who am a fellow-elder, and a witness of the sufferings
of Christ, and likewise a partaker of the glory which shall
2 be revealed: Feed the flock of God which is among you,
overseeing *it*, not by constraint, but willingly; not for filthy
3 gain, but of a ready mind; Neither as lording over the heri-

* Prov. xi. 31.

God first visits his church, and that both in justice and mercy. *What shall the end be of them that obey not the gospel*—How terribly will he visit them! The judgments which are milder at the beginning, grow more and more severe. But good men, having already sustained their part, are only spectators of the miseries of the wicked.

Verse 18. *If the righteous scarcely be saved*—Escape with the utmost difficulty. *Where shall the ungodly*—The man who knows not God. *And the* open *sinner appear*—In that day of vengeance The salvation here primarily spoken of is of a temporal nature. But we may apply the words to eternal things, and then they are still more awful.

Verse 19. *Let them that suffer according to the will of God*—Both for a good cause, and in a right spirit. *Commit to him their souls*—(Whatever becomes of the body) as a sacred depositum. *In well doing*—Be this your care, to do and suffer well: He will take care of the rest. *As unto a faithful Creator*—In whose truth, love, and power, ye may safely trust.

Verse 1. *I who am a fellow-elder*—So the first though not the head of the apostles appositely and modestly styles himself. *And a witness of the sufferings of Christ*—Having seen him suffer, and now suffering for him.

Verse 2. *Feed the flock*—Both by doctrine and discipline. *Not by constraint*—Unwillingly, as a burden. *Not for filthy gain*—Which, if it be the motive of acting, is *filthy* beyond expression. O consider this, ye that leave one flock and go to another, merely because there is more gain, a large salary! Is it not astonishing that men can see no harm in this? that it is not only practised, but avowed, all over the nation?

Verse 3. *Neither as lording over the heritage*—Behaving in a haughty, domineering manner, as though you had dominion over their conscience The word translated *heritage*, is, literally, *the portions*. There is one flock under the one chief Shepherd; but many *portions* of this, under many pastors. *But being examples to the flock*—This procures the most ready and free obedience.

4 tage, but being examples to the flock. And when the
chief Shepherd shall appear, ye shall receive the crown
5 of glory that fadeth not away. In like manner, ye younger,
be subject to the elder. Yea, being all subject to each
other, be clothed with humility: * for God resisteth the
6 proud, but giveth grace to the humble. Humble yourselves
therefore under the mighty hand of God, that he may exalt
7 you in due time: Casting all your care upon him; for he
8 careth for you. Watch; be vigilant; for your adversary
the devil walketh about as a roaring lion, seeking whom he
9 may devour: Whom resist steadfast in the faith, knowing
that the same afflictions are accomplished in your brethren
that are in the world.

10 Now the God of all grace, who hath called us by Christ
Jesus to his eternal glory, after ye have suffered a while, him-
11 self shall perfect, stablish, strengthen, settle you. To him
be the glory and the might for ever and ever. Amen.

12 By Silvanus, a faithful brother, as I suppose, I have

* James iv 6; Prov. iii. 34

Verse 5. *Ye younger, be subject to the elder*—In years. *And be all*—Elder or younger. *Subject to each other*—Let every one be ready, upon all occasions, to give up his own will. *Be clothed with humility*—*Bind it on,* (so the word signifies,) so that no force may be able to tear it from you.

Verse 6. *The hand of God*—Is in all troubles.

Verse 7 *Casting all your care upon him*—In every want or pressure.

Verse 8. But in the mean time *watch.* There is a close connexion between this, and the duly *casting our care* upon him. How deeply ha, St. Peter himself suffered for want of watching! *Be vigilant*—As if he had said, Awake, and keep awake. Sleep no more: be this your care. *As a roaring lion*—Full of rage. *Seeking*—With all subtilty likewise *Whom he may devour* or *swallow up*—Both soul and body.

Verse 9. Be the more *steadfast,* as ye *know the same* kind of *afflictions are accomplished in*—That is, suffered by, *your brethren,* till the measure allotted them is filled up.

Verse 10. *Now the God of all grace*—By which alone the whole work is begun, continued, and finished in your soul. *After ye have suffered a while*—A very little while compared with eternity. *Himself*—Ye have only to watch and resist the devil: the rest God will perform. *Perfect*—That no defect may remain. *Stablish*—That nothing may overthrow you. *Strengthen*—That ye may conquer all adverse power. *And settle you*—As an house upon a rock. So the apostle, being converted, does now "strengthen his brethren."

Verse 12. *As I suppose*—As I judge, upon good grounds, though not

written briefly to you, exhorting, and adding my testimony
13 that this is the true grace of God wherein ye stand. The
church that is at Babylon, elected together with *you*, saluteth
14 you; and Mark my son. Salute ye one another with a kiss
of charity. Peace *be* with you all that are in Christ.

by immediate inspiration. *I have written*—That is, sent my letter by him. *Adding my testimony*—To that which ye before heard from Paul, *that this is the true* gospel of the *grace of God.*

Verse 13. *The church that is at Babylon*—Near which St. Peter probably was, when he wrote this epistle. *Elected together with you*—Partaking of the same faith with you. *Mark*—It seems the evangelist. *My son*—Probably converted by St. Peter And he had occasionally served him, "as a son in the gospel."

NOTES

ON

THE SECOND EPISTLE GENERAL OF ST. PETER

THE parts of this epistle, wrote not long before St. Peter's death, and the destruction of Jerusalem, with the same design as the former, are likewise three:—

I. The inscription,	C. i.	1, 2
II. A farther stirring up of the minds of true believers, in which,		
1. He exhorts them, having received the precious gift, to give all diligence to "grow in grace,"		3—11
2. To this he incites them,		
1. From the firmness of true teachers,		12—21
2. From the wickedness of false teachers,	C. ii.	1—22
3. He guards them against impostors,		
1. By confuting their error,	C. iii.	1— 9
2. By describing the great day, adding suitable exhortations,		10—14
III. The conclusion, in which he,		
1. Declares his agreement with St. Paul,		15, 16
2. Repeats the sum of the epistle,		17, 18

II. ST. PETER.

CHAPTER I. 1 SIMON PETER, a servant and an apostle of Jesus Christ, to them that have obtained like precious
faith with us through the righteousness of our God and

Verse 1. *To them that have obtained*—Not by their own works, but by the free grace of God. *Like precious faith with us*—The apostles. The faith of those who have not seen, being equally precious with that of those who saw our Lord in the flesh. *Through the righteousness*—Both active and passive. *Of our God and Saviour*—It is this alone by which the justice of God is satisfied, and for the sake of which he gives this precious faith.

2 Saviour Jesus Christ: Grace and peace be multiplied unto
you through the knowledge of God, and of Jesus our Lord,
3 As his divine power hath given us all things that pertain to
life and godliness, through the knowledge of him that hath
4 called us by glory and virtue: Through which he hath
given us precious and exceeding great promises: that by
these, having escaped the corruption which is in the world
through desire, ye may become partakers of the divine
5 nature: For this very reason, giving all diligence, add to
6 your faith courage; and to courage knowledge; And to

Verse 2. *Through the* divine, experimental *knowledge of God and of Christ.*

Verse 3. *As his divine power has given us all things*—There is a wonderful cheerfulness in this exordium, which begins with the exhortation itself. *That pertain to life and godliness*—To the present, natural life, and to the continuance and increase of spiritual life. *Through* that divine *knowledge of him*—Of Christ. *Who hath called us by*—His own glorious power, to eternal *glory*, as the end; by Christian *virtue* or *fortitude*, as the means.

Verse 4. *Through which*—Glory and fortitude. *He hath given us exceeding great*, and inconceivably *precious promises*—Both the promises and the things promised, which follow in their due season, that, sustained and encouraged by the promises, we may obtain all that he has promised. *That, having escaped the* manifold *corruption which is in the world*—From that fruitful fountain, evil *desire. Ye may become partakers of the divine nature*—Being renewed in the image of God, and having communion with him, so as to dwell in God and God in you

Verse 5. *For this very reason*—Because God hath given you so great blessings. *Giving all diligence*—It is a very uncommon word which we render *giving*. It literally signifies, *bringing in by the by*, or *over and above:* implying, that God works the work; yet not unless we are diligent. Our diligence is to follow the gift of God, and is followed by an increase of all his gifts. *Add to*—And *in* all the other gifts of God. Superadd the latter, without losing the former. The Greek word properly means *lead up*, as in dance, one of these after the other, in a beautiful order. *Your faith*, that "evidence of things not seen," termed before "the knowledge of God and of Christ," the root of all Christian graces. *Courage*—Whereby ye may conquer all enemies and difficulties, and execute whatever faith dictates. In this most beautiful connexion, each preceding grace leads to the following; each following, tempers and perfects the preceding. They are set down in the order of nature, rather than the order of time. For though every grace bears a relation to every other, yet here they are so nicely ranged, that those which have the closest dependence on each other are placed together. *And to your courage knowledge*—Wisdom, teaching how to exercise it on all occasions.

Verse 6. *And to your knowledge temperance; and to your temperance*

knowledge temperance; and to temperance patience; and to
7 patience godliness; And to godliness brotherly kindness;
8 and to brotherly kindness love. For these being in you, and
abounding, make *you* neither slothful nor unfruitful in the
9 knowledge of our Lord Jesus Christ. But he that wanteth

patience—Bear and forbear; sustain and abstain; deny yourself and take up your cross daily The more knowledge you have, the more renounce your own will; indulge yourself the less. "Knowledge puffeth up," and the great boasters of knowledge (the Gnostics) were those that "turned the grace of God into wantonness." But see that *your* knowledge be attended with *temperance.* Christian temperance implies the voluntary abstaining from all pleasure which does not lead to God. It extends to all things inward and outward: the due government of every thought, as well as affection. "It is using the world," so to use all outward, and so to restrain all inward things, that they may become a means of what is spiritual; a scaling ladder to ascend to what is above. Intemperance is to abuse the world. He that uses anything below, looking no higher, and getting no farther, is intemperate. He that uses the creature only so as to attain to more of the Creator, is alone temperate, and walks as Christ himself walked. *And to patience godliness*—Its proper support: a continual sense of God's presence and providence, and a filial fear of, and confidence in, him; otherwise your patience may be pride, surliness, stoicism; but not Christianity.

Verse 7. *And to godliness brotherly kindness*—No sullenness, sternness, moroseness: "sour godliness," so called, is of the devil. Of Christian godliness it may always be said,

"Mild, sweet, serene, and tender is her mood,
Nor grave with sternness, nor with lightness free:
Against example resolutely good,
Fervent in zeal, and warm in charity."

And to brotherly kindness love—The pure and perfect love of God and of all mankind. The apostle here makes an advance upon the preceding article, *brotherly kindness,* which seems only to relate to the love of Christians toward one another.

Verse 8. *For these being* really *in you*—Added to your faith. *And abounding*—Increasing more and more, otherwise we fall short. *Make you neither slothful nor unfruitful*—Do not suffer you to be faint in your mind, or without fruit in your lives. If there is less faithfulness, less care and watchfulness, since we were pardoned, than there was before, and less diligence, less outward obedience, than when we were seeking remission of sin, we are both *slothful and unfruitful in the knowledge of Christ,* that is, in the faith, which then cannot work by love.

Verse 9. *But he that wanteth these*—That does not add them to his faith. *Is blind*—The eyes of his understanding are again closed. He cannot see God, or his pardoning love. He has lost the evidence of things not seen. *Not able to see afar off*—Literally, purblind. He has

these is blind, not able to see afar off, having forgotten the
10 purification from his former sins. Wherefore, brethren,
be the more diligent to make your calling and election firm;
11 for if ye do these things, ye shall never fall: For so an
entrance shall be ministered to you abundantly into the
everlasting kingdom of our Lord and Saviour Jesus Christ.
12 Wherefore I will not neglect always to remind you of these
things, though ye know them, and are established in the
13 present truth. Yea, I think it right, so long as I am in
14 this tabernacle, to stir you up by reminding *you;* Knowing
that shortly I must put off my tabernacle, even as our Lord
15 Jesus Christ showed me. But I will endeavour that ye
may be able after my decease to have these things always in
remembrance.
16 For we have not followed cunningly devised fables, while

lost sight of the precious promises: perfect love and heaven are equally out of his sight. Nay, he cannot now see what himself once enjoyed. *Having,* as it were, *forgot the purification from his former sins*—Scarce knowing what he himself then felt, when his sins were forgiven.

Verse 10. *Wherefore*—Considering the miserable state of these apostates. *Brethren*—St. Peter nowhere uses this appellation in either of his epistles, but in this important exhortation. *Be the more diligent*—By courage, knowledge, temperance, &c. *To make your calling and election firm*—God hath called you by his word and his Spirit; he hath elected you, separated you from the world, through sanctification of the Spirit. O cast not away these inestimable benefits! *If ye* are thus *diligent to make your election firm, ye shall never* finally *fall.*

Verse 11. *For* if ye do *so, an entrance shall be ministered to you abundantly into the everlasting kingdom*—Ye shall go in full triumph to glory.

Verse 12. *Wherefore*—Since everlasting destruction attends your sloth, everlasting glory your diligence, *I will not neglect always to remind you of these things*—Therefore he wrote another, so soon after the former, epistle. *Though ye are established in the present truth*—That truth which I am now declaring.

Verse 13. *In this tabernacle*—Or tent. How short is our abode in the body! How easily does a believer pass out of it!

Verse 14. *Even as the Lord Jesus showed me*—In the manner which he foretold, John xxi. 18, &c. It is not improbable, he had also showed him that the time was now drawing nigh.

Verse 15. *That ye may be able*—By having this epistle among you

Verse 16. *These things* are worthy to be *always had in remembrance For* they are *not cunningly devised fables*—Like those common among the heathens. *While we made known to you the power and coming*—That is, the powerful coming *of Christ* in glory. But if what they advanced of Christ was not true, if it was of their own invention, then

we made known to you the power and coming of our Lord
17 Jesus Christ, but were eyewitnesses of his majesty. For
he received honour and glory from God the Father, when
there came such a voice to him from the excellent glory,*
18 This is my beloved Son, in whom I delight. And we being
with him in the holy mountain, heard this voice coming
19 from heaven. And we have the word of prophecy more
confirmed; to which ye do well that ye take heed, as to a
lamp that shone in a dark place, till the day should dawn,
20 and the morning star arise in your hearts: Knowing this
before, that no scripture prophecy is of private interpreta-
21 tion. For prophecy came not of old by the will of man

* Matt. xvii. 5.

to impose such a lie on the world as it was, in the very nature of things, above all human power to defend, and to do this at the expense of life and all things only to enrage the whole world, Jews and gentiles, against them, was no cunning, but was the greatest folly that men could have been guilty of. *But were eyewitnesses of his majesty*—At his transfiguration, which was a specimen of his glory at the last day.

Verse 17. *For he received* divine *honour and* inexpressible *glory*—Shining from heaven above the brightness of the sun *When there came such a voice from the excellent glory*—That is, from God the Father

Verse 18. *And we*—Peter, James, and John. St. John was still alive. *Being with him in the holy mount*—Made so by that glorious manifestation, as mount Horeb was of old, Exod. iii. 4, 5.

Verse 19. *And we*—St. Peter here speaks in the name of all Christians. *Have the word of prophecy*—The words of Moses, Isaiah, and all the prophets, are one and the same word, every way consistent with itself. St. Peter does not cite any particular passage, but speaks of their entire testimony. *More confirmed*—By that display of his glorious majesty. *To which* word *ye do well that ye take heed, as to a lamp which shone in a dark place*—Wherein there was neither light nor window. Such anciently was the whole world, except that little spot where this lamp shone. *Till the day should dawn*—Till the full light of the gospel should break through the darkness. As is the difference between the light of a lamp and that of the day, such is that between the light of the Old Testament and of the New. *And the morning star*—Jesus Christ, Rev. xxii. 16. *Arise in your hearts*—Be revealed in you.

Verse 20. Ye do well, as *knowing this, that no scripture prophecy is of private interpretation*—It is not any man's own word. It is God, not the prophet himself, who thereby interprets things till then unknown.

Verse 21. *For prophecy came not of old by the will of man*—Of any mere man whatever. *But the holy men of God*—Devoted to him, and set apart

but the holy men of God spake, being moved by the Holy Ghost.

CHAP. II. 1 But there were false prophets also among
the people, as there shall likewise be false teachers among
you, who will privately bring in destructive heresies, even
denying the Lord that bought them, and bring upon them-
2 selves swift destruction. And many will follow their pernicious ways; by means of whom the way of truth will be
3 evil spoken of. And through covetousness will they with
feigned speeches make merchandise of you: whose judgment now of a long time lingereth not, and their destruction
4 slumbereth not. For if God spared not the angels that
sinned, but having cast *them* down to hell, delivered them
into chains of darkness, to be reserved unto judgment;

by him for that purpose, *spake* and wrote. *Being moved*—Literally, *carried.* They were purely passive therein.

Verse 1. *But there were false prophets also*—As well as true. *Among the people*—Of Israel. Those that spake even the truth, when God had not sent them; and also those that were truly sent of him, and yet corrupted or softened their message, were false prophets. *As there shall be false*—As well as true. *Teachers among you, who will privately bring in*—Into the church. *Destructive heresies*—They first, by denying the Lord, introduced destructive heresies, that is, divisions; or they occasioned first these divisions, and then were given up to a reprobate mind, even to deny the Lord that bought them. Either the heresies are the effect of denying the Lord, or the denying the Lord was the consequence of the heresies. *Even denying*—Both by their doctrine and their works. *The Lord that bought them*—With his own blood. Yet these very men perish everlastingly. Therefore Christ bought even them that perish.

Verse 2. *The way of truth will be evil spoken of*—By those who blend all false and true Christians together.

Verse 3. *They will make merchandise of you*—Only use you to gain by you, as merchants do their wares. *Whose judgment now of a long time lingereth not*—Was long ago determined, and will be executed speedily. All sinners are adjudged to destruction; and God's punishing some proves he will punish the rest.

Verse 4. *Cast them down to hell*—The bottomless pit, a place of unknown misery. *Delivered them*—Like condemned criminals to safe custody, as if bound with the strongest *chains* in a dungeon of *darkness, to be reserved unto* the *judgment* of the great day. Though still those chains do not hinder their often walking up and down seeking whom they may devour.

5 And spared not the old world, (but he preserved Noah the
eighth *person*, a preacher of righteousness,) bringing a
6 flood on the world of the ungodly; And condemned the
cities of Sodom and Gomorrha to destruction, turning *them*
into ashes, setting them *as* an example to them that should
7 afterwards live ungodly; And delivered righteous Lot,
8 grieved with the filthy behaviour of the wicked: (For that
righteous man dwelling among them, by seeing and hearing
tormented his righteous soul from day to day with *their*
9 unlawful deeds) The Lord knoweth how to deliver the
godly out of temptation, and to reserve the unrighteous to
10 the day of judgment to be punished: But chiefly them that
walk after the flesh in the lust of uncleanness, and despise
government. Daring, self-willed, they are not afraid to rail
11 at dignities. Whereas angels, who are greater in strength
and power, bring not a railing accusation against them before
12 the Lord. But these men, as natural brute beasts, born to
be taken and destroyed, speaking evil of the things they
13 understand not, shall perish in their own corruption; Receiving the reward of unrighteousness. They count it pleasure
to riot in the day time. Spots and blemishes, sporting themselves with their own deceivings while they feast with you;
14 Having eyes full of adultery, and that cease not from sin;

Verse 5. *And spared not the old,* the antediluvian, *world, but he preserved Noah the eighth person*—that is, Noah and seven others, *a preacher* as well as practiser, *of righteousness. Bringing a flood on the world of the ungodly*—Whose numbers stood them in no stead.

Verse 9. It plainly appears, from these instances, that *the Lord knoweth,* hath both wisdom and power and will, *to deliver the godly out of* all *temptations, and to* punish the ungodly.

Verse 10. *Chiefly them that walk after the flesh*—Corrupt nature; particularly *in the lust of uncleanness. And despise government*—The authority of their governors. *Dignities*—Persons in authority.

Verse 11. *Whereas angels*—When they appear *before the Lord,* Job i. 6, ii. 1, to give an account of what they have seen and done on the earth.

Verse 12. Savage *as brute beasts*—Several of which, in the present disordered state of the world, seem *born to be taken and destroyed.*

Verse 13. *They count it pleasure to riot in the day time*—They glory in doing it in the face of the sun. They are *spots* in themselves, *blemishes* to any church. *Sporting themselves with their own deceivings*—Making a jest of those whom they deceive, and even jesting while they are deceiving their own souls.

ensnaring unstable souls: having an heart exercised with
15 covetousness; accursed children: Who have forsaken the
right way, and are gone astray, following the way of Balaam
the son of Bosor, who loved the reward of unrighteousness;
16 But he had a rebuke for his iniquity: the dumb beast speaking with man's voice forbad the madness of the prophet.
17 These are fountains without water, clouds driven by a tempest; to whom the blackness of darkness is reserved for
18 ever. For by speaking swelling *words* of vanity, they
ensnare in the desires of the flesh, in wantonness, those that
19 were entirely escaped from them that live in error. While
they promise them liberty, themselves are the slaves of corruption: for by whom a man is overcome, by him he is also
20 brought into slavery. For if after they have escaped the
pollutions of the world through the knowledge of the Lord
and Saviour Jesus Christ, they are again entangled therein,
21 and overcome, their last state is worse than the first. For
it had been better for them not to have known the way
of righteousness, than, having known *it*, to turn from the
22 holy commandment delivered to them. But it has befallen

Verse 15. *The way of Balaam the son of Bosor*—So the Chaldeans pronounced what the Jews termed *Beor;* namely, the way of covetousness. *Who loved*—Earnestly desired, though he did not dare to take, *the reward of unrighteousness*—The money which Balak would have given him for cursing Israel.

Verse 16. *The beast*—Though naturally *dumb.*

Verse 17. *Fountains* and *clouds* promise water so do these promise, but do not perform.

Verse 18. *They ensnare in the desires of the flesh*—Allowing them to gratify some unholy desire. *Those who were* before *entirely escaped from* the spirit, custom, and company of *them that live in error*—In sin.

Verse 19. *While they promise them liberty*—From needless restraints and scruples; from the bondage of the law. *Themselves are slaves of corruption*—Even sin, the vilest of all bondage.

Verse 20. *For if after they*—Who are thus ensnared. *Have escaped the pollutions of the world*—The sins which pollute all who know not God. *Through the knowledge of Christ*—That is, through faith in him, 2 Peter i. 3. *They are again entangled therein, and overcome, their last state is worse than the first*—More inexcusable, and causing a greater damnation.

Verse 21. *The commandment*—The whole law of God, *once* not only *delivered* to their ears, but written in their hearts.

Verse 22. *The dog, the sow*—Such are all men in the sight of God

them according to the true proverb, * The dog *is* turned to
his own vomit, and the sow that was washed to her wallowing in the mire.

CHAP. III. 1 This second epistle, beloved, I now write
to you; in *both* which I stir up your pure minds by way
2 of remembrance: That ye may be mindful of the words
which were spoken before by the holy prophets, and of the
commandment of us the apostles of the Lord and Saviour:
3 Knowing this first, that there will come scoffers in the last
4 days, walking after their own desires, And saying, Where is
the promise of his coming? for ever since the fathers fell
asleep, all things continue as *they were* from the beginning
5 of the creation. For this they are willingly ignorant of,
that by the word of God the heavens were of old, and the
6 earth standing out of the water and in the water: Through

* Prov. xxvi. 11.

before they receive his grace, and after they have made shipwreck of the faith.

Verses 2, 3. *Be* the more *mindful* thereof, because ye *know scoffers will come first*—Before the Lord comes. *Walking after their own evil desires* —Here is the origin of the error, the root of libertinism. Do we not see this eminently fulfilled?

Verse 4 *Saying, Where is the promise of his coming*—To judgment (They do not even deign to name him.) We see no sign of any such thing. *For ever since the fathers*—Our first ancestors. *Fell asleep, all things*—Heaven, water, earth. *Continue as they were from the beginning of the creation*—Without any such material change as might make us believe they will ever end

Verse 5. *For this they are willingly ignorant of*—They do not care to know or consider. *That by the* almighty *word of God*—Which bounds the duration of all things, so that it cannot be either longer or shorter *Of old*—Before the flood. *The* aerial *heavens were, and the earth*—Not as it is now, but *standing out of the water and in the water*—Perhaps the interior globe of earth was fixed *in the* midst of the great deep, the abyss of *water; the* shell or exterior globe *standing out of the water,* covering the great deep. This, or some other great and manifest difference between the original and present constitution of the terraqueous globe, seems then to have been so generally known, that St. Peter charges their ignorance of it totally upon their wilfulness.

Verse 6. *Through which*—Heaven and earth, the windows of heaven being opened, and the fountains of the great deep broken up. *The world that then was*—The whole antediluvian race *Being overflowed with*

which the world that then was, being overflowed with water,
7 perished. But the heavens and the earth, that are now,
are by his word treasured up, reserved unto fire at the day
8 of judgment and destruction of ungodly men. * But, beloved,
be not ye ignorant of this one thing, that one day *is* with
the Lord as a thousand years, and a thousand years as one
9 day. The Lord is not slow concerning his promise; (though
some men count it slowness;) but is longsuffering for your
sake, not willing that any should perish, but that all should
10 come to repentance. But the day of the Lord will come as

* Psalm xc. 4.

water, perished—And the heavens and earth themselves, though they did not perish, yet underwent a great change. So little ground have these scoffers for saying that *all things continue as they were from the creation.*

Verse 7. *But the heavens and the earth, that are now*—Since the flood. *Are reserved unto fire at the day* wherein God will *judge* the world, and punish the ungodly with everlasting *destruction.*

Verse 8. *But be not ye ignorant*—Whatever they are. *Of this one thing*—Which casts much light on the point in hand. *That one day is with the Lord as a thousand years, and a thousand years as one day*—Moses had said, Psalm xc. 4, "A thousand years in thy sight are as one day;" which St. Peter applies with regard to the last day, so as to denote both his eternity, whereby he exceeds all measure of time in his essence and in his operation; his knowledge, to which all things past or to come are present every moment; his power, which needs no long delay, in order to bring its work to perfection; and his longsuffering, which excludes all impatience of expectation, and desire of making haste. *One day is with the Lord as a thousand years*—That is, in one day, in one moment, he can do the work of a thousand years. Therefore he "is not slow:" he is always equally ready to fulfil his promise. *And a thousand years are as one day*—That is, no delay is long to God. A thousand years are as one day to the eternal God. Therefore "he is longsuffering:" he gives us space for repentance, without any inconvenience to himself. In a word, with God time passes neither slower nor swifter than is suitable to him and his economy; nor can there be any reason why it should be necessary for him either to delay or hasten the end of all things. How can we comprehend this? If we could comprehend it, St. Peter needed not to have added, *with the Lord.*

Verse 9. *The Lord is not slow*—As if the time fixed for it were past *Concerning his promise*—Which shall surely be fulfilled in its season. *But is longsuffering towards us*—Children of men. *Not willing that any* soul which he hath made *should perish.*

Verse 10. *But the day of the Lord will come as a thief*—Suddenly, unexpectedly. *In which the heavens shall pass away with a great noise*—Sur

a thief; in which the heavens shall pass away with a great
noise, the elements shall melt with fervent heat, and the
earth and the works that are therein shall be burned up.
11 Seeing then all these things are dissolved, what manner
of persons ought ye to be in all holy conversation and godli-
12 ness, Looking for and hastening on *the* coming of the day
of God, wherein the heavens being on fire shall be dissolved,
13 and the elements shall melt with fervent heat? Nevertheless
we look for new heavens and a new earth, according to

prisingly expressed by the very sound of the original word. *The elements shall melt with fervent heat*—*The elements* seem to mean, the sun, moon, and stars; not the four, commonly so called; for air and water cannot melt, and the earth is mentioned immediately after. *The earth and* all *the works*—Whether of nature or art. *That are therein shall be burned up*—And has not God already abundantly provided for this? 1. By the stores of subterranean fire which are so frequently bursting out at Ætna, Vesuvius, Hecla, and many other burning mountains. 2. By the ethereal (vulgarly called electrical) fire, diffused through the whole globe; which, if the secret chain that now binds it up were loosed, would immediately dissolve the whole frame of nature. 3. By comets, one of which, if it touch the earth in its course toward the sun, must needs strike it into that abyss of fire; if in its return from the sun, when it is heated, as a great man computes, two thousand times hotter than a red-hot cannon-ball, it must destroy all vegetables and animals long before their contact, and soon after burn it up.

Verse 11. *Seeing then that all these things are dissolved*—To the eye of faith it appears as done already. *All these things*—Mentioned before; all that are included in that scriptural expression, "the heavens and the earth;" that is, the universe. On the fourth day God made the stars, Gen. i. 16, which will be dissolved together with the earth. They are deceived, therefore, who restrain either the history of the creation, or this description of the destruction, of the world to the earth and lower heavens; imagining the stars to be more ancient than the earth, and to survive it. Both the dissolution and renovation are ascribed, not to the one heaven which surrounds the earth, but to the heavens in general, verses 10, 13, without any restriction or limitation. *What persons ought ye to be in all holy conversation*—With men. *And godliness*—Toward your Creator.

Verse 12. *Hastening on*—As it were by your earnest desires and fervent prayers. *The coming of the day of God*—Many myriads of days he grants to men: one, the last, is the day of God himself.

Verse 13. *We look for new heavens and a new earth*—Raised as it were out of the ashes of the old; we look for an entire new state of things *Wherein dwelleth righteousness*—Only righteous spirits. How great a mystery!

14 his * promise, wherein dwelleth righteousness Wherefore,
beloved, seeing ye look for these things, labour to be found
15 of him in peace, without spot, and blameless. And account
the longsuffering of the Lord salvation; as our beloved brother Paul also according to the wisdom given him † hath
16 written to you; As also in all his epistles, speaking therein
of these things; in which are some things hard to be understood, which the unlearned and unstable wrest, as *they do*
also the other scriptures, to their own destruction.
17 Ye therefore, beloved, knowing *these things* before, beware
lest ye also, being led away by the error of the wicked, fall
18 from your own steadfastness. But grow in grace, and *in* the

* Isaiah lxv. 17; lxvi. 22. † Rom. ii. 4.

Verse 14. *Labour* that whenever he cometh *ye may be found in peace*—May meet him without terror, being sprinkled with his blood, and sanctified by his Spirit, so as to be *without spot and blameless*

Verse 15 *And account the longsuffering of the Lord salvation*—Not only designed to lead men to repentance, but actually conducing thereto: a precious means of saving many more souls. *As our beloved brother Paul also hath written to you*—This refers not only to the single sentence preceding, but to all that went before. St. Paul had written to the same effect concerning the end of the world, in several parts of his epistles, and particularly in his Epistle to the Hebrews.

Verse 16. *As also in all his epistles*—St. Peter wrote this a little before his own and St. Paul's martyrdom. St. Paul therefore had now written all his epistles; and even from this expression we may learn that St. Peter had read them all, perhaps sent to him by St. Paul himself Nor was he at all disgusted by what St. Paul had written concerning him in the Epistle to the Galatians *Speaking of these things*—Namely, of the coming of our Lord, delayed through his longsuffering, and of the circumstances preceding and accompanying it. *Which* things *the unlearned*—They who are not taught of God. *And the unstable*—Wavering, double-minded, unsettled men. *Wrest*—As though Christ would not come. *As they do also the other scriptures*—Therefore St Paul's writings were now part of the scriptures. *To their own destruction*—But that some use the scriptures ill, is no reason why others should not use them at all.

Verse 18. *But grow in grace*—That is, in every Christian temper There may be, for a time, grace without growth; as there may be natural life without growth. But such sickly life, of soul or body, will end in death, and every day draw nigher to it. Health is the means of both natural and spiritual growth. If the remaining evil of our fallen nature be not daily mortified, it will, like an evil humour in the body, destroy the whole man. But "if ye through the Spirit do mortify the deeds of the body," (only so far as we do this,) "ye shall live" the life of faith,

knowledge of our Lord and Saviour Jesus Christ. To him *be* the glory both now and to the day of eternity. Amen.

holiness, happiness. The end and design of grace being purchased and bestowed on us, is to destroy the image of the earthy, and restore us to that of the heavenly. And so far as it does this, it truly profits us; and also makes way for more of the heavenly gift, that we may at last be filled with all the fulness of God. The strength and well-being of a Christian depend on what his soul feeds on, as the health of the body depends on whatever we make our daily food. If we feed on what is according to our nature, we grow; if not, we pine away and die. The soul is of the nature of God, and nothing but what is according to his holiness can agree with it. Sin, of every kind, starves the soul, and makes it consume away. Let us not try to invert the order of God in his new-creation: we shall only deceive ourselves. It is easy to forsake the will of God, and follow our own; but this will bring leanness into the soul. It is easy to satisfy ourselves without being possessed of the holiness and happiness of the gospel. It is easy to call these frames and feelings, and then to oppose faith to one and Christ to the other. Frames (allowing the expression) are no other than heavenly tempers, "the mind that was in Christ." Feelings are the divine consolations of the Holy Ghost shed abroad in the heart of him that truly believes. And wherever faith is, and wherever Christ is, there are these blessed frames and feelings. If they are not in us, it is a sure sign that though the wilderness became a pool, the pool is become a wilderness again. *And in the knowledge of Christ*—That is, in faith, the root of all. *To him be the glory to the day of eternity*—An expression naturally flowing from that sense which the apostle had felt in his soul throughout this whole chapter. Eternity is a day without night, without interruption, without end.

NOTES

ON

THE FIRST EPISTLE OF ST. JOHN.

The great similitude, or rather sameness, both of spirit and expression, which runs through St. John's Gospel and all his epistles, is a clear evidence of their being written by the same person. In this epistle he speaks not to any particular church, but to all the Christians of that age; and in them to the whole Christian church in all succeeding ages.

Some have apprehended that it is not easy to discern the scope and method of this epistle. But if we examine it with simplicity, these may readily be discovered. St. John in this letter, or rather tract, (for he was present with part of those to whom he wrote,) has this apparent aim, to confirm the happy and holy communion of the faithful with God and Christ, by describing the marks of that blessed state.

The parts of it are three:—

I. The preface, C. i. 1—4
II. The tract itself, 5—C. v. —12
III. The conclusion, 13—21

In the preface he shows the authority of his own preaching and writing, and expressly points out, verse 3, the design of his present writing. To the preface exactly answers the conclusion, more largely explaining the same design, and recapitulating those marks, by *we know* thrice repeated, v. 18—20.

The tract itself has two parts, treating,

I. Severally,
  1. Of communion with the Father, C. i. 5—10
  2. Of communion with the Son, C. ii. 1—12
    With a distinct application to fathers, young men, and little children, 13—27
    Whereto is annexed an exhortation to abide in him, 28—C. iii. 1—24
    That the fruit of his manifestation in the flesh may extend to his manifestation in glory.
  3. Of the confirmation and fruit of this abiding through the Spirit, C. iv. 1—21

II. Conjointly,

CHAPTER I.

Of the testimony of the Father, and Son, and Spirit: **on** which faith in Christ, the being born of God, love to God and his children, the keeping his commandments, and victory over the world, are founded, C. v. 1—12

The parts frequently begin and end alike. Sometimes there is an allusion in a preceding part, and a recapitulation in the subsequent. Each part treats of a benefit from God, and the duty of the faithful derived therefrom by the most natural inferences.

I. ST. JOHN.

CHAPTER I 1 THAT which was from the beginning,
which we have heard, which we have seen with our eyes,
which we have beheld, and our hands have handled of the
2 Word of life; (For the life was manifested, and we saw *it*,
and testify and declare to you the eternal life which was with
3 the Father, and was manifested to us;) That which we have
seen and heard declare we to you, that ye also may have
fellowship with us; and truly our fellowship *is* with the

Verse 1. *That which was*—Here means, He which was the Word himself; afterwards it means, that which they had heard from him. *Which was*—Namely, with the Father, verse 2, before he was manifested. *From the beginning*—This phrase is sometimes used in a limited sense; but here it properly means from eternity, being equivalent with, "in the beginning," John i. 1 *That which we*—The apostles. *Have* not only *heard*, but *seen with our eyes, which we have beheld*—Attentively considered on various occasions. *Of the Word of life*—He is termed *the Word*, John i. 1; *the Life*, John i. 4; as he is the living Word of God, who, with the Father and the Spirit, is the fountain of life to all creatures, particularly of spiritual and eternal life.

Verse 2. *For the life*—The living Word. *Was manifested*—In the flesh, to our very senses. *And we testify and declare*—We testify by declaring, by preaching, and writing, verses 3, 4. Preaching lays the foundation, verses 5—10: writing builds thereon. *To you*—Who have not seen. *The eternal life*—Which always was, and afterward *appeared to us*. This is mentioned in the beginning of the epistle. In the end of it is mentioned the same *eternal life*, which we shall always enjoy.

Verse 3 *That which we have seen and heard*—Of him and from him. *Declare we to you*—For this end. *That ye also may have fellowship with us*—May enjoy the same fellowship which we enjoy. *And truly our fellowship*—Whereby he is in us and we in him. *Is with the Father and with the Son*—Of the Holy Ghost he speaks afterwards.

4 Father, and with his Son Jesus Christ And these things
write we to you, that your joy may be full.
5 And this is the message which we have heard of him, and
declare to you, that God is light, and in him is no darkness
6 at all. If we say we have fellowship with him, and walk in
darkness, we lie, and do not the truth: But if we walk in the
7 light, as he is in the light, we have fellowship one with
another, and the blood of Jesus Christ his Son cleanseth us
8 from all sin. If we say we have no sin, we deceive ourselves.
9 and the truth is not in us. If we confess our sins, he is

Verse 4. *That your joy may be full*—So our Lord also, John xv. 11; xvi. 22. There is a joy of hope, a joy of faith, and a joy of love. Here the joy of faith is directly intended. It is a concise expression. *Your joy*—That is, your faith and the joy arising from it: but it likewise implies the joy of hope and love.

Verse 5 *And this is* the sum of *the message which we have heard of him*—The Son of God. *That God is light*—The light of wisdom, love, holiness, glory. What light is to the natural eye, that God is to the spiritual eye. *And in him is no darkness at all*—No contrary principle. He is pure, unmixed light.

Verse 6 *If we say*—Either with our tongue, or in our heart, if we endeavour to persuade either ourselves or others. *We have fellowship with him*, while we *walk*, either inwardly or outwardly, *in darkness*—In sin of any kind *We do not the truth*—Our actions prove, that the truth is not in us.

Verse 7. *But if we walk in the light*—In all holiness. *As God is* (a deeper word than *walk*, and more worthy of God) *in the light*, then we may truly say, *we have fellowship one with another*—We who have seen, and you who have not seen, do alike enjoy that fellowship with God. the imitation of God being the only sure proof of our having fellowship with him. *And the blood of Jesus Christ his Son*—With the grace purchased thereby. *Cleanseth us from all sin*—Both original and actual, taking away all the guilt and all the power.

Verse 8. *If we say*—Any child of man, before his blood has cleansed us. *We have no sin*—To be cleansed from, instead of *confessing our sins*, verse 9, *the truth is not in us*—Neither in our mouth nor in our heart.

Verse 9. But *if* with a penitent and believing heart, *we confess our sins, he is faithful*—Because he had promised this blessing, by the unanimous voice of all his prophets. *Just*—Surely then he will punish: no; for this very reason he will pardon. This may seem strange; but upon the evangelical principle of atonement and redemption, it is undoubtedly true; because, when the debt is paid, or the purchase made, it is the part of equity to cancel the bond, and consign over the purchased possession. *Both to forgive us our sins*—To take away all the guilt of them. *And to cleanse us from all unrighteousness*—To purify our souls from every kind and every degree of it

faithful and just to forgive us our sins, and to cleanse us
10 from all unrighteousness. If we say we have not sinned, we
make him a liar, and his word is not in us.

CHAP II. 1 My beloved children, I write these things
to you, that ye may not sin. But if any one sin, we have
an advocate with the Father, Jesus Christ the righteous.
2 And he is the propitiation for our sins: and not for ours
3 only, but also for *the sins* of the whole world. And hereby
we know that we know him, if we keep his commandments.
4 He that saith, I know him, and keepeth not his command-
5 ments, is a liar, and the truth is not in him. But whoso

Verse 10. Yet still we are to retain, even to our lives' end, a deep sense of our past sins. Still *if we say, we have not sinned, we make him a liar*—Who saith, all have sinned. *And his word is not in us*—We do not receive it; we give it no place in our hearts.

Verse 1. *My beloved children*—So the apostle frequently addresses the whole body of Christians. It is a term of tenderness and endearment, used by our Lord himself to his disciples, John xiii. 33. And perhaps many to whom St. John now wrote were converted by his ministry. It is a different word from that which is translated "little children," in several parts of the epistle, to distinguish it from which, it is here rendered *beloved children. I write these things to you, that ye may not sin*—Thus he guards them beforehand against abusing the doctrine of reconciliation. All the words, institutions, and judgments of God are levelled against sin, either that it may not be committed, or that it may be abolished. *But if any one sin*—Let him not lie in sin, despairing of help *We have an advocate*—We have for our advocate, not a mean person, but him of whom it was said, "This is my beloved son." Not a guilty person, who stands in need of pardon for himself; but *Jesus Christ the righteous;* not a mere petitioner, who relies purely upon liberality, but one that has merited, fully merited, whatever he asks.

Verse 2. *And he is the propitiation*—The atoning sacrifice, by which the wrath of God is appeased. *For our sins*—Who believe. *And not for ours only, but also for the sins of the whole world*—Just as wide as sin extends, the propitiation extends also.

Verse 3. *And hereby we know that we* truly and savingly *know him*—As he is the advocate, the righteous, the propitiation *If we keep his commandments*—Particularly those of faith and love.

Verse 5. *But whoso keepeth his word*—His commandments. *Verily in him the love of God*—Reconciled to us through Christ. *Is perfected*—Is perfectly known. *Hereby*—By our keeping his word. *We know that we are in him*—So is the tree known by its fruits. To "know him," to be "in him," to "abide in him," are nearly synonymous terms; only with a gradation,—knowledge, communion, constancy

keepeth his word, verily in him the love of God is perfected:
6 hereby we know that we are in him. He that saith he
abideth in him ought himself also so to walk, even as he
7 walked. Beloved, I write not a new commandment to you,
but the old commandment which ye have had from the
beginning. The old commandment is the word which ye
8 have heard from the beginning. Again, I do write a new commandment to you, which is true in him and in you: for the
9 darkness is passed away, and the true light now shineth. He
that saith he is in the light, and hateth his brother, is in
10 darkness until now. He that loveth his brother abideth in
11 the light, and there is no occasion of stumbling in him. But
he that hateth his brother is in darkness, and walketh in
darkness, and knoweth not whither he goeth, because dark-
12 ness hath blinded his eyes. I have written to you, beloved
children, because your sins are forgiven you for his name

Verse 6. *He that saith he abideth in him*—Which implies a durable state; a constant, lasting knowledge of, and communion with, him. *Ought himself*—Otherwise they are vain words. *So to walk, even as he walked*—In the world. *As he,* are words that frequently occur in this epistle. Believers having their hearts full of him, easily supply his name.

Verse 7. When I speak of keeping his word, *I write not a new commandment*—I do not speak of any new one. *But the old commandment, which ye had*—Even from your forefathers.

Verse 8 *Again, I do write a new commandment to you*—Namely, with regard to loving one another. A commandment *which,* though it also was given long ago, yet *is* truly new *in him and in you.* It was exemplified *in him,* and is now fulfilled by you, in such a manner as it never was before. For there is no comparison between the state of the Old Testament believers, and that which ye now enjoy: the *darkness* of that dispensation *is passed away; and* Christ *the true light now shineth* in your hearts.

Verse 9. *He that saith he is in the light*—In Christ, united to him. *And hateth his brother*—The very name shows the love due to him. *Is in darkness until now*—Void of Christ, and of all true light.

Verse 10. *He that loveth his brother*—For Christ's sake. *Abideth in the light*—Of God. *And there is no occasion of stumbling in him*—Whereas he that hates his brother is an occasion of stumbling to himself. He stumbles against himself, and against all things within and without; while he that loves his brother, has a free, disencumbered journey.

Verse 11. *He that hateth his brother*—And he must hate, if he does not love him: there is no medium. *Is in darkness*—In sin, perplexity, entanglement. He *walketh in darkness, and knoweth not* that he is in the high road to hell.

Verse 12. *I have written to you, beloved children*—Thus St. John

13 sake. I write to you, fathers, because ye have known him
that is from the beginning I write to you, young men,
because ye have overcome the wicked one. I write to you,
14 little children, because ye have known the Father. I have
written to you, fathers, because ye have known him that is
from the beginning. I have written to you, young men,
because ye are strong, and the word of God abideth in you,
15 and ye have overcome the wicked one. Love not the world,
neither the things that are in the world. If any one love
16 the world, the love of the Father is not in him. For all
that is in the world, the desire of the flesh, and the desire
of the eye, and the pride of life, is not of the Father, but is

bespeaks all to whom he writes. But from the thirteenth to the twenty-seventh verse, he divides them particularly into "fathers," "young men," and "little children." *Because your sins are forgiven you*—As if he had said, This is the sum of what I have now written. He then proceeds to other things, which are built upon this foundation.

Verse 13. The address to spiritual fathers, young men, and little children, is first proposed in this verse, wherein he says, *I write to you, fathers: I write to you, young men: I write to you, little children*: and then enlarged upon; in doing which he says, "I have written to you, fathers," verse 14. "I have written to you, young men," verses 14—17. "I have written to you, little children," verses 18—27. Having finished his address to each, he returns to all together, whom he again terms, (as verse 12,) "beloved children." *Fathers, ye have known him that is from the beginning*—Ye have known the eternal God, in a manner wherein no other, even true believers, know him. *Young men, ye have overcome the wicked one*—In many battles, by the power of faith. *Little children, ye have known the Father*—As your Father, though ye have not yet overcome, by "the Spirit witnessing with your spirit, that ye are the children of God."

Verse 14. *I have written to you, fathers*—As if he had said, Observe well what I but now wrote. He speaks very briefly and modestly to these, who needed not much to be said to them, as having that deep acquaintance with God which comprises all necessary knowledge. *Young men, ye are strong*—In faith. *And the word of God abideth in you*—Deeply rooted in your hearts, whereby ye have often foiled your great adversary.

Verse 15. To you all, whether fathers, young men, or little children, I say, *Love not the world*—Pursue your victory by overcoming the world. *If any man love the world*—Seek happiness in visible things, he does not love God.

Verse 16. *The desire of the flesh*—Of the pleasure of the outward senses, whether of the taste, smell, or touch. *The desire of the eye*—Of the pleasures of imagination, to which the eye chiefly is subservient;

17 of the world. And the world passeth away, and the desire
thereof: but he that doeth the will of God abideth for ever.
18 Little children, it is the last time: and as ye have heard
that antichrist cometh, *so* even now there are many anti-
19 christs; whereby we know that it is the last time. They
went out from us, but they were not of us; for if they had
been of us, they would have continued with us: but *they
went out*, that they might be made manifest that they were
20 not all of us. But ye have an anointing from the Holy
21 One, and know all things. I have not written to you
because ye know not the truth; but because ye know it,

of that internal sense whereby we relish whatever is grand, new, or beautiful. *The pride of life*—All that pomp in clothes, houses, furniture, equipage, manner of living, which generally procure honour from the bulk of mankind, and so gratify pride and vanity. It therefore directly includes the desire of praise, and, remotely, covetousness. All these desires are not from God, but from the prince of this world.

Verse 17. *The world passeth away, and the desire thereof*—That is, all that can gratify those desires passeth away with it. *But he that doeth the will of God*—That loves God, not the world. *Abideth*—In the enjoyment of what he loves, *for ever.*

Verse 18 *My little children, it is the last time*—The last dispensation of grace, that which is to continue to the end of time, is begun. *Ye have heard that antichrist cometh*—Under the term antichrist, or the spirit of antichrist, he includes all false teachers, and enemies to the truth; yea, whatever doctrines or men are contrary to Christ. It seems to have been long after this that the name of antichrist was appropriated to that grand adversary of Christ, "the man of sin," 2 Thess. ii. 3 Antichrist, in St. John's sense, that is, antichristianism, has been spreading from his time till now; and will do so, till that great adversary arises, and is destroyed by Christ's coming.

Verse 19. *They were not of us*—When they went; their hearts were before departed from God, otherwise, *they would have continued with us: but they went out, that they might be made manifest*—That is, this was made manifest by their going out.

Verse 20. *But ye have an anointing*—A chrism; perhaps so termed in opposition to the name of antichrist; an inward teaching *from the Holy Ghost,* whereby ye *know all things*—Necessary for your preservation from these seducers, and for your eternal salvation. St. John here but just touches upon the Holy Ghost, of whom he speaks more largely, 1 John iii. 24; iv. 13; v. 6.

Verse 21. *I have written*—Namely, verse 13. *To you because ye know the truth*—That is, to confirm you in the knowledge ye have already. *Ye know that no lie is of the truth*—That all the doctrines of these antichrists are irreconcilable to it

22 and that no lie is of the truth. Who is that liar but he that
denieth that Jesus is the Christ? He is antichrist who
23 denieth the Father and the Son. Whosoever denieth the
Son, he hath not the Father: he that acknowledgeth the
24 Son hath the Father also. Therefore let that abide in you
which ye heard from the beginning. If that which ye heard
from the beginning abide in you, ye also shall abide
25 in the Son, and in the Father. And this is the promise
26 which he hath promised us, eternal life. These things have
27 I written to you concerning them that seduce you. But the
anointing which ye have received of him abideth in you, and
ye need not that any should teach you, save as the same
anointing teacheth you of all things, and is true, and is no
lie, and as it hath taught you, ye shall abide in him.
28 And now, beloved children, abide in him: that, when he
shall appear, we may have confidence, and not be ashamed

Verse 22. *Who is that liar*—Who is guilty of that lying, but he who denies that truth which is the sum of all Christianity? That Jesus is the Christ; that he is the Son of God; that he came in the flesh, is one undivided truth. and he that denies any part of this, in effect denies the whole. *He is antichrist*—And the spirit of antichrist, who in denying the Son denies the Father also.

Verse 23. *Whosoever denieth the* eternal *Son* of God, *he hath not* communion with *the Father;* but *he that* truly and believingly *acknowledgeth the Son, hath* communion with *the Father also.*

Verse 24. *If that* truth concerning the Father and the Son, *which ye* have *heard from the beginning, abide* fixed and rooted *in you, ye also shall abide in* that happy communion with *the Son and the Father.*

Verse 25. *He*—The Son. *Hath promised us*—If we abide in him.

Verse 26. *These things*—From verse 21. *I have written to you*—St. John, according to his custom, begins and ends with the same form, and having finished a kind of parenthesis, verses 20—26, continues, verse 27, what he said in the twentieth verse, *concerning them that* would *seduce you.*

Verse 27. *Ye need not that any should teach you, save as that anointing teacheth you*—Which is always the same, always consistent with itself But this does not exclude our need of being taught by them who partake of the same anointing. *Of all things*—Which it is necessary for you to know. *And is no lie*—Like that which antichrist teaches. *Ye shall abide in him*—This is added both by way of comfort and of exhortation. The whole discourse, from verse 18 to this, is peculiarly adapted to little children.

Verse 28. *And now, beloved children*—Having finished his address to each, he now returns to all in general. *Abide in him, that we*—A

29 before him at his coming. Since ye know that he is righteous, ye know that every one who practiseth righteousness is
born of him.

CHAP. III. 1 Behold, what manner of love the Father
hath bestowed upon us, that we should be called the children
of God: therefore the world knoweth us not, because it
2 knoweth not him. Beloved, now are we the children of God,
and it doth not yet appear what we shall be: but we know,
when he shall appear, we shall be like him; for we shall see
3 him as he is. And every one that hath this hope in him
4 purifieth himself, even as he is pure. Whosoever committeth sin transgresseth also the law: for sin is the trans-
5 gression of the law. And ye know that he was manifested to
6 take away our sins; and in him is no sin. Whosoever abideth

modest expression. *May not be ashamed before him at his coming*—O how will ye, Jews, Socinians, nominal Christians, be ashamed in that day!

Verse 29. *Every one*—And none else. *Who practiseth righteousness*—From a believing, loving heart. *Is born of him*—For all his children are like himself.

Verse 1. *That we should be called*—That is, should be, *the children of God. Therefore the world knoweth us not*—They know not what to make of us. We are a mystery to them.

Verse 2. *It doth not yet appear*—Even to ourselves. *What we shall be*—It is something ineffable, which will raise the children of God to be, in a manner, as God himself. *But we know,* in general, that *when he,* the Son of God, *shall appear, we shall be like him*—The glory of God penetrating our inmost substance. *For we shall see him as he is*—Manifestly, without a veil. And that sight will transform us into the same likeness.

Verse 3. *And every one that hath this hope in him*—In God.

Verse 4. *Whosoever committeth sin*—Thereby transgresseth the holy, just, and good law of God, and so sets his authority at nought; for this is implied in the very nature of sin.

Verse 5. *And ye know that he*—Christ. *Was manifested*—That he came into the world for this very purpose. *To take away our sins*—To destroy them all, root and branch, and leave none remaining. *And in him is no sin*—So that he could not suffer on his own account, but to make us as himself.

Verse 6. *Whosoever abideth in* communion with *him,* by loving faith, *sinneth not*—While he so abideth. *Whosoever sinneth* certainly *seeth him not*—The loving eye of his soul is not then fixed upon God;

in him sinneth not: whosoever sinneth seeth him not, neither
7 knoweth him. Beloved children, let no one deceive you:
he that practiseth righteousness is righteous, even as he is
8 righteous. He that committeth sin is of the devil; for the
devil sinneth from the beginning. To this end the Son of God
9 was manifested, to destroy the works of the devil. Whosoever
is born of God doth not commit sin; for his seed abideth in
10 him: and he cannot sin, because he is born of God. Hereby
the children of God are manifested, and the children of the
devil: whosoever practiseth not righteousness is not of God,
11 neither he that loveth not his brother. For this is the message which ye have heard from the beginning, that we love
12 one another. Not as Cain, *who* was of the wicked one, and
slew his brother. And wherefore slew he him? Because his
13 own works were evil, and his brother's righteous. Marvel
14 not, my brethren, if the world hate you. We know that we
are passed from death to life, because we love the brethren.

neither doth he then experimentally *know him*—Whatever he did in time past.

Verse 7. *Let no one deceive you*—Let none persuade you that any man is righteous but *he that* uniformly *practises righteousness;* he alone is *righteous,* after the example of his Lord.

Verse 8. *He that committeth sin is* a child *of the devil; for the devil sinneth from the beginning*—That is, was the first sinner in the universe, and has continued to sin ever since. *The Son of God was manifested to destroy the works of the devil*—All sin. And will he not perform this in all that trust in him?

Verse 9. *Whosoever is born of God*—By living faith, whereby God is continually breathing spiritual life into his soul, and his soul is continually breathing out love and prayer to God, *doth not commit sin. For* the divine *seed* of loving faith *abideth in him; and,* so long as it doth, *he cannot sin, because he is born of God*—Is inwardly and universally changed.

Verse 10. *Neither he that loveth not his brother*—Here is the transition from the general proposition to one particular.

Verse 12. *Who was of the wicked one*—Who showed he was a child of the devil by killing his brother. *And wherefore slew he him*—For any fault? No, but just the reverse; for his goodness.

Verse 13 *Marvel not if the world hate you*—For the same cause.

Verse 14. *We know*—As if he had said, We ourselves could not love our brethren, unless we were *passed from* spiritual *death to life,* that is, born of God. *He that loveth not his brother abideth in death*—That is, is not born of God And he that is not born of God, cannot love his brother.

15 He that loveth not his brother abideth in death. Whosoever
hateth his brother is a murderer: and ye know no murderer
16 hath eternal life abiding in him. Hereby we know the love
of God, because he laid down his life for us: and we ought
17 to lay down our lives for the brethren. But whoso hath this
world's good, and seeth his brother have need, and shutteth
up his bowels of compassion from him, how dwelleth the love
18 of God in him? My beloved children, let us love not in
19 word, neither in tongue; but in deed and in truth. And
hereby we know that we are of the truth, and shall assure
20 our hearts before him. For if our heart condemn us, God

Verse 15. He, I say, abideth in spiritual death, is void of the life of God. For *whosoever hateth his brother*, and there is no medium between loving and hating him, *is*, in God's account, *a murderer:* every degree of hatred being a degree of the same temper which moved Cain to murder his brother. *And no murderer hath eternal life abiding in him*—But every loving believer hath. For love is the beginning of eternal life. It is the same, in substance, with glory.

Verse 16. The word *God* is not in the original. It was omitted by the apostle just as the particular name is omitted by Mary, when she says to the gardener, "Sir, if thou hast borne him hence;" and by the church, when she says, "Let him kiss me with the kisses of his mouth," Sol. Song, i. 1; in both which places there is a language, a very emphatical language, even in silence. It declares how totally the thoughts were possessed by the blessed and glorious subject. It expresses also the superlative dignity and amiableness of the person meant, as though He, and He alone, was, or deserved to be, both known and admired by all. *Because he laid down his life*—Not merely for sinners, but *for us* in particular. From this truth believed, from this blessing enjoyed, the love of our brethren takes its rise, which may very justly be admitted as an evidence that our faith is no delusion.

Verse 17. *But whoso hath this world's good*—Worldly substance, far less valuable than life. *And seeth his brother have need*—The very sight of want knocks at the door of the spectator's heart. *And shutteth up*—Whether asked or not. *His bowels of compassion from him, how dwelleth the love of God in him*—Certainly not at all, however he may talk, verse 18, of loving God.

Verse 18. *Not in word*—Only. *But in deed*—In action: not *in tongue* by empty professions, *but in truth.*

Verse 19. *And hereby we know*—We have a farther proof by this real, operative love. *That we are of the truth*—That we have true faith, that we are true children of God. *And shall assure our hearts before him*—Shall enjoy the assurance of his favour, and the "testimony of a good conscience toward God." The *heart*, in St. John's language, is the conscience. The word *conscience* is not found in his writings.

Verse 20. *For if* we have not this testimony, if in anything *our heart,*

21 is greater than our heart, and knoweth all things. Beloved,
if our heart condemn us not, *then* have we confidence toward
22 God. And whatsoever we ask, we receive of him, because
we keep his commandments, and do those things that are
23 pleasing in his sight. And this is his commandment, that we
should believe on the name of his Son Jesus Christ, and love
24 one another, as he hath given us commandment. And he
that keepeth his commandments abideth in him, and he in
him: and hereby we know that he abideth in us, by the Spirit
which he hath given us.

CHAP. IV. 1 Beloved, believe not every spirit, but try
the spirits whether they are of God: because many false
2 prophets are gone out into the world. Hereby ye know the
Spirit of God: Every spirit which confesseth Jesus Christ,

our own conscience, *condemn us*, much more does *God*, who *is greater than our heart*—An infinitely holier and a more impartial Judge. *And knoweth all things*—So that there is no hope of hiding it from him.

Verse 21. *If our heart condemn us not*—If our conscience, duly enlightened by the word and Spirit of God, and comparing all our thoughts, words, and works with that word, pronounce that they agree therewith. *Then have we confidence toward God*—Not only our consciousness of his favour continues and increases, but we have a full persuasion, that *whatsoever we ask we* shall *receive of him.*

Verse 23. *And this is his commandment*—All his commandments in one word. *That we should believe and love*—In the manner and degree which he hath taught. This is the greatest and most important command that ever issued from the throne of glory. If this be neglected, no other can be kept: if this be observed, all others are easy.

Verse 24. *And he that keepeth his commandments*—That thus believes and loves. *Abideth in him, and God in him: and hereby we know that he abideth in us, by the Spirit which he hath given us*—Which witnesses with our spirits that we are his children, and brings forth his fruits of peace, love, holiness. This is the transition to the treating of the Holy Spirit which immediately follows.

Verse 1. *Believe not every spirit*—Whereby any teacher is actuated. *But try the spirits*—By the rule which follows. We are to try all spirits by the written word: "To the law and to the testimony!" If any man speak not according to these, the spirit which actuates him is not of God.

Verse 2. *Every spirit*—Or teacher. *Which confesseth*—Both with heart and voice. *Jesus Christ, who is come in the flesh, is of God*—This his coming presupposes, contains, and draws after it, the whole doctrine of Christ.

3 who is come in the flesh, is of God: And every spirit which
confesseth not Jesus Christ who is come in the flesh is not
of God: and this is that *spirit* of antichrist, whereof ye have
4 heard that it cometh; and now already it is in the world. Ye
are of God, beloved children, and have overcome them.
because greater is he that is in you, than he that is in the
5 world. They are of the world: therefore speak they of the
6 world, and the world heareth them. We are of God: he that
knoweth God heareth us; he that is not of God heareth not
us. Hereby know we the spirit of truth, and the spirit
7 of error. Beloved, let us love one another: for love is
of God; and every one that loveth is born of God, and know-
8 eth God. He that loveth not knoweth not God; for God is
9 love. Hereby was manifested the love of God toward us,
because God sent his only begotten Son into the world, that
10 we might live through him. Herein is love, not that we
loved God, but that he loved us, and sent his Son a propiti-
11 ation for our sins. Beloved, if God so loved us, we ought
12 also to love one another. No man hath seen God at any
time. If we love one another, God abideth in us, and his
13 love is perfected in us. Hereby we know that we abide in

Verse 3. *Ye have heard*—From our Lord and us, *that it cometh.*

Verse 4. *Ye have overcome* these seducers, *because greater is the Spirit* of Christ *that is in you* than the spirit of antichrist that *is in the world.*

Verse 5. *They*—Those false prophets. *Are of the world*—Of the number of those that know not God. *Therefore speak they of the world*—From the same principle, wisdom, spirit; and, of consequence, *the world heareth them*—With approbation.

Verse 6. *We*—Apostles *Are of God*—Immediately taught, and sent by him. *Hereby we know*—From what is said, verses 2—6.

Verse 7. *Let us love one another*—From the doctrine he has just been defending he draws this exhortation. It is by the Spirit that the love of God is shed abroad in our hearts. *Every one that* truly *loveth* God and his neighbour *is born of God.*

Verse 8. *God is love*—This little sentence brought St. John more sweetness, even in the time he was writing it, than the whole world can bring. God is often styled holy, righteous, wise; but not holiness, righteousness, or wisdom in the abstract, as he is said to be love; intimating that this is his darling, his reigning attribute, the attribute that sheds an amiable glory on all his other perfections.

Verse 12. *If we love one another, God abideth in us*—This is treated of, verses 13—16. *And his love is perfected*—Has its full effect. *In us*—This is treated of, verses 17—19.

him, and he in us, because he hath given us of his Spirit.
14 And we have seen and testify that the Father sent the Son
15 *to be* the Saviour of the world. Whosoever shall confess that
Jesus is the Son of God, God abideth in him, and he in
16 God. And we know and believe the love that God hath to
us. God is love; and he that abideth in love abideth in
17 God, and God in him. Hereby is our love made perfect,
that we may have boldness in the day of judgment, because
18 as he is, so are we in this world. There is no fear in love;
but perfect love casteth out fear: because fear hath torment.
19 He that feareth is not made perfect in love. We love him,
20 because he first loved us. If any man say, I love God, and
hateth his brother, he is a liar: for he that loveth not his
brother whom he hath seen, how can he love God whom he
21 hath not seen? And this commandment have we from him,
that he who loveth God love his brother also.

Verse 14. *And* in consequence of this *we have seen and testify that the Father sent the Son*—These are the foundation and the criteria of our abiding in God and God in us, the communion of the Spirit, and the confession of the Son.

Verse 15. *Whosoever shall,* from a principle of loving faith, openly *confess* in the face of all opposition and danger, *that Jesus is the Son of God, God abideth in him.*

Verse 16. *And we know and believe*—By the same Spirit, *the love that God hath to us.*

Verse 17. *Hereby*—That is, by this communion with God. *Is our love made perfect; that we may*—That is, so that we shall *have boldness in the day of judgment*—When all the stout-hearted shall tremble. *Because as he*—Christ. *Is*—All love. *So are we*—Who are fathers in Christ, even *in this world.*

Verse 18. *There is no fear in love*—No slavish fear can be where love reigns. *But perfect,* adult *love casteth out* slavish *fear: because* such *fear hath torment*—And so is inconsistent with the happiness of love. A natural man has neither fear nor love; one that is awakened, fear without love; a babe in Christ, love and fear; a father in Christ, love without fear.

Verse 19. *We love him, because he first loved us*—This is the sum of all religion, the genuine model of Christianity. None can say more: why should any one say less, or less intelligibly?

Verse 20. *Whom he hath seen*—Who is daily presented to his senses, to raise his esteem, and move his kindness or compassion toward him.

Verse 21. *And this commandment have we from him*—Both God and Christ. *That he who loveth God love his brother*—Every one, whatever his opinions or mode of worship be, purely because he is the child, and

CHAP. V. 1 Whosoever believeth that Jesus is the
Christ is born of God: and every one who loveth him that
2 begat loveth him also that is begotten of him. Hereby we
know that we love the children of God, when we love God,
3 and keep his commandments. For this is the love of God,
that we keep his commandments: and his commandments
4 are not grievous. For whatsoever is born of God overcometh
the world: and this is the victory that overcometh the world,
5 *even* our faith. Who is he that overcometh the world, but
6 he that believeth that Jesus is the Son of God? This is

bears the image, of God. Bigotry is properly the want of this pure and universal love. A bigot only loves those who embrace his opinions, and receive his way of worship; and he loves them for that, and not for Christ's sake.

Verse 1. The scope and sum of this whole paragraph appears from the conclusion of it, verse 13: "These things have I written to you who believe, that ye may know that ye who believe have eternal life." So faith is the first and last point with St. John also. *Every one who loveth* God *that begat loveth him also that is begotten of him*—Hath a natural affection to all his brethren.

Verse 2. *Hereby we know*—This is a plain proof *That we love the children of God*—As his children.

Verse 3. *For this is the love of God*—The only sure proof of it. *That we keep his commandments: and his commandments are not grievous*—To any that are born of God.

Verse 4. *For whatsoever*—This expression implies the most unlimited universality. *Is born of God overcometh the world*—Conquers whatever it can lay in the way, either to allure or fright the children of God from keeping his commandments. *And this is the victory*—The grand means of overcoming. *Even our faith*—Seeing all things are possible to him that believeth.

Verse 5. *Who is he that overcometh the world*—That is superior to all worldly care, desire, fear? Every believer, and none else. The seventh verse (usually so reckoned) is a brief recapitulation of all which has been before advanced concerning the Father, the Son, and the Spirit. It is cited, in conjunction with the sixth and eighth, by Tertullian, Cyprian, and an uninterrupted train of Fathers. And, indeed, what the sun is in the world, what the heart is in a man, what the needle is in the mariner's compass, this verse is in the epistle. By this the sixth, eighth, and ninth verses are indissolubly connected; as will be evident, beyond all contradiction, when they are accurately considered.

Verse 6. *This is he*—St. John here shows the immovable foundation of that faith that Jesus is the Son of God; not only the testimony of man, but the firm, indubitable testimony of God. *Who came*—Jesus is

he that came by water and blood; *even* Jesus Christ; not
by the water only, but by the water and the blood. And it
7 is the Spirit who testifieth, because the Spirit is truth. For
there are three that testify on earth, the Spirit, and the
8 water, and the blood: and these three agree in one. And
there are three that testify in heaven, the Father, the Word,

he of whom it was promised that he should come; and who, accordingly, *is* come. And this the Spirit, and the water, and the blood testify. *Even Jesus*—Who, coming by water and blood, is by this very thing demonstrated to be the *Christ. Not by the water only*—Wherein he was baptized. *But by the water and the blood*—Which he shed when he had finished the work his Father had given him to do. He not only undertook at his baptism "to fulfil all righteousness," but on the cross accomplished what he had undertaken; in token whereof, when all was finished, blood and water came out of his side. *And it is the Spirit who* likewise *testifieth*—Of Jesus Christ, namely, by Moses and all the prophets, by John the Baptist, by all the apostles, and in all the writings of the New Testament. And against his testimony there can be no exception, *because the Spirit is truth*—The very God of truth.

Verse 7. What Bengelius has advanced, both concerning the transposition of these two verses, and the authority of the controverted verse, partly in his "*Gnomon*," and partly in his "*Apparatus Criticus*," will abundantly satisfy any impartial person. *For there are three that testify*—Literally, *testifying*, or *bearing witness*. The participle is put for the noun *witnesses*, to intimate that the act of testifying, and the effect of it, are continually present. Properly, persons only can testify; and that *three* are described *testifying on earth*, as if they were persons, is elegantly subservient to the *three* persons *testifying in heaven. The Spirit*—In the word, confirmed by miracles. *The water*—Of baptism, wherein we are dedicated to the Son, (with the Father and Spirit,) typifying his spotless purity, and the inward purifying of our nature. *And the blood*—Represented in the Lord's supper, and applied to the consciences of believers. *And these three* harmoniously *agree in one*—In bearing the same testimony,—that Jesus Christ is the divine, the complete, the only Saviour of the world.

Verse 8. *And there are three that testify in heaven*—The testimony of the Spirit, the water, and the blood, is by an eminent gradation corroborated by three, who give a still greater testimony. *The Father*—Who clearly testified of the Son, both at his baptism and at his transfiguration. *The Word*—Who testified of himself on many occasions, while he was on earth; and again, with still greater solemnity, after his ascension into heaven, Rev. i. 5; xix. 13. *And the Spirit*—Whose testimony was added chiefly after his glorification, 1 John ii. 27; John xv. 26; Acts v. 32; Rom. viii. 16. *And these three are one*—Even as those two, the Father and the Son, are one, John x. 30. Nothing can separate the Spirit from the Father and the Son If he were not one with the Father

9 and the Holy Ghost: and these three are one. If we receive
the testimony of men, the testimony of God is greater: and
this is the testimony of God which he hath testified of his
10 Son. He that believeth on the Son of God, hath the testimony in himself: he that believeth not God hath made him
a liar; because he believeth not the testimony which he
11 hath testified of his Son. And this is the testimony, that

and the Son, the apostle ought to have said, *The Father and the Word,* who are one, *and the Spirit, are two.* But this is contrary to the whole tenor of revelation. It remains that *these three are one.* They are one in essence, in knowledge, in will, and in their testimony.

It is observable, the three in the one verse are opposed, not conjointly, but severally, to the three in the other: as if he had said, Not only the Spirit testifies, but also the Father, John v. 37; not only the water, but also the Word, John iii. 11, x 41; not only the blood, but also the Holy Ghost, John xv. 26, &c. It must now appear, to every reasonable man, how absolutely necessary the eighth verse is. St. John could not think of the testimony of the Spirit, and water, and blood, and subjoin, "The testimony of God is greater," without thinking also of the testimony of the Son and Holy Ghost; yea, and mentioning it in so solemn an enumeration. Nor can any possible reason be devised, why, without *three testifying in heaven,* he should enumerate *three,* and no more, *who testify on earth.* The testimony of all is given on earth, not in heaven; but they who testify are part on earth, part in heaven. The witnesses who are on earth testify chiefly concerning his abode on earth, though not excluding his state of exaltation: the witnesses who are in heaven testify chiefly concerning his glory at God's right hand, though not excluding his state of humiliation.

The seventh verse, therefore, with the sixth, contains a recapitulation of the whole economy of Christ, from his baptism to pentecost; the eighth, the sum of the divine economy, from the time of his exaltation.

Hence it farther appears, that this position of the seventh and eighth verses, which places those who testify *on earth* before those who testify *in heaven,* is abundantly preferable to the other, and affords a gradation admirably suited to the subject.

Verse 9. *If we receive the testimony of men*—As we do continually, and must do in a thousand instances. *The testimony of God is greater*—Of higher authority, and much more worthy to be received; namely, *this* very *testimony* which God the Father, together with the Word and the Spirit, *hath testified of the Son,* as the Saviour of the world.

Verse 10. *He that believeth on the Son of God hath the testimony*—The clear evidence of this, *in himself: he that believeth not God,* in this, *hath made him a liar; because* he supposes that to be false which God has expressly testified.

Verse 11. *And this is the* sum of that *testimony, that God hath given us* a title to, and the real beginning of, *eternal life: and* that *this is* pur-

God hath given us eternal life, and this life is in his Son.
12 He that hath the Son hath life; and he that hath not the
Son of God hath not life.
13 These things have I written to you who believe on the
name of the Son of God; that ye may know that ye who
believe on the name of the Son of God have eternal life.
14 And this is the confidence which we have in him, that, if we
15 ask anything according to his will, he heareth us: And if we
know that he heareth us, whatsoever we ask, we know that
16 we have the petitions which we have asked of him. If any
one see his brother sin a sin *which is* not unto death, let him
ask, and he will give him life for them that sin not unto
death. There is a sin unto death: I do not say that he
17 shall pray for that. All unrighteousness is sin: but there
18 is a sin not unto death. We know that whosoever is born of

chased by, and treasured up *in, his Son,* who has all the springs and the fulness of it in himself, to communicate to his body, the church, first in grace and then in glory.

Verse 12. It plainly follows, *he that hath the Son*—Living and reigning in him by faith. *Hath* this *life; he that hath not the Son of God hath not* this *life*—Hath no part or lot therein. In the former clause, the apostle says simply, *the Son;* because believers know him: in the latter, *the Son of God;* that unbelievers may know how great a blessing they fall short of.

Verse 13. *These things have I written*—In the introduction, 1 John i. 4, he said, *I write:* now, in the close, *I have written. That ye may know*—With a fuller and stronger assurance, *that ye have eternal life.*

Verse 14. *And we*—Who believe. *Have this* farther *confidence in him, that he heareth*—That is, favourably regards, whatever prayer we offer in faith, *according to his* revealed *will.*

Verse 15 *We have*—Faith anticipates the blessings. *The petitions which we asked of him*—Even before the event. And when the event comes, *we know* it comes in answer to our prayer.

Verse 16. This extends to things of the greatest importance. *If any one see his brother*—That is, any man. *Sin a sin which is not unto death*—That is, any sin but total apostasy from both the power and form of godliness. *Let him ask, and God will give him life*—Pardon and spiritual life, for that sinner. *There is a sin unto death: I do not say that he shall pray for that*—That is, let him not pray for it. *A sin unto death* may likewise mean, one which God has determined to punish with death.

Verse 17. *All* deviation from perfect holiness is sin; but all sin is not unpardonable.

Verse 18. Yet this gives us no encouragement to sin: on the contrary, it is an indisputable truth, *he that is born of God*—That sees and loves

God sinneth not; but he that is born of God keepeth
19 himself, and the wicked one toucheth him not. We know
that we are of God, and the whole world lieth in the wicked
20 one. But we know that the Son of God is come, and he
hath given us an understanding, that we may know the true
one, and we are in the true one, *even* in his Son Jesus
21 Christ. This is the true God, and eternal life. Beloved
children, keep yourselves from idols.

God. *Sinneth not*—So long as that loving faith abides in him, he neither speaks nor does anything which God hath forbidden. *He keepeth himself*—Watching unto prayer. *And*, while he does this, *the wicked one toucheth him not*—So as to hurt him.

Verse 19. *We know that we are* children *of God*—By the witness and the fruit of his Spirit, 1 John iii. 24. *But the whole world*—All who have not his Spirit, not only is "touched" by him, but by idolatry, fraud, violence, lasciviousness, impiety, all manner of wickedness. *Lieth in the wicked one*—Void of life, void of sense. In this short expression the horrible state of the world is painted in the most lively colours; a comment on which we have in the actions, conversations, contracts, quarrels, and friendships of worldly men.

Verse 20. *And we know*—By all these infallible proofs. *That the Son of God is come*—Into the world. *And he hath given us* a spiritual *understanding, that we may know him, the true one*—"The faithful and true witness." *And we are in the true one*—As branches in the vine, even in Jesus Christ, the eternal Son of God. *This* Jesus *is the* only living and *true God*, together with the Father and the Spirit, and the original fountain of *eternal life*. So the beginning and the end of the epistle agree.

Verse 21. *Keep yourselves from idols*—From all worship of false gods, from all worship of images or of any creature, and from every inward idol; from loving, desiring, fearing anything more than God. Seek all help and defence from evil, all happiness in the true God alone.

NOTES

ON

THE SECOND EPISTLE OF ST. JOHN.

The parts of this epistle, written to some Christian matron and her religious children, are three:—

II. ST. JOHN.

1 The elder unto the elect Kuria and her children, whom
I love in the truth; and not I only, but likewise all who
2 know the truth; For the truth's sake, which abideth in us,
3 and shall be with us for ever. Grace be with you, mercy
and peace, from God the Father, and from Jesus Christ, the
Son of the Father, in truth and love.

Verse 1. *The elder*—An appellation suited to a familiar letter, but upon a weighty subject. *To the elect*—That is, Christian. *Kuria* is undoubtedly a proper name, both here and in verse 5; for it was not then usual to apply the title of lady to any but the Roman empress; neither would such a manner of speaking have been suitable to the simplicity and dignity of the apostle. *Whom*—Both her and her children. *I love in the truth*—With unfeigned and holy love.

Verse 2. *For the truth's sake, which abideth in us*—As a living principle of faith and holiness.

Verse 3. *Grace* takes away guilt; *mercy*, misery: *peace* implies the abiding in grace and mercy. It includes the testimony of God's Spirit, both that we are his children, and that all our ways are acceptable to him. This is the very foretaste of heaven itself, where it is perfected.

4 I rejoiced greatly that I found of thy children walking
in the truth, as we received commandment from the Father
5 And now I beseech thee, Kuria, not as writing a new commandment to thee, but that which we had from the begin-
6 ning, that we may love one another. And this is love, that
we walk after his commandments. This is the commandment, as ye have heard from the beginning, that ye may
7 walk in it. For many seducers are entered into the
world, who confess not Jesus Christ that came in the flesh.
8 This is the seducer and the antichrist. Look to yourselves,
that we lose not the things we have wrought, but receive a
9 full reward. Whosoever transgresseth and abideth not in
the doctrine of Christ, hath not God. He that abideth in
the doctrine of Christ, he hath both the Father and the
10 Son. If any come to you, and bring not this doctrine,
receive him not into your house, neither bid him God speed.

In truth and love—Or, *faith and love,* as St. Paul speaks. Faith and truth are here synonymous terms.

Verse 4. *I found of thy children*—Probably in their aunt's house, verse 13. *Walking in the truth*—In faith and love

Verse 5. *That which we had from the beginning*—Of our Lord's ministry. Indeed it was, in some sense, from the beginning of the world. *That we may love one another*—More abundantly.

Verse 6. *And this is* the proof of true *love,* universal obedience built on the love of God. *This*—Love. *Is the* great *commandment which ye have heard from the beginning*—Of our preaching.

Verse 7. Carefully keep what ye have heard from the beginning, *for many seducers are entered into the world, who confess not Jesus Christ that came in the flesh*—Who disbelieve either his prophetic, or priestly, or kingly office. Whosoever does *this is the seducer*—From God. *And the antichrist*—Fighting against Christ.

Verse 8. *That we lose not the things which we have wrought*—Which every apostate does. *But receive a full reward*—Having fully employed all our talents to the glory of him that gave them. Here again the apostle modestly transfers it to himself.

Verse 9. Receive this as a certain rule: *Whosoever transgresseth*—Any law of God. *Hath not God*—For his Father and his God. *He that abideth in the doctrine of Christ*—Believing and obeying it. *He hath both the Father and the Son*—For his God

Verse 10. *If any come to you*—Either as a teacher or a brother. *And bring not this doctrine*—That is, advance anything contrary to it. *Receive him not into your house*—As either a teacher or a brother—*Neither bid him God speed*—Give him no encouragement therein.

11 For he that biddeth him God speed is partaker of his evil
deeds.
12 Having many things to write to you, I was not minded *to*
write with paper and ink: but I trust to come to you, and
13 speak face to face, that our joy may be full. The children
of thy elect sister salute thee.

Verse 11. *For he that biddeth him God speed*—That gives him any encouragement, *is* accessory to *his evil deeds.*

Verse 12. *Having many things to write, I was not minded to write now*—Only of these, which were then peculiarly needful.

Verse 13. *The children of thy elect* or Christian *sister*—Absent, if not dead, when the apostle wrote this.

NOTES

ON

THE THIRD EPISTLE OF ST. JOHN.

THE third epistle has likewise three parts :—

I. The inscription,	V. 1, 2
II. The commendation of Caius,	3— 8
With a caution against Diotrephes,	9—11
And a recommendation of Demetrius,	12
III. The conclusion,	13—15

III. ST. JOHN.

1 THE elder unto the beloved Caius, whom I truly love.
2 Beloved, I pray that in every respect thou mayest prosper
and be in health, as thy soul prospereth.
3 For I rejoiced greatly, when the brethren came and testified of the truth that is in thee, as thou walkest in the truth.
4 I have no greater joy than this, to hear that my children
5 walk in the truth. Beloved, thou doest faithfully whatsoever

Verse 1. *Caius* was probably that Caius of Corinth whom St. Paul mentions, Rom. xvi. 23. If so, either he was removed from Achaia into Asia, or St. John sent this letter to Corinth.

Verse 3. *For*—I know thou usest all thy talents to his glory. *The truth that is in thee*—The true faith and love.

Verse 4. *I have no greater joy than this*—Such is the spirit of every true Christian pastor. *To hear that my children walk in the truth*—Caius probably was converted by St. Paul. Therefore when St. John speaks of him, with other believers, as his children, it may be considered as the tender style of paternal love, whoever were the instruments of their conversion. And his using this appellation, when writing under the character of *the elder*, has its peculiar beauty.

Verse 5. *Faithfully*—Uprightly and sincerely.

6 thou doest to the brethren, and to strangers; Who have testified of thy love before the church: whom if thou send forward on their journey after a godly sort, thou shalt do well:
7 For they went forth for his sake, taking nothing of the gen-
8 tiles. We ought therefore to receive such, that we may be
9 fellowhelpers to the truth. I wrote to the church: but
Diotrephes, who loveth to have the pre-eminence among
10 them, receiveth us not. Wherefore, if I come, I will remember his wicked deeds which he doeth, prating against us with
malicious words: and not content therewith, neither doth he
himself receive the brethren, and forbiddeth them that would,
11 and casteth them out of the church. Beloved, follow not
that which is evil, but that which is good. He that is a doer
of good is of God: he that is a doer of evil hath not seen
12 God. Demetrius hath a good testimony from all men, and
from the truth itself: yea, we also bear testimony; and ye
know that our testimony is true.
13 I had many things to write, but I will not write to thee
14 with ink and pen: But I trust to see thee shortly, and we
shall speak face to face. Peace *be* to thee. Our friends
salute thee. Salute the friends by name.

Verse 6. *Who have testified of thy love before the church*—The congregation with whom I now reside. *Whom if thou send forward on their journey*—Supplied with what is needful. *Thou shalt do well*—How tenderly does the apostle enjoin this!

Verse 7. *They went forth*—To preach the gospel.

Verse 8. *To receive*—With all kindness. *The truth*—Which they preach.

Verse 9. *I wrote to the church*—Probably that to which they came. *But Diotrephes*—Perhaps the pastor of it. *Who loveth to have the pre-eminence among them*—To govern all things according to his own will. *Receiveth us not*—Neither them nor me. So did the mystery of iniquity already work!

Verse 10. *He prateth against us*—Both them and me, thereby endeavouring to excuse himself.

Verse 11. *Follow not that which is evil*—In Diotrephes. *But that which is good*—In Demetrius. *He hath not seen God*—Is a stranger to him.

Verse 12. *And from the truth itself*—That is, what they testify is the very truth. *Yea, we also bear testimony*—I and they that are with me.

Verse 14. *Salute the friends by name*—That is, in the same manner as if I had named them one by one. The word *friend* does not often occur in the New Testament, being swallowed up in the more endearing one of brother.

NOTES

ON

THE GENERAL EPISTLE OF ST. JUDE.

This epistle has three parts :—

I. The inscription,	V.	1, 2
II. The treatise, in which,		
1. He exhorts them to contend for the faith,		3
2. Describes the punishment and the manners of its adversaries,		4—16
3. Warns the believers,		17—19
4. Confirms them,		20, 21
5. Instructs them in their duty to others,		22, 23
III. The conclusion,		24, 25

This epistle greatly resembles the second of St. Peter, which St. Jude seems to have had in view while he wrote. That was written but a very little before his death; and hence we may gather that St. Jude lived some time after it, and saw that grievous declension in the church which St. Peter had foretold. But he passes over some things mentioned by St. Peter, repeats some in different expressions and with a different view, and adds others; clearly evidencing thereby the wisdom of God which rested upon him. Thus St. Peter cites and confirms St. Paul's writings, and is himself cited and confirmed by St. Jude.

ST. JUDE.

1 JUDE, a servant of Jesus Christ, and brother of James,
to them that are beloved of God the Father, and preserved

Verse 1. *Jude, a servant of Jesus Christ*—The highest glory which any, either angel or man, can aspire to. The word *servant*, under the old covenant, was adapted to the spirit of fear and bondage that clave to that dispensation. But when the time appointed of the Father was come, for the sending of his Son to redeem them that were under the law, the word *servant* (used by the apostles concerning themselves and all the children of God) signified one that, having the Spirit of adoption, is made free by

2 through Jesus Christ, and called· Mercy unto you, and
peace, and love, be multiplied.
3 Beloved, when I gave all diligence to write to you of the
common salvation, it was needful for me to write to you, and
exhort you to contend earnestly for the faith which was once
4 delivered to the saints. For there are certain men crept in
unawares, who were of old described before with regard to
this condemnation, ungodly men, turning the grace of our
God into lasciviousness, and denying our only Master and
5 Lord, Jesus Christ. I am therefore willing to remind you,
you who once knew this, that the Lord, having saved the
people out of the land of Egypt, afterwards destroyed them
6 that believed not. And the * angels who kept not their first

* 2 Peter ii. 4.

the Son of God. His being a servant is the fruit and perfection of his being a son. And whenever the throne of God and of the Lamb shall be in the new Jerusalem, then will it be indeed that "his servants shall serve him," Rev. xxii. 3. *The brother of James*—St. James was the more eminent, usually styled, "the brother of the Lord." *To them that are beloved*—The conclusion, verse 21, exactly answers the introduction. *And preserved through Jesus Christ*—So both the spring and the accomplishment of salvation are pointed out. This is premised, lest any of them should be discouraged by the terrible things which are afterwards mentioned. *And called*—To receive the whole blessing of God, in time and eternity.

Verse 3. *When I gave all diligence to write to you of the common salvation*—Designed for all, and enjoyed by all believers. Here the design of the epistle is expressed; the end of which exactly answers the beginning. *It was needful to exhort you to contend earnestly*—Yet humbly, meekly, and lovingly; otherwise your contention will only hurt your cause, if not destroy your soul. *For the faith*—All the fundamental truths. *Once delivered*—By God, to remain unvaried for ever.

Verse 4. *There are certain men crept in, who were of old described before*—Even as early as Enoch; of whom it was foretold, that by their wilful sins they would incur *this condemnation. Turning the grace of God*—Revealed in the gospel. *Into lasciviousness*—Into an occasion of more abandoned wickedness.

Verse 5. He *afterwards destroyed*—The far greater part of that very *people* whom he had once saved. Let none therefore presume upon past mercies, as if he was now out of danger.

Verse 6. *And the angels, who kept not their first dignity*—Once assigned them under the Son of God *But* voluntarily *left their own habitation*—Then properly their own, by the free gift of God. *He reserved*—Delivered to be kept *In everlasting chains under darkness*—O how unlike their own habitation! When these fallen angels came out of the hands of God, they

dignity, but left their own habitation, he hath reserved in
everlasting chains under darkness to the judgment of the
7 great day. Even as Sodom and Gomorrah, and the cities
about them which in the same manner with these gave themselves over to fornication, and went after strange flesh, are
set forth for an example, suffering the vengeance of eternal
8 fire. In like manner these dreamers also defile the flesh,
9 * despise authority, rail at dignities. Yet Michael the archangel, when contending with the devil he disputed concerning the body of Moses, durst not bring against him a railing

* 2 Pet. ii. 10.

were holy; else God made that which was evil: and being holy, they were beloved of God; else he hated the image of his own spotless purity. But now he loves them no more; they are doomed to endless destruction. (for if he loved them still, he would love what is sinful:) and both his former love, and his present righteous and eternal displeasure towards the same work of his own hands, are because he changeth not; because he invariably loveth righteousness, and hateth iniquity.

Verse 7. *The cities which gave themselves over to fornication*—The word here means, *unnatural lusts. Are set forth as an example, suffering the vengeance of eternal fire*—That is, the vengeance which they suffered is an example or a type of eternal fire.

Verse 8. *In like manner these dreamers*—Sleeping and dreaming all their lives. *Despise authority*—Those that are invested with it by Christ, and made by him the overseers of his flock. *Rail at dignities*—The apostle does not seem to speak of worldly dignities. These they had "in admiration for the sake of gain," verse 16; but those holy men, who for the purity of their lives, the soundness of their doctrine, and the greatness of their labours in the work of the ministry, were truly honourable before God and all good men; and who were grossly vilified by those who turned the grace of God into lasciviousness. Probably they were the impure followers of Simon Magus, the same with the Gnostics and Nicolaitans, Rev. ii. 15.

Verse 9. *Yet Michael*—It does not appear whether St. Jude learned this by any revelation or from ancient tradition. It suffices, that these things were not only true, but acknowledged as such by them to whom he wrote. *The archangel*—This word occurs but once more in the sacred writings, 1 Thess. iv. 16. So that whether there be one archangel only, or more, it is not possible for us to determine. *When he disputed with the devil*—At what time we know not. *Concerning the body of Moses*—Possibly the devil would have discovered the place where it was buried, which God for wise reasons had concealed. *Durst not bring* even *against him a railing accusation*—Though so far beneath him in every respect. *But* simply *said,* (so great was his modesty!) *The Lord rebuke thee*—I leave thee to the Judge of all.

10 accusation, but said, The Lord rebuke thee. But these rail
at all things which they know not: and all the things which
they know naturally, as the brute beasts, in these they are
11 defiled. Woe to them! for they have gone in the way
of Cain, and ran greedily after the error of Balaam for
reward, and perished in the gainsaying of Korah.
12 These are spots in your feasts of love, while they banquet
with you, feeding themselves without fear: clouds without
water, driven about of winds; trees without leaves, without
13 fruit, twice dead, plucked up by the roots; Raging waves
of the sea, foaming out their own shame; wandering stars,
14 for whom is reserved the blackness of darkness for ever. And
of these also, Enoch, the seventh from Adam, prophesied,
saying, Behold, the Lord cometh with ten thousands of his
15 holy ones, To execute judgment upon all, and to convict all

Verse 10. *But these*—Without all shame *Rail at the things* of God *which they know not*—Neither can know, having no spiritual senses. *And the natural things, which they know*—By their natural senses, they abuse into occasions of sin.

Verse 11. *Woe unto them*—Of all the apostles St. Jude alone, and that in this single place, denounces a woe. St. Peter, to the same effect, pronounces them "cursed children." *For they have gone in the way of Cain*—The murderer. *And ran greedily*—Literally, *have been poured out,* like a torrent without banks. *After the error of Balaam*—The covetous false prophet. *And perished in the gainsaying of Korah*—Vengeance has overtaken them as it did Korah, rising up against those whom God had sent.

Verse 12. *These are spots*—Blemishes. *In your feasts of love*—Anciently observed in all the churches. *Feeding themselves without fear*—Without any fear of God, or jealousy over themselves. *Twice dead*—In sin, first by nature, and afterwards by apostasy *Plucked up by the roots*—And so incapable of ever reviving.

Verse 13. *Wandering stars*—Literally, *planets,* which shine for a time, but have no light in themselves, and will be soon cast into utter darkness. Thus the apostle illustrates their desperate wickedness by comparisons drawn from the air, earth, sea, and heavens.

Verse 14. *And of these also*—As well as the antediluvian sinners *Enoch*—So early was the prophecy referred to, verse 4. *The seventh from Adam*—There were only five of the fathers between Adam and Enoch, 1 Chron. i. 1. The first coming of Christ was revealed to Adam; his second, glorious coming, to Enoch; and *the seventh from Adam* foretold the things which will conclude the seventh age of the world. St. Jude might know this either from some ancient book, or tradition, or immediate revelation. *Behold*—As if it were already done, *the Lord cometh!*

Verse 15 *To execute judgment*—Enoch herein looked beyond the flood

the ungodly of all their ungodly deeds which they have
impiously committed, and of all the grievous things which
ungodly sinners have spoken against him.
16 These are murmurers, complainers, walking after their
own desires; and their mouth speaketh great swelling things,
17 having men's persons in admiration for the sake of gain. But
ye, beloved, remember the words which were spoken before
18 by the apostles of our Lord Jesus Christ; For they told you,
In the last time there will be mockers, walking after their own
ungodly desires.
19 These are they who separate themselves, sensual, not hav-
20 ing the Spirit. But ye, beloved, building yourselves up in
21 your most holy faith, praying through the Holy Spirit, Keep

Upon all—Sinners, in general. *And to convict all the ungodly*, in particular, *of all the grievous things which ungodly sinners* (a *sinner* is bad; but the *ungodly* who sin without fear are worse) *have spoken against him*, verses 8, 10, though they might not think, all those speeches were *against him.*

Verse 16. *These are murmurers*—Against men. *Complainers*—Literally, *complainers of* their *fate*, against God. *Walking*—With regard to themselves. *After their own* foolish and mischievous *desires. Having men's persons in admiration for the sake of gain*—Admiring and commending them only for what they can get.

Verse 17. *By the apostles*—He does not exempt himself from the number of apostles. For in the next verse he says, they told *you*, not *us*.

Verse 19. *These are they who separate themselves, sensual, not having the Spirit*—Having natural senses and understanding only, not the Spirit of God; otherwise they could not *separate*. For that it is a sin, and a very heinous one, "to separate from the church," is out of all question. But then it should be observed, 1. That by *the church* is meant a body of living Christians, who are "an habitation of God through the Spirit:" 2. That by *separating* is understood, renouncing all religious intercourse with them; no longer joining with them in solemn prayer, or the other public offices of religion: and, 3. That we have no more authority from scripture to call even this schism, than to call it murder.

Verse 20. *But ye, beloved*, not separating, but *building yourselves up in your most holy faith*—Than which none can be more holy in itself, or more conducive to the most refined and exalted holiness. *Praying through the Holy Spirit*—Who alone is able to build you up, as he alone laid the foundation. In this and the following verse St. Jude mentions the Father, Son, and Spirit, together with faith, love, and hope.

Verse 21. By these means, through his grace, *keep yourselves in the love of God*, and in the confident expectation of that *eternal life* which is purchased for you, and conferred upon you, through the mere *mercy of our Lord Jesus Christ.*

yourselves in the love of God, looking for the mercy of our
22 Lord Jesus Christ unto eternal life. And some, that are
23 wavering, convince; Some save, snatching *them* out of the
fire; on others have compassion with fear, hating even the
garment spotted by the flesh.

24 Now to him *who is* able to keep them from falling, and
to present *them* faultless in the presence of his glory with
25 exceeding joy, To the only God our Saviour, *be* glory and
majesty, might and authority, both now and to all ages.
Amen.

Verse 22. Meantime watch over others, as well as yourselves, and give them such help as their various needs require. For instance, 1. *Some, that are wavering* in judgment, staggered by others' or by their own evil reasoning, endeavour more deeply to *convince* of the whole truth as it is in Jesus. 2. *Some snatch,* with a swift and strong hand, *out of the fire* of sin and temptation. 3. *On others* show *compassion* in a milder and gentler way; though still *with* a jealous *fear,* lest yourselves be infected with the disease you endeavour to cure. See, therefore, that while you love the sinners, ye retain the utmost abhorrence of their sins, and of any the least degree of, or approach to, them.

Verse 24. *Now to him who* alone *is able to keep them from falling*—Into any of these errors or sins. *And to present them faultless in the presence of his glory*—That is, in his own presence, when he shall be revealed in all his glory.

NOTES

ON

THE REVELATION OF JESUS CHRIST

It is scarce possible for any that either love or fear God not to feel their hearts extremely affected in seriously reading either the beginning or the latter part of the Revelation. These, it is evident, we cannot consider too much; but the intermediate parts I did not study at all for many years; as utterly despairing of understanding them, after the fruitless attempts of so many wise and good men: and perhaps I should have lived and died in this sentiment, had I not seen the works of the great Bengelius. But these revived my hopes of understanding even the prophecies of this book; at least many of them in some good degree: for perhaps some will not be opened but in eternity. Let us, however, bless God for the measure of light we may enjoy, and improve it to his glory.

The following notes are mostly those of that excellent man; a few of which are taken from his *Gnomon Novi Testamenti,* but far more from his *Ekklarte Offenbarung,* which is a full and regular comment on the Revelation. Every part of this I do not undertake to defend. But none should condemn him without reading his proofs at large. It did not suit my design to insert these: they are above the capacity of ordinary readers Nor had I room to insert the entire translation of a book which contains near twelve hundred pages.

All I can do is, partly to translate, partly abridge, the most necessary of his observations; allowing myself the liberty to alter some of them, and to add a few notes where he is not full. His text, it may be observed, I have taken almost throughout, which I apprehend he has abundantly defended both in the *Gnomon* itself, and in his *Apparatus* and *Crisis in Apocalypsin.*

Yet I by no means pretend to understand or explain all that is contained in this mysterious book. I only offer what help I can to the serious inquirer, and shall rejoice if any be moved thereby more carefully to read and more deeply to consider the words of this prophecy. Blessed is he that does this with a single eye. His labour shall not be in vain

THE REVELATION.

CHAPTER I. 1 The Revelation of Jesus Christ, which God gave unto him, to show his servants the things which must shortly come to pass; and he sent and signified

Verse 1. *The Revelation*—Properly so called; for things covered before are here revealed, or unveiled. No prophecy in the Old Testament has this title; it was reserved for this alone in the New. It is, as it were, a manifesto, wherein the Heir of all things declares that all power is given him in heaven and earth, and that he will in the end gloriously exercise that power, maugre all the opposition of all his enemies. *Of Jesus Christ*—Not of "John the Divine," a title added in latter ages. Certain it is, that appellation, the Divine, was not brought into the church, much less was it affixed to John the apostle, till long after the apostolic age. It was St. John, indeed, who wrote this book, but the author of it is Jesus Christ *Which God gave unto him*—According to his holy, glorified humanity, as the great Prophet of the church. God gave the Revelation to Jesus Christ; Jesus Christ made it known to his servants. *To show*—This word recurs, Rev. xxii 6; and in many places the parts of this book refer to each other. Indeed the whole structure of it breathes the art of God, comprising, in the most finished compendium, things to come, many, various; near, intermediate, remote; the greatest, the least; terrible, comfortable; old, new; long, short; and these interwoven together, opposite, composite; relative to each other at a small, at a great, distance; and therefore sometimes, as it were, disappearing, broken off, suspended, and afterwards unexpectedly and most seasonably appearing again. In all its parts it has an admirable variety, with the most exact harmony, beautifully illustrated by those very digressions which seem to interrupt it. In this manner does it display the manifold wisdom of God shining in the economy of the church through so many ages. *His servants*—Much is comprehended in this appellation. It is a great thing to be a servant of Jesus Christ. This book is dedicated particularly to the servants of Christ in the seven churches in Asia; but not exclusive of all his other servants, in all nations and ages It is one single revelation, and yet sufficient for them all, from the time it was written to the end of the world. Serve thou the Lord Jesus Christ in truth: so shalt thou learn his secret in this book; yea, and thou shalt feel in thy heart whether this book be divine, or not. *The things which must shortly come to pass*—The things contained in this prophecy did begin to be accomplished shortly after it was given; and the whole might

2 *them* by his angel to his servant John: Who hath testified
the word of God, and the testimony of Jesus Christ, what-
3 soever things he saw. Happy is he that readeth, and they

be said to come to pass shortly, in the same sense as St. Peter says, "The end of all things is at hand;" and our Lord himself, "Behold, I come quickly." There is in this book a rich treasure of all the doctrines pertaining to faith and holiness. But these are also delivered in other parts of holy writ; so that the Revelation need not to have been given for the sake of these. The peculiar design of this is, *to show the things which must come to pass.* And this we are especially to have before our eyes whenever we read or hear it

It is said afterward, "Write what thou seest;" and again, "Write what thou hast seen, and what is, and what shall be hereafter;" but here, where the scope of the book is shown, it is only said, *the things which must come to pass.* Accordingly, the showing things to come, is the great point in view throughout the whole And St. John writes what he has seen, and what is, only as it has an influence on, or gives light to, what shall be. *And he*—Jesus Christ. *Sent and signified them*—Showed them by signs or emblems; so the Greek word properly means. *By his angel*—Peculiarly called, in the sequel, "the angel of God," and particularly mentioned, Rev. xvii. 1; xxi. 9; xxii. 6, 16. *To his servant John*—A title given to no other single person throughout the book.

Verse 2 *Who hath testified*—In the following book. *The word of God*—Given directly by God. *And the testimony of Jesus*—Which he hath left us, as the faithful and true witness. *Whatsoever things he saw*—In such a manner as was a full confirmation of the divine original of this book.

Verse 3. *Happy is he that readeth, and they that hear, the words of this prophecy*—Some have miserably handled this book. Hence others are afraid to touch it; and, while they desire to know all things else, reject only the knowledge of those which God hath shown. They inquire after anything rather than this; as if it were written, "Happy is he that doth *not* read this prophecy." Nay, but *happy is he that readeth, and they that hear, and keep the words thereof*—Especially at this time, when so considerable a part of them is on the point of being fulfilled.

Nor are helps wanting whereby any sincere and diligent inquirer may understand what he reads therein. The book itself is written in the most accurate manner possible. It distinguishes the several things whereof it treats by seven epistles, seven seals, seven trumpets, seven phials; each of which sevens is divided into four and three. Many things the book itself explains; as the seven stars; the seven candlesticks; the lamb, his seven horns and seven eyes; the incense; the dragon; the heads and horns of the beasts; the fine linen; the testimony of Jesus: and much light arises from comparing it with the ancient prophecies, and the predictions in the other books of the New Testament.

that hear the words of *this* prophecy, and keep the things which are written therein: for the time *is* near.

In this book our Lord has comprised what was wanting in those prophecies touching the time which followed his ascension and the end of the Jewish polity. Accordingly, it reaches from the old Jerusalem to the new, reducing all things into one sum, in the exactest order, and with a near resemblance to the ancient prophets. The introduction and conclusion agree with Daniel; the description of the man child, and the promises to Sion, with Isaiah; the judgment of Babylon, with Jeremiah; again, the determination of times, with Daniel; the architecture of the holy city, with Ezekiel; the emblems of the horses, candlesticks, &c., with Zechariah. Many things largely described by the prophets are here summarily repeated; and frequently in the same words. To them we may then usefully have recourse. Yet the Revelation suffices for the explaining itself, even if we do not yet understand those prophecies; yea, it casts much light upon them. Frequently, likewise, where there is a resemblance between them, there is a difference also; the Revelation, as it were, taking a stock from one of the old prophets, and inserting a new graft into it. Thus Zechariah speaks of two olive trees; and so does St. John, but with a different meaning. Daniel has a beast with ten horns; so has St. John; but not with quite the same signification. And here the difference of words, emblems, things, times, ought studiously to be observed.

Our Lord foretold many things before his passion; but not all things; for it was not yet seasonable. Many things, likewise, his Spirit foretold in the writings of the apostles, so far as the necessities of those times required: now he comprises them all in one short book; therein presupposing all the other prophecies, and at the same time explaining, continuing, and perfecting them in one thread. It is right therefore to compare them; but not to measure the fulness of these by the scantiness of those preceding.

Christ, when on earth, foretold what would come to pass in a short time; adding a brief description of the last things. Here he foretells the intermediate things; so that both put together constitute one complete chain of prophecy. This book is therefore not only the sum and the key of all the prophecies which preceded, but likewise a supplement to all; the seals being closed before. Of consequence, it contains many particulars not revealed in any other part of scripture. They have therefore little gratitude to God for such a revelation, reserved for the exaltation of Christ, who boldly reject whatever they find here which was not revealed, or not so clearly, in other parts of scripture. *He that readeth and they that hear*—St. John probably sent this book by a single person into Asia, who read it in the churches, while many heard. But this, likewise, in a secondary sense, refers to all that shall duly read or hear it in all ages. *The words of this prophecy*—It is a revelation with regard to Christ who gives it; a prophecy, with regard to John who delivers it to

4 John to the seven churches which are in Asia: Grace be
unto you, and peace, from him who is, and who was, and
who cometh; and from the seven spirits that are before his
5 throne: And from Jesus Christ, the faithful witness, the
first begotten from the dead, and the prince of the kings

the churches. *And keep the things which are written therein*—In such a manner as the nature of them requires; namely, with repentance, faith, patience, prayer, obedience, watchfulness, constancy. It behoves every Christian, at all opportunities, to read what is written in the oracles of God; and to read this precious book in particular, frequently, reverently, and attentively. *For the time*—Of its beginning to be accomplished. *Is near*—Even when St. John wrote. How much nearer to us is even the full accomplishment of this weighty prophecy!

Verse 4. *John*—The dedication of this book is contained in the fourth, fifth, and sixth verses; but the whole Revelation is a kind of letter. *To the seven churches which are in Asia*—That part of the Lesser Asia which was then a Roman province. There had been several other churches planted here; but it seems these were now the most eminent; and it was among these that St. John had laboured most during his abode in Asia. In these cities there were many Jews. Such of them as believed in each were joined with the gentile believers in one church. *Grace be unto you, and peace*—The favour of God, with all temporal and eternal blessings. *From him who is, and who was, and who cometh*, or, *who is to come*—A wonderful translation of the great name Jehovah: he *was* of old, he *is* now, he *cometh*; that is, will be for ever. *And from the seven spirits which are before his throne*—Christ is he who "hath the seven spirits of God." "The seven lamps which burn before the throne are the seven spirits of God." "The lamb hath seven horns and seven eyes, which are the seven spirits of God." *Seven* was a sacred number in the Jewish church: but it did not always imply a precise number. It sometimes is to be taken figuratively, to denote completeness or perfection. By these *seven spirits*, not seven created angels, but the Holy Ghost is to be understood. The angels are never termed *spirits* in this book; and when all the angels stand up, while the four living creatures and the four and twenty elders worship him that sitteth on the throne, and the Lamb, *the seven spirits* neither stand up nor worship. To these "seven spirits of God," the seven churches, to whom the Spirit speaks so many things, are subordinate; as are also their angels, yea, and "the seven angels which stand before God." He is called *the seven spirits*, not with regard to his essence, which is one, but with regard to his manifold operations.

Verse 5. *And from Jesus Christ, the faithful witness, the first begotten from the dead, and the prince of the kings of the earth*—Three glorious appellations are here given him, and in their proper order. He was *the faithful witness* of the whole will of God before his death, and in death, and remains such in glory He rose from the dead, as "the first-

6 of the earth. To him that loveth us, and hath washed us
from our sins with his own blood, and hath made us kings
and priests unto his God and Father; to him be the glory
and the might for ever.
7 Behold, he cometh with clouds; and every eye shall see
him, and they who have pierced him: and all the tribes
8 of the earth shall wail because of him. Yea, Amen. I am

fruits of them that slept;" and now hath all power both in heaven and earth. He is here styled a *prince:* but by and by he bears his title of *king;* yea, "King of kings, and Lord of lords." This phrase, *the kings of the earth,* signifies their power and multitude, and also the nature of their kingdom. It became the Divine Majesty to call them kings with a limitation; especially in this manifesto from his heavenly kingdom; for no creature, much less a sinful man, can bear the title of king in an absolute sense before the eyes of God.

Verse 6. *To him that loveth us, and,* out of that free, abundant love, *hath washed us from* the guilt and power of *our sins with his own blood, and hath made us kings*—Partakers of his present, and heirs of his eternal, kingdom. *And priests unto his God and Father*—To whom we continually offer ourselves, an holy, living sacrifice. *To him be the glory*—For his love and redemption. *And the might*—Whereby he governs all things.

Verse 7. *Behold*—In this and the next verse is the proposition, and the summary of the whole book. *He cometh*—Jesus Christ. Throughout this book, whenever it is said, *He cometh,* it means his glorious coming. The preparation for this began at the destruction of Jerusalem, and more particularly at the time of writing this book; and goes on, without any interruption, till that grand event is accomplished. Therefore it is never said in this book, He *will* come; but, *He cometh.* And yet it is not said, He cometh *again:* for when he came before, it was not like himself, but in "the form of a servant." But his appearing in glory is properly his coming; namely, in a manner worthy of the Son of God. *And every eye*—Of the Jews in particular. *Shall see him*—But with what different emotions, according as they had received or rejected him! *And they who have pierced him*—They, above all, who pierced his hands, or feet, or side. Thomas saw the print of these wounds even after his resurrection; and the same, undoubtedly, will be seen by all, when he cometh in the clouds of heaven. *And all the tribes of the earth*—The word *tribes,* in the Revelation, always means the Israelites: but where another word, such as *nations* or *people,* is joined with it, it implies likewise (as here) all the rest of mankind. *Shall wail because of him*—For terror and pain, if they did not wail before by true repentance. *Yea, Amen*—This refers to, *every eye shall see him.* He that cometh saith, *Yea;* he that testifies it, *Amen.* The word translated *yea* is Greek; *Amen* is Hebrew: for what is here spoken respects both Jew and gentile.

Verse 8. *I am the Alpha and the Omega, saith the Lord God*—*Alpha* is the first, *Omega,* the last, letter in the Greek alphabet. Let his enemies

the Alpha and the Omega, saith the Lord God, who is, and
who was, and who cometh, the Almighty.
9 I John, your brother, and companion in the affliction,
and in the kingdom and patience of Jesus, was in the island
Patmos, for the word of God, and for the testimony of Jesus.
10 I was in the Spirit on the Lord's day, and heard behind me

boast and rage ever so much in the intermediate time, yet the Lord God is both *the Alpha*, or beginning, and *the Omega*, or end, of all things. God is the beginning, as he is the Author and Creator of all things, and as he proposes, declares, and promises so great things: he is the end, as he brings all the things which are here revealed to a complete and glorious conclusion. Again, the beginning and end of a thing is in scripture styled the whole thing. Therefore God is *the Alpha and the Omega*, the beginning and the end; that is, one who is all things, and always the same.

Verse 9. *I John*—The instruction and preparation of the apostle for the work are described from the ninth to the twentieth verse. *Your brother*—In the common faith. *And companion in the affliction*—For the same persecution which carried him to *Patmos* drove them into Asia. This book peculiarly belongs to those who are under the cross. It was given to a banished man; and men in affliction understand and relish it most. Accordingly, it was little esteemed by the Asiatic church, after the time of Constantine; but highly valued by all the African churches, as it has been since by all the persecuted children of God. *In the affliction, and kingdom and patience of Jesus*—The kingdom stands in the midst. It is chiefly under various afflictions that faith obtains its part in the kingdom; and whosoever is a partaker of this kingdom is not afraid to suffer for Jesus, 2 Tim. ii. 12. *I was in the island Patmos*—In the reign of Domitian and of Nerva. And there he saw and wrote all that follows. It was a place peculiarly proper for these visions. He had over-against him, at a small distance, Asia and the seven churches; going on eastward, Jerusalem and the land of Canaan; and beyond this, Antioch, yea, the whole continent of Asia. To the west, he had Rome, Italy, and all Europe, swimming, as it were, in the sea; to the south, Alexandria and the Nile with its outlets, Egypt, and all Africa; and to the north, what was afterwards called Constantinople, on the straits between Europe and Asia. So he had all the three parts of the world which were then known, with all Christendom, as it were, before his eyes; a large theatre for all the various scenes which were to pass before him: as if this island had been made principally for this end, to serve as an observatory for the apostle. *For* preaching *the word of God* he was banished thither, and *for the testimony of Jesus*—For testifying that he is the Christ.

Verse 10. *I was in the Spirit*—That is, in a trance, a prophetic vision; so overwhelmed with the power, and filled with the light, of the Holy Spirit, as to be insensible of outward things, and wholly taken up with spiritual and divine. What follows is one single, connected vision, which

11 a great voice, as of a trumpet, Saying, What thou seest,
write in a book, and send to the seven churches; to Ephesus, and to Smyrna, and to Pergamos, and to Thyatira, and
12 to Sardis, and to Philadelphia, and to Laodicea. And I
turned to see the voice that spake with me And being turned,

St. John saw in one day; and therefore he that would understand it should carry his thought straight on through the whole, without interruption. The other prophetic books are collections of distinct prophecies, given upon various occasions: but here is one single treatise, whereof all the parts exactly depend on each other. Chapter iv. 1 is connected with chapter i. 19; and what is delivered in the fourth chapter goes on directly to the twenty-second. *On the Lord's day*—On this our Lord rose from the dead: on this the ancients believed he will come to judgment. It was, therefore, with the utmost propriety that St. John on this day both saw and described his coming. *And I heard behind me*—St. John had his face to the east: our Lord, likewise, in this appearance looked eastward toward Asia, whither the apostle was to write. *A great voice, as of a trumpet*—Which was peculiarly proper to proclaim the coming of the great King, and his victory over all his enemies.

Verse 11. *Saying, What thou seest*—And hearest. He both saw and heard. This command extends to the whole book. All the books of the New Testament were written by the will of God; but none were so expressly commanded to be written. *In a book*—So all the Revelation is but one book: nor did the letter to the angel of each church belong to him or his church only; but the whole book was sent to them all. *To the churches*—Hereafter named; and through them to all churches, in all ages and nations. *To Ephesus*—Mr. Thomas Smith, who in the year 1671 travelled through all these cities, observes, that from Ephesus to *Smyrna* is forty-six English miles; from Smyrna to *Pergamos*, sixty-four; from Pergamos to *Thyatira*, forty-eight; from Thyatira to *Sardis*, thirty-three; from Sardis to *Philadelphia*, twenty-seven; from Philadelphia to *Laodicea*, about forty-two miles.

Verses 12, 13. *And I turned to see the voice*—That is, to see him whose voice it was. *And being turned, I saw*—It seems, the vision presented itself gradually. First he heard a voice; and, upon looking behind, he saw the *golden candlesticks*, and then, in the midst of the candlesticks, which were placed in a circle, he saw *one like a son of man*—That is, in an human form. As a man likewise our Lord doubtless appears in heaven: though not exactly in this symbolical manner, wherein he presents himself as the head of his church. He next observed that our Lord was *clothed with a garment down to the foot, and girt with a golden girdle*—Such the Jewish high priests wore. But both of them are here marks of royal dignity likewise. *Girt about at the breast*—He that is on a journey girds his loins. Girding the breast was an emblem of solemn rest. It seems that the apostle having seen all this, looked up to behold the face of our Lord: but was beat back by the appearance of his flaming eyes, which occa-

13 I saw seven golden candlesticks; And in the midst of the
candlesticks *one*, like a son of man, clothed with a garment
down to the foot, and girt about at the breast with a golden
14 girdle. His head and hair *were* white as white wool, as
15 snow, and his eyes as a flame of fire; And his feet like fine
brass, as if they burned in a furnace; and his voice as the
16 voice of many waters. And he had in his right hand seven
stars: and out of his mouth went a sharp two-edged sword·
and his countenance was as the sun shineth in his strength.
17 And when I saw him, I fell at his feet as dead. And he laid

sioned his more particularly observing his feet Receiving strength to raise his eyes again, he saw the stars in his right hand, and the sword coming out of his mouth: but upon beholding the brightness of his glorious countenance, which probably was much increased since the first glance the apostle had of it, he "fell at his feet as dead." During the time that St. John was discovering these several particulars, our Lord seems to have been speaking. And doubtless even his voice, at the very first, bespoke the God: though not so insupportably as his glorious appearance.

Verse 14. *His head and* his *hair*—That is, the hair of his head, not his whole head. *Were white as white wool*—Like the Ancient of Days, represented in Daniel's vision, Dan. vii. 9. Wool is commonly supposed to be an emblem of eternity. *As snow*—Betokening his spotless purity. *And his eyes as a flame of fire*—Piercing through all things; a token of his omniscience.

Verse 15. *And his feet like fine brass*—Denoting his stability and strength. *As if they burned in a furnace*—As if having been melted and refined, they were still red hot. *And his voice*—To the comfort of his friends, and the terror of his enemies. *As the voice of many waters*—Roaring aloud, and bearing down all before them.

Verse 16. *And he had in his right hand seven stars*—In token of his favour and powerful protection *And out of his mouth went a sharp two-edged sword*—Signifying his justice and righteous anger, continually pointed against his enemies as a sword; *sharp*, to stab; *two-edged*, to hew. *And his countenance was as the sun shineth in his strength*—Without any mist or cloud.

Verse 17. *And I fell at his feet as dead*—Human nature not being able to sustain so glorious an appearance. Thus was he prepared (like Daniel of old, whom he peculiarly resembles) for receiving so weighty a prophecy. A great sinking of nature usually precedes a large communication of heavenly things. St. John, before our Lord suffered, was so intimate with him, as to lean on his breast, to lie in his bosom. Yet now, near seventy years after, the aged apostle is by one glance struck to the ground. What a glory must this be! Ye sinners, be afraid cleanse your hands: purify your hearts. Ye saints, be humble prepare: rejoice.

his right hand upon me, saying, Fear not; I am the first
18 and the last: And he that liveth and was dead; and, behold.
I am alive for evermore; and have the keys of death and
19 of hades. Write the things which thou hast seen, and which
20 are, and which shall be hereafter; The mystery of the
seven stars which thou sawest in my right hand, and *of* the
seven golden candlesticks. The seven stars are angels of the
seven churches: and the seven candlesticks are seven
churches.

But rejoice unto him with reverence an increase of reverence towards this awful majesty can be no prejudice to your faith. Let all petulancy, with all vain curiosity, be far away, while you are thinking or reading of these things. *And he laid his right hand upon me*—The same wherein he held the seven stars. What did St. John then feel in himself? *Saying, Fear not*—His look terrifies, his speech strengthens. He does not call John by his name, (as the angels did Zechariah and others,) but speaks as his well known master. What follows is also spoken to strengthen and encourage him. *I am*—When in his state of humiliation he spoke of his glory, he frequently spoke in the third person, as Matt. xxvi. 64. But he now speaks of his own glory, without any veil, in plain and direct terms. *The first and the last*—That is, the one, eternal God, who is from everlasting to everlasting, Isaiah xli. 4.

Verse 18. *And he that liveth*—Another peculiar title of God. *And I have the keys of death and of hades*—That is, the invisible world. In the intermediate state, the body abides in death, the soul in hades. Christ hath the keys of, that is, the power over, both; killing or quickening of the body, and disposing of the soul, as it pleaseth him. He gave St. Peter the keys of the kingdom of heaven; but not the keys of death or of hades. How comes then his supposed successor at Rome by the keys of purgatory?

From the preceding description, mostly, are taken the titles given to Christ in the following letters, particularly the four first.

Verse 19. *Write the things which thou hast seen*—This day: which accordingly are written, Rev i. 11—18. *And which are*—The instructions relating to the present state of the seven churches. These are written, Rev. i. 20—iii. 22. *And which shall be hereafter*—To the end of the world; written, Rev. iv. 1, &c.

Verse 20. Write first *the mystery*—The mysterious meaning *of the seven stars*—St. John knew better than we do, in how many respects these stars were a proper emblem of those angels: how nearly they resembled each other, and how far they differed in magnitude, brightness, and other circumstances. *The seven stars are angels of the seven churches*—Mentioned in the eleventh verse. In each church there was one pastor or ruling minister, to whom all the rest were subordinate. This pastor, bishop, or overseer, had the peculiar care over that flock: on him the prosperity of that congregation in a great measure depended, and he was

CHAP. II. 1 To the angel of the church at Ephesus write; These things saith he that holdeth the seven stars in his right hand, that walketh in the midst of the seven golden

to answer for all those souls at the judgment seat of Christ. *And the seven candlesticks are seven churches*—How significant an emblem is this! For a candlestick, though of gold, has no light of itself. neither has any church, or child of man. But they receive from Christ the light of truth, holiness, comfort, that it may shine to all around them.

As soon as this was spoken St. John wrote it down, even all that is contained in this first chapter. Afterwards what was contained in the second and third chapters was dictated to him in like manner.

CHAP. II. Of the following letters to the angels of the seven churches it may be necessary to speak first in general, and then particularly.

In general we may observe, when the Israelites were to receive the law at Mount Sinai, they were first to be purified; and when the kingdom of God was at hand, John the Baptist prepared men for it by repentance In like manner we are prepared by these letters for the worthy reception of this glorious revelation. By following the directions given herein, by expelling incorrigibly wicked men, and putting away all wickedness, those churches were prepared to receive this precious depositum. And whoever in any age would profitably read or hear it, must observe the same admonitions.

These letters are a kind of sevenfold preface to the book. Christ now appears in the form of a man, (not yet under the emblem of a lamb,) and speaks mostly in proper, not in figurative, words. It is not till Rev. iv. 1, that St. John enters upon that grand vision which takes up the residue of the book.

There is in each of these letters,

1. A command to write to the angel of the church;
2. A glorious title of Christ;
3 An address to the angel of that church, containing
   A testimony of his mixed, or good, or bad state;
   An exhortation to repentance or steadfastness;
   A declaration of what will be; generally, of the Lord's coming;
4. A promise to him that overcometh, together with the exhortation, "He that hath an ear to hear, let him hear"

The address in each letter is expressed in plain words, the promise, in figurative In the address our Lord speaks to the angel of each church which then was, and to the members thereof directly; whereas in the promise he speaks of all that should overcome, in whatever church or age, and deals out to them one of the precious promises, (by way of anticipation,) from the last chapters of the book.

Verse 1 *Write*—So Christ dictated to him every word. *These things saith he who holdeth the seven stars in his right hand*—Such is his mighty power! Such his favour to them and care over them, that they may indeed shine as stars, both by purity of doctrine and holiness of life!

2 candlesticks; I know thy works, and thy labour, and thy
patience, that thou canst not bear evil men. and thou hast
tried those who say they are apostles, and are not, and hast
3 found them liars: And hast patience, and hast borne for my
4 name's sake, and hast not fainted. But I have against thee,
5 that thou hast left thy first love. Remember therefore from
whence thou art fallen, and repent and do the first works;

Who walketh—According to his promise, "I am with you always, even to the end of the world." *In the midst of the golden candlesticks*—Beholding all their works and thoughts, and ready to "remove the candlestick out of its place," if any, being warned, will not repent. Perhaps here is likewise an allusion to the office of the priests in dressing the lamps, which was to keep them always burning before the Lord.

Verse 2. *I know*—Jesus knows all the good and all the evil, which his servants and his enemies suffer and do. Weighty word, "I know," how dreadful will it one day sound to the wicked, how sweet to the righteous! The churches and their angels must have been astonished, to find their several states so exactly described, even in the absence of the apostle, and could not but acknowledge the all-seeing eye of Christ and of his Spirit. With regard to us, to every one of us also he saith, "I know thy works" Happy is he that conceives less good of himself, than Christ knows concerning him. *And thy labour*—After the general, three particulars are named, and then more largely described in an inverted order,

1. Thy labour·	6. Thou hast borne for my name's sake and hast not fainted.
2. Thy patience:	5. Thou hast patience:
3. Thou canst not bear evil men:	4. Thou hast tried those who say they are apostles and are not, and hast found them liars.

And thy patience—Notwithstanding which *thou canst not bear* that incorrigibly wicked men should remain in the flock of Christ. *And thou hast tried those who say they are apostles, and are not*—For the Lord hath not sent them.

Verse 4. *But I have against thee, that thou hast left thy first love*—That love for which all that church was so eminent when St. Paul wrote his epistle to them. He need not have *left* this. He might have retained it entire to the end. And he did retain it in part, or there could not have remained so much of what was commendable in him. But he had not kept, as he might have done, the first tender love in its vigour and warmth. Reader, hast thou?

Verse 5 It is not possible for any to recover the first love, but by taking these three steps, 1 *Remember:* 2. *Repent:* 3. *Do the first works. Remember from whence thou art fallen*—From what degree of faith, love, holiness, though perhaps insensibly. *And repent*—Which in the very lowest sense implies a deep and lively conviction of thy fall. Of the seven angels, two, at Ephesus and at Pergamos, were in a mixed state; two, at Sardis and at Laodicea, were greatly corrupted: all these are

if not, I come to thee, and will remove thy candlestick out
6 of its place, unless thou repent. But thou hast this, that
thou hatest the works of the Nicolaitans, which I also hate.
7 He that hath an ear, let him hear what the Spirit saith to

exhorted to repent; as are the followers of Jezebel at Thyatira: two, at Smyrna and Philadelphia, were in a flourishing state, and are therefore only exhorted to steadfastness.

There can be no state, either of any pastor, church, or single person, which has not here suitable instructions. All, whether ministers or hearers, together with their secret or open enemies, in all places and all ages, may draw hence necessary self-knowledge, reproof, commendation, warning, or confirmation. Whether any be as dead as the angel at Sardis, or as much alive as the angel at Philadelphia, this book is sent to him, and the Lord Jesus hath something to say to him therein. For the seven churches with their angels represent the whole Christian church, dispersed throughout the whole world, as it subsists, not, as some have imagined, in one age after another, but in every age. This is a point of deep importance, and always necessary to be remembered: that these seven churches are, as it were, a sample of the whole church of Christ, as it was then, as it is now, and as it will be in all ages. *Do the first works*—Outwardly and inwardly, or thou canst never regain the first love. *But if not*—By this word is the warning sharpened to those five churches which are called to repent; for if Ephesus was threatened, how much more shall Sardis and Laodicea be afraid! And according as they obey the call or not, there is a promise or a threatening, Rev. ii. 5, 16, 22; iii. 3, 20. But even in the threatening the promise is implied, in case of true repentance. *I come to thee, and will remove thy candlestick out of its place*—I will remove, unless thou repent, the flock now under thy care to another place, where they shall be better taken care of. But from the flourishing state of the church of Ephesus after this, there is reason to believe he did repent.

Verse 6. *But thou hast this*—Divine grace seeks whatever may help him that is fallen to recover his standing. *That thou hatest the works of the Nicolaitans*—Probably so called from Nicolas, one of the seven deacons, Acts vi. 5. Their doctrines and lives were equally corrupt. They allowed the most abominable lewdness and adulteries, as well as sacrificing to idols; all which they placed among things indifferent, and pleaded for as branches of Christian liberty.

Verse 7. *He that hath an ear, let him hear*—Every man, whoever can hear at all, ought carefully to hear this. *What the Spirit saith*—In these great and precious promises. *To the churches*—And in them to every one that overcometh; that goeth on from faith and by faith to full victory over the world, and the flesh, and the devil.

In these seven letters twelve promises are contained, which are an extract of all the promises of God. Some of them are not expressly mentioned again in this book, as "the hidden manna," the inscription of "the

the churches; To him that overcometh will I give to eat
of the tree of life, which is in the paradise of my God.
8 And to the angel of the church at Smyrna write; These
things saith the first and the last, who was dead and is alive;
9 I know thy affliction, and poverty, (but thou art rich,) and
the reviling of those who say they are Jews, and are not, but
10 a synagogue of Satan. Fear none of those things which thou
art about to suffer: behold, the devil is about to cast some

name of the new Jerusalem," the "sitting upon the throne." Some resemble what is afterwards mentioned, as "the hidden name," Rev. xix. 12; "the ruling the nations," Rev. xix. 15; "the morning star," Rev. xxii. 16. And some are expressly mentioned, as "the tree of life," Rev. xxii. 2; freedom from "the second death," Rev. xx. 6; the name in "the book of life," Rev. xx. 12; xxi. 27; the remaining "in the temple of God," . vii. 15; the inscription of "the name of God and of the Lamb," Rev. xiv. 1; xxii. 4. In these promises sometimes the enjoyment of the highest goods, sometimes deliverance from the greatest evils, is mentioned. And each implies the other, so that where either part is expressed, the whole is to be understood. That part is expressed which has most resemblance to the virtues or works of him that was spoken to in the letter preceding. *To eat of the tree of life*—The first thing promised in these letters is the last and highest in the accomplishment, Rev. xxii. 2, 14, 19. *The tree of life* and *the water of life* go together, Rev. xxii. 1, 2; both implying the living with God eternally. *In the paradise of my God*—The word *paradise* means a garden of pleasure. In the earthly paradise there was one tree of life: there are no other trees in the paradise of God.

Verse 8. *These things saith the first and the last, who was dead and is alive*—How directly does this description tend to confirm him against the fear of death! verses 10, 11. Even with the comfort wherewith St. John himself was comforted, Rev. i. 17, 18, shall the angel of this church be comforted.

Verse 9. *I know thy affliction and poverty*—A poor prerogative in the eyes of the world! The angel at Philadelphia likewise had in their sight but "a little strength." And yet these two were the most honourable of all in the eyes of the Lord. *But thou art rich*—In faith and love, of more value than all the kingdoms of the earth. *Who say they are Jews*—God's own people. *And are not*—They are not Jews inwardly, not circumcised in heart. *But a synagogue of Satan*—Who, like them, was a liar and a murderer from the beginning.

Verse 10. The first and last words of this verse are particularly directed to the minister; whence we may gather, that his suffering and the affliction of the church were at the same time, and of the same continuance. *Fear none of those things which thou art about to suffer*—Probably by means of the false Jews. *Behold*—This intimates the nearness of the affliction Perhaps the *ten days* began on the very day that the Revelation was read at Smyrna, or at least very soon after. *The devil*—Who sets all persecu-

of you into prison, that ye may be tried; and ye shall have
affliction ten days: be thou faithful unto death, and I will
11 give thee the crown of life. He that hath an ear, let him
hear what the Spirit saith to the churches; He that overcometh shall not be hurt by the second death.
12 And to the angel of the church at Pergamos write; These
13 things saith he who hath the sharp two-edged sword; I know
where thou dwellest, where the throne of Satan *is*: and thou
holdest fast my name, and hast not denied my faith, even in
the days wherein Antipas *was* my faithful witness, who was
14 slain among you, where Satan dwelleth. But I have a few
things against thee, that thou hast there them that hold the
doctrine of Balaam, who taught Balak to cast a stumblingblock before the sons of Israel, to eat things sacrificed to

tors to work; and these more particularly. *Is about to cast some of you*—Christians at Smyrna; where, in the first ages, the blood of many martyrs was shed. *Into prison, that ye may be tried*—To your unspeakable advantage, 1 Pet. iv. 12, 14. *And ye shall have affliction*—Either in your own persons, or by sympathizing with your brethren. *Ten days*—(Literally taken) in the end of Domitian's persecution, which was stopped by the edict of the emperor Nerva. *Be thou faithful*—Our Lord does not say, "till I come," as in the other letters, but *unto death*—Signifying that the angel of this church should quickly after seal his testimony with his blood; fifty years before the martyrdom of Polycarp, for whom some have mistaken him. *And I will give thee the crown of life*—The peculiar reward of them who are *faithful unto death.*

Verse 11. *The second death*—The lake of fire, the portion of the fearful, who do not overcome, Rev. xxi. 8.

Verse 12. *The sword*—With which I will cut off the impenitent, verse 16.

Verse 13. *Where the throne of Satan is*—Pergamos was above measure given to idolatry: so Satan had his throne and full residence there. *Thou holdest fast my name*—Openly and resolutely confessing me before men. *Even in the days wherein Antipas*—Martyred under Domitian. *Was my faithful witness*—Happy is he to whom Jesus, the faithful and true witness, giveth such a testimony!

Verse 14. *But thou hast there*—Whom thou oughtest to have immediately cast out from the flock. *Them that hold the doctrine of Balaam*—Doctrine nearly resembling his. *Who taught Balak*—And the rest of the Moabites. *To cast a stumblingblock before the sons of Israel*—They are generally termed, *the children*, but here, *the sons, of Israel*, in opposition to the *daughters* of Moab, by whom Balaam enticed them to fornication and idolatry. *To eat things sacrificed to idols*—Which, in so idolatrous a city as Pergamos, was in the highest degree hurtful to Christianity. *And*

15 idols, and to commit fornication. In like manner thou also
hast them that hold the doctrine of the Nicolaitans, which I
16 hate. Repent therefore; if not, I come to thee, and will
17 fight against them with the sword of my mouth. He that
hath an ear let him hear what the Spirit saith to the
churches; To him that overcometh will I give of the hidden
manna, and will give him a white stone, and on the stone a
new name written, which none knoweth but he that
receiveth it.
18 And to the angel of the church at Thyatira write; These
things saith the Son of God, who hath eyes as a flame of

to commit fornication—Which was constantly joined with the idol-worship of the heathens.

Verse 15. *In like manner thou also*—As well as the angel at Ephesus. *Hast them that hold the doctrine of the Nicolaitans*—And thou sufferest them to remain in the flock.

Verse 16. *If not, I come to thee*—Who wilt not wholly escape when I punish them. *And will fight with them*—Not with the Nicolaitans, who are mentioned only by the by, but the followers of Balaam. *With the sword of my mouth*—With my just and fierce displeasure. Balaam himself was first withstood by the angel of the Lord with "his sword drawn," Num. xxii. 23, and afterwards "slain with the sword," Num. xxxi. 8.

Verse 17. *To him that overcometh*—And eateth not of those sacrifices. *Will I give of the hidden manna*—Described, John vi. The new name answers to this: it is now "hid with Christ in God." The Jewish manna was kept in the ancient ark of the covenant. The heavenly ark of the covenant appears under the trumpet of the seventh angel, Rev. xi. 19, where also the hidden manna is mentioned again. It seems properly to mean, the full, glorious, everlasting fruition of God. *And I will give him a white stone*—The ancients, on many occasions, gave their votes in judgment by small stones; by black, they condemned; by white ones they acquitted. Sometimes also they wrote on small smooth stones. Here may be an allusion to both. *And a new name*—So Jacob, after his victory, gained the new name of Israel. Wouldest thou know what thy new name will be? The way to this is plain,—overcome. Till then all thy inquiries are vain. Thou wilt then read it on the white stone.

Verse 18. *And to the angel of the church at Thyatira*—Where the faithful were but a little flock. *These things saith the Son of God*—See how great he is, who appeared "like a son of man!" Rev. i. 13. *Who hath eyes as a flame of fire*—"Searching the reins and the heart," verse 23. *And feet like fine brass*—Denoting his immense strength. Job comprises both these, his wisdom to discern whatever is amiss, and his power to avenge it, in one sentence, Job xlii. 2, "No thought is hidden from him, and he can do all things."

19 fire, and feet like fine brass; I know thy love and faith,
and thy service and patience; and thy last works more than
20 the first. But I have against thee, that thou sufferest that
woman Jezebel, who calleth herself a prophetess, and teacheth and seduceth my servants to commit fornication, and
21 to eat things sacrificed to idols. And I gave her time to
22 repent of her fornication; but she will not repent. Behold,
I will cast her into a bed, and them that commit adultery
with her into great affliction, unless they repent of her
23 works. And I will kill her children with death; and all the
churches shall know that I am he who searcheth the reins

Verse 19. *I know thy love*—How different a character is this from that of the angel of the church at Ephesus! The latter could not bear the wicked, and hated the works of the Nicolaitans; but had left his first love and first works. The former retained his first love, and had more and more works, but did bear the wicked, did not withstand them with becoming vehemence. Mixed characters both; yet the latter, not the former, is reproved for his fall, and commanded to repent. *And faith, and thy service, and patience*—Love is shown, exercised, and improved by serving God and our neighbour; so is faith by patience and good works.

Verse 20. *But thou sufferest that woman Jezebel*—Who ought not to teach at all, 1 Tim. ii. 12. To *teach and seduce my servants*—At Pergamos were many followers of Balaam; at Thyatira, one grand deceiver. Many of the ancients have delivered, that this was the wife of the pastor himself. Jezebel of old led the people of God to open idolatry. This Jezebel, fitly called by her name, from the resemblance between their works, led them to partake in the idolatry of the heathens. This she seems to have done by first enticing them to fornication, just as Balaam did: whereas at Pergamos they were first enticed to idolatry, and afterwards to fornication.

Verse 21. *And I gave her time to repent*—So great is the power of Christ! *But she will not repent*—So, though repentance is the gift of God, man may refuse it; God will not compel.

Verse 22. *I will cast her into a bed—into great affliction—and them that commit* either carnal or spiritual *adultery with her, unless they repent*—She had her time before. *Of her works*—Those to which she had enticed them and which she had committed with them.

It is observable, the angel of the church at Thyatira was only blamed for suffering her. This fault ceased when God took vengeance on her. Therefore he is not expressly exhorted to repent, though it is implied.

Verse 23. *And I will kill her children*—Those which she hath borne in adultery, and them whom she hath seduced. *With death*—This expression denotes death by the plague, or by some manifest stroke of God's hand. Probably the remarkable vengeance taken on her children was

and hearts: and I will give you every one according to your
24 works. But I say to you, the rest that are at Thyatira, as
many as do not hold this doctrine, who have not known the
depths of Satan, as they speak; I will lay upon you no
25 other burden. But what ye have hold fast till I come.
26 And he that overcometh, and keepeth my works unto the
27 end, to him will I give power over the nations: And he
shall rule them with a rod of iron; they shall be dashed in
pieces like a potter's vessels: as I also have received from
28 my Father. And I will give him the morning star. He
29 that hath an ear, let him hear what the Spirit saith to the
churches.

CHAP. III. 1 And to the angel of the church at Sardis

the token of the certainty of all the rest. *And all the churches*—To which thou now writest. *Shall know that I search the reins*—The desires. *And hearts*—Thoughts.

Verse 24. *But I say to you* who *do not hold this doctrine*—Of Jezebel. *Who have not known the depths of Satan*—O happy ignorance! *As they speak*—That were continually boasting of the deep things which they taught. Our Lord owns they were deep, even deep as hell: for they were the very *depths of Satan.* Were these the same of which Martin Luther speaks? It is well if there are not some of his countrymen now in England who know them too well! *I will lay upon you no other burden*—Than that you have already suffered from Jezebel and her adherents.

Verse 25. *What ye*—Both the angel and the church *have.*

Verse 26. *My works*—Those which I have commanded. *To him will I give power over the nations*—That is, I will give him to share with me in that glorious victory which the Father hath promised me over all the nations who as yet resist me, Psalm ii. 8, 9.

Verse 27. *And he shall rule them*—That is, shall share with me when I do this. *With a rod of iron*—With irresistible power, employed on those only who will not otherwise submit; who will hereby *be dashed in pieces*—Totally conquered.

Verse 28. *I will give him the morning star*—Thou, O Jesus, art the morning star! O give thyself to me! Then will I desire no sun, only thee, who art the sun also. He whom this star enlightens has always morning and no evening. The duties and promises here answer each other; the valiant conqueror has power over the stubborn nations. And he that, after having conquered his enemies, keeps the works of Christ to the end, shall have the morning star,—an unspeakable brightness and peaceable dominion in him.

Verse 1. *The seven spirits of God*—The Holy Spirit, from whom alone

write; These things saith he that hath the seven spirits
of God, and the seven stars; I know thy works, that thou
2 hast a name that thou livest, but art dead. Be watchful,
and strengthen the things which remain, which were ready
to die; for I have not found thy works complete before my
3 God. Remember therefore how thou hast received and
heard, and hold fast, and repent. If thou watch not, I will
come as a thief, and thou shalt not know at what hour I
4 will come upon thee. Yet thou hast a few names in Sardis
who have not defiled their garments; and they shall walk
5 with me in white: they are worthy. He that overcometh,
he shall be clothed in white raiment; and I will not blot
his name out of the book of life, and I will confess his
6 name before my Father, and before his angels. He that
hath an ear, let him hear what the Spirit saith to the
churches.
7 And to the angel of the church at Philadelphia write;

all spiritual life and strength proceed. *And the seven stars*—Which are subordinate to him. *Thou hast a name that thou livest*—A fair reputation, a goodly outside appearance. But that Spirit seeth through all things, and every empty appearance vanishes before him.

Verse 2. *The things which remain*—In thy soul; knowledge of the truth, good desires, and convictions. *Which were ready to die*—Where-ever pride, indolence, or levity revives, all the fruits of the Spirit are *ready to die.*

Verse 3. *Remember how*—Humbly, zealously, seriously. *Thou* didst *receive* the grace of God once, *and hear*—His word. *And hold fast*—The grace thou hast received. *And repent*—According to the word thou hast heard.

Verse 4. *Yet thou hast a few names*—That is, persons. But though few, they had not separated themselves from the rest; otherwise, the angel of Sardis would not have had them. Yet it was no virtue of his, that they were unspotted; whereas it was his fault that they were but few. *Who have not defiled their garments*—Either by spotting themselves, or by partaking of other men's sins. *They shall walk with me in white*—In joy; in perfect holiness; in glory. *They are worthy*—A few good among many bad are doubly acceptable to God. O how much happier is this worthiness than that mentioned, Rev. xvi. 6!

Verse 5. *He shall be clothed in white raiment*—The colour of victory, joy, and triumph. *And I will not blot his name out of the book of life*—Like that of the angel of the church at Sardis: but he shall live for ever. *I will confess his name*—As one of my faithful servants and soldiers.

Verse 7 *The holy one, the true one*—Two great and glorious names

CHAPTER III

These things saith the holy one, the true one, he that hath
the key of David, he that openeth, and none shutteth ; and
8 shutteth, and none openeth ; I know thy works, (behold, I
have given before thee an opened door, none can shut it,)
that thou hast a little strength, and hast kept my word,
9 and hast not denied my name. Behold, I bring them
of the synagogue of Satan, who say they are Jews, and are
not, but lie ; behold, I will make them come and bow down
10 before thy feet, and know that I have loved thee. Because
thou hast kept the word of my patience, I also will keep
thee from the hour of temptation, which shall come upon

He that hath the key of David—A master of a family, or a prince, has one or more keys, wherewith he can open and shut all the doors of his house or palace. So had David a key, a token of right and sovereignty, which was afterward adjudged to Eliakim, Isaiah xxii. 22. Much more has Christ, the Son of David, the key of the spiritual city of David, the New Jerusalem ; the supreme right, power, and authority, as in his own house. He *openeth* this to all that overcome, *and none shutteth :* he *shutteth* it against all the fearful, *and none openeth.* Likewise when he openeth a door on earth for his works or his servants, none can shut ; and when he shutteth against whatever would hurt or defile, none can open.

Verse 8. *I have given before thee an opened door*—To enter into the joy of thy Lord ; and, meantime, to go on unhindered in every good work. *Thou hast a little strength*—But little outward human strength ; a little, poor, mean, despicable company. Yet thou *hast kept my word*—Both in judgment and practice.

Verse 9. *Behold, I*—Who have all power ; and they must then comply *I will make them come and bow down before thy feet*—Pay thee the lowest homage. *And know*—At length, that all depends on my love, and that thou hast a place therein. O how often does the judgment of the people turn quite round, when the Lord looketh upon them ! Job xlii. 7, &c.

Verse 10. *Because thou hast kept the word of my patience*—The word of Christ is indeed a *word of patience. I also will keep thee*—O happy exemption from that spreading calamity ! *From the hour of temptation*—So that thou shalt not enter into temptation ; but it shall pass over thee. *The hour* denotes the short time of its continuance ; that is, at any one place. At every one it was very sharp, though short ; wherein the great tempter was not idle, Rev. ii. 10. *Which* hour *shall come upon the whole earth*—The whole Roman empire. It went over the Christians, and over the Jews and heathens ; though in a very different manner. This was the time of the persecution under the seemingly virtuous emperor Trajan The two preceding persecutions were under those monsters, Nero and Domitian ; but Trajan was so admired for his goodness, and his persecution was of such a nature, that it was a temptation indeed, and did throughly *try them that dwelt upon the earth.*

11 the whole world, to try them that dwell upon the earth. I
come quickly: hold fast what thou hast, that none take thy
12 crown. He that overcometh, I will make him a pillar in
the temple of my God, and he shall go out no more: and
I will write upon him the name of my God, and the name
of the city of my God, the new Jerusalem, which cometh
13 down out of heaven from my God; and my new name. He
that hath an ear, let him hear what the Spirit saith to the
churches.
14 And to the angel of the church at Laodicea write; These
things saith the Amen, the faithful and true witness, the
15 beginning of the creation of God; I know thy works, that
16 thou art neither cold nor hot: O that thou wert cold or hot!
So because thou art lukewarm, and neither cold nor hot, I am
17 about to spue thee out of my mouth. Because thou sayest, I
am rich, and have enriched myself, and have need of nothing;

Verse 11. *Thy crown*—Which is ready for thee, if thou endure to the end.

Verse 12. *I will make him a pillar in the temple of my God*—I will fix him as beautiful, as useful, and as immovable as a pillar in the church of God *And he shall go out no more*—But shall be holy and happy for ever. *And I will write upon him the name of my God*—So that the nature and image of God shall appear visibly upon him. *And the name of the city of my God*—Giving him a title to dwell in the *New Jerusalem* *And my new name*—A share in that joy which I entered into, after overcoming all my enemies.

Verse 14. *To the angel of the church at Laodicea*—For these St. Paul had had a great concern, Col. ii. 1. *These things saith the Amen*—That is, the True One, the God of truth. *The beginning*—The Author, Prince, and Ruler. *Of the creation of God*—Of all creatures; *the beginning*, or Author, by whom God made them all.

Verse 15. *I know thy works*—Thy disposition and behaviour, though thou knowest it not thyself. *That thou art neither cold*—An utter stranger to the things of God, having no care or thought about them. *Nor hot*—As boiling water: so ought we to be penetrated and heated by the fire of love. *O that thou wert*—This wish of our Lord plainly implies that he does not work on us irresistibly, as the fire does on the water which it heats. *Cold or hot*—Even if thou wert *cold*, without any thought or profession of religion, there would be more hope of thy recovery.

Verse 16. *So because thou art lukewarm*—The effect of lukewarm water is well known. *I am about to spue thee out of my mouth*—I will utterly cast thee from me; that is, unless thou repent.

Verse 17. *Because thou sayest*—Therefore "I counsel thee," &c. *I am rich*—In gifts and grace, as well as worldly goods. *And knowest not that thou art*—In God's account, *wretched and pitiable.*

and knowest not that thou art wretched, and pitiable, and
18 poor, and blind, and naked: I counsel thee to buy of me
gold purified in the fire, that thou mayest be rich; and
white raiment, that thou mayest be clothed, and the shame
of thy nakedness may not appear; and eyesalve to anoint
19 thine eyes, that thou mayest see. Whomsoever I love, I
20 rebuke and chasten be zealous, and repent. Behold, I
stand at the door, and knock: if any man hear my voice,
and open the door, I will come in to him, and sup with him,
21 and he with me. He that overcometh, I will give him to
sit with me on my throne, as I also have overcome, and sat
22 down with my Father on his throne. He that hath an ear,
let him hear what the Spirit saith to the churches.

Verse 18. *I counsel thee*—Who art poor, and blind, and naked. *To buy of me*—Without money or price. *Gold purified in the fire*—True, living faith, which is purified in the furnace of affliction. *And white raiment*—True holiness *And eyesalve*—Spiritual illumination; the "unction of the Holy One," which teacheth all things.

Verse 19. *Whomsoever I love*—Even thee, thou poor Laodicean! O how much has his unwearied love to do! *I rebuke*—For what is past. *And chasten*—That they may amend for the time to come.

Verse 20. *I stand at the door, and knock*—Even at this instant; while he is speaking this word. *If any man open*—Willingly receive me. *I will sup with him*—Refreshing him with my graces and gifts, and delighting myself in what I have given. *And he with me*—In life everlasting

Verse 21. *I will give him to sit with me on my throne*—In unspeakable happiness and glory. Elsewhere, heaven itself is termed the throne of God: but this throne is in heaven.

Verse 22. *He that hath an ear, let him hear*, &c.—This stands in the three former letters before the promise; in the four latter, after it; clearly dividing the seven into two parts; the first containing three, the last, four letters. The titles given our Lord in the three former letters peculiarly respect his power after his resurrection and ascension, particularly over his church; those in the four latter, his divine glory, and unity with the Father and the Holy Spirit. Again, this word being placed before the promises in the three former letters, excludes the false apostles at Ephesus, the false Jews at Smyrna, and the partakers with the heathens at Pergamos, from having any share therein. In the four latter, being placed after them, it leaves the promises immediately joined with Christ's address to the angel of the church, to show that the fulfilling of these was near; whereas the others reach beyond the end of the world. It should be observed, that the overcoming, or victory, (to which alone these peculiar promises are annexed,) is not the ordinary victory obtained by every believer; but a special victory over great and peculiar temptations, by those that are strong in faith.

CHAP IV. 1 After these things I saw, and, behold, **a door**
opened in heaven: and the first voice which I had heard, **as**
of a trumpet talking with me, said, Come up hither, and I
2 **will show thee things** which must be hereafter. And imme-
diately I was in the spirit: and, behold, a throne was set in

CHAP. IV We are now entering upon the main prophecy. The whole Revelation may be divided thus:—

The first, second, and third chapters contain the introduction;

The fourth and fifth, the proposition;

The sixth, seventh, eighth, and ninth describe things which are already fulfilled;

The tenth to the fourteenth, things which are now fulfilling;

The fifteenth to the nineteenth, things which will be fulfilled shortly;

The twentieth, twenty-first, and twenty-second, things at a greater distance.

Verse 1. *After these things*—As if he had said, After I had written these letters from the mouth of the Lord. By the particle *and*, the several parts of this prophecy are usually connected: by the expression, *after these things*, they are distinguished from each other, Rev. vii. 9; xix. 1. By that expression, *and after these things*, they are distinguished, and yet connected, Rev. vii. 1; xv. 5; xviii. 1. St. John always saw and heard, and then immediately wrote down one part after another: and one part is constantly divided from another by some one of these expressions. *I saw*—Here begins the relation of the main vision, which is connected throughout; as it appears from "the throne, and him that sitteth thereon;" "the Lamb;" (who hitherto has appeared in the form of a man;) "the four living creatures;" and "the four and twenty elders," represented from this place to the end. From this place, it is absolutely necessary to keep in mind the genuine order of the texts, as it stands in the preceding table. *A door opened in heaven*—Several of these openings are successively mentioned. Here *a door* is *opened;* afterward, "the temple of God in heaven," Rev xi. 19; xv. 5; and, at last, "heaven" itself, Rev. xix. 11. By each of these St John gains a new and more extended prospect. *And the first voice which I had heard*—Namely, that of Christ: afterward, he heard the voices of many others. *Said, Come up hither*—Not in body, but in spirit; which was immediately done.

Verse 2. *And immediately I was in the spirit*—Even in an higher degree than before, Rev. i. 10. *And, behold, a throne was set in heaven*—St. John is to write "things which shall be;" and, in order thereto, he is here shown, after an heavenly manner, how whatever "shall be," whether good or bad, flows out of invisible fountains; and how, after it is done on the visible theatre of the world and the church, it flows back again into the invisible world, as its proper and final scope Here commentators divide some proceed theologically; others, historically; whereas the right way is, to join both together.

The court of heaven is here laid open; and the throne of God is, as it

3 **heaven, and one sitting on the throne. And he that sat was**
in appearance like a jasper and a sardine stone: and a rainbow
***was* round about the throne, in appearance like an emerald**
4 **And round about the throne *are* four and twenty thrones**
and on the thrones four and twenty elders sitting, clothed
in white raiment; and upon their heads crowns of gold.

were, the centre from which everything in the visible world goes forth, and to which everything returns. Here, also, the kingdom of Satan is disclosed; and hence we may extract the most important things out of the most comprehensive and, at the same time, most secret history of the kingdom of hell and heaven. But herein we must be content to know only what is expressly revealed in this book. This describes, not barely what good or evil is successively transacted on earth, but how each springs from the kingdom of light or darkness, and continually tends to the source whence it sprung: so that no man can explain all that is contained therein, from the history of the church militant only.

And yet the histories of past ages have their use, as this book is properly prophetical. The more, therefore, we observe the accomplishment of it, so much the more may we praise God, in his truth, wisdom, justice, and almighty power, and learn to suit ourselves to the time, according to the remarkable directions contained in the prophecy. *And one sat on the throne*—As a king, governor, and judge. Here is described God, the Almighty, the Father of heaven, in his majesty, glory, and dominion

Verse 3. *And he that sat was in appearance*—Shone with a visible lustre, like that of sparkling precious stones, such as those which were of old on the high priest's breastplate, and those placed as the foundations of the new Jerusalem, Rev. xxi. 19, 20. If there is anything emblematical in the colours of these stones, possibly the *jasper*, which is transparent and of a glittering white, with an intermixture of beautiful colours, may be a symbol of God's purity, with various other perfections, which shine in all his dispensations. The *sardine stone*, of a blood-red colour, may be an emblem of his justice, and the vengeance he was about to execute on his enemies. *An emerald*, being green, may betoken favour to the good; *a rainbow*, the everlasting covenant. See Gen. ix. 9. And this being *round about the* whole breadth of the *throne*, fixed the distance of those who stood or sat round it.

Verse 4. *And round about the throne*—In a circle, *are four and twenty thrones, and on the thrones four and twenty elders*—The most holy of all the former ages, Isai. xxiv. 23; Heb. xii. 1; representing the whole body of the saints. *Sitting*—In general; but falling down when they worship. *Clothed in white raiment*—This and their *golden crowns* show, that they had already finished their course and taken their place among the citizens of heaven. They are never termed *souls*, and hence it is probable that they had glorified bodies already Compare Matt. xxvii. 52.

5 And out of the throne go forth lightnings and voices and
thunders: and seven lamps of fire burn before the throne,
6 which are the seven Spirits of God. And before the throne
is a sea as of glass, like crystal: and in the midst of the
throne, and round about the throne, four living creatures,
7 full of eyes before and behind. And the first living creature

Verse 5. *And out of the throne go forth lightnings*—Which affect the sight. *Voices*—Which affect the hearing. *Thunderings*—Which cause the whole body to tremble. Weak men account all this terrible; but to the inhabitants of heaven it is a mere source of joy and pleasure, mixed with reverence to the Divine Majesty. Even to the saints on earth these convey light and protection; but to their enemies, terror and destruction.

Verse 6. *And before the throne is a sea as of glass, like crystal*—Wide and deep, pure and clear, transparent and still. Both the "seven lamps of fire" and this sea are *before the throne;* and both may mean "the seven spirits of God," the Holy Ghost; whose powers and operations are frequently represented both under the emblem of fire and of water. We read again, Rev. xv. 2, of "a sea as of glass," where there is no mention of "the seven lamps of fire;" but, on the contrary, the sea itself is "mingled with fire." We read also, Rev. xxii. 1, of "a stream of water of life, clear as crystal." Now, the sea which is before the throne, and the stream which goes out of the throne, may both mean the same; namely, the Spirit of God. *And in the midst of the throne*—With respect to its height. *Round about the throne*—That is, toward the four quarters, east, west, north, and south. *Were four living creatures*—Not beasts, no more than birds. These seem to be taken from the cherubim in the visions of Isaiah and Ezekiel, and in the holy of holies. They are doubtless some of the principal powers of heaven; but of what order, it is not easy to determine. It is very probable that the twenty-four elders may represent the Jewish church: their harps seem to intimate their having belonged to the ancient tabernacle service, where they were wont to be used. If so, the *living creatures* may represent the Christian church. Their number, also, is symbolical of universality, and agrees with the dispensation of the gospel, which extended to all nations under heaven. And the "new song" which they all sing, saying, "Thou hast redeemed us out of every kindred, and tongue, and people, and nation," Rev. v. 9, could not possibly suit the Jewish without the Christian church. *The first living creature was like a lion*—To signify undaunted courage. *The second, like a calf*—Or ox, Ezek. i. 10, to signify unwearied patience. *The third, with the face of a man*—To signify prudence and compassion. *The fourth, like an eagle*—To signify activity and vigour. *Full of eyes*—To betoken wisdom and knowledge. *Before*—To see the face of him that sitteth on the throne. *And behind*—To see what is done among the creatures.

Verse 7. *And the first*—Just such were the four cherubim in Ezekiel, who supported the moving throne of God; whereas each of those that

is like a lion, and the second living creature *is* like a calf,
and the third living creature hath a face as a man, and the
8 fourth *is* like a flying eagle. And the four living creatures
hath each of them six wings; round about and within they
are full of eyes: and they rest not day and night, saying,
Holy, holy, holy is the Lord God, the Almighty, who was,

overshadowed the mercy-seat in the holy of holies had all these four faces: whence a late great man supposes them to have been emblematic of the Trinity, and the incarnation of the second Person. *A flying eagle*—That is, with wings expanded.

Verse 8. *Each of them hath six wings*—As had each of the seraphim in Isaiah's vision. "Two covered his face," in token of humility and reverence: "two his feet," perhaps in token of readiness and diligence for executing divine commissions. *Round about and within they are full of eyes. Round about*—To see everything which is farther off from the throne than they are themselves. *And within*—On the inner part of the circle which they make with one another. First, they look from the centre to the circumference, then from the circumference to the centre. *And they rest not*—O happy unrest! *Day and night*—As we speak on earth. But there is no night in heaven. *And say, Holy, holy, holy*—Is the Three-One God.

There are two words in the original, very different from each other; both which we translate *holy*. The one means properly *merciful;* but the other, which occurs here, implies much more. This holiness is the sum of all praise, which is given to the almighty Creator, for all that he does and reveals concerning himself, till the new song brings with it new matter of glory.

This word properly signifies *separated,* both in Hebrew and other languages. And when God is termed holy, it denotes that excellence which is altogether peculiar to himself; and the glory flowing from all his attributes conjoined, shining forth from all his works, and darkening all things besides itself, whereby he is, and eternally remains, in an incomprehensible manner separate and at a distance, not only from all that is impure, but likewise from all that is created.

God is separate from all things. He is, and works from himself, out of himself, in himself, through himself, for himself. Therefore, he is the first and the last, the only one and the Eternal, living and happy, endless and unchangeable, almighty, omniscient, wise and true, just and faithful, gracious and merciful.

Hence it is, that *holy* and *holiness* mean the same as *God* and *Godhead:* and as we say of a king, "His Majesty;" so the scripture says of God, "His Holiness," Heb. xii. 10. The Holy Spirit is the Spirit of God. When God is spoken of, he is often named "the Holy One:" and as God swears by his name, so he does also by his holiness; that is, by himself.

This holiness is often styled *glory:* often his holiness and glory are celebrated together, Lev. x. 3; Isai. vi. 3. For holiness is covered glory,

9 and who is, and who cometh. And when the living creatures
give glory and honour and thanks to him that sitteth upon
10 the throne, that liveth for ever and ever, The four and
twenty elders fall down before him that sitteth upon the
throne, and worship him that liveth for ever and ever, and
11 cast their crowns before the throne, saying, Worthy art
thou, O Lord our God, to receive the glory, and the honour,
and the power: for thou hast created all things, and through
thy will they were and are created.

CHAP. V. 1 And I saw in the right hand of him that
sat upon the throne a book written within and without,

and glory is uncovered holiness The scripture speaks abundantly of the holiness and glory of the Father, the Son, and the Holy Ghost And hereby is the mystery of the Holy Trinity eminently confirmed.

That is also termed *holy* which is consecrated to him, and for that end separated from other things: and so is that wherein we may be like God, or united to him.

In the hymn resembling this, recorded by Isaiah, chap. vi. 3, is added, "The whole earth is full of his glory." But this is deferred in the Revelation, till the glory of the Lord (his enemies being destroyed) fills the earth.

Verses 9, 10. *And when the living creatures give glory—the elders fall down*—That is, as often as the living creatures give glory, immediately the elders fall down. The expression implies, that they did so at the same instant, and that they both did this frequently. The living creatures do not say directly, "Holy, holy, holy art thou;" but only bend a little, out of deep reverence, and say, "Holy, holy, holy is the Lord." But the elders, when they are *fallen down,* may say, "Worthy art thou, O Lord our God."

Verse 11. *Worthy art thou to receive*—This he receives not only when he is thus praised, but also when he destroys his enemies and glorifies himself anew. *The glory and the honour and the power*—Answering the thrice-holy of the living creatures, verse 9. *For thou hast created all things*—Creation is the ground of all the works of God: therefore, for this, as well as for his other works, will he be praised to all eternity. *And through thy will they were*—They began to be. It is to the free, gracious, and powerfully-working will of Him who cannot possibly need anything that all things owe their first existence. *And are created*—That is, continue in being ever since they were created.

Verse 1. *And I saw*—This is a continuation of the same narrative. *In the right hand*—The emblem of his all-ruling power. He held it openly, in order to give it to him that was worthy. It is scarce needful to observe, that there is not in heaven any real book of parchment or paper

2 sealed with seven seals. And I saw a strong angel proclaiming with a loud voice, Who *is* worthy to open the book, and
3 to loose the seals thereof? And none in heaven, or on earth,
neither under the earth, was able to open the book, neither
4 to look thereon. And I wept much, that none was found

or that Christ does not really stand there, in the shape of a lion or of a lamb. Neither is there on earth any monstrous beast with seven heads and ten horns. But as there is upon earth something which, in its kind, answers such a representation; so there are in heaven divine counsels and transactions answerable to these figurative expressions. All this was represented to St. John at Patmos, in one day, by way of vision. But the accomplishment of it extends from that time throughout all ages. Writings serve to inform us of distant and of future things. And hence things which are yet to come are figuratively said to be "written in God's book;" so were at that time the contents of this weighty prophecy. But the book was sealed. Now comes the opening and accomplishing also of the great things that are, as it were, the letters of it. *A book written within and without*—That is, no part of it blank, full of matter. *Sealed with seven seals*—According to the seven principal parts contained in it, one on the outside of each. The usual books of the ancients were not like ours, but were volumes or long pieces of parchment, rolled upon a long stick, as we frequently roll silks. Such was this represented, which was *sealed with seven seals.* Not as if the apostle saw all the seals at once; for there were seven volumes wrapped up one within another, each of which was sealed: so that upon opening and unrolling the first, the second appeared to be sealed up till that was opened, and so on to the seventh. The book and its seals represent all power in heaven and earth given to Christ. A copy of this book is contained in the following chapters. By "the trumpets," contained under the seventh seal, the kingdom of the world is shaken, that it may at length become the kingdom of Christ. By "the vials," under the seventh trumpet, the power of the beast, and whatsoever is connected with it, is broken. This sum of all we should have continually before our eyes: so the whole Revelation flows in its natural order.

Verse 2. *And I saw a strong angel*—This proclamation to every creature was too great for a man to make, and yet not becoming the Lamb himself. It was therefore made by an angel, and one of uncommon eminence.

Verse 3. *And none*—No creature; no, not Mary herself. *In heaven, or in earth, neither under the earth*—That is, none in the universe. For these are the three great regions into which the whole creation is divided. *Was able to open the book*—To declare the counsels of God. *Nor to look thereon*—So as to understand any part of it.

Verse 4. *And I wept much*—A weeping which sprung from greatness of mind. The tenderness of heart which he always had appeared more clearly now he was out of his own power. The Revelation was not

5 worthy to open the book, neither to look thereon. And
one of the elders saith to me, Weep not: behold, the Lion
of the tribe of Judah, the root of David, hath prevailed to
6 open the book, and the seals thereof. And I beheld in the
midst of the throne and of the four living creatures, and in
the midst of the elders, a Lamb standing as if he had been
slain, having seven horns and seven eyes, which are the seven
7 spirits of God sent forth into all the earth. And he came
and took the book out of the right hand of him that sat upon

written without tears; neither without tears will it be understood. How far are they from the temper of St. John who inquire after anything rather than the contents of this book! yea, who applaud their own clemency if they excuse those that do inquire into them!

Verse 5. *And one of the elders*—Probably one of those who rose with Christ, and afterwards ascended into heaven. Perhaps one of the patriarchs. Some think it was Jacob, from whose prophecy the name of *Lion* is given him, Gen. xlix. 9. *The Lion of the tribe of Judah*—The victorious prince who is, like a lion, able to tear all his enemies in pieces. *The root of David*—As God, *the root* and source of David's family, Isai. xi. 1, 10. *Hath prevailed to open the book*—Hath overcome all obstructions, and obtained the honour to disclose the divine counsels.

Verse 6. *And I saw*—First, Christ *in* or on *the midst of the throne;* secondly, *the four living creatures* making the inner circle round him; and, thirdly, *the four and twenty elders* making a larger circle round him and them. *Standing*—He lieth no more; he no more falls on his face; the days of his weakness and mourning are ended. He is now in a posture of readiness to execute all his offices of prophet, priest, and king. *As if he had been slain*—Doubtless with the prints of the wounds which he once received. And because *he was slain,* he is worthy to open the book, verse 9, to the joy of his own people, and the terror of his enemies. *Having seven horns*—As a king, the emblem of perfect strength. *And seven eyes*—The emblem of perfect knowledge and wisdom. By these he accomplishes what is contained in the book, namely, by his almighty and all-wise Spirit. To these seven horns and seven eyes answer the seven seals and the sevenfold song of praise, verse 12. In Zechariah, likewise, iii 9, iv. 10, mention is made of "the seven eyes of the Lord, which go forth over all the earth." *Which*—Both the horns and the eyes. *Are the seven spirits of God sent forth into all the earth*—For the effectual working of the Spirit of God goes through the whole creation; and that in the natural, as well as spiritual, world. For could mere matter act or move? Could it gravitate or attract? Just as much as it can think or speak.

Verse 7. *And he came*—Here was "Ask of me," Psalm ii. 8, fulfilled in the most glorious manner. *And took*—It is one state of exaltation that reaches from our Lord's ascension to his coming in glory. Yet this

8 the throne. And when he took the book, the four living
creatures and the four and twenty elders fell down before the
Lamb, having every one an harp, and golden phials full
9 of incense, which are the prayers of the saints. And they
sing a new song, saying, Worthy art thou to take the book,
and to open the seals thereof: for thou wast slain, and hast
redeemed us to God by thy blood out of every tribe, and
10 tongue, and people, and nation; And hast made them unto
our God kings and priests: and they shall reign over the
11 earth. And I saw and heard a voice of many angels, round

state admits of various degrees. At his ascension, "angels, and principalities, and powers were subjected to him" Ten days after, he received from the Father and sent the Holy Ghost And now he *took the book out of the right hand of him that sat upon the throne*—Who gave it him as a signal of his delivering to him all power in heaven and earth. He received it, in token of his being both able and willing to fulfil all that was written therein.

Verse 8. *And when he took the book, the four living creatures fell down*—Now is homage done to the Lamb by every creature. These, together with the elders, make the beginning; and afterward, verse 14, the conclusion. They are together surrounded with a multitude of angels, verse 11, and together sing the new song, as they had before praised God together, Rev. iv 8, &c. *Having every one*—The elders, not the living creatures. *An harp*—Which was one of the chief instruments used for thanksgiving in the temple service: a fit emblem of the melody of their hearts. *And golden phials*—Cups or censers. *Full of incense, which are the prayers of the saints*—Not of the elders themselves, but of the other saints still upon earth, whose prayers were thus emblematically represented in heaven.

Verse 9. *And they sing a new song*—One which neither they nor any other had sung before. *Thou hast redeemed us*—So the living creatures also were of the number of the redeemed. This does not so much refer to the act of redemption, which was long before, as to the fruit of it; and so more directly to those who had finished their course, "who were redeemed from the earth," (Rev. xiv. 1,) *out of every tribe, and tongue, and people, and nation*—That is, out of all mankind.

Verse 10. *And hast made them*—The redeemed. So they speak of themselves also in the third person, out of deep self-abasement. *They shall reign over the earth*—The new earth: herewith agree the golden crowns of the elders. The reign of the saints in general follows, under the trumpet of the seventh angel; particularly after the first resurrection, as also in eternity, Rev. xi. 18; xv. 7; xx. 4; xxii. 5; Dan. vii. 27; Psalm xlix. 14.

Verse 11 *And I saw*—The many angels. *And heard*—The voice and the number of them. *Round about the elders*—So forming the third cir

about the throne and the living creatures and the elders: and
the number of them was ten thousand times ten thousand,
12 and thousands of thousands; Saying with a loud voice,
Worthy is the Lamb that was slain to receive the power, and
riches, and wisdom, and strength, and honour, and glory, and
13 blessing. And every creature which is in the heaven, and
on the earth, and under the earth, and on the sea, and all that
are in them, I heard them all saying, To him that sitteth on
the throne, and to the Lamb, *is* the blessing, and the honour,
14 and the glory, and the strength, for ever and ever. And the
four living creatures said, Amen. And the elders fell down
and worshipped

cle. It is remarkable, that men are represented through this whole vision as nearer to God than any of the angels. *And the number of them was*—At least two hundred millions, and two millions over. And yet these were but a part of the holy angels. Afterward, Rev. vii. 11, St. John heard them all.

Verse 12. *Worthy is the Lamb*—The elders said, verse 9, "Worthy art thou." They were more nearly allied to him than the angels. *To receive the power*, &c.—This sevenfold applause answers the seven seals, of which the four former describe all visible, the latter all invisible, things, made subject to the Lamb. And every one of these seven words bears a resemblance to the seal which it answers.

Verse 13. *And every creature*—In the whole universe, good or bad *In the heaven, on the earth, under the earth, on the sea*—With these four regions of the world, agrees the fourfold word of praise. What is *in heaven*, says *blessing;* what is *on earth, honour;* what is *under the earth, glory;* what is *on the sea, strength; is unto him.* This praise from all creatures begins before the opening of the first seal; but it continues from that time to eternity, according to the capacity of each. His enemies must acknowledge his *glory;* but those in heaven say, *Blessed* be God and the Lamb.

This royal manifesto is, as it were, a proclamation, showing how Christ fulfils all things, and "every knee bows to him," not only *on earth*, but also *in heaven, and under the earth.* This book exhausts all things, 1 Cor. xv. 27, 28, and is suitable to an heart enlarged as the sand of the sea. It inspires the attentive and intelligent reader with such a magnanimity, that he accounts nothing in this world great; no, not the whole frame of visible nature, compared to the immense greatness of what he is here called to behold, yea, and in part, to inherit.

St. John has in view, through the whole following vision, what he has been now describing, namely, the four living creatures, the elders, the angels, and all creatures, looking together at the opening of the seven seals

CHAPTER VI.

CHAP. VI. 1. And I saw when the Lamb opened one of the seven seals, and I heard one of the four living crea-

CHAP. VI. The seven seals are not distinguished from each other by specifying the time of them. They swiftly follow the letters to the seven churches, and all begin almost at the same time. By the four former is shown, that all the public occurrences of all ages and nations, as empire, war, provision, calamities, are made subject to Christ. And instances are intimated of the first in the east, the second in the west, the third in the south, the fourth in the north and the whole world.

The contents, as of the phials and trumpets, so of the seals, are shown by the songs of praise and thanksgiving annexed to them. They contain therefore "the power, and riches, and wisdom, and strength, and honour, and glory, and blessing," which the Lamb received. The four former have a peculiar connexion with each other; and so have the three latter seals. The former relate to visible things, toward the four quarters to which the four living creatures look.

Before we proceed, it may be observed, 1. No man should constrain either himself or another to explain everything in this book. It is sufficient for every one to speak just so far as he understands. 2. We should remember that, although the ancient prophets wrote the occurrences of those kingdoms only with which Israel had to do, yet the Revelation contains what relates to the whole world, through which the Christian church is extended. Yet, 3. We should not prescribe to this prophecy, as if it must needs admit or exclude this or that history, according as we judge one or the other to be of great or small importance. "God seeth not as a man seeth;" therefore what we think great is often omitted, what we think little inserted, in scripture history or prophecy. 4. We must take care not to overlook what is already fulfilled; and not to describe as fulfilled what is still to come.

We are to look in history for the fulfilling of the four first seals, quickly after the date of the prophecy. In each of these appears a different horseman. In each we are to consider, first, the horseman himself; secondly, what he does.

The horseman himself, by an emblematical prosopopœia, represents a swift power, bringing with it either, 1. A flourishing state; or, 2. Bloodshed; or, 3. Scarcity of provisions; or, 4. Public calamities. With the quality of each of these riders the colour of his horse agrees. The fourth horseman is expressly termed "death;" the first, with his bow and crown, "a conqueror;" the second, with his great sword, is a warrior, or, as the Romans termed him, Mars; the third, with the scales, has power over the produce of the land. Particular incidents under this or that Roman emperor are not extensive enough to answer any of these horsemen.

The action of every horseman intimates farther, 1. Toward the east, wide spread empire, and victory upon victory: 2. Toward the west, much bloodshed: 3. Toward the south, scarcity of provisions: 4 Toward the north, the plague and various calamities.

tures saying, as the voice of thunder, Come *and* see.
2 And I saw, and behold a white horse: and he that sat on
him had a bow; and a crown was given him: and he went
forth conquering and to conquer.
3 And when he opened the second seal, I heard the second
4 living creature saying, Come. And there went forth another
horse *that was* red: and to him that sat thereon it was given
to take peace from the earth, that they should kill one
another; and there was given him a great sword.

Verse 1. *I heard one*—That is, the first *Of the living creatures*—Who looks forward toward the east.

Verse 2. *And I saw, and behold a white horse, and he that sat on him had a bow*—This colour, and the bow shooting arrows afar off, betoken victory, triumph, prosperity, enlargement of empire, and dominion over many people.

Another horseman, indeed, and of quite another kind, appears on a white horse, Rev. xix. 11. But he that is spoken of under the first seal must be so understood as to bear a proportion to the horsemen in the second, third, and fourth seal.

Nerva succeeded the emperor Domitian at the very time when the Revelation was written, in the year of our Lord 96. He reigned scarce a year alone; and three months before his death he named Trajan for his colleague and successor, and died in the year 98. Trajan's accession to the empire seems to be the dawning of the seven seals. *And a crown was given him*—This, considering his descent, Trajan could have no hope of attaining. But God gave it him by the hand of Nerva; and then the east soon felt his power. *And he went forth conquering and to conquer*—That is, from one victory to another In the year 108 the already victorious Trajan went forth toward the east, to conquer not only Armenia, Assyria, and Mesopotamia, but also the countries beyond the Tigris, carrying the bounds of the Roman empire to a far greater extent than ever. We find no emperor like him for making conquests. He aimed at nothing else; he lived only to conquer. Meantime, in him was eminently fulfilled what had been prophesied of the fourth empire, Dan ii. 40, vii. 23, that he should "devour, tread down, and break in pieces the whole earth."

Verse 3. *And when he had opened the second seal, I heard the second living creature*—Who looked toward the west. *Saying, Come*—At each seal it was necessary to turn toward that quarter of the world which it more immediately concerned.

Verse 4. *There went forth another horse that was red*—A colour suitable to bloodshed. *And to him that sat thereon it was given to take peace from the earth*—Vespasian, in the year 75, had dedicated a temple to Peace; but after a time we hear little more of peace. All is full of war and bloodshed, chiefly in the western world, where the main business of men seemed to be, to kill one another.

To this horseman *there was given a great sword;* and he had much to

CHAPTER VI.

5 And when he opened the third seal, I heard the third
living creature say, Come. And I saw, and behold a black
horse: and he that sat on him had a pair of scales in his
6 hand. And I heard a voice in the midst of the four living

do with it; for as soon as Trajan ascended the throne, peace was taken from the earth. Decebalus, king of Dacia, which lies westward from Patmos, put the Romans to no small trouble. The war lasted five years, and consumed abundance of men on both sides; yet was only a prelude to much other bloodshed, which followed for a long season. All this was signified by the great sword, which strikes those who are near, as the bow does those who are at a distance.

Verse 5. *And when he had opened the third seal, I heard the third living creature*—Toward the south. *Saying, Come. And behold a black horse*—A fit emblem of mourning and distress; particularly of black famine, as the ancient poets term it. *And he that sat on him had a pair of scales in his hand*—When there is great plenty, men scarce think it worth their while to weigh and measure everything, Gen. xli. 49. But when there is scarcity, they are obliged to deliver them out by measure and weight, Ezek. iv. 16. Accordingly, these scales signify scarcity. They serve also for a token, that all the fruits of the earth, and consequently the whole heavens, with their courses and influences; that all the seasons of the year, with whatsoever they produce, in nature or states, are subject to Christ. Accordingly his hand is wonderful, not only in wars and victories, but likewise in the whole course of nature.

Verse 6. *And I heard a voice*—It seems, from God himself. *Saying*—To the horseman, "Hitherto shalt thou come, and no farther." Let there be *a measure of wheat for a penny*—The word translated *measure,* was a Grecian measure, nearly equal to our quart. This was the daily allowance of a slave. The Roman penny, as much as a labourer then earned in a day, was about sevenpence halfpenny English. According to this, wheat would be near twenty shillings per bushel. This must have been fulfilled while the Grecian measure and the Roman money were still in use; as also where that measure was the common measure, and this money the current coin. It was so in Egypt under Trajan. *And three measures of barley for a penny*—Either barley was, in common, far cheaper among the ancients than wheat, or the prophecy mentions this as something peculiar. *And hurt not the oil and the wine*—Let there not be a scarcity of everything. Let there be some provision left to supply the want of the rest.

This was also fulfilled in the reign of Trajan, especially in Egypt, which lay southward from Patmos. In this country, which used to be the granary of the empire, there was an uncommon dearth at the very beginning of his reign; so that he was obliged to supply Egypt itself with corn from other countries. The same scarcity there was in the thirteenth year of his reign, the harvest failing for want of the rising of the Nile: and that not only in Egypt, but in all those other parts of Afric, where the Nile uses to overflow.

creatures saying, A measure of wheat for a penny, and
three measures of barley for a penny; and hurt not the oil
and the wine.
7 And when he opened the fourth seal, I heard the voice
8 of the fourth living creature saying, Come. And I saw, and
behold a pale horse, and he that sat on him, his name is
Death; (and hades followeth even with him;) and power was
given him over the fourth part of the earth, to kill with the
scimitar, and with famine, and with death, and by the wild
beasts of the earth.

Verse 7 *I heard the voice of the fourth living creature*—Toward the north.

Verse 8. *And I saw, and behold a pale horse*—Suitable to pale death, his rider. *And hades*—The representative of the state of separate souls *Followeth even with him*—The four first seals concern living men. Death therefore is properly introduced. Hades is only occasionally mentioned as a companion of death. So the fourth seal reaches to the borders of things invisible, which are comprised in the three last seals. *And power was given to him over the fourth part of the earth*—What came single and in a lower degree before, comes now together, and much more severely The first seal brought victory with it: in the second was "a great sword;" but here a *scimitar*. In the third was moderate dearth; here *famine*, and *plague*, and *wild beasts* beside. And it may well be, that from the time of Trajan downwards, the fourth part of men upon the earth, that is, within the Roman empire, died by sword, famine, pestilence, and wild beasts. "At that time," says Aurelius Victor, "the Tyber overflowed much more fatally than under Nerva, with a great destruction of houses; and there was a dreadful earthquake through many provinces, and a terrible plague and famine, and many places consumed by fire." *By death*—That is, by pestilence *Wild beasts* have, at several times, destroyed abundance of men; and undoubtedly there was given them, at this time, an uncommon fierceness and strength. It is observable that war brings on scarcity, and scarcity pestilence, through want of wholesome sustenance; and pestilence, by depopulating the country, leaves the few survivors an easier prey to the wild beasts. And thus these judgments make way for one another in the order wherein they are here represented.

What has been already observed may be a fourfold proof that the four horsemen, as with their first entrance in the reign of Trajan, (which does by no means exhaust the contents of the four first seals,) so with all their entrances in succeeding ages, and with the whole course of the world and of visible nature, are in all ages subject to Christ, subsisting by his power, and serving his will, against the wicked, and in defence of the righteous Herewith, likewise, a way is paved for the trumpets, which

CHAPTER VI.

9 And when he opened the fifth seal, I saw under the altar
the souls of them that had been slain for the word of God,
10 and for the testimony which they held: And they cried
with a loud voice, saying, How long, O Lord, thou Holy
One and true, dost thou not judge and avenge our blood on
11 them that dwell upon the earth? And there was given to

regularly succeed each other; and the whole prophecy, as to what is future, is confirmed by the clear accomplishment of this part of it.

Verse 9. *And when he opened the fifth seal*—As the four former seals, so the three latter, have a close connexion with each other These all refer to the invisible world; the fifth, to the happy dead, particularly the martyrs; the sixth, to the unhappy; the seventh, to the angels, especially those to whom the trumpets are given. *And I saw*—Not only the church warring under Christ, and the world warring under Satan; but also the invisible hosts, both of heaven and hell, are described in this book. And it not only describes the actions of both these armies upon earth; but their respective removals from earth, into a more happy or more miserable state, succeeding each other at several times, distinguished by various degrees, celebrated by various thanksgivings; and also the gradual increase of expectation and triumph in heaven, and of terror and misery in hell. *Under the altar*—That is, at the foot of it. Two altars are mentioned in the Revelation, "the golden altar" of incense, chap. ix. 13; and the altar of burnt-offerings, mentioned here, and chap. viii. 5. xiv. 18, xvi. 7. At this the souls of the martyrs now prostrate themselves. By and by their blood shall be avenged upon Babylon; but not yet. whence it appears that the plagues in the fourth seal do not concern Rome in particular.

Verse 10. *And they cried*—This cry did not begin now, but under the first Roman persecution. The Romans themselves had already avenged the martyrs slain by the Jews on that whole nation. *How long*—They knew their blood would be avenged; but not immediately, as is now shown them. *O Lord*—The Greek word properly signifies the *master of a family*: it is therefore beautifully used by these, who are peculiarly of the household of God. *Thou Holy One and true*—Both the holiness and truth of God require him to execute judgment and vengeance. *Dost thou not judge and avenge our blood?*—There is no impure affection in heaven: therefore, this desire of theirs is pure and suitable to the will of God. The martyrs are concerned for the praise of their Master, of his holiness and truth: and the praise is given him, Rev. xix. 2, where the prayer of the martyrs is changed into a thanksgiving:—

Thou holy One and true:	"True and right are thy judgments."
How long dost thou not judge and avenge our blood?	"He hath judged the great whore, and hath avenged the blood of his servants."

Verse 11. *And there was given to every one a white robe*—An emblem of innocence, joy, and victory, in token of honour and favourable accept-

them, to every one, a white robe: and it was said to them,
that they should rest yet for a time, till their fellowservants
also and their brethren should be fulfilled, who should be
killed even as they *were*.
12 And I saw when he opened the sixth seal, and there was
a great earthquake, and the sun became black as sackcloth
13 of hair, and the moon became as blood; And the stars of
heaven fell to the earth, as a fig tree casteth its untimely
14 figs, when it is shaken by a mighty wind. And the heaven
departed as a book that is rolled together; and every moun-
15 tain and island were moved out of their places. And the

ance. *And it was said to them*—They were told how long. They were not left in that uncertainty. *That they should rest*—Should cease from crying. They rested from pain before. *A time*—This word has a peculiar meaning in this book, to denote which, we may retain the original word *chronos*. Here are two classes of martyrs specified the former killed under heathen Rome; the latter, under papal Rome. The former are commanded to rest till the latter are added to them. There were many of the former in the days of John: the first fruits of the latter died in the thirteenth century Now, *a time*, or *chronos*, is 1111 years. This *chronos* began A. C. 98, and continued to the year 1209; or from Trajan's persecution, to the first crusade against the Waldenses. *Till*—It is not said, Immediately after this time is expired, vengeance shall be executed; but only, that immediately after this time *their brethren and fellow-servants* will come to them. This event will precede the other; and there will be some space between.

Verse 12. *And I saw*—This sixth seal seems particularly to point out God's judgment on the wicked departed. St. John saw how the end of the world was even then set before those unhappy spirits. This representation might be made to them, without anything of it being perceived upon earth. The like representation is made in heaven, Rev xi. 18. *And there was a great earthquake*—Or shaking, not of the earth only, but the heavens. This is a farther description of the representation made to those unhappy souls.

Verse 13. *And the stars fell to*, or towards, *the earth*—Yea, and so they surely will, let astronomers fix their magnitude as they please. *As a fig tree casteth its untimely figs, when it is shaken by a mighty wind*—How sublimely is the violence of that shaking expressed by this comparison!

Verse 14. *And the heavens departed as a book that is rolled together*—When the scripture compares some very great with a little thing, the majesty and omnipotence of God, before whom great things are little, is highly exalted. *Every mountain and island*—What a mountain is to the land, that an island is to the sea.

Verse 15. *And the kings of the earth*—They who had been so in their day. *And the great men and chief captains*—The generals and nobles

kings of the earth, and the great men, and the chief captains,
and the rich, and the mighty, and every slave, and freeman,
hid themselves in the caves and in the rocks of the moun-
16 tains; And said to the mountains and to the rocks, Fall on
us, and hide us from the face of him that sitteth on the
17 throne, and from the wrath of the Lamb· For the great
day of his wrath is come; and who is able to stand?

CHAP. VII. 1 And after these things I saw four angels
standing on the four corners of the earth, holding the four
winds, that the wind should not blow upon the earth, nor
2 on the sea, nor on any tree. And I saw another angel
ascending from the *rising of the sun*, having the seal of the

Hid themselves—So far as in them lay. *In the rocks of the mountains*—There are also rocks on the plains; but they were rocks on high, which they besought to fall upon them.

Verse 16. *To the mountains and the rocks*—Which were tottering already, verse 12. *Hide us from the face of him*—Which "is against the ungodly," Psalm xxxiv. 116.

Verse 1 *And after these things*—What follows is a preparation for the seventh seal, which is the weightiest of all. It is connected with the sixth by the particle *and;* whereas what is added, verse 9, stands free and unconnected. *I saw four angels*—Probably evil ones. They have their employ with the four first trumpets, as have other evil angels with the three last; namely, the angel of the abyss, the four bound in the Euphrates, and Satan himself. These four angels would willingly have brought on all the calamities that follow without delay. But they were restrained till the servants of God were sealed, and till the seven angels were ready to sound: even as the angel of the abyss was not let loose, nor the angels in the Euphrates unbound, neither Satan cast to the earth, till the fifth, sixth, and seventh angels severally sounded. *Standing on the four corners of the earth*—East, west, south, north. In this order proceed the four first trumpets. *Holding the four winds*—Which else might have softened the fiery heat, under the first, second, and third trumpet. *That the wind should not blow upon the earth, nor on the sea, nor on any tree*—It seems, that these expressions betoken the several quarters of the world; that *the earth* signifies that to the east of Patmos, Asia, which was nearest to St. John, and where the trumpet of the first angel had its accomplishment. Europe swims in *the sea* over against this; and is accordingly termed by the prophets, "the islands." The third part, Afric, seems to be meant, Rev. viii. 7, 8, 10, by "the streams of water," or "the trees," which grow plentifully by them.

Verse 2. *And I saw another* (a good) *angel ascending from the east*—The plagues begin in the east; so does the sealing *Having the seal of the*

living God: and he cried with a loud voice to the four
angels, to whom it was given to hurt the earth and the sea,
3 Saying, Hurt ye not the earth, neither the sea, neither the
trees, till we have sealed the servants of our God on their
4 foreheads. And I heard the number of them that were
sealed: an hundred forty four thousand were sealed out of all
5 the tribes of the children of Israel. Of the tribe of Judah
were sealed twelve thousand. Of the tribe of Reuben *were*
sealed twelve thousand. Of the tribe of Gad *were* sealed
6 twelve thousand. Of the tribe of Asher *were* sealed twelve
thousand. Of the tribe of Napthali *were* sealed twelve thousand. Of the tribe of Manasseh *were* sealed twelve thou-
7 sand. Of the tribe of Simeon *were* sealed twelve thousand.
Of the tribe of Levi *were* sealed twelve thousand. Of the
8 tribe of Issachar *were* sealed twelve thousand. Of the tribe
of Zebulon *were* sealed twelve thousand. Of the tribe
of Joseph *were* sealed twelve thousand. Of the tribe
of Benjamin *were* sealed twelve thousand.
9 After these things I saw, and, behold, a great multitude,

only *living* and true *God: and he cried with a loud voice to the four angels*—Who were hasting to execute their charge. *To whom it was given to hurt the earth and the sea*—First, and afterwards "the trees."

Verse 3. *Hurt not the earth, till we*—Other angels were joined in commission with him. *Have sealed the servants of our God on their foreheads*—Secured the servants of God of the twelve tribes from the impending calamities; whereby they shall be as clearly distinguished from the rest, as if they were visibly marked on their foreheads.

Verse 4. *Of the children of Israel*—To these will afterwards be joined a multitude out of all nations But it may be observed, this is not the number of all the Israelites who are saved from Abraham or Moses to the end of all things; but only of those who were secured from the plagues which were then ready to fall on the earth. It seems as if this book had, in many places, a special view to the people of Israel.

Verse 5. *Judah* is mentioned first, in respect of the kingdom, and of the Messiah sprung therefrom.

Verse 7. After the Levitical ceremonies were abolished, *Levi* was again on a level with his brethren.

Verse 8. *Of the tribe of Joseph*—Or Ephraim; perhaps not mentioned by name, as having been, with Dan, the most idolatrous of all the tribes It is farther observable of Dan, that it was very early reduced to a single family; which family itself seems to have been cut off in war, before the time of Ezra; for in the Chronicles, where the posterity of the patriarchs is recited, Dan is wholly omitted.

Verse 9 *A great multitude*—Of those who had happily finished their

which no man could number, of all nations, and tribes, and
people, and tongues, standing before the throne, and before
the Lamb, clothed with white robes, and palms in their
10 hands; And they cry with a loud voice, saying, Salvation
to our God who sitteth on the throne, and to the Lamb.
11 And all the angels stood round about the throne, and the
elders, and the four living creatures, and they fell before
the throne on their faces, and worshipped God, saying,
12 Amen: The blessing, and the glory, and the wisdom, and
the thanksgiving, and the honour, and the power, and the
13 strength, *be* to our God for ever and ever. And one of the
elders answered, saying to me, Who are these that are

course. Such multitudes are afterwards described, and still higher degrees of glory which they attain after a sharp fight and magnificent victory, Rev. xiv. 1; xv. 2; xix. 1; xx. 4. There is an inconceivable variety in the degrees of reward in the other world. Let not any slothful one say, "If I get to heaven at all, I will be content:" such an one may let heaven go altogether. In worldly things, men are ambitious to get as high as they can. Christians have a far more noble ambition. The difference between the very highest and the lowest state in the world is nothing to the smallest difference between the degrees of glory. But who has time to think of this? Who is at all concerned about it? *Standing before the throne*—In the full vision of God. *And palms in their hands*—Tokens of joy and victory

Verse 10. *Salvation to our God*—Who hath saved us from all evil into all the happiness of heaven. The salvation for which they praise God is described, verse 15; that for which they praise the Lamb, verse 14; and both, in the sixteenth and seventeenth verses.

Verse 11. *And all the angels stood*—In waiting. *Round about the throne, and the elders and the four living creatures*—That is, *the living creatures,* next *the throne; the elders,* round these; and *the angels,* round them both. *And they fell on their faces*—So do the elders, once only, Rev. xi 16. The heavenly ceremonial has its fixed order and measure.

Verse 12. *Amen*—With this word all the angels confirm the words of the "great multitude;" but they likewise carry the praise much higher. *The blessing, and the glory, and the wisdom, and the thanksgiving, and the honour, and the power, and the strength, be unto our God for ever and ever*—Before the Lamb began to open the seven seals, a sevenfold hymn of praise was brought him by many angels, Rev. v. 12. Now he is upon opening the last seal, and the seven angels are going to receive seven trumpets, in order to make the kingdoms of the world subject to God All the angels give sevenfold praise to God.

Verse 13. *And one of the elders*—What stands, verses 13—17, might have immediately followed the tenth verse; but that the praise of the angels, which was at the same time with that of the "great multitude,"

14 clothed in white robes? and whence are they come? And
I said to him, My lord, thou knowest. And he said to me,
These are they who come out of great affliction, and they
have washed their robes, and made them white in the blood
15 of the Lamb. Therefore are they before the throne of God,
and serve him day and night in his temple: and he that
16 sitteth upon the throne shall have his tent over them. They
shall hunger no more, neither thirst any more; neither shall
17 the sun light on them, nor any heat. For the Lamb who
is in the midst of the throne will feed them, and will lead
them to living fountains of water and God will wipe away
all tears from their eyes.

CHAP. VIII. 1 And when he had opened the seventh
seal, there was silence in heaven about half an hour.

came in between. *Answered*—He answered St. John's desire to know, not any words that he spoke.

Verse 14. *My lord*—Or, *my master;* a common term of respect. So Zechariah, likewise, bespeaks the angel, Zech. i. 9; iv. 4; vi. 4. *Thou knowest*—That is, I know not; but thou dost. *These are they*—Not martyrs; for these are not such a multitude as no man can number. But as all the angels appear here, so do all the souls of the righteous who had lived from the beginning of the world. *Who come*—He does not say, who *did* come; but, *who come* now also: to whom, likewise, pertain all who will come hereafter. *Out of great affliction*—Of various kinds, wisely and graciously allotted by God to all his children. *And have washed their robes*—From all guilt. *And made them white*—In all holiness. *By the blood of the Lamb*—Which not only cleanses, but adorns us also.

Verse 15. *Therefore*—Because they came out of great affliction, and have washed their robes in his blood. *Are they before the throne*—It seems, even nearer than the angels. *And serve him day and night*—Speaking after the manner of men; that is, continually. *In his temple*—Which is in heaven. *And he shall have his tent over them*—Shall spread his glory over them as a covering.

Verse 16. *Neither shall the sun light on them*—For God is there their sun. *Nor any* painful *heat,* or inclemency of seasons.

Verse 17. *For the Lamb will feed them*—With eternal peace and joy; so that they shall hunger no more. *And will lead them to living fountains of water*—The comforts of the Holy Ghost; so that they shall thirst no more. Neither shall they suffer or grieve any more; for God "will wipe away all tears from their eyes."

Verse 1. *And when he had opened the seventh seal, there was silence in heaven*—Such a silence is mentioned but in this one place. It was uncommon, and highly observable for praise is sounding in heaven day and

CHAPTER VIII

2 And I saw the seven angels who stood before God; and seven

night. In particular, immediately before this silence, all the angels, and before them the innumerable multitude, had been crying with a loud voice; and now all is still at once: there is an universal pause. Hereby the seventh seal is very remarkably distinguished from the six preceding. This silence before God shows that those who were round about him were expecting, with the deepest reverence, the great things which the Divine Majesty would farther open and order. Immediately after, the seven trumpets are heard, and a sound more august than ever. Silence is only a preparation: the grand point is, the sounding the trumpets to the praise of God. *About half an hour*—To St. John, in the vision, it might seem a common half hour.

Verse 2. *And I saw*—The seven trumpets belong to the seventh seal, as do the seven phials to the seventh trumpet. This should be carefully remembered, that we may not confound together the times which follow each other. And yet it may be observed, in general, concerning the times of the incidents mentioned in this book, it is not a certain rule, that every part of the text is fully accomplished before the completion of the following part begins. All things mentioned in the epistles are not fully accomplished before the seals are opened; neither are all things mentioned under the seals fulfilled before the trumpets begin; nor yet is the seventh trumpet wholly past before the phials are poured out. Only the beginning of each part goes before the beginning of the following. Thus the epistles begin before the seals, the seals before the trumpets, the trumpets before the phials. One epistle begins before another, one seal before another, one trumpet especially before another, one phial before another. Yet, sometimes, what begins later than another thing ends sooner; and what begins earlier than another thing ends later: so the seventh trumpet begins earlier than the phials, and yet extends beyond them all. *The seven angels which stood before God*—A character of the highest eminence. *And seven trumpets were given them*—When men desire to make known openly a thing of public concern, they give a token that may be seen or heard far and wide; and, among such, none are more ancient than trumpets, Lev. xxv. 9; Num. x. 2; Amos iii. 6. The Israelites, in particular, used them, both in the worship of God and in war; therewith openly praising the power of God before, after, and in, the battle, Josh. vi. 4; 2 Chron. xiii. 14, &c. And the angels here made known by these trumpets the wonderful works of God, whereby all opposing powers are successively shaken, till the kingdom of the world becomes the kingdom of God and his Anointed.

These trumpets reach nearly from the time of St. John to the end of the world; and they are distinguished by manifest tokens The place of the four first is specified; namely, east, west, south, and north successively: in the three last, immediately after the time of each, the place likewise is pointed out

The seventh angel did not begin to sound, till after the going forth of the second woe: but the trumpets were given to him and the other

3 trumpets were given them. And another angel came and
stood at the altar, having a golden censer; and much
incense was given him, that he might place *it* with the
prayers of all the saints upon the golden altar which is
4 before the throne. And the smoke of the incense ascended
before God out of the angel's hand with the prayers of the
5 saints. And the angel took the censer, and filled it with
the fire of the altar, and threw it upon the earth: and there
were thunderings, and lightnings, and voices, and an earthquake.
6 And the seven angels who had the seven trumpets pre-
7 pared themselves to sound. And the first sounded, and

six together; (as were afterward the phials to the seven angels;) and it is accordingly said of all the seven together, that "they prepared themselves to sound." These, therefore, were not men, as some have thought, but angels, properly so called.

Verse 3. *And*—In the second verse, the "trumpets were given" to the seven angels; and in the sixth, they "prepared to sound." But between these, the incense of this angel and the prayers of the saints are mentioned; the interposing of which shows, that the prayers of the saints and the trumpets of the angels go together. and these prayers, with the effects of them, may well be supposed to extend through all the seven. *Another angel*—Another created angel. Such are all that are here spoken of. In this part of the Revelation, Christ is never termed *an angel;* but, "the Lamb." *Came and stood at the altar*—Of burnt-offerings *And there was given him a golden censer*—*A censer* was a cup on a plate or saucer. This was the token and the business of the office. *And much incense was given*—*Incense* generally signifies prayer: here it signifies the longing desires of the angels, that the holy counsel of God might be fulfilled. And there was *much incense;* for as the prayers of all the saints in heaven and earth are here joined together: so are the desires of all the angels which are brought by this angel. *That he might place it*—It is not said, *offer it;* for he was discharging the office of an angel, not a priest. *With the prayers of all the saints*—At the same time; but not *for* the saints. The angels are fellowservants with the saints, not mediators for them.

Verse 4. *And the smoke of the incense came up before God, with the prayers of the saints*—A token that both were accepted.

Verse 5. *And there were thunderings, and lightnings, and voices, and an earthquake*—These, especially when attended with *fire,* are emblems of God's dreadful judgments, which are immediately to follow.

Verse 6. *And the seven angels prepared themselves to sound*—That each, when it should come to his turn, might sound without delay. But while they do sound, they still stand before God.

Verse 7. *And the first sounded*—And every angel continued to sound, till all which his trumpet brought was fulfilled, and till the next began

there was hail and fire mingled with blood, and they were
cast upon the earth: and the third part of the earth was
burned up, and the third part of the trees was burned up,
and all the green grass was burned up.
8 And the second angel sounded, and as it were a great
mountain burning with fire was cast into the sea: and the

There are intervals between the three woes, but not between the four first trumpets. *And there was hail and fire mingled with blood, and they were cast upon the earth*—The earth seems to mean Asia; Palestine, in particular. Quickly after the Revelation was given, the Jewish calamities under Adrian began: yea, before the reign of Trajan was ended. And here the trumpets begin. Even under Trajan, in the year 114, the Jews made an insurrection with a most dreadful fury; and in the parts about Cyrene, in Egypt, and in Cyprus, destroyed four hundred and sixty thousand persons. But they were repressed by the victorious power of Trajan, and afterward slaughtered themselves in vast multitudes. The alarm spread itself also into Mesopotamia, where Lucius Quintius slew a great number of them. They rose in Judea again in the second year of Adrian; but were presently quelled. Yet in 133 they broke out more violently than ever, under their false messiah Barcochab; and the war continued till the year 135, when almost all Judea was desolated. In the Egyptian plague also *hail* and *fire* were together. But here *hail* is to be taken figuratively, as also *blood,* for a vehement, sudden, powerful, hurtful invasion; and *fire* betokens the revenge of an enraged enemy, with the desolation therefrom. *And they were cast upon the earth*—That is, the *fire* and *hail* and *blood.* But they existed before they were cast upon the *earth.* The storm fell, the blood flowed, and the flames raged round Cyrene, and in Egypt, and Cyprus, before they reached Mesopotamia and Judea. *And the third part of the earth was burnt up*—Fifty well-fortified cities, and nine hundred and eighty-five well-inhabited towns of the Jews, were wholly destroyed in this war. Vast tracts of land were likewise left desolate and without inhabitant. *And the third part of the trees was burned up, and all the green grass was burned up*—Some understand by *the trees,* men of eminence among the Jews; by *the grass,* the common people. The Romans spared many of the former: the latter were almost all destroyed

Thus vengeance began at the Jewish enemies of Christ's kingdom; though even then the Romans did not quite escape. But afterwards it came upon them more and more violently: the second trumpet affects the Roman heathens in particular; the third, the dead, unholy Christians; the fourth, the empire itself.

Verse 8. *And the second angel sounded, and as it were a great mountain burning with fire was cast into the sea*—By *the sea,* particularly as it is here opposed to the earth, we may understand the west, or Europe; and chiefly the middle parts of it, the vast Roman empire. *A mountain* here seems to signify a great force and multitude of people. Jer. li. 25; so

9 third part of the sea became blood; And the third part
of the creatures that were in the sea which had life, died;
and the third part of the ships were destroyed.
10 And the third angel sounded, and there fell from heaven
a great star burning as a torch, and it fell on the third part
of the rivers, and on the fountains of waters.

this may point at the irruption of the barbarous nations into the Roman empire. The warlike Goths broke in upon it about the year 250: and from that time the irruption of one nation after another never ceased till the very form of the Roman empire, and all but the name, was lost. *The fire* may mean the fire of war, and the rage of those savage nations. *And the third part of the sea became blood*—This need not imply, that just a third part of the Romans was slain; but it is certain an inconceivable deal of blood was shed in all these invasions.

Verse 9. *And the third part of the creatures that were in the sea*—That is, of all sorts of men, of every station and degree. *Died*—By those merciless invaders. *And the third part of the ships were destroyed*—It is a frequent thing to resemble a state or republic to a ship, wherein many people are embarked together, and share in the same dangers. And how many states were utterly destroyed by those inhuman conquerors! Much likewise of this was literally fulfilled. How often was the sea tinged with blood! How many of those who dwelt mostly upon it were killed! And what number of ships destroyed!

Verse 10. *And the third angel sounded, and there fell from heaven a great star, and it fell on the third part of the rivers*—It seems Afric is meant by the *rivers*; (with which this burning part of the world abounds in an especial manner;) Egypt in particular, which the Nile overflows every year far and wide. In the whole African history, between the irruption of the barbarous nations into the Roman empire, and the ruin of the western empire, after the death of Valentinian the Third, there is nothing more momentous than the Arian calamity, which sprung up in the year 315. It is not possible to tell how many persons, particularly at Alexandria, in all Egypt, and in the neighbouring countries, were destroyed by the rage of the Arians. Yet Afric fared better than other parts of the empire, with regard to the barbarous nations, till the governor of it, whose wife was a zealous Arian, and aunt to Genseric, king of the Vandals, was, under that pretence, unjustly accused before the empress Placidia. He was then prevailed upon to invite the Vandals into Afric; who under Genseric, in the year 428, founded there a kingdom of their own, which continued till the year 533. Under these Vandal kings the true believers endured all manner of afflictions and persecutions. And thus Arianism was the inlet to all heresies and calamities, and at length to Mahometanism itself.

This *great star* was not an angel, (angels are not the agents in the two preceding or the following trumpet,) but a teacher of the church, one of the stars in the right hand of Christ. Such was Arius. He fell from

11 And the name of the star is called Wormwood: and the
third part of the waters became wormwood; and many men
12 died of the waters, because they were made bitter. And the
fourth angel sounded, and the third part of the sun was
smitten, and the third part of the moon, and the third part
the stars; so that the third part of them was darkened,
and the day shone not for the third part thereof, and the
night likewise.

on high, as it were *from heaven*, into the most pernicious doctrines, and made in his fall a gazing on all sides, being *great*, and now *burning as a torch*. He *fell on the third part of the rivers*—His doctrine spread far and wide, particularly in Egypt. *And on the fountains of water*—Wherewith Afric abounds.

Verse 11. *And the name of the star is called Wormwood*—The unparalleled bitterness both of Arius himself and of his followers show the exact propriety of his title. *And the third part of the waters became wormwood*—A very considerable part of Afric was infected with the same bitter doctrine and spirit. *And many men* (though not a third part of them) *died*—By the cruelty of the Arians.

Verse 12. *And the fourth angel sounded, and the third part of the sun was smitten*—Or struck After the emperor Theodosius died, and the empire was divided into the eastern and the western, the barbarous nations poured in as a flood. The Goths and Hunns in the years 403 and 405 fell upon Italy itself with an impetuous force; and the former, in the year 410, took Rome by storm, and plundered it without mercy. In the year 452 Attila treated the upper part of Italy in the same manner. In 455 Valentinian the Third was killed, and Genseric invited from Afric. He plundered Rome for fourteen days together. Recimer plundered it again in 472. During all these commotions, one province was lost after another, till, in the year 476, Odoacer seized upon Rome, deposed the emperor, and put an end to the empire itself.

An eclipse of the sun or moon is termed by the Hebrews, a stroke. Now, as such a darkness does not come all at once, but by degrees, so likewise did the darkness which fell on the Roman, particularly the western empire; for the stroke began long before Odoacer, namely, when the barbarians first conquered the capital city. *And the third part of the moon, and the third part of the stars; so that the third part of them was darkened*—As under the first, second, and third trumpets by "the earth," "sea," and "rivers," are to be understood the men that inhabit them; so here by *the sun, moon*, and *stars*, may be understood the men that live under them, who are so overwhelmed with calamities in those days of darkness, that they can no longer enjoy the light of heaven: unless it may be thought to imply their being killed; so that the sun, moon, and stars shine to them no longer. The very same expression we find in Ezekiel, chap. xxxii. 8 "I will darken all the lights of heaven over them." As then the fourth seal transcends the

13 And I saw, and heard an angel flying in the midst of
heaven, saying with a loud voice, Woe, woe, woe, to the
inhabitants of the earth by reason of the other voices of the
trumpets of the three angels, who are yet to sound!

CHAP. IX. 1 And the fifth angel sounded, and I saw
a star falling from heaven to the earth: and to him was

ree preceding seals, so does the fourth trumpet the three preceding trumpets. For in this not the third part of the earth, or sea, or rivers only, but of all who are under the sun, are affected. *And the day shone not for a third part thereof*—That is, shone with only a third part of its usual brightness. *And the night likewise*—The moon and stars having lost a third part of their lustre, either with regard to those who, being dead, saw them no longer, or those who saw them with no satisfaction.

The three last trumpets have the time of their continuance fixed, and between each of them there is a remarkable pause: whereas between the four former there is no pause, nor is the time of their continuance mentioned; but all together these four seem to take up a little less than four hundred years

Verse 13. *And I saw, and heard an angel flying*—Between the trumpets of the fourth and fifth angel. *In the midst of heaven*—The three woes, as we shall see, stretch themselves over the earth from Persia eastward, beyond Italy, westward; all which space had been filled with the gospel by the apostles. In the midst of this lies Patmos, where St. John saw this angel, *saying, Woe, woe, woe*—Toward the end of the fifth century, there were many presages of approaching calamities. *To the inhabitants of the earth*—All without exception. Heavy trials were coming on them all. Even while the angel was proclaiming this, the preludes of these three woes were already in motion. These fell more especially on the Jews. As to the prelude of the first woe in Persia, Isdegard II., in 454, was resolved to abolish the sabbath, till he was, by Rabbi Mar, diverted from his purpose. Likewise in the year 474, Phiruz afflicted the Jews much, and compelled many of them to apostatize. A prelude of the second woe was the rise of the Saracens, who, in 510, fell into Arabia and Palestine. To prepare for the third woe, Innocent I., and his successors, not only endeavoured to enlarge their episcopal jurisdiction beyond all bounds, but also their worldly power, by taking every opportunity of encroaching upon the empire, which as yet stood in the way of their unlimited monarchy.

Verse 1. *And the fifth angel sounded, and I saw a star*—Far different from that mentioned, Rev. viii. 11. This star belongs to the invisible world. The third woe is occasioned by the dragon cast out of heaven; the second takes place at the loosing of the four angels who were bound in the Euphrates. The first is here brought by the angel of the abyss, which is opened by this star, or holy angel. *Falling to the earth*—Coming swiftly and with great force. *And to him was given*—When he was come

2 given the key of the bottomless pit And he opened the
bottomless pit; and there ascended a smoke out of the pit,
as the smoke of a great furnace; and the sun and the air
3 were darkened by the smoke of the pit. And out of the
smoke there came forth locusts upon the earth: and power
was given them, as the scorpions of the earth have power.
4 And it was commanded them not to hurt the grass of the
earth, neither any green thing, neither any tree; but only
the men who have not the seal of God on their foreheads.
5 And it was given them not to kill them, but that they should
be tormented five months; and the torment of them *is* as

The key of the bottomless pit—A deep and hideous prison; but different from "the lake of fire."

Verse 2. *And there arose a smoke out of the pit*—The locusts, who afterwards rise out of it, seem to be, as we shall afterwards see, the Persians; agreeable to which, this smoke is their detestable idolatrous doctrine, and false zeal for it, which now broke out in an uncommon paroxysm. *As the smoke of a great furnace*—Where the clouds of it rise thicker and thicker, spread far and wide, and press one upon another, so that the darkness increases continually. *And the sun and the air were darkened*—A figurative expression, denoting heavy affliction. This smoke occasioned more and more such darkness over the Jews in Persia.

Verse 3. *And out of the smoke*—Not out of the bottomless pit, but from the smoke which issued thence. *There went forth locusts*—A known emblem of a numerous, hostile, hurtful people. Such were the Persians, from whom the Jews, in the sixth century, suffered beyond expression. In the year 540 their academies were stopped, nor were they permitted to have a president for near fifty years. In 589 this affliction ended; but it began long before 540. The prelude of it was about the year 455 and 474: the main storm came on in the reign of Cabades, and lasted from 483 to 532. Toward the beginning of the sixth century, Mar Rab Isaac, president of the academy, was put to death. Hereon followed an insurrection of the Jews, which lasted seven years before they were conquered by the Persians. Some of them were then put to death, but not many; the rest were closely imprisoned. And from this time the nation of the Jews were hated and persecuted by the Persians, till they had well nigh rooted them out. *The scorpions of the earth*—The most hurtful kind. The scorpions of the air have wings.

Verse 4. *And it was commanded them*—By the secret power of God *Not to hurt the grass, neither any green thing, nor any tree*—Neither those of low, middling, or high degree, *but only* such of them as were *not sealed*—Principally the unbelieving Israelites. But many who were called Christians suffered with them.

Verse 5. *Not to kill them*—Very few of them were killed: in general, they were imprisoned and variously tormented.

6 the torment of a scorpion when he stingeth a man. And in
those days the men shall seek death, but not find it; and
7 shall desire to die, but death will flee from them. And the
appearances of the locusts *are* like horses made ready for
battle; and on their heads *are* as it were crowns like gold,
8 and their faces *are* as the faces of men. And they had hair
as the hair of women, and their teeth were as the *teeth*
9 of lions. And they had breastplates, as it were breastplates
of iron; and the noise of their wings *was* as the noise
10 of chariots of many horses running to battle. And they have
tails like scorpions, and stings were in their tails: their
11 power *is*, to hurt men five months. And they have over
them a king, the angel of the bottomless pit: his name in the
Hebrew is Abaddon, but in the Greek he hath the name
12 Apollyon. One woe is past; behold, there come yet two
woes after these things.

Verse 6. *The men*—That is, the men who are so tormented.

Verse 7. *And the appearances*—This description suits a people neither throughly civilized, nor entirely savage; and such were the Persians of that age. *Of the locusts are like horses*—With their riders. The Persians excelled in horsemanship. *And on their heads are as it were crowns*—Turbans. *And their faces are as the faces of men*—Friendly and agreeable.

Verse 8. *And they had hair as the hair of women*—All the Persians of old gloried in long hair. *And their teeth were as the teeth of lions*—Breaking and tearing all things in pieces.

Verse 9. *And the noise of their wings was as the noise of chariots of many horses*—With their war-chariots, drawn by many horses, they, as it were, flew to and fro

Verse 10. *And they have tails like scorpions*—That is, each tail is like a scorpion, not like the tail of a scorpion. *To hurt the* unsealed *men five months*—Five prophetic months; that is, seventy-nine common years So long did these calamities last.

Verse 11. *And they have over them a king*—One by whom they are peculiarly directed and governed. *His name is Abaddon*—Both this and *Apollyon* signify a destroyer. By this he is distinguished from the dragon, whose proper name is Satan.

Verse 12. *One woe is past; behold, there come yet two woes after these things*—The Persian power, under which was the first woe, was now broken by the Saracens: from this time the first pause made a wide way for the two succeeding woes. In 589, when the first woe ended, Mahomet was twenty years old, and the contentions of the Christians with each other were exceeding great. In 591 Chosroes II. reigned in Persia, who, after the death of the emperor, made dreadful disturbances in the east.

CHAPTER IX.

13 And the sixth angel sounded, and I heard a voice from
the four corners of the golden altar which is before God,
14 Saying to the sixth angel who had the trumpet, Loose the
four angels who are bound in the great river Euphrates.
15 And the four angels were loosed, who were prepared for the
hour, and day, and month, and year, to kill the third part

Hence Mahomet found an open door for his new religion and empire. And when the usurper Phocas had, in the year 606, not only declared the Bishop of Rome, Boniface III., universal bishop, but also the church of Rome the head of all churches, this was a sure step to advance the Papacy to its utmost height. Thus, after the passing away of the first woe, the second, yea, and the third, quickly followed; as indeed they were both on the way together with it before the first effectually began.

Verse 13. *And the sixth angel sounded*—Under this angel goes forth the second woe. *And I heard a voice from the four corners of the golden altar*—This golden altar is the heavenly pattern of the Levitical altar of incense. This voice signified that the execution of the wrath of God, mentioned verses 20, 21, should, at no intercession, be delayed any longer.

Verse 14. *Loose the four angels*—To go every way; to the four quarters. These were evil angels, or they would not have been bound. Why, or how long, they were bound we know not.

Verse 15. *And the four angels were loosed, who were prepared*—By loosing them, as well as by their strength and rage. *To kill the third part of men*—That is, an immense number of them. *For the hour, and day, and month, and year*—All this agrees with the slaughter which the Saracens made for a long time after Mahomet's death. And with the number of angels let loose agrees the number of their first and most eminent caliphs. These were Ali, Abubeker, Omar, and Osman. Mahomet named Ali, his cousin and son-in-law, for his successor; but he was soon worked out by the rest, till they severally died, and so made room for him. They succeeded each other, and each destroyed innumerable multitudes of men. There are in a prophetic

	Com. Years.	*Com. Days.*	
Hour		8	in all 212 years.
Day		196	
Month	15	318	
Year	196	117	

Now, the second woe, as also the beginning of the third, has its place between the ceasing of the locusts and the rising of the beast out of the sea, even at the time that the Saracens, who were chiefly cavalry, were in the height of their carnage; from their first caliph, Abubeker, till they were repulsed from Rome under Leo IV. These 212 years may therefore be reckoned from the year 634 to 847. The gradation in reckoning the time, beginning with *the hour* and ending with a *year*, corresponds with their small beginning and vast increase. Before and after Mahomet's

16 of men. And the number of the army of horsemen *was* two
17 hundred millions: I heard their number. And thus I saw
the horses in the vision, and them that sat on them, having
breastplates of fire, and hyacinth, and brimstone: and the
heads of the horses *are* as the heads of lions; and out
18 of their mouths goeth fire and smoke and brimstone. By
these three plagues were the third part of men killed, by the
fire, and the smoke, and the brimstone, which went out
19 of their mouths. For the power of the horses is in their
mouths, and in their tails: for their tails *are* like serpents,

death, they had enough to do to settle their affairs at home. Afterwards Abubeker went farther, and in the year 634 gained great advantage over the Persians and Romans in Syria. Under Omar was the conquest of Mesopotamia, Palestine, and Egypt made. Under Osman, that of Afric, (with the total suppression of the Roman government in the year 647,) of Cyprus, and of all Persia in 651. After Ali was dead, his son Ali Hasen, a peaceable prince, was driven out by Muavia; under whom, and his successors, the power of the Saracens so increased, that within four-score years after Mahomet's death they had extended their conquests farther than the warlike Romans did in four hundred years.

Verse 16. *And the number of the horsemen was two hundred millions*—Not that so many were ever brought into the field at once, but (if we understand the expression literally) in the course of "the hour, and day, and month, and year." So neither were "the third part of men killed" at once, but during that course of years.

Verse 17. *And thus I saw the horses and them that sat on them in the vision*—St. John seems to add these words, *in the vision*, to intimate that we are not to take this description just according to the letter. *Having breastplates of fire*—Fiery red. *And hyacinth*—Dun blue. *And brimstone*—A faint yellow. Of the same colour with the *fire and smoke and brimstone*, which *go out of the mouths of their horses. And the heads of their horses are as the heads of lions*—That is, fierce and terrible. *And out of their mouth goeth fire and smoke and brimstone*—This figurative expression may denote the consuming, blinding, all-piercing rage, fierceness, and force of these horsemen.

Verse 18. *By these three*—Which were inseparably joined. *Were the third part of men*—In the countries they over-ran. *Killed*—Omar alone, in eleven years and a half, took thirty-six thousand cities or forts. How many men must be killed therein!

Verse 19. *For the power of these horses is in their mouths, and in their tails*—Their riders fight retreating as well as advancing: so that their rear is as terrible as their front. *For their tails are like serpents, having heads*—Not like the tails of serpents only. They may be fitly compared to the amphisbena, a kind of serpent, which has a short tail, not unlike a head; from which it throws out its poison, as if it had two heads

20 having heads, and with them they do hurt. And the rest
of the men who were not killed by these plagues yet repented
not of the works of their hands, that they should not worship
devils, and idols of gold, and silver, and brass, and stone,
and wood: which can neither see, nor hear, nor walk:
21 Neither repented of their murders, nor of their sorceries, nor
of their fornications, nor of their thefts.

CHAP. X. 1 And I saw another mighty angel coming
down from heaven, clothed with a cloud and a rainbow

Verse 20. *And the rest of the men who were not killed*—Whom the Saracens did not destroy. It is observable, the countries they over-ran were mostly those where the gospel had been planted. *By these plagues*—Here the description of the second woe ends. *Yet repented not*—Though they were called Christians. *Of the works of their hands*—Presently specified. *That they should not worship devils*—The invocation of departed saints, whether true, or false, or doubtful, or forged, crept early into the Christian church, and was carried farther and farther; and who knows how many who are invoked as saints are among evil, not good, angels; or how far devils have mingled with such blind worship, and with the wonders wrought on those occasions? *And idols*—About the year 590, men began to venerate images; and though upright men zealously opposed it, yet, by little and little, images grew into manifest idols. For after much contention, both in the east and west, in the year 787, the worship of images was established by the second Council of Nice Yet was image worship sharply opposed some time after, by the emperor Theophilus. But when he died, in 842, his widow, Theodora, established it again; as did the Council at Constantinople in the year 863, and again in 871.

Verse 21. *Neither repented of their murders, nor of their sorceries*—Whoever reads the histories of the seventh, eighth, and ninth centuries, will find numberless instances of all these in every part of the Christian world. But though God cut off so many of these scandals to the Christian name, yet the rest went on in the same course. Some of them, however, might repent under the plagues which follow.

CHAP. X. From the first verse of this chapter to chap. xi. 13, preparation is made for the important trumpet of the seventh angel. It consists of two parts, which run parallel to each other: the former reaches from the first to the seventh verse of this chapter; the latter, from the eighth of this to the thirteenth verse of the eleventh chapter: whence, also, the sixth verse of this chapter is parallel to the eleventh verse. The period to which both these refer begins during the second woe, as appears, chap. xi. 14; but, being once begun, it extends in a continued course far into the trumpet of the seventh angel. Hence many things are represented here which are not fulfilled till long after. So the joyful "consumma-

upon his head, and his face as the sun, and his feet as pillars
2 of fire: And he had in his hand a little book opened: and
he set his right foot upon the sea, and his left upon the
3 earth. And he cried with a loud voice, as a lion roareth:
and while he cried, seven thunders uttered their voices.
4 And when the seven thunders had uttered their voices, I was
about to write: and I heard a voice from heaven, saying,
Seal up the things which the seven thunders have uttered,

tion of the mystery of God" is spoken of in the seventh verse of this chapter, which yet is not till after "the consummation of the wrath of God," Rev. xv. 1. So the ascent of the beast "out of the bottomless pit" is mentioned, Rev. xi. 7, which nevertheless is still to come, Rev. xvii. 8; and so "the earthquake," by which a tenth part of the great city falls, and the rest are converted, Rev. xi. 13, is really later than that by which the same city is "split into three parts," Rev. xvi. 19. This is a most necessary observation, whereby we may escape many and great mistakes.

Verse 1. *And I saw another mighty angel*—Another from that "mighty angel," mentioned, Rev. v. 2; yet he was a created angel; for he did not swear by himself, verse 6. *Clothed with a cloud*—In token of his high dignity. *And a rainbow upon his head*—A lovely token of the divine favour. And yet it is not too glorious for a creature: the woman, Rev. xii. 1, is described more glorious still. *And his face as the sun*—Nor is this too much for a creature: for all the righteous "shall shine forth as the sun," Matt. xiii. 43. *And his feet as pillars of fire*—Bright as flame.

Verse 2. *And he had in his hand*—His left hand: he swore with his right. He stood with his right foot on the sea, toward the west; his left, on the land, toward the east: so that he looked southward. And so St. John (as Patmos lies near Asia) could conveniently take the book out of his left hand. This sealed book was first in the right hand of him that sat on the throne: thence the Lamb took it, and opened the seals. And now this *little book*, containing the remainder of the other, is given *opened*, as it was, to St. John. From this place the Revelation speaks more clearly and less figuratively than before. *And he set his right foot upon the sea*—Out of which the first beast was to come. *And his left foot upon the earth*—Out of which was to come the second. *The sea* may betoken Europe; *the earth*, Asia; the chief theatres of these great things.

Verse 3. *And he cried*—Uttering the words set down, verse 6. *And while he cried*, or *was crying*—At the same instant. *Seven thunders uttered their voices*—In distinct words, each after the other. Those who spoke these words were glorious, heavenly powers, whose voice was as the loudest thunder.

Verse 4. *And I heard a voice from heaven*—Doubtless from him who had at first commanded him to write, and who presently commands him to take the book; namely, Jesus Christ. *Seal up those things which the seven thunders have uttered, and write them not*—These are the only things

5 and write them not. And the angel whom I saw standing
upon the sea and upon the earth lifted up his right hand
6 toward heaven, And sware by him that liveth for ever and
ever, who created the heaven, and the things that are
therein, and the earth, and the things that are therein, and
the sea, and the things that are therein, there shall be no
7 more a time· But in the days of the voice of the seventh

of all which he heard that he is commanded to keep secret: so something peculiarly secret was revealed to the beloved John, besides all the secrets that are written in this book. At the same time we are prevented from inquiring what it was which these thunders uttered: suffice that we may know all the contents of the opened book, and of the oath of the angel.

Verse 5. *And the angel*—This manifestation of things to come under the trumpet of the seventh angel hath a twofold introduction: first, the angel speaks for God, verse 7; then Christ speaks for himself, Rev. xi. 3. The angel appeals to the prophets of former times; Christ, to his own two witnesses. *Whom I saw standing upon the earth and upon the sea, lifted up his right hand toward heaven*—As yet the dragon was in heaven. When he is cast thence he brings the third and most dreadful woe on the earth and sea: so that it seems as if there would be no end of calamities. Therefore the angel comprises, in his posture and in his oath, both heaven, sea, and earth, and makes, on the part of the eternal God and almighty Creator, a solemn protestation, that he will assert his kingly authority against all his enemies. *He lifted up his right hand toward heaven*—The angel in Daniel, chap. xii. 7, (not improbably the same angel,) lifted up both his hands.

Verse 6. *And sware*—The six preceding trumpets pass without any such solemnity. It is the trumpet of the seventh angel alone which is confirmed by so high an oath *By him that liveth for ever and ever*—Before whom a thousand years are but a day. *Who created the heaven, the earth, the sea, and the things that are therein*—And, consequently, has the sovereign power over all: therefore, all his enemies, though they rage a while in heaven, on the sea, and on the earth, yet must give place to him *That there shall be no more a time*—"But in the days of the voice of the seventh angel, the mystery of God shall be fulfilled:" that is, *a time*, a *chronos*, shall not expire before that mystery is fulfilled. A *chronos* (1111 years) will nearly pass before then, but not quite. The period, then, which we may term a *non-chronos* (not a whole *time*) must be a little, and not much, shorter than this. The *non-chronos* here mentioned seems to begin in the year 800, (when Charles the Great instituted in the west a new line of emperors, or of "many kings,") to end in the year 1836; and to contain, among other things, the "short time" of the third woe, the "three times and a half" of the woman in the wilderness, and the "duration" of the beast.

Verse 7. *But in the days of the voice of the seventh angel*—Who sounded not only at the beginning of those days, but from the beginning to the

angel, while he shall sound, the mystery of God shall be
fulfilled, as he hath declared to his servants the prophets.
8 And the voice which I heard from heaven spake with me
again, and said, Go, take the book which is open in the
hand of the angel who standeth on the sea and on the earth.
9 And I went to the angel, saying to him, Give me the book
And he saith to me, Take and eat it up; and it will make
thy belly bitter, but it will be sweet as honey in thy mouth.
10 And I took the book out of the angel's hand and eat it up;
and it was in my mouth sweet as honey: but when I had
11 eaten it, my belly was bitter. And he saith to me, Thou
must prophesy again concerning people, and nations, and

end. *The mystery of God shall be fulfilled*—It is said, Rev. xvii. 17, "The word of God shall be fulfilled." The word of God is fulfilled by the destruction of the beast; *the mystery*, by the removal of the dragon. But these great events are so near together, that they are here mentioned as one. The beginning of them is in heaven, as soon as the seventh trumpet sounds; the end is on the earth and the sea. So long as the third woe remains on the earth and the sea, the mystery of God is not fulfilled. And the angel's swearing is peculiarly for the comfort of holy men, who are afflicted under that woe. Indeed the wrath of God must be first fulfilled, by the pouring out of the phials: and then comes the joyful fulfilling of the mystery of God. *As he hath declared to his servants the prophets*—The accomplishment exactly answering the prediction. The ancient prophecies relate partly to that grand period, from the birth of Christ to the destruction of Jerusalem; partly to the time of the seventh angel, wherein they will be fully accomplished. To the seventh trumpet belongs all that occurs from Rev. xi. 15, to xxii. 5. And the third woe, which takes place under the same, properly stands, Rev. xii 12, xiii. 1—18.

Verse 8. *And*—What follows from this verse to chap. xi. 13, runs parallel with the oath of the angel, and with "the fulfilling of the mystery of God," as it follows under the trumpet of the seventh angel; what is said, verse 11, concerning St. John's "prophesying again," is unfolded immediately after; what is said, verse 7, concerning "the fulfilling the mystery of God," is unfolded, Rev. xi. 15—19, and in the following chapters.

Verse 9. *Eat it up*—The like was commanded to Ezekiel. This was an emblem of thoroughly considering and digesting it. *And it will make thy belly bitter, but it will be sweet as honey in thy mouth*—The sweetness betokens the many good things which follow, Rev. xi. 1, 15, &c.; the bitterness, the evils which succeed under the third woe.

Verse 11. *Thou must prophesy again*—Of the mystery of God; of which the ancient prophets had prophesied before. And he did prophesy, by "measuring the temple," Rev. xi. 1; as a prophecy may be

CHAPTER XI.

XI. 1 tongues, and many kings. And there was given me a
reed like a measuring rod: and he said, Arise, and measure
the temple of God, and the altar, and them that worship
2 therein. But the court which is about the temple cast out,
and measure it not; for it is given to the gentiles: and they
3 shall tread the holy city forty-two months. And I will give to

delivered either by words or actions. *Concerning people, and nations, and tongues, and many kings*—The *people, nations, and tongues* are contemporary; but the *kings*, being *many*, succeed one another. These kings are not mentioned for their own sake, but with a view to the "holy city," Rev. xi. 2. Here is a reference to the great kingdoms in Spain, England, Italy, &c., which arose from the eighth century; or at least underwent a considerable change, as France and Germany in particular; to the Christian, afterward Turkish, empire in the east; and especially to the various potentates, who have successively reigned at or over Jerusalem, and do now, at least titularly, reign over it.

CHAP. XI. In this chapter is shown how it will fare with "the holy city," till the mystery of God is fulfilled; in the twelfth, what will befal the woman, who is delivered of the man-child; in the thirteenth, how it will be with the kingdom of Christ, while the "two beasts" are in the height of their power. *And there was given me*—By Christ, as appears from the third verse. *And he said, Arise*—Probably he was sitting to write. *And measure the temple of God*—At Jerusalem, where he was placed in the vision. Of this we have a large description by Ezekiel, chap. xl.—xlviii.; concerning which we may observe,

1. Ezekiel's prophecy was not fulfilled at the return from the Babylonish captivity.

2. Yet it does not refer to the "New Jerusalem," which is far more gloriously described.

3. It must infallibly be fulfilled even then "when they are ashamed of all that they have done," Ezek. xliii. 11.

4. Ezekiel speaks of the same temple which is treated of here.

5. As all things are there so largely described, St. John is shorter and refers thereto.

Verse 2. *But the court which is without the temple*—The old temple had a court in the open air, for the heathens who worshipped the God of Israel. *Cast out*—Of thy account. *And measure it not*—As not being holy in so high a degree. *And they shall tread*—Inhabit. *The holy city*—Jerusalem, Matt. iv. 5. So they began to do, before St. John wrote. And it has been trodden almost ever since by the Romans, Persians, Saracens, and Turks. But that severe kind of treading which is here peculiarly spoken of, will not be till under the trumpet of the seventh angel, and toward the end of the troublous times. This will continue but *forty-two* common *months*, or twelve hundred and sixty common days; being but a small part of the *non-chronos*.

Verse 3 *And I*—Christ. *Will give to my two witnesses*—These seem

my two witnesses, to prophesy twelve hundred *and* sixty days,
4 clothed in sackcloth. These are the two olive trees, and the
5 two candlesticks, standing before the Lord of the earth. And
if any one would hurt them, fire proceedeth out of their mouth,
and devoureth their enemies: and if any would kill them, he
6 must thus be killed. These have power to shut heaven,
that it rain not in the days of their prophesying: and have
power over the waters to turn them into blood, and to smite
7 the earth with all plagues, as often as they will. And when

to be two prophets; two select, eminent instruments. Some have supposed (though without foundation) that they are Moses and Elijah, whom they resemble in several respects. *To prophesy twelve hundred and sixty days*—Common days, that is, an hundred and eighty weeks. So long will they *prophesy*, (even while that last and sharp treading of the holy city continues,) both by word and deed, *witnessing* that Jesus is the Son of God, the heir of all things, and exhorting all men to repent, and fear, and glorify God. *Clothed in sackcloth*—The habit of the deepest mourners, out of sorrow and concern for the people.

Verse 4. *These are the two olive trees*—That is, as Zerubbabel and Joshua, *the two olive trees* spoken of by Zechariah, chap. iii. 9, iv. 10, were then the two chosen instruments in God's hand, even so shall these be in their season. Being themselves full of the unction of the Holy One, they shall continually transmit the same to others also. *And the two candlesticks*—Burning and shining lights. *Standing before the Lord of the earth*—Always waiting on God, without the help of man, and asserting his right over the earth and all things therein.

Verse 5. *If any would kill them*—As the Israelites would have done Moses and Aaron, Numb. xvi. 41. *He must be killed thus*—By that devouring fire.

Verse 6. *These have power*—And they use that power. See verse 10. *To shut heaven, that it rain not in the days of their prophesying*—During those "twelve hundred and sixty days." *And have power over the waters*—In and near Jerusalem. *To turn them into blood*—As Moses did those in Egypt. *And to smite the earth with all plagues, as often as they will*—This is not said of Moses or Elijah, or any mere man besides. And how is it possible to understand this otherwise than of two individual persons?

Verse 7. *And when they shall have finished their testimony*—Till then they are invincible. *The wild beast*—Hereafter to be described. *That ascendeth*—First out of the sea, Rev. xiii. 1, and then *out of the bottomless pit*, Rev. xvii. 8. *Shall make war with them*—It is at his last ascent, not out of the sea, but the bottomless pit, that the beast makes war upon the two witnesses. And even hereby is fixed the time of "treading the holy city," and of the "two witnesses." That time ends after the ascent of the *beast* out of the abyss, and yet before the fulfilling of the mystery. *And shall conquer them*—The fire no longer proceeding

they shall have finished their testimony, the wild beast that
ascendeth out of the bottomless pit shall make war with
8 them, and conquer them, and kill them. And their dead
bodies *shall be* in the street of the great city, which is
called spiritually Sodom and Egypt, where also their Lord
9 was crucified. And *some* of the people and tribes and
tongues and nations behold their dead bodies three days and
a half, and they shall not suffer their dead bodies to be put
10 in a grave. And they that dwell upon the earth rejoice over
them, and they shall make merry, and send gifts to one
another; because these two prophets tormented them that
11 dwelt upon the earth. And after the three days and an
half the spirit of life from God came into them, and they
stood upon their feet; and great fear fell upon them that
12 saw them. And I heard a great voice saying from heaven
to them, Come up hither. And they went up to heaven in
13 a cloud; and their enemies beheld them. And in that hour

out of their mouth when they have finished their work. *And kill them*—These will be among the last martyrs, though not the last of all.

Verse 8. *And their bodies shall be*—Perhaps hanging on a cross *In the street of the great city*—Of Jerusalem, a far greater city, than any other in those parts. This is described both spiritually and historically: spiritually, as it is called *Sodom* (Isai. i.) *and Egypt;* on account of the same abominations abounding there, at the time of the witnesses, as did once in Egypt and Sodom. Historically: *Where also their Lord was crucified*—This possibly refers to the very ground where his cross stood. Constantine the Great inclosed this within the walls of the city. Perhaps on that very spot will their bodies be exposed.

Verse 9. *Three days and a half*—So exactly are the times set down in this prophecy. If we suppose this time began in the evening, and ended in the morning, and included (which is no way impossible) Friday, Saturday, and Sunday, the weekly festival of the Turkish people, the Jewish tribes, and the Christian tongues; then all these together, with the heathen nations, would have full leisure to gaze upon and rejoice over them.

Verse 10. *And they that dwell upon the earth*—Perhaps this expression may peculiarly denote earthly-minded men. *Shall make merry*—As did the Philistines over Samson. *And send gifts to one another*—Both Turks, and Jews, and heathens, and false Christians.

Verse 11. *And great fear fell upon them that saw them*—And now knew that God was on their side

Verse 12. *And I heard a great voice*—Designed for all to hear. *And they went up to heaven, and their enemies beheld them*—Who had not taken notice of their rising again; by which some had been convinced before.

Verse 13. *And there was a great earthquake, and the tenth part of the*

there was a great earthquake, and the tenth part of the city fell, and there were slain in the earthquake seven thousand men, and the rest were terrified, and gave glory to the God

city fell—We have here an unanswerable proof that this city is not Babylon or Rome, but Jerusalem. For Babylon shall be wholly burned before the fulfilling of the mystery of God. But this city is not burned at all; on the contrary, at the fulfilling of that mystery, a tenth part of it is destroyed by an earthquake, and the other nine parts converted. *And there were slain in the earthquake seven thousand men*—Being a tenth part of the inhabitants, who therefore were seventy thousand in all. *And the rest*—The remaining sixty-three thousand were converted: a grand step toward the fulfilling of the mystery of God. Such a conversion we no where else read of. So there shall be a larger as well as holier church at Jerusalem than ever was yet. *Were terrified*—Blessed terror! *And gave glory*—The character of true conversion, Jer. xiii. 16. *To the God of heaven*—He is styled, "The Lord of the earth," verse 4, when he declares his right over the earth by the two witnesses; but *the God of heaven,* when he not only gives rain from heaven after the most afflicting drought, but also declares his majesty from heaven, by taking his witnesses up into it. When the whole multitude gives glory to the God of heaven, then that "treading of the holy city" ceases. This is the point so long aimed at, the desired "fulfilling of the mystery of God," when the divine promises are so richly fulfilled on those who have gone through so great afflictions. All this is here related together, that whereas the first and second woe went forth in the east, the rest of the eastern affairs being added at once, the description of the western might afterwards remain unbroken.

It may be useful here to see how the things here spoken of, and those hereafter described, follow each other in their order.

1. The angel swears; the *non-chronos* begins; John eats the book; the many kings arise.

2. The *non-chronos* and the "many kings" being on the decline, that "treading" begins, and the "two witnesses" appear.

3. The beast, after he has with the ten kings destroyed Babylon, wars with them and kills them. After three days and an half they revive and ascend to heaven. There is a great earthquake in the holy city: seven thousand perish, and the rest are converted. The "treading" of the city by the gentiles ends.

4. The beast, and the kings of the earth, and their armies are assembled to fight against the Great King.

5. Multitudes of his enemies are killed, and the beast and the false prophet cast alive into the lake of fire.

6. While John measures the temple of God and the altar with the worshippers, the true worship of God is set up. The nations who had trodden the holy city are converted. Hereby the mystery of God is fulfilled.

7. Satan is imprisoned. Being released for a time, he, with Gog and Magog, makes his last assault upon Jerusalem.

14 of heaven. The second woe is past behold, the third
woe cometh quickly.
15 And the seventh angel sounded; and there were great voices
in heaven, saying, The kingdom of the world is become *the*
kingdom of our Lord and of his Christ; and he shall reign
16 for ever and ever. And the four and twenty elders, who

Verse 14. *The second woe is past*—The butchery made by the Saracens ceased about the year 847, when their power was so broken by Charles the Great that they never recovered it. *Behold, the third woe cometh quickly*—Its prelude came while the Roman see took all opportunities of laying claim to its beloved universality, and enlarging its power and grandeur. And in the year 755 the bishop of Rome became a secular prince, by king Pepin's giving him the exarchate of Lombardy. The beginning of the third woe itself stands, Rev. xii. 12.

Verse 15. *And the seventh angel sounded*—This trumpet contains the most important and joyful events, and renders all the former trumpets matter of joy to all the inhabitants of heaven. The allusion therefore in this and all the trumpets is to those used in festal solemnities. All these seven trumpets were heard in heaven: perhaps the seventh shall once be heard on earth also, 1 Thess. iv. 16. *And there were great voices*—From the several citizens of heaven. At the opening of the seventh seal "there was silence in heaven;" at the sounding of the seventh trumpet, *great voices*. This alone is sufficient to show that the seven seals and seven trumpets do not run parallel to each other. As soon as the seventh angel sounds, the kingdom falls to God and his Christ. This immediately appears in heaven, and is there celebrated with joyful praise. But on earth several dreadful occurrences are to appear first. This trumpet comprises all that follows from these voices to Rev. xxii. 5. *The kingdom of the world*—That is, the royal government over the whole world, and all its kingdoms, Zech. xiv. 9. *Is become the kingdom of the Lord*—This province has been in the enemy's hands: it now returns to its rightful Master. In the Old Testament, from Moses to Samuel, God himself was the King of his own people. And the same will be in the New Testament: he will himself reign over the Israel of God. *And of his Christ*—This appellation is now first given him, since the introduction of the book, on the mention of the kingdom devolving upon him, under the seventh trumpet. Prophets and priests were anointed, but more especially kings: whence that term, *the anointed*, is applied only to a king. Accordingly, whenever the Messiah is mentioned in scripture, his kingdom is implied. *Is become*—In reality, all things (and so the kingdom of the world) are God's in all ages: yet Satan and the present world, with its kings and lords, are risen against the Lord and against his Anointed. God now puts an end to this monstrous rebellion, and maintains his right to all things. And this appears in an entirely new manner, as soon as the seventh angel sounds.

Verse 16. *And the four and twenty elders*—These shall reign over the

sat before God on their thrones, fell on their faces and
17 worshipped God, Saying, We give thee thanks, O Lord
God, the Almighty, who is, and who was; because thou hast
18 taken thy great power, and hast reigned. And the nations
were wroth, and thy wrath is come, and the time of the
dead, that they be judged, and to give a reward to thy

earth, Rev. v. 10. *Who sit before God on their thrones*—Which we do not read of any angel.

Verse 17. *The Almighty*—He who hath all things in his power, as the only Governor of them. *Who is, and who was*—God is frequently styled, "He who is, and who was, and who is to come." but now he is actually come, the words, "who is to come," are, as it were, swallowed up. When it is said, *We thank thee that thou hast taken thy great power*, it is all one as, "We thank thee that thou art come." This whole thanksgiving is partly an enlargement on the two great points mentioned in the fifteenth verse; partly a summary of what is hereafter more distinctly related. Here it is mentioned, how the kingdom is the Lord's; afterwards, how it is the kingdom of his Christ. *Thou hast taken thy great power*—This is the beginning of what is done under the trumpet of the seventh angel. God has never ceased to use his power; but he has suffered his enemies to oppose it, which he will now suffer no more.

Verse 18. *And the* heathen *nations were wroth*—At the breaking out of the power and kingdom of God. This wrath of the heathens now rises to the highest pitch; but it meets the wrath of the Almighty, and melts away In this verse is described both the going forth and the end of God's wrath, which together take up several ages. *And the time of the dead is come*—Both of the quick and dead, of whom those already dead are far the more numerous part. *That they be judged*—This, being infallibly certain, they speak of as already present. *And to give a reward*—At the coming of Christ, Rev. xxii. 12; but of free grace, not of debt, 1. *To his servants the prophets:* 2. *To his saints:* to them who were eminently holy: 3. *To them that fear his name:* these are the lowest class. Those who do not even fear God will have no reward from him. *Small and great*—All universally, young and old, high and low, rich and poor. *And to destroy them that destroyed the earth*—The earth was destroyed by the "great whore" in particular, Rev. xix. 2; xvii. 2, 5; but likewise in general, by the open rage and hate of wicked men against all that is good; by wars, and the various destruction and desolation naturally flowing therefrom; by such laws and constitutions as hinder much good, and occasion many offences and calamities; by public scandals, whereby a door is opened for all dissoluteness and unrighteousness; by abuse of secular and spiritual powers; by evil doctrines, maxims, and counsels; by open violence and persecution; and by sins crying to God to send plagues upon the earth.

This great work of God, destroying the destroyers, under the trumpet of the seventh angel, is not the third woe, but matter of joy, for which

servants the prophets, and to the saints, and to them that
fear thy name, small and great; and to destroy them that
destroyed the earth.
19 And the temple of God was opened in heaven, and the
ark of the covenant was seen in the temple and there were
lightnings, and voices, and thunders, and an earthquake.
and great hail.

CHAP. XII. 1 And a great sign was seen in heaven;
a woman clothed with the sun, and the moon under her feet,

the elders solemnly give thanks. All the woes, and particularly the third, go forth over those "who dwell upon the earth;" but this destruction, over those "who destroy the earth," and were also instruments of that woe.

Verse 19. *And the temple of God*—The inmost part of it. *Was opened in heaven*—And hereby is opened a new scene of the most momentous things, that we may see how the contents of the seventh trumpet are executed; and, notwithstanding the greatest opposition, (particularly by the third woe,) brought to a glorious conclusion. *And the ark of the covenant was seen in his temple*—The ark of the covenant which was made by Moses was not in the second temple, being probably burnt with the first temple by the Chaldeans. But here is the heavenly ark of the everlasting covenant, the shadow of which was under the Old Testament, Heb ix. 4. The inhabitants of heaven saw the ark before: St. John also saw it now; for a testimony, that what God had promised, should be fulfilled to the uttermost. *And there were lightnings, and voices, and thunders, and an earthquake, and great hail*—The very same there are, and in the same order, when the seventh angel has poured out his phial; Rev. xvi. 17—21: one place answers the other. What the trumpet here denounces in heaven, is there executed by the phial upon earth. First it is shown what will be done; and afterwards it is done.

CHAP. XII. The great vision of this book goes straight forward, from the fourth to the twenty-second chapter. Only the tenth, with part of the eleventh chapter, was a kind of introduction to the trumpet of the seventh angel; after which it is said, "The second woe is past: behold, the third woe cometh quickly." Immediately the seventh angel sounds, under whom the third woe goes forth. And to this trumpet belongs all that is related to the end of the book.

Verse 1. *And a great sign was seen in heaven*—Not only by St. John, but many heavenly spectators represented in the vision. *A sign* means something that has an uncommon appearance, and from which we infer that some unusual thing will follow. *A woman*—The emblem of the church of Christ, as she is originally of Israel, though built and enlarged on all sides by the addition of heathen converts; and as she will here-

2 and on her head a crown of twelve stars. And being with
child she crieth, travailing in birth, and pained to be deli-
3 vered. And another sign was seen in heaven; and behold
a great red dragon, having seven heads and ten horns, and
4 seven diadems on his heads. And his tail draweth the third
part of the stars of heaven, and casteth them to the earth.

after appear, when all her "natural branches are again "grafted in." She is at present on earth; and yet, with regard to her union with Christ, may be said to be in heaven, Eph. ii. 6. Accordingly, she is described as both assaulted and defended in heaven, verses 4, 7. *Clothed with the sun, and the moon under her feet, and on her head a crown of twelve stars*—These figurative expressions must be so interpreted as to preserve a due proportion between them. So, in Joseph's dream, the sun betokened his father; the moon, his mother; the stars, their children. There may be some such resemblance here; and as the prophecy points out the "power over all nations," perhaps *the sun* may betoken the Christian world; *the moon*, the Mahometans, who also carry the moon in their ensigns; and the *crown of twelve stars*, the twelve tribes of Israel; which are smaller than the sun and moon. The whole of this chapter answers the state of the church from the ninth century to this time.

Verse 2. *And being with child she crieth, travailing in birth*—The very pain, without any outward opposition, would constrain a woman in travail to cry out. These cries, throes, and pains to be delivered, were the painful longings, the sighs, and prayers of the saints for the coming of the kingdom of God. The woman groaned and travailed in spirit, that Christ might appear, as the Shepherd and King of all nations.

Verse 3. *And behold a great red dragon*—His fiery-red colour denoting his disposition. *Having seven heads*—Implying vast wisdom. *And ten horns*—Perhaps on the seventh head; emblems of mighty power and strength, which he still retained. *And seven diadems on his heads*—Not properly crowns, but costly bindings, such as kings anciently wore; for, though fallen, he was a great potentate still, even "the prince of this world."

Verse 4. *And his tail*—His falsehood and subtilty. *Draweth*—As a train *The third part*—A very large number. *Of the stars of heaven*—The Christians and their teachers, who before sat in heavenly places with Christ Jesus. *And casteth them to the earth*—Utterly deprives them of all those heavenly blessings. This is properly a part of the description of the dragon, who was not yet himself on earth, but in heaven: consequently, this casting them down was between the beginning of the seventh trumpet and the beginning of the third woe; or between the year 847 and the year 947; at which time pestilent doctrines, particularly that of the Manichees in the east, drew abundance of people from the truth *And the dragon stood before the woman, that when she had brought forth, he might devour the child*—That he might hinder the kingdom of Christ from spreading abroad, as it does under this trumpet.

and the dragon stood before the woman who was ready to
be delivered, that when she had brought forth, he might
5 devour the child. And she brought forth a man child, who
was to rule all the nations with a rod of iron: and her child
6 was caught up to God, and to his throne. And the woman
fled into the wilderness, where she hath a place prepared
by God, that they may feed her there twelve hundred *and*
sixty days.
7 And there was war in heaven: Michael and his angels

Verse 5. *And she brought forth a man child*—Even Christ, considered not in his person, but in his kingdom. In the ninth age, many nations with their princes were added to the Christian church. *Who was to rule all nations*—When his time is come. *And her child*—Which was already in heaven, as were the woman and the dragon. *Was caught up to God*—Taken utterly out of his reach.

Verse 6. *And the woman fled into the wilderness*—This wilderness is undoubtedly on earth, where the woman also herself is now supposed to be. It betokens that part of the earth where, after having brought forth, she found a new abode. And this must be in Europe; as Asia and Afric were wholly in the hands of the Turks and Saracens; and in a part of it where the woman had not been before. In this wilderness, God had already *prepared a place;* that is, made it safe and convenient for her. The wilderness is, those countries of Europe which lie on this side the Danube; for the countries which lie beyond it had received Christianity before. *That they may feed her*—That the people of that place may provide all things needful for her. *Twelve hundred and sixty days*—So many prophetic days, which are not, as some have supposed, twelve hundred and sixty, but seven hundred and seventy-seven, common years. This Bengelius has shown at large in his German Introduction. These we may compute from the year 847 to 1524. So long the woman enjoyed a safe and convenient place in Europe, which was chiefly Bohemia; where she was fed, till God provided for her more plentifully at the Reformation.

Verse 7. *And there was war in heaven*—Here Satan makes his grand opposition to the kingdom of God; but an end is now put to his accusing the saints before God The cause goes against him, verses 10, 11, and Michael executes the sentence. That Michael is a created angel, appears from his not daring, in disputing with Satan, Jude 9, to bring a railing accusation; but only saying, "The Lord rebuke thee." And this modesty is implied in his very name; for Michael signifies, "Who is like God?" which implies also his deep reverence toward God, and distance from all self-exaltation. Satan would be like God: the very name of Michael asks, "Who is like God?" Not Satan; not the highest archangel. It is he likewise that is afterward employed to seize, bind, and imprison that proud spirit.

warred with the dragon; and the dragon warred and his
8 angels, But he prevailed not; neither was his place found
9 any more in heaven. And the great dragon was cast out,
the ancient serpent, who is called the Devil, and Satan, who
deceiveth the whole world: he was cast out unto the earth,
10 and his angels were cast out with him. And I heard a loud
voice saying in heaven, Now is come the salvation, and the
might, and the kingdom of our God, and the power of his
Christ: for the accuser of our brethren is cast out, who
11 accused them before our God day and night. And they

Verse 8. *And he prevailed not*—The dragon himself is principally mentioned; but his angels, likewise, are to be understood. *Neither was his place found any more in heaven*—So till now he had a place in heaven. How deep a mystery is this! One may compare this with Luke x. 18; Eph. ii. 2; iv. 8; vi. 12.

Verse 9. *And the great dragon was cast out*—It is not yet said, *unto the earth*—He was cast out of heaven; and at this the inhabitants of heaven rejoice. He is termed *the great dragon*, as appearing here in that shape, to intimate his poisonous and cruel disposition. *The ancient serpent*—In allusion to his deceiving Eve in that form. Dragons are a kind of large serpent. *Who is called the Devil and Satan*—These are words of exactly the same meaning; only the former is Greek; the latter, Hebrew; denoting the grand adversary of all the saints, whether Jews or gentiles. He has *deceived the whole world*—Not only in their first parents, but through all ages, and in all countries, into unbelief and all wickedness; into the hating and persecuting faith and all goodness. *He was cast out unto the earth*—He was cast out of heaven; and being cast out thence, himself came to the earth Nor had he been unemployed on the earth before, although his ordinary abode was in heaven.

Verse 10. *Now is come*—Hence it is evident that all this chapter belongs to the trumpet of the seventh angel. In the eleventh chapter, from the fifteenth to the eighteenth verse, are proposed the contents of this extensive trumpet; the execution of which is copiously described in this and the following chapters. *The salvation*—Of the saints. *The might*—Whereby the enemy is cast out. *The kingdom*—Here the majesty of God is shown. *And the power of his Christ*—Which he will exert against the beast; and when he also is taken away, then will the kingdom be ascribed to Christ himself, Rev. xix. 16; xx. 4. *The accuser of our brethren*—So long as they remained on earth. This great voice, therefore, was the voice of men only. *Who accused them before our God day and night*—Amazing malice of Satan, and patience of God!

Verse 11. *And they have overcome him*—Carried the cause against him *By the blood of the Lamb*—Which cleanses the soul from all sin, and so leaves no room for accusing. *And by the word of their testimony*—The word of God, which they believed and testified, even unto death

have overcome him by the blood of the Lamb, and by the
word of their testimony; and they loved not their lives unto
12 the death. Therefore rejoice, ye heavens, and ye that dwell
in them. Woe to the earth and the sea! for the devil is
come down to you, having great wrath, because he knoweth
he hath but a little time.

So, for instance, died Olam, king of Sweden, in the year 900, whom his own subjects would have compelled to idolatry; and, upon his refusal, slew as a sacrifice to the idol which he would not worship. So did multitudes of Bohemian Christians, in the year 916, when queen Drahomire raised a severe persecution, wherein many "loved not their lives unto the death"

Verse 12. *Woe to the earth and the sea*—This is the fourth and last denunciation of the third woe, the most grievous of all. The first was only, the second chiefly, on the earth, Asia; the third, both on the earth and the sea, Europe. The earth is mentioned first, because it began in Asia, before the beast brought it on Europe. *He knoweth he hath but a little time*—Which extends from his casting out of heaven to his being cast into the abyss.

We are now come to a most important period of time. The non-chronos hastens to an end. We live in the *little time* wherein Satan hath great wrath; and this *little time* is now upon the decline. We are in the "time, times, and half a time," wherein the woman is "fed in the wilderness;" yea, the last part of it, "the half time," is begun. We are, as will be shown, towards the close of the "forty-two months" of the beast; and when his number is fulfilled, grievous things will be.

Let him who does not regard the being seized by the wrath of the devil; the falling unawares into the general temptation; the being borne away, by the most dreadful violence, into the worship of the beast and his image, and, consequently, drinking the unmixed wine of the wrath of God, and being tormented day and night for ever and ever in the lake of fire and brimstone; let him also who is confident that he can make his way through all these by his own wisdom and strength, without need of any such peculiar preservative as the word of this prophecy affords; let him, I say, go hence. But let him who does not take these warnings for senseless outcries, and blind alarms, beg of God, with all possible earnestness, to give him his heavenly light herein.

God has not given this prophecy, in so solemn a manner, only to show his providence over his church, but also that his servants may know at all times in what particular period they are. And the more dangerous any period of time is, the greater is the help which it affords. But where may we fix the beginning and end of the *little time?* which is probably four-fifths of a chronos, or somewhat above 888 years This, which is the time of the third woe, may reach from 947, to the year 1836 For,

13 And when the dragon saw that he was cast to the earth,
he persecuted the woman that had brought forth the male
14 child. And there were given to the woman the two wings
of the great eagle, that she might fly into the wilderness, to
her place, where she is fed for a time, and times, and half a

1. The short interval of the second woe, (which woe ended in the year 840,) and the 777 years of the woman, which began about the year 847, quickly after which followed the war in heaven, fix the beginning not long after 864: and thus the third woe falls in the tenth century, extending from 900 to 1000; called the dark, the iron, the unhappy age. 2. If we compare the length of the third woe with the period of time which succeeds it in the twentieth chapter, it is but a *little time* to that vast space which reaches from the beginning of the non-chronos to the end of the world.

Verse 13. *And when the dragon saw*—That he could no longer accuse the saints in heaven, he turned his wrath to do all possible mischief on earth. *He persecuted the woman*—The ancient persecutions of the church were mentioned, Rev. i. 9, ii. 10, vii. 14; but this persecution came after her flight, verse 6, just at the beginning of the third woe. Accordingly, in the tenth and eleventh centuries, the church was furiously persecuted by several heathen powers. In Prussia, king Adelbert was killed in the year 997, king Brunus in 1008; and when king Stephen encouraged Christianity in Hungary, he met with violent opposition. After his death, the heathens in Hungary set themselves to root it out, and prevailed for several years. About the same time, the army of the emperor, Henry the Third, was totally overthrown by the Vandals. These, and all the accounts of those times, show with what fury the dragon then persecuted the woman.

Verse 14. *And there were given to the woman the two wings of the great eagle, that she might fly into the wilderness to her place*—Eagles are the usual symbols of great potentates. So Ezekiel, xvii. 3, by "a great eagle" means the king of Babylon. Here *the great eagle* is the Roman empire; *the two wings*, the eastern and western branches of it. A place in the wilderness was mentioned in the sixth verse also; but it is not the same which is mentioned here. In the text there follow one after the other,

1. The dragon's waiting to devour the child.
2. The birth of the child, which is caught up to God.
3. The fleeing of the woman into the wilderness.
4. The war in heaven, and the casting out of the dragon.
5. The beginning of the third woe.
6. The persecution raised by the dragon against the woman
7. The woman's flying away upon the eagle's wings.

In like manner there follow one after the other,

1. The beginning of the twelve hundred and sixty days.
2. The beginning of the little time.
3. The beginning of the time, times, and half a time. This third

15 time, from the face of the serpent. And the serpent **cast**
out of his mouth after the woman water as a river, that he

period partly coincides both with the first and the second. After the beginning of the twelve hundred and sixty days, or rather of the third woe, Christianity was exceedingly propagated, in the midst of various persecutions About the year 948 it was again settled in Denmark; in 965, in Poland and Silesia; in 980, through all Russia. In 997 it was brought into Hungary; into Sweden and Norway, both before and after. Transylvania received it about 1000; and, soon after, other parts of Dacia.

Now, all the countries in which Christianity was settled between the beginning of the twelve hundred and sixty days, and the imprisonment of the dragon, may be understood by *the wilderness*, and by *her place* in particular. This place contained many countries; so that Christianity now reached, in an uninterrupted tract, from the eastern to the western empire; and both the emperors now lent their wings to the woman, and provided a safe abode for her. *Where she is fed*—By God rather than man; having little human help. *For a time, and times, and half a time*—The length of the several periods here mentioned seems to be nearly this:—

	Years.
1. The non-chronos contains less than	1111
2. The little time	888
3. The time, times, and half a time	777
4. The time of the beast	666

And comparing the prophecy and history together, they seem to begin and end nearly thus:—

1 The non-chronos extends	from about	800 to 1836
2. The 1260 days of the woman	from	847 — 1524
3. The little time	——	947 — 1836
4. The time, time, and half	——	1058 — 1836

5. The time of the beast is between the beginning and end of the three times and a half. In the year 1058 the empires had a good understanding with each other, and both protected the woman. The bishops of Rome, likewise, particularly Victor II., were duly subordinate to the emperor. We may observe, the twelve hundred and sixty days of the woman, from 847 to 1524, and the three times and a half, refer to the same wilderness. But in the former part of the twelve hundred and sixty days, before the three times and an half began, namely, from the year 847 to 1058, she was fed by others, being little able to help herself; whereas, from 1058 to 1524, she is both fed by others, and has food herself. To this the sciences transplanted into the west from the eastern countries much contributed; the scriptures, in the original tongues, brought into the west of Europe by the Jews and Greeks, much more; and most of all, the Reformation, grounded on those scriptures.

Verse 15 *Water* is an emblem of a great people; this water, of the

16 might cause her to be carried away by the stream. But the
earth helped the woman, and opened her mouth, and swallowed up the river which the dragon had cast out of his
17 mouth. And the dragon was wroth with the woman, and
went forth to make war with the rest of her seed, who keep
the commandments of God, and retain the testimony of
Jesus.

CHAP. XIII. 1 And I stood on the sand of the sea,

Turks in particular. About the year 1060 they overran the Christian part of Asia. Afterward, they poured into Europe, and spread farther and farther, till they had overflowed many nations.

Verse 16. *But the earth helped the woman*—The powers of the earth and indeed she needed help through this whole period. "The time" was from 1058 to 1280; during which the Turkish flood ran higher and higher, though frequently repressed by the emperors, or their generals, helping the woman. "The" two "times" were from 1280 to 1725 During these likewise the Turkish power flowed far and wide; but still from time to time the princes of the earth *helped the woman,* that she was not carried away by it. "The half time" is from 1725 to 1836 In the beginning of this period the Turks began to meddle with the affairs of Persia: wherein they have so entangled themselves, as to be the less able to prevail against the two remaining Christian empires. Yet this flood still reaches the woman "in her place;" and will, till near the end of the "half time," itself be swallowed up, perhaps by means of Russia, which is risen in the room of the eastern empire.

Verse 17. *And the dragon was wroth*—Anew, because he could not cause her to be carried away by the stream. *And he went forth*—Into other lands. *To make war with the rest of her seed*—Real Christians, living under heathen or Turkish governors.

Verse 1. *And I stood on the sand of the sea*—This also was in the vision. *And I saw*—Soon after the woman flew away. *A wild beast coming up*—He comes up twice; first from the sea, then from the abyss. He comes from the sea before the seven phials; "the great whore" comes after them.

O reader, this is a subject wherein we also are deeply concerned, and which must be treated, not as a point of curiosity, but as a solemn warning from God! The danger is near. Be armed both against force and fraud, even with the whole armour of God. *Out of the sea*—That is, Europe So the three woes (the first being in Persia, the second about the Euphrates) move in a line from east to west This beast is the Romish Papacy, as it came to a point six hundred years since, stands now, and will for some time longer. To this, and no other power on earth, agrees the whole text, and every part of it in every point; as we may see, with the utmost evidence, from the propositions following:—

CHAPTER XIII.

and saw a wild beast coming up out of the sea, having

Prop. 1. It is one and the same beast, having seven heads, and ten horns, which is described in this and in the seventeenth chapter. Of consequence, his heads are the same, and his horns also.

Prop. 2. This beast is a spiritually secular power, opposite to the kingdom of Christ. A power not merely spiritual or ecclesiastical, nor merely secular or political: but a mixture of both. He is a secular prince; for a crown, yea, and a kingdom are ascribed to him. And yet he is not merely secular; for he is also a false prophet.

Prop. 3. The beast has a strict connexion with the city of Rome. This clearly appears from the seventeenth chapter

Prop. 4. The beast is now existing. He is not past. for Rome is now existing; and it is not till after the destruction of Rome that the beast is thrown into the lake. He is not altogether to come: for the second woe is long since past, after which the third came quickly; and presently after it began, the beast rose out of the sea. Therefore, whatever he is, he is now existing.

Prop. 5. The beast is the Romish Papacy This manifestly follows from the third and fourth propositions; the beast has a strict connexion with the city of Rome; and the beast is now existing: therefore, either there is some other power more strictly connected with that city, or the Pope is the beast.

Prop. 6. The Papacy, or papal kingdom, began long ago.

The most remarkable particulars relating to this are here subjoined; taken so high as abundantly to show the rise of the beast, and brought down as low as our own time, in order to throw a light on the following part of the prophecy:—

A. D. 1033. Benedict the Ninth, a child of eleven years old, is bishop of Rome, and occasions grievous disorders for above twenty years.

A. D. 1048. Damasus II. introduces the use of the triple crown.

A. D. 1058. The church of Milan is, after long opposition, subjected to the Roman.

A. D. 1073. Hildebrand, or Gregory VII., comes to the throne

A. D. 1076. He deposes and excommunicates the emperor

A. D. 1077. He uses him shamefully and absolves him.

A. D. 1080. He excommunicates him again, and sends a crown to Rodulph, his competitor.

A. D. 1083. Rome is taken. Gregory flees. Clement is made Pope, and crowns the emperor.

A. D. 1085. Gregory VII. dies at Salerno.

A. D. 1095. Urban II. holds the first Popish council, at Clermont, and gives rise to the crusades.

A. D. 1111. Paschal II. quarrels furiously with the emperor.

A. D. 1123. The first western general council in the Lateran. The marriage of priests is forbidden.

A. D. 1132. Innocent II declares the emperor to be the Pope's liege-man, or vassal.

seven heads and ten horns, and upon his horns ten

A D. 1143. The Romans set up a governor of their own, independent on Innocent II. He excommunicates them, and dies. Celestine II. is, by an important innovation, chosen to the Popedom without the suffrage of the people; the right of choosing the Pope is taken from the people, and afterward from the clergy, and lodged in the Cardinals alone.

A. D. 1152. Eugene II. assumes the power of canonizing saints.

A. D. 1155. Adrian IV. puts Arnold of Brixia to death for speaking against the secular power of the Papacy.

A. D. 1159. Victor IV. is elected and crowned. But Alexander III. conquers him and his successor.

A. D 1168. Alexander III. excommunicates the emperor, and brings him so low, that,

A. D. 1177. he submits to the Pope's setting his foot on his neck.

A. D. 1204. Innocent III. sets up the Inquisition against the Vaudois.

A. D. 1208. He proclaims a crusade against them.

A. D. 1300. Boniface VIII. introduces the year of jubilee.

A. D. 1305. The Pope's residence is removed to Avignon.

A. D. 1377. It is removed back to Rome.

A. D. 1378. The fifty years' schism begins.

A. D. 1449. Felix V., the last Antipope, submits to Nicholas V.

A. D. 1517. The Reformation begins.

A. D. 1527. Rome is taken and plundered.

A. D. 1557. Charles V. resigns the empire; Ferdinand I. thinks the being crowned by the Pope superfluous.

A. D 1564. Pius IV. confirms the Council of Trent.

A. D. 1682. Doctrines highly derogatory to the Papal authority are openly taught in France.

A.D. 1713. The constitution *Unigenitus*.

A. D. 1721. Pope Gregory VII. canonized anew.

He who compares this short table with what will be observed, verse 3, and Rev. xvii. 10, will see that the ascent of the beast out of the sea must needs be fixed toward the beginning of it; and not higher than Gregory VII., nor lower than Alexander III.

The secular princes now favoured the kingdom of Christ; but the bishops of Rome vehemently opposed it. These at first were plain ministers or pastors of the Christian congregation at Rome, but by degrees they rose to an eminence of honour and power over all their brethren: till, about the time of Gregory VII. (and so ever since) they assumed all the ensigns of royal majesty; yea, of a majesty and power far superior to that of all other potentates on earth.

We are not here considering their false doctrines, but their unbounded power When we think of those, we are to look at the false prophet, who is also termed a *wild beast* at his ascent out of the earth. But the first beast then properly arose, when, after several preludes thereto, the Pope raised himself above the emperor.

diadems, and upon his heads a name of blasphemy.

PROP. 7. Hildebrand, or Gregory VII., is the proper founder of the papal kingdom. All the patrons of the Papacy allow that he made many considerable additions to it; and this very thing constituted the beast, by completing the spiritual kingdom: the new maxims and the new actions of Gregory all proclaim this. Some of his maxims are,

1. That the bishop of Rome alone is universal bishop.
2. That he alone can depose bishops, or receive them again.
3. That he alone has power to make new laws in the church
4. That he alone ought to use the ensigns of royalty.
5. That all princes ought to kiss his foot.
6. That the name of Pope is the only name under heaven; and that his name alone should be recited in the churches.
7. That he has a power to depose emperors.
8. That no general synod can be convened but by him
9. That no book is canonical without his authority.
10. That none upon earth can repeal his sentence, but he alone can repeal any sentence.
11. That he is subject to no human judgment
12. That no power dare to pass sentence on one who appeals to the Pope.
13. That all weighty causes everywhere ought to be referred to him.
14. That the Roman church never did, nor ever can, err.
15 That the Roman bishop, canonically ordained, is immediately made holy, by the merits of St. Peter.
16 That he can absolve subjects from their allegiance.

These the most eminent Romish writers own to be his genuine sayings. And his actions agree with his words Hitherto the Popes had been subject to the emperors, though often unwillingly; but now the Pope began himself, under a spiritual pretext, to act the emperor of the whole Christian world: the immediate dispute was, about the investiture of bishops, the right of which each claimed to himself. And now was the time for the Pope either to give up or establish his empire for ever: to decide which, Gregory excommunicated the emperor Henry IV.; "having first," says Platina, "deprived him of all his dignities." The sentence ran in these terms: "Blessed Peter, prince of the apostles, incline, I beseech thee, thine ears, and hear me thy servant. In the name of the omnipotent God, Father, Son, and Holy Ghost, I cast down the emperor Henry from all imperial and regal authority, and absolve all Christians, that were his subjects, from the oath whereby they used to swear allegiance to true kings. And moreover, because he had despised mine, yea, thy admonitions, I bind him with the bond of an anathema."

The same sentence he repeated at Rome in these terms: "Blessed Peter, prince of the apostles, and thou Paul, teacher of the gentiles, incline, I beseech you, your ears to me, and graciously hear me. Henry, whom they call emperor, hath proudly lifted up his horns and his head against the church of God,—who came to me, humbly imploring to be

2 And the wild beast which I saw *was* like a leopard, and his

absolved from his excommunication,—I restored him to communion, but not to his kingdom,—neither did I allow his subjects to return to their allegiance. Several bishops and princes of Germany, taking this opportunity, in the room of Henry, justly deposed, chose Rodulph emperor, who immediately sent ambassadors to me, informing me that he would rather obey me than accept of a kingdom, and that he should always remain at the disposal of God and us. Henry then began to be angry, and at first intreated us to hinder Rodulph from seizing his kingdom. I said I would see to whom the right belonged, and give sentence which should be preferred. Henry forbad this. Therefore I bind Henry and all his favourers with the bond of an anathema, and again take from him all regal power. I absolve all Christians from their oath of allegiance, forbid them to obey Henry in anything, and command them to receive Rodulph as their king. Confirm this, therefore, by your authority, ye most holy princes of the apostles, that all may now at length know, as ye have power to bind and loose in heaven, so we have power to give and take away on earth, empires, kingdoms, principalities, and whatsoever men can have."

When Henry submitted, then Gregory began to reign without control. In the same year, 1077, on September 1, he fixed a new era of time, called the Indiction, used at Rome to this day.

Thus did the Pope claim to himself the whole authority over all Christian princes. Thus did he take away or confer kingdoms and empires, as a king of kings. Neither did his successors fail to tread in his steps It is well known, the following Popes have not been wanting to exercise the same power, both over kings and emperors. And this the later Popes have been so far from disclaiming, that three of them have sainted this very Gregory, namely, Clement VIII., Paul V., and Benedict XIII. Here is then the beast, that is, the king: in fact such, though not in name: according to that remarkable observation of Cardinal Bellarmine, "Antichrist will govern the Roman empire, yet without the name of Roman emperor." His spiritual title prevented his taking the name, while he exerciseth all the power Now Gregory was at the head of this novelty. So Aventine himself, "Gregory VII was the first founder of the pontifical empire."

Thus the time of the ascent of the beast is clear. The apostasy and mystery of iniquity gradually increased till he arose, "who opposeth and exalteth himself above all." (2 Thess. ii 4.) Before the seventh trumpet the adversary wrought more secretly; but soon after the beginning of this, the beast openly opposes his kingdom to the kingdom of Christ.

Prop 8. The empire of Hildebrand properly began in the year 1077 Then it was, that upon the emperor's leaving Italy, Gregory exercised his power to the full. And on the first of September, in this year, he began his famous epocha.

This may be farther established and explained by the following observations:—

feet *were* as *the feet* of a bear, and his mouth as the mouth

Obs 1. The beast is the Romish Papacy, which has now reigned for some ages.

Obs. 2. The beast has seven heads and ten horns.

Obs. 3. The seven heads are seven hills, and also seven kings. One of the heads could not have been, "as it were, mortally wounded," had it been only a hill.

Obs. 4. The ascent of the beast out of the sea is different from his ascent out of the abyss . the Revelation often mentions both the sea and the abyss; but never uses the terms promiscuously.

Obs. 5. The heads of the beast do not begin before his rise out of the sea, but with it.

Obs. 6. These heads, as kings, succeed each other.

Obs. 7. The time which they take up in this succession is divided into three parts. "Five" of the kings signified thereby "are fallen: one is, the other is not yet come."

Obs. 8. "One is:" namely, while the angel was speaking this.

He places himself and St. John in the middlemost time, that he might the more commodiously point out the first time as past, the second as present, the third as future.

Obs. 9. The continuance of the beast is divided in the same manner The beast "was, is not, will ascend out of the abyss," Rev. xvii., verses 8 and 11. Between these two verses, that is interposed as parallel with them, "Five are fallen, one is, the other is not yet come."

Obs. 10. Babylon is Rome. All things which the Revelation says of Babylon, agree to Rome, and Rome only. It commenced "Babylon," when it commenced "the great." When Babylon sunk in the east, it arose in the west; and it existed in the time of the apostles, whose judgment is said to be "avenged on her."

Obs. 11. The beast reigns both before and after the reign of Babylon First, the beast reigns, Rev. xiii. 1, &c.; then Babylon, Rev. xvii. 1, &c.; and then the beast again, Rev. xvii. 8, &c.

Obs 12. The heads are of the substance of the beast; the horns are not. The wound of one of the heads is called "the wound of the beast" itself, verse 3; but the horns, or kings, receive the kingdom "with the beast," Rev. xvii. 12 That word alone, "the horns and the beast," Rev. xvii. 16, sufficiently shows them to be something added to him.

Obs. 13. The forty-two months of the beast fall within the first of the three periods. The beast rose out of the sea in the year 1077. A little after, power was given him for forty-two months. This power is still in being.

Obs. 14. The time when the beast "is not," and the reign of "Babylon," are together. The beast, when risen out of the sea, raged violently, till "his kingdom was darkened" by the fifth phial. But it was a kingdom still; and the beast having a kingdom, though darkened, was the beast still. But it was afterwards said, "the beast was," (was the beast, that is, reigned,) "and is not;" is not the beast: does not reign, having

›f a lion. and the dragon gave him his power, and his

lost his kingdom. Why? because "the woman sits upon the beast," who "sits a queen," reigning over the kings of the earth: till the beast, rising out of the abyss, and taking with him the ten kings, suddenly destroys her.

Obs. 15. The difference there is between Rome and the Pope, which has always subsisted, will then be most apparent. Rome, distinct from the Pope, bears three meanings; the city itself, the Roman church, and the people of Rome. In the last sense of the word, Rome with its dutchy, which contained part of Tuscany and Campania, revolted from the Greek emperor in 726, and became a free state, governed by its senate. From this time the senate, and not the Pope, enjoyed the supreme civil power. But in 796, Leo III., being chosen Pope, sent to Charles the Great, desiring him to come and subdue the senate and people of Rome, and constrain them to swear allegiance to him. Hence arose a sharp contention between the Pope and the Roman people, who seized and thrust him into a monastery. He escaped and fled to the emperor, who quickly sent him back in great state. In the year 800 the emperor came to Rome, and shortly after, the Roman people, who had hitherto chosen their own bishops, and looked upon themselves and their senate as having the same rights with the ancient senate and people of Rome, chose Charles for their emperor, and subjected themselves to him, in the same manner as the ancient Romans did to their emperors. The Pope crowned him, and paid him homage on his knees, as was formerly done to the Roman emperors: and the emperor took an oath "to defend the holy Roman church in all its emoluments." He was also created consul, and styled himself thenceforward Augustus, Emperor of the Romans. Afterwards he gave the government of the city and dutchy of Rome to the Pope, yet still subject to himself.

What the Roman church is, as distinct from the Pope, appears, 1. When a council is held before the Pope's confirmation; 2. When upon a competition, judgment is given which is the true Pope; 3. When the See is vacant; 4. When the Pope himself is suspected by the Inquisition

How Rome, as it is a city, differs from the Pope, there is no need to show.

Obs. 16. In the first and second period of his duration, the beast is a body of men; in the third, an individual. The beast with seven heads is the Papacy of many ages: the seventh head is the man of sin, antichrist. He is a body of men from Rev. xiii. 1, to xvii. 7; he is a body of men and an individual, chap. xvii., from the eighth to the eleventh verse; he is an individual, from chap. xvii. 12, to xix. 20.

Obs. 17. That individual is the seventh head of the beast, or, the other king after the five and one, himself being the eighth, though one of the seven. As he is a Pope, he is one of the seven heads. But he is the eighth, or not a head, but the beast himself, not, as he is a Pope, but as he bears a new and singular character at his coming from the abyss. To illustrate this by a comparison: suppose a tree of seven branches, one of which is much larger than the rest; if those six are cut away, and the seventh remain, that is the tree

3 throne, and great authority And *I saw* one of his heads

Obs. 18. "He is the wicked one, the man of sin, the son of perdition," usually termed antichrist.

Obs. 19. The ten horns, or kings, "receive power as kings with the wild beast one hour," Rev. xvii. 12; with the individual beast, "who was not." But he receives his power again, and the kings with it, who quickly give their new power to him.

Obs. 20. The whole power of the Roman monarchy, divided into ten kingdoms, will be conferred on the beast, Rev. xvii. 13, 16, 17.

Obs. 21. The ten horns and the beast will destroy the whore, verse 16.

Obs. 22. At length the beast, the ten horns, and the other kings of the earth, will fall in that great slaughter, chap. xix. 19.

Obs. 23. Daniel's fourth beast is the Roman monarchy, from the beginning of it, till the thrones are set. This, therefore, comprises both the apocalyptic beast, and the woman, and many other things. This monarchy is like a river which runs from its fountain in one channel, but in its course sometimes takes in other rivers, sometimes is itself parted into several streams, yet is still one continued river. The Roman power was at first undivided; but it was afterwards divided into various channels, till the grand division into the eastern and western empires, which likewise underwent various changes. Afterward the kings of the Heruli, Goths, Lombards, the exarchs of Ravenna, the Romans themselves; the emperors, French and German, besides other kings, seized several parts of the Roman power. Now whatever power the Romans had before Gregory VII., that Daniel's beast contains; whatever power the Papacy has had from Gregory VII., this the apocalyptic beast represents. But this very beast (and so Rome with its last authority) is comprehended under that of Daniel. *And upon his heads a name of blasphemy*—To ascribe to a man what belongs to God alone is blasphemy. Such a name the beast has, not on his horns, nor on one head, but on all. The beast himself bears that name, and indeed through his whole duration. This is the name of Papa or Pope; not in the innocent sense wherein it was formerly given to all bishops, but in that high and peculiar sense wherein it is now given to the bishop of Rome by himself, and his followers: a name which comprises the whole pre-eminence of the highest and most holy father upon earth. Accordingly among the above cited sayings of Gregory, those two stand together, that his "name alone should be recited in the churches;" and that it is "the only name in the world." So both the church and the world were to name no other father on the face of the earth.

Verse 2 The three first beasts in Daniel are like "a leopard," "a bear," and "a lion." In all parts, except his feet and mouth, this beast was like a leopard or female panther; which is fierce as a lion or bear, but is also swift and subtle. Such is the Papacy, which has partly by subtilty, partly by force, gained power over so many nations. The extremely various usages, manners, and ways of the Pope, may likewise

as it were wounded to death; and his deadly wound was healed: and the whole earth wondered after the wild beast,

be compared to the spots of the leopard. *And his feet were as the feet of a bear*—Which are very strong, and armed with sharp claws. And, as clumsy as they seem, he can therewith walk, stand upright, climb, or seize anything. So does this beast seize and take for his prey whatever comes within the reach of his claws. *And his mouth was as the mouth of a lion*—To roar, and to devour. *And the dragon*—Whose vassal and vicegerent he is. *Gave him his power*—His own strength and innumerable forces. *And his throne*—So that he might command whatever he would, having *great,* absolute *authority.* The dragon had his throne in heathen Rome, so long as idolatry and persecution reigned there. And after he was disturbed in his possession, yet would he never wholly resign, till he gave it to the beast in Christian Rome, so called.

Verse 3. *And I saw one*—Or the first. *Of his heads as it were wounded*—So it appeared as soon as ever it rose. The beast is first described more generally, then more particularly, both in this and in the seventeenth chapter. The particular description here respects the former parts; there, the latter parts of his duration: only that some circumstances relating to the former are repeated in the seventeenth chapter

This deadly wound was given him on his first head by the sword, verse 14; that is, by the bloody resistance of the secular potentates, particularly the German emperors. These had for a long season had the city of Rome, with her bishop, under their jurisdiction. Gregory determined to cast off this yoke from his own, and to lay it on the emperor's shoulders. He broke loose, and excommunicated the emperor, who maintained his right by force, and gave the Pope such a blow, that one would have thought the beast must have been killed thereby, immediately after his coming up. But he recovered, and grew stronger than before. The first head of the beast extends from Gregory VII., at least to Innocent III. In that tract of time the beast was much wounded by the emperors. But, notwithstanding, *the wound was healed.*

Two deadly symptoms attended this wound: 1. Schisms and open ruptures in the church. For while the emperors asserted their right, there were from the year 1080 to the year 1176 only, five open divisions, and at least as many antipopes, some of whom were, indeed, the rightful Popes. This was highly dangerous to the papal kingdoms. But a still more dangerous symptom was, 2. The rising of the nobility at Rome, who would not suffer their bishop to be a secular prince, particularly over themselves. Under Innocent II. they carried their point, re-established the ancient commonwealth, took away from the Pope the government of the city, and left him only his episcopal authority. "At this," says the historian, "Innocent II. and Celestine II. fretted themselves to death: Lucius II., as he attacked the capitol, wherein the senate was, sword in hand, was struck with a stone, and died in a few days: Eugene III., Alexander III., and Lucius III., were driven out of the city: Urban III. and Gregory VIII. spent their days in banishment At length they

4 And worshipped the dragon, because he gave the authority to
the wild beast; and worshipped the wild beast, saying, Who
5 *is* like the wild beast? and who can war with him? And
there was given him a mouth speaking great things and
blasphemy; and authority was given him forty and two
6 months. And he opened his mouth in blasphemy against
God, to blaspheme his name and his tabernacle, even them
7 that dwell in heaven. And it was given him to make war with
the saints, and to overcome them: and authority was given
him over every tribe, and people, and tongue, and nation

came to an agreement with Clement III., who was himself a Roman." *And the whole earth*—The whole western world. *Wondered after the wild beast*—That is, followed him with wonder, in his councils, his crusades, and his jubilees This refers not only to the first head, but also to the four following.

Verse 4. *And they worshipped the dragon*—Even in worshipping the beast, although they knew it not. *And worshipped the wild beast*—Paying him such honour as was not paid to any merely secular potentate. That very title, "Our most holy Lord," was never given to any other monarch on earth. *Saying, Who is like the wild beast*—"Who is like him?" is a peculiar attribute of God; but that this is constantly attributed to the beast, the books of all his adherents show.

Verse 5. *And there was given him*—By the dragon, through the permission of God. *A mouth speaking great things and blasphemy*—The same is said of the little horn on the fourth beast in Daniel. Nothing greater, nothing more blasphemous, can be conceived, than what the Popes have said of themselves, especially before the Reformation. *And authority was given him forty-two months*—The beginning of these is not to be dated immediately from his ascent out of the sea, but at some distance from it.

Verse 6. *To blaspheme his name*—Which many of the Popes have done explicitly, and in the most dreadful manner *And his tabernacle, even them that dwell in heaven*—(For God himself dwelleth in the inhabitants of heaven.) Digging up the bones of many of them, and cursing them with the deepest execrations.

Verse 7. *And it was given him*—That is, God permitted him. *To make war with his saints*—With the Waldenses and Albigenses. It is a vulgar mistake, that the Waldenses were so called from Peter Waldo of Lyons. They were much more ancient than him; and their true name was Vallenses or Vaudois from their inhabiting the valleys of Lucerne and Agrogne. This name, Vallenses, after Waldo appeared about the year 1160, was changed by the Papists into Waldenses, on purpose to represent them as of modern original. The Albigenses were originally people of Albigeois, part of Upper Languedoc, where they considerably prevailed, and possessed several towns in the year 1200. Against these

8 And all that dwell upon the earth will worship him, whose
name is not written in the book of life of the Lamb who
9 was slain from the foundation of the world. If any one have
10 an ear, let him hear. If any leadeth into captivity, he goeth
into captivity: if any man kill with the sword, he must be
killed with the sword. Here is the patience and the faithfulness of the saints.
11 And I saw another wild beast coming up out of the earth;
and he had two horns like a lamb, but he spake like a
12 dragon. And he exerciseth all the authority of the first

many of the Popes made open war. Till now the blood of Christians had been shed only by the heathens or Arians; from this time by scarce any but the Papacy. In the year 1208 Innocent III. proclaimed a crusade against them In June, 1209, the army assembled at Toulouse; from which time abundance of blood was shed, and the second army of martyrs began to be added to the first, who had cried "from beneath the altar." And ever since, the beast has been warring against the saints, and shedding their blood like water. *And authority was given him over every tribe and people*—Particularly in Europe. And when a way was found by sea into the East Indies, and the West, these also were brought under his authority.

Verse 8. *And all that dwell upon the earth will worship him*—All will be carried away by the torrent, but the little flock of true believers. The name of these only is *written in the Lamb's book of life*. And if any even of these "make shipwreck of the faith," he will blot them "out of his book;" although they were written therein *from* (that is, *before*) *the foundation of the world*, Rev. xvii. 8.

Verse 9. *If any one have an ear, let him hear*—It was said before, "He that hath an ear, let him hear." This expression, *if any*, seems to imply, that scarce will any that *hath an ear* be found. *Let him hear*—With all attention the following warning, and the whole description of the beast.

Verse 10. *If any man leadeth into captivity*—God will in due time repay the followers of the beast in their own kind. Meanwhile, *here is the patience and faithfulness of the saints* exercised: their patience, by enduring captivity or imprisonment; their faithfulness, by resisting unto blood.

Verse 11. *And I saw another wild beast*—So he is once termed to show his fierceness and strength; but in all other places, "the false prophet." He comes to confirm the kingdom of the first beast. *Coming up*—After the other had long exercised his authority. *Out of the earth*—Out of Asia. But he is not yet come, though he cannot be far off for he is to appear at the end of the forty-two months of the first beast. *And he had two horns like a lamb*—A mild, innocent appearance. *But he spake like a dragon*—Venemous, fiery, dreadful. So do those who are zealous for the beast.

Verse 12. *And he exerciseth all the authority of the first wild beast*—

wild beast before him, and he causeth the earth and them
that dwelt therein to worship the first wild beast, whose deadly
13 wound was healed. And he doeth great wonders, so that he
even maketh fire to come down out of heaven to the earth
14 in the sight of men. And he deceiveth them that dwell on
the earth by the wonders which it is given him to do before
the wild beast; saying to them that dwell on the earth, to
make an image to the wild beast, which had the wound by
15 the sword, and yet lived. And it was given him to give
breath to the image of the wild beast, so that the image
of the wild beast should speak: and he will cause, that as
many as will not worship the image of the wild beast shall
16 be killed. And he causeth all, small and great, both rich
and poor, both free and slaves, to receive a mark on the right
17 hand, or on the forehead: That no man might buy or sell,
but he that had the mark, the name of the wild beast, or the

Described in the second, fourth, fifth, and seventh verses. *Before him*—For they are both together. *Whose deadly wound was healed*—More throughly healed by means of the second beast.

Verse 13. *He maketh fire*—Real fire. *To come down*—By the power of the devil.

Verse 14. *Before the wild beast*—Whose usurped majesty is confirmed by these wonders. *Saying to them*—As if it were from God. *To make an image to the wild beast*—Like that of Nebuchadnezzar, whether of gold, silver, or stone The original image will be set up where the beast himself shall appoint. But abundance of copies will be taken, which may be carried into all parts, like those of Diana of Ephesus.

Verse 15. *So that the image of the wild beast should speak*—Many instances of this kind have been already among the Papists, as well as the heathens. *And as many as will not worship*—When it is required of them; as it will be of all that buy or sell. *Shall be killed*—By this the Pope manifests that he is antichrist, directly contrary to Christ. It is Christ who shed his own blood; it is antichrist who sheds the blood of others. And yet, it seems, his last and most cruel persecution is to come. This persecution, the reverse of all that preceded, will, as we may gather from many scriptures, fall chiefly on the outward-court worshippers, the formal Christians. It is probable that few real, inward Christians shall perish by it: on the contrary, those who "watch and pray always" shall be "accounted worthy to escape all these things, and to stand before the Son of man," Luke xxi. 36.

Verse 16. *On their forehead*—The most zealous of his followers will probably choose this. Others may receive it *on their hand.*

Verse 17. *That no man might buy or sell*—Such edicts have been published long since against the poor Vaudois *But he that had the mark,*

18 number of his name. Here is the wisdom. Let him that
hath understanding count the number of the wild beast: for
it is the number of a man: and his number is six hundred
sixty-six.

CHAP. XIV. 1 And I looked, and, behold, the Lamb
standing on mount Sion, and with him an hundred forty-four
thousand, having his name and the name of his Father writ-

namely, *the name of the first beast, or the number of his name*—*The name of the beast* is that which he bears through his whole duration; namely, that of *Papa* or *Pope*: *the number of his name* is the whole time during which he bears this name. Whosoever, therefore, receives the mark of the beast does as much as if he said expressly, "I acknowledge the present Papacy, as proceeding from God;" or, "I acknowledge that what St. Gregory VII. has done, according to his legend, (authorized by Benedict XIII.,) and what has been maintained in virtue thereof, by his successors to this day, is from God." By the former, a man hath *the name of the beast* as a mark; by the latter, *the number of his name*. In a word, to have *the name of the beast* is, to acknowledge His papal Holiness; to have *the number of his name* is, to acknowledge the papal succession. The second beast will enforce the receiving this mark under the severest penalties.

Verse 18. *Here is the wisdom*—To be exercised. "The patience of the saints" availed against the power of the first beast: *the wisdom* God giveth them will avail against the subtilty of the second. *Let him that hath understanding*—Which is a gift of God, subservient to that wisdom *Count the number of the wild beast*—Surely none can be blamed for attempting to obey this command. *For it is the number of a man*—A number of such years as are common among men. *And his number is six hundred* and *sixty-six* years—So long shall he endure from his first appearing.

Verse 1. *And I saw on mount Sion*—The heavenly *Sion*. *An hundred forty-four thousand*—Either those out of all mankind who had been the most eminently holy, or the most holy out of the twelve tribes of Israel: the same that were mentioned, Rev. vii. 4, and perhaps also, Rev xv. 2. But they were then in the world, and were sealed *in their foreheads*, to preserve them from the plagues that were to follow. They are now in safety, and have *the name of the Lamb and of his Father written on their foreheads*, as being the redeemed of God and of the Lamb, his now unalienable property. This prophecy often introduces the inhabitants of heaven as a kind of chorus with great propriety and elegance. The church above, making suitable reflections on the grand events which are foretold in this book, greatly serves to raise the attention of real Christians, and to teach the high concern they have in them. Thus is the church on earth instructed, animated, and encouraged, by the sentiments temper, and devotion of the church in heaven.

2 ten on their foreheads. And I heard a sound out of heaven,
as a sound of many waters, and as a sound of a great
thunder: and the sound which I heard *was* as of harpers
3 harping on their harps: And they sing a new song before
the throne, and before the four living creatures, and the
elders: and none could learn the song but the hundred
forty-four thousand, who were redeemed from the earth
4 These are they who had not been defiled with women; for
they are virgins: these are they who follow the Lamb
whithersoever he goeth. These were redeemed from among
5 men, firstfruits to God and the Lamb. And in their mouth
there was found no guile: they are without fault.
6 And I saw another angel flying in the midst of heaven,
having an everlasting gospel to preach to them that dwell on
the earth, and to every nation, and tribe, and tongue, and

Verse 2. *And I heard a sound out of heaven*—Sounding clearer and clearer: first, at a distance, *as the sound of many waters* or *thunders*; and afterwards, being nearer, it *was as of harpers harping on their harps*. It sounded vocally and instrumentally at once.

Verse 3. *And they*—The hundred forty-four thousand—*Sing a new song—and none could learn that song*—To sing and play it in the same manner. *But the hundred forty-four thousand who were redeemed from the earth*—From among men; from all sin

Verse 4. *These are they who had not been defiled with women*—It seems that the deepest defilement, and the most alluring temptation, is put for every other. *They are virgins*—Unspotted souls; such as have preserved universal purity. *These are they who follow the Lamb*—Who are nearest to him. This is not their character, but their reward. *Firstfruits*—Of the glorified spirits Who is ambitious to be of this number?

Verse 5. *And in their mouth there was found no guile*—Part for the whole Nothing untrue, unkind, unholy. *They are without fault*—Having preserved inviolate a virgin purity both of soul and body.

Verse 6. *And I saw another angel*—A second is mentioned, verse 8; a third, verse 9. These three denote great messengers of God with their assistants; three men who bring messages from God to men. The first exhorts to the fear and worship of God; the second proclaims the fall of Babylon; the third gives warning concerning the beast. Happy are they who make the right use of these divine messages! *Flying*—Going on swiftly. *In the midst of heaven*—Breadthways. *Having an everlasting gospel*—Not *the* gospel, properly so called; but *a* gospel, or joyful message, which was to have an influence on all ages. *To preach to every nation, and tribe, and tongue, and people*—Both to Jew and gentile, even as far as the authority of the beast had extended.

7 people, Saying with a loud voice, Fear God and give glory
to him ; for the hour of his judgment is come : and worship
him that made the heaven, and the earth, and the sea, and
fountains of water.
8 And another angel followed, saying, Babylon the great
is fallen, is fallen, she that hath made all nations drink
of the wine of her fornication

Verse 7 *Fear God and give glory to him ; for the hour of his judgment is come*—The joyful message is properly this, that *the hour of* God's *judgment is come.* And hence is that admonition drawn, *Fear God and give glory to him.* They who do this will not worship the beast, neither any image or idol whatsoever. *And worship him that made*—Whereby he is absolutely distinguished from idols of every kind. *The heaven, and the earth, and the sea, and fountains of water*—And they who worship him shall be delivered when the angels pour out their phials on the earth, sea, fountains of water, on the sun, and in the air.

Verse 8. *And another angel followed, saying, Babylon is fallen*—With the overthrow of Babylon, that of all the enemies of Christ, and, consequently, happier times, are connected. *Babylon the great*—So the city of Rome is called upon many accounts. Babylon was magnificent, strong, proud, powerful. so is Rome also Babylon was first, Rome afterwards, the residence of the emperors of the world. What Babylon was to Israel of old, Rome hath been both to the literal and spiritual "Israel of God" Hence the liberty of the ancient Jews was connected with the overthrow of the Babylonish empire. And when Rome is finally overthrown, then the people of God will be at liberty.

Whenever Babylon is mentioned in this book, *the great* is added, to teach us that Rome then commenced Babylon, when it commenced the great city; when it swallowed up the Grecian monarchy and its fragments, Syria in particular; and, in consequence of this, obtained dominion over Jerusalem about sixty years before the birth of Christ. Then it began, but it will not cease to be Babylon till it is finally destroyed. Its spiritual greatness began in the fifth century, and increased from age to age. It seems it will come to its utmost height just before its final overthrow.

Her fornication is her idolatry; invocation of saints and angels; worship of images; human traditions; with all that outward pomp, yea, and that fierce and bloody zeal, wherewith she pretends to serve God. Bu with spiritual fornication, as elsewhere, so in Rome, fleshly fornication is joined abundantly. Witness the stews there, licensed by the Pope, which are no inconsiderable branch of his revenue. This is fitly compared to wine, because of its intoxicating nature.

Of this wine *she hath,* indeed, *made all nations drink*—More especially by her later missions. We may observe, this making them drink is not ascribed to the beast, but to Babylon. For Rome itself, the Roman inquisitions, congregations, and Jesuits, continually propagate their

9 And a third angel followed them, saying with a loud
voice, If any one worship the wild beast and his image, and
10 receive *his* mark on his forehead, or on his hand, He shall
also drink of the wine of the wrath of God, which is poured
unmixed into the cup of his indignation; and shall be tormented with fire and brimstone, in the presence of the
11 angels, and in the presence of the Lamb: And the smoke
of their torments ascendeth for ever and ever: and they
have no rest day or night, who worshipped the wild beast
and his image, and whosoever receiveth the mark of his
12 name. Here is the patience of the saints; who keep the
commandments of God, and the faith of Jesus.
13 And I heard a voice out of heaven saying, Write, From

idolatrous doctrines and practices, with or without the consent of this or that Pope, who himself is not secure from their censure.

Verse 9. *And a third angel followed*—At no great distance of time *Saying, If any one worship the wild beast*—This worship consists, partly in an inward submission, a persuasion that all who are subject to Christ must be subject to the beast or they cannot receive the influences of divine grace, or, as their expression is, there is no salvation out of their church; partly in a suitable outward reverence to the beast himself, and consequently to his image.

Verse 10. *He shall drink*—With Babylon, Rev. xvi. 19. *And shall be tormented*—With the beast, Rev. xx. 10 In all the scripture there is not another so terrible threatening as this. And God by this greater fear arms his servants against the fear of the beast. *The wrath of God, which is poured unmixed*—Without any mixture of mercy; without hope *Into the cup of his indignation*—And is no real anger implied in all this? O what will not even wise men assert, to serve an hypothesis!

Verse 11. *And the smoke*—From the fire and brimstone wherein they are tormented. *Ascendeth for ever and ever*—God grant thou and I may never try the strict, literal eternity of this torment!

Verse 12. *Here is the patience of the saints*—Seen, in suffering all things rather than receive this mark. *Who keep the commandments of God*—The character of all true saints; and particularly the great command to believe in Jesus.

Verse 13. *And I heard a voice*—This is most seasonably heard when the beast is in his highest power and fury. *Out of heaven*—Probably from a departed saint. *Write*—He was at first commanded to write the whole book. Whenever this is repeated it denotes something peculiarly observable. *Happy are the dead—From henceforth* particularly: 1. Because they escape the approaching calamities: 2. Because they already enjoy so near an approach to glory. *Who die in the Lord*—In the faith of the Lord Jesus. *For they rest*—No pain, no purgatory follows; but pure, unmixed happiness. *From their labours*—And the more laborious their

henceforth happy are the dead who die in the Lord: Yea,
saith the Spirit, that they may rest from their labours. Their
works follow them.
14 And I looked, and behold a white cloud, and on the cloud
one sitting like a son of man, having a golden crown on his
15 head, and a sharp sickle in his hand. And another angel
came out of the temple, crying with a loud voice to him that
sat on the cloud, Thrust in thy sickle, and reap: for the
time to reap is come; for the harvest of the earth is ripe.
16 And he that sat on the cloud thrust in his sickle upon the
earth; and the earth was reaped.
17 And another angel came out of the temple which is in
18 heaven, and he also had a sharp sickle. And another angel
came out from the altar, who had power over fire; and cried
with a loud cry to him that had the sharp sickle, saying,
Thrust in thy sickle, and lop off the clusters of the vine

life was, the sweeter is their rest. How different this state from that of those, verse 11, who "have no rest day or night!" Reader, which wilt thou choose? *Their works*—Each one's peculiar works. *Follow*—Or accompany them; that is, the fruit of their works. Their works do not go before to procure them admittance into the mansions of joy; but they follow them when admitted.

Verse 14. In the following verses, under the emblem of an harvest and a vintage, are signified two general visitations; first, many good men are taken from the earth by the harvest; then many sinners during the vintage. The latter is altogether a penal visitation; the former seems to be altogether gracious. Here is no reference in either to the day of judgment, but to a season which cannot be far off. *And I saw a white cloud*—An emblem of mercy. *And on the cloud sat one like a son of man*—An angel in an human shape, sent by Christ, the Lord both of the vintage and of the harvest. *Having a golden crown on his head*—In token of his high dignity. *And a sharp sickle in his hand*—The sharper the welcomer to the righteous.

Verse 15. *And another angel came out of the temple*—"Which is in heaven," verse 17. Out of which came the judgments of God in the appointed seasons.

Verse 16. *Crying*—By the command of God. *Thrust in thy sickle, for the harvest is ripe*—This implies an high degree of holiness in those good men, and an earnest desire to be with God.

Verse 18. *And another angel from the altar*—Of burnt offering; from whence the martyrs had cried for vengeance. *Who had power over fire*—As "the angel of the waters," Rev. xvi. 5, had over water. *Cried, saying, Lop off the clusters of the vine of the earth*—All the wicked are considered as constituting one body

19 of the earth; for her grapes are fully ripe. And the angel
thrust in his sickle upon the earth, and lopped off the vine
of the earth, and cast *it* into the great winepress of the
20 wrath of God. And the winepress was trodden without the
city, and blood came out of the winepress, even to the
horses' bridles, one thousand six hundred furlongs.

CHAP. XV. 1 And I saw another sign in heaven, great
and wonderful, seven angels having the seven last plagues;
2 for by them the wrath of God is fulfilled. And I saw
as it were a sea of glass mingled with fire; and them that
gained the victory over the wild beast, and over his image,
and over the number of his name, standing at the sea
3 of glass, and having the harps of God. And they sing the
song of Moses the servant of God, and the song of the Lamb,

Verse 20. *And the winepress was trodden*—By the Son of God, Rev. xix. 15. *Without the city*—Jerusalem. They to whom St. John writes, when a man said, "The city," immediately understood this. *And blood came out of the winepress, even to the horses' bridles*—So deep at its first flowing from the winepress! *One thousand six hundred furlongs*—So far! at least two hundred miles, through the whole land of Palestine

Verse 1. *And I saw seven* holy *angels having the seven last plagues*—Before they had the phials, which were as instruments whereby those plagues were to be conveyed. They are termed *the last*, because *by them the wrath of God is fulfilled*—Hitherto God had borne his enemies with much longsuffering; but now his wrath goes forth to the uttermost, pouring plagues on the earth from one end to the other, and round its whole circumference. But, even after these plagues, the holy wrath of God against his other enemies does not cease, Rev. xx. 15.

Verse 2. The song was sung while the angels were coming out with their plagues, who are therefore mentioned both before and after it, verses 1—6. *And I saw as it were a sea of glass mingled with fire*—It was before "clear as crystal," Rev. iv. 6, but now *mingled with fire*, which devours the adversaries. *And them that gained*, or *were gaining, the victory over the wild beast*—More of whom were yet to come. *The mark of the beast, the mark of his name*, and *the number of his name*, seem to mean here nearly the same thing. *Standing at the sea of glass*—Which was before the throne. *Having the harps of God*—Given by him, and appropriated to his praise.

Verse 3 *And they sing the song of Moses*—So called, partly from its near agreement with the words of that song which he sung after passing the Red Sea, Exod. xv. 11, and of that which he taught the children of Israel a little before his death, Deut. xxxii. 3, 4 But chiefly because

saying, Great and wonderful *are* thy works, Lord God
Almighty; righteous and true are thy ways, O King of the
4 nations. Who would not fear thee, O Lord, and glorify thy
name? for thou only *art* gracious: for all the nations shall
come and worship before thee; for thy judgments are made
manifest.
5 And after these things I looked, and the temple of the
6 tabernacle of the testimony was open in heaven: And the
seven angels that had the seven plagues came out of the
temple, clothed in pure white linen, and having their breasts

Moses was the minister and representative of the Jewish church, as Christ is of the church universal. Therefore it is also termed *the song of the Lamb.* It consists of six parts, which answer each other:—

1. *Great and wonderful are thy works, Lord God Almighty.*	2. *For thou only art gracious.*
3. *Just and true are thy ways, O King of the nations.*	4. *For all the nations shall come and worship before thee.*
5 *Who would not fear thee, O Lord, and glorify thy name?*	6. *For thy judgments are made manifest.*

We know and acknowledge that all *thy works* in and toward all the creatures are *great and wonderful;* that *thy ways* with all the children of men, good and evil, are *just and true. For thou only art gracious*—And this grace is the spring of all those wonderful works, even of his destroying the enemies of his people. Accordingly in Psalm cxxxvi., that clause, "For his mercy endureth for ever," is subjoined to the thanksgiving for his works of vengeance as well as for his delivering the righteous. *For all the nations shall come and worship before thee*—They shall serve thee as their king with joyful reverence. This is a glorious testimony of the future conversion of all the heathens. The Christians are now a little flock: they who do not worship God, an immense multitude. But *all the nations shall come,* from all parts of the earth, to *worship him and glorify his name. For thy judgments are made manifest*—And then the inhabitants of the earth will at length learn to fear him.

Verse 5. *After these things the temple of the tabernacle of the testimony*—The holiest of all. *Was opened*—Disclosing a new theatre for the coming forth of the judgments of God now made manifest.

Verse 6. *And the seven angels came out of the temple*—As having received their instructions from the oracle of God himself. St. John saw them in heaven, verse 1 before they went into the temple. They appeared in habits like those the high priest wore when he went into the most holy place to consult the oracle. In this was the visible testimony of God's presence. *Clothed in pure white linen*—*Linen* is the habit of service and attendance. *Pure*—Unspotted, unsullied. *White*—Or *bright* and *shining,* which implies much more than bare innocence. *And having their breasts girt with golden girdles*—In token of their high dignity and glorious rest.

7 girt with golden girdles. And one of the four living creatures
gave the seven angels seven golden phials full of the wrath
8 of God, who liveth for ever. And the temple was filled with
smoke from the glory of God, and from his power; and none
could go into the temple, till the seven plagues of the seven
angels were fulfilled.

CHAP. XVI. 1 And I heard a loud voice out of the
temple saying to the seven angels, Go, pour out the seven
2 phials of the wrath of God upon the earth. And the first
went, and poured out his phial upon the earth; and there
came a grievous ulcer on the men that had the mark of the

Verse 7. *And one of the four living creatures gave the seven angels*—After they were come out of the temple. *Seven golden phials*—Or *bowls.* The Greek word signifies vessels broader at the top than at the bottom. *Full of the wrath of God, who liveth for ever and ever*—A circumstance which adds greatly to the dreadfulness of his wrath.

Verse 8. *And the temple was filled with smoke*—The cloud of glory was the visible manifestation of God's presence in the tabernacle and temple. It was a sign of protection at erecting the tabernacle and at the dedication of the temple. But in the judgment of Korah the glory of the Lord appeared, when he and his companions were swallowed up by the earth. So proper is the emblem of smoke from the glory of God, or from the cloud of glory, to express the execution of judgment, as well as to be a sign of favour Both proceed from the power of God, and in both he is glorified. *And none*—Not even of those who ordinarily stood before God. *Could go into the temple*—That is, into the inmost part of it. *Till the seven plagues of the seven angels were fulfilled*—Which did not take up a long time, like the seven trumpets, but swiftly followed each other.

Verse 1 *Pour out the seven phials*—The epistles to the seven churches are divided into three and four: the seven seals, and so the trumpets and phials, into four and three. The trumpets gradually, and in a long tract of time, overthrow the kingdoms of the world: the phials destroy chiefly the beast and his followers, with a swift and impetuous force. The four first affect the earth, the sea, the rivers, the sun; the rest fall elsewhere, and are much more terrible.

Verse 2. *And the first went*—So the second, third, &c., without adding *angel,* to denote the utmost swiftness; of which this also is a token, that there is no period of time mentioned in the pouring out of each phial They have a great resemblance to the plagues of Egypt, which the Hebrews generally suppose to have been a month distant from each other. Perhaps so may the phials; but they are all yet to come. *And poured out his phial upon the earth*—Literally taken. *And there came a grievous ulcer*—As in Egypt, Exod. ix. 10, 11. *On the men who had the mark of the*

3 wild beast, and that worshipped his image. And the second
poured out his phial upon the sea; and it became blood, as
the blood of a dead man: and every living soul in the sea
4 died. And the third poured out his phial on the rivers and
5 on fountains of waters; and they became blood. And I heard
the angel of the waters saying, Righteous art thou, who art,
and who wast, the Gracious one, because thou hast judged
6 thus. For they have shed the blood of saints and prophets,
and thou hast given them blood to drink: they are worthy.
7 And I heard *another* from the altar saying, Yea, Lord God
8 Almighty, true and righteous *are* thy judgments. And the
fourth poured out his phial upon the sun; and it was given
9 him to scorch the men with fire. And the men were scorched
exceedingly, and blasphemed the name of God, who had
power over these plagues: but they repented not to give

wild beast—All of them, and them only. All these plagues seem to be described in proper, not figurative, words.

Verse 3. *The second poured out his phial upon the sea*—As opposed to the dry land. *And it became blood, as of a dead man*—Thick, congealed, and putrid. *And every living soul*—Men, beasts, and fishes, whether on or in the sea, *died.*

Verse 4. *The third poured out his phial on the rivers and fountains of water*—Which were over all the earth. *And they became blood*—So that none could drink thereof.

Verse 5. *The Gracious one*—So he is styled when his judgments are abroad, and that with a peculiar propriety. In the beginning of the book he is termed "The Almighty." In the time of his patience, he is praised for his power, which otherwise might then be less regarded. In the time of his taking vengeance, for his mercy Of his power there could then be no doubt.

Verse 6. *Thou hast given them blood to drink*—Men do not drink out of the sea, but out of fountains and rivers. Therefore this is fitly added here. *They are worthy*—Is subjoined with a beautiful abruptness.

Verse 7. *Yea*—Answering the angel of the waters, and affirming of God's judgments in general, what he had said of one particular judgment.

Verse 8. *The fourth poured out his phial upon the sun*—Which was likewise affected by the fourth trumpet. There is also a plain resemblance between the first, second, and third phials, and the first, second, and third trumpet. *And it was given him*—The angel. *To scorch the men*—Who had the mark of the beast. *With fire*—As well as with the beams of the sun. So these four phials affected earth, water, fire, and air.

Verse 9. *And the men blasphemed God, who had power over these plagues*—They could not but acknowledge the hand of God, yet did they harden themselves against him

10 him glory. And the fifth poured out his phial upon the
throne of the wild beast; and his kingdom was darkened;
11 and they gnawed their tongues for pain, And blasphemed
the God of heaven, because of their pains and because
12 of their ulcers, and repented not of their works. And the
sixth poured out his phial upon the great river Euphrates
and the water of it was dried up, that the way of the kings
13 from the east might be prepared. And I saw out of the
mouth of the dragon, and out of the mouth of the wild

Verse 10. The four first phials are closely connected together; the fifth concerns the throne of the beast, the sixth the Mahometans, the seventh chiefly the heathens. The four first phials and the four first trumpets go round the whole earth; the three last phials and the three last trumpets go lengthways over the earth in a straight line

The fifth poured out his phial upon the throne of the wild beast—It is not said, "on the beast and his throne." Perhaps the see will then be vacant. *And his kingdom was darkened*—With a lasting, not a transient, darkness. However the beast as yet has his kingdom. Afterward the woman sits upon the beast, and then it is said, "The wild beast is not," Rev xvii 3, 7, 8.

Verse 11. *And they*—His followers. *Gnawed their tongues*—Out of furious impatience. *Because of their pains and because of their ulcers*—Now mentioned together, and in the plural number, to signify that they were greatly heightened and multiplied.

Verse 12. *And the sixth poured out his phial upon the great river Euphrates*—Affected also by the sixth trumpet. *And the water of it*—And of all the rivers that flow into it. *Was dried up*—The far greater part of the Turkish empire lies on this side the Euphrates. The Romish and Mahometan affairs ran nearly parallel to each other for several ages. In the seventh century was Mahomet himself; and, a little before him, Boniface III., with his universal bishopric. In the eleventh, both the Turks and Gregory VII. carried all before them. In the year 1300, Boniface appeared with his two swords at the newly-erected jubilee. In the self-same year arose the Ottoman Porte; yea, and on the same day. And here the phial, poured out on the throne of the beast, is immediately followed by that poured out on the *Euphrates; that the way of the kings from the east might be prepared*—Those who lie east from the Euphrates, in Persia, India, &c., who will rush blindfold upon the plagues which are ready for them, toward the Holy Land, which lies west of the Euphrates

Verse 13. *Out of the mouth of the dragon, the wild beast, and the false prophet*—It seems, *the dragon* fights chiefly against God; *the beast*, against Christ; *the false prophet*, against the Spirit of truth; and that the three unclean spirits which come from them, and exactly resemble them, endeavour to blacken the works of creation, of redemption, and of sanc-

beast, and out of the mouth of the false prophet, three
14 unclean spirits like frogs go forth, (They are spirits of devils,
working miracles,) to the kings of the whole world, to gather
them unto the battle of the great day of God the Almighty.
15 (Behold, I come as a thief. Happy is he that watcheth, and
keepeth his garments, lest he walk naked, and they see his
16 shame.) And they gathered them together to the place
17 which is called in the Hebrew Armageddon. And the
seventh poured out his phial upon the air; and there went
forth a loud voice, out of the temple from the throne, say-
18 ing, It is done. And there were lightnings, and voices, and
thunders; and a great earthquake, such as had not been
since men were upon the earth, such an earthquake, so
19 great. And the great city was *split* into three parts, and
the cities of the nations fell: and Babylon the great was
remembered before God, to give her the cup of the wine

tification. *The false prophet*—So is the second beast frequently named, after the kingdom of the first is darkened; for he can then no longer prevail by main strength, and so works by lies and deceit. Mahomet was first a false prophet, and afterwards a powerful prince: but this beast was first powerful as a prince; afterwards a false prophet, a teacher of lies. *Like frogs*—Whose abode is in fens, marshes, and other unclean places. *To the kings of the whole world*—Both Mahometan and pagan. *To gather them*—To the assistance of their three principals.

Verse 15. *Behold, I come as a thief*—Suddenly, unexpectedly. Observe the beautiful abruptness. *I*—Jesus Christ. Hear him. *Happy is he that watcheth*—Looking continually for him that "cometh quickly." *And keepeth* on *his garments*—Which men use to put off when they sleep. *Lest he walk naked, and they see his shame*—Lest he lose the graces which he takes no care to keep, and others see his sin and punishment.

Verse 16 *And they gathered them together to Armageddon*—Mageddon, or Megiddo, is frequently mentioned in the Old Testament. *Armageddon* signifies *the city* or *the mountain of Megiddo;* to which the valley of Megiddo adjoined. This was a place well known in ancient times for many memorable occurrences; in particular, the slaughter of the kings of Canaan, related, Judges v. 19 Here the narrative breaks off. It is resumed, Rev. xix. 19.

Verse 17. *And the seventh poured out his phial upon the air*—Which encompasses the whole earth. This is the most weighty phial of all, and seems to take up more time than any of the preceding. *It is done*—What was commanded, verse 1. The phials are poured out.

Verse 18. *A great earthquake, such as had not been since men were upon the earth*—It was therefore a literal, not figurative, earthquake.

Verse 19. *And the great city*—Namely, Jerusalem, here opposed to the

20 of the fierceness of his wrath. And every island fled away,
21 and the mountains were not found. And a great hail, every
hail-stone about the weight of a talent, falleth out of heaven
upon the men · and the men blasphemed God, because
of the plague of the hail; for the plague thereof is exceeding great.

CHAP. XVII. 1 And there came one of the seven angels
who had the seven phials, and talked with me, saying, Come
hither; I will show thee the judgment of the great whore
2 that sitteth upon many waters: With whom the kings of the
earth have committed fornication, and the inhabitants of the
earth have been made drunk with the wine of her fornica-
3 tion. And he carried me away in the spirit into a wilderness . and I saw a woman sitting upon a scarlet wild beast,

heathen cities in general, and in particular to Rome. *And the cities of the nations fell*—Were utterly overthrown. *And Babylon was remembered before God*—He did not forget the vengeance which was due to her, though the execution of it was delayed.

Verse 20. *Every island and mountain* was "moved out of its place," Rev. vi. 14; but here they all *flee away*. What a change must this make in the face of the terraqueous globe! And yet the end of the world is not come.

Verse 21 *And a great hail falleth out of heaven*—From which there was no defence. From the earthquake men would fly into the fields; but here also they are met by the hail: nor were they secure if they returned into the houses, when each hail-stone weighed sixty pounds.

Verse 1. *And there came one of the seven angels, saying, Come hither*—This relation concerning the great whore, and that concerning the wife of the Lamb, Rev. xxi. 9, 10, have the same introduction, in token of the exact opposition between them. *I will show thee the judgment of the great whore*—Which is now circumstantially described. *That sitteth as a queen*—In pomp, power, ease, and luxury. *Upon many waters*—Many people and nations, verse 15.

Verse 2. *With whom the kings of the earth*—Both ancient and modern, for many ages. *Have committed fornication*—By partaking of her idolatry and various wickedness. *And the inhabitants of the earth*—The common people. *Have been made drunk with the wine of her fornication*—No wine can more thoroughly intoxicate those who drink it, than false zeal does the followers of the great whore.

Verse 3. *And he carried me away*—In the vision. *Into a wilderness*—The campagna di Roma, the country round about Rome, is now a wilderness, compared to what it was once. *And I saw a woman*—Both

full of names of blasphemy, having seven heads and ten
4 horns. And the woman was arrayed in purple and scarlet,
and adorned with gold and precious stone and pearls, having
in her hand a golden cup, full of abomination and filthiness
5 of her fornication: And on her forehead a name written,
MYSTERY, BABYLON THE GREAT, THE
MOTHER OF HARLOTS AND ABOMINATIONS

the scripture and other writers frequently represent a city under this emblem. *Sitting upon a scarlet wild beast*—The same which is described in the thirteenth chapter. But he was there described as he carried on his own designs only: here, as he is connected with the whore. There is, indeed, a very close connexion between them; the *seven heads* of the beast being "seven hills on which the woman sitteth." And yet there is a very remarkable difference between them,—between the papal power and the city of Rome. This woman is the city of Rome, with its buildings and inhabitants; especially the nobles. The beast, which is now scarlet-coloured, (bearing the bloody livery, as well as the person, of the woman,) appears very different from before. Therefore St. John says at first sight, *I saw a beast*, not *the beast, full of names of blasphemy*—He had before "a name of blasphemy upon his head," Rev. xiii. 1: now he has many. From the time of Hildebrand, the blasphemous titles of the Pope have been abundantly multiplied. *Having seven heads*—Which reach in a succession from his ascent out of the sea to his being cast into the lake of fire. *And ten horns*—Which are contemporary with each other, and belong to his last period.

Verse 4. *And the woman was arrayed*—With the utmost pomp and magnificence. *In purple and scarlet*—These were the colours of the imperial habit: the purple, in times of peace; and the scarlet, in times of war. *Having in her hand a golden cup*—Like the ancient Babylon, Jer. li. 7. *Full of abominations*—The most abominable doctrines as well as practices.

Verse 5. *And on her forehead a name written*—Whereas the saints have the name of God and the Lamb on their foreheads. *Mystery*—This very word was inscribed on the front of the Pope's mitre, till some of the Reformers took public notice of it. *Babylon the great*—Benedict XIII., in his proclamation of the jubilee, A.D. 1725, explains this sufficiently. His words are, "To this holy city, famous for the memory of so many holy martyrs, run with religious alacrity. Hasten to the place which the Lord hath chose. Ascend to this new Jerusalem, whence the law of the Lord and the light of evangelical truth hath flowed forth into all nations, from the very first beginning of the church: the city most rightfully called 'The Palace,' placed for the pride of all ages, the city of the Lord, the Sion of the Holy One of Israel. This catholic and apostolical Roman church is the head of the world, the mother of all believers, the faithful interpreter of God and mistress of all churches." But God somewhat varies the style. *The mother of harlots*—The parent, ringleader, patroness, and nourisher of many daughters, that closely copy after her. *And abomi-*

6 OF THE EARTH. And I saw the woman drunk with
the blood of the saints, and with the blood of the witnesses
of Jesus. And when I saw, I wondered exceedingly.
7 And the angel said to me, Wherefore didst thou wonder?
I will tell thee the mystery of the woman, and of the wild
beast that carrieth her, which hath the seven heads and
8 the ten horns. The wild beast which thou sawest was, and
is not, and shall ascend out of the bottomless pit, and go
into perdition: and they that dwell on the earth (whose
names are not written in the book of life from the foundation of the world) shall wonder, when they behold the wild
9 beast, that he was, and is not, and yet will be. Here *is* the
mind that hath wisdom The seven heads are seven hills

nations—Of every kind, spiritual and fleshly. *Of the earth*—In all lands. In this respect she is indeed catholic or universal.

Verse 6. *And I saw the woman drunk with the blood of the saints*—So that Rome may well be called, "The slaughter-house of the martrys." She hath shed much Christian blood in every age; but at length she is even drunk with it, at the time to which this vision refers. *The witnesses of Jesus*—The preachers of his word. *And I wondered exceedingly*—At her cruelty and the patience of God.

Verse 7. *I will tell thee the mystery*—The hidden meaning of this.

Verse 8. *The beast which thou sawest* (namely, verse 3) *was*, &c.—This is a very observable and punctual description of the beast, verses 8, 10, 11 His whole duration is here divided into three periods, which are expressed in a fourfold manner.

I. He, 1. Was; 2 And is not; 3. And will ascend out of the bottomless pit, and go into perdition.

II. He, 1. Was; 2. And is not; 3. And will be again.

III. The seven heads are seven hills and seven kings: 1. Five are fallen; 2. One is; 3. The other is not come; and when he cometh, he must continue a short space.

IV. He, 1. Was; 2. And is not; 3 Even he is the eighth, and is one of the seven, and goeth into perdition.

The first of these three is described in the thirteenth chapter. This was past when the angel spoke to St. John. The second was then in its course; the third was to come. *And is not*—The fifth phial brought darkness upon his kingdom: the woman took this advantage to seat herself upon him. Then it might be said, He *is not*. Yet shall he afterwards *ascend out of the bottomless pit*—Arise again with diabolical strength and fury. But he will not reign long: soon after his ascent he goeth *into perdition* for ever.

Verse 9. *Here is the mind that hath wisdom*—Only those who are wise will understand this. *The seven heads are seven hills*.

10 on which the woman sitteth. And they are seven kings:
five are fallen, one is, the other is not yet come; when he
11 cometh, he must continue a short space. And the wild
beast that was, and is not, even he is the eighth, and is

Verse 10. *And they are seven kings*—Anciently there were royal palaces on all the seven Roman hills. These were the Palatine, Capitoline, Cœlian, Exquiline, Viminal, Quirinal, Aventine hills. But the prophecy respects the seven hills at the time of the beast, when the Palatine was deserted and the Vatican in use. Not that the seven heads mean hills distinct from kings; but they have a compound meaning, implying both together.

Perhaps the first head of the beast is the Cœlian hill, and on it the Lateran, with Gregory VII. and his successors; the second, the Vatican with the church of St. Peter, chosen by Boniface VIII.; the third, the Quirinal, with the church of St. Mark, and the Quirinal palace built by Paul II.; and the fourth, the Exquiline hill, with the temple of St. Maria Maggiore, where Paul V reigned. The fifth will be added hereafter. Accordingly, in the papal register, four periods are observable since Gregory VII. In the first almost all the bulls made in the city are dated in the Lateran; in the second, at St. Peter's; in the third, at St. Mark's, or in the Quirinal; in the fourth, at St. Maria Maggiore. But no fifth, sixth, or seventh hill has yet been the residence of any Pope. Not that one hill was deserted, when another was made the papal residence; but a new one was added to the other sacred palaces.

Perhaps the times hitherto mentioned might be fixed thus:—

1058. Wings are given to the woman
1077. The beast ascends out of the sea
1143. The forty-two months begin
1810. The forty-two months end.
1832. The beast ascends out of the bottomless pit
1836. The beast finally overthrown.

The fall of those five kings seems to imply, not only the death of the Popes who reigned on those hills, but also such a disannulling of all they had done there, that it will be said, The beast *is not;* the royal power, which had so long been lodged in the Pope, being then transferred to the city. *One is, the other is not yet come*—These two are remarkably distinguished from the five preceding, whom they succeed in their turns. The former of them will continue not *a short space,* as may be gathered from what is said of the latter: the former is under the government of Babylon; the latter is with the beast.

In this second period, *one is,* at the same time that the beast *is not.* Even then there will be a Pope, though not with the power which his predecessors had. And he will reside on one of the remaining hills, leaving the seventh for his successor.

Verse 11. *And the wild beast that was, and is not, even he is the eighth*—When the time of his not being is over. The beast consists, as it were,

12 of the seven, and goeth into perdition. And the ten horns
which thou sawest are ten kings, who have not received the
kingdom; but receive authority as kings one hour with the
13 wild beast. These have one mind, and give their power and
14 authority to the wild beast. These shall make war with the
Lamb, and the Lamb shall overcome them: for he is Lord
of lords, and King of kings; and they that *are* with him
are called, and chosen, and faithful.

15 And he saith to me, The waters which thou sawest, where
the whore sitteth, are people, and multitudes, and nations,
16 and tongues. And the ten horns which thou sawest, and
the wild beast, these shall hate the whore, and shall make
her desolate and naked, and shall eat her flesh, and burn her

of eight parts. The seven heads are seven of them; and the eighth is his whole body, or the beast himself. Yet the beast himself, though he is in a sense termed the eighth, *is of the seven,* yea, contains them all. The whole succession of Popes from Gregory VII. are undoubtedly antichrist. Yet this hinders not, but that the last Pope in this succession will be more eminently the antichrist, the man of sin, adding to that of his predecessors a peculiar degree of wickedness from the bottomless pit. This individual person, as Pope, is the seventh head of the beast; as the man of sin, he is the eighth, or the beast himself.

Verse 12. *The ten horns are ten kings*—It is nowhere said that these horns are on the beast, or on his heads. And he is said to have them, not as he is one of the seven, but as he is the eighth. They are ten secular potentates, contemporary with, not succeeding, each other, who *receive authority as kings with the beast,* probably in some convention, which, after a very short space, they will deliver up to the beast. Because of their short continuance, only *authority as kings,* not a *kingdom,* is ascribed to them. While they retain this authority together with the beast, he will be stronger than ever before; but far stronger still, when their power is also transferred to him.

Verse 13. In the thirteenth and fourteenth verses is summed up what is afterwards mentioned, concerning the horns and the beast, in this and the two following chapters. *These have one mind, and give*—They all, with one consent, *give their* warlike *power and* royal *authority to the wild beast*

Verse 14. *These*—Kings with the beast. *He is Lord of lords*—Rightful sovereign of all, and ruling all things well. *And King of kings*—As a king he fights with and conquers all his enemies. *And they that are with him*—Beholding his victory, *are* such as were, while in the body, *called,* by his word and Spirit. *And chosen*—Taken out of the world, when they were enabled to believe in him. *And faithful*—Unto death.

Verse 15. *People, and multitudes, and nations, and tongues*—It is not said *tribes;* for Israel hath nothing to do with Rome in particular.

Verse 16 *And shall eat her flesh*—Devour her immense riches

17 with fire. For God hath put *it* into their hearts to execute
his sentence, and to agree, and to give their kingdom to the
18 wild beast, till the words of God shall be fulfilled. And the
woman whom thou sawest is the great city, which reigneth
over the kings of the earth

CHAP. XVIII. 1 And after these things I saw another
angel coming down out of heaven, having great power; and
2 the earth was enlightened with his glory. And he cried
mightily with a loud voice, saying, Babylon the great is
fallen, is fallen, and is become an habitation of devils, and
an hold of every unclean spirit, and a cage of every unclean
3 and hateful bird. For all nations have drank of the wine
of her fornication, and the kings of the earth have committed
fornication with her, and the merchants of the earth are
waxed rich through the abundance of her delicacies.
4 And I heard another voice out of heaven, saying, Come

Verse 17. *For God hath put it into their heart*—Which indeed no less than almighty power could have effected. *To execute his sentence—till the words of God*—Touching the overthrow of all his enemies, *should be fulfilled.*

Verse 18. *The woman is the great city, which reigneth*—Namely, while the beast "is not," and the woman "sitteth upon him."

Verse 1. *And I saw another angel coming down out of heaven*—Termed another, with respect to him who "came down out of heaven," Rev. x. 1. *And the earth was enlightened with his glory*—To make his coming more conspicuous. If such be the lustre of the servant, what images can display the majesty of the Lord, who has "thousand thousands" of those glorious attendants "ministering to him, and ten thousand times ten thousand standing before him?"

Verse 2. *And he cried, Babylon is fallen*—This fall was mentioned before, Rev. xiv. 8; but is now declared at large. *And is become an habitation*—A free abode. *Of devils, and an hold*—A prison. *Of every unclean spirit*—Perhaps confined there where they had once practised all uncleanness, till the judgment of the great day. How many horrid inhabitants hath desolate Babylon! of invisible beings, devils, and unclean spirits; of visible, every unclean beast, every filthy and hateful bird. Suppose, then, Babylon to mean heathen Rome; what have the Romanists gained, seeing from the time of that destruction, which they say is past, these are to be its only inhabitants for ever.

Verse 4. *And I heard another voice*—Of Christ, whose people, secretly scattered even there, are warned of her approaching destruction. *That ye be not partakers of her sins*—That is, of the fruits of them.

out of her, my people, that ye be not partakers of her sins,
5 and that ye receive not of her plagues. For her sins have
reached even to heaven, and God hath remembered her ini-
6 quities. Reward her even as she hath rewarded, and give
her double according to her works: in the cup which she
7 mingled, mingle to her double. As much as she hath glorified herself, and lived deliciously, so much torment and
sorrow give her: because she saith in her heart, I sit as a
8 queen, and am no widow, and shall see no sorrow. Therefore shall her plagues come in one day, death, and sorrow,
and famine; and she shall be burned with fire: for strong *is*
9 the Lord God who judgeth her. And the kings of the earth,
who had committed fornication and lived deliciously with
her, shall weep and mourn over her, when they see the
10 smoke of her burning, Standing afar off for fear of her tor-

What a remarkable providence it was that the Revelation was printed in the midst of Spain, in the great Polyglot Bible, before the Reformation! Else how much easier had it been for the Papists to reject the whole book, than it is to evade these striking parts of it!

Verse 5. *Even to heaven*—An expression which implies the highest guilt.

Verse 6 *Reward her*—This God speaks to the executioners of his vengeance *Even as she hath rewarded*—Others; in particular, the saints of God. *And give her double*—This, according to the Hebrew idiom, implies only a full retaliation.

Verse 7. *As much as she hath glorified herself*—By pride, and pomp, and arrogant boasting. *And lived deliciously*—In all kinds of elegance, luxury, and wantonness. *So much torment give her*—Proportioning the punishment to the sin. *Because she saith in her heart*—As did ancient Babylon, Isai. xlvii. 8, 9 *I sit*—Her usual style. Hence those expressions, "The chair, the see of Rome: he sat so many years." *As a queen*—Over many kings, "mistress of all churches; the supreme; the infallible; the only spouse of Christ; out of which there is no salvation." *And am no widow*—But the spouse of Christ. *And shall see no sorrow*—From the death of my children, or any other calamity; for God himself will defend "the church."

Verse 8. *Therefore*—as both the natural and judicial consequence of this proud security *Shall her plagues come*—The *death* of her children, with an incapacity of bearing more *Sorrow*—of every kind. *And famine*—In the room of luxurious plenty: the very things from which she imagined herself to be most safe. *For strong is the Lord God who judgeth her*—Against whom therefore all her strength, great as it is, will not avail

Verse 10 *Thou strong city*—Rome was anciently termed by its inha-

ment, saying, Alas, alas, thou great city Babylon, thou
11 strong city! In one hour is thy judgment come. And the
merchants of the earth weep and mourn over her; for none
12 buyeth their merchandise any more: Merchandise of gold,
and silver, and precious stone, and pearl, and fine linen,
and purple, and silk, and scarlet, and all sorts of thyine
wood, and all sorts of vessels of ivory, and all sorts of vessels
of most precious wood, and of brass, and iron, and
13 marble, And cinnamon, and amomum, and odours, and
ointment, and frankincense, and wine, and oil, and fine
flour, and wheat, and beasts, and sheep, and *merchandise*
of horses and of chariots, and of bodies and souls of men.
14 And the fruits which thy soul desireth are departed from
thee, and all things that were dainty and splendid are
perished from thee, and thou shalt find them no more.
15 The merchants of these things, who became rich by her,
shall stand afar off, for fear of her torment, weeping and
16 mourning, Saying, Alas, alas the great city, that was clothed
in fine linen, and purple, and scarlet, and adorned with
gold, and precious stone, and pearl! in one hour so great
17 riches are become desolate. And every ship-master, and all

bitants, Valentia, that is, *strong*. And the word Rome itself, in Greek, signifies strength. This name was given it by the Greek strangers.

Verse 12. *Merchandise of gold, &c.*—Almost all these are still in use at Rome, both in their idolatrous service, and in common life. *Fine linen*—The sort of it mentioned in the original is exceeding costly. *Thyine wood*—A sweet-smelling wood not unlike citron, used in adorning magnificent palaces. *Vessels of most precious wood*—Ebony, in particular, which is often mentioned with ivory: the one excelling in whiteness, the other in blackness; and both in uncommon smoothness.

Verse 13. *Amomum*—A shrub whose wood is a fine perfume. *And beasts*—Cows and oxen. *And of chariots*—a purely Latin word is here inserted in the Greek. This St. John undoubtedly used on purpose, in describing the luxury of Rome. *And of bodies*—A common term for slaves. *And souls of men*—For these also are continually bought and sold at Rome. And this of all others is the most gainful merchandise to the Roman traffickers.

Verse 14. *And the fruits*—From what was imported they proceed to the domestic delicates of Rome; none of which is in greater request there, than the particular sort which is here mentioned. The word properly signifies, pears, peaches, nectarines, and all of the apple and plum kinds. *And all things that are dainty*—To the taste. *And splendid*—To the sight; as clothes, buildings, furniture

the company belonging to ships, and sailors, and all who
18 trade by sea, stood afar off, And cried when they saw the
smoke of her burning, saying, What *city was* like the great
19 city! And they cast dust on their heads, and cried, weeping and mourning, saying, Alas, alas the great city, wherein
were made rich all that had ships in the sea, by reason of
her magnificence! for in one hour she is made desolate.
20 Rejoice over her, thou heaven, and ye saints, and apostles,
and prophets; for God hath avenged you on her.
21 And a mighty angel took up a stone like a great mill-stone,
and threw *it* into the sea, saying, Thus with violence shall
Babylon, the great city, be thrown down, and shall be found
no more at all. And the voice of harpers, and musicians,
and pipers, and trumpeters, shall be heard no more at all in
thee; and no artificer of any kind shall be found any more
in thee; and the sound of a mill-stone shall be heard no more

Verse 19. *And they cast dust on their heads*—As mourners. Most of the expressions here used in describing the downfal of Babylon are taken from Ezekiel's description of the downfal of Tyre, Ezek. xxvi., xxvii

Verse 20. *Rejoice over her, thou heaven*—That is, all the inhabitants of it; and more especially, *ye saints;* and among the saints still more eminently, *ye apostles and prophets.*

Verse 21. *And a mighty angel took up a stone, and threw it into the sea*—By a like emblem Jeremiah fore-showed the fall of the Chaldean Babylon, Jer. li. 63, 64.

Verse 22. *And the voice of harpers*—Players on stringed instruments. *And musicians*—Skilful singers in particular. *And pipers*—Who played on flutes, chiefly on mournful, whereas *trumpeters* played on joyful, occasions. *Shall be heard no more in thee; and no artificer*—Arts of every kind, particularly music, sculpture, painting, and statuary, were there carried to their greatest height. No, nor even *the sound of a mill-stone shall be heard any more in thee*—Not only the arts that adorn life, but even those employments without which it cannot subsist, will cease from thee for ever. All these expressions denote absolute and eternal desolation. *The voice of harpers*—Music was the entertainment of the rich and great; trade, the business of men of middle rank; preparing bread and the necessaries of life, the employment of the lowest people: marriages, in which lamps and songs were known ceremonies, are the means of peopling cities, as new births supply the place of those that die. The desolation of Rome is therefore described in such a manner, as to show that neither rich nor poor, neither persons of middle rank, nor those of the lowest condition, should be able to live there any more. Neither shall it be repeopled by new marriages, but remain desolate and uninhabited for ever.

23 at all in thee; And the light of a candle shall shine no more
at all in thee; and the voice of the bridegroom and the
bride shall be heard no more in thee: for thy merchants
were the great men of the earth; for by thy sorceries were
24 all nations deceived. And in her was found the blood
of prophets, and saints, and of all that had been slain upon
the earth.

CHAP. XIX. 1 After these things I heard a loud
voice of a great multitude in heaven, saying, Hallelujah;

Verse 23. *For thy merchants were the great men of the earth*—A circumstance which was in itself indifferent, and yet led them into pride, luxury, and numberless other sins.

Verse 24. *And in her was found the blood of the prophets and saints*—The same angel speaks still, yet he does not say "in thee," but *in her*, now so sunk as not to hear these last words. *And of all that had been slain*—Even before she was built. See Matt. xxiii. 35. There is no city under the sun which has so clear a title to catholic blood-guiltiness as Rome. The guilt of the blood shed under the heathen emperors has not been removed under the Popes, but hugely multiplied. Nor is Rome accountable only for that which hath been shed in the city, but for that shed in *all the earth*. For at Rome under the Pope, as well as under the heathen emperors, were the bloody orders and edicts given: and wherever the blood of holy men was shed, there were the grand rejoicings for it. And what immense quantities of blood have been shed by her agents! Charles IX., of France, in his letter to Gregory XIII., boasts, that in and not long after the massacre of Paris, he had destroyed seventy thousand Hugonots. Some have computed, that, from the year 1518, to 1548, fifteen millions of Protestants have perished by the Inquisition. This may be overcharged; but certainly the number of them in those thirty years, as well as since, is almost incredible. To these we may add innumerable martyrs, in ancient, middle, and late ages, in Bohemia, Germany, Holland, France, England, Ireland, and many other parts of Europe, Afric, and Asia.

Verse 1. *I heard a loud voice of a great multitude*—Whose blood the great whore had shed. *Saying, Hallelujah*—This Hebrew word signifies, *Praise ye Jah*, or *Him that is*. God named himself to Moses, *EHEIEH*, that is, *I will be*, Exod. iii. 14; and at the same time, "Jehovah," that is, "He that is, and was, and is to come:" during the trumpet of the seventh angel, he is styled, "He that is and was," Rev xvi. 5; and not "He that is to come;" because his long-expected coming is under this trumpet actually present. At length he is styled, "Jah," "He that is;" the past together with the future being swallowed up in the present, the former things being no more mentioned, for the greatness of those that now are. This title is of all others the most peculiar to the everlasting God. *The salvation*—Is opposed to the destruction which the great whore

the Salvation, and the glory, and the power to our God
2 For true and righteous *are* his judgments: for he hath
judged the great whore, who corrupted the earth with her
fornication, and hath avenged the blood of his servants at
3 her hand. (And again they said, Hallelujah.) And her
4 smoke ascendeth for ever and ever. And the four and
twenty elders and the four living creatures fell down, and
worshipped God that sat on the throne, saying, Amen;
5 Hallelujah. And a voice came forth from the throne, saying,
Praise our God, all ye his servants, and ye that fear him,
6 small and great. And I heard as it were a voice of a great
multitude, and as a voice of many waters, and as a voice of
mighty thunders, saying, Hallelujah; for the Lord God,
7 the Almighty reigneth. Let us be glad and rejoice, and
give the glory to him. for the marriage of the Lamb is

had brought upon the earth *His power and glory*—Appear from the judgment executed on her, and from the setting up his kingdom to endure through all ages.

Verse. 2 *For true and righteous are his judgments*—Thus is the cry of the souls under the altar changed into a song of praise.

Verse 4. *And the four and twenty elders, and the four living creatures fell down*—*The living creatures* are nearer the throne than *the elders* Accordingly they are mentioned before them, with the praise they render to God, Rev. iv. 9, 10; v. 8, 14; inasmuch as there the praise moves from the centre to the circumference. But here, when God's judgments are fulfilled, it moves back from the circumference to the centre. Here, therefore, *the four and twenty elders* are named before *the living creatures.*

Verse 5. *And a voice came forth from the throne*—Probably from the four living creatures, *saying, Praise our God*—The occasion and matter of this song of praise follow immediately after, verses 6, &c.; God was praised before, for his judgment of the great whore, verses 1—4. Now for that which follows it: for that the Lord God, the Almighty, takes the kingdom to himself, and avenges himself on the rest of his enemies. Were all these inhabitants of heaven mistaken? If not, there is real, yea, and terrible anger in God.

Verse 6. *And I heard the voice of a great multitude.* So all his servants did praise him. *The Almighty reigneth*—More eminently and gloriously than ever before.

Verse 7. *The marriage of the Lamb is come*—Is near at hand, to be solemnized speedily. What this implies, none of "the spirits of just men," even in paradise, yet know. O what things are those which are yet behind! And what purity of heart should there be, to meditate upon them! *And his wife hath made herself ready*—Even upon earth; but in a far higher sense, in that world. After a time allowed for this,

8 come, and his wife hath made herself ready. And it is
given to her to be arrayed in fine linen, white and clean;
the fine linen is the righteousness of the saints.
9 And he saith to me, Write, Happy *are* they who are invited to the marriage supper of the Lamb. And he saith
10 to me, These are the true sayings of God. And I fell
before his feet to worship him. But he saith to me, See
thou do it not: I am thy fellowservant, and of thy brethren
that keep the testimony of Jesus. Worship God: the
testimony of Jesus is the spirit of prophecy.
11 And I saw the heaven opened, and behold a white horse,
and he that sitteth on him, called Faithful and True, and
12 in righteousness he judgeth and maketh war. His eyes *are*
a flame of fire, and upon his head *are* many diadems, and he
hath a name written, which none knoweth but himself.

the new Jerusalem comes down, both made ready and adorned, Rev. xxi. 2.

Verse 8. *And it is given to her*—By God The bride is all holy men, the whole invisible church. *To be arrayed in fine linen, white and clean*—This is an emblem of *the righteousness of the saints*—Both of their justification and sanctification

Verse 9. *And he*—The angel, *saith to me, Write*—St. John seems to have been so amazed at these glorious sights, that he needeth to be reminded of this *Happy are they who are invited to the marriage supper of the Lamb*—Called to glory *And he saith*—After a little pause.

Verse 10. *And I fell before his feet to worship him*—It seems, mistaking him for the angel of the covenant. *But he saith, See thou do it not*—In the original, it is only, *See not,* with a beautiful abruptness. To pray to or worship the highest creature is flat idolatry. *I am thy fellowservant, and of thy brethren that have the testimony of Jesus*—I am now employed as your fellowservant, to testify of the Lord Jesus, by the same Spirit which inspired the prophets of old.

Verse 11 *And I saw the heaven opened*—This is a new and peculiar opening of it, in order to show the magnificent expedition of Christ and his attendants, against his great adversary. *And behold a white horse*—Many little regarded Christ, when he came meek, "riding upon an ass;" but what will they say, when he goes forth upon his white horse, with the sword of his mouth? *White*—Such as generals use in solemn triumph. *And he that sitteth on him, called Faithful*—In performing all his promises. *And True*—In executing all his threatenings. *And in righteousness*—With the utmost justice. *He judgeth and maketh war*—Often the sentence and execution go together.

Verse 12. *And his eyes are a flame of fire*—They were said to be as or like a flame of fire, before, Rev. i. 14; an emblem of his omniscience. *And upon his head are many diadems*—For he is king of all nations. *And*

13 And he *is* clothed in a vesture dipped in blood: and his name
14 is called The Word of God. And the armies which were in
heaven followed him on white horses, clothed in clean, fine
15 linen. And out of his mouth goeth forth a sharp two-edged
sword, that with it he might smite the nations: And he
shall rule them with a rod of iron; and he treadeth the
winepress of the fierceness of the wrath of God, the
16 Almighty. And he hath on his vesture and on his thigh a
name written, KING OF KINGS, AND LORD OF
17 LORDS And I saw an angel standing in the sun; and he
cried with a loud voice, saying to all the birds that fly in
the midst of heaven, Come, and gather yourselves together
18 to the great supper of God; That ye may eat the flesh of
kings, and the flesh of chief captains, and the flesh of
mighty men, and the flesh of horses, and of those that sit
on them, and the flesh of all men, both freemen and slaves,

he hath a name written, which none knoweth but himself—As God he is incomprehensible to every creature.

Verse 13. *And he is clothed in a vesture dipped in blood*—The blood of the enemies he hath already conquered. Isaiah lxiii. 1, &c

Verse 15. *And he shall rule them*—Who are not slain by his sword *With a rod of iron*—That is, if they will not submit to his golden sceptre. *And he treadeth the wine-press of the wrath of God*—That is, he executes his judgments on the ungodly.

This ruler of the nations was born (or appeared as such) immediately after the seventh angel began to sound. He now appears, not as a child, but as a victorious warrior. The nations have long ago felt his "iron rod," partly while the heathen Romans, after their savage persecution of the Christians, themselves groaned under numberless plagues and calamities, by his righteous vengeance; partly, while other heathens have been broken in pieces by those who bore the Christian name. For although the cruelty, for example, of the Spaniards in America, was unrighteous and detestable, yet did God therein execute his righteous judgment on the unbelieving nations; but they shall experience his iron rod as they never did yet, and then will they all return to their rightful Lord.

Verse 16. *And he hath on his vesture and on his thigh*—That is, on the part of his vesture which is upon his thigh. *A name written*—It was usual of old, for great personages in the eastern countries, to have magnificent titles affixed to their garments.

Verse 17. *Gather yourselves together to the great supper of God*—As to a great feast, which the vengeance of God will soon provide; a strongly figurative expression, (taken from Ezekiel xxxix. 17,) denoting the vastness of the ensuing slaughter

19 both small and great. And I saw the wild beast, and the
kings of the earth, and their armies, gathered together to
make war with him that sat on the horse, and with his army.
20 And the wild beast was taken, and with him the false
prophet who had wrought the miracles before him, with
which he had deceived them who had the mark of the wild
beast, and them who had worshipped his image. These
two were cast alive into the lake of fire burning with brim-
21 stone. And the rest were slain by the sword of him that sat
upon the horse, which went forth out of his mouth; and all
the birds were satisfied with their flesh.

CHAP XX. 1 And I saw an angel descending out

Verse 19. *And I saw the kings of the earth*—The ten kings mentioned Rev. xvii. 12; who had now drawn the other kings of the earth to them, whether Popish, Mahometan, or pagan. *Gathered together to make war with him that sat upon the horse*—All beings, good and evil, visible and invisible, will be concerned in this grand contest. See Zech. xiv verses 1, &c.

Verse 20. *The false prophet, who had wrought the miracles before him*—And therefore shared in his punishment; *these two* ungodly men *were cast alive*—Without undergoing bodily death. *Into the lake of fire*—And that before the devil himself, Rev. xx. 10. Here is the last of *the beast.* After several repeated strokes of omnipotence, he is gone alive into hell. There were two that went alive into heaven; perhaps there are two that go alive into hell. It may be, Enoch and Elijah entered at once into glory, without first waiting in paradise; the *beast* and the *false prophet* plunge at once into the extremest degree of torment, without being reserved in chains of darkness till the judgment of the great day. Surely, none but the beast of Rome would have hardened himself thus against the God he pretended to adore, or refused to have repented under such dreadful, repeated visitations! Well is he styled a *beast,* from his carnal and vile affections; a *wild beast,* from his savage and cruel spirit! *The rest were slain*—A like difference is afterwards made between the devil, and Gog and Magog, Rev. xx. 9, 10.

Verse 21. Here is a most magnificent description of the overthrow of the beast and his adherents. It has, in particular, one exquisite beauty that, after exhibiting the two opposite armies, and all the apparatus for a battle, verses 11—19; then follows immediately, verse 20, the accoun of the victory, without one word of an engagement or fighting. Here is the most exact propriety; for what struggle can there be between omnipotence, and the power of all the creation united against it! Every description must have fallen short of this admirable silence.

CHAP. XX. Verse 1 *And I saw an angel descending out of heaven*—

of heaven, having the key of the bottomless pit and a great
2 chain in his hand. And he laid hold on the dragon, the old
serpent, who is the devil, and Satan, and bound him a thou-
3 sand years, And cast him into the bottomless pit, and shut
him up, and set a seal upon him, that he might deceive the

Coming down with a commission from God. Jesus Christ himself overthrew the beast. the proud dragon shall be bound by an angel; even as he and his angels were cast out of heaven by Michael and his angels *Having the key of the bottomless pit*—Mentioned before, Rev. ix. 1. *And a great chain in his hand*—*The angel of the bottomless pit* was shut up therein before the beginning of the first woe. But it is now first that Satan, after he had occasioned the third woe, is both chained and shut up.

Verse 2. *And he laid hold on the dragon*—With whom undoubtedly his angels were now cast into the bottomless pit, as well as finally "into everlasting fire," Matt. xxv. 41. *And bound him a thousand years*—That these thousand do not precede, or run parallel with, but wholly follow, the times of the beast, may manifestly appear, 1. From the series of the whole book, representing one continued chain of events. 2. From the circumstances which precede. The woman's bringing forth is followed by the casting of the dragon out of heaven to the earth. With this is connected the third woe, whereby the dragon through, and with, the beast, rages horribly. At the conclusion of the third woe the beast is overthrown and cast into "the lake of fire." At the same time the other grand enemy, the dragon, shall be bound and shut up. 3. These thousand years bring a new, full, and lasting immunity from all outward and inward evils, the authors of which are now removed, and an affluence of all blessings. But such a time the church has never yet seen. Therefore it is still to come. 4. These thousand years are followed by the last times of the world, the letting loose of Satan, who gathers together Gog and Magog, and is thrown to the beast and false prophet "in the lake of fire." Now Satan's accusing the saints in heaven, his rage on earth, his imprisonment in the abyss, his seducing Gog and Magog, and being cast into the lake of fire, evidently succeed each other. 5. What occurs from Rev. xx. 11, to xxii. 5, manifestly follows the things related in the nineteenth chapter. The thousand years came between; whereas if they were past, neither the beginning nor the end of them would fall within this period. In a short time those who assert that they are now at hand will appear to have spoken the truth. Meantime let every man consider what kind of happiness he expects therein. The danger does not lie in maintaining that the thousand years are yet to come; but in interpreting them, whether past or to come, in a gross and carnal sense. The doctrine of the Son of God is a mystery. So is his cross; and so is his glory. In all these he is a sign that is spoken against. Happy they who believe and confess him in all!

Verse 3. *And set a seal upon him*—How far these expressions are to be taken literally, how far figuratively only, who can tell? *That he might*

nations no more, till the thousand years should be fulfilled:
after this he must be loosed for a small time.
4 And I saw thrones, and they that sat on them, and judgment was given to them: and *I saw* the souls of them who
had been beheaded for the testimony of Jesus, and for the
word of God, and those who had not worshipped the wild

deceive the nations no more—One benefit only is here expressed, as resulting from the confinement of Satan. But how many and great blessings are implied! For the grand enemy being removed, the kingdom of God holds on its uninterrupted course among the nations; and the great mystery of God, so long foretold, is at length fulfilled; namely, when the beast is destroyed and Satan bound. This fulfilment approaches nearer and nearer; and contains things of the utmost importance, the knowledge of which becomes every day more distinct and easy. In the mean time it is highly necessary to guard against the present rage and subtilty of the devil. Quickly he will be bound. when he is loosed again, the martyrs will live and reign with Christ. Then follow his coming in glory, the new heaven, new earth, and new Jerusalem. *The bottomless pit* is properly the devil's prison: afterwards he is cast into the lake of fire. He can deceive the nations no more till the "thousand years," mentioned before, verse 2, are *fulfilled. Then he must be loosed*—So does the mysterious wisdom of God permit. *For a small time*—Small comparatively: though upon the whole it cannot be very short, because the things to be transacted therein, verses 8, 9, must take up a considerable space. We are very shortly to expect, one after another, the calamities occasioned by the second beast, the harvest and the vintage, the pouring out of the phials, the judgment of Babylon, the last raging of the beast and his destruction, the imprisonment of Satan. How great things these! and how short the time! What is needful for us? Wisdom, patience, faithfulness, watchfulness. It is no time to settle upon our lees. This is not, if it be rightly understood, an acceptable message to the wise, the mighty, the honourable, of this world Yet that which is to be done, shall be done: there is no counsel against the Lord.

Verse 4. *And I saw thrones*—Such as are promised the apostles, Matt. xix. 28; Luke xxii. 30. *And they*—Namely, the saints, whom St. John saw at the same time, Dan. vii. 22, *sat upon them; and judgment was given to them.* 1 Cor. vi. 2. Who, and how many, these are, is not said. But they are distinguished from *the souls,* or *persons,* mentioned immediately after; and from the saints already raised. *And I saw the souls of them who had been beheaded—With the axe:* so the original word signifies. One kind of death, which was particularly inflicted at Rome, is mentioned for all. *For the testimony of Jesus, and for the word of God*—The martyrs were sometimes killed *for the word of God* in general; sometimes particularly *for the testimony of Jesus:* the one, while they refused to worship idols; the other, while they confessed the name of Christ. *And those who had not worshipped the wild beast, nor his image*—

beast, nor his image, neither had received the mark on their
forehead, or on their hand; and they lived and reigned with
5 Christ a thousand years. The rest of the dead lived not
again till the thousand years were ended. This *is* the first
6 resurrection. Happy and holy *is* he that hath a part in the
first resurrection: over these the second death hath no power,
but they shall be priests of God and of Christ, and shall
reign with him a thousand years.

These seem to be a company distinct from those who appeared, Rev. xv. 2. Those overcame, probably, in such contests as these had not. Before the number of the beast was expired, the people were compelled to worship him, by the most dreadful violence. But when the beast "was not," they were only seduced into it by the craft of the false prophet. *And they lived*—Their souls and bodies being re-united. *And reigned with Christ*—Not on earth, but in heaven. The "reigning on earth" mentioned, Rev. xi. 15, is quite different from this. *A thousand years*—It must be observed, that two distinct thousand years are mentioned throughout this whole passage. Each is mentioned thrice; the thousand wherein Satan is bound, verses 2, 3, 7; the thousand wherein the saints shall reign, verses 4—6. The former end before the end of the world; the latter reach to the general resurrection. So that the beginning and end of the former thousand is before the beginning and end of the latter. Therefore as in the second verse, at the first mention of the former; so in the fourth verse, at the first mention of the latter, it is only said, *a thousand years;* in the other places, "*the* thousand," verses 3, 5, 7, that is, the thousand mentioned before. During the former, the promises concerning the flourishing state of the church, Rev. x. 7, shall be fulfilled; during the latter, while the saints reign with Christ in heaven, men on earth will be careless and secure.

Verse 5. *The rest of the dead lived not till the thousand years*—Mentioned, verse 4. *Were ended*—The thousand years during which Satan is bound both begin and end much sooner.

The small time, and the second thousand years, begin at the same point, immediately after the first thousand. But neither the beginning of the first nor of the second thousand will be known to the men upon earth, as both the imprisonment of Satan and his loosing are transacted in the invisible world.

By observing these two distinct thousand years, many difficulties are avoided. There is room enough for the fulfilling of all the prophecies, and those which before seemed to clash are reconciled; particularly those which speak, on the one hand, of a most flourishing state of the church as yet to come; and, on the other, of the fatal security of men in the last days of the world

Verse 6. *They shall be priests of God and of Christ*—Therefore Christ is God. *And shall reign with him*—With Christ, *a thousand years.*

7 And when the thousand years are fulfilled, Satan shall be
8 loosed out of his prison, And shall go forth to deceive the
nations, which are in the four corners of the earth, Gog and
Magog, to gather them together to battle: whose number is
9 as the sand of the sea. And they went up on the breadth
of the earth, and surrounded the camp of the saints, and the
beloved city: and fire came down from God out of heaven,
10 and devoured them. And the devil that deceived them was
cast into the lake of fire and brimstone, where both the wild
beast and the false prophet *are:* and they shall be tormented
day and night for ever and ever.
11 And I saw a great white throne, and him that sat thereon,
from whose face the earth and the heaven fled away; and

Verse 7. *And when the* former *thousand years are fulfilled, Satan shall be loosed out of his prison*—At the same time that the first resurrection begins. There is a great resemblance between this passage and Rev. xii. 12 At the casting out of the dragon, there was joy in heaven, but there was woe upon earth: so at the loosing of Satan, the saints begin to reign with Christ; but the nations on earth are deceived.

Verse 8. *And shall go forth to deceive the nations in the four corners of the earth*—(That is, in all the earth)—the more diligently, as he hath been so long restrained, and knoweth he hath but a small time. *Gog and Magog—Magog,* the second son of Japhet, is the father of the innumerable northern nations toward the east. The prince of these nations, of which the bulk of that army will consist, is termed *Gog* by Ezekiel also, Ezek. xxxviii. 2 Both *Gog* and *Magog* signify *high* or *lifted up;* a name well suiting both the prince and people. When that fierce leader of many nations shall appear, then will his own name be known. *To gather them*—Both Gog and his armies. Of *Gog,* little more is said, as being soon mingled with the rest in the common slaughter. The Revelation speaks of this the more briefly, because it had been so particularly described by Ezekiel. *Whose number is as the sand of the sea*—Immensely numerous: a proverbial expression.

Verse 9. *And they went up on the breadth of the earth,* or *the land*—Filling the whole breadth of it. *And surrounded the camp of the saints*—Perhaps the gentile church, dwelling round about Jerusalem. *And the beloved city*—So termed, likewise, Ecclesiasticus xxiv. 11.

Verse 10. *And they*—All these. *Shall be tormented day and night*—That is, without any intermission. Strictly speaking, there is only night there: no day, no sun, no hope!

Verse 11. *And I saw*—A representation of that great day of the Lord. *A great white throne*—How great, who can say? *White* with the glory of God, of him that sat upon it,—Jesus Christ. The apostle does not attempt to describe him here; only adds that circumstance, far above all description, *From whose face the earth and the heaven fled away*—Pro-

12 there was found no place for them. And I saw the dead,
great and small, standing before the throne; and the books
were opened: and another book was opened, which is *the
book* of life: * and the dead were judged out of the things
that were written in the books, according to their works.
13 And the sea gave up the dead that were therein; and death
and hades gave up the dead that were in them: and they
14 were judged every one according to their works. And death
and hades were cast into the lake of fire. This is the second
15 death. And whosoever was not found written in the book
of life was cast into the lake of fire.

* Mal. iii. 16, &c

bably both the aerial and the starry heaven; which "shall pass away with a great noise." *And there was found no place for them*—But they were wholly dissolved, the very "elements melting with fervent heat." It is not said, they were thrown into great commotions, but they *fled* entirely *away;* not, they started from their foundations, but they "fell into dissolution;" not, they removed to a distant place, but *there was found no place for them;* they ceased to exist; they were no more. And all this, not at the strict command of the Lord Jesus; not at his awful presence, or before his fiery indignation; but at the bare presence of his Majesty, sitting with severe but adorable dignity on his throne.

Verse 12. *And I saw the dead, great and small*—Of every age and condition. This includes, also, those who undergo a change equivalent to death, 1 Cor. xv. 51. *And the books*—Human judges have their books written with pen and ink · how different is the nature of these books! *Were opened*—O how many hidden things will then come to light; and how many will have quite another appearance than they had before in the sight of men! With the book of God's omniscience, that of conscience will then exactly tally. The book of natural law, as well as of revealed, will then also be displayed. It is not said, The books will be read: the light of that day will make them visible to all. Then, particularly, shall every man know himself, and that with the last exactness This will be the first true, full, impartial, universal history. *And another book*—Wherein are enrolled all that are accepted through the Beloved; all who lived and died in the faith that worketh by love. *Which is the book of life, was opened*—What manner of expectation will then be, with regard to the issue of the whole!

Verse 13. *Death and hades gave up the dead that were in them*—*Death* gave up all the bodies of men; and *hades*, the receptacle of separate souls, gave them up, to be re-united to their bodies

Verse 14. *And death and hades were cast into the lake of fire*—That is, were abolished for ever; for neither the righteous nor the wicked were to die any more: their souls and bodies were no more to be separated Consequently, neither *death* nor *hades* could any more have a being

CHAP. XXI. 1 And I saw a new heaven and a new
earth: for the first heaven and the first earth were passed
2 away; and there was no more sea. And I saw the holy
city, the new Jerusalem, coming down from God out of hea-
3 ven, prepared as a bride adorned for her husband. And I
heard a loud voice out of heaven, saying, Behold, the tabernacle of God with men, and he will pitch his tent with
them, and they shall be his people, and God himself *shall*
4 *be* with them, *and be* their God. And he shall wipe away
all tears from their eyes; and death shall be no more, neither shall sorrow, or crying, or pain be any more because
5 the former things are gone away. And he that sat upon
the throne said, Behold, I make all things new. And he

Verse 1 *And I saw*—So it runs, Rev. xix. 11, xx. 1, 4, 11, in a succession. All these several representations follow one another in order: so the vision reaches into eternity *A new heaven and a new earth*—After the resurrection and general judgment. St. John is not now describing a flourishing state of the church, but a new and eternal state of all things *For the first heaven and the first earth*—Not only the lowest part of heaven, not only the solar system, but the whole ethereal heaven, with all its host, whether of planets or fixed stars, Isai xxxiv. 4; Matt. xxiv. 29. All the former things will be done away, that all may become new, verses 4, 5; 2 Peter iii. 10, 12 *Are passed away*—But in the fourth verse it is said, "are gone away." There the stronger word is used; for death, mourning, and sorrow go away all together: the former heaven and earth only *pass away*, giving place to the *new heaven and* the *new earth*.

Verse 2. *And I saw the holy city*— The new heaven, the new earth, and the new Jerusalem, are closely connected. This city is wholly new, belonging not to this world, not to the millennium, but to eternity. This appears from the series of the vision, the magnificence of the description, and the opposition of this city to the second death, Rev. xx. 11, 12; xxi. 1, 2, 5, 8, 9; xxii 5. *Coming down*—In the very act of descending.

Verse 3 *They shall be his people, and God himself shall be with them, and be their God*—So shall the covenant between God and his people be executed in the most glorious manner

Verse 4. *And death shall be no more*—This is a full proof that this whole description belongs not to time, but eternity. *Neither shall sorrow, or crying, or pain, be any more: for the former things are gone away*—Under the former heaven, and upon the former earth, there was death and sorrow, crying and pain; all which occasioned many tears: but now pain and sorrow are fled away, and the saints have everlasting life and joy.

Verse 5. *And he that sat upon the throne said*—Not to St. John only. From the first mention of "him that sat upon the throne,' Rev. iv. 2, this is the first speech which is expressly ascribed to him. *And he*—

saith to me, Write. these sayings are faithful and true.
6 And he said to me, It is done. I am the Alpha and the
Omega, the beginning and the end. I will give to him that
7 thirsteth of the fountain of the water of life freely. He that
overcometh shall inherit these things; and I will be to him
8 a God, and he shall be to me a son. But the fearful, and
unbelieving, and abominable, and murderers, and whoremongers, and sorcerers, and idolaters, and all liars, their part *is*
in the lake that burneth with fire and brimstone; which is
the second death.
9 And there came one of the seven angels that had the
seven phials full of the seven last plagues, and talked with
me, saying, Come hither, I will show thee the bride, the
10 Lamb's wife. And he carried me away in the spirit to a

The angel. *Saith to me, Write*—As follows. *These sayings are faithful and true*—This includes all that went before. The apostle seems again to have ceased writing, being overcome with ecstasy at the voice of him that spake.

Verse 6. *And he*—That sat upon the throne. *Said to me, It is done*—All that the prophets had spoken; all that was spoken, Rev. iv. 1. We read this expression twice in this prophecy: first, Rev. xvi. 17, at the fulfilling of the wrath of God; and here, at the making all things new. *I am the Alpha and the Omega, the beginning and the end*—The latter explains the former: the Everlasting. *I will give to him that thirsteth*—The Lamb saith the same, Rev. xxii. 17.

Verse 7. *He that overcometh*—Which is more than, "he that thirsteth." *Shall inherit these things*—Which I have made new. *I will be his God, and he shall be my son*—Both in the Hebrew and Greek language, in which the scriptures were written, what we translate *shall* and *will* are one and the same word. The only difference consists in an English translation, or in the want of knowledge in him that interprets what he does not understand.

Verse 8. *But the fearful and unbelieving*—Who, through want of courage and faith, do not overcome. *And abominable*—That is, sodomites. *And whoremongers, and sorcerers, and idolaters*—These three sins generally went together; *their part is in the lake.*

Verse 9. *And there came one of the seven angels that had the seven phials*—Whereby room had been made for the kingdom of God. *Saying, Come, I will show thee the bride*—The same angel had before showed him Babylon, Rev. xvii. 1, which is directly opposed to the new Jerusalem.

Verse 10. *And he carried me away in the spirit*—The same expression as before, Rev. xvii. 3. *And showed me the holy city Jerusalem*—The old city is now forgotten, so that this is no longer termed the new, but absolutely Jerusalem. O how did St. John long to enter in! but the time

great and high mountain, and showed me the holy city
11 Jerusalem, descending out of heaven from God, Having the
glory of God: her window was like the most precious stone,
12 like a jasper stone, clear as crystal; Having a wall great and
high, having twelve gates, and at the gates twelve angels,
and the names written thereon, which are *the names* of the
13 twelve tribes of the children of Israel: On the east three
gates; and on the north three gates; and on the south three
14 gates; and on the west three gates. And the wall of the
city had twelve foundations, and upon them the twelve
15 names of the twelve apostles of the Lamb. And he that
talked with me had a measure, a golden reed, to measure the

was not yet come. Ezekiel also describes "the holy city," and what pertains thereto, xl.—xlviii.; but a city quite different from the old Jerusalem, as it was either before or after the Babylonish captivity The descriptions of the prophet and of the apostle agree in many particulars; but in many more they differ. Ezekiel expressly describes the temple, and the worship of God therein, closely alluding to the Levitical service. But St. John saw no temple, and describes the city far more large, glorious, and heavenly than the prophet. Yet that which he describes is the same city; but as it subsisted soon after the destruction of the beast. This being observed, both the prophecies agree together, and one may explain the other.

Verse 11. *Having the glory of God*—For her light, verse 23, Isaiah lx. 1, 2, Zech. ii. 5. *Her window*—There was only one, which ran all round the city. The light did not come in from without through this; for the glory of God is within the city. But it shines out from within to a great distance, verses 23, 24.

Verse 12. *Twelve angels*—Still waiting upon the heirs of salvation.

Verse 14. *And the wall of the city had twelve foundations, and on them the names of the twelve apostles of the Lamb*—Figuratively showing that the inhabitants of the city had built only on that faith which the apostles once delivered to the saints.

Verse 15. *And he measured the city, twelve thousand furlongs*—Not in circumference, but on each of the four sides. Jerusalem was thirty-three furlongs in circumference; Alexandria thirty in length, ten in breadth. Nineveh is reported to have been four hundred furlongs round; Babylon four hundred and eighty. But what inconsiderable villages were all these compared to the new Jerusalem! By this measure is understood the greatness of the city, with the exact order and just proportion of every part of it; to show, figuratively, that this city was prepared for a great number of inhabitants, how small soever the number of real Christians may sometimes appear to be; and that everything relating to the happiness of that state was prepared with the greatest order and exactness.

16 city, and the gates thereof, and the wall thereof. And the
city lieth foursquare, and the length is as large as the
breadth: and he measured the city with the reed, twelve
thousand furlongs. The length and the breadth and the
17 height of it are equal. And he measured the wall thereof
an hundred and forty-four *reeds*, the measure of a man, that
18 is, of an angel. And the building of the wall thereof was
jasper: and the city *was* of pure gold, like clear glass
19 And the foundations of the wall of the city were adorned
with all manner of precious stones. The first foundation
was a jasper; the second, a sapphire; the third, a chal-
20 cedony; the fourth, an emerald; The fifth, a sardonyx; the

The city is *twelve thousand furlongs* high; the wall, *an hundred and forty-four reeds.* This is exactly the same height, only expressed in a different manner. The twelve thousand furlongs, being spoken absolutely, without any explanation, are common, human furlongs: the hundred forty-four reeds are not of common human length, but of angelic, abundantly larger than human. It is said, *the measure of a man, that is, of an angel,* because St. John saw the measuring angel in an human shape. The reed therefore was as great as was the stature of that human form in which the angel appeared. In treating of all these things a deep reverence is necessary; and so is a measure of spiritual wisdom; that we may neither understand them too literally and grossly, nor go too far from the natural force of the words. The gold, the pearls, the precious stones, the walls, foundations, gates, are undoubtedly figurative expressions; seeing the city itself is in glory, and the inhabitants of it have spiritual bodies: yet these spiritual bodies are also real bodies, and the city is an abode distinct from its inhabitants, and proportioned to them who take up a finite and a determinate space. The measures, therefore, above mentioned are real and determinate

Verse 18 *And the building of the wall was jasper*—That is, the wall was built of jasper. *And the city*—The houses, *was of pure gold.*

Verse 19. *And the foundations were adorned with precious stones*—That is, beautifully made of them. The precious stones on the high priest's breastplate of judgment were a proper emblem to express the happiness of God's church in his presence with them, and in the blessing of his protection. The like ornaments on the foundations of the walls of this city may express the perfect glory and happiness of all the inhabitants of it from the most glorious presence and protection of God. Each precious stone was not the ornament of the foundation, but the foundation itself. The colours of these are remarkably mixed. *A jasper* is of the colour of white marble, with a light shade of green and of red; *a sapphire* is of a sky-blue, speckled with gold; *a chalcedony,* or carbuncle, of the colour of red-hot iron; *an emerald,* of a grass green.

Verse 20. *A sardonyx* is red streaked with white; *a sardius,* of a deep

sixth, a sardius; the seventh, a chrysolite; the eighth, a
beryl; the ninth, a topaz; the tenth, a chrysoprase; the
21 eleventh, a jacinth; the twelfth, an amethyst. And the
twelve gates *were* twelve pearls; each of the gates was of one
pearl: and the street of the city *was* pure gold, transparent
22 as glass. And I saw no temple therein; for the Lord God
23 Almighty and the Lamb are the temple of it. And the city
hath no need of the sun, neither of the moon, to shine on it
for the glory of God hath enlightened it, and the Lamb *is*
24 the lamp thereof. And the nations shall walk by the light
thereof: and the kings of the earth bring their glory into it.
25 And the gates of it shall not be shut by day: and there shall
26 be no night there. And they shall bring the glory and the
27 honour of the nations into it. But there shall in nowise
enter into it anything common, or that worketh abomination,
or *maketh* a lie: but they who are written in the Lamb's
book of life.

CHAP XXII. 1 And he showed me a river of the water of life, clear as crystal, proceeding out of the throne

red; *a chrysolite,* of a deep yellow; *a beryl,* sea-green; *a topaz,* pale yellow; *a chrysoprase* is greenish and transparent, with gold specks; *a jacinth,* of a red purple; *an amethyst,* violet purple.

Verse 22. *The Lord God and the Lamb are the temple of it*—He fills the new heaven and the new earth. He surrounds the city and sanctifies it, and all that are therein. He is "all in all."

Verse 23 *The glory of God*—Infinitely brighter than the shining of the sun.

Verse 24. *And the nations*—The whole verse is taken from Isaiah lx. 3. *Shall walk by the light thereof*—Which throws itself outward from the city far and near. *And the kings of the earth*—Those of them who have a part there. *Bring their glory into it*—Not their old glory, which is now abolished; but such as becomes the new earth, and receives an immense addition by their entrance into the city

Verse 26. *And they shall bring the glory of the nations into it*—It seems, a select part of each nation; that is, all which can contribute to make this city honourable and glorious shall be found in it; as if all that was rich and precious throughout the world was brought into one city.

Verse 27. *Common*—That is, unholy. *But those who are written in the Lamb's book of life*—True, holy, persevering believers. This blessedness is enjoyed by those only; and, as such, they are registered among them who are to inherit eternal life

Verse 1 *And he showed me a river of the water of life*—The

2 of God and of the Lamb. In the midst of the street of it,
and on each side of the river, *is* the tree of life, bearing
twelve sorts of fruits, yielding its fruit every month: and the
3 leaves of the tree *are* for the healing of the nations. And
there shall be no more curse: but the throne of God and
of the Lamb shall be in it; and his servants shall worship
4 him, And shall see his face; and his name *shall be* on
5 their foreheads. And there shall be no night there; neither

ever fresh and fruitful effluence of the Holy Ghost. See Ezek. xlvii. 1—12; where also the trees are mentioned which "bear fruit every month," that is, perpetually. *Proceeding out of the throne of God, and of the Lamb*—"All that the Father hath," saith the Son of God, "is mine;" even the throne of his glory.

Verse 2. *In the midst of the street*—Here is the paradise of God, mentioned, Rev. ii. 7. *Is the tree of life*—Not one tree only, but many *Every month*—That is, in inexpressible abundance. The variety, likewise, as well as the abundance of the fruits of the Spirit, may be intimated thereby. *And the leaves are for the healing of the nations*—For the continuing their health, not the restoring it; for no sickness is there

Verse 3 *And there shall be no more curse*—But pure life and blessing; every effect of the displeasure of God for sin being now totally removed *But the throne of God and the Lamb shall be in it*—That is, the glorious presence and reign of God *And his servants*—The highest honour in the universe *Shall worship him*—The noblest employment

Verse 4. *And shall see his face*—Which was not granted to Moses. They shall have the nearest access to, and thence the highest resemblance of, him. This is the highest expression in the language of scripture to denote the most perfect happiness of the heavenly state, 1 John iii. 2. *And his name shall be on their foreheads*—Each of them shall be openly acknowledged as God's own property, and his glorious nature most visibly shine forth in them. *And they shall reign*—But who are the subjects of these kings? The other inhabitants of the new earth. For there must needs be an everlasting difference between those who when on earth excelled in virtue, and those comparatively slothful and unprofitable servants, who were just saved as by fire. The kingdom of God is taken by force; but the prize is worth all the labour. Whatever of high, lovely, or excellent is in all the monarchies of the earth is all together not a grain of dust, compared to the glory of the children of God. God "is not ashamed to be called their God, for whom he hath prepared this city." But who shall come up into his holy place? "They who keep his commandments," verse 14.

Verse 5. *And they shall reign for ever and ever*—What encouragement is this to the patience and faithfulness of the saints, that, whatever their sufferings are, they will work out for them "an eternal weight of glory!" Thus ends the doctrine of this Revelation, in the everlasting happiness

is there need of a lamp, or of the light of the sun; for the
Lord God will enlighten them: and they shall reign for
ever.
6 And he said to me, These sayings *are* faithful and true:
the Lord, the God of the spirits of the prophets hath sent
his angel to show his servants the things which must be
7 done shortly. Behold, I come quickly: happy *is* he that
8 keepeth the words of the prophecy of this book. And *it was*
I John who heard and saw these things. And when I had
heard and seen, I fell down to worship at the feet of the
9 angel who showed me these things. But he saith to me,
See *thou do it* not: I am thy fellowservant, and of thy
brethren the prophets, and of them who keep the sayings
10 of this book: worship God. And he saith to me, Seal not
the sayings of the prophecy of this book: the time is nigh.
11 He that is unrighteous, let him be unrighteous still: and he

of all the faithful. The mysterious ways of Providence are cleared up, and all things issue in an eternal Sabbath, an everlasting state of perfect peace and happiness, reserved for all who endure to the end.

Verse 6. *And he said to me*—Here begins the conclusion of the book, exactly agreeing with the introduction, (particularly verses 6, 7, 10, with chap. i. 1, 3,) and giving light to the whole book, as this book does to the whole scripture. *These sayings are faithful and true*—All the things which you have heard and seen shall be faithfully accomplished in their order, and are infallibly true. *The Lord, the God of the holy prophets*—Who inspired and authorised them of old *Hath* now *sent* me *his angel, to show his servants*—By thee. *The things which must be done shortly*—Which will begin to be performed immediately.

Verse 7. *Behold, I come quickly*—Saith our Lord himself, to accomplish these things. *Happy is he that keepeth*—Without adding or diminishing, verses 18, 19, *the words of this book.*

Verse 8 *I fell down to worship at the feet of the angel*—The very same words which occur, Rev. xix. 10. The reproof of the angel, likewise, *See thou do it not,* for *I am thy fellowservant,* is expressed in the very same terms as before. May it not be the very same incident which is here related again? Is not this far more probable, than that the apostle should commit a fault again, of which he had been so solemnly warned before?

Verse 9. *See thou do it not*—The expression in the original is short and elliptical, as is usual in showing vehement aversion.

Verse 10. *And he saith to me*—After a little pause. *Seal not the sayings of this book*—Conceal them not, like the things that are sealed up. *The time is nigh*—Wherein they shall begin to take place.

Verse 11. *He that is unrighteous*—As if he had said, The final judgment

that is filthy, let him be filthy still: and he that is righteous
let him be righteous still. and he that is holy, let him be
12 holy still Behold, I come quickly; and my reward *is* with
13 me, to render to every one as his work shall be. I am
the Alpha and the Omega, the first and the last, the beginning and the end.
14 Happy *are* they that do his commandments, that they
may have right to the tree of life, and may enter in by
15 the gates into the city. Without *are* dogs, and sorcerers,
and whoremongers, and murderers, and idolaters, and every
one that loveth and maketh a lie.
16 I Jesus have sent my angel to testify to you, to the
churches, these things. I am the root and the offspring of
17 David, the bright, the morning-star And the Spirit and
the bride say, Come. And let him that heareth say, Come.

is at hand; after which the condition of all mankind will admit of no change for ever. *Unrighteous*—Unjustified. *Filthy*—Unsanctified, unholy

Verse 12. *I*—Jesus Christ. *Come quickly*—To judge the world. *And my reward is with me*—The rewards which I assign both to the righteous and the wicked are given at my coming. *To give to every man according as his work*—His whole inward and outward behaviour *shall be.*

Verse 13. *I am the Alpha and the Omega, the first and the last*—Who exist from everlasting to everlasting How clear, incontestable a proof, does our Lord here give of his divine glory!

Verse 14. *Happy are they that do his commandments*—His, who saith, *I come*—He speaks of himself. *That they may have right*—Through his gracious covenant. *To the tree of life*—To all the blessings signified by it. When Adam broke his commandment, he was driven from *the tree of life.* They "who keep his commandments" shall eat thereof.

Verse 15. *Without are dogs*—The sentence in the original is abrupt, as expressing abhorrence. The gates are ever open; but not for *dogs;* fierce and rapacious men.

Verse 16. *I Jesus have sent my angel to testify these things*—Primarily. *To you*—The seven angels of the churches; then *to* those *churches*—and afterwards to all other churches in succeeding ages. *I*—as God. *Am the root*—And source of *David's* family and kingdom; as man, am descended from his loins. "I am the star out of Jacob," Num. xxiv. 17; like *the bright morning star,* who put an end to the night of ignorance, sin, and sorrow, and usher in an eternal day of light, purity, and joy

Verse 17. *The Spirit and the bride*—The Spirit of adoption in the bride, in the heart of every true believer. *Say*—With earnest desire and expectation. *Come*—And accomplish all the words of this prophecy. *And let him that thirsteth, come*—Here they also who are farther off are invited *And whosoever will, let him take the water of life*—He may partake of my spiritual and unspeakable blessings, as freely as he makes use of the

And let him that thirsteth, come. Let him that willeth, take the water of life freely.
18 I testify to every one that heareth the words of the pro-
phecy of this book, If any man add to them, God shall add
19 to him the plagues that are written in this book: And if any
man shall take away from the words of the book of this
prophecy, God shall take away his part of the tree of life,
and the holy city, which are written in this book.
20 He that testifieth these things saith, Yea, I come
quickly. Amen. Come, Lord Jesus!
21 The grace of the Lord Jesus *be* with all.

most common refreshments; as freely as he drinks of the running stream.

Verses 18, 19. *I testify to every one,* &c.—From the fulness of his heart, the apostle utters this testimony, this weighty admonition, not only to the churches of Asia, but to all who should ever hear this book. He that *adds,* all the plagues shall be added to him; he that *takes* from it, all the blessings shall be taken from him; and, doubtless, this guilt is incurred by all those who lay hinderances in the way of the faithful, which prevent them from hearing their Lord's "I come," and answering, "Come, Lord Jesus." This may likewise be considered as an awful sanction, given to the whole New Testament; in like manner as Moses guarded the law, Deut. iv 2, and xii. 32; and as God himself did, Mal. iv. 4, in closing the canon of the Old Testament.

Verse 20. *He that testifieth these things*—Even all that is contained in this book. *Saith*—For the encouragement of the church in all her afflictions. *Yea*—Answering the call of the Spirit and the bride. *I come quickly*—To destroy all her enemies, and establish her in a state of perfect and everlasting happiness. The apostle expresses his earnest desire and hope of this, by answering, *Amen. Come, Lord Jesus!*

Verse 21. *The grace*—The free love. *Of the Lord Jesus*—And all its fruits. *Be with all*—Who thus long for his appearing!

REVELATION

It may be proper to subjoin here a short view of the whole contents of this book.

In the year of the world,

3940. Jesus Christ is born, three years before the common computation
In that which is vulgarly called, the thirtieth year of our Lord, Jesus Christ dies; rises; ascends.

A. D. 96. The Revelation is given; the coming of our Lord is declared to the seven churches in Asia, and their angels, Rev i., ii., iii.

97, 98. The seven seals are opened, and under the fifth the chronos is declared, C. iv.—vi.

Seven trumpets are given to the seven angels, C vii. viii.

Century, 2d, 3d, 4th, 5th, the trumpet of the 1st, 2d, 3d, 4th angel, C viii.

510—589 The first woe,
589—634 The interval after the first woe,
634—840 The second woe, } Ch. ix.

800 The beginning of the non-chronos many kings,
840—947 The interval after the second woe, } C. ix., x.

847—1521 The twelve hundred and sixty days of the woman, after she had brought forth the man child, C xii. 6

947—1836 The third woe, 12

1058—1836 The time, times, and half a time, and within that period, the beast, his forty-two months, his number 666, } to C. xiii. 5

1209 War with the saints: the end of the chronos, 7

1614 An everlasting gospel promulged, C. xiv. 6

1810 The end of the forty-two months of the beast; after which, and the pouring out of the phials, he is not, and Babylon reigns queen, C. xv., xvi.

1832 The beast ascends from the bottomless pit, C. xvii., xviii.

1836 The end of the non-chronos, and of the many kings; the fulfilling of the word, and of the mystery of God; the repentance of the survivors in the great city; the end of the "little time," and of the three times and a half; the destruction of the beast; the imprisonment of Satan, C. xix., xx.

Afterward The loosing of Satan for a small time; the beginning of the thousand years' reign of the saints; the end of the small time, C. xx.

The end of the world; all things new, C. xx., xxii.

The several ages, from the time of St. John's being in Patmos, down to the present time, may, according to the chief incidents mentioned in the Revelation, be distinguished thus:—

Age II. The destruction of the Jews by Adrian, C viii. 7

III The inroads of the barbarous nations, 8

REVELATION.

IV The Arian bitterness, 10
V. The end of the western empire, 12
VI. The Jews tormented in Persia, C. ix. 1
VII. The Saracen cavalry, 13
VIII. Many kings, C. x. 11
IX. The ruler of the nations born, C. xii. 5
X. The third woe, 12
XI. The ascent of the beast out of the sea, C. xiii. 1
XII. Power given to the beast, 5
XIII. War with the saints, 7
XIV. The middle of the third woe,
XV. The beast in the midst of his strength, 8
XVI. The Reformation ; the woman better fed, 9
XVII. An everlasting gospel promulged, C. xiv. 6
XVIII. The worship of the beast and of his image, 9

O God, whatsoever stands or falls, stands or falls by thy judgment Defend thy own truth ! Have mercy on me and my readers ! To thee be glory for ever !

AN INDEX

CHIEFLY OF WORDS EXPLAINED IN THE PRECEDING COMMENT.

INDEX.

INDEX.

W9-ASU-958

REVELATION

WERNER BULST, S.J.

REVELATION

TRANSLATED BY
BRUCE VAWTER, C.M.

SHEED AND WARD
NEW YORK

Originally published as *Offenbarung*
Biblischer und theologischer Begriff,

Library of Congress Catalog Card Number 65-12200

Nihil obstat:
Patrick A. Barry
Censor Librorum

Imprimatur:
Patrick C. Brennan
Vicar General
Diocese of Burlington

The Nihil Obstat and Imprimatur are official declarations that a book or pamphlet is free of doctrinal or moral error. No implication is contained therein that those who have granted the Nihil Obstat and Imprimatur agree with the contents, opinions or statements expressed.

Manufactured in the United States of America

TRANSLATOR'S PREFACE

This little work deserves reading by a larger public than it is likely to have in its original German. It deals, sometimes repetitiously and sometimes schematically, but always adequately, with a subject of crucial importance which must inevitably loom larger in the Catholic consciousness with the increasing influence exercised by the biblical and ecumenical movements within the Church. To my knowledge, no one has attempted in English for the theologically-minded precisely what Father Bulst has done here.

Let this, then, serve as the justification of this translation. The technical language of theology is never likely to produce great literature, and there is necessarily a certain amount of technical language in this book. But since it will be of interest chiefly to readers who have some familiarity with such terms, I have not thought it advisable to modify them for the general reader. Neither have I felt called on to offer substitutions for the mainly German sources on which the author has drawn and to which he refers in his text and notes, even though these may not be available to the reader who requires this translation. For the most part, the names and the positions involved will already be familiar, even if the citations are not.

To the extent possible I have noted the existence of English translations (indicated as ET) and have adapted my translation to the existing ones. Otherwise the footnotes are for the most part precisely as the author wrote them. In the exceptional footnote that I have thought it advisable to recast, I have placed a *Tr.* at the end.

DTC is, of course, the *Dictionnaire de Théologie Catholique*. *ANET* is *Ancient Near Eastern Texts Relating to the Old Testament* ([2]1955), edited by James B. Pritchard, which I have substituted for the standard German translation employed by the author. *EDB* refers to the *Encyclopedic Dictionary of the Bible* (ET 1963), edited by Louis F. Hartman. This is a translation of the second edition of a Dutch original, preferable in every way to the German version used by the author, which was made from the first edition. Denz. indicates the paragraph numbers of the well-known Denzinger-Bannwart *Enchiridion Symbolorum*, a new English translation of which is now available. *ThWNT* gives the volume and page numbers of the indispensable Kittel-Friedrich *Theologisches Wörterbuch zum Neuen Testament*. A few of the articles in this monumental work have been translated (and sometimes abbreviated) in a series of small books called *Bible Key Words*. The entire *Wörterbuch*, however, is now being translated into English.

CONTENTS

REVELATION

INTRODUCTION

In the past two or three decades apologetics has been little discussed. In contrast with other departments of theology where significant advances could be noted, there were for a long time hardly any major publications of significance in this area. Today we see ever more clearly that even in our time justification of faith is a necessity if we seek to engage in serious dialogue with our opponents and those who disagree with us rather than simply to reject their views from a position of *possessio veritatis*.[1] However, still more essential is that justification of faith which has as its purpose to offer positive proof of the reasonableness of faith, which therefore at the same time—and primarily—has a properly theological task to perform. As such, as *Fundamental Theology*, apologetics has its own meaning, independent of whatever the opposition of the time may be, although it must always keep in view, even more than other theological disciplines, the intellectual world of the existing present, especially the concerns and arguments of non-Christians or non-Catholics.[2]

If, therefore, any department of theology must be up-to-date, this is true above all of apologetics, or fundamental theology, from the very nature of its particular function. It must be abreast of the many new dimensions in knowledge, the viewpoints, and the formulations of questions that have developed in other departments of theology (especially, perhaps, in exegesis and biblical theology) in order to re-examine the customary ways by which faith is justified. Here we shall be concerned with the fundamental and central concept of fundamental theology, the concept of *revelation*.

The task of fundamental theology in relation to the whole of theology is to secure its logical foundations and prove them scientifically. This it must do because, over and above the natural revelation which is given with creation, God has revealed himself in a supernatural way: provisionally in the old covenant, definitively in Christ; further, this revelation has been entrusted to the Church to be communicated to mankind, and it is deposited in those "sources" of revelation from which theology (as positive theology) is obliged to seek its proofs.

The central concept bound up with this reality is therefore that of *revelation*. In every living religion, of course, there is some concern for "revelation" or "revelations," often in quite diverse senses. It is therefore necessary that fundamental theology should begin its demonstration by clarifying this concept. Afterwards, quite naturally, will follow the questions of the possibility (very often such a possibility is simply denied), the knowability, the necessity, and the fitness of revelation, of man's capability of receiving revelation, etc.

We shall not be primarily concerned with making an historical investigation, involving such questions as the origin of the concept of revelation which has become common in Catholic theology, "attesting divine speech" (*locutio Dei attestans*), how in the course of time this concept prevailed, and the like. In order to set forth the problem and its urgency, however, we must first of all present a summary view of how *revelation* is understood in Catholic theology, especially in the theology of more recent times. By this means it will be shown that the concept of revelation in present-day Catholic theology must be considered a *quaestio disputata.*

It is, of course, true that the theologians of the Middle Ages, and especially Thomas Aquinas, were much concerned with revelation, and in more recent centuries this concern has continued: first in the controversies of the Reformation (where it was a question of the *sources* of revelation rather than of its essential nature), then, especially, in the controversy with rationalism; and later with Immanentism. Finally in most recent times, with the return of the leading Protestant theologians to a strong "revelation theology," the *concept of revelation itself* has become properly the object of theological reflection. What is its nature? What are its forms? What is its essential content? What is therefore entailed in the response of man to God so revealing himself, that is, in *faith?*

Notes

1. The author refers here to two works well known in the German world of apologetics: *Essai sur Dieu, l'Homme et l'Univers,* edited by J. de Bivost de la Saudée (now in its third German edition), and A. Riedmann, *Die Wahrheit des Christentums,* Freiburg ^{2}1952. English-language equivalents of modern times can be found, for example, in several of the volumes of the *Twentieth Century Encyclopedia of Catholicism* (Faith and Fact Books). *Tr.*
2. Here we may mention especially the important *Fundamentaltheologie* of A. Lang (Munich 1954, ^{2}1957/58), which retains what has been proved good while remaining open to new knowledge and new formulations.

PART I

THE CONCEPT OF REVELATION IN PRESENT-DAY THEOLOGY

1

REVELATION IN CATHOLIC SYSTEMATIC THEOLOGY

In Catholic Scholastic theology, both fundamental and dogmatic, supernatural revelation is defined with highly consistent unanimity as *locutio Dei* (*attestans*), that is, "God speaking out of the treasury of his own understanding, communicating to men truths which otherwise would be attainable by them only with difficulty or not at all." This is, moreover, an "attesting" speech: it does not produce understanding of the matter communicated but commands faith in it.

The concept of speech involved here does not embrace the wider sense of the word (as might in itself be conceivable) but is confined to the strict sense of conceptual speech as it is defined by St. Thomas: To speak to someone means to make known to him the idea in one's mind (*Nihil aliud est loqui ad alterum, quam conceptum mentis manifestare: S. Th.* 1,107, *a.* 1). H. Dieckmann, for example, holds, along with C. Pesch, that: Revelation consists in this, that God communicates to men something of what he himself knows. . . . This manifestation of the divine mind is by its nature something intellectual and conceptual (*Deus nimirum ex iis, quae cognoscit, quaedam cum hominibus communicat. . . . Haec autem manifestatio mentis divinae natura sua est intellectualis et conceptualis*).[1] The means of communication is the spoken or written word. Revelation is "the word of God teaching and attesting."[2] "Divine revelation [is] the communication of those truths which are necessary and profitable for human salvation . . . in the form of ideas."[3] Supernatural revelation "consists in the spoken communication to man of those truths whose knowledge and attainment serve his supernatural destiny. . . . [It] offers higher instruction in the forms of human speech."[4] Revelation is "direct discourse and instruction on the part of God"; it is "in its inmost being an authoritative utterance of God's . . . i.e., an act by which God exhibits to the created mind his judgments in their formal expression, in internal or external words."[5] "In the form of speech" God makes known in revelation supernatural mysteries and truths of natural religion. "Formally, therefore, revelation is speaking (*locutio* or *testimonium*) which is specified by its object."[6]

R. Garrigou-Lagrange defines the formal cause of revelation in this way: Divine speech which manifests supernatural mysteries and natural religious truths (*Locutio divina manifestans mysteria supernaturalia et veritates nat-*

urales religionis). As public revelation it must find its expression in the common and unchanging concepts of natural reason . . . , such as the concepts of being, unity, truth . . . , nature, and person (*notiones communes et immutabiles rationis naturalis . . . Huiusmodi sunt notiones entis, unitatis, veritatis . . . , naturae et personae*).[7] According to A. Tanquerey, revelation takes place in this manner: The correspondence between two concepts is made known in a proposition outside the natural manner of knowledge (*Convenientia inter duos conceptus in propositione praeter naturales cognoscendi modos manifestatur*).[8] This revelatory divine speech need not be external; it is not necessarily implied that it is heard with fleshly ears. God can also act immediately on the soul of man: "God makes use of the means adapted to the recipient (speech or similar signs) in order to express externally a thought (judgment) in an understandable way, or he acts internally on the powers of the soul through visions or the perceptions of hearing, sometimes also in dreams."[9] When authors enter more specifically into the various possibilities of divine speech, they often follow the exposition of St. Thomas in the *Summa Theologica* (II-II, q. 171–174) concerning prophetical inspiration. There three degrees of revelation are distinguished: first, *revelatio sensibilis,* which occurs by means of the senses: God produces a physical sign, either a corporeal, visible thing, or a voice. Examples adduced are the writing hand in the vision of Belshazzar (Dn 5), the voice from the burning bush (Ex 3), etc. In *revelatio imaginaria* God acts instead on the imagination of man and produces impressions in it. A good example of this is the dream-vision of Jacob's ladder. In *revelatio intellectualis,* finally, God acts immediately on man's intellect through the "infusion" of mental images (*species intelligibiles infusae*).[10]

The first of these three degrees, *revelatio sensibilis,* could suggest to the theologians, one might think, that a form of revelation might be seen also in God's works as such, in his "great deeds" in the liberation of Israel from Egypt, in the miracles of Jesus, and so forth. However, this is not the case. The theologians we have mentioned, who are representative of many others, often explicitly exclude these supernatural works from the concept of "speech" and therefore from the concept of "revelation" as such. The (supernatural) revelation in *word* is carefully distinguished from the (natural) revelation in *works* and from the revelation in *vision* of the state of beatitude.[11] The supernatural *works* of God are related to supernatural revelation purely as *criteria* which enter into revelation "extrinsically" (*ab extra*) as its "concomitants." The miracles of Jesus also, even his personality and his resurrection, are in this sense qualified only as criteria of revelation, often with intentional exclusion of any other aspect. To the extent that anything immediately pertaining to revelation is acknowledged in these events themselves, it is generally reckoned as natural (sic!) revelation. The reason for this is that in these events there has been no formal speech, and therefore no supernatural revelation. B. Goebel believes that this is the general teaching of theologians.[12]

Locutio Dei attestans: by what procedures has this definition—narrow in its scope, however arresting—been obtained, and how is it justified? Many authors simply set it at the beginning of their treatment of the possibility, the need and the criteria of revelation; they may add numerous clarifications and definitions, but they do not actually explain how they have arrived at the preliminary statement itself. J. V. Bainvel, for example, includes revelation among those concepts which are universally understood as self-evident (*passim obvia*): Revelation is the manifestation of a hidden thing through speech properly so called (*Revelatio est manifestatio rei occultae per proprie dictam locutionem*). H. Straubinger, C. Pesch, and others, have similar views.[13]

Most authors, however, proceed from the concept of revelation derived from the Church's magisterium, or at least refer to it, especially to the first *Vatican* Council, which treated revelation in the second chapter of its third session, though without giving a proper definition of it. In a recent study R. Latourelle has shown that the interpretation of revelation as divine speech is either stated or presupposed in numerous pronouncements of the Church's magisterium from the time of *Trent* on. Among the most obvious examples are the formulations in the so-called *oath against Modernism*, where faith is defined as "a true assent of the understanding to truth that has been received from without through hearing, according to which we hold as true on the authority of the all-true God what has been said, attested, and revealed to us by a personal God, our Creator and Lord" (Denz. 2145).[14]

The emphasis of these theologians is almost always on making an exclusively rational analysis of the concept of revelation; this is especially evident in Dieckmann and Garrigou-Lagrange. The Scriptures serve only as the point of departure for the analysis of the concept or to provide proof texts, which in turn—as in Tanquerey—frequently appear only as footnotes. Hardly anywhere in Scholastic fundamental theology is there any extensive investigation of the concept of revelation on the basis of biblical theology.[15]

The *content of revelation* is defined in a quite standard form: "something" (*aliquid*), "concepts," "teaching," "truths which otherwise would be unattainable to man or understood only with difficulty," etc. Nevertheless P. Althaus is not justified in saying that "Roman Catholic theology has entirely de-personalized and materialized the concept of revelation . . . The de-personalization of the idea of revelation is evident from the fact that they never say, 'God has revealed himself.' Revelation is intellectualized."[16] On the contrary, the content of the revealed "truths," however generically and formally this may be expressed in the definition, remains first and foremost God himself and his work of salvation, as is clear from the whole of Catholic theology. Even in the most standard text, namely in the definition of *Vatican I, it is said explicitly:* It has pleased God *to reveal himself and the eternal decrees of his will to the human race* (Denz. 1785).

In summary we can say that in systematic Catholic theology there is a preponderant unanimity of opinion in favor of the concept of revelation as (*attesting*) *divine speech.* Furthermore, this concept apparently rests on very good grounds: the pronouncements of the Church's magisterium, explicit texts of St. Thomas and other great theologians (among whom De Lugo can serve as an example),[17] a host of important Scripture passages, especially Heb 1,1, and above all the relation of revelation to faith, which in the mind of St. Paul is based on "hearing." Also, rational analysis yields a clear division: Natural revelation consists in *works,* the revelation of salvation in this world is that of *the word,* and the final revelation is that of *vision.*

Notes

1. H. Dieckmann, *De Revelatione Christiana* (1930), No. 198f.
2. N. Jung, *DTC* XIII, 2586.
3. P. Schanz, *Apologie des Christentums* II [3](1905), p. 414.
4. I. Brunsmann, *Lehrbuch der Apologetik* I [2](1930), p. 147.
5. B. Goebel, *Katholische Apologetik* (1930), pp. 30f.
6. J. Brinktrine, *Offenbarung und Kirche* I [2](1947), p. 38.

7. R. Garrigou-Lagrange, *De revelatione per Ecclesiam catholicam proposita* [3](1925), pp. 58f.
8. A. Tanquerey, *Synopsis Theologiae dogmaticae fundamentalis* [26](1949), p. 125.
9. Pohle-Gummersbach, *Lehrbuch der Dogmatik* I [10](1952), p. 35.
10. Cf. *inter alios* Dieckmann, *op. cit.*, no. 205; S. Tromp, *De revelatione christiana* [6](1950), p. 73; Brinktrine, *op. cit.*, p. 52.
11. C. Pesch, *Praelectiones dogmaticae* I [6,7](1924), no. 151. Similarly Dieckmann, Pohle-Gummersbach, *et al.*
12. B. Goebel, *op. cit.*, p. 30, note 3.
13. J. V. Bainvel, *De vera religione et apologetica* (1914), p. 152. H. Straubinger, *Fundamentaltheologie* (1936), pp. 37ff.
14. R. Latourelle, "Notion de révélation et magistère de l'Église," *Sciences ecclésiastiques* 9 (1957), pp. 201–261.
15. Only isolated authors attempt a departure from the word "revelation" (*apokalyptō, phaneroō*) as it is found in the NT. However, this remains supplementary. Furthermore, the *fact* can be present where the *word* is lacking. See further below p. 62.
16. Paul Althaus, *Die christliche Wahrheit* I (1947), p. 286.
17. De Lugo, *Tractatus de virtute fidei divinae, disp.* I, *sectio* 10: *In quo formaliter consistat revelatio Dei.*

2

REVELATION IN CATHOLIC BIBLICAL THEOLOGY

Considering the unanimity of opinion that has been noted in the foregoing summary of the views of systematic theology, it is at first glance very surprising to find that Catholic theologians who have attempted to set forth the concept of revelation according to Sacred Scripture have arrived at quite contrary results. A brief survey which makes no pretence of completeness will suffice to show this.

We do not claim that all the theologians we propose to cite are biblical theologians in the strict sense of the word with regard to the totality of their work. Neither do we exclude the possibility that some of those cited in the previous chapter are biblical in their theological approach to other questions. We are concerned here solely with the present-day treatment and explanation of the concept of revelation.

Since in biblical theology in general and in the concept of revelation in particular Catholic theology during the past few decades has profited from many insights of Protestant theology, either directly or through controversy, we shall end with a short treatment of the concept of revelation in present-day Protestant theology (Chapter 3).

It goes without saying that no biblical theologian would deny that the divine word plays a decisive role in the whole of revelation. However, it also becomes immediately evident that hardly any single event of revelation can be formulated exclusively in the category of conceptual speech. Though "God's word" is used as the customary designation of the revelatory event, "word" is understood as the Hebrew *dābār*—often in direct antithesis to the intellectual "Greek" understanding—in a much fuller sense than merely as a means of communication. The word of God in the biblical sense is first and foremost an expression of the divine will: it is filled with might and power, it is immediately creative, it is what lies behind all that occurs, especially salvation history. In the deepest sense, the "word" of God is definitively the eternal Word become man in Christ.[1]

As a synthesis of the attempts at a biblical elaboration of the concept of revelation in recent theology we can cite the first words of Romano Guardini in his study *Die Offenbarung: Ihr Wesen und ihre Formen* (1940): "The first statement of any doctrine of revelation must be: What revelation is, only revelation itself can say. It is produced by no development in the course of natural occurrences, but is of a purely divine origin. Neither is it brought about by any necessary self-communication of the highest Being, but is a free action of a personal God. As a preliminary to its understanding, the thought must enter into the school of the Scriptures and run the risk of understanding God in too 'human' a fashion rather than too 'philosophically.'" Guardini does not mean to give "a conceptual definition" but wishes to bring out "the living totality" of revelation. He wants to "set forth that context of reality and meaning which constitutes the foundations of Christian existence and which is called 'revelation.'" Behind this lies the recognition that the manifold reality of revelation as it is described in the Sacred Scriptures of Old and New Testaments cannot perhaps be so easily compressed into a brief formal definition. As Guardini emphatically repeats: "God reveals himself basically not in the form of teaching but of doing; it is this doing that conveys his teaching. . . Never does revelation manifest itself as an abstract system, but always as living event" (118f.). "What is essential in Old Testament revelation consists in this, that it is unfolded through a history" (69). "At the end of the history of revelation stands the figure of the incarnate God." "What is revealed in Christ consists above all in what he himself is. . . That Jesus, the God-man, is precisely what he is—this God reveals" (119, 78f.).

Much earlier H. Schell had accurately observed the vast

complexity of revelation and attempted to reduce it to speculative terms. Through supernatural revelation one has possession of the fact of God's existence, which hitherto has been only the product of inference, "the power of a living fact of experience. . . As the powerful and living God, [God manifests himself] in the education of mankind, in the great deeds of its spiritual direction, wholly above and beyond the natural course of things. . . The personality of God is seen in revelation immediately and in its proper character as it exists in living historical reality."[2] Schell emphasizes that miracles in salvation history are not only external signs for faith, criteria, but "signs" standing in intimate connexion with the invisible realities they represent: "The reality is the epiphany of being and the proof of its worth and origin." "The divine origin [of the Christian religion] is to be recognized, therefore, in the successful realization of the kingdom of God in the world, in the victorious conquest of all evil forces, of all powers of corporeal and spiritual corruption, whether in nature or the spiritual world. Hence revelation itself is a miracle of divine power and accordingly is rendered acceptable to individual credence by deeds and events in the miraculous order."[3] Thus Schell accords a universal precedence to revelation in word: "The word, in distinction to works, manifests not only the content of the thought it expresses, but also the intentions and motives of the author, the circumstances and conditions of the reality itself. The word is the interpreter of the works and of the reality in its inner disposition and significance."[4]

Among present-day dogmatic theologians M. Schmaus has made the most careful exposition of the historical character of all forms of supernatural revelation entirely in the sense of biblical theology. "God reveals himself to the extent that he intervenes, acting and speaking in a determined, precisely datable moment within human history." "The historical self-manifestation of God occurs either through divine action or through divine speech or through both together." The fulfillment of the history of revelation is Christ, the incarnate Logos: "Christ was, both in his historical appearance and in his message, in his work even to the death on the cross—yes, especially here in his humiliation—and in his teaching (which, according to the mysterious laws of God, is received obscurely and in a veiled manner), the fulfilment and the completion of all divine revelations. . . . Precisely what he does and says is done and said by God." In him, therefore, "the word of God has not only been heard but also shown. . . God's personal Word has been incarnated in a human nature. It has appeared." Christ also speaks over the centuries not merely in his committed word, but "in his bodily form of existence effected through the Holy Spirit. . . , transfigured" in the Church.[5]

The "factual character" of revelation and "the inner unity of word and deed in God's works of salvation" have also been treated by G. Söhngen, who has dealt with the concept of revelation in various contexts—biblical and speculative as well (which in turn have been derived from the Bible). He, too, shows how above all this element becomes evident in the completion of revelation in Christ: "Jesus Christ. . . *is* revelation itself, the revealed God himself; and that he is the revealed image of the invisible God (cf. Col 1,15) is first fully revealed in his resurrection and exaltation (thus in a divine *act*)."[6]

In many specialized studies of biblical theology we find the same picture. In his significant work *Jesus der Christus* (1951), J. R. Geiselmann has shown how in the apostolic preaching the resurrection-and-ascension of Jesus was understood as the decisive revelatory event which illumined the passion event and the entire earthly life of Jesus. The disciples are witnesses to "the revelatory work of God in Jesus from his baptism in the Jordan through his suffering and death till his resurrection" (34). He does not minimize the significance of the words of the risen Christ which interpret the event for the disciples; however, the resurrection does not become a revelatory event only through the word of Jesus. As understood by the primitive apostolic preaching, there is also an inner relation between the prophetic word and the events of revelation which is manifest particularly as it takes place in the fulfilment of the messianic prophecies in Jesus, a fulfilment which at the same time is an interpretation of this reality. W. Hillman comes to similar conclusions after a careful analysis of the sermons of Acts. There is throughout a "continual correlation between occurrence and word" in the events of revelation. In the correspondence between the activity and the word of God in Peter's sermons there "is expressed the essential of Christian faith, that the history of Jesus from the beginning of his public ministry till his resurrection and exaltation is a single consistent event of revelation in which the word of God within the context of history and the historical activity of God mutually interpret each other."[7]

A special form of divine revelation which by its very name proclaims itself to be something more than mere revelation in word has been investigated by E. Pax in his study *Epiphaneia* (1955). Though in the Old Testament the "message character" of theophanies is of decisive significance—"God appears first and foremost to speak, not to be seen"—still, seeing and hearing form "an indivisible unity and thus make up the proper nature of an epiphany" (111). Especially, however, the epiphanies of the Old Testament universally stand in essential relation to the revelatory activity of God in the history of his people: "If God permits himself to be known, this is not merely a display, but an intervention in history and a revelation of his will" (128). For the christophanies as well (transfiguration, resurrection appearances), "the verbal material with its parallelism of seeing and hearing proper to the New Testament" shows "that appearance and message stand on the same plane and that both together make up revelation" (191f.). For John the incarnation is already "the decisive event of salvation, an epiphany, indeed, which has eclipsed all other kinds of epiphany" (214).

Heinrich Schlier has something similar to say with regard to the Johannine concept of revelation: "Revelation according to John is essentially the entry of the Logos into all that pertains to the 'flesh' and the working of the Logos through everything 'fleshly' that he took unto himself, to which, naturally and even especially, the spoken word also belongs!" It is revelation "that he, the eternal Logos. . . now hides himself in the 'fleshly' history of this world and reveals himself throughout the fleshly history of this world, so that in this and in no other way. . . his Doxa, his life-enlightening reality, may be encountered and experienced." In brief: "The Word became 'flesh' and not Word." This decisive essential of the New Testament expressed by John is confirmed by all the other apostolic authors, each in his own fashion.[8]

The same view is presented by the more recent commentaries on the Bible whenever they treat the concept of revelation: Jesus is "the final revealer of God, not merely through his preaching, but also through his deeds, his death, and his resurrection. . . . In his activity the kingdom of God whose coming he announced stands revealed (cf. Mt 12,28; Lk 11,20)." However, "Even his deeds, his miracles, he completes by his word. . . , and therefore it can be said that the word is the pre-eminent means by which Jesus acts as revealer of God, just as God in the Old Testament acts through his all-powerful word." But "word" even in this case is not to be understood merely as a conceptual utterance. "What is proper to the miracles of Jesus is their character as 'signs' (cf. Jn 2,11; 20,30f.; Acts 2,22). They, no less than his preaching, are revelations of the imminent coming of the kingdom of God. It is God who in both issues the call to faith."[9] "In John's view God is revealed above all in the person of Jesus Christ. . . . Jesus is the revealer precisely because in him the invisible God has become accessible to men as visible."[10]

That supernatural revelation is not merely a communication to man of "truths," but a personal event in which God meets man and summons him to dialogue, Otto Semmelroth has set forth for special theological treatment.[11] "Christ's first and fundamental function is revelation. This must, however, be rightly understood: not only as a deepening of the knowledge of the human understanding but as the coming of the invisible and remote God into visibility and the establishment of personal intimacy by the God-man with men. . . This is the prophetical function of Christ: to reveal the invisible God to us corporeal men. This revelation he is himself, who through the incarnation became the visible image of the invisible God (Col 1,15). But he carries the revelation further in the express word of his teaching. . . . The mysteries of God have become disclosed to us since the incarnate Son of God has spoken to us of them."[12] In revelation God encounters man concretely in his historical condition. Thus follows the "sacramental principle" of revelation, the unity of visible figure and revelatory word.[13]

This personal character of the revelatory event has been treated very perceptively by A. Lang in a manual of fundamental theology, *Die Sendung Christi* ([2] 1957): God is "encountering subject," revelation is "living encounter" in which God "transmits himself." Nevertheless Lang still holds fundamentally to the definition of revelation as God speaking. It consists in "formal communications, teachings, appeals, and summonses." The miracles of Jesus, even his resurrection and his very person, are therefore considered exclusively (or almost exclusively) as miracles to establish faith. This is, it is true, a valid and necessary point of view for the systematic proof of fundamental theology. The inner pertinence of these criteria to the revelatory event itself, however—namely, how by their means the divine salvific will also becomes immediately manifest—should have been better clarified.[14]

The concept of revelation took on a new fullness in the discussion of tradition and the development of dogma which arose in connexion with the definition of the Assumption. Karl Rahner said in this context that the proposition that revelation was closed with the death of the last apostle does not imply that therefore "a numerical sum of definite propositions" has been stored up. For "revelation is not the communication of a definite number of propositions . . ., but an historical dialogue between God and man in which something *happens* and in which the communication is related to the continuous 'happening' and enterprise of God. The dialogue moves to a quite definite term in which first the *happening* and *consequently* the communication comes to its never to be surpassed climax and so to its conclusion. Revelation is a saving Happening and only then, and in relation to this, a communication of 'truths.' This continuous Happening of saving history has now reached its never to be surpassed climax in Jesus Christ: God himself has definitively given himself to the world in his only Son."[15] "Properly and precisely, we know *who* God is, not from ourselves and the world, but only from the activity in history of the free and living God, through which he showed us who he wished to be to us. Consequently the teaching of the New Testament in the ultimate analysis is not an ontology of God's attributes, not a theory, but an historical account of the experiences in which man has come to know God."[16]

Notes

1. Paul Heinisch, *Das Wort im Alten Testament und im Alten Orient* (1922); G. Söhngen, "Das Mysterium des lebendigen Christus und der lebendige Glaube," *Die Einheit in der Theologie* (1952), pp. 354f.; Jean Daniélou, *God and the Ways of Knowing* (ET 1957); cf. *EDB*: "Logos," "Word"; J. B. Bauer, *Bibeltheologisches Wörterbuch*: "Wort" (G. Ziener); cf. also pp. 61f.
2. H. Schell, *Religion und Offenbarung* [3](1907), p. 214.
3. *Op. cit.*, pp. 263, 266.
4. *Op. cit.*, p. 215.
5. M. Schmaus, *Katholische Dogmatik* I [5](1953), pp. 8–14.
6. G. Söhngen, "Überlieferung und apostolische Verkündigung" (1949), *Die Einheit in der Theologie* (1952), p. 316, see also 354f., 359, etc.
7. W. Hillmann, "Grundzüge der urkirchlichen Glaubensverkündigung," *Wissenschaft und Weisheit* 20 (1957), pp. 163ff.
8. Heinrich Schlier, "Kurze Rechenschaft," *Bekenntnis zur katholischen Kirche* [5](1956), pp. 179ff.
9. Josef Schmid, *Das Evangelium nach Matthäus* [3](1956), excursus on Mt 11, 30: "Der Begriff und Inhalt der Offenbarung nach der synoptischen Überlieferung." See also, *Das Evangelium nach Markus* [3](1954), excursus on Mk 1, 45: "Die Wunder Jesu."
10. Alfred Wikenhauser, *Das Evangelium nach Johannes* [2](1957), excursus on Jn 8,20: "Jesus als der Offenbarer Gottes."
11. O. Semmelroth, *Gott und Mensch in Begegnung* (1956).
12. O. Semmelroth, *Das geistliche Amt* (1958), pp. 116f.
13. E. H. Schillebeeckx, "The Sacraments: an Encounter with God," in *Christianity Divided* (1961), pp. 245–275 (ET of

an article of 1957, a summary of the themes of his *Christ, Sacrament of Encounter with God* [1963], Tr.).

14. A. Lang, *Fundamentaltheologie* I: *Die Sendung Christi*[2] (1957), pp. 38ff.
15. Karl Rahner, "The Development of Dogma," *Theological Investigations* (New York, Taplinger, 1961), p. 48.
16. *Ib.*, "Theos in the New Testament," p. 117.

3

REVELATION IN PROTESTANT THEOLOGY

At the end of a long process of ever increasing disintegration of Christian substance—in the rationalistic Enlightenment which no longer left room for revelation coming from above; in F. Schleiermacher's religion of feeling and in Protestant idealism, where revelation became a subjective, immanent process; in the ethicism of A. Ritschl and finally in the naturalization of Christian revelation in the historicism of *Religionsgeschichte*—the investigation of what is peculiar to Christian revelation, and therefore to Christian faith, still remained a question for those Protestant theologians who wished their confession of faith to specify a belonging to Christ in the true sense. In a number of special studies, including many works of systematic theology, especially those of Emil Brunner and Karl Barth, the question of the nature of divine revelation has been raised. Since there are some who are consciously in search of a "revelation theology," the word "revelation" is not understood in all these studies in precisely the same sense.

It is not possible to enter here into every detail or even to give a complete picture of the whole field. We can only bring out those stresses which are to some extent characteristic and which appear especially relevant to our present study, in relation to the classic Catholic definition of revelation as *divine speech*. The opinions of Protestant theologians will merit our attention to the extent that they make an evident attempt to set forth the biblical understanding of revelation, especially that of the New Testament, from the Bible itself, and the less they concern themselves with philosophical expositions and speculations. (A particular example of the latter is Rudolf Bultmann's existential interpretation of biblical statements; but another is found in the works of Karl Barth, especially his earlier writings in which he upholds with so much emphasis the wholly unbiblical idea that by the very fact of his creation man is absolutely incapable of knowing God, and equally incapable of hearing God's word as such.)

In a sharp contradiction of the concept of revelation in Catholic theology, and also that of the older Protestant orthodoxy, it is insistently stated that revelation is not "teaching," not "communication of knowledge." Emil Brunner especially has taken it as his task to inveigh against the "intellectualizing" of faith and therefore of revelation. P. Althaus, as we have seen, condemns Roman Catholic theology for having "thoroughly de-personalized, materialized" the conception of revelation. Revelation "is not communication of a material truth, a 'teaching,' but a personal encounter of God with us. . . There are, in the strict sense of the word, no *credenda,* but only the *credendus.*"[1] It will be generally conceded, it is true, that the content of revelation—in a secondary way—can also be expressed doctrinally, as in knowledge and dogma. The beginnings of such "doctrine" are already found within the canon, or on "the margin of the canon"—that is to say, in the Pastoral letters. However, it is often added that dogmatic formulations can possess only an approximative value.

In present-day Protestant theology the *historical character of revelation* and of the redemption is very strongly emphasized, often in conscious opposition to liberal Protestantism, which sought after universally valid fundamental religious "principles" that were realized in the Old Testament and in Christ uniquely or in a purer fashion. Revelation occurs not merely *in* history but *as* history, as "event." A. Oepke maintains that, beginning with the fundamental revelatory act in the Old Testament, the liberation from Egypt, all the way to the revelatory event in Christ, the characteristic of the biblical understanding of revelation is "precision in history." "Revelation is *not* communication of supernatural knowledge and *not* a stirring up of religious feeling. True, a knowledge concerning revelation can develop and the revelation of God is necessarily accompanied by perceptions divinely induced. . . But revelation is not this, but is in its proper sense the *doing of Yahweh*, the lifting of his essential hiddenness, the offering of himself to the community."[2] "God so orders the facts of history as to manifest himself. That is the telling characteristic of the revelation attested by the Bible, of the revelation which took place in Israel and in Christ."[3]

In contrast to the conceptions of revelation and tradition in recent Catholicism and in Protestant orthodoxy, G. Gloege also stresses this historical quality of the revelatory event: From all the witnesses to the events of revelation this "fundamental property" can be recognized: "God's revelation constantly signifies a God-event, a God-act: God *comes*, God *intervenes*. God deals with man when he reveals his will to him. In intervening and taking possession by means of revelatory act, God invariably makes use of concrete means which allow the revelation to come forth only *veiled* and *piecemeal*. God's revelation is thus historical revelation, and this in a threefold sense: (a) Firstly—seen from God's viewpoint—revelation is historical since it is accomplished as a factual occurrence. It is historical in its character as *event*. (b) Secondly—seen from man's viewpoint—revelation is historical as it approaches man in a concrete setting, man as he is endowed and defined in history. It is historical in its character of *decision.* (c) Revelation is also historical, however, in the sense that it interprets history (*Geschichte*) within the context of a course of events (*Historie*) which occurs on the stage of worldly reality and receives concrete expression in earthly institutions and ordinances, in the cult and law of a community. It is historical (*geschichtlich*) in its historic (*historisch*) character. What God reveals according to the Old Testament is never (as it might have been in the Greek conception of revelation) an insight into his supernatural essence and being, or (as it is in the Catholic principle of revelation) the knowledge of hitherto unknown truths or facts, but his guiding will (a) for historical decision (b) and historic involvement (c)." Hence: "The original character of tradition is not that of dogmatic teaching, but that of historical message which sets forth in narrative God's former historic action, especially the miraculous liberation from Egypt." The same historical characteristic holds for the understanding of revelation in the New Testament. It is true that "In the place of theophany we now have christophany." This, however, is to be understood "as a new form of theophany."[4]

For the Old Testament in particular, Walther Eichrodt has fully explored the historical character of revelation by taking as the leading idea of his Old Testament theology the concept of the covenant. "First of all it must be noted that the establishment of a covenant through the work of

Moses especially emphasizes one basic element in the whole Israelite experience of God, namely *the factual nature of the divine revelation.* God's disclosure of himself is not grasped speculatively, not expounded in the form of a lesson; it is as he breaks in on the life of his people in his dealings with them and moulds them according to his will that he grants them knowledge of his being."[5] In like manner E. Stauffer has ordered his theology of the New Testament according to historical categories. At the centre stands the "Christ-event."[6]

More than any other, however, O. Cullmann has made the historical character of revelation the fundamental principle of his theology: "*All Christian theology in its innermost essence is Biblical history;* on a straight line of an ordinary process in time God here reveals himself." God's revelation, his "Word," is a deed: "The Word, the Logos, is God *in his revelatory action.* Nowhere, however, is God's action more concretely revealed to man than in history." The climax and centre of all revelation means, according to primitive Christian theology, "that the self-revealing God, that is, his Word, his Logos, *once* entered so completely into history that this unique entrance can be designated by dates just as can every other historical event. . . . The same Word of God who proclaims himself as creative action and will proclaim himself at the end in the new creation 'became flesh' in Jesus Christ."[7] Cullmann has rightly singled out the resurrection as the decisive event of revelation and therefore placed it at the centre of all history.

Naturally no Protestant theologian denies that in the totality of the revelation-event, the spoken revelatory word also has an essential importance: it accompanies the works of revelation, refers to them, elucidates their true meaning, draws them out of the ambiguity in which the bare action (often) stands, and gives them their univocal sense, so that man is allowed to perceive the divine will in the divine act. But, on the one hand, they insist on the essentially derivative quality of this revelation *in word* in relation to the revelatory *act* of God in the history of his people and in Christ. And on the other hand, when *God's word* is used by preference as the summary designation of divine revelation, this *word* is never understood as a mere word of *teaching*, but in the fullness of meaning of the Hebrew *dābār*, as *word of action,*[8] and over and above that—with special emphasis—as a summons to man. God's word is not an "it" truth but a "thou" truth, not *revealed doctrine* but *personal truth, self-communication,* a living encounter of the incarnate Word of God with sinful man (E. Brunner).[9] The objective side of the revelatory event as such does not stand as revelation, but only the truth contained in it, "the truth of my Lord which reaches me."[10] In revelation, therefore, there is never a question simply of "God in himself"; God discloses himself to mankind for its salvation or, in case man rejects him, for perdition. The *soteriological* character of revelation is increasingly stressed, even to the identification of the two elements: Revelation is redemption taken place, brought to completion.[11]

The heavy emphasis placed on revelation as summons easily leads to a more or less *actualistic interpretation of revelation*: The word of God (spoken or written or incarnate in an event) is not already in itself revelation, but is revelation only when, and to the extent that, it is received by man as such: "If there is no faith, then the revelation has not been consummated: it has not actually happened, so to speak, but is only at the first stage."[12] With Bultmann the emphasis on the summons in itself is expressed in terms as absolute as possible: Only the word as address, and as address here and now, is revelation. The message does not communicate "something that happened in a certain place and at a certain time," but says only what has happened to the one addressed, or rather, what is happening to him. Consequently, faith is not "being convinced, but rather the response to an address." This, however, represents the intrusion of existential ideas, alien to its thought forms, into the world of the New Testament.[13]

The self-disclosure of God that has taken place in history, and especially in Christ, reaches man, after Christ, in the witness of the apostles, and postapostolic generations in the written word of the apostles and the contemporary preaching of the Church. The older Protestant orthodoxy, in identifying the word of the Bible as such with revelation, misapprehended the nature of revelation. The Bible is only human, for all that it is a divinely authorized witness of the revelation that has taken place in the old covenant and in Christ. But through this human word of the Bible and of the Church's preaching God's revelation nevertheless comes through as an actual summons to men. Therefore "derivatively" the *knowledge* of the Christ-event can also be called *revelation, word of God*, as it has already become in the New Testament.[14]

In a sharp reversal of the ethicizing of Christianity in the school of A. Ritschl and of a this-worldly culture-Protestantism, the essential *eschatological direction of all revelation* has once again been recognized—though with a bias which leads to extreme consequences. On the liberal side the "unrealized parousia" has been designated by the so-called consequent eschatologists (J. Weiss, A. Schweitzer, M. Werner, *et al.*) as the key to the development of early Christian doctrine and to the emergence of a "Church" from the primitive community. But also in general, in so far as the resurrection has once more been placed as the central event of revelation, marking the beginning of the end-time, to the same extent the eschatological character of the revelation in Christ has been recognized. Even Bultmann's theology is, though in an existential interpretation, eschatologically orientated: In faith, and only in faith, does the Christian achieve death and resurrection with Christ.

Notes

1. P. Althaus, *Die christliche Wahrheit* I (1947), pp. 285f.
2. A. Oepke, "*apokalyptō*," *ThWNT* 3, 565–597, esp. p. 575.
3. P. Althaus, *op. cit.*, p. 31.
4. Gerhard Gloege, *Offenbarung und Überlieferung* (Theologische Forschung, Wissenschaftliche Beiträge zur kirchen-evangelischen Lehre, Nr. 6, 1954), pp. 23f., 26, 29.
5. From *Theology of the Old Testament* by Walther Eichrodt. Tr. A. J. Baker. Copyright © 1961, SCM Press Ltd. Published U.S.A. 1961, The Westminster Press. Used by permission. P. 37.
6. Ethelbert Stauffer, *New Testament Theology* (1948) (ET 1955), pp. 103ff.
7. From *Christ and Time* by Oscar Cullmann, revised ed. Copyright © 1964, W. L. Jenkins. The Westminster Press. Used by permission. Pp. 23f.
8. Cf. here, *inter al.*, O. Procksch, "*legō, Wort Gottes im AT*," *ThWNT* IV, 89–100.
9. Cf. W. Stolz, "Theologisch-dialektischer Personalismus und kirchliche Einheit. Apologetisch-kritische Studie zu Emil Brunners Lehre von der Kirche . . . ," *Studia Friburgensia* N.F. 6 (1953), pp. 7ff., 91, etc.
10. P. Althaus, *Die christliche Wahrheit* I (1947), pp. 31f.
11. For K. Barth in his earlier writings, the word of God is the central concept. It would seem to be significant, however, for his understanding of revelation, that as the volumes of his *Church Dogmatics* (ET 1956–) have succeeded one another, "imperceptibly but irresistibly" he has substituted the more concrete and more embracing "Jesus Christ, God-man." Cf. H. U. von Balthasar, *Karl Barth, Darstellung und Deutung seiner Theologie* (1951), p. 124.

12. From *The Christian Doctrine of God,* Vol. 1, by Emil Brunner. Tr. Olive Wyon. Copyright 1950, W. L. Jenkins. The Westminster Press. Used by permission. P. 19.
13. Rudolf Bultmann, "The Concept of Revelation in the New Testament," *Existence and Faith, Shorter Writings* (New York, Meridian, 1960), pp. 86f. (ET of an article of 1929.)
14. Cf. A. Oepke, "*apokalyptō*," *ThWNT* III, 595f.

PART II

A "SYSTEMATIC" OR A "BIBLICAL" CONCEPT?

4

METHODOLOGICAL CONSIDERATIONS

WITHOUT question, as is evident from the foregoing summary, extraordinarily important views have been elaborated in biblical theology—Catholic as well as Protestant—which have received little or no attention in the treatment of revelation presented by Catholic systematic theology and have sometimes even been expressly excluded from it, at least from the treatment of supernatural revelation as a formal concept. The tension surrounding this issue becomes especially evident in the monograph of H. Niebecker, *Wesen und Wirklichkeit der übernaturlichen Offenbarung: Eine Besinnung auf die Grundlagen der Theologie* (1940), an investigation which is of particular interest to us since Niebecker attempts to set forth precisely "the concept of revelation in the magisterium of the Church (and therefore also that of Catholic theology) and its biblical basis." "As corresponding to the magisterium of the Church," he gives the following definition: "Supernatural revelation is a free divine act which is essentially supernatural and consists in this, that God has spoken to us through the prophets and Jesus Christ and, with a certain obscurity, has communicated supernatural mysteries and likewise truths of natural religion, to be taught by the Church without alteration of their sense until the end of time, by means of which those who give credence to God's revelation can attain the supernatural goal of mankind, the vision of God" (57f.). In brief: Revelation "coincides with God speaking in the various organs of revelation" (50f.). But in his subsequent chapters on the concept of revelation in the Old and New Testaments (where this doctrinal conception of revelation is to be justified!), in conformity with biblical theology, he develops in general a rather significantly different picture: Revelation in the sense of the Scriptures simply does not coincide with "God speaking in the various organs of revelation" (whatever bearing such divine speech may have on the revelatory event). If this is true for the Old Testament (Niebecker refers here to the various theophanies, but overlooks almost entirely the revelation effected in the divine dealing with Israel in history), it is even more true for the New Testament: "In the incarnation God's revelation *ad extra* reaches its culmination. It takes place now no longer in word or work alone, but assumes a personal form: The Logos comes in person and dwells among us. . . . In the Logos become flesh the divine glory has shone upon the earth" (149). "The Word of the Father has become flesh and therefore *is in his person the revelation of God,* whose glory could be seen by those who lived with Jesus Christ. In this personal revelation of the Logos his revelation in word takes root" (155).

As Sacred Scripture understands it, therefore, revelation takes place also in "word," in "vision," and in "personal form"—how, then, is traditional Scholastic theology justified in restricting the concept of revelation to "speech" (in the formal sense)? A definition must always be exclusive! By his own conclusions Niebecker has obviously created a problem.[1]

DIVERGENCE OF TRADITIONAL CONCEPT AND BIBLICAL DATA

Moreover, this discrepancy between the traditional concept of revelation and the biblical data is already evident in the work of M. J. Scheeben, who at the beginning of his theological manual (*Handbuch der Dogmatik* §1–6) treats the concept of revelation in detail. First, in traditional fashion, he distinguishes the *revelatio naturae* as revelation in work, the *revelatio gratiae,* whose "vehicle" is the formal word, and the *revelatio gloriae,* which consists in vision. Later, however, he produces another schema in which "the three historical degrees" of the *revelatio gratiae* are paralleled with the "forms of revelation" just named:

The patriarchal revelation is preponderantly *revelatio per naturam;* the Mosaic revelation, as pedagogy leading to Christ, is *revelatio per fidem,* thus revelation in word; and, finally, Christian revelation represents the *revelatio gloriae,* since in Christ God revealing himself becomes visible (No. 54). Scheeben, therefore, rightly saw that the reality of revelation attested in the Bible transcends the formal traditional concept of supernatural revelation as *locutio formalis.* However, his book goes no further into the tension he had discovered.

The comparison of the concept of revelation traditional in Catholic systematic theology with the concept of revelation in modern biblical theology shows that we have to deal not merely with a *fundamentally important theological fact* but also with a *problem of considerable urgency.* Furthermore, this one point is merely illustrative of a more general situation in our theological work today: Systematic and biblical theology (and the same holds true for moral, ascetical theology, etc.) have grown apart from one another to a dangerous degree. This divergence amounts, as the example of the concept of revelation shows, to the development of a difference in theological language.

True, we should not exaggerate this tension between the traditional and the biblical concepts of revelation. In such an important matter, it can hardly be that Catholic theology has simply fallen into error, whatever the strictures made against it from the Protestant side. Nevertheless we must enquire seriously into the relationship between the traditional and the biblical understandings of revelation. With what justification has the traditional Catholic concept selected, from the fullness of the reality attested by the Bible, simply the idea of God speaking?

It will be unanimously agreed today, at least theoretically, that a purely philosophical, aprioristic determination or elaboration of the concept should not be considered, even though many contemporary treatises on the concept of revelation, with their concise, neat formulas and multiple distinctions, can seem somewhat rationalistic, especially when they fail to base themselves on positive sources, or do so only inadequately. Since the revelation in Christ and the preceding revelation of the old covenant is a *supernatural* reality, a completely free gift of God's grace, we can only proceed from this reality itself (or from positive, either immediately divine or divinely authorized utterances concerning this reality), in which that which is proper to this revelation consists. "It is produced by no development in the course of natural occurrences, but is of purely divine origin. Neither is it brought about by any necessary self-communication of the highest Being, but is a free action of a personal God. As a preliminary to its understanding the thought must enter into the school of the Scriptures and run the risk of understanding God in too 'human' a fashion rather than too 'philosophically.' "[2]

More specifically, in view of the two classical approaches of fundamental theology, the empirical and the genetico-historical, there are two possibilities when we come to decide how the concept of revelation should be set forth. We can, on the one hand, begin with the teaching of the Church and establish what it understands by the revelation it claims to communicate to mankind. Many fundamental theologians do this, almost always contenting themselves with references to the first Vatican Council. If then they were to develop their proof by restricting themselves to the empirical method—that is, to a consideration of the Church as it now exists, demonstrating itself to be a "divine sign"—no logical complaint could be raised against such a presentation of the concept of revelation, even though the resolution of the tension between the ecclesiastical and biblical concepts would remain a pressing concern.

As a matter of fact, however, hardly any fundamental theologian today makes use of the empirical method of proof either exclusively or primarily. With good reason almost all fundamental theologians prefer to begin not with the Church but with Christ, or even with the revelation of the old covenant that preceded him; hence with the revelatory event, not as it is made present for us *today* through the mediation of the Church, but as it took place *originally*, and as it is attested in Scripture (as an historical source).[3] But is it proper, from the standpoint of correct methodology, in this *genetic* proof simply to take over the concept of revelation as it has been derived from the formulations of the Church's magisterium? The very fact that the process of biblical theology has led to a not inconsiderably divergent concept of revelation should give us pause. This consideration raises the question whether the Church's magisterium does not treat revelation from a somewhat different perspective than that described in Sacred Scripture, perhaps not as far as content is concerned, but at least with a different method of procedure. We should also consider whether, owing to controversy with non-Catholic formulations of revelation—and, indeed, all the formulations of the magisterium occurred as a consequence of such controversies—certain viewpoints have not been emphasized to the extent that others, perhaps no less important but not at issue in the discussion, have retired into the background. This is the case, for example, in the controversy with Protestantism over the specific question of what the sources of revelation are for us: Sacred Scripture alone or Scripture and tradition?[4] Obviously, however, the theme of revelation is by no means exhausted by this one question. In controversy with modern heresies, Immanentism, Relativism, etc., the same thing has taken place with regard to the objectivity of revelation, its unchanging truth, its reasonableness, and therefore also the probative force of its criteria.[5]

THE CHURCH: A TEACHING WORD

The Church considers revelation as something committed to her, as something to be communicated through her to mankind. Revelation is committed to her, however, and is transmitted by her (especially) in the character of a teaching *word.*[6] In this sense—and only in this sense—can Sacred Scripture and tradition be called the *sources* in which revelation (precisely in the character of the word) is *contained,* as repeated utterances of the Church's magisterium have indicated: "This supernatural revelation is contained, according to the faith of the universal Church . . . in written books and unwritten traditions" (Vatican, s. III, cap. 2: Denz. 1787).

However, never has it been said unconditionally that the revelation transmitted to later generations in the word of Scripture and tradition and through the living word of the Church occurred *exclusively* in this form at its origin. Only then would one be able to say that the nature of revelation consists absolutely in (formal) divine speech; for a definition must be exclusive. Rather, the fact is that the revelation now presented to us in word goes back to an original revelatory event which did not occur exclusively in word but also—as will be shown in greater detail —in the revelatory activity of God in history and in multiple theophanies, both of the latter reaching their term in the incarnation of the eternal Word.

An evident difficulty in defining the concept of revelation lies in the fact that the concept *word* or *speech* which plays such an important role in it is not perfectly univocal. As a rule, we understand it to mean the *conceptual utterance* of something contained in the mind; thus, a thought, a judgment, to be communicated to another person by means of vocal signs, in whose stead other signs, such as those of writing, can also serve. Speech in this sense therefore lies essentially in the dimension of the conceptual and of its signs. What is properly meant is the thought expressed in the vicarious sign.[7] As we have already shown, it is in this sense, as conceptual communication, that the idea of "God *speaking*" is usually understood in the traditional definition of revelation.

It is, however, possible of itself to define the concept *speech* in a broader way, namely as *any* message of an intelligent being. A person *speaks* not only in his words, but also in his actions, in the entire giving of himself; above all, he speaks when this action and self-giving are directed toward another person, and more than ever when the purpose of the message is to reveal his intentions towards this other person. One could therefore arrive at the idea (in order to be more faithful to the biblical understanding of revelation) that the concept of divine *speech* could also embrace the *acts of God* in *salvation history*, in which Israel had to "know Yahweh," in which Christ made known his goodness, etc. But such a broader concept of *speech* is not sufficient to define supernatural revelation, at least not without further distinctions. For God also makes himself known in his natural work of creation, and this not only as a matter of fact but from the deliberate intention of making himself known. In accord with the manifold witness of Scripture, the Vatican Council said of natural creation that God made all things "in order to reveal his perfection through the good things which he communicated to creatures" (*ad manifestandam perfectionem suam per bona, quae creaturis impertitur*: Vatican s. III, cap. 1: Denz. 1783). In a completely acceptable sense, therefore, we can talk of a *message of creation*, or better, of *God speaking through his creation*. As a consequence, supernatural revelation cannot be separated from natural revelation merely by the fact that the latter is revelation in *work* and the former is revelation in *word*. The matter is not as simple as that. Supernatural revelation is not only given in revelation of the word (at least when *word* is set in opposition to *work*), but also, as we shall go on to show, essentially includes revelation in work, and, indeed, supernatural revelation in work. On the other hand, natural revelation can also be designated in a wider sense as the word of God to man.

SPEECH: THE BIBLICAL CONCEPT

It is also extremely important to note (though this is often overlooked) that our ordinary concept of *word* or *speech* does not coincide with the biblical concept of *word* or *speech*, or that it only partly coincides with it. The Hebrew *dābār*, unlike the Greek *logos* and our *word*, means not only intelligible utterance (whether in the strict sense of conceptual utterance or in the wider sense of any personal communication), but over and above this the *word as effective power*. It includes, therefore, a dynamic as well as a dianoetic significance. By his *word* God has called the world into existence. The *word of Yahweh* is the distinctive determining power in Israel's history. *Word* often enough also means simply the occurrence itself, the thing. In many biblical passages this fullness of meaning is primarily the key to correct interpretation, as, for example, when the shepherds say in the infancy narrative: "Let us go unto Bethlehem and see this *word* that has *taken place* there, which the Lord has made known to us" (Lk 2,15). Or when it is said in Heb 1,3 that the Son "upholds the universe by the *word* of his power."[8]

We must not, therefore—though this has in fact been done often enough—use Bible texts to justify the definition of revelation as (formal) divine speech, simply because they have to do with the *word* or *speech* of God; this is to ignore the fact that individual scriptural texts, at least when they are employed without attention to their context —very often Heb 1,1 alone is cited—have little probative value.[9]

Neither is it sound procedure to take a philosophical point of departure in the elaboration of the concept of revelation which has been developed from the terms *revelation, reveal,* or whatever corresponds to them in the primitive language of the Bible.[10] For the *fact* of revelation can exist and be described throughout univocally without the use of a distinct *terminus technicus.* The Old Testament has, in general, no *terminus technicus* for *reveal.* Also, it can only come as a surprise that, for example, in the Johannine writings where we are presented with a theology of revelation in an eminent sense, the word *apokalyptō* nevertheless occurs only a single time, and then only in a citation of Isaiah (Jn 12,38), while the word *apokalypsis* is found only in Ap 1,1. Nor is *phaneroō,* closely related in meaning, very frequent. Even *phaneroō,* moreover (and similarly *apokalyptō*!), is used in Rom 1,18f. for natural revelation! The vocabulary, therefore, will not serve as a point of departure. This is not to say, of course, that it cannot provide many insights.

A NECESSARY PRE-CONCEPTION OF REVELATION

Thus it is evident that no other way remains than that of a *phenomenological consideration and analysis* of those situations which in the Old and New Testaments are described as God's revelation. That is, it is first of all necessary to examine in their fullness these occurrences which represent revelation as the Bible knows it; we must bring out the essential characteristics, what is the *unique* element in the event which makes it certain that it is God's revelation; and all this must be seen precisely as the Bible itself sees it. It is therefore necessary at first to prescind from questions of value and truth. To prove that this biblical conception in fact contains truth, that therefore God has really made himself known in the way that the Bible understands and describes, is the further task of fundamental theology. It is clear that in taking up the question: What is revelation in the biblical sense? a clear *preliminary understanding* of revelation is necessary. Otherwise we could hardly ask the question. Such a preliminary understanding is the presupposition for any attempt at a definition. This pre-conception of revelation is extremely important. It must not be so rigid and fixed as to rule out any aspects or viewpoints that may emerge from the analysis of the revelatory event.

REVELATION

To a most generic, quite basic understanding of revelation belongs the idea that in every *revelation* something is *unveiled,* becomes known, which before—at least in some measure—was *veiled,* hidden. In the religious use of the word—the only one with which we are concerned here—it is a question of *divine* revelation: about God himself, his "thoughts," his judgments, the determinations of his will for man, especially about God's relation to man and man's to God, etc. Furthermore—and this, too, belongs to the preliminary conception of revelation with which we are concerned—it is not a question of that *general* revelation which is given along with creation and is accessible to any reasoning person (though in the concrete it may be difficult to understand it rightly). It is a question only of that *special* and (not as yet in any closely defined sense) *supernatural* revelation which—over and above the natural revelation—has taken place *in Israel* and which, according to the conviction of our faith, attained its completion in *Christ* and has subsequently been communicated to mankind through the *Church.*

It must not be overlooked that this revelatory event, as it is described in the Bible, is complex and many-sided, extending over many centuries. Hence it can very well be asked whether the Bible, a collection of such diverse writings from such diverse times, contains a single concept of revelation throughout. As a conceptual distinction, it certainly does not. Moreover, it is certain that there are real diversities in the conceptions of the Bible (which are explained by the historical character of the revelation of salvation and its various stages). But seen as a whole there does exist an all-embracing unity—in this, at least, that the Bible is always thinking of the same God who has made himself known, and what is made known are not isolated points of information; the various occurrences of revelation always seem to be somehow contributing to the totality of a salvation history leading to an end-revelation which, according to the witness of the New Testament, has occurred in Christ.

The pre-conception of supernatural revelation with which we begin must, therefore, say something like this: The hidden God has, over and above the *general* revelation given with and in creation, made himself known to man in a *special* way in *Israel* and above all in *Christ*. What are the characteristics of this revelation?

The question can be raised whether it is necessary in fundamental theology (or even advisable) to develop this essential of supernatural revelation to its ultimate theological depth—that is, to advance to the inner-trinitarian archetype of that revelation in the generation of the divine Word. It must suffice at first to content ourselves with a —theologically speaking—provisional concept of revelation, one which, however, remains open to theological deepening. It will indeed be sufficient to recognize revelation rightly as an historical phenomenon which, as an encounter with man, is characterized above all by the fact that it places a claim on man and demonstrates itself to man as divine. By this means we can pierce through the obvious externals into the inmost mystery of revelation. In the end it will lead us—not merely in its content, but also of itself—into the depths of the triune God. Thus in this concept—and the same is true of other central theological concepts, such as the incarnation, grace, etc.—the organic interdependence of the various tracts in theology becomes evident, since here what is final and most profound must also stand at the beginning. However, we can approach it only step by step.

Notes

1. Quite similar is the impression created by W. Grossouw, "Offenbarung," *Bibellexikon* (German edition, Einsiedeln 1951ff.; in the *EDB* the revision of the article, "Revelation," by J. de Fraine has considerably bettered the presentation [*Tr.*]): While at the outset it is maintained that "the essential characteristic of all biblical revelation" is that "it is God speaking" (citing Heb 1,1), the subsequent exposition, especially on revelation according to Paul and John, shows that in the biblical sense revelation is not always identical with "God speaking."
2. Guardini, *Die Offenbarung*: *Ihr Wesen und ihre Formen* (1940), p. 1.
3. The genetico-historical approach gives a more circumstanced

view and a better explanation of the truth of the Catholic religion. A judgment on the Church as a divine sign, moreover, is not possible without a consideration of its history. It is this history which brings out what is divine in the Church, which at times is very much obscured by the human.

4. Trent, s. IV: Denz. 783.
5. Vatican, s. III, cap. 2–3: Denz. 1785–94. Decree *Lamentabili* (1907), Denz. 2001ff.; encycl. *Humani Generis* (1950), Denz. 2305ff.
6. We say *especially* in word, since the Church does not hand on revelation exclusively in its expressed word, but also in its life, and in an especial way also in the sacraments. Furthermore, in the indefectibility of the Church, its holiness, its fruitfulness for all good, etc., the revealed salvific will of God should and does become visible in the present.
7. The author refers the reader to the recognized philosophical dictionaries for the clarification of "word," "speak," "speech," etc. *Tr.*
8. Cf. O. Procksch, "*logos I: Das 'Wort Gottes' im AT*," *ThWNT* IV, 89ff. Also W. Eichrodt, *Theologie des AT*, II[5], §14, II. To what extent the logos-concept of the Johannine prologue has its conceptual and historical roots in Hellenism (certainly not in the philosophical logos-doctrine, but rather in the philosophy of religion of Hellenistic Judaism) or in the area of Gnosticism, or whether it is not rather to be explained from the OT world of thought, especially from the wisdom literature (G. Kittel, F. Büchsel), is very much debated and need not be decided here (see, *inter al.*, A. Wikenhauser, *Evangelium nach Johannes*,[2] [1957], excursus on Jn 1, 18).
9. That Heb 1,1 should not be taken as defining revelation as "God speaking" in the exclusive sense of conceptual speech, and that such a definition cannot be extracted from the text,

is shown by the immediately following verses, where the Son is called "the brightness of the glory (of God) and the stamp of his nature"—formulations which certainly do not refer exclusively or even primarily to the metaphysical being of the Son but which belong to the concept involved in the revelatory event (and which cannot be simply subsumed under conceptual speech). Furthermore: By his "powerful word he upholds the universe." "Word" here again has the fullness of meaning of the Hebrew *dābār*. Cf. on this G. Söhngen, "Die biblische Lehre von der Gottebenbildlichkeit des Menschen," *Die Einheit in der Theologie*, pp. 185ff.

10. For the NT the terms involved are *apokalyptō, apokalypsis, phaneroō, gnōrizō*. H. Dieckmann made an effort to begin with the biblical vocabulary (*De revelatione christiana*, no. 193ff.); however, the studies into the history of the concepts now available in *ThWNT* were then lacking to him.

PART III

REVELATION IN THE BIBLICAL SENSE

5

NATURAL AND SUPERNATURAL REVELATION

THE HIDDENNESS OF GOD

IT IS a presupposition for divine revelation that God and the divine as such are hidden from earthly man, or at least that they are not accessible to him in the same way as the things of his world of experience. This hiddenness of God is spoken of in Sacred Scripture often and in many ways. Here a few references must suffice.

God dwells in *heaven*. It is from heaven that he looks down upon the earth. He sees all things but himself remains hidden. As far as man is concerned, God remains by nature invisible. But when he does, by exception, appear to their sight, men become filled with awe and with the fear of imminent death. This is true both in early Israelite times and in the consciousness of the prophets (cf. Ex 3,6; 33,20; Jgs 13,22; Is 6,5).[1]

As regards the New Testament, we shall refer only to two classic texts. Jn 1, 18: "No one has ever seen God. The Only-begotten, who is in the bosom of the Father, has made him known to us"; and 1 Tim 6,16: God, "who dwells in unapproachable light, whom no man has ever seen or can see, to him be honor and eternal dominion. Amen."

The hiddenness of God naturally extends also to his thoughts and judgments. This is not only bound up with his invisibility but is rooted in the fact that he is *Lord.* Borrowing words from Isaiah and the wisdom books, Paul praises the unsearchable depths of the thoughts and ways of God (Rom 11,33). His plan of salvation—in the pregnant sense, *the* mystery—has been hidden from all eternity; but now through God's grace freely bestowed in Christ, in his cross and his exaltation, it has been realized and is revealed to the nations in the apostolic message.[2]

Moreover, the hiddenness of God is by no means entirely removed even in supernatural revelation. The divine deeds of salvation history, the visible phenomena in the theophanies, are not God in his proper existence, and even the explicit word of God, since it is expressed in human concepts and images, can never represent the divine reality other than by analogy. The veiled character of God's revelation is stated or implied in many ways in Scripture.[3]

NATURAL REVELATION

It would, however, be too partial a view, and contrary to the clear witness of the Bible, were we to speak of a total hiddenness of God—as Karl Barth does to some extent.[4] Before the special revelation received in Israel and through Christ and outside it, God has not been entirely unknown to men (however incomplete their actual knowledge of him may always have remained). The notion of a *natural* revelation is, as a matter of fact, perfectly consonant with the sense of Sacred Scripture, even though the explicit texts concerning it are few (see especially the two classic texts of Wis 13 and Rom 1, 18ff.; cf. also Rom 2,14f.).[5] It happens that there are few *theoretical* utterances of any kind in Scripture. Nevertheless, quite often and in various ways the fact of natural revelation is presupposed as a self-evident truth or is implicitly stated, as, for example, when it is said that the world in its beauty and order shows forth the *glory of Yahweh:* Ps 8; 19; 104, etc. Furthermore, there is no indication in Sacred Scripture that man's ability to know God in some fashion through his works has been destroyed by sin. Therefore Paul can count it as guilt that men, "though they have known God," have nevertheless not honored him as God (Rom 1,21). Natural revelation is also recognized throughout Sacred Scripture as a fundamental fact to the extent that the message of revelation has created no strictly new words, but has made use of the general religious concepts of mankind, though it has greatly enriched these concepts and filled them with much new content.[6]

The great truths of the natural knowledge of God, such

as the fact of God's existence, his essential veracity, etc., are not only the theoretical bases for the surer knowledge given through the fact of revelation; they also constitute—more or less expressly—a connecting link with the preaching of the good news of salvation to the Gentiles, as is shown in the New Testament in the Areopagus speech (Acts 17,16–31).

SUPERNATURAL REVELATION

Natural revelation, which has been given in the creation and in man's nature itself, is—or at least can be—generally accessible to every man (though in the concrete it may present its difficulties). But over and above this, according to the Bible's representation of things, God has made himself known in an especial manner, among a particular people, at definite times and in definite situations. This initial and quite obvious distinction is not merely external and incidental, but introduces us immediately to the essence of this special revelation, that is, to its historical character.

Its Historical Character

Natural revelation takes place in the realm of *nature*, without immediate relation to the history of mankind. Mediately, of course, there is a relation to history, since the individual man is aided or hindered in his ability to know by many historical factors: tradition, education, environment, etc. Supernatural revelation, on the other hand, takes place *as such* in the area of *history*: first and foremost in the sense that the individual revelations described in the Bible are presented as genuine occurrences[7] and not merely as belonging to the kind of mythology in which something otherworldly is of necessity conveyed in the visual media of this world, after the fashion of an historical happening.

Over and above this, however, revelation itself in the biblical sense implies history: it is event *as* history, indeed as salvation history, which claims to be in every case the divinely intended meaning of all history. Biblical history is at the same time revelation history, and vice versa. In it God progressively makes known to mankind himself and his divine plan. The formula "God's plan" as summarizing the essence of revelation is found first in Amos (3,7) and repeatedly thereafter.[8] "The contemplation of the plan of Yahweh, in varying inflections but with increasingly sharper definition, is the underlying motive power of both the great outlines of the history (of the Old Testament) and its smaller unities." "In the motif of 'plan' the sovereignty, reality, and universality of the revelatory action becomes more and more expressive."[9] Despite all opposition—both on the part of his own chosen people and of the world—God carries through his plan concerning mankind.

The climax of revelation is Christ Jesus, the goal and

fulfilment of all previous revelations. Especially in his cross and his resurrection, he becomes the centre of world history, as is evident not only in the New Testament but also in the Christian mentality which, since the sixth century, has led us to count the years of history as either *before* or *after Christ*. In Christ God has "made known to us the mystery of his will, according to his good pleasure, as he purposed in him for the *oikonomia* of the fullness of the times: to sum up in Christ all things in heaven and on earth. In him we also have been called to inherit, we who have been predestined according to the counsel of his will" (Eph. 1,9ff.). In the New Testament view everything that has taken place in the past, from the creation on, is already salvation history; but this meaning of the whole of history is unveiled only in Christ (Rom 16,25ff.). In him God himself has entered immediately as the one who acts in human history. Therefore all Christian theology is necessarily at the same time biblical history.[10] Nevertheless, the revealed "truths" of theology in the more restricted sense are implied in statements of the divine work of salvation in history.

The transmission of revelation to men of later generations likewise occurs in an historical way: in the Old Testament in the *people Israel:* in the evidence it gives of being a chosen people, in its religious doctrine, its cult, etc.; in the time after Christ in the *Church,* which carries revelation on in the form of teaching, but which at the same time in its whole diversified life, in its entire historical manifestation—in the indefectibility of its existence, its holiness, its fruitfulness in all good things, etc.—shows forth the salvific will of God in the present time.

This essential of historicity distinguishes the revelation described in the Bible both from natural revelation and from the revelation of the *end-time*, in which history in the proper sense will have attained its goal, since then the individual and the race of man will have entered into their consummation.

This characteristic of historicity also strictly distinguishes the biblical concept of revelation from the forms of revelation in the *Gentile* religions. In these, revelation is either considered as an isolated occurrence unrelated to anything else or finds its place in the thinking bound up with the cyclic, constantly recurring events of nature, as in the Oriental and Hellenistic mystery cults.

In an equally fundamental way the historical character of the biblical concept of revelation distinguishes it from the conceptions of the modern liberal theology of Schleiermacher, according to whom there is in the last analysis no revelation of God that has taken place in history, but only a religious *principle* that has emerged with especial clarity, or in some sense uniquely, in the religion of the Old or New Testament.[11] Here revelation is understood no longer as an objective set of circumstances but as something occurring in the individual consciousness, or—as in the case of

Rudolf Bultmann—in the final analysis only man's *self-understanding,* for which something that "took place at a distinct time and place" fundamentally has no relevance.

Personal Revelation

Natural revelation is within the sphere of the factual: it is identical with creation, which in itself witnesses to the grandeur, the wisdom and goodness of its Creator. By contemplation and reflection on the things and experiences of his world man works back to the first cause of all things hidden behind all world events. By inference (even though not necessarily of a reflexive kind) man can thereby arrive in some fashion also at the knowledge that God is a person, even though the precise nature of this personality, namely the fact of three persons in God, still necessarily remains unknown to him.

The revelation described in the Bible, on the contrary, is personally defined through and through. After the fashion of an encounter between men, God *encounters* man in this revelation, even though still in a veiled manner. Revelations as they were understood by the Gentiles, on the other hand, were either simply applied to an individual god or were recognized as the message of an individual god only through special circumstances (e.g., the geographical). What the Gentile was concerned about, generally speaking, was not which god had revealed himself; what was important to him basically were the attitudes he should adopt in illness, in his undertakings in war and peace, etc. For revelation as the Bible understands it, the uniquely personal origin is always characteristic. Never, for example, in the revelatory experiences of the prophets was there room for the slightest doubt that it was Yahweh who had made himself known to them.[12] He *comes;* he makes known his nearness, his presence in visible, unmistakable signs; he *appears.* He utters his *name*—in which, according to ancient Oriental conceptions, the essence of the person is contained.[13] God *speaks* to men he has chosen; and not in omens which must be interpreted,[14] but in plain human speech comprehensible to all. In clear words he has made known his will to his people.[15] God thereby permits himself to become the partner of man: He enters into a *covenant* with him: with individual men, with a people, with all mankind. He permits himself to enter into speech with men, to Moses he speaks "face to face, just as a man speaks with his friend" (Ex 33, 11); likewise the revelation experiences of the prophets, especially those of Jeremiah, are to a great extent carried out in the form of dialogue.

This personal character of revelation attains its climax in the incarnation: *Christ Jesus* is in his person the completion of all divine revelation. "What is revealed in Christ consists above all in what he himself is. . . . That Jesus, the God-man, is precisely what he is—this God reveals. . . . The living God is himself hidden; only in Christ does he stand revealed. Christ is God's epiphany. Who 'sees him, sees God' (Jn 1,14.18; 14,9; 1 Jn 1,1–3)."[16] It is one of the essential traits of the revelation of salvation, precisely as it is God's manifestation of himself, that—not unlike the personal activity of man—it is not calculable, deducible, as are the metaphysical conceptions of God at which we arrive through strict deduction from the data and meaning we find in the world about us.

Revelation is also most profoundly personal because in it God speaks to man in his inmost being. Revelation is never a mere communication of truth, it is always *address.* It never consists merely in an enrichment of man's understanding, it concerns his inner self and therefore his salvation. Even the most sublime mysteries of the inner life of God, therefore, are not set forth as abstract doctrine. For example, in the whole of Scripture there is not to be found a single doctrinal formulation of the mystery of the most Holy Trinity. Everything said on this question is contained in pronouncements that concern our salvation, as in the farewell discourses where Jesus speaks of the sending of "another Paraclete" (Jn 14–16), in the baptismal commission (Mt 28,19), or in blessing formulas (2 Cor 13,13; 1 Pt 1,2). God revealing himself demands of man not understanding but *faith,* that is, the wholehearted yes of the entire man, personal commitment to him as eternal truth: "the complete obedience of understanding and will" (Vatican, s. III, cap. 3: Denz. 1789).

We have now come to the heart of the object of revelation. It is unfortunate, to say the least, that the theological manuals so often formulate revelation as God's communication to man of "something" (*aliquid*), "concepts," "judgments," "doctrines," etc. For the content of revelation pertains to man's innermost being and thereby profoundly distinguishes biblical revelation from revelation as it was understood in the rest of the ancient world.

The Object of Revelation

God reveals "himself and the eternal decrees of his will" (Vatican, s. III, cap. 2: Denz, 1785). Everything else in revelation is subsumed in this. Thus God reveals himself as the one *who is* when he communicates his name, *Yahweh*. Indeed this name was not originally intended to be understood in a metaphysical sense but rather in the sense of one who is present, who is near his people at all times. Nevertheless, the name provided the possibility of a deepened understanding of the divine being and an invitation to it. God therefore reveals himself in the history of his people time and time again as the living one, the powerful one, the Lord of the whole earth and Lord of history, as the faithful one who keeps the covenant he has made, as the holy one who himself enters into judgment with his own people, but also as the one who is always merciful. That he may be "known as Yahweh" is the aim of all his acts of revelation, as is said so often in the Old Testament. And the knowledge of Yahweh is foretold by the prophets as the great good of the end-time (Is 11,9; 52,6; Jer 31,34).

Most intimately bound up with this self-revelation of God is the revelation of his *will* to men: Precisely in the commandments of their God does his nature become evident to the Israelites: He is the *one* God, a *jealous* God who will tolerate no foreign gods beside himself; a God exalted to the utmost above all that is visible, so that no one can make any kind of an image of him; a *holy* God who demands of his people: "Be holy, as I am holy!" (Lv 19,1, etc.). This will at the same time signifies *salvation for* men: From the Protoevangelion to the fulfilment in Christ, the history of revelation is a salvation history. But it is also, for men who are ill-disposed and for an ever faithless people, a history of the divine *anger*.

The divine self-revelation is completed—within the limits of this age—in the incarnate image of the eternal Father: *Christ Jesus*. Through the power of his word and deed the kingdom of God comes into being, and men ask themselves: "Who, then, is this?" (Mk 4,41). By his moral irreproachability and superiority he enlightens us with the holiness of God. The divine salvific will, moreover, has found its figuration in him: In him "has appeared the goodness and kindness of God our savior" (Tit 3,4). In his person, finally, in his relation to the Father in heaven, and above all through his express word, we are permitted to gaze into the mysterious *trinitarian inner-life of God,* in which we have a share through grace as heirs of God and co-heirs with Christ. Thus the most exalted thing is said that can be said by any revelation. And here we find a characteristic that is proper to revelation from its beginnings till its fulfilment in Christ, and afterwards in glory: it is a grace.

Revelation as Grace

Natural revelation has been given along with the nature of man and with the world in which God created him. God was free to create a world and to create it as in fact he did create it. But there would have been an inner contradiction had he created the world and man in it without at the same time giving a *natural revelation.* Natural revelation as such, therefore, is not a gift of grace bestowed on man over and above his human nature.

The revelation of salvation history, on the other hand, is a free, entirely undeserved, divine gift. This is already evident from the fact that it is bestowed at distinct moments in historical time and not simply once for all and to all mankind. In the Old Testament the character of revelation as a grace is clearly expressed in the *idea of election,* from which the entire religious consciousness of the Old Testament has been drawn and is developed. Abraham is called from his homeland into a special intimacy with God; later the same thing takes place with his descendants, now grown into a people, through the mediation of Moses, whom God summons to be the redeemer of *his* people. Subsequently within this people more and more individuals are chosen as instruments of divine revelation. In the nature of these calls[17] and in the way in which revelation is received it becomes ever clearer how this salvific revelation is a grace: The initiative rests wholly and at all times with God—a complete reversal of the notion of revelation widely prevalent in the Gentile world, where men sought to penetrate the mysteries of the gods and of destiny by many diverse means, often quite *technical* means, as through the liver-divination in use among many ancient peoples, through cup-divination, etc.

In the fullness of time revelation as grace achieves its culmination in the mystery of the *incarnation:* "God so loved the world that he gave his only begotten Son for it" (Jn 3,16). In him, in his person, "has appeared the grace of God, our Savior" (Tit 2,11). "No one has ever seen God; the Only-begotten, who is in the bosom of the Father, has made him known to us" (Jn 1,18), but only to him to whom he himself intends to reveal him (cf. Mt 11,27). Above all Paul, who himself had experienced the complete gratuity of grace but also its overwhelming power, continually testifies to the grace that is in revelation, in the call to Christ, in justification: "It pleased him who from my mother's womb set me apart and called me by his grace, to reveal his Son in me" (Gal 1,15f.).

Notes

1. Once and for all let it be noted here that in the use of such texts as these we are not concerned with the historicity of the details of the narratives, but only with the conception which Scripture itself has of the various occurrences of revelation.
2. Rom 16,25ff.; Col 2,2; Eph 1,9ff.; 3,4–11. Cf. Also G. Bornkamm, "*mystērion*," *ThWNT* IV, 823ff.
3. Cf. p. 124.
4. K. Barth, *Church Dogmatics* I, 1.
5. See also Acts 14,16f.; 17,24ff.
6. E. Brunner rightly brought this out in his controversy with Karl Barth over natural revelation: *Natur und Gnade* (1934), p. 20.
7. That some texts, despite their form, need not be understood (and were not intended to be understood) as historical accounts in the strict sense of the word (such as Job, Tobit), we do not deny.
8. Cf. Ps 33,11; Is 5,19; 28,29; 46,10; Jer 23,20.
9. G. Gloege, *Offenbarung und Überlieferung*, p. 24f.
10. To this extent the formulation of Oscar Cullmann is acceptable, "that all Christian theology in its innermost essence is Biblical history" (*Christ and Time*, p. 23).
11. In his fifth discourse on religion Schleiermacher raised the idea of "principle" and thereby the problem which has epitomized the liberal Christology for generations: What redeems,

the person of Jesus or a principle (such as the idea of divine sonship)? Cf. M. Huber, *Jesus Christus als Erlöser in der liberalen Theologie* (1956).

12. At the conclusion of his investigation of "the criterion of the word of God," Ivar P. Seierstad rightly says in *Die Offenbarungserlebnisse der Propheten Amos, Jesaja, und Jeremia* (1946), pp. 236f.: "The prophetic experience of revelation was never a mere emergence of thought, a seizing of truths, a recognition of hidden truths, but always simultaneously a discovery of God. Its constitutive was the living perception of an immediate contact with God. That their Lord was the acting and speaking subject, belonged to their experience of the word itself; they did not need to infer this only after they had tested the content of their revelation in the forum of a religious-moral judgment. . . . The divine provenance was not concluded to, but immediately experienced." This fact alone explains the invincible dynamism of their preaching; from it alone may we understand their rock-firm confidence that they have God's word.
13. The religion of the OT always considered this revelation a signal grace: Israel, and only Israel, knows the *name* of Yahweh.
14. In Israel's more ancient history there are some traces of such a manifestation of the divine will (Gn 24,14; 1 Sm 14,9f.; 2 Sm 5,24). A greater role, it is true, was played by the casting of lots, but even quite early its use began to decline; in the postexilic period the *ephod* with the *urim* and *thummim* are only a symbolic garment of the highpriest (Ezr 2,63). The prophets waged a war unique in world history against all heathen divination in Israel, and in the end it was victorious.
15. What this knowledge of the will of God signified for the men of the OT becomes especially evident when it is compared with the distressful ignorance of the purposes, moods, and demands of God or the gods in the Gentile world. A striking example

of this can be seen in a Babylonian penitential psalm translated in *ANET*, pp. 391f. ("prayer to every god"). *Tr.*

16. Guardini, *Die Offenbarung*, pp. 78f.
17. Cf. the accounts in Ex 3; Am 7,14f.; Is 6; and in the NT: Mk 3, 13ff.; Mt 9,9; Acts 9,15.

6

THE FORMS OF SUPERNATURAL REVELATION

We have already dealt with the essentials concerning the nature and the manner of supernatural revelation. Now we must consider these more in detail, in view of what we have seen of that oversimplification which commonly defines the salvific revelation of the present life as attesting divine speech and identifies revelation in act with natural revelation and revelation in vision with the revelation of the world to come. It is true, of course, that natural revelation takes place with a divine act: the work of creation, and this is revelation to the extent that God thereby makes himself known to man and makes known also that he intends this disclosure. But man must interpret this revelation himself, for it contains no interpretative word of God: it is revelation in act only. The revelation of beatitude essentially consists in this, that we see God "as he is": in this sense it is revelation of vision.

That God speaks to us *in express words,* in our conceptual speech, is doubtless the specific mark of earthly salvific revelation. But it does not therefore follow that this revelation consists exclusively in words. In conformity with man's sensible and intellectual nature and his existence in history, this revelation does not take place in a purely intellectual dimension, solely in a communication of truth by words—a revelation in which, as Scheeben says, the physically spoken word would be merely the "vehicle"; it is likewise quite essentially contained in historical events within our world of experience and in many visible figures. It is *also,* therefore, *revelation in act:* but it is a different act from that which occurs in God's natural revelation. It is *also revelation in vision:* but it remains a vision of God containing much obscurity, not yet the full disclosure it will some time be.

Supernatural revelation taken as a whole is an extraordinarily complex and many-sided event. When, in the following pages, we distinguish in the event revelation in act, vision, and word, we are not implying that these are three distinct forms in which the event of revelation can be isolated in a given case. As a matter of fact, always at least two of these forms, and often all three, must be intimately connected to make up the totality of any given revelation.

REVELATION IN ACT

Every revelation is at the same time a divine act. In the various revelations of salvation history this becomes quite evident when they are explicitly characterized as *events* having an always evident divine origin. The revelation narratives of Sacred Scripture frequently indicate this by beginning with the words "And it came to pass . . .," or "The word of Yahweh came . . .," or some similar formula. It is never simply a matter of acquiring knowledge, but always and primarily of an encounter with God revealing himself.[1]

Here, however, we are taking revelation in act in a restricted sense, to distinguish it on the one hand from the visible *appearance of God*, and on the other hand from his *speech* (in which, it is true, in the wider sense, an act of God is also involved). According to the witness of Scripture, the acts of God in salvation history are not only the "concomitant" criteria of revelation, as they are regarded almost exclusively in traditional fundamental theology, but also and essentially a form of revelation itself.

Basic to this understanding of the divine activity in history, and therefore for the knowledge of Yahweh among his people, are his *great deeds* in the liberation of Israel from Egypt: "I will take you as my own people, and you shall have me as your God. You will know that I, Yahweh, am your God when I free you from the labor of the Egyptians" (Ex 6,7; cf. Dt 4,32ff.; 29,1ff., etc.). Already in the very ancient Song of the Reed Sea, Israel's rescue from the Egyptians is celebrated as the revelation of Yahweh's goodness and fidelity (Ex 15,1–21).[2] For all coming generations Israel's historical consciousness has received the impress of these experiences: The redemption from the "house of slavery" has become the pattern of Yahweh's loving kindness and powerful aid. "The historical occurrences were written up not merely as the chronicle of factual events but as revelation, and they thus form the religious consciousness of subsequent ages."[3] They are referred to in prayer, again and again.[4] In later times it is especially the liberation of Jerusalem from Sennacherib that is celebrated as the revelation of Yahweh's fidelity and power: Ps 46; 48; 76. This view of the events is especially featured by the Deuteronomic history. God is hardly ever described in the Old Testament according to his attributes, but almost exclusively in what he *does* and what he *commands*.

Not Yahweh's help only, but also his judgment on Israel stands as revelation: "The Lord of hosts shall be exalted by his judgment, and God the Holy shall be shown holy by his justice" (Is 5,16). Ezekiel especially teaches the afflicted people to recognize this meaning in all the fearful events of their time. More than fifty times he makes use of the formula: "Thus you shall know that I am Yahweh!"

Even though it is one of the major contributions of the prophets that they have singled out this divine activity in the history of their people and have interpreted it, it is not true that these acts acquire the character of revelation only through the interpretation given them by the prophets.

Rather, the Old Testament understands the divine acts themselves to be the means whereby Yahweh revealed himself to his people and thereby also to the Gentiles. It is the people's fault when they do not understand this: "What Yahweh does they regard not; the work of his hands they see not. Therefore my people go into exile, because they do not understand!" (Is 5,12f.)[5] However, the prophets, Isaiah especially, do prophesy, beyond the revelatory acts of God in the past and present, concerning the coming revelation of his power and his grace in the messianic age.

Also *Christ the Lord* reveals himself before men in his acts: in the very way in which he encounters men—sinners, the sick, the simple people; in the manner of his speech: He speaks as "one having power" (Mk 1,22,etc.). Especially in his miracles "he reveals his glory" (Jn 2,11), so that men ask one another: "Who, then, is this?" (Mk 4,41). His miracles signal the beginning of the messianic age (Mt 11,1ff., cf. Is 35,5f.). In them, and especially in the exorcisms of demons, the inauguration of the kingdom of God is revealed (Mt 12, 28). All his miracles, with the single exception of the withering of the figtree, are the works of a merciful love: In Jesus' acts, and not primarily and certainly not exclusively in his words, the divine mercy is made known to us. Such of his parables as those of the lost son and the lost sheep form a running commentary on his own actions: the answer to the question of the scandalized Pharisees, why he consorted with sinners and tax-gatherers. From Jesus' words to the messengers of the Baptist it becomes clear that he considered his works themselves a sufficient revelation of his messiahship. He does not answer the Baptist's question about his mission with an explicit yes, but refers to his miracles. By clothing his reference in the words of Isaiah (Is 35,5f.), however, he also gives the Baptist an aid to the right interpretation of the miracles.

Still more, when we have the eyes of faith, do God and his merciful love stand revealed to us in the works of salvation in the strict sense: in the incarnation, in the cross and resurrection of Jesus: "In this has the love of God been shown—become visible—in our case, that God has sent his only-begotten Son into the world that we may live through him" (1 Jn 4,9). "Thus has God shown his love for us, that Christ died for us when we were yet sinners" (Rom 5,8). True, this divine act takes place in a manner hidden in Christ's condition as a slave (Phil 2,7); but still in such a way that in his personal holiness, in his power and goodness, and in his superhuman majesty even in the midst of his profound humiliation, the divine shows through every concealment, so that the eyewitnesses can say: "We have seen his glory, the glory of an Only-begotten of the Father, full of grace and truth" (Jn 1,14).

The New Testament considers the resurrection of Jesus above all to be an act of divine revelation. It was "understood by the primitive Church not simply as a miracle to establish faith, on whose basis the words of Jesus would be proved God's words and therefore binding. . . . Rather is it spoken of entirely from a consciousness that this attesting work of God in history is as such and in itself the decisive and all-embracing *event* of revelation, because of which the words and works of Jesus in the history of his earthly life and also the words and works of God in the history of the old covenant acquire their essential understanding in Christian faith."[6]

Supernatural revelation is closed with Christ, the incarnate Son of God, and his witnesses, the apostles; only an unfolding, a deeper understanding, now remains possible. But in the Church, which mediates revelation to us in the name of Christ, the divine salvific will is continually being brought to our experience. Because of God working in her the Church is, as she herself says, echoing the words of Isaiah, *a sign raised among the nations* (Vatican, s. II, cap. 3: Denz. 1794). Neither is she such a sign in just a generic way, but in the most substantial sense of the word: In her indefectible continuity despite all human opposition, God's fidelity endures as a present reality, the fidelity of a God who never goes back on his promises; in her holiness and fruitfulness in all good can be seen his will to make us holy, and thus his own holiness; in her catholicity is seen the universality of the divine salvific will; in the unity of the Church's teaching in all times and among all peoples is seen the unwavering continuity of divine truth. Thus the divine revelation in act is not something exclusively pertaining to the past; it is present. No new content is thereby made known to us, but the divine salvific will revealed once and for all in Christ and realized in time is revealed in the Church as present. In her, as part of her, can be recognized, as the Jews once recognized in the acts of Jesus, that the kingdom of God has come to us in truth. This divine revelatory act will be evidenced in a new and impressive manner in the *end-time*. The prophets, the eschatological discourse of the synoptic Gospels, and especially the Apocalypse portray this fact dramatically and visually.

One can ask where in this supernatural revelation in act there is room for the personal element which—in distinction to natural revelations—must be one of the characteristics of supernatural revelation. It consists in this, that this divine act is similar to the human act by which man reveals himself as a person. It is, unlike the occurrences of nature's laws, unpredictable; it is always in some fashion unexpected, surprising, often shocking; it is, however, always deeply filled with meaning both as an individual event and, above all, in the context of the totality of saving history, so that in this act the divine purposes, in the personal categories of grace, wrath, etc., become intelligible, revealed. The personal character of the revelatory act becomes even more explicit, again in a way similar to the personal activity of man, through the word which accompanies or follows it.

Together with the word, the divine act in saving history builds *one* complex event of revelation. But even considered in itself, the miraculous divine act has its own value as a statement, as Augustine repeatedly emphasizes: "Let us enquire into the miracles themselves, what they have to tell us about Christ; for they have, rightly understood, their own speech. For since Christ is the Word of God, an act of the Word is also a word for us."[7]

REVELATION IN VISION

In the formal sense, the final goal of all revelation is, of course, the vision of God. But in the earthly revelation of salvation man has already been given a manifold, though still obscure, vision. In the divine acts of salvation history the man who experiences them already *sees* the *glory* of God, as it is so often called in the Old Testament and by John, speaking of the miracles of Jesus (Jn 2,11). Here, however, we must speak of visionary revelation in a restricted sense—namely, as it occurs when God shows himself to men not only in his acts but in some way in a visionary *figure*, when he *appears* to them.

Already in the Old Testament, beginning with primeval history (which we pass over here), we are told of numerous, quite varied *theophanies*. It is true that in the history of Abraham God's word stands in the foreground, but from many texts one must conclude that the sense of the narrative is that not only auricular experiences were involved in the revelations given him; these were, at the same time, visual encounters with God. Thus it is said in Gn 15,1: "The word of Yahweh came to Abram in a *vision*"; Gn 17,1: "Yahweh *appeared* to Abram"; at the end of this experience of revelation, "he departed from him" (v. 22). Difficult to interpret and much debated is the divine appearance at the terebinths of Mamre (Gn 18–19): God comes to Abraham in human form; two of the *three men* are later designated *angels*, but at the same time are identified with Yahweh (Gn 19,18ff.). The Church Fathers, as is well known, interpreted the text in a trinitarian sense; however, such an understanding lay entirely beyond the grasp of the Old Testament reader.

In many texts, all of which belong to the period of ancient Israel (the Pentateuch, the Book of Judges), we read of the appearances of the *angel of Yahweh*.[8] This *angel*, evidently differentiated from the angels of the later biblical books by his special qualities, is in a striking manner identified with Yahweh and yet at the same time distinguished from him. Thus it is the *angel of Yahweh* that appears to Moses in the burning bush; yet the text goes on to say that "When Yahweh saw him coming over, . . . God called out to him from the bush, 'Moses! Moses!' . . . Then Moses hid his face, for he was afraid to look at God" (Ex 3,1ff.). We cannot enter further into this much-studied problem here; in any case, a theophany is certainly involved.[9]

Throughout, God's transcendence is maintained: What is seen is not God in his proper being, though he shows his presence in a visible form and permits himself to be seen in it.[10] It is worthy of note that the speaker in these appearances is always Yahweh himself.

We are informed of an entirely different kind of theophany from the Mosaic age: God appears in his *kābôd:* "Yahweh, our God, has indeed let us see his glory and his greatness! We have heard his voice from the midst of the fire" (Dt 5,24). The abstract *glory,* like the *doxa* of the Septuagint, only imperfectly reproduces the sense of *kābôd. Kābôd* is not a mere abstraction but something concrete, a thing that can be seen with bodily eyes.[11] Ex 24,17 describes its *visibility:* "The *kābôd* of Yahweh showed itself to the eyes of the sons of Israel like a consuming fire on the mountaintop." Doubtless here too it is not God who is seen in his proper being—nor is this the meaning of the writer. The light and the fire together are the guise in which Yahweh veils himself: In fire he comes down upon the mountain (cf. Ex 19,18; cf. also Ps 104,2); but it is still Yahweh who *therein* permits himself to be seen. Ex 19,11ff. states: "On the third day Yahweh will come down on Mount Sinai before the eyes of all the people." And at that time the people see the *kābôd of Yahweh* (Ex 19, 16ff.)[12]

In the prophets, revelation in word stands emphatically in the foreground; the prophets can even be defined as *men of God's word.* Nevertheless, we are also told of numerous visions in which they experienced revelation. The ancient traditional name *seer,* together with the fact that experiences in which only the hearing of God's word is spoken of are nevertheless called *visions,* proves that originally the visionary element must have been predominant. With the literary prophets revelation in vision becomes more and more the mere framework for revelation in word. It is also significant in this respect that what is heard is always, or almost always, God himself; what is seen is mainly symbolic objects, animals, persons, etc.[13] In some very important revelations, however, it is Yahweh himself who manifests himself in visible, though still veiled form, as in the visions of Isaiah's and Ezekiel's calls to prophecy. Isaiah cries out in fear: "My eyes have seen the King, Yahweh of hosts!" (Is 6,5). Ezekiel describes in detail the glory of Yahweh which he was permitted to see at his prophetical call (Ez 1). In the consciousness of the prophets the theophany here is not, therefore, something merely secondary.

A new, more complete and universal appearance of the glory of Yahweh is prophesied for the end-time: "Prepare the way of Yahweh . . . Then shall the glory of Yahweh be revealed, and all mankind shall see it together" (Is 40,3ff.).

This promise found its fulfilment in Christ Jesus. In him has God's only Son descended into our world of touch and of sight (Jn 1,1ff.; 1 Jn 1,1). He is "the image of the invisible God" (Col 1,15) now become visible to us: The glory of God shines upon us from the countenance of Christ (cf. 2 Cor 4,3–6). Christ has been "given to us as the image of God . . . in which we recognize what God wills and does. . . . Paul also employs the concept of image of God to make known to the community what it possesses in Jesus."[14] The *doxa*-passages of the Old Testament are applied, suitably modified, to Jesus. He is the "Lord of glory" (*kyrios tēs doxēs,* 1 Cor 2,8). True, he comes to his encounter with man under a veil, "manifested in the flesh" (1 Tim 3,16), in the "form of a slave" (Phil 2,7); nevertheless, the manner of the vision is such that the eyes of faith see in him "the glory of the Only-begotten of the Father, full of grace and truth" (Jn 1,14). And he himself can therefore say: "Blessed the eyes which see what you see!" (Lk 10,23), and: "He who sees me sees the Father also" (Jn 14,9). Once, on the mountain of transfiguration, he allows three chosen disciples to "see his glory" with bodily eyes (Lk 9,32; cf. 2 Pt 1,16ff.).

By his resurrection Christ has entered in a mysterious manner even in his flesh "into his glory" (Lk 24,26). Only the chosen witnesses were able to see him at this time. In all the Easter narratives this "seeing" is emphasized, and usually also the tangible corporeality of the resurrected Christ. It is the proper calling of the apostles to bear witness of what they have *seen and heard.*[15] When Christ eventually returns, he will appear before the whole world in his glory (Mt 24,30). Thereby will the completion of all revelation take place.

How is such a revelation perceptible with bodily eyes possible at all for earthly man? Our first presupposition must be, naturally, that through his sensible experiences man is capable of perceiving reality (what Scholasticism expresses by the axiom *intelligibile in sensibili*). It is further presupposed that the various phenomena of our world of experience are already suited by their nature to be the symbols of transcendent realities and values. Thus the figure of a storm, a tempest, can remind man of the sovereign power of God; a ray of light can remind him of the sublimity and invisibility of the divine. Man himself, because of his lordship over created things, and by purity in his moral conduct, can serve as an image referring back to God as its original. The phenomenology of religion contributes countless and quite varied examples of the same kind. It is worthy of note that all the elements of truth in the pagan religions (even though they may often appear obscured and corrupted) stem from natural revelation; also, that the same symbols—e.g., light, fire, tempest, darkness, rain—have always signified essentially the same realities. There must be, therefore, between the symbol and the divine reality, a relation that is rooted in the order of things (and at the same time in the intellectual structure of man); it is not just an arbitrary construction. Metaphysically it is rooted in the general analogy of being, according to which everything that is represents a participation in God and therefore bears in itself some trace of him. The world itself is a "book" which speaks to us of God, and it is the only book which pagan humanity had to read.[16]

In the revelation of his salvation God can put this natural power of apprehension and experience on the part of man to use. Especially the Old Testament, but in another fashion the New Testament as well, shows that to a great extent God has done so. We can consider, for example, the manifestations of God in the storm (Ex 19,16; Ps 77,17ff.; Is 29,6; Hb 3,10f.). That it is *God* who so intends to reveal himself is made unequivocal for the witnesses by what is extraordinary in the occurrence, its miraculous character—as in the burning bush or in the transfiguration of Christ on the mountain or the appearances of the resurrected Christ. The more precise significance of the revelation is further clarified by its proper character as an appearance, its fundamental symbolic character which pertains to it in the order of being and corresponds to man's natural conceptions. It often becomes even plainer through its historical context. We also have to reckon with the possibility of a mystical-intellectual vision. The final, univocal sense, as far as the revelations in vision of saving history are concerned, is always given through the express word. It is clear that the possibilities of revelation in vision within man's earthly life remain in the realm of analogy. This is also true in a similar way of revelation in word; here, however, thanks to the possibility of negation, things can be expressed which could not be made known immediately in a sensible vision.

REVELATION IN WORD IN RELATION TO ACT AND VISION

The divine act and God's self-manifestation in the order of vision are of such significance within the supernatural revelation of Sacred Scripture that they cannot be simply passed over, and still less expressly excluded from any definition of revelation. It is, however, incontestable that in the revelation of salvation taken as a whole the explicit word has the place of preference.

The history of Abraham's call begins with the words: "And Yahweh spoke to Abram . . ." (Gn 12,1), thus with a formula that we shall encounter again and again in the Old Testament. Also, however powerful may have been the impact in the consciousness of Old Testament man of Yahweh's momentous appearances and his mighty ways, above all those of the Mosaic age, still they all refer to a revelation in word. In the theophany of the burning bush, as in that of Sinai, God appears not so much to be seen as to speak. What is seen is passed over quickly; what remains and is to be repeated is the divine word. God makes known his name; he reveals his will to his people—above all in the "ten words" (Ex 34,28). In the course of the history of prophecy, revelation in vision recedes even more. Revelation in word becomes increasingly the "purest expression of revelation."[17] "The word of Yahweh came upon. . . ." This formula stands as the foreword to all the prophetical books or to their various divisions (Hos 1,1; Mi 1,1; Is 2,1, etc.). The entire collection of the sacred writings is finally known simply as "the word of God." The religion of the Old Testament, and even more of Judaism, is a religion of the word of God, heard and to be heard, and of the act of man grounded in it: An eloquent witness of this is the *Shema,* the daily remembrance of the pious Jew: "Hear, O Israel! Yahweh is our God, Yahweh alone . . ." (Dt 6,4ff.).

Christ, also, is sent "to bear witness to the truth" (Jn 18,37), "to reveal the name of the Father to men" (cf. Jn 17,6; Mt 11,27). "No one has ever seen God; the Only-begotten, who is in the bosom of the Father, has made him known to us" (Jn 1,18). The Synoptic Gospels recount to us concretely this preaching of the word by Jesus. As *teacher* he appears before men, gathering about him a circle of *disciples.* It is true, he never allows himself to be placed on the same level with other rabbis: he speaks "with power." Above all, the content of his message is in the last analysis the revelation which he himself is. And his word is not simply the word of teaching; it is at the same time a real act: a creative word in his miracles, a pardoning word in respect to sinners; it is a summoning word; it is a seed which bears in itself its own power to bring forth fruit a hundredfold; his words are "spirit and life" (Jn 6,63).

In Christ, God and his saving will are visible to us, but the major emphases of this revelation to be contemplated are, as in the theophanies of the Old Testament, conditioned by the divine word: the transfiguration on the mountain by the word of the Father: "This is my beloved Son; hear him!" (Mk 9,7); the resurrection appearances (however decisively important vision is here) by the word of peace, by the instruction of the disciples, and above all by the meaning of Christ's suffering and the kingdom of God, and by their mission. In this mission they continue the work of the Master. The service of the word is their commission (Lk 1,2; Acts 6,4). By their word the event of salvation is prolonged. "Not as the word of man" is it received by their hearers, "but as what, in truth, it is, the word of God" (1 Thes 2,13). Thus in the word of the apostles and of the Church the revelation of Christ and his salvation comes to men. Faith, which justifies man, comes from hearing—namely, the apostolic preaching (Rom 10,17). Not infrequently the revelation of salvation, as it is mediated by the Church, is now simply expressed in the formula: *'o logos*—the word, the word of God, the word of the Lord (1 Thes 1,6; 1 Cor 14,36; 2 Tim 4,2).

Thus a quick inventory and comparison of the biblical concepts already shows an obvious pre-eminence of the divine word in the totality of saving revelation. We could content ourselves with the conclusion that so it was decreed by God. However, we should enquire into the deeper reasons for this precedence and see them in the following.

The Word is Express Self-Revelation

The word is the most *personal* form of self-revelation. Here the person does not reveal himself merely in his conduct and activity or in his bodily appearance. That kind of revelation must always first be interpreted and permits only indirect inference with regard to his dispositions (even though this process is usually spontaneous, intuitive, not a matter of conscious reflection). In the word, the person makes known his inner being *expressly:* his thoughts, his will, his feelings, his inner self. This is what takes place in God's self-manifestation to us men. Only the explicit divine word makes known to us in full clarity the divine plan of salvation. It is true that visible realities and occurrences within our world, those at least which obviously transcend the bounds of mere this-worldly causality, can manifest divine truths to us through the analogy which God intends to reveal to us in them. But the further removed these analogies are from the divine reality they express, the more necessary is the presence of the interpreting divine word. As for mysteries in the proper sense, both of the inner divine life and of the event of salvation, they can be revealed to us in general only by the divine word. That in God who in his nature is absolutely one there is nevertheless a fullness of three-personal life; that the man Jesus is "the Son"; that his death is an act of obedience to the Father and redemption for us sinners; that we have been called in grace to be children of God and co-heirs with Christ; that in the visible, entirely human community of the Church Christ extends the mystery of his incarnation to redeemed mankind as his mystical "body"; that sinful man dies with Christ in baptism and rises with him to new life; that Christ under the species of bread and wine, present as God and man, renews his redemptive sacrifice among us, etc.—all of this only the explicit word of God tells us. It is only this word, moreover, that reveals to us in some fashion the mysteries of the future.

Man, however, is not a pure spirit but a psychosomatic being, spirit limited by incorporation in a world of place and time. Thus, on the one hand, he can come to an intellectual understanding of his temporal world, but on the other he is under the necessity of reducing the spiritual things he wants to understand or share to corporeal representations and processes. It means much more to man when not only does he hear the voice of another or receive his written or printed word, but this other comes to him in person, so that his word takes on solid reality in his countenance, in his whole conduct and activity.

Revelation in act, vision, and word, therefore, do not

merely stand side by side in salvation history, external to one another; on the contrary, their association is grounded in man's nature as a body-soul unity and in his mode of understanding, to which God accommodates himself in revelation. Here, just as in human communication, the visible appearance, the works, and the word of God make up a complex unity, both in the individual revelation and in revelation history as a whole. They mutually interpret one another. This confluence of corporeal figure, divine reality, and divine word can be called the "sacramental principle" of revelation, and it is also at work in the mediation of revelation and salvation through the Church.[18] Doubtless it is the explicit word that gives a revelation its final univocal determination, comparable perhaps, in Scholastic terminology, to the *causa formalis* in its relation to the *causa materialis*.[19] The "material" event of revelation, taken by itself, often remains in an apparent ambiguity. But the divine act and appearance show us the full import of the divine word. Thus the sense and the consequence of Jesus' words, the greatness of his love, etc., have become plain to us in his concrete appearance among us. Moreover, this alone has given us the final clarification of the discordant prophecies of the Old Testament, which must often be understood only in a transferred sense. And above all: Only the divine act of the resurrection has cast the definitive light on Jesus' whole teaching, action, and suffering in his earthly life. Rightly does present-day exegesis say that the Gospels have all been written in the light of Easter—that is, in the perspective of the events which has come to the witnesses only through their Easter experience.

The Word is Communicable to Later Generations

Of decisive importance is this also: What could be made known in revelation by word can be communicated to later generations substantially in the same form, even though the encounter with God given in the reception of the word remains a unique grace of the first recipient. Revelations in act and vision, on the other hand, are as such accessible only to the one who immediately experiences them. Therein lies what is unique about the great events in the history of revelation, above all those of the Mosaic age and of the fullness of time in Christ. "Blessed are the eyes which see what you see!" (Lk 10,23). It is proper to the genuine historical character of revelation that fundamentally it is not accessible to every man in the same way. For all those who cannot be the immediate witnesses, that which was revealed in act and vision must first be translated *into the form of words*, to the extent that the essential content of revelation was not already expressed in the divine act or appearance accompanying the word of revelation. In word, therefore, revelation is promulgated. In this form it is, as the Church says, "contained" in Sacred Scripture and tradition. It is the Church which is the "custodian and teacher of the word of revelation."[20] In the course of many centuries, obviously, considerable changes can occur in human modes of expression and concepts; this is especially true when people of other cultural backgrounds make their contribution to a stream of tradition. From essential errors, however, the Church is protected by the presence of the Holy Spirit. Through this presence the Church is "the pillar and mainstay of the truth" (1 Tim 3, 15).

In the New Testament this (formal) distinction between the original event of revelation and the revelation continued in the word already becomes evident. Thus the activity of the apostles is often designated as *service of the word,* or something similar. It is their function to announce the word of God. But hardly ever is the activity of Jesus described with this or any similar formula, although Jesus also appeared as a teacher and announced the word. This fact makes it plain that there is in the New Testament a consciousness that the mission and coming of Jesus cannot properly be expressed in the same terms applied to the mission of the apostles: as *word* or *service of the word.* Jesus is not merely a preacher of the word. To the word he also contributes his activity. It is not merely heard but also seen.[21] When Paul says that *faith comes from hearing* (Rom 10,14 ff.), this applies universally to those who come to faith in Christ through the word of the apostles and the word of those who come after them (cf. Jn 17,20). It does not apply in the same sense to the first witnesses of revelation: These believe not merely what they hear but also what they see and experience. This change in the conditions for faith becomes fully apparent in the words of the risen Christ to Thomas: "Since you have seen me, you believe; blessed are they who do not see [or, who only hear: namely, the revelation as attested in the word] and yet believe!" (Jn 20,29). Similarly, Luke speaks in the prologue of his Gospel of those who from the beginning were *eyewitnesses* (*autoptai*) of all that has been revealed in Christ, and then of the *ministers of the word* (*hypēretai tou logou*). By the testimony received from them by Luke, Theophilus, to whom the Gospel is dedicated, will be convinced of the trustworthiness of the word in which he has been instructed. The—formal—transformation of revelation on its way to men is thereby implicitly indicated: What took place in Christ (including, of course, as of great moment, also his word),[22] is communicated by the word of the eyewitnesses and the Church. When Paul says in Tit 1,3: God "has in due times revealed his word through the preaching committed to my trust," it is clear that the revelation given in preaching is only revelation in a secondary sense; it refers back to the original event of revelation and proclaims it.

Indeed it is not necessarily, and in general not primarily, in the form of *teaching* (in the strict sense of this word) that revelation is communicated. Therefore we should not say, even when we have in mind the revelation mediated through the Church, that supernatural revelation consists in this: that God has made known to us "certain teachings" (*quasdam doctrinas*), or the like. It is rather, primarily, the immediate *witness* of those things that were seen and heard, as it is set forth, for example, in the sermons of Acts, the *narrative* of the event of revelation; which, most especially, is given to us in the Gospels. Afterwards, witness and narrative are further developed into teaching in the proper sense—a process already at work in the New Testament, particularly in the Pastoral Epistles[23]—and this in turn results in the structure of binding *dogmas* of the Church and is scientifically formulated in *theology*.[24] This progressively conceptual interpretation is essential to the deeper understanding of divine revelation. In it is manifested the dynamism of the (divinely elevated) human understanding, and above all the working of the Holy Spirit which, in fulfilment of Christ's promise, continues to lead the Church deeper into his truth (Jn 16,13). In the course of the history of the Church this intellectual grasp of the truths of divine revelation has proved to be a necessity, particularly in the face of heretical misinterpretations.

On the other hand, development should not lead one-sidedly to ever more abstract formulations of revelation. For, according to the divine will, what the Church teaches has been given to us also in full clarity and as a concrete experience in the very life of charity within the Church and in its sacramental and cultic expression (cf. the following chapter). Through the creative energies of the human spirit, which are at the same time part of the dynamic life of the Church, the revelation communicated by the Church's word obtains even more eloquent expression in artistic representations of the events of revelation and salvation. The possibility of this is grounded in the incarnational character of the whole of saving revelation, above all in the incarnation of the eternal Word himself: the eternal, essential image of the Father has become visible to us in the man Christ Jesus. More than in western Christianity "the honoring of icons, the icons of Christ and the Saints, in the Eastern Church. . . [has] remained something living from the biblical concept of image. The reason that the struggle with iconoclasm had such profound repercussions in the Eastern Church's piety and science of faith was that it was a conflict involving revelation itself, its continuous working in the present. From the icons of Christ and his Saints still shines on the Christians of the East the radiance of God's revelation in the face of Christ and his Saints."[25]

But all these forms in which revelation comes to us or is brought near to us: tradition and Sacred Scripture which "contain" it, the Church which proclaims it to us in its word, communicates the revealed salvation to us in the sacraments as real signs, brings it to visual representation in its art—all these, always and necessarily, refer back to the original event of revelation and salvation of which they are the witness, narration, teaching, participation, representation.

Notes

1. Cf. especially here Abraham J. Heschel, *The Prophets*, 1962, pp. 435ff. *Tr.*
2. At least the "Song of Miriam" (Ex 15,21-15,1b) must be very ancient. Even by many critical exegetes it is ascribed to the Mosaic age.
3. Guardini, *Die Offenbarung*, p. 72.
4. Cf. Ps 78; 105; 135,8ff.; Jdt 9,6ff.; Neh 9,9ff.
5. Cf. also Is 22,11; 41,20, etc.
6. W. Hillmann, "Grundzüge der urkirchlichen Glaubensverkündigung," *Wissenschaft und Weisheit* 20 (1957), pp. 176f.
7. Augustine, *in Johannis Ev.*, Tract. 24, *PL* 35, 1593 (= Corp. Christ., ser. Lat. XXXVI, 244): "*Miracula quae fecit Dominus noster Jesus Christus sunt quidem divina opera, et ad intelligendum Deum de visibilibus admonent humanam mentem . . . Nec tamen sufficit haec intueri in miraculis Christi. Interrogemus ipsa miracula, quid nobis loquantur de Christo; habent enim, si intelligantur, linguam suam. Nam quia ipse Christus Verbum Dei est, etiam factum Verbi verbum nobis est.*" Cf. also *Serm. XCVIII (De Luc.* 7,11–15), *PL* 5, 591ff.; *De Civ. Dei* 22, 8, 22, *PL* 41, 770: The divine act has "*quamdam Dei eloquentiam.*"

8. Here we can include Gn 18–19, though an exception is formed in this account in the use of the threefold number.
9. Another interpretation, which however does not do justice to the text in its entirety, has been suggested by Fridolin Stier: There is no theophany, but the angel of Yahweh is merely a messenger of God, similar to other such angels. When he speaks as Yahweh himself, this is to be explained simply from the literary form of message in which the usual introductory formula ("Thus says . . . ," etc.) has been lost (*Gott und sein Engel im AT*, Münster 1934).
10. It is a further question whether in the original narratives sensible appearances of God had been naively described, and the angel of Yahweh was introduced only in a later redaction, in order to bring out the obscurity of the appearances. Thus, for example, G. von Rad, "*angelos*," *ThWNT* I,76. On the Catholic side Lagrange had already offered this literary critical solution to the problem in *Revue biblique* 12 (1903), 212–225.
11. B. Stein has suggested the translation "majesty," which like *kābôd* designates as an abstract honor and eminence, as a concrete the person of the king (*Der Begriff Kebod Jahweh und seine Bedeutung für die alttestamentliche Gotteserkenntnis*, 1939).
12. In a wider sense Yahweh's *glory* can already be seen in creation: Ps 8; 19; 29; cf. Ps 104,1f.
13. The manner of these visions—mostly it is a question of mental rather than of sensible perceptions—need not concern us here. In any case they are, in the sense of the narratives, visions divinely caused.
14. Thus G. Kittel with A. Schlatter, "*eikōn*," *ThWNT* II, 394. G. Söhngen also rightly says: "The NT *eikōn* is . . . univocally a concept of the history of revelation." It is not a question,

however (at least primarily), "of the metaphysical nature of the God-man, but of the activity of God revealing himself in salvation history. Only from the meaning of such a concept as *eikōn* in salvation history can theology begin to derive its metaphysical fullness. *Eikōn* is appearance or revelation of God and his power which works within history, and in its midst forms a history of God, namely, salvation history. . . . The *eikōn* consists in this, that it shows forth its power, that is, the power and glory of God revealed" ("Die biblische Lehre von der Gottebenbildlichkeit des Menschen," *Münchener Theologische Zeitschrift* 2 (1951), pp. 60f.; cf. *Die Einheit in der Theologie*, p. 186).

15. Cf. Jn 20,20; Acts 4,20; 1 Cor 9,1, etc. That in the *ōphthē* of 1 Cor 15,5ff. the vision of the resurrected Christ "in the sense of a perception with the eyes" is directly involved, is rightly emphasized by K. H. Rengstorf, *Die Auferstehung Jesu* (1952), pp. 83ff., against W. Michaelis, who takes it to mean not a visualization but rather as a general term for "being revealed" (*Die Erscheinungen des Auferstandenen* [1944], pp. 107f.; cf. *ThWNT* V, 360).
16. Cf. here Jean Daniélou, *Der Gott der Heiden, der Juden und der Christen* (1956), pp. 17ff.; in specie: Gerardus van der Leeuw, *Religion in Essence and Manifestation* (ET 1963); M. Eliade, *The Sacred and the Profane* (ET 1961).
17. O. Procksch, *ThWNT* IV, 93f.
18. The formulation is that of E. H. Schillebeeckx, cf. pp. 34, 36.
19. Cf. also the relation (which is not wholly easy to determine) between "matter" (the sensible material or the sensible action) and "form" (the determining word or sign) in the sacraments.
20. Thus in the so-called oath against Modernism: Denz. 2145.
21. Cf. G. Kittel, "*logos*," *ThWNT* IV, 121f.

22. Therefore the "eyewitnesses from the beginning" are also "ear-witnesses from the beginning" (Heb 2,3); therefore is it said: "Blessed are your eyes, that they see; and your ears, that they hear" (Mt 13,16).

23. Rom 16,17; Acts 2,42; 1 Tim 5,17; 2 Tim 4,3; Tit 1,9. Also Jesus' own proclamation is occasionally called "teaching": Mk 1,27; Mt 7,28; Lk 4,32; Jn 7,16

24. The doctrinal formulation of revelation can (but should not!) lead to an exclusively intellectual understanding of revelation. This took place especially in *Judaism*, which with the extinction of prophecy saw itself bereft of the presence of revelation. The codification of revelation, which above all could be seen in the Torah, brought it about that religion became book-religion. All that remained was rightly to understand and interpret it. No longer the prophet but now the scribe presided over religious life. Even concerning the revelation of the end-time the Jews expected in the first place simply "teaching," namely, the explanation of difficult particulars (cf. A. Oepke, "*apokalyptō*," *ThWNT* III, 580; W. Bousset—H. Gressmann, *Die Religion des Judentums* [[3] 1926], pp. 394f.). The understanding of revelation in the Qumrân literature is similarly intellectual. The highest authority of the community is the "teacher of justice," whom God "brings to knowledge of all secrets of the words of his servants, the prophets," that is, he reveals to him the right interpretation. The goal of this knowledge, however, as is true of Judaism in general, is seen in right conduct before God (cf. F. Nötscher, *Zur theologischen Terminologie der Qumrantexte* [1956], pp. 15–78, esp. pp. 50f., 68ff.).

Also in Catholic theology there has prevailed at times, especially in the age of rationalism, a one-sided intellectualistic understanding of revelation. The Church itself, however, has been protected from an essentially erroneous understanding of revelation by the presence of the Holy Spirit.

25. G. Söhngen, "Die biblische Lehre von der Gottebenbildlichkeit des Menschen," *Münchener Theologische Zeitschrift* 2 (1951), 61; cf. *Die Einheit in der Theologie*, pp. 186f.

7

THE ECCLESIOLOGICAL ASPECT AND ESCHATOLOGY

According to God's plan, divine revelation comes to most men only mediately. We say mediately not merely in the sense that God himself does not personally make himself known, but in the sense that he manifests himself in created obscurity: in his revelatory activity, in that he allows himself to be seen in the medium of a visible figure, in that he employs earthy-human words to utter his divine truth to us. Even more, in the sense that over and above this he makes use of the mediation of men and human communities and their institutions and functions. In the time of the old covenant these were the prophets and the Old Testament people of God with its institutions, above all its temple and worship.

THE CHURCH

In the fullness of time the mediator is the Man Christ Jesus (1 Tim 2,5). He is this pre-eminently: for this man is God himself, the connatural Son of the eternal Father become man. Furthermore, the revelation that has taken place in him is now further communicated in a human fashion: in the testimony of the witnesses called by him who at the same time represent the beginning of the new Israel, the *Church*. In the Church revelation is now made present to men.

It is true that in inspiration God has called into his service the written word of chosen men—above all the prophets and the first witnesses of the Christ-revelation—in such a way that their word in a proper, formal sense is *his* word, through which as a living and responsible instrument he has spoken to us. But even this written word is given to us only in the Church. The Church alone says to us and can say to us—by virtue of its living tradition and its divine authority—that there *is* a written word in the first place, what writings belong to it, and in what sense they are God's word. The Church alone is empowered to interpret the word of Scripture authoritatively and to bring it to men in living proclamation. On the other hand, the Church is also bound to the word of God in Scripture as the norm of its teaching.

For the fulfillment of this commission Christ has given to his Church the Spirit of truth who will remain with her forever. Through the Spirit the Church is "the pillar and groundstay of the truth" (1 Tim 3,15). Only because of this can she, and dare she, summon men to unconditional obedience to her message. This position has been strongly emphasized in the statements of the Church's magisterium, above all since the Reformation.

But the Church is more than a mere "custodian and teacher" of the revelation that has been brought to an end and committed to her as a *depositum*. The event of salvation of which revelation speaks in express word, and which became accessible to human sight and experience in the *mirabilia* of divine act and in the many theophanies of salvation history, gains greater fullness, even though in a new fashion, in the Church and her sacramental life.

The Old Testament revelation itself did not take place just anywhere, but in the sphere of the saving history of the *ekklēsia*, as Israel is repeatedly called in the Old Testament.[1] In the history of his people and through this history, God revealed himself: from the call of Abraham to the liberation of his descendants, who had now become a people; in the divine guidance given this people, including the punishments by which it was tested and purified; in the inner character of this people (despite its human failures): in its faith in Yahweh, in the distinctive nature of its worship, in its sanctification through the law, in its consciousness of election, in the incomparable phenomenon of prophetism embracing many centuries. In all of this, God and his salvific plan were revealed to the people then and are revealed to us now.

The same thing is true of the people of God of the new

covenant. The difference is that the fullness of time has come and the Church is the final figure of God's covenant in the earthly realm. Revelation has been closed with Christ and his witnesses. In him God has said and committed all to us: himself. But this completed revelation and the final salvific plan of God achieved in the sacrifice of Christ are still present in the Church. If Christ in the incarnation is the image of the eternal Father made visible for us, so, by analogy, is his Church; for in her as his mystical Body the mystery of his incarnation is extended to all of redeemed mankind in an imponderable way. The Church "does not possess a word about the thing instead of the thing itself. Consequently her hearing of the Word and her reflection upon the Word heard are not merely a logical activity." She lives "in living contact with the thing itself."[2] The Church possesses the revealed reality itself. She herself is the present and visible form of this reality, namely, of the salvation which God has revealed and effected.

Therefore the Church is also "through herself . . . an incontestable witness of her divine mission . . . a sign raised among the nations" (Vatican, s. III, cap. 3: Denz. 1794). Those marks of divine activity in the Church to which the first Vatican Council referred are not simply some kind of "concomitant" criteria (which could just as easily be lacking), but arise from the nature, the mission, and the divine endowment of the Church: her indefectible continuity, her wonderful holiness and fruitfulness in all good, the unity of her teaching and her life spanning the millennia and the continents. In all of this, just as in ancient Israel, God's salvation is brought to our experience in the present: his fidelity to his promises, his power overcoming all the forces of evil (even in the Church), the inerrancy of his truth, his holiness laying hold of man in his command and his grace, his salvific will for us sinners. The Church as an historically tangible reality is therefore—throughout all that is human in her—an "epiphany of her being" (H. Schell). The final key to a recognition of her nature, it is true, is given only by the explicit word of Christ and her own word. The mystery of the Church as the mystical body of Christ enters as an essential element into her proclamation.

Thus the Church stands in a manifold relationship to revelation: she is custodian and teacher of the revelation consigned to her as a *depositum*. She is, as divine mystery, herself the object of this revelation. She is at the same time the manner in which God's revelation and salvation are present to us. She is, to the extent that her inner nature is visible to us in the realm of historical experience, also the criterion of revelation.

This, however, must be kept in view: As far as content is concerned, nothing new is revealed to us in the Church. Revelation was brought to its term with Christ and his witnesses. But in the Church this closed revelation (and the revealed salvation itself) is brought to us in an ever new way, as an experienced, living reality.

The Obscurity of Revelation

The hiddenness of God is not completely removed even in supernatural revelation. God comes to his encounter with man not in his own divine being, but always in some kind of obscurity proper to creatures: in his activity in the realm of saving history, in figurative phenomena which indicate his presence visibly, in human words which make known to us the mysteries of the divine being and will.

That God himself remains hidden in the theophanies of salvation history is always more or less plainly stated in Sacred Scripture. Thus in the narratives of the appearances of the angel of Yahweh the transcendence of God is emphasized, even when he manifests himself visibly (see above pp. 97f.). The same is true of the *kābôd*-appearances of the Mosaic age, the revelations of the divine "glory." The phenomena that are seen, the light and the fire, are not God himself but indicate his presence. The problem of the visibility of God in his self-revelation is set forth especially in the Old Testament in the prayer of Moses that God should show himself (Ex 33,18ff.). Even Moses can see only the "back" of the Lord who passes by. However difficult a precise interpretation of the text may be, the sense is clear: Even for Moses, and therefore *a fortiori* for all other men, God remains invisible in his own being: "My face no man may see."[3] This hiddenness of God, the New Testament tells us, was not completely removed even in the Christ-revelation. Revelation and obscurity co-exist here in a mysterious tension. Thus Paul can say of the earthly Jesus: "He emptied himself, took on the condition of a slave, and appeared in the form of man" (Phil 2,7), while John can speak of the Word made man as a beneficent theophany: "We have seen his glory, glory as of the Only-begotten of the Father, full of grace and truth" (Jn 1,14). For the "saints" the mystery of God, that is, Christ, is now revealed through the Holy Spirit (Col 1,25ff.; Eph 3,2ff.); yet we still live in "the hope of glory"; the treasures of wisdom and knowledge are still hidden from us (and for us) in Christ (Eph 3,2ff.; Col 1,25ff.; 2,2f.); we now see only as in a mirror, a reflection (1 Cor 13,12).

The same is true of the Church. Through its quite human manifestation in history, through its operation, and especially through its word spoken by men, the revelation completed in Christ becomes present for us and is made part of our experience (cf. above pp. 119f.).

Even when the divine truth is given to us in the formal word of God, obscurity remains. Since the concepts of the language of revelation derive from our earthly world, they can never express the divine truth other than analogously. But an analogy, even though remote, between these concepts and the divine mystery to be uttered is a necessary presupposition for the fact that the mystery can be uttered in this fashion at all.[4]

From what has been said certain definite conclusions follow. First, the possibility of misunderstanding and of scandal. God's revelation is never so evident to us here below (perhaps with the exception of those who receive the revelation immediately) that no evasions remain possible. His works can be judged as works of the devil (Mt 12,24), the theophanies—even the appearances of the resurrected Christ—can be dismissed as delusions, his revealed word as the wisdom or error of men. From the obscurity of revelation, therefore, follows the necessity of criteria from which we can recognize its divine provenance with sufficient certainty. This does not mean that these criteria must be sought entirely outside the event of revelation. There are within the revelatory event characteristics whereby its divine origin shines forth through its earthly form in obvious clarity—e.g., in the miracles of Christ, in the wonder of his person, etc. There is, further, everything essential for man's response to the God who reveals himself. Earthly realities in which God makes himself known and earthly concepts can never adequately correspond to the divine truth; that is, no intrinsic understanding of the revealed fact is committed to us. Therefore—and not merely from a positive divine decree—God's revelatory speech is an attesting speech (*locutio attestans*): This characteristic of God speaking in revelation is often emphasized in theology, but in the main, no intrinsic cause is assigned for the fact. God's word gives us, though it is stated in human concepts, no intrinsic understanding, but demands of us the *obedience of faith*. And, finally, it becomes evident from this that the earthly revelation of salvation is not yet the final form of supernatural revelation. It is ordered towards a completion in the beyond.

ESCHATOLOGICAL REVELATION

From its first beginnings supernatural revelation as it is described for us in Sacred Scripture is directed towards the future, beginning with the mysterious Protoevangelion. Likewise in the revelation to Abraham it is said at the beginning: "I will make a great nation of you . . . so that you shall be a blessing. . . In you shall all the nations of the earth be blessed!" (Gn 12,2f.). In the Mosaic age this element bearing on the future of Abraham's descendants, now grown into a people and constituted by divine initiative the people of God, is the pledge and concession of the promised land; after David's time it is the promise of everlasting duration for his kingdom. The *day of the Lord* was awaited, when he would destroy all the enemies of his name and give a final salvation to his people. The prophets had to correct this expectation again and again: the Lord will begin his judgment with his own people. But none of the prophets was simply a prophet of doom. All of them proclaimed as well the unwavering fidelity and the salvific will of the God of the covenant. At least for a remnant of his people he will fulfil his promises with the establishment of his reign. In Old Testament Israel, Yahweh was already the only true king, or was supposed to be. The contemporary incumbent of the Davidic throne was only a steward. The prophets, however, refer to a more perfect kingdom of God in the future, when all will know and love Yahweh and walk in his ways, when there will be peace and salvation. Not infrequently this promise expressly transcends all national boundaries. Through his Anointed, Yahweh will rule over his people and over the nations for their salvation. He himself will come and bring redemption (Is 35,4).

In Jesus of Nazareth the messianic promises, many and diverse as they are, seeming even contradictory in their immediate sense, came to a fulfilment beyond all human anticipation: God himself came in his only Son and revealed himself to us, in that he was among us as man and wrought our salvation. In him has the absolutely free and, for us, incalculable God spoken his last, definitive word to mankind. He undertook to do this by making himself known to us as the one who loves us. In his Son God has bestowed on us himself, and therefore "all" (*ta panta;* Rom 8,32). That is the insurpassable climax of the whole of revelation. Everything else was only a prelude. Therefore with Christ necessarily "the final time" is here (Heb 1,2, etc.). Revelation is concluded.

But all still remains for us in earthly form, in "the condition of a slave," veiled in earthly, even though divinely filled, events and spoken in earthly, human words—which, even though chosen by God himself, still express the divine reality only incompletely and with the possibility of misunderstanding on our part. We "see," but only "as in a mirror, as a reflection" (1 Cor 13,12). We know only in faith, in a faith which, therefore, is beset with many difficulties.

Thus even the revelation in Christ still looks beyond itself. We look for the coming of Christ in his glory, to that completion of all divine revelation in which we shall know face to face just as we ourselves are known.

Notes

1. Israel is called in the LXX *ekklēsia* (= almost always the Hebrew *qahal*) about 100 times. Cf. K. L. Schmidt, "*ekklēsia*," *ThWNT* III, 530ff. (*Bible Key Words: The Church*, ET 1950.)
2. Rahner, "The Development of Dogma," *Theological Investigations* I, p. 50.
3. As is known, some Fathers, such as Augustine, and later Thomas (*S. Th.* I, 9. 12, a. 11, ad 2; II-II, 8. 175, a.3), were of the opinion that in this theophany Moses was granted a transitory immediate vision of God.
4. One cannot say with S. Tromp, *De revelatione* [6](1950), p. 81, that it belongs to the nature of a mystery in the strict sense that it should have no analogies at all in the area of creation. Such a mystery could not be revealed to us in human concepts.

As a matter of fact, all the mysteries revealed to us have their analogies in the earthly, e.g., the mystery of the Most Holy Trinity in the relation of nature and person in man, in human fatherhood, sonship, etc. But these earthly analogies are not such that we naturally could conclude from them to the divine reality as *analogatum primarium*. Only through revelation are these earthly analogies recognized as such.

PART IV

BIBLICAL AND THEOLOGICAL CONCEPTS: IN SEARCH OF A SYNTHESIS

8

BROADENING THE CLASSIC DEFINITION

There is no doubt that supernatural revelation as it is described for us in Sacred Scripture is a very complex reality. The Bible itself, as usual, gives us no handy formula which we can use as a universally valid definition of revelation. But it is the task of theology to achieve a deeper comprehension, through reason enlightened by faith, of that which is attested in Scripture, and thereby also to clarify it conceptually. It goes without saying that the concept of revelation in systematic theology may not contradict the understanding of revelation found in the Scripture. Furthermore, an abstract concept of revelation will never exhaust the existential fullness of the reality of revelation. And an oversimplified formula may too easily lead to misunderstandings, even one which is correct to the extent that it includes what is essential and, from a given viewpoint, accurately conveys the nature of revelation; for it may exclude other factors that are no less essential when another line of enquiry is taken.

The classic formulation of revelation in systematic Catholic theology: "God speaking"—more precisely: "attesting divine speech" (*locutio Dei attestans*)—cannot therefore be considered simply false, since it is encountered in plain statements of the Church's magisterium and has support in Sacred Scripture itself. But from the standpoint of revelation as it is understood by the Bible it obviously needs explanation and a more precise determination of its area of validity.

First of all, *locutio Dei*—even in the strict sense of conceptual and attesting speech, in distinction to revelation in act and vision—can be accepted as a correct definition of supernatural revelation *to the extent* that revelation has been consigned to the Church in the form of the word and is thus communicated by her. It is in this sense, at least usually, that the Church's magisterium speaks of revelation. Only of revelation in this sense can it be said that it is "contained" in Sacred Scripture and tradition (Vatican). To revelation thus understood corresponds, on the part of man, faith "from hearing" (Rom 10,17).

LIVING CONTACT WITH THE THING ITSELF

Of course we cannot say even of revelation as communicated by the Church that it consists exclusively and in every respect in the conceptual word. The believing and likewise the teaching Church certainly cannot comprehend the reality of salvation "leaving the word behind." But the Church "does not possess a word about the thing instead of the thing itself. Consequently her hearing of the Word and her reflection upon the Word heard are not *merely* a logical activity." "She lives in living contact with the thing itself."[1] The Church possesses the revealed reality itself and *is* something of this supernatural reality that she proclaims; still in obscurity, it is true, but in such a way that the reality of salvation as such is manifested through all the obscurities of the created order, that is, through the empirical form of the Church. Of such a nature, as we have already said, are those "criteria" which make the Church in the world credible to us as the mediatrix of God's revelation and constitute the Church itself a divine sign among the nations: her wonderful propagation, her victorious endurance, her holiness and fruitfulness in all good, the unity and purity of her teaching, etc.—all these are not merely the "concomitant" criteria of revelation (as has been said so often) but are themselves a realization of the divine salvific will present to us in the Church and accessible to our experience: an epiphany, even though incomplete and never unalloyed, of the inner nature of the Church.

The word of the Church in which revelation comes to us, moreover, as likewise the word of Scripture and of tradition, never rests in itself alone; it always and necessarily looks back to the original event of revelation of which it gives testimony. The conceptual proposition in which revelation is presented to us is "always a kind of window through which a view may be gained of the thing itself, and implies in its full sense . . . this view of the thing through the proposition (in its 'stated' sense)," namely, the vision of the incarnate, crucified, resurrected One who in his Church and its sacraments is present and acting, the vision of his grace, and so on.[2]

Locutio Dei also, however, conveys the *totality* of revelation to the extent that in the original event the divine word plays a decisive role not merely *along with* act and vision (though these three forms are to be distinguished one from the other), but above all because the divine word in explicit utterance embraces the entire event of revelation, even that which occurs in divine act and in theophanies, and expresses its final significance.

But the original event of revelation is as such not merely God's conceptual speech directed to us. Therefore when we enquire into supernatural revelation absolutely, into its nature, possibility, and actuality, as is done in fundamental theology (at least when we seek to establish the fact of revelation by the genetico-historical way, from its historical origins), we cannot content ourselves merely with the formula *locutio Dei* (*attestans*). If we were to do this, we would have to understand the formula in an unaccustomed fullness, as including God's (visible) coming to us and his revealing and salvific activity. Such a wide conception, embracing revelation in act and vision, is of course possible; but it would no longer be sufficient as a definition of the earthly revelation of salvation. It would have to be distinguished from the natural revelation in act and from the revelation in vision of eternity.

In practice, however, there is no doubt that *locutio Dei* is not understood in this broad sense in systematic Catholic theology, but almost always in the sense of conceptual speech. It can hardly be denied that the formula thus understood can lead to a more or less intellectualized understanding of revelation, a danger which is especially clear when the content of revelation is presented not as something real, but purely in the abstract, as "concepts," "judgments," "teachings." Man by his nature can state the content of revelation only in concepts and judgments, but this content itself cannot be fully contained in them. We should not, it is true, exaggerate the harm caused by formulating revelation as such an intellectual thing, for it is undeniable that in the concepts and doctrines of Catholic preaching and theology the revealing salvific act of God is also expressed.

SUMMARIZING THE ESSENTIALS

Revelation is such a complex reality that it is impossible to capture it completely in a short abstract formula. Historical realities can never be adequately defined in a simple concept. Therefore, if we are to view the reality of revelation as it is attested in the Bible we must seek a more descriptive definition which will summarize all the essentials as briefly as possible. We can, then, perhaps say: *Supernatural revelation is an act of grace, the personal, salvific self-manifestation of God to man in the realm of his history; it takes place in supernatural divine activity, in visible appearance, and above all, as interpreting and embracing the others, in his attesting word; first of all in Israel, then definitively in Christ Jesus, and present to us in the word and work of the Church; here below remaining in considerable obscurity (therefore to be received by man in faith), but ordered towards the immediate vision of God in eternity.*

All the points given would be necessary for the fullest possible comprehension of what is essential in supernatural revelation, though we would not pretend that every point is equally central. However, it is not always necessary to say everything explicitly. Depending on the various problems and questions involved, we can and should content ourselves with shorter formulas which express supernatural revelation with relative completeness and set forth its essentials—e.g., earthly revelation of salvation, personal self-manifestation, act of grace, word of God, etc.

Since it is the special property of the divine word in relation to revelation as a whole to contain within itself

—specifically, in its form as explicit utterance—the totality of revelation (including what is revealed in deed and vision), many questions which in themselves have broad reference to revelation as a whole can validly be confined to revelation as the word of God. An example is the question, discussed in fundamental theology, of the possibility of revelation: Is it possible to express otherworldly and "supernatural" realities—which as such are absolutely unknowable to natural man—correctly, even though only analogously, in our conceptuology stemming from the visible world? If that is possible, and if such a verbal revelation can be verified as a fact, then immediately we establish the possibility and actuality of the reality intended by the words.

For a right understanding of what supernatural revelation actually is, it still remains indispensable to see it whole. This is true specifically for the evaluation of the criteria of revelation, and therefore for revelation as something knowable. The prophecies and miracles of salvation history, in particular the miracle of Christ's person and the miracle of the Church as a sign of God present to us, are not merely "extrinsically" (*ab extra*) connected with revelation; they belong within the revealed reality itself. They are signs in which God says something to us. They attain, therefore, to an intrinsic credibility, as integral components within the larger context of salvation history. C. S. Lewis has rightly brought out the importance of this viewpoint for the interpretation of the biblical miracle stories.[3] In the revealed word God's salvific will is given *expressly*, though in the language of our world of ideas; in the deeds and visions of revelation, however, it is revealed to us *implicitly*, since the divine provenance of God's act intervening in our world is manifest to us, and we encounter the divine salvific will existentially and experientially.

REVELATION IS CHRIST HIMSELF

In the language of abstract concepts we cannot adequately state in a few words what supernatural revelation is and how it has taken place. There is, however, one *concrete* formula which says everything that is essential in all brevity and accuracy: *Revelation* (in its definitive form) *is Christ himself*. Everything in revelation beforehand is only a reference to him and a preparation for him. Everything after—the reality of the Church—is only the way in which Christ is near to us men here today and encounters us. Everything that can and must be said of revelation in circumstantial, abstract concepts is said concretely and univocally with this one name *Christ*. In Christ we have *God's self-manifestation* to us men and for our *salvation;* it is *personal*: in this person encountering us and addressing himself to each individual; it is *historical*: as historical fact at a distinct moment in time in the course of the centuries, as the centre of all history, and as a concrete event defined by many historical factors; it is a *grace*: since in this man God himself comes to us as one of us in order to bestow on us his salvation; and therefore it is *eschatological*: with the coming of God in person the insurpassable climax of every revelation is already present; the last times have begun; all that remains is only a further unfolding.

Visible coming, revelatory activity, and express word are in Christ most profoundly united, not only to the extent that his word is necessarily truth—that is, it expresses the uttered reality completely—but also, and above all, in the much deeper sense *that he himself is the Word*—word now no longer to be understood merely as conceptual utterance. He is, as the second divine person, the eternal, living Word in whom God the Father in the divine "now" utters and communicates his own divine nature. And this divine Word has been given to us made man, and thereby has become revealed to us as our salvation. In him God has said everything to us and accomplished everything. "In this centre of Christian faith the whole contrast, as current among us, between word and work, between knowing and living, ceases to have any meaning. But the Word, the Logos, is actually the work, the *ergon*, as well, the *verbum* is also the *opus*. . . The very Word with which we are here concerned is an act, this act, which as such is the Word, is Revelation."[4] The entire divine life destined for us is shown in him, the historical man Jesus of Nazareth, when he appears and acts. "In this has the love of God been shown in our case, that God has sent his only-begotten Son into the world that we may live through him" (1 Jn 4,9). But all of that happened, and continues to happen, provisionally, concealed by the "flesh" which never permits the divine truth and reality to be recognized except as in a mirror; and only faith—a faith corresponding to human nature raised into the order of salvation but not dispensed with, therefore a reasonable faith—sees this divine thing and receives it. Only in the consummation of the world beyond will man see God face to face and thereby see and possess his own salvation, and—recognizing the witness of the eternal Word through the Father in the Holy Spirit—also the archetype and ultimate origin of divine revelation.

Notes

1. Karl Rahner, "The Development of Dogma," *Theological Investigations* I, p. 50.
2. *Ib.*, p. 59.
3. C. S. Lewis, *Miracles: A Preliminary Study* (1948), pp. 159ff.
4. K. Barth, *Dogmatics in Outline* (New York, Harper, 1959), p. 67.

9

REVELATION AND FAITH

The concept of revelation is essentially relative: revelation always occurs in relation to a person or a community of persons. Therefore the nature of divine revelation can be clarified by a consideration of the response it demands from man—that is, faith. Also the other way round—by an analysis of this response we can confirm the concept of revelation as it has been developed. Here we shall not undertake any investigation in detail of the nature of faith; of the many aspects of the problem we shall discuss briefly only those which immediately concern the relation of revelation to faith—which are thus informative for the concept of revelation.

Corresponding to *natural revelation,* there is in man a genuine *knowledge of God* developed from a recognition of the nature of things, which can also be made a reflexive inferential process. The world of our (external and internal) experience necessarily calls for the existence of the absolute, and indeed the personal Being we call God. This knowledge is, of course, profoundly differentiated from the rest of our inner-worldly knowledge: first of all, since God ever remains for us one who is entirely "other," our knowledge of him must always be at the same time an unknowing; secondly, even this natural knowledge of God already lays a claim on man, elicits awe, and demands a response.[1]

To the *supernatural revelation in the beyond* our response will be the *contemplation of God.* In the light of glory, participating in God's own knowledge, we shall see him as he is and know ourselves as we are known by him.

To the *supernatural revelation on earth,* according to the witness of Sacred Scripture, our response, as the fundamental religious act—that is, the fundamental attitude of man in the order of salvation—is *faith.* Faith is therefore absolutely necessary for salvation. In this all Christians are at one. But there is no unity of belief among Christians concerning the nature of this fundamental attitude. Against the Reformation thesis of "fiducial faith," a confident trust of the sinner in the imputation of the righteousness of Christ, as well as against various kinds of Modernistic irrationalism, Catholic theology has emphasized the *intellectual* character of faith. But even within Catholic theology, just as there are tensions between systematic theology on the one hand and biblical theology on the other regarding the concept of revelation, so it is with the concept of faith

—and given the close correlation between the two this is not surprising.

THE CONCEPT OF FAITH IN SYSTEMATIC THEOLOGY

In systematic theology, faith is generally defined as "the firm adherence of the mind to the truths revealed by God (and presented by the Church)." This is in accordance with the definition of the first Vatican Council, in which the supernatural quality of faith is taught along with other essentials: "This faith, which is the beginning of human salvation, the Catholic Church teaches to be a supernatural virtue, through which, by the grace of God inspiring and helping us, we believe those things revealed by him to be true, not because of the intrinsic truth of the things perceived by the natural light of human reason, but because of the authority of God himself revealing, who can neither deceive nor be deceived" (s. III; cap. 3: Denz. 1789). The intellectual character of faith is set forth most pronouncedly in the oath against Modernism: ". . . I profess that faith is not a blind religious feeling . . . but a true assent of the mind to a truth accepted from without through hearing, by which we believe to be true on the authority of the most true God those things which have been said, testified, and revealed by the personal God, our Creator and Lord" (Denz. 2145).

THE BIBLICAL CONCEPT OF FAITH

Catholic and non-Catholic biblical theology are, on the other had, now at one in the conviction that in the biblical understanding of faith, besides the noetic aspect (never lacking, but not always standing in the foreground), the essentials are obedience, trust, hope, and personal commitment to God or Christ. Can we simply distinguish, as is often done, between faith in the strict sense—that is, the fundamental religious act of man in the supernatural order as it is understood in systematic theology—and faith in a wider sense—that is, the same fundamental act taken together with the whole complex of attitudes intimately associated with it and following from it or commanded by it, which is faith in the scriptural sense, viewed in the usual way, not in the theoretical and abstract order but as a living and concrete reality? As will be shown, this distinction, while it is not absolutely false, does not entirely come to grips with the problem.

In Sacred Scripture "faith"—in the New Testament *pistis* or *pisteuō*—is the religious attitude of man towards God revealing himself. Through faith (with baptism) man becomes a Christian. Very often the members of the Church in the New Testament are called simply "the believers." From among the many word-roots used in the

Old Testament for "believe," the New Testament has adhered by preference to *'āman* for its understanding of faith. In the Septuagint only this root is regularly translated by *pistis* or *pisteuō*. Actually, in *'āman* is to be found the ultimate that the Old Testament can say about the attitude of man to the revelation of God, so that it can be used absolutely in theologically important passages such as Is 7,9: "If you will not believe, you shall not endure!," and Hb 2,4: "The just man, because of his faith, shall live." When said of God *'āman* means (in the *nifal*) "firm," "reliable," "trustworthy." To this corresponds the fact that God's "truth" in the Old Testament is also understood in the first place as his unconditional reliability, his fidelity. The symbol of truth is not, as for the Greeks, "light," but rather "rock." The causal form of *'āman* (the *hifil*: *he'ĕmîn*) is used of man and signifies his responsive attitude to God's revelation: faith.

It is true that, according to the particular mode under which revelation is viewed, various aspects of "faith" may enter into the foreground. To the God giving himself to be known corresponds the element of *knowledge* in faith: Man contributes faith to revelation and is thereby made participant of a knowledge otherwise inaccessible to him. This element is always the deepest stratum (even though not always explicitly expressed) of the attitude of faith, since revelation means first of all that something has been made known to man by God. In faith man makes this thing his own. The "bestowal of faith" in this sense is especially stressed whenever God reveals himself in explicit words; but the same holds true for the self-manifestation of God in his doing and his appearing: By his activity in the history of his people shall Israel know its God, as the Old Testament says again and again. And this knowing also presupposes the attitude of faith in man: it is a knowledge of faith. Thus Jesus reveals his glory in his works, and his disciples believe in him. Knowledge as part of the structure of faith is seen in the New Testament especially in John, where the terms faith and knowledge can sometimes be used interchangeably: cf. Jn 6,69 and 1 Jn 4,16.[2] Also in Heb 11—the famous chapter on faith—in two passages this noetic significance is expressly brought out: "By faith we understand that the world was fashioned by the word of God. . ." (11,3), and "He who comes to God must believe that God exists and is a rewarder to those who seek him" (11,6). Similarly it is said—in almost Johannine terminology—in Is 43,10f., "You are my witnesses, says the Lord . . . to know and believe in me and understand that it is I . . . It is I, I the Lord; there is no savior but me!"

To God commanding, man's response in faith is *obedience*. This is true when the content of a revelation essentially consists in a commandment of God—e.g., God's command to Abraham to depart from his homeland, to sacrifice his son Isaac, etc. Abraham's faith—and Abraham is "the father of believers" (cf. Gal 3,7)—has therefore the aspect of obedience: Gn 12,1; Heb 11,8: "In faith (or *by* his faith: *pistei*) Abraham obeyed the call to go out" (cf. also Gn 22,1ff. and Heb 11,17).[3] But revelation of itself, even independently of its actual content, is also always a divine commandment to man, who is not left free to say yes or no to revelation. Therefore faith itself is as such always an act of obedience on man's part. This is evident above all to Paul, who speaks of the "obedience of faith" (Rom 1,5) and not infrequently uses "faith" and "obedience" in the same sense (cf. Rom 1,8 and Rom 16,19 for example). Similarly in 1 Pt 1,22 we read of "obedience to the (divine) truth."

The object of revelation as Sacred Scripture understands it is God himself and his salvific will for mankind. From this fact faith as the fundamental religious attitude towards this revelation necessarily takes on the character of *trust* and *hope*. As a matter of fact, no other aspect of faith as understood by the Old Testament is stressed so much as this. This applies especially to the "faith" of Abraham which tirelessly adheres to God's "truth" and fidelity to his promises and "believes against all hope" (Gn 15,6; Rom 4,18). In "faith"—that is, in its trust in the Lord rather than in "horses and chariots" and alliances with the Gentiles—must Israel seek its welfare: Ps 20,8f.; Is 31,1ff.; 40,31, etc. The piety of the Psalms especially is instinct with this attitude. In many New Testament texts faith has also the sense of unshakable trust. Thus in the Synoptic Gospels: the "little faith" for which Jesus has to rebuke his disciples again and again is pre-eminently a lack of trust. When any man "believes" that whatever he says will be done, it shall be done for him (Mk 11,23). As trust and hope, faith is seen again especially in Heb 11: "Faith is the firm assurance of what is hoped for . . ." (11,1). To this the many examples further on in the chapter correspond, especially including that of Abraham once more. Faith is response to God's promises: cf. 11,9ff.; 11,13f.; 11,17ff. Christian faith, says 1 Pt 1,21, is at the same time hope in God; for this hope the Christian should "be ready at all times to give an account" (3,15). According to Pauline theology it is of the essence of faith that man should not build on his own works but on the grace of God entrusted to him in Christ Jesus.

Wherever revelation comes to man in the mediating message of the prophet, the apostle, or the Church, his faith is primarily *acceptance of this message*. The missionary activity of the primitive Church explains the fact that in the New Testament faith is so often viewed under this aspect.[4] Faith means to accept the message of Jesus as the Christ, the Son of God, the Kyrios and Savior: Acts 2,41; 4,4; 8,12; 1 Cor 15,11 Eph 1,13, etc. "Faith comes from hearing (the message)": Rom 10,17. It goes without saying that the New Testament does not put this in contradiction to what has been previously said. Acceptance of the Christ-message is only the formal side of faith. This acceptance is essentially obedience to God, who offers his salvation in the message; in this faith man knows and acknowledges Jesus as Christ and God's Son; in this faith he places his whole trust in God, abandoning all reliance on himself. Since God himself reveals himself and his salvation to us in Christ, this faith in Christ is at the same time faith in God, as is explicitly said in Jn 12,44. Faith in the one, true, living God is the presupposition for the right understanding and acceptance of the message of his revelation in Christ (cf. 1 Thes 1,9).

Thus in the New Testament, as already in the Old Testament, the essentially *personal character of faith* is brought out. Since God reveals himself as our salvation—in the New Testament in Christ—therefore faith is also faith "in him," faith "in Christ." Ever and again the New Testament speaks of "belief in Christ," and even when it says simply "believe" or "faithful," almost always we are to supply the words "in Christ." Faith is to acknowledge him as our Lord and Savior, to adhere to him: Jn 20;28; Rom 1,4; 8,35; Gal 3,29, etc. Relatively seldom does faith appear as a belief *about* God: the disciples must believe *that* Christ is who he is (Jn 8,24); the Gospel has been written "that you may believe *that* Jesus is the Christ" (Jn 20,30; cf. 1 Cor 15,3–5; Heb 11,6). But even here this belief "that" is not as such the proper object of faith, but rather what is asserted in it: Jesus as the Christ, as the one who died and rose for our sins, for my sins. This gives us the key to a synthesis of the biblical understanding of faith with that of dogmatic theology.

SYNTHESIS OF THE BIBLICAL AND DOGMATIC UNDERSTANDINGS OF FAITH

Where divine revelation meets man in the message and teaching of the Church, faith has primarily the form of acceptance of this message: "I believe what God has revealed and teaches us to believe through his Church." This act of faith is without doubt an intellectual act (made with the grace of God and in freedom): assent to the Christ-proclamation of the Church. Rightly has the Church emphasized this intellectual character of faith against misinterpretations or denials of it. By doing so, however, it has also made it possible for this aspect of the reality of faith to be stressed somewhat one-sidedly. For it must never be overlooked that "believing that" is *only the formal side* of faith as it exists in the Church. Faith, if it is a perfection of the interior man, rests "in the heart" (Rom 10,9)—not in the assertion as such; rather, by the assertion it extends to the reality itself, that is, to God and to his salvation in Christ Jesus.[5] Thus faith, even when it is expressed as a statement about something (and therefore formulated intellectually), is still a *personal avowal* of

Christ, a personal response to him, an engagement with him who has revealed himself as our salvation, as my salvation; it is a personal acceptance of the salvation made known to me and announced to me in revelation, the "beginning of salvation." In any interiorly completed act of faith there is, to the same extent, already a beginning of love. Therefore Christ continues to speak to us not in an impersonal institution or merely in a dead letter, but in a Church, his mystical Body, in which he himself is present to us.

From this fact, namely that faith is the personal response of man to the God revealing himself and offering his salvation (that is, participation in his own divine life), it becomes evident also that for this act man must be *supernaturally* elevated. For a merely intellectual assent to the propositions of revelation set forth as worthy of faith no supernatural elevation is yet needed. But man must be raised into the divine order if he is to encounter him personally in his response of faith. Only thus can faith be the beginning of a life-dispensing salvific encounter between God and man.

Since not the understanding, but the understanding *man* believes, *man* performs freely and responsibly the act of faith which God demands of him through the Church; our faith is also and, indeed, by its very nature, essentially an *act of obedience*, as the first Vatican Council also explicitly teaches: "Full submission of the intellect and will" (s. III, cap. 3: Denz. 1789).

It is true, genuine supernatural faith according to the teaching of the Church—in accord with Scripture—is a "reasonable" faith, since God makes his revelation credible to us through the signs in which he reveals himself and with which he accompanies his explicit word. Since, however, the content of revelation (to the extent that it deals with divine mysteries, the proper objects of revelation) remains beyond the grasp of human intelligence, faith as such is always at the same time an act of *trust* in which man abandons himself to the truth of God in a *sacrificium intellectus.* In addition to this, faith is also an act of trust because of its actual content, since it takes God's promises seriously and affirms God's fidelity. He who affirms with inner assent that God has called us to eternal life through Christ accomplishes *eo ipso* an act of trust. Faith and trust are in this act only logical aspects of the same act, not to be distinguished as two acts related to each other. However, this does not imply that in addition to this trust inhering in the act of faith itself there is not also a relatively independent virtue of trust (though even this is impossible without faith).

Thus a deepened understanding of revelation also leads to a deepened understanding of faith. All the essentials of revelation have their correlatives in the response of faith. Christian faith is the response of man to God's revealing and saving activity in *history*: that in the heart of time he has wrought our salvation in his Son become man and has made this known to us. It is a *personal* response of man to God and his Son, who in revelation manifests and gives himself to us as our salvation. It is a response to God of man elevated in the divine order of *grace*, a revelation which is an ineffable gift of God's grace. It is essentially *ecclesiological*, since revelation and salvation are present to us only in the Church, and only in her can they be received. It is *eschatological*, since it is man's assent to the God-given salvation from sin and at the same time his hope for its completion in the return of Christ and in eternal life.

Notes

1. Therefore, though only analogously to supernatural faith, even the recognition of God founded on natural revelation can be called "faith in God."
2. However, we cannot speak of an absolute identification of faith and knowledge in John. Knowledge is more perfect; Jesus "knows" the Father. "Faith" is never spoken of in connexion with him. The Jews who *believe* in Jesus are promised: "You shall *know* the truth" (8,31f.). For men there is only (here below) a knowledge in faith.
3. In Judaism, which excessively restricted the content of revelation to the law alone, faith also, as a consequence, took on a legal note: obedience of faith became obedience to the law.

4. Rudolf Bultmann points out in this connexion that "faith" (*pistis*) was also a catch-word of the propagandizing religions of the Hellenistic age. Every missionary sermon demanded "belief" in the deity it proclaimed. cf. *ThWNT* V, 205. (*Bible Key Words: Faith*, ET 1961, p. 41.)
5. *Actus credentis non terminatur ad enuntiabile, sed ad rem*: S. Thomas, *S. Th*. II-II, 1, 2 ad 2m.

INDEX OF AUTHORS